CONTENTS

MUSIC in the
BAROQUE ERA

FROM *Monteverdi* TO *Bach*

By

MANFRED F. BUKOFZER
PROFESSOR OF MUSIC, THE UNIVERSITY OF CALIFORNIA

New York

W · W · NORTON & COMPANY · INC·

BY

W. W. NORTON & COMPANY, INC.

NEW YORK, N. Y.

2 00 6 001 709

PRINTED IN THE UNITED STATES OF AMERICA
FOR THE PUBLISHERS BY THE VAIL-BALLOU PRESS

IN MEMORY OF
ANDRÉ PIRRO
(1869–1943)
A Pioneer of Baroque Music

ILLUSTRATIONS

THE FIRST book in the English language on the history of baroque music does not need either apology or justification. Histories of music have been written usually as quick surveys of the entire field and if they specialize at all they concentrate as a rule on a single composer. It is a strange though incontestable fact that by far the great majority of music books deal with composers rather than their music. This attitude is a survival of the hero-worship that characterizes the nineteenth-century approach to music as well as the other arts. In a history of a single musical period the shortcomings of such an approach become particularly obvious. A musical era receives its inner unity from the musical style and can be historically understood only in terms of stylistic development. It is for this reason that in the present history of baroque music the stylistic approach has consistently been adopted. Biographical information, easily accessible in musical dictionaries, has been reduced to a minimum in order to leave space for the discussion of stylistic trends and characteristics of style, usually ignored in the dictionaries.

I have written this book for the music student and music lover with the aim of acquainting him with a great period of musical history and helping him to gain a historical understanding of music without which baroque music cannot fully be appreciated and enjoyed. If the history of music is to have more than an antiquarian interest and significance, it must be seen as a history of musical styles, and the history of styles in turn as a history of ideas. The ideas that underlie musical styles can only be shown in a factual stylistic analysis that takes music apart as a mechanic does a motor and that shows how musical elements are combined, how they achieve their specific effect, and what constitutes the difference between externally similar factors. This analysis is at once historical and "technological" and takes beauty for granted. Those writers to whom the description of music is no more than a matter of elegant variation in judiciously chosen adjectives may be shocked to learn that the word "beautiful" does not occur in this book. My aim has been not the expatiation on the obvious but the explanation of the specific musical results of baroque style. This explanation must of necessity rely on words, but it must be clearly understood that words cannot render the aesthetic experience of music itself, let alone replace it. Familiarity with the rudiments of music is assumed in this book though it is not designed for specialists nor has it been written, for that matter, by a specialist of the period. But even the specialized musicologist will find a few new facts, new interpretations, and a number of hitherto unpublished examples. In the organization of material I have departed from the usual practice by not making the book a strictly chronological report. The main principle of organization is style in its various manifestations. Chapters II–IX comprise the actual history of baroque style. The first and the three last chapters cut across the field and complement the subject: the first gives a general comparison between renaissance and baroque style, the three last deal with aspects of form, theory, and sociology, rarely, if ever, discussed in histories of music. Several chapters were first presented publicly in a lecture series at the University of Chicago in 1945, and for the Northern California Chapter of the American Musicological Society in 1946.

For reasons of space the bibliographical footnotes have been restricted essentially to references to musical reprints. Through the courtesy of Dr. Willi Apel I was able to incorporate references to the second volume, as yet unpublished, of the *Historical Anthology of Music* which contains many valuable examples of baroque music. It goes without saying that the material presented in this book is based largely on the special studies listed in the bibliography. Unfortunately for the music student the majority of these books and articles is written in languages other than English. Such excellent stylistic studies as those by J. A. Westrup (*Purcell*) and Ernst Meyer (*English Chamber Music*) are all too rare exceptions. The bibliography stresses style-criticism and includes only those biographies that consider the musical style of the composer. Although it is the largest bibliography of baroque music ever printed it is far from being complete. The inclusion of local and archives studies would have doubled its size. The checklist of baroque books on music represents a new bibliographical venture the aim of which has not been completeness, but comprehensive coverage of the various aspects of musical literature in a given period, the detailed study of which raises fascinating problems. Prolific writers like Mattheson and others appear in the list only with their most important titles. Items that appear in a footnote in incomplete form are more fully cited in the bibliography. It should be noted that throughout the book major and minor keys are differentiated by means of small and capital letters; for example, c and C stand for C-minor and C-major, respectively.

It is my pleasant duty to acknowledge the help and advice I received from many friends and colleagues. I am especially grateful to Dr. Alfred Einstein of Smith College who took a fatherly interest in my book and permitted me to use some examples from his rich treasure of early baroque music, and to Professor Edward Lawton of the University of California who put his scores of the works of Gesualdo and several photostats at my disposal. I gratefully recall the assistance of the following institutions: the Music Division of the Library of Congress, New York Public Library, Newberry Library, British Museum, Metropolitan Museum of Art, Union Theological Seminary, and the library of the University of California. Last but not least my thanks go to my wife. Without her unflagging encouragement and help this book would not have been possible.

Manfred F. Bukofzer

Berkeley, California

CHAPTER ONE

Renaissance Versus Baroque Music

DISINTEGRATION OF STYLISTIC UNITY

WHEN Monteverdi in his fifth book of madrigals (1605) asserted that he did not follow the precepts of the old school, but was guided by what he called the *seconda prattica*, he spoke with the self-assertion of an artist fully conscious of a fundamental change in the conception of music. Monteverdi was retorting in his statement to an abusive attack of Artusi, in which this conservative critic and theorist found fault with Monteverdi's treatment of dissonance. By opposing the second practice to the first, and by implying that the standards of the old school could not be applied to the new, Monteverdi challenged the whole basis of the argument. Thus the eternal controversy between artist and critic about the standards of art criticism flamed up in the violent manner that is indicative of all periods of transition.

It was not the first time, nor was it to be the last, that the transition from one musical era to another was accompanied by claims of the progressive and counterclaims of the conservative camp. The title *Nuove Musiche*, which became the battle cry of the baroque period, has its parallels in the late Gothic *ars nova* (proclaimed by Philippe de Vitry), in the *ars nova* of the renaissance (described by Tinctoris), in the *goût galant* of the early classic period, and in the "modern music" of our own day. Old music or *stile antico* was identified, at the time of Monteverdi, with renaissance music, new music or *stile moderno* with baroque music.

The term *baroco* [1] had originally a derogatory meaning that clearly reflects the light in which former generations have seen the seventeenth century. The baroque was taken to be a degenerate form of the renaissance, another "dark age" between the limpid *cinquecento* and the classicism

---

[1] For a history of the term see the special issue on baroque style of the *Journal of Aesthetics and Art Criticism* V (1946), no. 2.

of the eighteenth century. Even Jacob Burckhardt still defined in his
Cicerone the baroque as "a corrupt dialect" of the renaissance. Today our
concepts have radically changed. The baroque is recognized as a period
in its own right, with its own intrinsic development and its own aesthetic
standards. The period covers roughly the seventeenth century and the
first half of the eighteenth century. Signs of the stylistic change became
noticeable as early as the late sixteenth century, and for some time renaissance and baroque traits ran side by side. Likewise, the new forces at the
end of the baroque era that led ultimately to the classic period appeared
early in the eighteenth century simultaneously with the most monumental
and lasting manifestations of baroque music.

The terms "renaissance" and "baroque" music have been borrowed
from art history as convenient labels for periods which apply equally well
to music history and other fields of civilization. The transposition to music
history of terms developed in art history has its dangers if performed too
literally. Since the days of Wölfflin's *Principles of Art History* attempts have
been made to apply his terminology to music in wholesale fashion. The
concepts of Wölfflin, the linear, closed form, etc., are abstractions distilled
from the live development of art, indeed very useful abstractions, but so
general in nature that they can be applied to all periods indiscriminately,
although they were originally found in the comparison of renaissance and
baroque. If used as eternal principles, however, they defeat their own purpose, namely, the historical understanding of one particular period which
never repeats itself in art or music history. Only a historical terminology
able to recognize the uniqueness of each stylistic era can further such understanding. The application of the term "baroque" to music has been
criticized because baroque qualities cannot be found in the musical notes.
Indeed, whoever hopes to discover baroque qualities in music as though
they were a mysterious chemical substance misunderstands the meaning of
the term which essentially denotes the inner stylistic unity of the period.

That the development of baroque music runs parallel with that of baroque
art, and that music does not, as legend has it, lag behind the other arts can
be shown only by a technical analysis that penetrates the last detail, not
by general comparative abstractions. On the other hand, the theory that
the baroque manifests itself so uniformly in all fields that every work
of art of the time is "typically baroque" must be examined on the merits
of the individual case. There are undercurrents of opposed forces that do
not conform to the "spirit of the time," which is itself another abstraction.
The concrete life of a period knows internal contradictions, conflicts of

prevalent and suppressed ideas, survivals from the
tions of the following periods. In spite of these co
ideas of an era stand out and must receive the mai
trends in baroque music correspond to those in b
this is an inevitable by-product of any investig

The change from renaissance to baroque music
stylistic changes in music history in one important aspect. As
musical style of the old school fell into oblivion. The new style took ov
and transformed the last vestiges of previous musical techniques, so that
the unity of style in each period was assured. However, at the beginning
of the baroque era the old style was not cast aside, but deliberately preserved as a second language, known as the *stile antico* of church music.
The hitherto unchallenged unity of style disintegrated, and composers
were obliged to become bilingual. The *stile antico* was fashioned after
the style of Palestrina, who became the idol of those who followed the
strict a-cappella style of baroque music. The more the actual knowledge of
Palestrina's music faded away, the more powerful became the legend of the
alleged savior of church music.

Mastery of the *stile antico* became the indispensable equipment in the
composer's education. He was now at liberty to choose in which style he
wanted to write, whether in the *moderno*, the vehicle of his spontaneous
expression, or in the strict *antico* which he acquired by academic training.
This choice of styles was the first significant step toward the musical historicism that perplexes modern music education. Our much discussed and
often cursed division of musical instruction into "strict" and "free" writing
goes back ultimately to the distinction between *stile antico* and *moderno*.
The rules of the *stile antico* were diligently codified by such theorists as
Bontempi and Fux whose works furnish a drastic example of the contrast
between the old and modern manner. However, recent investigations have
shown that the "Palestrina style" of the baroque actually differs from its
model; the theorists eternalized in their rules a fictitious strict style which
bears the semblance of renaissance music, but which, in fact, is subtly in-
fected with modern licenses. Although this unintentional transformation
took place, as it were, behind the backs of the composers, they continued
to speak of the *stile alla Palestrina*. The tension between the *stile antico*,
however fictitious it may be, and the *stile moderno* has left its mark on
baroque music and all subsequent periods. The conflict has been dealt
with in various ways but has never been completely removed. Thus the
renaissance stands out as the last era of stylistic unity, and for this reason

Music in the Baroque Era

glorified as the paradise lost of music. This stylistic unity ex-
self also in the self-reliant attitude of renaissance composers toward
al style. They took style for granted, whereas it became a problem
baroque composers. The baroque era is the era of style-consciousness.

Many attempts have been made to bring the contrast of renaissance and
baroque music down to a short formula. Early baroque theorists, especially,
have been guilty of aggressive oversimplifications that served their tenden-
tious purpose at the time, but that have unfortunately been taken seriously
by modern historians. With the beginning of the baroque we hear for the
first time of elaborate classifications of music according to styles, an indication that the unity of style has been lost. The fundamental pair of styles
which underlies the new style-consciousness has already been discussed:
the *stile antico* and *moderno,* also known respectively as *stylus gravis* and
luxurians, or *prima* and *seconda prattica.* Another distinction, emerging
later in the century, divides the field into church, chamber, and theatre
music (*musica ecclesiastica, cubicularis, theatralis*). These terms classify
music according to its sociological function and do not necessarily imply
differences in musical technique. It is significant that the main stylistic
terms were not mutually exclusive. Church music, for example, could not
be categorically classified because it was composed either in the old or in
the modern style. The numerous stylistic distinctions of the time have been
the cause of much confusion; the apparent inconsistencies can only be
removed if the word "style" is understood in a wider sense than the modern,
merely technical, interpretation admits.

How profoundly the consciousness of style had sharpened the senses for
the contrast of renaissance and baroque can be seen in Berardi's *Miscellanea Musicale* (1689), where he says: "the old masters [of the renaissance]
had only one style and one practice, the moderns have three styles, church,
chamber, and theatre style, and two practices, the first and the second."
According to Berardi and his teacher Scacchi, the essential difference between first and second practice lay in the changed relations between music
and word. In renaissance music, "harmony is the master of the word"; in
baroque music "the word is the master of harmony." This neat antithesis,
which merely paraphrases Monteverdi's distinction of first and second
practice, touches, indeed, upon one fundamental aspect of baroque music,
the musical expression of the text or what was called, at the time, *expressio
verborum.* This term does not have the modern, emotional connotation of
"expressive music" and can more accurately be rendered as "musical repre-

sentation of the word." The means of verbal representation in baroque music were not direct, psychological, and emotional, but indirect, that is, intellectual and pictorial. The modern psychology of dynamic emotions did not yet exist in the baroque era. Feelings were classified and stereotyped in a set of so-called affections, each representing a mental state which was in itself static. It was the business of the composer to make the affection of the music correspond to that of the words. According to the lucid rationalism of the time, the composer had at his disposal a set of musical figures which were pigeonholed like the affections themselves and were designed to represent these affections in music.

However, the principle of the doctrine of affections and figures was already known to the renaissance, and a writer of that period refers in particular to the Penitential Psalms of Lasso as an outstanding example of powerful representation of the words. He uses, in this connection, the controversial term *musica reservata* which probably derives its name from the faithful observance of the words. The *musica reservata* belongs primarily to the Netherlands orbit. But Italian composers also developed a refined technique of pictorial representation in the Italian madrigal. Since both renaissance and baroque music know the representation of words in music, Berardi oversimplified matters with the implication that it was unknown in the renaissance. The two periods actually operated under the same principle, but they differed fundamentally in the method of its application. The renaissance favored the affections of restraint and noble simplicity, the baroque the extreme affections, ranging from violent pain to exuberant joy. It is obvious that the representation of extreme affections called for a richer vocabulary than had been required before.

Berardi's sweeping distinction merely echoes opinions already expressed, around 1590, by a noisy group of literati that, under the leadership of the Counts Bardi and Corsi, established itself in Florence under the name of *Camerata*. This group based its attack on renaissance music on the handling of the words. They claimed that in contrapuntal music the poetry was literally "torn to pieces" (*laceramento della poesia*), because the individual voices sang different words simultaneously. Words like "heaven" and "wave" were frequently depicted by high notes and wavy lines. The *Camerata* scornfully objected to this "pedantry" and insisted that the sense of an entire passage rather than that of a single word should be imitated in music. As a result of such theoretical discussions, the recitative was created, in which contrapuntal writing was altogether abandoned. In the speech-song of the recitative, the music was completely subordinated to the words, so that the words governed the musical rhythm and even the place of the cadences. The recitative was sung from its very beginning with a hitherto unknown realistic pathos and with an affective violence in which the singer resorted to grimaces, acting, and the imitation of the inflections of natural speech, like crying and gasping. In the eyes of the *Camerata* it was precisely the extremely affective quality of the recitative that gave it its measure of distinction and made it superior to the "pedantic" methods of renaissance music. But, in the eyes of the renaissance composer, the recitative was hardly more than a ridiculous experiment which showed that its author was "not a good musician," to use the words by which Schumann characterized Wagner. From the point of view of renaissance composers, nothing was easier than the composition of a recitative since it required only a most superficial familiarity with musical technique. It is symptomatic that the leading spirits of the *Camerata*, Bardi and Corsi, were, indeed, aristocratic amateurs who tried their hands at composition. Amateurs are less likely to be hidebound by tradition, and less likely to be hampered by facts in the pursuit of new ideas. The influence of dilettanti was as decisive a factor in the formation of baroque music as in that of the classic style in the days of the Bach sons.

Amateurish, then, was the assertion of the *Camerata* that renaissance music was unable to imitate the affection of the words; and renaissance theorists were quick to deny this claim. The reason why the advocates of the old and new schools could not settle their issue and were unable to understand each other can be easily seen. When the baroque composer spoke about affections, he referred to the extreme and violent ones, considered improper by the renaissance composer; so the whole argument was carried out on two levels that did not even touch each other.

The invention of the recitative was intimately connected with the birth of opera, in which the *Camerata* tried to resuscitate the ancient Greek tragedy. Since opera was prompted by an enthusiasm for ancient music, and since the revival of the classics passes as a "typical renaissance" feature, historians of past generations have regarded the opera as the last flowering of renaissance music. To follow the logic of this specious argument, opera would come at least two or three generations "too late" to fit into the picture. It is this allegedly "belated" arrival of the opera that has produced the unfortunate theory that music lags behind the other arts. However, the preoccupation with ancient Greek music is not an exclusive characteristic of the renaissance. Medieval treatises literally abound with lengthy quotations from ancient authors and religiously perpetuate the reports about the magical powers of Greek music; and likewise do the innumerable baroque books on music. Enthusiasm for ancient music is in itself as insufficient an indication of a renaissance attitude as the desire to represent affections in music. These ideas can be observed in medieval, renaissance, and baroque music alike and only the various methods by which they were realized give us the key to the specific character of each individual period.

The opera serves, in fact, as one of the most striking examples of the realization of extreme affections in music, and thus must be regarded as one of the foremost innovations of the baroque era. We know of performances of Greek tragedies in translation during the renaissance in which music was, characteristically, restricted to polyphonic choruses. None of these revivals envisaged the idea, inconceivable at the time, of setting the entire tragedy to music, or, in a manner of speaking, under music. The *Camerata* justified the introduction of the continuous recitative on the theory that music should imitate the delivery of an orator and his manner of moving the affections of the audience. In spite of Galilei's discovery of the hymn of Mesomedes, the first original of Greek music known at the time, the nature of Greek music was a sealed book to the *Camerata,* since its notation could not be deciphered. In the invention of the recitative the chimera of ancient music served only a catalytic function; the primary impulse came from the baroque desire to represent affections of violence.

The composers of the *Camerata* repeatedly insisted on the oratorical nature of the recitative—for example, Caccini, who called it "speaking in music," and Peri, who admitted that he tried "to imitate a speaking person in song." Also Galilei and Bardi maintained that the musician should learn from the orator how to move the affections. The recitative actually fused together the stylized accents of natural speech and those of music. The tendency to merge the disparate elements of poetry and music finds its exact parallel in the mutual assimilation of architecture and painting, of which baroque architecture provides so many amusing examples.

For the renaissance composers it was absurd to imitate the orator because a speech-song depended on an extra-musical law, that of speech. For them the recitative was a song-speech rather than a speech-song. Zarlino, the authoritative spokesman of the old school, objected precisely to the fusion of music and poetry. He maintained in his *Sopplimenti* that the composer must indeed excite the affections of the words, but insisted on the fundamental difference between the method of the orator and that of the musician. He emphasized the fact that poetry and music had distinct modes of imitation which should not be confused, and that the musician who emulated the orator would become a histrion or clown. It is amusing to note that Marsilio Ficino, long before Zarlino, had summarized the renaissance attitude in one of his letters, in which he asserted that the orator and poet took the musician as their model—as we see, the exact reverse of the baroque position.

Renaissance and early baroque concepts of music stand, at this point, clearly opposed. The renaissance artist saw in music a self-contained autonomous art, subject only to its own laws. The baroque artist saw in music a heteronomous art, subordinated to words and serving only as musical means to a dramatic end that transcended music. It should not confuse us that both renaissance and baroque concepts were founded on the ancient theory: art imitates nature, and that the advocates of both schools fortified themselves with quotations of identical passages from Plato and Aristotle. The imitation of the "nature of the words" formed only the springboard from which both periods took off. It is, again, the method by which the theory was put into effect which constitutes the difference between renaissance and baroque.

The violent attacks against counterpoint by the *Camerata,* especially by Galilei, furnish another example of the manner in which baroque authors tried to establish their opposition against the renaissance period. The first composers of recitatives, Galilei, Peri, and Caccini, all attest to the stimulation they received in regard to the recitative from the musical amateur Bardi. Caccini tells us himself that he learned, in the short years with Bardi, more about music "than in thirty years of contrapuntal study." It is true that, at first, Caccini did not write in the new recitative style, but his works clearly disprove his exaggerated claim of prolonged contrapuntal study. The extant compositions of Galilei, on the other hand, disclose a skilful madrigal- and motet-composer who did not forego the pleasures of contrapuntal fireworks of which the madrigalists were so fond, and which the *Camerata* despised. On the evidence of his own compositions, Galilei's utter contempt for counterpoint reveals itself as an academic pose assumed under the influence of Bardi. Bardi was also responsible for the sweeping statement that the renaissance was the age of counterpoint, the baroque the age of the art of singing. In modified form this distinction has survived to the present day in the opposition of counterpoint and harmony, or polyphony and homophony.

Bardi's definition of the renaissance as the age of counterpoint pure and simple ignored an essential part of its musical literature. The contrast between contrapuntal and note-against-note writing existed in the renaissance just as strongly as in the baroque. This contrast, moreover, was recognized by renaissance theorists, and one glance at the masses of Josquin shows how consciously it was employed. Actually both eras had in common the conflict of contrapuntal and chordal textures; they differed, however, in its solution. The renaissance solved the problem by part-writing—that is, by a set of balanced voices of almost equal importance, regardless of the texture. Thus the chordal and contrapuntal sections of a renaissance composition were united by the underlying principle of part-writing. Similarly, the baroque cannot be called the age of harmony pure and simple. The baroque found the solution of the conflict in a new interpenetration of contrapuntal and harmonic strands which led finally to the fusion of functional harmony and linear counterpoint in Bach's works, the crowning monuments of baroque music.

STYLISTIC COMPARISON BETWEEN RENAISSANCE AND BAROQUE MUSIC

The foregoing critique of renaissance and baroque theorists and their attempts to formulate the contrast of the periods in a nutshell makes plain why the generalizations of the time do not give us a true picture. The advocates of both schools had their axes to grind and bothered little about inconvenient facts. It must be admitted, however, that their generalizations contain a grain of truth, and can serve as excellent sources for understanding the trend of prevalent ideas that prompted the change from one period to the other. Yet the study of these sources would be of little value if it were not complemented by a rigorous stylistic analysis of the compositions themselves. The findings of both theoretical and practical studies must be checked against each other in order to arrive at a genuine understanding of the inherent traits of either period. In the following, the outstanding structural features of renaissance and baroque music will be briefly submitted to a comparative analysis.

The most striking difference between renaissance and baroque music comes to light in the treatment of dissonance, to which also Berardi drew attention in his books. The dissonance treatment is indeed the touchstone of the stylistic contrast, and it is here that changes in harmony and counterpoint manifest themselves most conspicuously. In renaissance music all dissonances came either in passing on the weak beat or else as suspensions on the strong beat. The harmonic result of the combination of voices was conceived as a conjunction of intervals rather than as the unfolding of one chord. This intervallic harmony of the renaissance was diametrically opposed to the chordal harmony of the baroque. If harmony was chordally conceived, it became possible to introduce a dissonant note against the chord at any time, provided that the chord as such was clearly outlined. The bass, which in baroque music supplied the chords, thus enabled the upper voices to form dissonances more freely than before. The resolution of the dissonance could be effected by leading the dissonant voice to the next chord tone by either downward or upward motion. This alternative illustrates the new melodic freedom of baroque music, which was no longer bound to the renaissance rule to resolve all dissonances by descending motion.

It is obvious that the treatment of dissonance in the renaissance put severe restrictions on the harmonic rhythm, that is, the change of harmony per unit of time. In a fast harmonic rhythm the renaissance composer could hardly use any dissonances, and for this reason all fast sections in triple time stood out for the sparseness of dissonances. The dissonance treatment of baroque music not only permitted a fast harmonic rhythm, but supplied the main technical means for the affective style of the recitative. The old dissonance treatment was conserved in baroque music only in the domain of the *stile antico*. Since the *stile antico* was bound up with church music, the absence of modern dissonance treatment was interpreted by baroque musicians as typical of the sacred style. Berardi criticized renaissance music from the viewpoint of this new standard and declared renaissance music to be inferior to baroque music because there was, as he says, "little or no difference in style between a motet and a madrigal." Here lies the root of the opposition between the sacred and the secular in music. The misleading idea that a certain style is in itself more proper for the church than any other came forth in the style-conscious baroque period, and the same idea continues to afflict us today. Berardi's statement of fact was correct only with regard to dissonance treatment, and his conclusion was based on an inapplicable standard. He was unable to see that the unity of style in renaissance music was the secret of its strength, not its weakness.

The baroque dissonance treatment depended upon a voice able to carry chords, and consequently the bass received more attention than ever before. Indeed the peculiar form in which the bass was made to serve the new function was as characteristic of the baroque period as its name: thorough-bass, or *basso continuo*. The baroque era begins and ends almost exactly with the thorough-bass era. For this reason, Riemann has not hesitated to call the baroque era *Generalbass-Zeitalter*. However, this term, if strictly interpreted, would not include the harpsichord and organ works of Bach which have no continuo, and is therefore too restricted. Nevertheless, the presence of the continuo is a clear indication of baroque style, and its absence, aside from keyboard works, is so exceptional as to require a special note by the composer.

The invention of the continuo was a symptom rather than a cause. With it all aspects of melody, harmony, and counterpoint appeared in a fundamentally changed perspective. For the first time there emerged in music history a harmonic polarity between bass and soprano, between harmonic support and a new type of melody dependent on such support. This polarity is the essence of the monodic style. With the new function of "accompaniment" relegated to the bass, the melody gained freedom and agility. How quickly the baroque composers realized the import of the polarity can be seen in Agazzari's novel distinction between fundamental and ornamental instruments. The fundamental ones were primarily the keyboard instruments and such others as could be used for the continuo. The ornamental ones were the melody instruments. The division of fundamental and ornamental function in the field of instruments directly paralleled the dualism of bass accompaniment and melody. The outermost voices acquired, in baroque music, a domineering position: bass and soprano furnished the skeleton of the composition. This structural contour was the essential part of the music, the rest could be filled in at the discretion of the improvising continuo player. It is significant that the filling-in could be left to improvisation because the structural contour was assured by the polarity of the outer voices.

The new type of melody differed from renaissance melody mainly in its internal structure and its rhythm. The limitations imposed on the renaissance composer as to upward and downward skips were no longer valid. The new dissonance treatment implied also new melodic intervals. Chromatic steps and, especially, augmented and diminished progressions were the earmarks of the early baroque style. All of these intervals were experimentally tested in the late madrigal which led from the renaissance to the baroque. The new intervals then became the stock in trade of the affective theatre style.

The change of melody and its interval structure was directly bound up with the new harmonic concepts. The intervallic harmony of the renaissance admitted only triads and sixth chords while all other combinations required suspensions. The polarity of bass and soprano opened the door to numerous novel harmonic possibilities which appeared to the conservatives of the time as the beginning of chaos. If the favorite augmented and diminished intervals were employed simultaneously, a rich vocabulary of altered chords resulted, highly characteristic of early baroque style. Seventh chords appeared on the strong beat without preparation. Early baroque harmony lacked tonal direction, it was fully occupied with the experimental exploration of chordal effects as such. The experiments in pre-tonal harmony led finally to a clarification in the creation of tonality.

Tonality may be defined as a system of chordal relations based on the attraction of a tonal center. This tonic formed the center of gravitation for the other chords. It is no mere metaphor if tonality is explained in terms of gravitation. Both tonality and gravitation were discoveries of the baroque period made at exactly the same time. The profound effects of the recognition of tonality persist even in the present-day search for a new and wider conception of tonality. In the period of tonal or functional harmony, musical interest was concentrated on the regulation of chord progressions. In renaissance music, harmony was restricted to the regulation of intervallic combinations. The progressions from any one combination to any other, or what in modern terminology would be called the chord progressions, were dictated not by a tonal or harmonic principle, but by the melodic laws of part-writing. Since the individual parts were in turn guided by the rules of the melodic modes, the intervallic harmony was indirectly governed by modality. The intervallic harmony of renaissance music was directed by modality, the chordal harmony of the late baroque by tonality. The experimental harmony of the early baroque strikingly exemplifies the transition from the earlier to the later conception of harmony. The harmony of the early baroque was already clearly conceived in terms of chords and therefore "modern," but it was as yet free from the directive force of tonality, and thus preserved a vestige of the renaissance tradition.

The rhythm of renaissance music was regulated by an even flow of beats, the so-called *tactus*. The movements of the parts and the various tempi were strictly bound up with the *tactus* by a mathematical system of proportions, in sacred music as well as in dance music. Syncopations and accents were achieved by duration rather than by dynamic stress. The baroque composers did not altogether discontinue this kind of rhythm, but they moved characteristically toward rhythmic extremes hardly, if ever, touched by the renaissance. In the affective recitative style the music was subservient to the spoken word so that the *tactus* became unimportant. A radical composer like Monteverdi at times discarded the beat completely and prescribed in his recitatives an affective delivery *senza battuta* (without measure). In the ears of the renaissance composer, such outrageous music had no musical rhythm at all because he was not able even to imagine a rhythm divorced from the regularity of the *tactus*. To the baroque composer the newly gained, extra-musical flexibility of rhythm deserved the highest praise because it allowed for the most slavish representation of the affections. But this is only one aspect of baroque rhythm. The composer also explored the other extreme in which the *tactus* was transformed to mechanically recurrent pulsations. They appeared first in dance music and then also in the stylized instrumental music. The concerto style of the late baroque, especially, exemplifies an almost ruthless exploitation of beats. Between the extremes of a free and a strictly mechanical rhythm, all intermediate stages of rhythm were used in baroque music.

With the change of renaissance to baroque all elements of musical structure gained new specific qualities, even if the single elements were common to both styles. Since the single elements depended on the structure of the whole, each one acquired a new meaning, as has been shown here in the discussion of dissonance treatment, the function of the bass, melody, harmony, and rhythm.

At the beginning of the baroque period, a novel stylistic element made its appearance: idiomatic writing. The baroque era consciously developed the idiomatic possibilities inherent in the instrumental and vocal media. The idiom-consciousness of the baroque era must be understood as another aspect of its style-consciousness, and nowhere does the difference between renaissance and baroque music come more openly to the surface than here. The renaissance conception of musical structure was premised upon part-writing which embraced vocal and instrumental music alike. By its very nature this conception did not stress musical styles idiomatic for particular instruments, and consequently the voices of renaissance music could be performed vocally or instrumentally, or, conversely, instrumental parts were often designated "to be played or sung" although no words were given. The fact that voice or instrument were interchangeable shows how strongly the emphasis rested not on the medium, but on the realization of the single parts.

Since the structure of the linear parts was more essential than the medium in which it was realized, the renaissance cannot be regarded as the age of the a-cappella style, as popular opinion has it. Renaissance and baroque have often been set apart, one as the age of the a-cappella ideal and the other as the age of the instrumental ideal. Like every oversimplification, this one, also, contained some truth, but it imputed a standard of medium-consciousness to renaissance music that was foreign to it. That voice and instruments were interchangeable even in church music can be proved by innumerable title pages calling explicitly for "the 'live voice' or instruments." The manner of performance was flexible and a matter of little concern so long as the part-structure was left untouched. Renaissance music allowed, principally, three possibilities: performance by voices alone, by instruments alone, and by the combination of voices and instruments, the most common of the three. A-cappella performance was only one possibility among others. Any classification of renaissance music that does not consider the doubling or replacement of voices by instruments is too narrow.

It was the baroque composer who developed the idiomatic characteristics of voice and instrument, and it was he who deployed them first in the *concertato* style of the early baroque. With his flair for coloristic effects, he also discovered the sensuous appeal of the a-cappella chorus, which would be ruined if instruments doubled the voices. Since doubling the voices was a common practice among the renaissance composers, they obviously did not yet fully recognize this appeal of the medium. The a-cappella ideal, which finds its most dignified expression in the *stile antico*, was a creation of the baroque. Moreover, the term a-cappella itself was coined in the baroque period. The example of the Sistine Chapel, so often quoted by historians as a typical case, is actually exceptional. The utilization of the pure a-cappella effect represented only one extreme of the idiom-conscious baroque, complemented by the other extreme: the strictly instrumental idiom.

Since *stile antico* and a-cappella style were practically identical in the baroque, it is easily understandable why the model of *stile antico*, the Palestrina style, was also seen in the light of the a-cappella ideal. It is an ironic misunderstanding that the sensuous effect of the a-cappella style, for which the renaissance showed little interest, has contributed to the mythical glorification of renaissance music. The modern controversy about the a-cappella ideal owes part of its confusion to the powerful survival of baroque ideas and prejudices.

The glowing sonorities of the a-cappella chorus were only one color on the rich palette of baroque idioms. The idiomatic possibilities of the solo voice were explored in the remarkable virtuoso singing of the early baroque, and then crystallized in the refined methods of the Italian *bel canto*. Vocal and instrumental ensembles sharpened the ear for the difference of vocal and instrumental idioms, consciously juxtaposed in opera, oratorio, and cantata. After Gabrieli and Schütz the choral idiom was distinctly divorced from that of the solo ensemble. The instruments, especially, gradually developed specific styles, notably the violin family, and to a lesser degree the wind instruments. Lute and keyboard music, too, became more idiomatic than before, and composers showed great resourcefulness in taking advantage of the peculiar aptitudes and weaknesses of the respective instruments. In renaissance music it cannot be decided categorically on the basis of the style whether the music was intended for voices or instruments, except for lute and keyboard pieces. In baroque music the musical style and, sometimes, even certain forms were bound up with the medium in novel fashion. Nobody can mistake the violin character of a concerto grosso by Vivaldi, which was conceived from the outset in this medium.

With the discovery of idioms in the baroque, new possibilities arose from the deliberate exchange of idioms between different instruments, or between instrument and voice. This transfer of idioms forms one of the most fascinating aspects of baroque music. Lute ornaments could be transferred to the harpsichord, vocal techniques could be imitated by the violin, and violin figuration could appear in organ music. In the late baroque a rich interchange and interpenetration of idioms can be observed which reached almost incredible complexity. Vocal and instrumental idioms were not fixed entities; they constantly influenced one another, developed analogous techniques, and the new idiom could in turn influence the original one. In the late baroque, voice and instrument often competed on equal terms and their idioms became almost undistinguishable. Here the exchange of idioms was carried to an extreme that seems to contradict the principle itself. However, paradoxically enough, the instrumental handling of the voice must be recognized as one of the vocal idioms of the time. The same paradox can be seen in baroque garden architecture, which forced shrubs and trees to grow in geometrical patterns or in the shapes of animals.

Baroque composers went a step further in the exchange of idioms and transposed entire forms, with all their stylistic peculiarities, from one medium to another. The church sonata could be transferred to the keyboard, the recitative could become an instrumental form, and the organ prelude could be projected into the choral medium. The transpositions presented each time a special stylistic problem which challenged the ingenuity of the composer. We cannot properly understand the impressive range of musical techniques in late baroque music without recognizing the tremendous importance of these transfer forms.

The preceding discussion has been summarized in the following table, in which renaissance and baroque music are contrasted in outline fashion. It will be seen that some of the old terms have been retained, but they can now be applied without being misunderstood. It goes without saying that the outline juxtaposes only the pre-eminent elements of each style and does not permit such misleading generalizations as "counterpoint *versus* harmony" which single out elements present in both styles.

RENAISSANCE	BAROQUE
One practice, one style	Two practices, three styles
Restrained representation of the words, *musica reservata* and madrigalism	Affective representation of the words, textual absolutism
All voices equally balanced	Polarity of the outermost voices
Diatonic melody in small range	Diatonic and chromatic melody in wide range.
Modal counterpoint	Tonal counterpoint
Intervallic harmony, and intervallic dissonance treatment	Chordal harmony and chordal dissonance treatment
Chords are by-products of the part-writing	Chords are self-contained entities
Chord progressions are governed by modality	Chord progressions are governed by tonality
Evenly flowing rhythm regulated by the *tactus*	Extremes of rhythm, free declamation and mechanical pulsations
No pronounced idioms, voice and instrument are interchangeable	Vocal and instrumental idioms, the idioms are interchangeable

The above outline seems to imply that the two styles can be contrasted as two disconnected and static units that have no internal development of their own. This implication is incorrect, but unavoidable. It must be remembered that the term "baroque era" is in itself an abstraction. A comparison that involves two abstractions must of necessity be general. For this reason it ignores the internal development of either era and also the works of transition which frequently show characteristics of both eras.

THE PHASES OF BAROQUE MUSIC

The music of the baroque era covers such contrasting figures as Monteverdi and Bach, or Peri and Handel. What these composers have in common seems rather insignificant in the light of what separates them. Yet what they share are, besides minor traits, the recitative and the continuo, two fundamental devices of baroque music. In their artistic application, however, the differences are again more important than the similarities. Only the internal history of the baroque era can offer a satisfactory explanation of the striking developments that unfold in the span between Gabrieli and Handel. The baroque style went through several phases that do not even coincide in different countries. They can be grouped into three major periods: early, middle, and late baroque. Although the periods actually overlap in time, they can roughly be dated as follows: the first from 1580 to 1630, the second from 1630 to 1680, and the last from 1680 to 1730. These spans indicate only the formative periods of the new concepts with which the previous ones may run parallel for some time. It must also be clearly understood that the dates apply only to Italy, from which baroque music received its main impulses. In the other countries, the respective periods began about ten or twenty years later than in Italy. Thus it becomes understandable that around 1730, when Italy had already turned to the *style galant*, Germany brought baroque music to its consummation.

A short characterization of the three periods will serve to elucidate their important differences with regard to style. In early baroque style two ideas prevailed: the opposition to counterpoint and the most violent interpretation of the words, realized in the affective recitative in free rhythm. With it appeared an extraordinary desire for dissonance. The harmony was experimental and pre-tonal, that is, its chords were not yet tonally directed. For this reason the power to sustain a longer movement was lacking, and in consequence all forms were on a small scale and sectional. The differentiation of vocal and instrumental idioms began, vocal music being in the leading position.

The middle baroque period brought above all the *bel-canto* style in the cantata and opera, and with it the distinction between aria and recitative. The single sections of musical forms began to grow and contrapuntal texture was reinstituted. The modes were reduced to major and minor, and the chord progressions were governed by a rudimentary tonality which restrained the free dissonance treatment of the early baroque. Vocal and instrumental music were of equal importance.

The late baroque style is distinguished by a fully established tonality which regulated chord progressions, dissonance treatment, and the formal structure. The contrapuntal technique culminated in the full absorption of tonal harmony. The forms grew to large dimensions. The concerto style appeared and with it the emphasis on mechanical rhythm. The exchange of idioms reached its highest point. Vocal music was dominated by instrumental music.

These phases of the baroque style must be kept in sight if the gap between Monteverdi and Bach is to be discussed. It might be argued that, in view of the stylistic differences within the baroque era, there is no need to retain the larger term "baroque era" at all. However, the comparison of renaissance and baroque music has shown that the baroque era as a whole differs from the renaissance era much more fundamentally than early, middle, and late baroque styles do among themselves. In spite of their particular qualities, the three styles are linked together by the inner unity of the period which comes to light only in a comparison on a higher level. It should also be noted that the distinction of the three stylistic groups within the baroque is made even more complex by the national styles which cut across the styles of the period. The recognition of national styles by baroque writers further illustrates their style-consciousness.

The question of renaissance *versus* baroque has been discussed so far on the basis of a comparative analysis. There remain, however, some characteristics of the baroque that do not fall into this category. They are incomparable with the renaissance because they are unique. A great variety of forms, techniques, and idioms was created in the baroque era for the first time in music history, providing a fund of musical material that has survived in various transformations to the present day. The baroque saw the first development of the opera, the oratorio, and the cantata; and the creation of the solo sonata, the trio sonata, and the chamber duet. It was the age of the prelude and fugue, the chorale prelude, and the chorale fantasy. It instituted the important forms of the concerto grosso and the solo concerto. The baroque reached the first peak in the history of opera in the works of Scarlatti and Handel, the first peak of the concerto in the works of Vivaldi and Bach, and the first peak of the oratorio in the works of Handel. The baroque created the unique dramatic *concertato* style of which Gabrieli, Monteverdi, and Schütz were the leading masters. It represents, finally, in the works of Bach, the greatest period of organ music, and likewise the greatest period of Protestant church music.

The heritage of baroque music has been so stupendous that it has, time and again, been a challenge to later generations. The recognition of the greatness of baroque music has developed slowly, beginning in piecemeal fashion at the end of the classic period. It rose during the romantic period, paradoxically, by way of misunderstandings, and has assumed impressive proportions today in the revival of baroque music. The relevancy of this revival to our musical life should not be explained as the result of a freak coincidence, nor by the fact that industrious musicologists have happened to unearth such music. It is significant that modern composers, consciously and unconsciously, return to formal and technical devices of the baroque style and make them serve a new function in modern music.

It must be pointed out, however, that the modern revival of baroque music is limited almost exclusively to works in late baroque style, and the music historian cannot help wondering whether a new legend is in the making which mistakes the late baroque style for baroque music in general. It is devoutly to be wished that the qualities of early baroque music, so frequently obscured by touched-up performances, will receive their well-deserved attention. Whether or not the new legend of baroque music will stand in the way of a more enlightened evaluation cannot yet be decided. However this may be, the revival of Handel operas, and the controversies about the "correct" performance of Bach, demonstrate that baroque music has ceased to be merely a historical issue. It has become a living force in the music of our day.

CHAPTER TWO

Early Baroque in Italy

THE BEGINNINGS OF THE *Concertato* STYLE: GABRIELI

MUSIC at the turn of the sixteenth century discloses a bewildering diversity of conflicting techniques, styles, forms, and terms which always characterizes a period of transition in music history. This diversity was gathered into a more unified style in the works of three pre-eminent composers who decided the future course of music: Giovanni Gabrieli, the master of church music; Monteverdi, the most universal composer of the early baroque; and Frescobaldi, the genius of keyboard music.

The first intimations of a stylistic change can be discerned in the Venetian school during the latter half of the sixteenth century. The music for double chorus, or *cori spezzati*, was brought to fame (not invented, as it is frequently claimed) by Willaert, choirmaster at San Marco, the architecture of which lent itself singularly well to such experiments. He introduced into music the elements of space and contrast, and the fashion of echo effects which was to become an important device in the hands of baroque composers. The spatial organization of a composition into two opposing bodies of sound was accentuated by the use of instruments together or in alternation with the voices. Whereas the *colla-parte* practice of the renaissance permitted that instruments substitute for or double vocal parts, a new practice appeared under the name of *concertato* or *concerto*, a term that became the veritable watchword of early baroque music. The term, probably derived from *concertare* = to compete, had at first various connotations and usually referred to competing or contrasted groups, or, most important, to the combination of voices and instruments. It occurred sporadically throughout the sixteenth century, but served as a title first in the *Concerti . . . per voci et stromenti* (1587) by Andrea and Giovanni Gabrieli. In the preface to his Penitential Psalms (1583) Andrea Gabrieli prescribed the use of instruments and voices "together and separately," but in both collections the particulars of the combination were left to the discretion of the performer, in keeping with the *ad-libitum* tradition of the renaissance. Toward the end of the century the term became fashionable, as for example in the *Intermedii et Concerti*, edited by Malvezzi (1591), and in three collections with the favorite title *Concerti ecclesiastici*, one with works by Andrea Gabrieli and other composers (1590), another by Banchieri (1595), and the third by Viadana (1602).

Malvezzi, who gave in his collection an unusually precise and illuminating account of the music for the wedding festivities of Ferdinand of Medici, recorded not only the colorful, varied vocal and instrumental combinations, but even the embellishments that the performers had improvised. The music ranged from instrumentally accompanied solo songs to polychoral compositions for instruments and voices.[1] Instrumental ensembles were called here "concerto" or even "concerto grosso." In his *Concerti ecclesiastici* for double chorus Banchieri supplied a rudimentary organ score for the first chorus only. The fact that there was an organ accompaniment justified in itself the title concerto, and all works with a chordal accompaniment were called "in *concertato* style" with the general implication of "modern style." It is symptomatic, however, that the *concertato* style developed first in the many-voiced compositions of the Venetian school where the aid of instruments was needed first. In the early *concertato* [2] a stylistic differentiation between instrumental and vocal writing did not yet exist. It took a composer of eminent genius like Gabrieli to realize the possibilities inherent in the new medium.

Giovanni Gabrieli (1557–1612) received his musical education from his uncle Andrea in Venice, probably served for a time in Munich under Lasso, and, when only twenty-seven years of age, became organist at San Marco, after he had·brilliantly passed the severe tests that every applicant to the coveted position had to take. Only comparatively few of Gabrieli's works appeared in print during his lifetime, notably Part I of the *Sacrae Symphoniae* (1597) containing vocal and instrumental compositions for six to sixteen voices. A definite stylistic change can be observed in his later works, all printed posthumously in 1615, as if by secret agreement. They comprise Part II of the *Sacrae Symphoniae* (six to nineteen voices), *Canzoni et Sonate* (three to twenty voices), and *Reliquae Sacrorum Concentum*. The last collection presents works by Gabrieli and Hassler, who maintained

---

[1] Examples in Kinkeldey, *Orgel und Klavier;* Goldschmidt, *Studien,* I; Schneider, *Anfänge des Basso Continuo;* and Haas, *Aufführungspraxis,* 119.

[2] Although there exists a definite if tenuous relation between the early and the late baroque meaning of "concerto," it seems advisable in view of the important stylistic differences to retain the form *concertato* for early baroque compositions and to reserve the other term for the concerto proper.

a lifelong friendship that began during their years of study with Andrea Gabrieli, and who died in the same year.

In his earlier works Gabrieli showed himself a consummate master of the magical effects of many-voiced texture. With an uncanny sense for color he wrote for as many as seven or eight real voices, interwoven in infinite variety. He combined choruses of different registers, thus heightening the element of space with that of color. Although instruments were not specified, the extreme range of the compositions from the low *C* to the high *a″* made them necessary, even if they had not been implicitly prescribed in the *Concerti* of 1587. A report of the time [3] specifically mentioned the "grand harmony" that was brought about by the mixture of voices and instruments in the Venetian church service. The early works preserved the even pulse of renaissance music; and in the harmonic and melodic progressions also there were only occasional hints of the future break with the renaissance tradition.

Gabrieli's later works, composed probably after 1600, breathe a revolutionary spirit affecting all aspects of composition: dissonance treatment, melodic design, rhythmic flow, the attitude toward the words, and the disposition of vocal and instrumental parts. The composer now seized upon the words with a fervor and intensity of affection unprecedented in sacred music. In the motet *Timor et Tremor* (Ex. 1 a) "fear and trembling" is represented in

Ex. 1.a. Giovanni Gabrieli: *Timor et tremor.*

[3] Pirro, *Schütz*, 19.

graphic fashion with literally "breathtaking" rests, jagged figures, descending sixths, augmented "false" intervals, and strong dissonances; this music violates nearly all rules of sixteenth-century counterpoint. The beginning is based on a contrast motive characterized by closely juxtaposed notes of very long and very short time value. The nervous and discontinuous rhythm of these motives is totally at variance with the continuous flow of the old style. The motet *Exaudi deus* (1565) by Andrea Gabrieli (Ex. 1 b) shows by comparison the restraint with which a true renaissance composer set the same words.[4]

Ex. 1.b. Andrea Gabrieli: *Timor et tremor.*

The radical stylistic change in the works of Giovanni Gabrieli can also be observed if his two settings of *O Jesu mi dulcissime* are compared.[5] In Part I of the *Sacrae Symphoniae* the text is conservatively treated as double-chorus; in Part II it appears again, set this time in modern fashion with contrast motives. The invocative gesture of the beginning contains rhythmic and melodic tensions unknown to renaissance composers. Contrast motives with their intricate and crotchety rhythms represent one of the characteristics of the *concertato* style. They appeared first in the madrigal of the late sixteenth century and were then transplanted to sacred music by Gabrieli. He conferred on the playful and experimental motives of the madrigal an affective profundity not dreamed of before.

With regard to dissonant combinations, too, Gabrieli ventured boldly into uncharted regions, as can be seen in his insistent use of "false" intervals—that is melodic dissonances not tolerated in renaissance music. He underlined significant words by diminished fourths, tritones, and augmented triads which appear usually in first inversion. This chord-form, which presents the diminished fourth between the upper voices, became a commonplace, if not a hackneyed, device in the pre-tonal phase of baroque

---

[4] Compare also Lasso's motet on these words, CE 19, 673.
[5] Winterfeld, *Gabrieli* III, 122, and *Chorwerk*, 10.

harmony to which the works of Monteverdi, Frescobaldi, and Schütz attest. The favorite place for sharp dissonances was the cadence.

Gabrieli's late works contain specific directions as to the combination of voices and instruments although they do not appear very consistently. Several compositions are scored for voices and instrumental ensembles, consisting of violins, *cornetti* (wooden trumpets), trombones, bassoons, and bass viols in highly coloristic combinations. In *Suscipe clementissime* a six-voice chorus stands against a second chorus for six trombones; and in *O gloriosa virgo* he combined three choruses in the bass register which set a model for similarly somber compositions of Monteverdi and, especially, Schütz. Each chorus was a self-contained unit that could be placed separately in the various lofts and galleries of the church.

The magnificent twelve-voice motet *In Ecclesiis* [6] calls for an orchestra of three *cornetti*, viola, and two trombones, and contrasts a full chorus or *cappella* with a solo quartet. Here Gabrieli took the first step toward a differentiation between choral and solo ensemble, fully developed by later baroque composers. The end of the composition should be noted as one of the rare occasions where he tentatively differentiated the choral idiom from intricate soloistic *concertato* sections that could be performed only by trained virtuosi.

The instruments sometimes doubled the voices at the octave and sometimes moved independently in a concerted ensemble. The technique of extensive doublings in highest and lowest registers was first suggested by the mixture stops of the organ which Gabrieli transferred to the vocal setting. In compositions without specified orchestration, the selection of instruments was left to the arranger who made his choice according to the clefs, as we learn from a detailed account in Praetorius' *Syntagma Musicum*. In compositions for three and even four choruses Gabrieli achieved vibrant sonorities and sweeping color effects that remind one of the monumental paintings of Tintoretto. The motets were punctuated by ritornelli, and joyful refrain passages on *Alleluia* in a lively triple meter, as indicated by the *proportio tripla*.[7] Repetitions of words, so ridiculed by the *Camerata*, served, like the sudden changes in tempo and the contrast

---

[6] HAM, no. 157; also in Winterfeld, *op. cit.*

[7] The meaning of the *proportio tripla* has been frequently misunderstood by modern conductors, as for example in the recording of *In ecclesiis* by Gabrieli. The change to triple meter always coincides with an accelerated tempo because the three beats of the new meter take only the same time as the two beats of the preceding meter.

motives, the purpose of emphatic intensification. Gabrieli's style was on the whole still contrapuntal, although the many-voiced settings tended toward a chordal, though not yet tonal, conception of voice-leading. With the increase of voices the harmonies became more and more static, but they were vivified by cascades of figuration and coalescent imitations within a stable chord. This neatly imitative "miniature" or "open" work, one of the main devices of the *concertato*, presents in spite of its contrapuntal appearance an essentially rhythmic sham-polyphony.

The fervor of word interpretation breathed the mystic and aggressive spirit of the counter-reformation which overwhelmed the faithful with gigantic structures, be it in architecture, painting, or music. The nervous sensibility of Gabrieli's novel style inspired only a few kindred Italian composers to continue his path, notably Monteverdi, and among lesser figures Bernardi, Capello, Giovanni Bassani, and Leoni. The true heir to Gabrieli was his greatest German disciple, Schütz, and it is not without symbolic significance that Gabrieli on his deathbed bequeathed his sealing ring to him as if he had a premonition that this pupil would carry the torch that he had lighted.

MONODY: PERI AND CACCINI

The emergence of the *stile rappresentativo* or recitative about the year 1600 has often been regarded as the most important turning point in the entire history of music. The deliberate renunciation of polyphonic style set an end to the renaissance and brought to the fore a new principle: the solo melody with a chordally conceived accompaniment. Doni, one of the theorists of the new style, called it *monodia* in analogy to the music of the Greeks which the opera had ostensibly revived. However, the change was not entirely so abrupt as is commonly assumed. Solo singing with lute (or viol) accompaniment was a well-established practice in the renaissance, as shown in the collection of Bossinensis (1509, printed by Petrucci) and in numerous later publications in Italy, France, England, Spain, and Germany. These solo songs should not be regarded as monodies because the style of accompaniment was, at least potentially, polyphonic. The early examples of solo singing lacked both the harmonically conceived melody and the supporting bass, designed from the outset to carry harmonies. Likewise absent were the affective approach to the words and the virtuoso embellishments. Only the aggregate of these characteristics makes solo song a monody. While it is true that the renaissance musicians knew solo song, they had no monodic style; however, it is within the orbit of the solo song of the renaissance that monody was first experimentally approached.

Monody counts among the few musical innovations in which theory antedates practice. It was a creation of learned intellectuals, the *Camerata* in Florence. The first manifesto of the monodic style is contained in the *Dialogo della musica antica e della moderna* (1581) by Vincenzo Galilei, the father of the astronomer Galileo. The emphatic praise of Greek music and the equally emphatic condemnation of counterpoint herald the change with regard to music and word. Caccini says in a passage, based on Plato, that the composer had to start with the consideration of "word, rhythm, and then tone, not the other way around." It is amusing that Greek music, completely unknown at the time, served merely as a foil for the new affective approach. In his first experiments with monody Galilei set two strikingly expressive texts, the lament of Ugolino from the *Divine Comedy* and a passage from the lamentations of Jeremiah. The music is not extant, but we know that it was greeted with a mixture of enthusiasm and ridicule. The most active musical members of the *Camerata* were, besides the Roman gentleman-composer Cavalieri, Peri and Caccini, both, significantly, virtuoso singers. In their operas the recitative assumed its definitive form, and the *basso continuo* appeared for the first time. These represent the main technical devices of the monodic style.

The *basso continuo* or thorough-bass, easily the most successful system of musical shorthand ever devised, outlined a chordal accompaniment by a figured bass line, the realization of which was left to improvisation. It required at least two players, one to sustain the bass line (string bass, or wind instrument) and the other for the chordal accompaniment (keyboard instruments, lute, theorboe, and the popular guitar). Frequently, however, there were more than two fundamental instruments; massed ensembles in fact characterize the early baroque continuo practice.

The roots of the continuo accompaniment lie in the organ scores, such as we have met with Banchieri. The organ doubled whatever happened to be the lowest part in a polyphonic composition. The primitive organ score consisted of this composite bass line and the highest part and naturally needed no figures. The slavishly doubling bass, known as *basso seguente,* can be traced back well into the sixteenth century. Unlike the *basso seguente,* the continuo was essentially an instrumental support that did not necessarily double the lowest voice but furnished a foundation of sustained harmonies to it. The transition from the *basso seguente* to the thorough-bass can be seen in the *Concerti* of Viadana who restricted the figures of the bass to accidentals and who depended more on the old polyphonic style than on the monody. The evolution of the *basso continuo* was a slow process in which many composers participated and did not result from the ingenuity of Viadana alone, as the early German theorists assumed who drew their information exclusively from Italian sources.

The realization of the bass called for diminutions of the ornamental instruments which lent "beauty to the concerto," as Agazzari puts it. He gave as the main reason for the adoption of the continuo that it was convenient and highly suitable for the recitative in *stile moderno*. The care with which the bass was figured varies greatly from fully figured parts over sparse figuration to completely unfigured basses that vex modern editors. Not by any means does an unfigured continuo imply that the bass should not be realized; it merely leaves the entire responsibility to the performer, as occurs regularly in the Italian opera of the middle baroque. Italian composers were generally far laxer in this respect than their German and French colleagues.

The embellishments in the continuo realization were only part of the general practice of improvised ornamentation, the vocal form of which was known at the time as *gorgia*.[8] A monody would remain a bare skeleton were it not for the affective delivery of the singer and his embellishments, which served here not merely an ornamental but a structural function. The ornamental diminutions of contrapuntal compositions, which noticeably increased toward the end of the renaissance, adumbrated the heavily embellished baroque style. The ornaments that Malvezzi recorded for the *Intermedii e Concerti* in Florence illustrate the virtuoso performance of madrigals by such famous singers as Vittoria Archilei who also sang the title role in *Euridice*. It is significant that the music of the *intermedii* was composed not only by masters of the madrigal like Marenzio, but in part also by the creators of monody.

In the lengthy introduction to the *Nuove Musiche* Caccini gave a survey of the *gorgia* practice not without vainly exaggerating claims as to his own part in the "invention" of the ornaments, many of which he merely borrowed from renaissance treatises on diminution. The ornaments may be

[8] Examples in Goldschmidt, *Lehre von der vokalen Ornamentik*.

divided into five groups: 1) the *passaggi* or scale passages, in wide use
during the renaissance; 2) the *accenti* which consisted in breaking up the
full length of the note by *ports de voix* or *portamenti*, beginning usually
a third below the written note; 3) the *esclamatione*, the attack and release
of a tone by means of dynamic nuances like increase and decrease on a
sustained note; 4) the *groppo*, our modern trill; and 5) the *trillo*, a rapid
measured tremolo on the same note, not to be confused with what we
call trill today. In addition to these stereotyped ornaments, characteristic
figures, such as the Lombard rhythm ♫. ♫., further enhanced the
affective style of singing by their sobbing effect.

The accumulation of intricate embellishments so strongly affected the
rhythm that the music could no longer be performed in strict time. Whereas
the ruffled rhythms of Gabrieli's contrast motives were still based on an
even beat, the monody destroyed the continuity of the beat and thus arrived at what we call the *tempo rubato*. It is highly significant that Caccini
actually called for the *tempo rubato* by the name of *sprezzatura* (non-
chalance), a term that has been frequently misunderstood.[9] In a model
recitative of the *Nuove Musiche* (Ex. 2) Caccini made precise indications
where and how ornaments should be applied. At a parlando section he

Ex. 2. Caccini: Monody *Deh, dove son.*

prescribed "not in strict time, as if speaking in music with the above mentioned *rubato*." The recitative cadences, which always emphasized the

[9] Winterfeld, *Gabrieli*, Haas B, and Dorian, *History of Music in Performance* give
an erroneous explanation of the term.

divisions of the text by conspicuously slow note-values and stereotyped suspensions of the fourth, time and again interrupted the flow of the declamation and gave it a very sluggish pace.

The monodic style varied between two extremes: it appeared either as a recitative with a static bass that amounted practically to a series of pedal points, or as a song-like melody with a more vivid bass line. The first was typical of the emphatic style of the opera from which the *stile rappresentativo* (theatrical or actor's style) derived its name. Peri was the first to handle the pedal-point basses in masterly fashion.

Although monody was established in the opera, the main stream of musical life flowed through the innumerable collections of monodies that publishers threw on the market. The opera reached only the small, if select, audiences at the courts. How quickly monody gained a foothold in musical life can be inferred from the fact that many singers, dilettanti, and women suddenly emerged as composers of monodies.

Luzzaschi's *Madrigali per cantare e sonare* for one to three voices (1601), although composed in a conservative style, are characteristic of the trend toward few-voiced composition. His collection marks the transition from polyphony to monody. The solo madrigals are accompanied by a fully written-out harpsichord part which doubles the voice part except for the written-out *gorgia*.[10] Aside from the opera, monodies proper began with Caccini's *Nuove Musiche* (1602).[11] This famous publication opens a long procession of similar collections of which only the outstanding ones are here listed by title:[12] Megli (1602), Brunetti, Rasi (1608), India, Peri (*Varie Musiche*, 1609), Bellanda, Benedetti (1611), Rasi (*Musica di camera e chiesa*, 1612), Pace (1613), Saracini (1614), Marco da Gagliano, Falconieri (1616), Giovanni Steffani,[18] Belli, Filippo Vitali, Monteverdi (Seventh madrigal book, 1619), Landi, Grandi (*Cantade ed Arie*, 1620), Tarditi, Frescobaldi (*Arie*, 1630), and Ferrari. Most of these composers published their works in Florence, the center of the early monodic style, or in Venice.

[10] Examples in Kinkeldey SIMG IX; GMB no. 166; Wolf, *Music of Earlier Times*, no. 48.

[11] The imprint gives the year 1601 according to the old calendar. For examples see ICMI, 4 and HAM no. 184.

[12] See the bibliographical list of monodic publications in Ambros-Leichtentritt, *Geschichte der Musik* IV, 777. For emendations and additions see Eugen Schmitz, *Jahrbuch Peters*, 1911, 35 ff.

[18] Steffani's *Affetti amorosi* (1618) have been reprinted by Chilesotti, *Biblioteca di rarità musicali* III.

The third, though more conservative center was Rome with Cifra, Fres-cobaldi, Quagliati, and Vitali. The collections were, of course, most un-even with regard to musical value; the pre-eminent masters were Peri, Monteverdi, Grandi, Saracini, and the Roman Frescobaldi.

Although Claudio Monteverdi (1567–1643) was not associated with the early monody, his dramatic genius gave it the spark that turned it into living music. He was taught in the severe school of Ingegneri and acquired here the respect for polyphonic part-writing that he never entirely forsook throughout his life. He served first as string player and singer at the court of Mantua (after 1590) and from 1613 to his death he held the position of greatest prestige in Italy, that of chapel master at San Marco in Venice. Aside from the *Orfeo* all his printed secular music was published in only nine madrigal books and a few smaller collections. His non-operatic mono-dies appeared in his late madrigal books, especially the seventh and eighth.

The expressive power of his monodic style became proverbial through his *Lamento d'Arianna*,[14] published at the time as an independent monody. The seventh madrigal book contains among other monodies the *Partenza amorosa* and the famous "love letter," to be sung in free tempo and speech rhythm, *senza battuta*. They are distinguished by an austere and impas-sioned tone, noble declamation, and somber inflections of the key note by the lower major second, characteristic of Monteverdi's recitative begin-nings. In *Con che soavità* he combined the monody with a *concertato* ac-companiment of three instrumental choruses which demonstrate in their strikingly sensuous effect his superb sense of color.

Peri was perhaps the only one of the early monodists who could com-pare with Monteverdi's solemn monodic style. The affective handling of lugubrious subjects was recognized by Bonini as the peculiar talent of Peri whose immovable pedal basses set the model for Monteverdi. One of the most radical composers of monodies was the gentleman-composer Saracini; strongly under the spell of Monteverdi, he surpassed him in the unconventional use of dissonances. Only a dilettant would show so little concern about the accepted standards of harmony. His works abound in experimental clashes, cross-relations, and appoggiature, sounded not only in succession but even simultaneously. In the monody *Tu parti* (Ex. 3) he imaginatively expanded the Phrygian cadence on *ahi lasso* by a simul-

---

[14] GMB no. 177. No references to reprints will be given if the works of the com-poser have appeared in a complete edition. For these consult the list of editions in the appendix. Recently an anonymous *Lamento d'Erminia* has been found (in a manu-script also containing Arianna's lament) which Torrefranca and Bonaccorsi (*Inedito*, Rome, 1944, no. 2) ascribe to Monteverdi.

taneous cross-relation (*b* against *b* flat) which almost obliterates the underlying chord progression. Monteverdi rarely went to such extremes, but
even he could not avoid a certain monotony for which the recitative was
openly reproved by Mazzocchi and della Valle. Another fault of the
recitative was its lack of formal distinction. Whereas on the opera stage
action and vivid rendition mitigated the monotony and made up for the
amorphous structure, it soon became apparent that, if performed in the
chamber, the recitative needed some formal clarification.

Ex. 3. Saracini: Monody *Tu parti.*

Tu par - ti,   tu par-ti   ahi las - so,   ahi las - so!

Three methods of achieving musical coherence can be found in the early
monodic literature. The first consisted of recurrent refrain sections or
repetitions, as appear in Caccini's celebrated *Amarilli* [15] and in the *Lamento
d'Arianna*. The second method introduced snatches of imitation between
bass and melody, which not only integrated the parts but also freed the
bass from the rigid pedal-point style. It represents the first encroachment
of polyphonic devices on the monody and can be found more frequently
in sacred than in secular monodies. The third and most characteristic
method was what may be called strophic variation. Here the same bass
was retained for every stanza while progressive variations of the melody
created the impression of a through-composed composition. Although
the recurrent bass could be slightly varied, it guaranteed practically the
same harmony for each strophe. The first statement of a strophic variation
should not be mistaken for the "theme" of subsequent variations because
all strophes stood on the same level. On the other hand, the bass cannot
be regarded as a true ostinato because it still lacked distinctive rhythm
and the easily recognizable profile of a ground bass. The strophic variation
holds a place of its own halfway between theme and variation and the
ostinato bass.

Nearly all monodic collections contained at least a few strophic variations. Caccini divided his *Nuove Musiche* into twelve madrigals and ten
arie. All compositions of the first group are through-composed, in keeping
with the tradition of the madrigal. Upon closer examination most of the

[15] GMB no. 173.

arie turn out to be strophic variations.[16] In Grandi's musically most attractive *Cantade ed Arie* the "cantatas" are strophic variations, the "arias," however, strophic continuo songs. Grandi presented in his strophic variations as many as nine more or less free statements of the bass, above which the melody could unfold with remarkable ease (Ex. 4).[17] Although Cac-

Ex. 4. Alessandro Grandi: Strophic variation (cantata) *Apre l'huomo.*

cini and Frescobaldi called strophic variations simply *arie,* Grandi's term cantata soon found acceptance in the collections of Berti, Turini (both 1624), Rovetta, and Sances. The emergence of the term was not without significance since these variations did indeed foreshadow the chamber cantata, especially if instrumental ritornelli separated the single statements. Such ritornelli occur often in the collections of Peri, Monteverdi, and Berti.[18] The very first "madrigal" of Monteverdi's seventh book, the monody *Tempro la cetra,* is cast in form of a fourfold strophic variation, preceded and concluded by an instrumental sinfonia. Between each statement of the bass a ritornello, taken from the second part of the sinfonia, intervenes. The whole represents a diminutive chamber cantata to which many parallels can be found in the monodies of the time.

[16] See GMB no. 172, and Riemann HMG 2:2, 25.
[17] For another example see Lavignac E II:5, 3395.
[18] Example in Adler HMG, 437.

The strong trend toward the chamber cantata was also manifested in dramatic dialogues in which two singers alternated in recitative style or even joined in short duets. The dialogues also were often punctuated by ritornelli or "toccatas," as Quagliati called them, which consisted at times of nothing more than a section for continuo alone. Pastoral or moral subjects familiar from the madrigal and lauda literature, like *Tirsi e Filli* (Megli, Bellanda), *Tirsi e Clori* (Monteverdi), *Anima e Corpo* (Bellanda), *Anima e Caronte* (Barbarino), *Anima ed Amore* (Grandi), or even *Adone, Venere e Pastore* (Grandi) now invaded the monodic style, and even in strict solo songs the composers hinted at the dialogue by means of playful echoes. In all phases of baroque music the echo had an important dramatic, and even structural, function.

TRANSFORMATION OF THE MADRIGAL: MONTEVERDI

Toward the end of the sixteenth century two factors impinged on the madrigal style: on the one hand, the simple rhythm and chordal texture of the dance song, the villanella, and canzonetta; and on the other hand, deliberate harmonic experiments that destroyed the balance of voices and led to the polarity of bass and soprano. Both factors precipitated the disintegration of the madrigal proper. Only the last stage of its development, represented by the latest period of Marenzio, and by the works of Gesualdo and Monteverdi, belongs to the history of baroque music. In this phase the dramatic and expressive tendencies, always latent in the form, were pushed to affective extremes. These reveal a conception of dissonance no longer consistent with renaissance ideas, as Monteverdi recognized when he spoke of the *seconda prattica* in music. He and his follower, the theorist Berardi, insisted on the fact that the new dissonance treatment was the essence of the new style.

Unlike the monodists Monteverdi approached his stylistic crisis through the madrigal. Like the *Camerata,* he laid down the axiom of the dominance of the words over the harmony (see the postscript to his *Scherzi musicali*), but it led to a diametrically opposed result because he applied it *to* polyphony, not *against* it, as the Florentines did. Monteverdi thus appears as a Janus-faced composer between two eras, conservative with regard to the preservation of polyphony in principle, but revolutionary with regard to its transformation in practice.

The fundamental turn from intervallic to chordal harmony, from prepared to unprepared dissonance, took place around 1600. Dissonances, notably sevenths and ninths, needed no preparation, if justified by affective words such as *crudo, acerbo, lasso,* and all the other household words of the madrigal vocabulary. The chromaticism of the earlier madrigal had paved the way for melodic dissonances, but even the daring and highly chromatic madrigals of Cipriano de Rore and the startling enharmonic ventures of Marenzio were couched in terms of triads and the traditional dissonance treatment. It is only in the works of the Prince Gesualdo di Venosa (c. 1560–1614) that the madrigal went through its crisis.

This singularly individual composer was passionately interested in radical harmonic experiments which, though still prompted by affective words, actually became an end in themselves. Gesualdo traced each nuance of the text so slavishly that the entire musical fabric fell into small fractions of diffuse musical ideas. The lack of musical continuity was reinforced by two distinct textures, the one characterized by an interplay of rapid motives in the simplest triadic harmony, and the other by extreme harmonic combinations, paralleled only in the modern music of our own day. The contrast of textures corresponded to Gesualdo's two manners of textual representation: notions of space and movement were depicted by vivid rhythmic motives, whereas affective notions were set with melodic and harmonic chromaticism. He did not omit any of the rhythmic and harmonic figures, musical similes, and intellectual contrivances that the madrigalists had made famous. His advanced dissonance treatment resulted from the cumulative effect of passing notes employed simultaneously in the different voices, and extreme melodic steps, including even such exacting intervals as diminished octaves (*Ardita Zanzaretta,* sixth madrigal book). In the absence of a direct key-feeling Gesualdo experimented with the limitless possibilities of pre-tonal harmony. It is, however, symptomatic that his most outlandish chord progressions involved consonant chords, and that his pungently dissonant combinations were, as a rule, achieved by suspensions. He clung to contrapuntal part-writing, even if worn thin by harmonic experimentation. Of his six books of madrigals [19] the first four showed the gradual complication of the harmonic idiom, but only the last two presented unprepared combinations more frequently.

Monteverdi did not emulate Gesualdo's radical chord progressions but, in his later works, surpassed him in the freedom of dissonance treatment. Like Gesualdo he approached the new style step by step. While the first four books of madrigals merely hinted at the future, the turn became

[19] Examples in ICMI, 14; GMB no. 167; Torchi AM IV; HAM no. 161.

obvious in *Cruda Amarilli* (c. 1600), which achieved notoriety by the vitriolic criticism it provoked in *L'Artusi overo delle imperfettioni della moderna musica*. Monteverdi countered Artusi's objections to unprepared dissonances with the reference to the "second practice." He defiantly put the contested madrigal at the head of his fifth madrigal book (1605) and promised to expound his views in a treatise with the pointed title *Seconda Prattica overo delle perfettioni della moderna musica*—a promise that he unfortunately did not keep.

The new harmonic approach to the madrigal which made unprepared dissonances possible inevitably obliterated the equivalence of voices and thus exploded the madrigal from within. The continuo exploded the madrigal from without. Both factors were responsible for the structural transformation of the form to what may be called the *concertato* or continuo madrigal. Monteverdi used the continuo for the first time in his fifth book, in which all madrigals have a continuo,[20] though it is obligatory only for the last six. Optional use of the thorough-bass was typical of the transition period. Many times composers "revised" their early works by adding a continuo in order to bring them up to date, as Monteverdi did when his fourth book was reprinted (1613). The added part was usually nothing more than a *basso seguente* that did not substantially alter the old madrigal texture.

In the continuo madrigal proper the musical structure depended on the harmonic support of the instrumental part, and on such polyphonic features as had survived from the old madrigal. The fusion of these elements resulted in the typical texture of the continuo madrigal: an imitative, open-work and airy dialogue of voices that were no longer bound to form a complete harmony by themselves. Like the old madrigal, the continuo madrigal favored five voices, but with the general trend to the few-voiced *concertato,* those for two or three voices also became fashionable. These few-voiced continuo madrigals, also known as chamber duet and chamber trio, combined two or three highly integrated voices in the same register with a continuo. The trio setting of the chamber duet must be regarded as one of the happiest and most influential innovations of baroque music.

As a collection by Salomone Rossi (1602) shows, the continuo madrigal arose almost coincidentally with monodic publications. It flourished throughout the first half of the century, especially in Venice with Grandi and Rovetta; in Rome, where the old madrigal survived longer than per-

---

[20] The continuo of all but the last six madrigals has been omitted in the complete edition.

haps any other center, with Anerio, Sances, and Tarditi; and in other places with Agazzari, Rasi, Pace, and Priuli. The last two may be singled out as especially talented composers of *concertato* madrigals, but none in the above list runs a close second to Monteverdi.

In his first continuo madrigal, *Ahi come a un vago sol* (fifth book, no. 8), Monteverdi seized with marvellous assuredness on the possibilities of the trio setting and the contrast between delicate solos and full choral sections. The soloistic nature of the few-voiced sections can be inferred from the intricate part-writing and the written-out *gorgia*. The interpenetration of monodic and madrigalistic features came naturally to Monteverdi because he arrived at the continuo through the madrigal. How close the seemingly unrelated fields were for him is demonstrated in his fascinating arrangement of the *Lamento d'Arianna* as a five-voice madrigal (sixth book) which gives revealing hints as to his own realization of the celebrated monody.

Instruments were used frequently, either for sinfonie and ritornelli, or for the *concertato* accompaniment of the voices, as for example in *A quest'olmo* (seventh book). The seventh book, not accidentally entitled "Concerto," presents, aside from the monodic cantatas, expansive continuo madrigals for four to six voices, and chamber duets and trios in a sparkling *concertato* style. Not a single madrigal in the old sense is represented here.

The chamber duets fall into two categories. The one betrays its derivation from the monody by its declamatory rhythm and its static basses. The other is written in a much steadier rhythm on a sequentially running bass of obviously instrumental origin; it occurs so frequently with Monteverdi that it can almost be taken as his trademark. The chamber duets of the Florentine, Venetian, and Roman monodists parallel and sometimes even antedate those of Monteverdi. Brunetti's *Euterpe* (1606) contains a very early example of the form (Ex. 5), and others can be found with Peri (*Varie Musiche*), Caccini (*Fuggilotio*), Quagliati (*Sfera armoniosa*), Belli, Giovanni Valentini, Frescobaldi, and Sances. Some of these pieces were only nominally duets and stood closer to monody than to the continuo madrigal because they called for a soprano, and a bass that merely doubled the continuo.

The Roman composer Quagliati made the unique, though hardly successful, attempt to bridge the gap between monodic and madrigal literature with hybrid madrigals (1608) [21] that could be performed either as

---

[21] See the example in Einstein, AM VI. 115.

continuo madrigals or else as monodies. Eager to satisfy both the conservative and the progressive taste, Quagliati lost in these "double-duty" madrigals the *concertato* texture of the parts without gaining the flexibility of the monodic style. He neatly contrasted the choral performance (*musica piena*) with the solo performance (*musica vota*), fully aware of the possibilities of the vocal medium. The first explicit document illustrating the

Ex. 5. Brunetti: Chamber duet *Amor s'io non.*

polarity between *concertato* and a-cappella performance in secular music was Domenico Mazzocchi's madrigal book of 1638 containing both continuo and a-cappella madrigals. In the preface the composer rather diffidently advocated a-cappella performance and, symptomatically, we find here, for the first time in print, symbols for such choral idioms as crescendo and decrescendo. The fact that the madrigals appeared in score for study purposes, not for actual performance, discloses that Mazzocchi sang the swan song of the old madrigal. From now on it held an essentially antiquarian interest, characteristic of the *stile antico* in secular music. Cenci also pleaded in his madrigals (1647) for a-cappella singing. Mazzocchi and Cenci did not yet use the term "a cappella," which originated in church music, but they advocated an a-cappella ideal in conscious opposition to the *concertato* ideal.

The *Madrigali Guerrieri et Amorosi* (eighth book, 1638) acquaint us with the fully developed *concertato* style of the mature Monteverdi. Considerable progress in dissonance treatment comes to light in passages with simultaneous cross-relations, not otherwise frequent in his harmonic vocabulary.[22] Monteverdi enriched the *concertato* style by an important innovation: the *stile concitato* (style of agitation) in which he turned the measured tremolo of the *gorgia* to dramatic effect. As the title of the madrigal book suggests, the first part of the collection deals with terror, ire, and bellicose affections, represented by exclusively triadic melodies and fanfare motives in rapidly repeated notes. In its vocal form the *stile concitato* was characterized by a Rossini-like parlando; it gained, however, its greatest and truly elemental force as orchestral tremolo, ever since Monteverdi the favorite (and by now rather threadbare) device for dramatic agitation. The principle of the *stile concitato* was so simple and so devoid of harmonic interest that only a composer of Monteverdi's imagination could make something of it. Sometimes he presented a single triad for more than thirty measures in a measured tremolo or in other rhythmic patterns.

Although the string tremolo occurred even before Monteverdi in the sonatas of Marini, Usper, and Riccio, he was the first to realize its dramatic possibilities. His *Combattimento di Tancredi e Clorinda* (composed 1624, published in the eighth madrigal book) is noteworthy not only for the introduction of the *stile concitato* and such other dramatic devices as *pizzicato* and *morendo,* but primarily for its form. The tragic story, based on the famous passage from Tasso, is related by a *testo* or narrator, and is articulated by an orchestral *concitato* accompaniment that depicts the prancing of the horses and the battle noise in a highly stylized, yet uncannily suggestive manner. At climactic points the actors themselves begin to sing in *stile rappresentativo.* With the *Combattimento* Monteverdi established the secular oratorio; its partly narrated and partly enacted, semi-operatic performance is clear testimony to the all-embracing influence of the opera on other vocal forms.

THE INFLUENCE OF THE DANCE ON VOCAL MUSIC

Beside the higher forms of vocal art music we find, in the early baroque period, less demanding types, all in varying degree affected by dance music. The unpretentious canzonettas and villanellas of the late renaissance, which had found in Gastoldi and Vecchi their most spirited masters, had never seriously been touched by polyphonic writing. The addition of

[22] See for example CE VIII, 242 where a simultaneous cross relation appears to the words *dolorosi guai* (painful wails).

the continuo transformed the canzonetta to the continuo song, the vogue of which continued to the end of the seventeenth century. The favorite medium of the continuo song was the trio setting in which the voices were no longer bound by the melodic restrictions of the sixteenth century. The strophes were usually separated by ritornelli, written on typical instrumental basses in brisk rhythms. With the trend toward monody solo songs also became popular, sharing with the monodic style only the combination for voice and continuo, but not its affective character. Continuo songs can be found even with Caccini and Peri under a confusing variety of traditional names, such as canzonetta, villanella, madrigal, or aria. Monteverdi, whose early canzonettas still reflect the renaissance tradition, published numerous continuo songs, mostly for two voices, in his *Scherzi musicali* (1607) and in his later madrigal books. The strongly rhythmic character of these compositions points toward the French chanson; the rigidly maintained verse patterns may be a reflection of the *vers mesuré* with which Monteverdi came in contact during his stay in France. He expressly acknowledged his debt to French music not only in the preface to the *Scherzi* but also in the designation *canzonetta alla francese*.

One of the most intriguing patterns of the dance song was the hemiola rhythm, an old feature of the Burgundian chanson, faithfully preserved in baroque music. It consists of a more or less regular alternation between 3/4 and 6/8, or 3/2 and 6/4 time, not indicated by the meter signature. Since six units in a bar can always be felt as either 3 x 2 or 2 x 3 beats, the hemiola should not be misrepresented as syncopation. In his drinking song *Damigella* Monteverdi consistently alternated between 6/8 and 3/4 on the basis of the following text pattern:

The hemiola rhythm is often obscured by the signature C which in early baroque music had not yet necessarily a metrical, but rather a mensural meaning. It signified merely that the beats were divided by two, but it did not determine the number of beats in the measure. The harmonic rhythm and the cadences must be carefully examined in order to establish whether the piece moves in duple or triple meter. Modern editors have too often neglected this precaution with the result that they have overlooked upbeats and forced triple meter into the straitjacket of 4/4.[23] Mon-

---

[23] Nearly half of all the *Scherzi musicali* have been incorrectly barred by Malipiero, the editor of the complete edition which leaves much to be desired with regard to accuracy. The mistakes are not always so obvious as that in *Lidia spina* (CE X, 56)

teverdi's canzonetta *Amarilli* (Ex. 6) illustrates the hemiola alternation of 3/2 and 6/4 time. The bouncing repeated notes at the end of each phrase, and the dissonant cadences with parallel seconds or *échappé* notes belong to the stock in trade of the continuo song.

Ex. 6. Monteverdi: Canzonetta *Amarilli onde.*

The canzonetta style increasingly affected both the monodic and the *concertato* literature. In the few-voiced collections all transitional stages between the plain dance song and the monody can be observed. In these compositions relics of short imitative sections in madrigal style, affective recitative passages, and snatches of dance-like melodies were fused together within a single composition, *e.g.* Monteverdi's *Eri già.*[24] This juxtaposition of recitative and canzonetta anticipated the future distinction between recitative and aria in the opera. The influence of canzonetta style can also be felt in certain ground basses of the chamber cantata. In contrast to the stagnant basses of the strophic variations, they betrayed their closeness to the dance by a lively rhythm, concise melody, and sequential structure, as can be seen in Monteverdi's canzonetta *Amor che deggio far.*[25]

Aside from the freely invented ground basses of the chamber cantata, certain traditional bass melodies, some of which went back to renaissance music,[26] served as the basis for vocal and instrumental variations or furnished the harmonic foundation for the improvised singing of popular

which must be barred, in spite of its C signature, in 3/4 time with upbeat. The edition illustrates better than any other example the pitfalls of editing old music. It shows that even a person of unquestioned musicianship fails to grasp the musical essentials if confronted with patterns not familiar from later styles.

Riemann, who was the first to draw attention to the conflict between meter signature and rhythm, pressed his point when he tried to force it also on music that lacks the regularity of beat, such as the monody and the opera recitative. The ostensible 5/4 time that Leichtentritt (Ambros, *Geschichte der Musik,* IV, 563) reads into Monteverdi is due to a misinterpretation of the hemiola. Real 5/4 and 7/8 time does, however, occur with Giovanni Valentini.

[24] CE X, 80.
[25] CE VII, 182.
[26] See Einstein, SIMG XIII (1912), 444, and RMI 41 (1937), 163; Gombosi, *Rassegna Musicale* VII (1934), 14.

poetry (*ottave rime*), described in Calestani's *Modo di cantar ottave* (1617). The most frequently used basses included the *passamezzo antico*, the *romanesca*, the *folia*, the *passamezzo moderno*, and the *ruggiero*, the first three of which were obviously closely related (Ex. 7).

Ex. 7. Traditional ground-bass melodies.

The basses were only skeletal melodies each note of which appeared on the first beat of every measure or every other measure, thus guiding the succession of harmonies. In each statement of the variation melody and bass were strongly varied by figuration. Since this variation technique combined in singular fashion elements of the strophic variation and of the *basso ostinato*, it cannot easily be classified. In view of the fact that the harmonic scheme was the only stable element, the procedure may be called a variation on ostinato harmonies.

The long list of early baroque composers who wrote vocal variations on ostinato harmonies includes Caccini, India, Cifra, Dognazzi, Domenico Mazzocchi, Monteverdi, Landi, Giovanni Steffani, Filippo Vitali, Milanuzzi, Frescobaldi, and Sances. Caccini's *romanesca* in the *Nuove Musiche* and that of Landi [27] represent the florid type of variation that called for a solo virtuoso. In Monteverdi's four variations on the *romanesca* (seventh book) the freely treated bass supports an exceptionally fine *concertato* duet with skilfully handled dissonances. The *folia* occurs in the vocal collections of Steffani and Milanuzzi.

A more recent group of ground basses appeared around 1600 under the name of *ciacona* (chaconne) or *passacaglia*. They consisted of concise and often sequentially constructed ideas. Unlike the melodies of the *passamezzo*

[27] Riemann HMG 2:2, 91.

family the chaconnes were unquestionably strict ostinato basses, relentlessly repeated a great many times throughout the entire composition with
little or no melodic variation. Transpositions of the ground bass occurred
only exceptionally in early baroque chaconnes. Although obviously instrumental in nature, they could serve equally well as the basis for a continuously varied vocal melody. The chaconne basses moved in triple meter and
were governed by the interval of the fourth. The archetype was the descending tetrachord in its three forms: minor, major, or chromatic, of which
the chromatic was the latest to be used extensively. A fourth type consisted
of a sequence of fourths and a cadence formula (Ex. 8). Other basses combined the four types, varied the rhythms, inverted the direction of the intervals, or used lively figuration.

Ex. 8. Chaconne bass patterns.

It is striking that no early baroque theorist is known to have commented
on the widespread use of chaconne basses. The composers often used the
terms chaconne and passacaglia indiscriminately and modern attempts to
arrive at a clear distinction are arbitrary and historically unfounded.[28]
Although it seems certain that the chaconne was an exotic dance of the
Spanish colonies, its musical origin and its name have not yet been satis-
factorily elucidated. The first type of bass may have been originally the
discant of the *romanesca* beginning, which in turn became a bass itself.
The minor form of the tetrachord (the first type) appeared preferably in

---

[28] The *Harvard Dictionary of Music* proposes an equally arbitrary, but perhaps
useful, distinction according to which the term chaconne would be reserved for ostinato harmonies, the term passacaglia for ground basses. It should be noted, however,
that the early baroque usage seems to favor exactly the opposite distinction. Most
chaconnes adhere to the four types of basses mentioned above, whereas the passacaglia has often no recognizable ostinato, but merely recurrent rhythmic patterns and
harmonies, as for example the *Cento Partite sopra Passacaglio* by Frescobaldi (TAM
V).

In middle and late baroque music the chaconne often assumed the characteristic
dotted rhythm of the saraband in contrast with the smooth ternary rhythm of the
passacaglia themes, but there was no difference in the technique of variation. The
first book of Frescobaldi's *Toccate d'Intavolatura* (1637) contains a piece remarkable
for its dissonances and for the fact that the composer consistently alternates between
chaconne and passacaglia. In this case neither one has a clearly stated ground bass.
The reason why Frescobaldi took pains to designate the parts as chaconne and passacaglia respectively is obscure.

mournful pieces and plaints, as for example in Monteverdi's pathetic *Lamento della Ninfa* [29] which carries the significant remark: to be sung "not in strict time, but according to the affection." Equally noteworthy is his highly imaginative chamber duet *Zeffiro torna*,[30] which Schütz later arranged in a *contrafactum* setting. It is built on the fourth type, also used for vocal chaconnes by Frescobaldi, Sances, Negri, Manelli, and Ferrari.[31] In these variations the voice moved with striking independence; its phrase divisions often overlapped those of the bass and lent to the setting a flowing, if complex, continuity.

Vocal dance music was also incorporated in the stage ballets of the period which, fashioned after the French *ballet de cour*, were transplanted to Italy by Rinuccini, the first librettist of the opera. In contrast to the spectacular intermezzi of the renaissance these *balletti* had a continuous plot, or at least dramatic episodes, and were composed in monodic style and interspersed with instrumental and choral dances. The ballets began with an *intrada* and were concluded by a *retirada* for the dancers; they contained, of course, a great deal of dance music for the stage, which, however, did not fall into the stereotyped patterns of the social ballroom dance. Of Monteverdi's numerous ballets only a few have come down to us. The *Ballo delle Ingrate* (eighth madrigal book), the grisly plot of which may have prompted some remarkable dissonance in the music, leans heavily, in its somber recitatives and pathetic choruses, toward the opera. The pastoral dialogue *Tirsi e Clori* (seventh book) is rounded off by a choral dance. The *ballo* for Emperor Ferdinand III (eighth book) presents after the *"entrata"* strophic variations in monodic style. Its imposing ballet for five voices and two instruments, a masterpiece of choral variations on a recurrent, slightly varied bass, eloquently bespeaks Monteverdi's most mature *concertato* style.

EMANCIPATION OF INSTRUMENTAL MUSIC: FRESCOBALDI

Three general principles govern the instrumental music of the early baroque: multisectional structure with regard to form, extensive variation

[29] CE VIII, 288.
[30] CE IX, 9. The text of this duet is not identical with the sonnet by Petrarch that Monteverdi set in his sixth book of madrigals. Only the first words are the same.
[31] Riemann HMG 2:2, 64.

with regard to melodic procedure, and polarity between bass and upper voices with regard to texture. The advent of the thorough-bass brought only to completion what had lain latent in the dance music of the sixteenth century: a running and patterned bass above which the parts could freely unfold. This principle of the trio setting was generally adopted in instrumental music. Sequential bass patterns were so prominent that, were it not for the transpositions to the various degrees of the scale, they would actually have become ground basses. Such quasi-ostinato basses form one of the most important resources of baroque music. Wherever static, motionless basses appear in instrumental music of the period they are borrowed from the monodic style and attest to the lively interchange between instrumental and vocal idioms.

The immense variety of instrumental music can be reduced to three categories: (1) dance music, (2) idiomatic instrumental forms of rhapsodic character, and compositions on a *cantus firmus,* and (3) forms derived originally from vocal models. Baroque dance music consisted of dances that had survived from the renaissance and new types added in the course of the seventeenth century. We learn from the dancing masters Arbeau and Caroso not only that a great variety of dance and step patterns was often covered by the same name,[32] but also that the pavane and galliarde had gone out of fashion. Although they had ceased to be social ballroom dances or *balli* they persisted as stylized dance music characterized by complex melodic structure and sophisticated texture.

Social dances were, of old, performed in pairs, the "stepped dance" in a moderate duple meter and the "leapt dance" in a nimble triple meter; occasionally a third dance followed in a still faster tempo. Musically, the second dance was only a rhythmically varied transformation of the first. The basic pair, which may be called a "varied couple," formed the nucleus of what later became the variation suite. The oldest varied couples, the *passamezzo* and *saltarello,* and the pavane and galliarde, were succeeded by the more recent allemande and courante or *corrente.* Other types of the time included the *brando* (= French *branle*) in duple meter, the saraband in triple meter, and the *canario* in compound meter with dotted notes. The distinguishing characteristic of these dances was not their melody but their typified rhythmic pattern. The same melody served in the varied couple for both allemande and courante. The *polacca* and its *corrente* by Marini (1629), composed for chamber ensemble in the favorite trio setting, clearly illus-

---

[32] For a discussion of the individual dances and their steps see Sachs, *World History of the Dance.*

trate the melodic identity and rhythmic contrast in a typical varied couple (Ex. 9).

Ex. 9. Marini: Varied couple *Polacca* and *Corrente*.

In dances for keyboard instruments the variation was also applied to the single dance, each section of which was repeated in the manner of the English virginalists with ornamental variations, as the works by Picchi show.[88] Dance music was written for every conceivable medium, for an *ad-libitum* combination of strings, especially violins. This newcomer among the instruments was particularly appropriate for the dance because of its penetrating sound. Also wind ensembles (*cornetti*, flutes, recorders, and bassoons) or keyboard instruments, lutes, and guitars were used. Nearly all composers listed below in connection with the sonata published dance music along with their canzonas and sonatas. The innumerable dance collections of the time either presented the varied couples in their proper order, or lumped all dances of the same type together, leaving the selection to the discretion of the player. The latter practice shows that the dance suite was not yet conceived as a cyclic form; there was actually no generic name for a dance collection. The term "suite" did not yet exist and the term *sonata da camera* was not restricted to dance music. The latter term, already used in Merula's *Sonate concertate da chiesa e da camera* (1637), had no formal implication, but a purely functional one. *Da camera* denoted "fit for the chamber," as distinct from "fit for the church." Dances were the only type of instrumental music not tolerated in the church.

A set of sectional variations on bass melodies like the *monicha, ruggiero, tenori da Napoli,* and the *passamezzo* group, was fittingly called partita, a term that became synonymous with suite not before the late baroque period. Such instrumental bass variations and also the various strict

---

[88] TAM V, 90; Chilesotti, *Biblioteca di rarità musicali* II, HAM, no. 154 b.

chaconnes belonged largely to stylized dance music. Written for one or two concerting instruments, they formed an important part of early baroque chamber music. The elevated atmosphere is suggested by the contrapuntal interplay of the parts and the exacting demands on violin technique. The sonatas by Buonamente (1626) contain a number of variations, not always identified as to their origin, for example *Cavaletto zoppo* (Ex. 10), which turns out to be based on the *passamezzo antico*.[84] Buona-

Ex. 10. Buonamente: Variations *Cavaletto zoppo*.

mente's partita, which becomes progressively more lively and difficult, clearly illustrates the light-handed dialogue of the instrumental *concertato* and the integration of the bass into the trio setting.

Unlike the vocal variations, each section of the partita strictly maintained fixed patterns of figuration, such as dialogue in complementary rhythms, triplets, upbeat motives, and scale passages, which for the entire era furnished an inexhaustible reservoir of patterns. Also Merula's chaconne for two violins [85] (built on the fourth chaconne type) and the variations on the *romanesca* or the *ruggiero* by Salomone Rossi,[86] Merula,[87] Buonamente, Marini, and Frescobaldi deployed them with great imagination. It should be noted that the ternary rhythm of the *romanesca* was often disguised by the mensural signature C. Both Marini's *romanesca* for violin [88]

[84] The ritornello to Monteverdi's canzonetta *Dolci miei sospiri* (CE X, 52) is also based on the *passamezzo antico*.
[85] Riemann HMG 2:2, 123.
[86] *ib.* 88 and 94.
[87] Example in OCM.
[88] Torchi AM VII, 13; also HAM, no. 199.

and Frescobaldi's highly florid keyboard variations [39] are incorrectly barred in modern editions.

The dance music for chamber ensembles and for keyboard was far surpassed in quantity by the dance collections for lute and guitar which, like the sheet-music of our day, contributed most to the dissemination of popular dances. The Spanish fashion in Italy brought a speedy victory of the noisy guitar over the dignified lute. The simplified guitar notation which indicated in shorthand fashion a set of about a dozen chords by single letters is, perhaps, the most striking symptom of the change to chordal thinking. This primitive tablature, introduced by Montesardo (1606), replaced the tradition of the polyphonic *punteado* playing by the chordal strumming, the *rasgueado* playing, which enabled the dilettanti of modest ambition to play a continuo or the latest dance hit in a few easy lessons.

The rhapsodic forms of instrumental music, the toccata, *intonazione*, and prelude or preamble, were essentially improvisatory solo music. They represented the first really idiomatic forms of keyboard and lute music. Toccatas for ensembles of wind instruments, like the introduction to Monteverdi's *Orfeo,* were survivals of an earlier practice. The toccata or "touch piece" was characterized by rhapsodic sections with sustained chords, rambling scale passages, and broken figuration over powerful pedal points which abruptly alternated with fugal sections.

Giovanni Gabrieli and Diruta, the author of the important organ method *Il Transilvano,* were in their toccatas still dependent on the model of Andrea Gabrieli and Merulo. The new style appeared first with the Neapolitans Trabaci [40] and Mayone and, above all, with the greatest genius of Italian organ music, Frescobaldi (1583-1643). This eminent pupil of Luzzaschi made of the toccata a vehicle of great affective tensions. What used to be a mere alternation of chordal and fugal textures in the toccatas of Merulo became in the hands of Frescobaldi a calculated dramatic contrast, enhanced by the experimental dissonances or *durezze* that distinguish his keyboard style. His toccatas had several functions: they supplied music for the Mass (the elevation of the host) and other liturgical occasions; they served as rhapsodic preludes to larger pieces, or were compositions of considerable length in their own right. The introductory toccatas or *intonazione* were designed to set the pitch for the singers.

[39] TAM IV, 20.
[40] Torchi AM III, 365, and TAM V.

As organist at St. Peter's in Rome, Frescobaldi cultivated also the old form of organ improvisation on a Gregorian *cantus firmus*. Throughout the baroque period the organ alternated with the choir in the so-called *alternatim* practice which assigned to the organ an important liturgical function. The sections of the chant for which the instrument substituted, notably the alternate verses of the psalms and the magnificat, were known as versets. The versets treated the chant with considerable latitude; they varied from strict *cantus-firmus* settings with running counterpoint to fugal paraphrases of the plainsong in motet style. Frescobaldi's thoroughly contrapuntal approach, which may have been reinforced by a visit to Flanders in his youth, is best exemplified by the *Fiori Musicali* (1635), a strictly liturgical collection, the severity of which so much impressed Bach that he copied it in its entirety in spite of the difference in religious denomination. Frescobaldi presented here organ music for three Masses in form of *cantus-firmus* settings and free toccatas, ricercars, and capriccios. He transformed the traditional counterpoint by a highly sensitive chromaticism, a brilliant keyboard technique, and an affective *tempo rubato*. In his preface he exhorts the performer to "find out the affection of the passage" before playing it, to vary the tempo "in the madrigal manner," to give the rapid passages relief by phrasing, and to retard the cadences. In its lack of tonal direction the iridescent harmonic language of Frescobaldi can be compared with that of Gesualdo. In spite of the rich harmonies there was little modulation because the "wolf note" of the meantone tuning ruled out keys with numerous accidentals.

The fugal forms that originated in the imitation of vocal models constituted the core of the instrumental music of the time; they were the ultimate sources for the future development of both fugue and sonata. The motet and the French chanson served as prototypes for the ricercar and the canzona (*canzon da sonar*) respectively. Both forms finally merged in what we call fugue today, after the fugal procedure had crystallized in late baroque music. At the beginning of the baroque era instrumental music had become fully emancipated from vocal music. Ricercar and canzona, now instrumental compositions in their own right, were no longer dependent on the intavolation of vocal settings. While they retained the multisectional structure of their models, the absence of text made new methods of formal extension necessary. Here again, the answer was variation; if consistently applied it led to the variation ricercar and the variation canzona.

The strictly fugal ricercar, which was characterized by concise themes in long note values as used in the motet, could be either polythematic or monothematic. The first type consisted, like its vocal model, of as many sections as there were themes; each one was stated in a short fugal exposition, but with occasional recurrences of the first theme in augmentation or diminution, as suggested by the original meaning of the term *ricercar* = to seek again. The second type, often designated as *sopra un soggetto*, was the variation ricercar which subjected its theme to extensive variation in two distinct manners. In the first, the theme itself was modified rhythmically and melodically and stated in as many fugal expositions as there were variations. In the second, the theme was kept relatively constant, but was combined successively with new counter-subjects. The latter type came closest to the monothematic fugue of the Bach era. Both types of variation ricercar were established by Frescobaldi; he continued in his early works the tradition of the polythematic ricercar, represented by Giovanni Gabrieli and Merulo, but gave distinction to the form in his later collections [41] by his imaginative variation technique and his new harmonic vocabulary. The theme of his memorable *ricercare cromatico* (Ex. 11) which appears with various countersubjects seems to defy in its bold intervallic progressions any constriction of a mode or key.

Ex. 11. Frescobaldi: *Ricercare cromatico.*

Frescobaldi made no clear distinction between ricercar and fantasia, a term that at the time did not yet have the connotation of a rhapsodic free form, but merely implied the freedom from a vocal model. The same laxness of terminology can also be seen in a number of ricercars which would more properly be called toccatas or *intonazione* because of their nonimitative texture. Although the ricercars appeared in collections for harpsichord or organ they betrayed their organistic style by pedal points in the bass or a middle voice.

Ricercars were also printed in part books for chamber ensembles or even for voices; as the designation *da cantar o sonar* indicates the line of de-

[41] The three fugues, printed in Torchi AM III, 245 under the name of Frescobaldi, are spurious.

marcation between vocal and instrumental performance was as yet rather fluid. A special, but inferior, kind of ricercar for two or three textless voices without continuo was used for didactic purposes as vocalizations for singers (Metallo, 1624). It was a survival of the old-fashioned *bicinium* of the renaissance and should not be confused with the modern chamber duet.

The canzona differed from the ricercar in its sprightly themes which favored tone repetitions, typically "pianistic" figuration, and the stereotyped ♩♫♩ rhythm of the chanson beginning. Less rigidly contrapuntal than the ricercar, it contained several contrasted sections of imitative and chordal texture. The early baroque composers, especially Frescobaldi, pushed this contrast to such an extreme point that the canzona fell into a variegated quilt pattern of ten or more sections in varying character, tempo, and texture. The nervous discontinuity of these "quilt canzonas" was diametrically opposed to the even flow of the renaissance canzona. The canzonas by Merulo, Banchieri, Mayone, Trabaci, and Cifra, published before 1620, tended to be polythematic and those of Frescobaldi also followed at first the same trend. However, Frescobaldi gave new perspective to the form by the introduction of variation. In the variation canzona the contrasted sections were unified by the variation of a single theme, as in the variation ricercar. Frescobaldi separated the sections by expressive *adagio* cadences in free tempo with written-out trills and presented his themes in many imaginative transformations (Ex. 12).

Ex. 12. Frescobaldi: Thematic transformations of *Capriccio sopra un soggetto*, 1624.

Although countersubjects in double counterpoint were not uncommon in the canzona, it was on the whole written in a light-footed style and not by accident were its themes sometimes derived from popular songs. Canzonas contrived on such artifices as the solmisation hexachord, a clever *obbligo* and an ostinato motive with rapid counterpoint, were called "capriccios." A partita and a capriccio by Frescobaldi, both based on the *rug-*

giero, clearly show the difference between a set of formal variations and a fanciful contrapuntal treatment of the same subject.[42]

Canzonas for chamber ensembles appeared frequently under the title "sinfonia" or "sonata." These forms did not essentially differ from the canzona; they began, however, not necessarily in fugal style, but in a stately chordal manner. The many-voiced ensemble canzonas reached their highest development in Venice where sumptuous polychoral compositions for two to four choruses in a resplendent orchestration were used for occasions of state. The many-voiced canzonas were written for solo ensembles. The modern "orchestral" reinforcement of one part by a great number of players, was not yet in general use, and when it occurred it was especially marked *a cori,* as in Banchieri's *Moderna armonia* (1612). Giovanni Gabrieli's canzonas and sonatas called for as many as twenty-two voices and his famous sonata *Pian e Forte* [43] contrasted two choruses in echo manner. Besides Gabrieli a host of composers wrote in this brilliant style, notably Merulo, Guami, Massaini, Banchieri, Viadana, Canale, Mortaro, Merula, and Frescobaldi. Most of these names are represented in the Raveri collection (Venice, 1608) which contains among other remarkable compositions one for sixteen trombones. The modernists among these composers, such as Frescobaldi and Grillo,[44] leaned toward the quilt canzona. The ensemble canzonas were significant also from the formal point of view, because they sometimes anticipated in their echo technique the principle of the concerto. An eleven-voice canzona [45] by Gabrieli so clearly sets a "tutti" in rondo fashion against a highly figurative "concertino" of a few instruments that it may be called the first realization of the concerto-grosso principle. Another canzona [46] in which Gabrieli assigned the echo optionally to the organ, foreshadows the solo concerto.

By far the most important group was formed by the few-voiced canzonas from which the vast literature of the baroque sonata—the term is merely an abbreviation for *canzon da sonar*—took its origin. The few-voiced sonatas called for from one to four melody instruments and continuo. While the many-voiced canzonas hardly needed their optional *basso seguente,* the few-voiced sonatas were based in principle on a dualistic setting that could not dispense with the continuo.

The terminology of the sonata literature has created considerable con-

[42] TAM IV, 38 and 70.
[43] GMB no. 148.
[44] Riemann HMG 2:2, 127.
[45] IM II, 118.
[46] IM II, 180.

fusion. According to the most consistent usage the sonatas were distinguished by the number of essential parts, including the continuo, as sonatas *a due, a tre, a quattro*. Since, however, the continuo was often taken for granted, the sonata *a due* was also called solo sonata, a term that has a misleading connotation today. And while the sonata for two ornamental instruments was known usually as trio sonata or sonata *a tre*, the corresponding vocal form was inconsistently termed chamber duet, obviously because of the difference in medium between the upper parts and the bass. The performance even added to the confusion because the continuo required at least two players, so that the "solo sonata" called for three, the trio sonata for four players. It must be remembered that the number of structural parts in baroque chamber music did not coincide with the number of performers, and that the continuo was always understood, so much so that the exceptional sonatas for violin solo without accompaniment were always expressly marked *senza continuo*.

Stylistically, the sonata stood between two influences, the dance and the monody, and both in conjunction rapidly displaced what had survived of the original canzona elements. The sonata developed the virtuoso idiom of the violin, the brilliant tone of which supplanted the soft timbre of the viol family, better suited to a polyphonic than a dualistic setting. Only the agile *cornetto* could rival the newcomer.

Violinistic idioms were conspicuous especially in the sonatas for one violin and continuo, first written by Fontana [47] (d. 1630) and the resourceful Biago Marini (1597-1667), probably the pupil of the former. These two were soon followed by Frescobaldi, Farina, Buonamente, Nicolaus a Kempis and others. The virtuoso character of the solo violin sonata made itself felt not only in the fiery scale passages, the wide skips, the use of high positions, rarely used in ensemble music, but especially in the astonishing transfer of vocal idioms to the violin. In Marini's sonatas we find static basses, Lombard rhythms, recitative-like passages, and *gorgia* ornaments such as the *trillo* or tremolo that clearly bespeak the influence of the monody. The tremolo, which appeared first in the sonatas of Marini,[48] Usper, and Riccio, and slightly later also with Buonamente, Possenti, Giovanni Valentini, and Merula, was frequently only suggested by the characteristic term *affetti*. In spite of the absorption of monodic elements the sonatas retained an essentially instrumental style by virtue of the continuous rhythm of

---

[47] Example in Iselin *Biago Marini,* Appendix; Wasielewski, *Instrumentalsätze,* XIII; HAM no. 197.
[48] GMB no. 182 and 183.

the solo passages, upbeat patterns, idiomatic figuration, and such violinistic features as double and triple stops, *pizzicato, col legno,* and use of harmonics. These technical resources were turned by Farina to playful programmatic purposes; he liked to simulate animal sounds (crowing, caterwauling, and barking) on the violin. Multiple stops, called by Marini *a modo di lira* after the polyphonic playing of the viol, were cultivated more in the northern countries than in Italy, and their use in the music of Marini possibly reflects German influence.

The trio sonata, the classic medium of baroque chamber music, was established in the *Sinfonie e Galiarde* (1607) by Salomone Rossi Ebreo (Ex. 13) and was extensively cultivated by Marini (*Affetti musicali*, 1617) and a great many other composers, notably Belli, Riccio, Turini, Merula (1637), Usper, Bernardi, Ottavio Grandi, Possenti, Frescobaldi, and Buonamente.

Ex. 13. Salomone Rossi: Trio Sonata, 1607.

In the trio sonata violinistic virtuosity was less pronounced than in the solo sonata and most was made of a spirited *concertato* dialogue in complementary rhythmic patterns, in which the bass increasingly participated. The trio setting for a duet of strings in the same range was most common, but the duet was extended to include a string bass, trombone, or bassoon which doubled the continuo only at cadence points, but otherwise maintained an independent virtuoso figuration, as in the sonatas of Castello.[49] Frescobaldi's canzonas contain an unusual violin sonata in which the

[49] Haas, *Aufführungspraxis,* 167.

written-out spinet part, largely independent of the continuo, supplies the second voice.[50]

The formal characteristics of the canzona held true in the solo and trio sonata only with some modifications. The sections of the trio sonata frequently coincided with the contrast of imitative and chordal textures, but in the solo sonata imitative texture was less prominent. The thematic transformation of the variation canzona appeared in the sonata literature less often, and when it did, less consistently than in the keyboard canzona. The variegated structure of the quilt canzona prevailed only in the first three decades of the century, after which a process of clarification set in. The initial fugal section was often preceded by a chordal introduction, a feature that became a fixture in the church sonata, but the very common term *da chiesa* of the title-pages had, until about 1650, hardly a formal significance, merely affirming the fact, now often forgotten, that the sonatas were church music. The main aim of the composer was contrast effected by changes in tempo, texture, and melodic content. The order of the sections defies a valid generalization; all that can be stated is that the sections were not all of the same weight, and that there was always at least one fugal section, and a slow one in stylized dance rhythm. Marini sometimes wrote only three movements and Salomone Rossi accidentally anticipated the form of the late baroque church sonata in his sonata *La Moderna*.

Sonatas for three and four melody instruments and continuo merely expanded the dualistic setting by placing a trio or a quartet against the continuo. These works emphasized closely spaced sonorities in the high register with frequent part crossings, a technique the opera composers transferred to the overture. Gabrieli seems to have set the model, as he did in so many other cases, in a sonata for three violins,[51] his only work based on the dualistic continuo setting. Also Rossi, Fontana, Marini, Frescobaldi, and Giovanni Valentini published sonatas of this kind in their collections. The valuable canzonas and sonatas of Valentini include a noteworthy "enharmonic sonata" with many distant modulations.[52] In the sonatas for four violins the instruments were often paired into rivalling groups that alternated in the manner of a miniature concertino with solo passages in virtuoso style, as can be seen in the works of Usper,[53] Fontana, Castello,

[50] *ib.* 173.
[51] OCM; also in Winterfeld, *Gabrieli* III.
[52] OCM.
[53] Example in Einstein, *Kretzschmar Festschrift*, 1918, 26.

Bernardi, Buonamente, and Neri.[54] These composers transposed the concerto elements of the many-voiced Venetian canzona to the few-voiced medium in a highly successful fashion. Their works furnish the tenuous link between the ensemble canzona and the concerto proper of the late baroque period.

THE RISE OF OPERA: MONTEVERDI

The music of the opera, which combined all the styles thus far discussed, cannot compare in quantity—and sometimes even in quality—with the vocal and instrumental chamber music of the period. The rise of the opera can only be understood in view of its literary background, the intermezzo and the pastoral drama; in both forms music was an important component. The intermezzo or *intermedium*, the main form of renaissance entertainment, was a musico-dramatic insertion in the spoken dramas performed at courtly occasions. The detailed description of the *intermedii* in Florence by Malvezzi (1591) gives us a good idea of the form. The main difference between opera and intermezzo lay in the function of music. The latter presented madrigals, motets, instrumental music, and ballets as self-contained musical forms and thus kept drama and music apart. The distinction between musical and literary forms clearly comes to light in the practice of first reciting and then singing the poetry.[55] Poetry, stage sets, machines, ballet, and music were all on equal footing. Many characteristic features of the intermezzo, particularly the invisible orchestra, the massed instrumental ensembles, and the spectacular machines, were retained in early opera. However, in contrast to the intermezzo, the opera permeated the drama with music by means of the continuous recitative. Although the spoken drama thus lost its identity as a literary form, the subordination of music to the word gave the drama in turn an unprecedented importance over the music. While the intermezzo juxtaposed drama *and* music, the opera blended them as a drama *in* music or *dramma in musica*. It was exactly this baroque mixture of artistic media that prompted the oft-repeated objections against the "impossible form of art."

Rinuccini fashioned his first libretto after the model of the pastoral drama. Not by accident do several early operas carry the title *favola pastorale* and interpret the classic mythologies and heroic tragedies in the pastoral spirit of the madrigal. The history of the opera opens with the performance

---

[54] Wasielewski, *Instrumentalsätze.*
[55] Rubsamen, Walter. *Literary Sources of Secular Music in Italy* (1943), University of California Publications in Music I, 1, 32.

in Florence of Rinuccini's *Dafne* (1597?),[56] composed by Peri (1561–1633). The music is lost, save two pieces in very primitive style by the amateur Count Corsi (in whose house the memorable première took place) and two by Peri, one of which is a recitative.[57] The first complete opera to survive was Peri's *Euridice* (likewise on a libretto by Rinuccini), staged during the festivities for the marriage of Henry IV of France and Maria of Medici in 1600. The composer himself sang the role of Orfeo. The libretto was set in the same year also by the ambitious Caccini, who by obscure machinations succeeded in having sections of his own music sung at the first performance. Throughout the baroque period composers frequently collaborated in operas —it was the rule in the intermezzo—but this early instance of it was hardly intentional on the part of Peri. Both Peri and Caccini published their own versions of the opera in 1600. Caccini's unabashed jealousy of Peri, which transpires with amusing clarity from the prefaces of his publications, casts serious doubts on his insistent boasts of being the "inventor" of the new monodic style, and on his belated assertion that he had also composed a *Dafne,* a claim not confirmed by the early historians of the *Camerata* circle.

The two compositions of *Euridice* are strikingly similar not only in the general application of monody, but also with regard to musical form. Both are marked by a radical purism of style, typical of the Florentine reform ideas. In no other operatic work does the continuous recitative so exclusively dominate the scene, although even Florentine purism could not rule out closed forms altogether. In the careful observance of speech rhythm, key scheme, and modulation the two scores are at times in complete agreement. Similarly, both scores depart from the recitative style at the same places, both set the prologue as a strophic aria, and both use corresponding refrain choruses. The bass of the recitative is written predominantly in the slow pedal-point style, the dramatic purpose of which is attested by Peri. He stated in the preface that he sustained the bass even against the dissonances of the singer, and moved it "according to the affections" whenever they made a change of harmony necessary. This remark discloses how seriously the Florentine took the merging of word and music. A similar statement can be found in the preface to Caccini's *Nuove Musiche.*

The rigid pedal basses of Peri, who established this technique, far surpass in their dramatic impact those of his rival. On the other hand, Caccini's

[56] The date has not been definitely established. Peri himself gave it as 1594. For a list of operas see Riemann HMG 2:2, 273, and Loewenberg, *Annals of Opera.*
[57] See Ghisi, *Alle Fonti della Monodia.* Corsi's music has been reproduced in facsimile in Wotquenne, *Catalogue de la Bibliothèque du Conservatoire de Bruxelles, Annexe I,* 1901, 46.

bass line is more varied, and his florid melodic ornamentation shows that more often than not the virtuoso singer got the better of the dramatic composer. This difference will become clear if two representative scenes are compared,[58] such as the entrance of Dafne who relates the death of the heroine—one of the climactic "messenger scenes" that became extremely popular in the operas to come. At no place are there strictly periodic melodies in the canzonetta style; and strophic songs, too, are extremely rare, being at variance with the dogma of the continuous recitative. The few refrain choruses are, in both operas, preceded by a rudimentary strophic variation. The choruses of the shepherds seem to have been written with a deliberately anti-contrapuntal intent. Only at a few places is the recitative punctuated by a musical refrain, as in Orfeo's plaint in the underworld. The perpetual slow recitative cadences which emphasize each line of the text inevitably adduce a monotonous effect, relieved only by Peri's attempt to evolve melodic figures for questions and exclamations.

The staging of *Euridice* in Florence prompted, in the same year, the performance in Rome of the "sacred representation" *Anima e Corpo* by Cavalieri. Its allegorical subject and semi-operatic staging set the work apart from the secular opera, though it shares its most important principle: the continuity of the music. Textual relations to the lauda, on the other hand, point toward the oratorio, at this time not yet an established form. The hybrid work has aroused a good deal of controversy as to its classification which, however, seems much less important than the analysis of the disparate stylistic traits that make it a hybrid. Created for the Jesuits, it was one of the many attempts of the counter-reformation to salvage from secular art forms all those features that lent themselves to the promotion of the *ecclesia militans*. Could the unmistakably secular style of the opera be applied to a sacred subject? This vital question was answered by Cavalieri whose work proved, as the preface affirms, that the modern style "can also move to pious affections."

Peri politely named Cavalieri as the first composer of monody though he admitted that his own was of a different style. Indeed, Peri's affective tone is conspicuously absent in the music of Cavalieri who may, at best, claim temporal but not artistic priority in the genesis of the *stile rappresentativo*. *Anima e Corpo* has a rather dry recitative, and, unlike the Florentine opera, numerous choruses, written in a primitive chordal style. One of its few musically arresting features is the fact that strophic variation is applied here sometimes to the choral sections.

[58] Riemann HMG 2:2, 189; Adler HMG 418; and Haas B 36.

The line of allegorical plays with music was continued by Agazzari's *Eumelio* (1606) and Kapsberger's *Apotheosis of St. Ignatius* which open the long list of spectacular pageants and school dramas that the industrious Jesuits performed at their Seminars in Rome and later also in other Catholic parts of Europe. Another venture in Rome was Quagliati's *Carro di fedeltà d'amore* (1606), staged entirely on wheels after the model of the Thespian cart.

After the establishment of the opera in Florence, Mantua came to the fore with the performance of Monteverdi's *Orfeo* (1607) in the *Accademia degli Invaghiti*. The dramatic genius of Monteverdi that had expressed itself hitherto in the medium of madrigals, finally found its most congenial form in this opera, unquestionably the first masterpiece of operatic history. Its stylistic complexity sets it sharply apart from all earlier operas. Accepting the radical *stile rappresentativo* of the Florentines and infusing it with his intense pathos Monteverdi realized at the same time the dramatic possibilities of the closed musical forms, the strophic aria, the dance song, the chamber duet, the madrigal, and the instrumental interlude, which the *Camerata* had discarded. In spite of their adherence to strictly musical laws these forms were made subservient to the drama.

The lavish orchestration which called for more than three dozen instruments has aroused the misconception that the *Orfeo* was revolutionary with regard to orchestration. Yet a specific orchestration was prescribed only exceptionally at a few dramatically important places. With its massed ensembles the *Orfeo* merely continued the tradition of the intermezzo; Monteverdi transferred it even to the realm of the continuo, as can be seen in the tremendous accumulation of fundamental instruments, typical of the early baroque continuo practice. Actually therefore, the orchestration represents a rather conservative feature and, paradoxical though it may sound, the use of the traditional closed forms constitutes the revolutionary element in the opera.

Compared with Rinuccini's *Euridice,* Striggio's libretto of the *Orfeo* appears as a monumental work. The first two acts are pastoral, the next two infernal; the last act shows Orfeo's ascent to heaven with Apollo appearing as *deus ex machina*. Originally the poet had provided a stark tragic ending, presenting Orfeo's death through the raving bacchantes; the temperate heroic finale that Monteverdi set to music may have been suggested by the composer himself who is known to have made significant changes in his librettos, and whose letters, like those of Mozart, are documents of supreme dramaturgical interest.

The pastoral and infernal spheres are sharply profiled in Monteverdi's music by coloristic means; the infernal regions are overshadowed by somber choruses in the low register, dark brass instruments, and the reedy and nasal regal serving as continuo instrument. The first climax occurs in Act II after profuse choruses and pastoral songs in the famous messenger scene in which Euridice's death is reported. The second climax is Orfeo's invocation of Charon, *Possente spirto,* an unforgettable monument to the power of music on a subject that quite fittingly held a peculiar fascination for the librettists of the early opera.

Monteverdi manifested his overpowering musico-dramatic insight in the broad pull toward unity which pervade the scenes or even acts. The entire first act is organized as a large structure by two choruses and an intermediate ritornello, both of which are later repeated in reversed order, and then followed by a threefold strophic variation for chorus punctuated by an imitative and dissonant ritornello. The extension of the principle of strophic variation to the chorus goes far beyond Cavalieri's modest attempts in this direction and in fact represents such a novel feature that it has frequently escaped detection. The chorus rarely participates in the action and resembles, in its contemplative function, that of the Greek tragedy; it is either set as many-voiced *concertato,* or cast in one of the forms of few-voiced chamber music. For dramatic reasons Monteverdi fused in startling manner elements of the monodic and the many-voiced style; for example, the recitative of the messenger is literally taken up later as a chorus refrain in five-part harmonization which parallels Monteverdi's polyphonization of the *Lamento d'Arianna.* A remarkable anticipation of the beginning of Arianna's lament can be found in the *Orfeo* (Ex. 14) and,

Ex. 14. Monteverdi: Excerpt from *Orfeo.*

among the many forward-looking details, a hint of the *stile concitato* on the word "fury" [59] may be mentioned.

Of particular interest is the distribution of recitative and closed musical forms. All highly dramatic events, such as the rescue and the subsequent loss of Euridice are composed as recitatives in heated affective harmonies over static basses, and, whenever dramatically necessary, Monteverdi did

[59] CE XI, 125.

not hesitate to set the characters against one another by violent and abrupt key changes for which the messenger scene furnishes memorable examples. The main vocal forms are the strophic song, often strongly affected by the canzonetta style, and the strophic variation. Either one may appear with ritornelli between the stanzas. Only in Orfeo's *pièce de résistance Possente spirto*,[60] a masterpiece of fivefold strophic variation, do instruments actually support the singer—in the first four variations in a vivacious *concertato* dialogue, and in the final one in simple chords. The score preserves this aria in two versions, the one without embellishments, the other with all the coloratura ornaments of the *gorgia* illustrating the art of singing of the time better than any theoretical discussion. There are no da-capo arias in the entire opera, the only hint at a return occurring in a short canzonetta, the ternary phrase structure of which can hardly be called a da capo proper.

More than a dozen independent instrumental interludes are skilfully integrated into the drama, four of which recur at strategic moments, sometimes even in changed orchestration. The linking-together of scenes by the same music has been compared, though not too happily, with the Wagnerian *leitmotiv* technique, the psychological nature of which is worlds apart from Monteverdi. The numerous ritornelli of the arias and dance songs, which give ample room for ballets, move in steady rhythms and at times in typical hemiola patterns, not recognized by the modern editors of the *Orfeo* score. The harmonies of the instrumental sections are free from the chromatic ventures of the vocal style, but display sharp clashes between stern harmonic progressions and the passing tones or appoggiature of the melody. The stark simplicity of Monteverdi's instrumental style can best be described as elemental. It involves nothing more than a change of orchestration or the sudden entry of a new continuo instrument, used with profound effect in the messenger scene.

Transcending the narrow ideals of the Florentine purists Monteverdi in his *Orfeo* set the future course of the opera. His next work, *Arianna* (1608), is lost except for the celebrated *lamento* which provoked many imitations; Monteverdi himself arranged it not only as a madrigal, but also as a sacred *contrafactum*. Peri was chosen to compose the recitatives for *Arianna*—a significant choice in view of the stylistic affinity between the two composers.

The resounding success of the *Orfeo*, which made its composer famous with one stroke, is reflected in its influence on subsequent operas, especially Gagliano's *Dafne* (1607) [61] and Belli's *Orfeo Dolente*.[62] Using a revised

[60] CE XI, 84–100.
[61] Eitner PAM 10, see also Einstein, *Short History*, Example 24.
[62] Riemann HMG 2:2, 288.

version of Rinuccini's *Dafne* Gagliano composed the fight with the dragon as a choral ensemble with synchronized action, minutely prescribed in the highly illuminating preface to the opera. Gagliano was very fond of dissonant cadential formulas and simultaneous cross-relations (Ex. 15) which

Ex. 15. Marco da Gagliano: Duet from *Dafne*.

non vil pre - gio ancor sa - rà ster-mi - nar cru - do ser - pen - 'te

remained exemplary for middle baroque composers as late as Purcell. Certain sections in Belli's *Orfeo* surpassed Monteverdi in harmonic boldness, but neither Belli and Gagliano, nor Francesca Caccini,[63] the daughter of the singer, and the Bolognese Giacobi were able to sustain in their operas the dramatic function of the music as firmly as had Monteverdi.

After the flowering of the opera in Northern Italy the leadership passed after 1620 to Rome, and nearly twenty years later to Venice. It is customary to divide the early operas into three groups, the Florentine recitative opera, the Roman chorus opera, and the Venetian solo opera. The last two terms describe only external, if conspicuous, traits important less in stylistic than in sociological respect. The chorus formed also an integral part of Monteverdi's *Orfeo* and its presence or absence hardly suffices to define the difference between the types. In the sumptuous Roman opera the dramatic importance of the recitative was weakened by a shift of emphasis from the drama to the grand musical spectacle, and not by accident did the display of vocal virtuosity become an end in itself, as can be seen in the spectacular opera *La Galatea*[64] by the castrato-composer Loreto Vittori. The recitative gradually yielded its structural function to arias, elaborate but static choruses, ballets, and dance songs. The appearance of a-cappella madrigals in the opera is a telling sign of the Roman conservatism. Domenico Mazzocchi frankly admitted in the preface to his opera *Catena d'Adone* (1626)[65] that he inserted arias "to break the tediousness of the recitative"; as a result the recitative reached only at times the affective heights of the Florentine opera and adumbrated occasionally even the *secco* recitative of the middle baroque bel-canto style.

[63] See her ballet *La Liberazione di Ruggiero* in SCMA VII.
[64] Excerpts in Goldschmidt *Studien*, I, 273.
[65] *ib.* 155.

Landi's important opera *Sant' Alessio* (1632) [66] was performed in the new theater of the Palazzo Barberini with sets by Bernini. It belonged, with *Erminia* [67] by Michelangelo Rossi, to the numerous operas on sacred subjects, very characteristic of Rome, where the aristocratic clergy served as the main patron of music. Significantly, Landi's librettist was the Marchese Rospigliosi, the future Pope Clemens IX.

The sinfonie in *Sant' Alessio* [68]—actually canzonas for the sonorous combination of three violins and a heavily reinforced continuo—mark an important step in the evolution of an independent opera overture. Landi framed the action by big eight-voice choruses which displayed pompous polyphony. His recitatives, written partly in a remarkable pathetic Florentine style, partly in a tentative *secco* style, were frequently interrupted by duets, trios, and novel ensemble recitatives. Among the ensembles the mournful trio on the death of St. Alexis deserves special notice for its combination of poignant harmonies with great flexibility of line. As in most Roman operas, comic scenes with dance songs and ariettas in canzonetta style were scattered throughout the acts, in keeping with the idea of entertainment. In these episodes the stereotyped comic servants of the *commedia dell'arte* were first introduced into the opera. With their parlando sections and their flippant dialogue they anticipate with amazing clarity the tone of the future *opera buffa* (Ex. 16).

Ex. 16. Landi: Comic duet from *Sant' Alessio*.

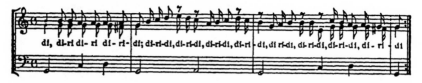

di, di-ri di- ri di-ri- ri | di; di-ri-di, di-ri-di, di-ri-di, di-ri | di, di ri-di, di-ri-di, di-ri-di, di - ri | di

The history of the Venetian opera began with the opening of the first commercial opera house in 1637. The composers of the first Venetian opera, Manelli and Ferrari, were Romans who continued at first the stylistic tradition of the Roman opera. During its early phase the Venetian opera was far from being a solo opera; its numerous choruses served, as in the Roman opera, a decorative rather than a dramatic purpose. It is most regrettable that all of Monteverdi's operas between the *Orfeo* and the two surviving Venetian works are lost. They would throw light on the striking

[66] *ib.* 202, also Torchi AM V.
[67] *ib.* 258.
[68] HAM no. 208; Riemann HMG 2:2, 255 and 263.

stylistic change evinced in both the *Ritorno d'Ulisse* [68a] (1641) and the *Incoronazione di Poppea* (1642). It is quite possible that Monteverdi wrote them under the influence of his pupil Cavalli whose first stage-work *Le Nozze di Teti e Peleo* (1639) united Monteverdian and novel features. How far the mutual give and take between master and disciple went cannot be decided as long as Monteverdi's first Venetian work, *Adone*, remains undiscovered.

The change in Monteverdi's style, already commented upon by Doni (1640), was most apparent in a new differentiation of the recitative style. The continuity of the recitative was broken up by *cantabile* sections or refrains in triple meter marking the incipient stage of the division between aria and recitative which was developed in the bel-canto style. The recitative was also loosened up by rapid tone repetitions and parlando sections *alla* Rossini, put either to dramatic use in form of the *stile concitato*, as in Nero's rage,[69] or to comic effect, as in Iro's parodistic lament.[70] Monteverdi inserted scenes like the flirtation of the page and the damsel (*Poppea*), and Iro's antics with excessively sustained notes (*Ritorno*) to give comic relief to the tragic action, in Shakespeare's manner. In his tragic recitatives Monteverdi maintained his customary intensity with undiminished power—for example in Ottavia's moving farewell to Rome in which her failing voice is depicted in highly realistic manner.[71] The musical unification of the drama reaches its peak in scenes like the drawing of the bow (*Ritorno*), or the marital dispute between the ambitious, unfaithful Poppea and her husband. In the latter scene Monteverdi contrasted the characters by means of two interlocked strophic variations with ritornello.[72] The outstanding aria form, the strophic variation, still prevailed, but in all closed forms the bass was less static than in *Orfeo* and more highly organized by rhythmic patterns, as can be seen in Penelope's great final aria with a five-voice ritornello.

An important novel trait of the late operas is the appearance of arias on short chaconne basses. The passionate duet finale of Poppea and Nero, the drink duet of Poppea,[73] and two duets from the *Ritorno* all depend

---

[68a] The authenticity of this work has been questioned by Vogel, Riemann, Kretzschmar, and, recently again, by Benvenuti, and Paoli (*Monteverdi*). However, Goldschmidt (SIMG IV, 671; X, 570) and Haas (StzMW 9) have adduced evidence that seems to confirm Monteverdi's authorship.

[69] CE XIII, 81.

[70] CE XII, 170, 175.

[71] CE XIII, 229.

[72] CE XIII, 95.

[73] CE XIII, 146.

to a greater or lesser degree on chaconne patterns. Comparatively little use is made of independent instrumental music, and such modest pieces as occur are obligated to the dance style. The overture to *Poppea* consists merely of a varied couple in stylized rhythmic transformation.

The two last operas show Monteverdi not only far removed from the polyphonic style of his youth, but also greatly at variance with his earlier dramatic style. With his restless and searching spirit he set out in his late years on the road to the bel-canto style the fulfilment of which he was not destined to see.

TRADITION AND PROGRESS IN SACRED MUSIC

The sacred music of the early baroque went through a stylistic crisis that the rise of the affective modern style had precipitated. This crisis was reflected in the momentous struggle between tradition and progress, between *stile antico* and *moderno*. The traditional vocal polyphony was securely anchored in sacred music and could not be overthrown by a group of enthusiasts like the *Camerata*. Yet the impact of the modern style was felt immediately. The stylistic unity of sacred music was split into a conservative and a progressive branch and gave way to a style-conscious historicism which made the composers bilingual. The lack of restraint in the modern secular style was viewed with suspicion by the church, and although Cavalieri transferred the recitative to sacred music in the very year in which it was definitely established, objections against "theatrical" music in the church persisted for a long time. Nevertheless, the vigorous and affective spirit of the baroque soon asserted itself in the liturgy also, forming a strange contrast with the official objectivity of the liturgy of our day.

In sacred music five styles can be distinguished: (1) the monody, (2) the few-voiced or small *concertato*, (3) the many-voiced or grand *concertato*, (4) the "colossal baroque," and (5) the *stile antico*. Cavalieri's mediocre recitatives in *Anima e Corpo* are, as far as is known, the earliest monodies. The sacred recitatives that Caccini supposedly composed are not extant. Viadana's *Concerti ecclesiastici a 1-4 voci* (1602) [74] adopted the monodic style only externally; they cannot be considered as monodies proper. The preface stated that it was highly unsatisfactory to sing only one voice of a polyphonic motet with the organ supplying the other parts. This was a

[74] Examples in Schneider, *Anfänge des Basso continuo;* Wolf, *Music of Earlier Times*, no. 52; Arnold, *The Art of Accompaniment*, II, 21–33; HAM no. 185.

widespread practice during the transition period that sought to give to the old style the semblance of the monody. Viadana's motets were works of transition that owed their importance to the fact that he substituted for the makeshift of the *basso seguente* an obligatory continuo.
The true monody forced its way into sacred music only after 1610 and can be recognized in titles such as *Affetti amorosi spirituali* (Quagliati).
Significantly enough, we meet with the affective style less frequently at first in strictly liturgical compositions with Latin text, than in devotional compositions with Italian words. It is again the universal Monteverdi who furnishes one of the earliest examples of true monody in liturgical music and, in addition, examples of all other styles of church music, except the colossal baroque the compromising attitude of which was not congenial to him. His first collection of church music in modern style was published in Mantua (1610). Unfortunately, only two publications have come down to us from his Venetian period, the *Selva morale e spirituale* (1641) and a collection containing psalms and a Mass, printed posthumously in 1650.
The liturgical collection of 1610 is characterized by a baffling variety of styles that Monteverdi contrasted with cool deliberation. It contains the complete service for vespers with psalms, antiphons, a hymn, and the magnificat. The antiphons, traditionally composed as polyphonic motets, were supplanted here by monodies, set *à la mode* with much virtuoso *gorgia* on significant words. He indulged also in echo effects with puns such as *gaudio-audio,* to which he was partial also in *Orfeo.* All this occurred, it must be repeated, in liturgical music; no Gregorian chants were used because the monodic style made the treatment of a *cantus firmus* impractical if not impossible. The only form in which the chant was absorbed by the modern style is illustrated by Viadana's experimental mass compositions [75] with *gorgia* ornaments for solo voice and organ continuo, and Banchieri's directions for the accompaniment of the chant by a continuo, a practice that survived to the days of Haydn and Mozart, and in the form of the Gregorian "harmonization," even to the present.
Liturgical monodies became very common in the first third of the century. Alessandro Grandi, a pupil of Gabrieli, must be singled out as a master whose contributions to the monodic motet and the sacred solo cantata can well be compared with those of Monteverdi. His *Motetti a voce sola* (1628) show the influence of the recitative in emphatic repetitions of words and declamatory contrast motives, but the static bass lines are enlivened by imitative sequences which tie both voices together. Such compromise

[75] Peter Wagner, *Geschichte der Messe*, Appendix.

between contrapuntal and monodic principles was more typical of monodic church music than were adaptations of the radical Florentine recitative which were sometimes bodily transferred to church music in form of *contrafacta*.

The monodic church composers fell into two groups, of which the first, including Grandi, Casati, Turini, Pace, Donati, Saracini, Bellanda, was in varying degree under the spell of the Florentine monodists or of Monteverdi. The other was formed by Roman composers, notably Durante who prescribed in his *Arie devote* (1608) the crescendo in Caccini's manner, Bonini, Severi, Kapsberger, the prolific Tarditi, Agazzari, Quagliati and Graziani.[76] Whereas the first school leaned toward unrestrained text interpretation by means of expressive *gorgia*, carefully indicated dynamics, and frequent tempo changes, the Roman school showed a marked proclivity toward vocal virtuosity, especially in the rather dry *motetti passeggiati* of Kapsberger and Severi.[77] One of the most memorable displays of vocal fireworks was the rendition by the castrato Vittori of Domenico Mazzocchi's plaint of the repentant Magdalen. He transported the audience by the realistic sobs of his singing, which strikingly correspond to the mixture of devotion and erotic realism that we find in certain sculptures of Bernini.

The few-voiced *concertato* with or without instruments represents one of the favorite forms of sacred music. Its texture was characterized by the open work or the *concertato* interplay of the voices, be it in the chamber duet or trio, dialogue, or cantata. The Catholic church cantata exactly paralleled the secular cantata in its flexible form, its rondo structure, and its instrumental ritornelli. Monteverdi's vespers contain several noteworthy specimens with a written-out organ part giving us an authentic picture of the modest continuo practice of the early baroque period. An early example of the juxtaposition of solo and tutti in the *concertato* occurs in the second part of Balestra's motet *Salve aeterni* (Ex. 17), published in Bonometti's *Parnassus Musicus* (Venice, 1615). The moderate use of affective intervals and *gorgia* figures, the integration of bass and melody, and the relatively steady rhythm clearly distinguish the sacred style of the piece from secular parallels.

---

[76] A bibliographical list of the sacred *concertato* in Italy from 1600 to 1630 can be found in Adrio, *Anfänge des geistlichen Konzerts*.
[77] Examples in Kuhn, *Die Verzierungskunst*.

Ex. 17. Balestra: From the *Concertato* motet *Salve aeterni.*

In the grand *concertato* the gigantic combinations of Gabrieli were reduced to smaller dimensions. The contrast between instrumental and vocal
idioms, and also that between solo ensemble and chorus, not yet clearly
observed in Gabrieli, became more pronounced with Monteverdi. He experimented with all the elements of the grand *concertato* and even tried
to combine them with the traditional use of *cantus firmus.* In his vespers,
designated as *sopra canti fermi,* the psalm tones are set with amazing resourcefulness. In the psalm *Dominus ad adiuvandum* a six-part chorus
sustains a D-major chord in simple declamatory fashion while six instruments dress up the static chord with a dazzling network of short-winded
imitations that are made to serve a purely coloristic purpose. Also in the
ten-voice *Nisi Dominus* for two choruses he made imaginative use of the
open work and supported the structure by the plainchant in long note
values. The formidable "sonata" *Sancta Maria,* noteworthy for its sumptuous orchestration, presents a psalmodic *cantus firmus,* repeated in varied
rhythmic shapes by a unison chorus.

The *cantus firmus* treatment all but disappeared in the grand *concertato* after Monteverdi. His Venetian followers, Pellegrini, Grandi, Merula, Rovetta, Usper, Donati, and even such late composers as Neri and Monferrato, were too much concerned with textual representation to be restricted by the shackles of a *cantus firmus*. Only intonations and short quotations of the chant were sometimes presented in contrapuntal fashion. In the absence of *cantus firmus* other constructive methods intruded into church music, notably the ostinato, and the strophic variation. This practice is illustrated by Merula's chaconne Mass, and by Donati's set of fifteen motets on the same bass (1629). The Masses could no longer be designated by the plainchant or the model from which they had formerly been derived, but received their titles from the special occasion for which they were composed. The dependence of the music on the word manifested itself in the fact that the declamatory rhythm of the word usually generated the rhythm of the contrast motives.

While Venice was the center of progress in sacred music, Rome was the bulwark of traditionalism. The followers of the Roman school such as Paolo Agostini, Abbatini, Benevoli, Domenico and Virgilio Mazzocchi, Massaini, and Crivelli took over the polychoral style of the Venetian school, but expanded it to unprecedented dimensions in compositions for four, six, and sometimes even twelve and more choruses that have justly been called the "colossal baroque" in analogy with the architecture of the time. The colossal baroque attempted to graft the polychoral techniques of the grand *concertato* on the *stile antico*. The resulting hybrid style was typical of the Roman conservatism. The profusion of vocal and instrumental means, the innumerable echos, solos, and tuttis, reflected the pomp of the church ritual in the counter-reformation, but the affective spirit of the Venetian *concertato* was conspicuously lacking. The inner fervor of Gabrieli was externalized to technical virtuosity. It is symbolic for the subordination of the liturgy to the display of glamour that the chorus no longer had its traditional place near the altar, but was distributed in the lofts and balconies that baroque church architecture supplied in abundance. Rarely again have music and architecture been as closely associated as in the baroque period where space as such became an essential component of musical structure.

Benevoli's polychoral Mass for fifty-three parts,[78] commissioned for the inauguration of the Salzburg cathedral, bears testimony to the stupendous

[78] DTOe X (vol. 20).

facility of spatial dispositions and, at the same time, the inflation of essentially modest music to mammoth dimensions. It is written for two eight-voice choruses, each with a continuo, and six instrumental ensembles, two for strings, one for wood winds, and three for brass instruments. Florid ensembles for the soloists, carefully marked as "solo" are set against choral *ripieno* sections, usually, though not always, distinguished by chordal texture. The Mass is held together by a master continuo which readily discloses how simple the underlying chord progressions actually are. As a matter of course the colossal baroque made even more extensive use of octave doublings than the Venetian model. This practice constituted a definite break with the tradition of renaissance music and was specifically approved by Viadana and other theorists of the time.

The colossal baroque represented the concession of Roman traditionalism to the modern trend. The staunchest conservatives among the composers perpetuated a living tradition of renaissance music under the name of *stile antico*, a term that in itself implied the awakening of a historical detachment from the current *stile concertato*. In the struggle between tradition and progress the old style became more and more the symbol of churchliness; this connotation was originally foreign to renaissance music and could only arise in conscious reaction to the modern style. As early as Agazzari, Palestrina was raised to the dignity of an infallible model. Palestrina's direct emulators and successors, Felice and Giovanni Anerio, Giovanelli, Soriano, Nanino, and Allegri, and also such later masters as Pier Valentini and Simonelli slowly transformed their model by applying the harmonies and accentuating rhythms of the time which distinguish the *stile antico* from the real Palestrina style. The works of Palestrina, Lasso, and other composers of the old school were now printed in "enriched" form with continuo, and famous pieces like the Marcellus Mass were subjected to various arrangements. Allegri's celebrated *Miserere* for double chorus, long a well-guarded secret of the Sistine chapel, belonged to the declamatory chordal type of *falso-bordone*, very popular during the renaissance. Its magical effect on the audience was due not to the composition as such but to its rendition with improvised embellishments, a custom that was carefully preserved to the time of Mozart and even of Mendelssohn, both of whom wrote them down from memory. Burney's story that Emperor Leopold I of Austria, who received the composition as a special favor from Rome, was disappointed with the music, may well be true because the "essentials," namely the ornaments, were not written down. The excessive ornamentation, the sustained chordal effects, the wide range of dynamics, and the essentially harmonic approach to polyphony were typical traits of the *stile antico* that demonstrated the baroque re-interpretation of renaissance music as clearly as the parading with learned *cantus firmus* treatment, contrapuntal stunts, puzzles, and colossal canons. Pier Valentini proved his learned showmanship in a canon for ninety-six voices which Kircher admiringly printed in his *Musurgia*.

The progressives of the seventeenth and eighteenth centuries, Monteverdi, Turini, Landi, Cifra, Schütz, Alessandro Scarlatti, Durante, Lotti, and Marcello also wrote in *stile antico* with skill and taste. It was not a sign of creative eclecticism, but a natural outgrowth of the polarity of styles which prevailed throughout the baroque period. Monteverdi showed his complete mastery of the *prima prattica* in his polyphonic Mass on motives of a motet by Gombert which resuscitated the old parody or paraphrase Mass, by this time an almost extinct form. It survived in the baroque era only in such isolated examples as Bernardi's Mass on Arcadelt's famous madrigal *Il bianco e dolce cigno*.[79]

The discovery of choral sonorities in the essentially vocal *stile antico* formed the logical complement to the discovery of instrumental idioms in the *concertato* style. Not by coincidence did the a-cappella ideal originate in the realm of the *stile antico*. The term "cappella" which denoted with Gabrieli merely a vocal or instrumental tutti, acquired now the special meaning "not accompanied by instruments" in pointed opposition to the *concertato* style. Symptomatically, this meaning of the term originated only in the first decades of the seventeenth century. A collection of Masses by Ghizzolo (Venice, 1619), composed *parte a cappella, parte da concerto*, is one of the earliest examples of the deliberate juxtaposition of the two styles. Curiously enough, the a-cappella performance did not necessarily preclude an organ continuo, which was, however, often only optional. Monteverdi, too, contrasted in his Mass (1650) and in the *Selva morale* a-cappella with accompanied *concertato* sections, while Turini, Landi, and many others observed the *stile antico* in strict a-cappella Masses, thus designated on the title-page.

It is not surprising that the a-cappella ideal, once discovered, should have been attached in retrospect to renaissance music. This interpretation has persisted to the present day, but whenever we refer to the renaissance as the "a-cappella period" we unwittingly apply a baroque term with questionable implications.

---

[79] DTOe XXXVI (vol. 69).

CHAPTER THREE

Early and Middle Baroque in the Northern Countries

THE NETHERLANDS SCHOOL AND ITS ENGLISH BACKGROUND

IN THE formation of the baroque style Italy represented only one pole. Her influence was decisive primarily in the development of vocal monody. The other pole was England. Her influence was decisive in the development of an abstract instrumental style which spread from England to the Netherlands and from there all over Europe. In England, as in all other non-Italian countries, the new style emerged almost imperceptibly. The great schools of the madrigalists, lutenists, and virginalists overlap the beginnings of the baroque era but do not stylistically belong to it. The belated flowering of the English madrigal explains why only the first generation of madrigal composers (Byrd and Morley) can be said to represent a pure renaissance style, while in the second (Weelkes and Wilbye) and especially in the third generation (Tomkins and Orlando Gibbons) undercurrents came to the surface that parallel the rapid development of the Italian madrigal from Marenzio to Monteverdi. It is characteristic that none of the madrigalists took the final step to the continuo madrigal, except Porter, the pupil of Monteverdi.

The school of lutenists which began to blossom with John Dowland (1597) as suddenly as it withered with Attey (*Ayres*, 1622) has erroneously been regarded as an "entirely original" prefiguration of monody in England. The English "ayre" was in fact, as even the name implies, dependent on the *air de cour*, the great popularity of which is proved by a great many English editions, either in the original French (Tessier, 1597) or in translation (Hilton: *French Court-Ayres with their ditties Englished*, 1629). Although the ayres were solo songs they had stylistically nothing in common with monody, and not by coincidence were they published in alternative versions as accompanied solos or part songs. In the *Musical Banquet* (1610) by Robert Dowland (the son of John) the difference in style between ayre and monody comes clearly to light; we find here English ayres side by side with Spanish and Italian monodies. It is, however, significant that the latter are supplied here with a written-out lute and viol accompaniment instead of with a continuo [1] which was not yet an established practice in England. John Dowland was far removed from a continuo style but he struck a new and personal note by cautious use of poignant "false" intervals. One of his finest songs, *Go nightly cares* from *A Pilgrimes Solace* (1612),[2] is steeped in deep melancholy like the somber ayre *In darkness let me dwell* and many other of his songs of death. He justly gave as his motto: Dowland *semper dolens*. Within a small frame Dowland achieved a perfection of song writing that none of his fellow composers could match. Among these the poet-musician Campion, the graceful Rosseter, and Danyel, noteworthy for his chromatic ventures, may be especially mentioned. Campion's ayre *Fain would I wed* (Book IV, no. 24) which exists also in a virginal arrangement by Richard Farnaby (Fitzwilliam Virginal Book) betrays Italian influence since it is built on a variant of the *passamezzo antico* which furnished the basis to several English ballad tunes.

ENGLISH ANTECEDENTS: THE ABSTRACT INSTRUMENTAL STYLE

The mechanical patterns in English solo music for keyboard instruments and in ensemble music for consorts were the only elements that had a direct bearing on the genesis of baroque style. The virginalists excelled in discant variations of secular tunes and patterned variations on plainsongs, ground basses, and melodies of the *passamezzo* family which all involved a purely instrumental *cantus firmus* technique. The ballads, dances, and popular songs were subjected to variation by means of abstract patterns that became increasingly more complex as the variation progressed. Under the flow of rapid scale passages, inexorably repeated rhythms, syncopated and dotted figures, arpeggios, broken octaves, and percussive chord successions the tunes were at times completely atomized. The typically clavieristic idiom of this music manifested itself in the "free-voiced" style in which the number of parts was not consistently maintained. In contrast to the dissolu-

---

[1] These accompaniments throw an interesting light on the continuo practice of the time. The collection also contains Caccini's *Amarilli* the accompaniment of which permits us to correct the faulty realization by Schering in GMB no. 173.
[2] Printed in Fellowes, *The English School of Lutenist Song-writers*.

tion of secular tunes in the variation, plainsongs were left essentially untouched by figuration. The favorite plainsongs included the hymn *Felix namque*, *Miserere*, and *In nomine*, the melody of the Trinity antiphon *Gloria tibi* which enjoyed universal favor, from Taverner to Purcell.[2a] The plainsong melodies served as the scaffolding for great instrumental structures, often wrongly regarded as dry-as-dust exercises without aesthetic importance. Actually, however, they established one of the essential elements of baroque music, namely, patterned figuration that relied on rhythmic consistency and the abstract interplay of patterns and lines. These specifically instrumental devices mark the final emancipation of instrumental music from vocal style. The idea of mechanical severity that underlay patterned figuration called for a peculiar kind of non-expressive, purely abstract musical imagination without which the future development of baroque organ music would not have been possible. That the imagination of Italian and English composers ran along entirely different lines can be seen in Peter Philips's revealing virginal arrangement of Caccini's madrigal *Amarilli* in which he grafted the English abstract figuration on an affective monody, certainly not in the spirit of the original.[3]

The fantasia, or fancy, of the virginalists covered a much wider range than the Italian fantasia; it combined, in fact, traits of the Italian ricercar, canzona, and toccata. The English composers paid particular attention to the returns of the main idea, which they often actually numbered in the virginal books. With the exception of Byrd, the virginalists belonged not to the Elizabethan but to the late Jacobean generation. They comprised beside Giles Farnaby and Peter Philips three prominent masters: Bull (d. 1628), a virtuoso of the first water, Orlando Gibbons (d. 1625), and Thomas Tomkins (d. 1656). Bull and Philips, who spent the latter part of their lives in the Netherlands, transmitted the English style to Sweelinck. The only printed collection of virginal music was *Parthenia* (1611) and its sequel, *Parthenia inviolata*, so called because it was supplied with a doubling viol part.

The composers of ensemble music for viols,[4] such as Ferrabosco, Lupo, Deering, Coperario (or Cooper), Gibbons, Hume, Ward, and East, were in their conservative attitude obligated to an essentially polyphonic renaissance style. The chamber ensembles or consorts for which they wrote consisted of either a "chest" of instruments of one family or a combination of

[2a] For the answer to the puzzling question why the antiphon was known as *In nomine* see Reese, *Music in the Renaissance* (in preparation) ch. 16.

[3] GMB no. 174; Fitzwilliam Virginal Book I, 329.

[4] For examples see Meyer, *English Chamber Music*.

different instruments ("broken consort"). Consort music was written without continuo in the familiar forms of virginal music, notably the fancy, the plainsong elaboration, and the dance. Hardly affected by the slight modernisms of the English madrigal and ayre the first two groups were rigidly contrapuntal and retrospective in style. The viol ensemble with its unemotional and remote color was particularly suitable for the abstract linear design of the fancy. It was "still music," as Shakespeare says, a music that did not call for an audience, that should be played rather than listened to since its structure became clear only from within, not from without.

The simple dance music of Brade,[5] Thomas Simpson, Harding, Rowe, Holborne, Edward Johnson, and Dowland, was widely disseminated through German collections since many of these composers were active on the Continent. Their consorts which consisted of varied couples, or single dances loosely strung together, exerted a considerable influence on the development of the orchestral suite. Its polyphonic tradition was eagerly pursued by the German masters of the dance suite, notably Melchior Franck and Schein.

Mixed ensemble music (for voices and instruments without continuo) enjoyed a great vogue in the first decades of the century. Coperario's *Funeral Tears* and *Songs of Mourning*, Leighton's *Tears or Lamentations*, and Peerson's *Private Musicke* (1620) and *Mottects or Grave Chamber Music* (1630) called for fairly large combinations of voices and instruments. In Peerson's *Private Musicke* the obligatory viol accompaniment could be replaced by a makeshift virginal part, another indication that the continuo was not yet common in England. With its slight contrapuntal texture and occasional hints of affective writing, mixed ensemble music had all the earmarks of a transition period. Convivial music was represented by Ravenscroft whose *Briefe discourse* contained songs for "Hunting, Hawking, Dauncing, Drinking, and Enamouring." His catch collections, *Pammelia, Deuteromelia,* and *Melismata,* "fitting for the Court, Citie, and Countrey Humours," aptly demonstrated the three types of music making in the Jacobean period.

THE NETHERLANDS: SWEELINCK

The religious separation of the Calvinist north from the Catholic south in the Netherlands had profound repercussions on music. The Calvinists

[5] For Brade see GMB no. 156, and Engelke, *Musik am Gottorfer Hofe* 1927; for Holborne see *Pavans* ed. by Sydney Beck, New York Public Library 1942.

ascetically restricted church music to the Huguenot psalter which had supplanted the traditional psalms or *Souterliedekens*. The main outlet of musical activity was instrumental music, especially the elaboration of sacred and secular tunes, which found its greatest master in Jan Pieters Sweelinck (1562–1621). He was the first of the famous quartet of S's in early baroque music: Sweelinck, Schütz, Schein, and Scheidt. Taught by Zarlino in Venice and thoroughly familiar with the works of the two Gabrielis and Merulo, he amalgamated in his music the modern Venetian forms with the figurative techniques of the English virginalists. His intimate relations to English music transpire in the fact that some of his pieces were included in the Fitzwilliam Virginal Book; that he wrote variations on compositions by Dowland and Philips; that Bull based a fantasia on one of his themes, and that he in turn quoted one of Bull's canons in the theoretical treatise he compiled after Zarlino. As organist at the Oude Kirk in Amsterdam he was sought as teacher by the young organists of Germany where he was affectionately nicknamed the "maker of organists."

The vocal works of Sweelinck, notably four books of psalms in the metrical French translation of Marot and Beza, were still written in renaissance style; only the *Cantiones sacrae* (1619) called for a continuo. Of far greater importance were his organ and harpsichord works which can be divided into three categories: sacred and secular variations, toccatas, and fantasias. Sweelinck's variations of psalm tunes and chorales open the long and brilliant history of the organ chorale. He made the essentially secular variation technique of the virginalists subservient to a liturgical purpose. The severity and gravity of these "spiritual exercises" was a direct reflection of the ethical convictions of the Reformed Church. The Calvinists firmly believed that worldly success was indicative of predestined salvation in the hereafter. The complete interpenetration of the secular and spiritual spheres was musically symbolized in the transference of a secular variation technique to sacred melodies. The liturgical significance of the psalm and the chorale bestowed on this technique a religious dignity that cannot be found in the English models. The sacred tunes were subjected to mechanical elaboration in abstract rhythmic patterns in the belief that the effort of elaboration was in itself a token of unceasing devotion. The patterns constantly challenged the imagination of the composer; only the great composers could deal with them successfully, the minor ones ran them into the ground. Consistent with the idea of mechanical severity which pervades the entire history of the organ chorale in the Protestant countries, Swee-

linck presented the lines of the chorale in a network of motives, rigidly
worked out for a certain time and then replaced by others (Ex. 18). Each
variation contained a great variety of upbeat patterns, complementary
rhythms, and motives in double counterpoint. In the course of the variation the *cantus firmus* changed its position, and the number of parts often

Ex. 18. Sweelinck: Chorale variations *Hertzlich lieb*.

increased in the English manner, resulting in a climactic, yet controlled,
effect of mounting complexity which Sweelinck liked to resolve by a
rhapsodic coda in toccata style. Because of their liturgical dignity the
tunes themselves kept aloof from the lively motivation of the surrounding
voices. They were real *cantus firmi* which were only exceptionally dissolved
by variation. This structural dualism could not be realized through the
blending stops of the renaissance organ; it called for a new type of instrument, the baroque organ, characterized by sharply differentiated stops that
permitted the *cantus firmus* to stand out. Catholic composers like Frescobaldi and his south German followers did not adopt the patterned variation
in their *cantus firmus* composition because to them the idea of organistic
severity had no religious associations and seemed therefore pedantic rather
than dignified.

    In his secular variations Sweelinck also leaned heavily on the technique
of the virginalists, but his motives were more rigidly developed, more neatly
organized, and, above all, rhythmically more square than was the custom
with English composers. If Sweelinck's variations on Dowland's famous
Lachrimae Pavan and on the pavan by Philips are compared with the Eng-

lish originals,[6] a revealing difference comes to light. Although Sweelinck also drew the melody into the variational patterns, it never lost its own identity in the process.

The toccatas carried the stamp of the Venetian school. They usually began with sustained harmonies and then rambled on in rhapsodic passages, but their flow was now disciplined by the mechanical rhythms of the English figuration. Sections of contrasted textures sometimes enclosed short fugal passages in Merulo's manner.

In musical importance the toccatas could not compare with the fantasias in which Sweelinck laid the foundation for the evolution of the fugue. The fantasias were based on a single idea, a real fugue subject of abstract design, such as the hexachord, the chromatic fourth, or similar patterns.[7] Variation played a prominent role, but, in contrast with the favorite method of Frescobaldi, Sweelinck varied not the subject, but the countersubjects. He sometimes gathered the numerous sections of the fantasia into a vast tripartite form. In the first part the subject was led through several ex-positions with various countersubjects, the second part brought the aug-mentation, the third the diminution of the theme with new or rhythmically varied countersubjects. The perpetual stretti, the piling-up of contrapuntal devices, and the increased pace led in the last part to a rhythmic climax which lent the fantasia a pervasive unity not found in Frescobaldi. The thorough craftsmanship and clear formal disposition of Sweelinck's fan-tasias were second only to Bach's fugues. Sweelinck's conception of counter-point was essentially rhythmic; in his countersubjects he utilized with amazing consistency and resourcefulness the untold possibilities of rhythmic subdivision and the interplay of slow and rapid patterns.

The fantasias that Sweelinck designated as "in the manner of an echo" belong to an entirely different type.[8] Only lightly contrapuntal, they were closely allied with the toccata. Here the technique of the Venetian double chorus, brilliantly adapted to the two manuals of the organ, was reduced to short upbeat motives which were tossed back and forth in terraced dy-namics, *forte* and *piano;* toward the end, the play of the echo subsided in rhapsodic toccata passages.

Sweelinck had scarcely a rival in his country. The only contemporary of note was the organist Pieter Cornet (d. 1626), active at the Catholic court in Brussels.[9] Sweelinck's contemporaries and successors included

[6] See TAM II and III, also the Fitzwilliam Virginal Book.
[7] GMB no. 158, TAM III, 17, Fitzwilliam Virginal Book II, 26.
[8] HAM no. 181.
[9] See Peeters: *Oudnederlandsche Meesters*, 1938, 59–80, and *Liber Fratrum Cruci-ferorum Leodiensium* (Guilmant, Archives, 10), 183 ff.

vocal composers, such as Padbrué (*Kruisbergh*, 1640),[10] and the organists Kerckhoven [11] and van Noordt. The *Tabulatuur Boeck* (1659) [12] by van Noordt was the first Dutch keyboard work to appear in print. The Dutch school of lutenists, noteworthy for its lute arrangements of psalm tunes for home use and a vast repertory of dance music is represented by the tablature books of Vallet (*Secretum Musarum*, 1615 ff.), van den Hove, Thysius, and Valerius (*Nederlandtsche Gedenckclanck*, 1626).[13] The last contains the famous Wilhelmus tune, a political song against the Spanish oppressor which has become the Dutch national anthem, distinguished not only for its antiquity but, unlike many other national anthems, for its musical quality. The tablature book of Thysius [14] discloses the strong dependence of the Dutch lutenists on English music. English titles appear here in fantastically corrupt spellings, *e.g.* "Pacce tou pon" for "Packington Pound," and "Inno myne" for *In nomine*. The opera arose in the Netherlands only in the middle baroque period. The first Dutch opera, *De triomfeerende Min* (1678), was written by Hacquaert for Amsterdam.

GERMANY AND AUSTRIA IN THE SEVENTEENTH CENTURY

German music of the early and middle baroque was inextricably interwoven with the paralyzing religious and political struggles of the nation. The Thirty Years' War deepened the rift between the denominations and widened the cultural gap between the Catholic south and the Protestant parts of northern and central Germany. The wave of Italian influence that rolled over Germany in the first half of the century was followed in its wake by a French one, and the assimilation and transformation of these stimuli gave German music its special problems. While the Catholic composers adopted the Italian style without essential changes the Protestant composers were faced with the task of bringing their precious heritage, the chorale, in harmony with the *concertato* style. The result of this fusion was the most original German contribution to the history of baroque music.

In the seventeenth century Protestantism passed through its "scholastic" period, a phase of rigid orthodoxy in which violent dogmatic quarrels were

[10] VNM 42.

[11] *Monumenta Musicae Belgicae* II.

[12] Printed in VNM 19, new edition by Seiffert, 1935; see also the clavier book of Eijl (1671), VNM 37.

[13] VNM 2, other reprints: Utrecht 1931, Amsterdam, 1942.

[14] See *Tijdschrift* VNM I, 129, and MfM 18.

fought, first with the Calvinists, and later with the Pietists. The orthodox Lutherans upheld the "artificial" figural music in the church, sung not by the congregation, but by a specially trained choir, the *Kantorei*. The Pietists, who sought a mystic union with God and stressed the private devotion of the layman, were, like the Calvinists, opposed to the artistic autarchy of music and insisted on rather shallow songs within the reach of everybody. The struggle between Orthodoxy and Pietism which began in the second half of the century continued throughout the period and even overshadowed the life of Bach. Consistent with the Lutheran idea of exegesis as the foundation of the liturgy, Protestant church music had the function of interpreting the "word" of the Gospel. This goal could be achieved in two ways: the word could be either objectively "presented" by a chorale, the quintessence of the dogma, or subjectively "interpreted" by a free *concertato* composition. The first course, that of *cantus firmus* treatment, was taken by the organists and cantors, the second by Schütz and his Italianate school. Both trends merged with Bach and found in his works their final consummation.

The music for the Protestant service fell into three fundamental categories: (1) Gregorian chant and motets in *stile antico;* (2) the chorale, and —in the Reformed Church—the psalter; (3) figural music, that is composed art music. In spite of the rift between the denominations a substantial part of Catholic church music was retained in the Lutheran service, notably the plainchant of the Mass, the magnificat, and certain hymns, which were sung in Latin or in German translation. In addition, a wide common ground was provided by motets in *stile antico,* disseminated in Germany by two huge and influential collections: the *Promptuarium* by Schadaeus (1611 ff.) and the *Florilegium Portense* (1603 ff.) by Bodenschatz; they contained almost the complete repertory of the old Roman, Venetian, and German schools known and performed in the seventeenth century, and appeared time and again in new editions well into the Bach period. Bach is known to have ordered a new copy of the *Florilegium* for Leipzig. The importance of the *stile antico* and the Gregorian chant began to fade only in the late baroque period.

CHORALE AND DEVOTIONAL SONG

The Protestant chorale was a German hymn sung in unison—that is *choraliter,* hence the name—by the congregation, originally without accompaniment. Polyphonic arrangements of the chorale were traditionally the prerogative of the *Kantorei.* These settings carried the chorale as *cantus firmus* either in the tenor or, since Osiander (1586), in the upper voice. The latter practice led to the organ accompaniment of the chorale, already present in the Hamburg *Melodeien-Gesangsbuch* (1604). It was definitely established as a formal organ continuo in Schein's *Cantional* (1627). The organ accompaniment of the chorale was an invention of the early baroque period.

In the course of the seventeenth century numerous chorale melodies were added to the body of traditional tunes, notably by Johann Crüger who set the texts of Paul Gerhardt, the only German poet able to rival Luther's terse language and mystic fervor. As in the renaissance, many of the baroque chorales were of secular origin, but they were not folksongs, as a persistent legend has it. The situation was remarkably, yet rather typically, complex in the case of the famous chorale *O Haupt voll Blut und Wunden.* The melody had its origin in Hassler's love song *Mein G'müt ist mir verwirret* from the *Lustgarten* (1601) and was soon spiritualized to the chorale *Herzlich tut mich verlangen.* The Catholics adopted the same tune in the Latin hymn *Salve caput cruentatum,* which in turn was translated and paraphrased by Paul Gerhardt and thus became *O Haupt voll Blut und Wunden.* The interactions between secular models and sacred *contrafacta* on the one hand, and Protestant and Catholic repertory on the other were very lively throughout the entire period.

While Crüger's chorales still breathed the collective, congregational spirit of the liturgical chorale, later compositions approached in their individual devotional spirit the sacred aria or song. The gradual qualitative decline of chorale composition in the latter part of the century coincided with a sharp increase in quantity. Under the influence of Pietism a veritable flood of devotional songbooks for private singing appeared containing chorale-like arias with sentimental and ecstatic texts of which only very few were ultimately accepted as liturgical chorales by the congregation. It is highly characteristic that Bach, whose harmonizations represented the peak of the harmonic chorale interpretation, did not compose any chorales in the orthodox sense, and contributed only very few melodies of his own to Schemelli's devotional songbook. In the following list the major chorale books of the baroque period are compiled in chronological order:

Osiander: *Fünfzig Geistliche Lieder,* 1586 [15]
Hamburger *Melodeien-Gesangbuch,* 1604

[15] Reprinted 1903.

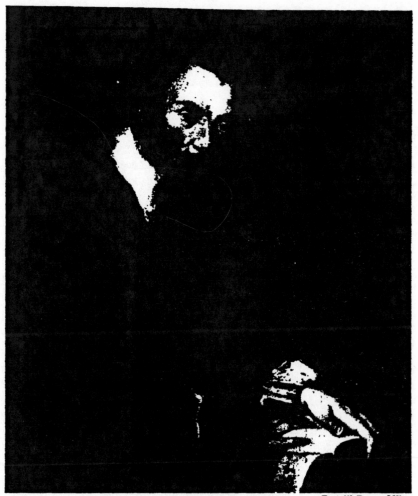

Claudio Monteverdi

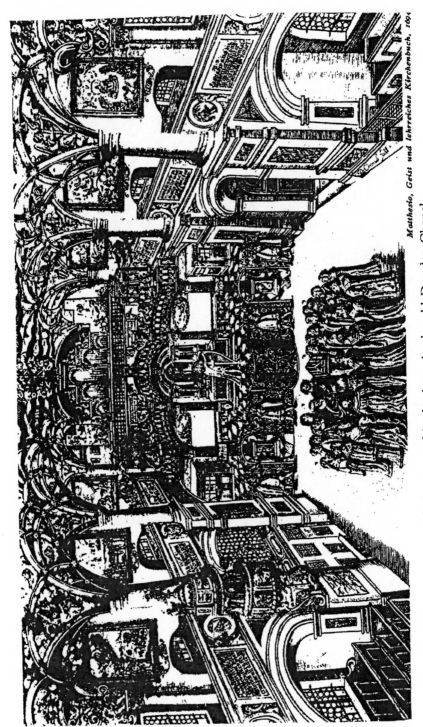

Mathesio, Geist und lehrreiches Kirchenbuch, 1604

Schütz among his choristers in the old Dresden Chapel

Praetorius: *Musae Sioniae*, V–VIII, 1607 ff.[16]
Hassler: *Kirchengesäng . . . simpliciter*, 1608 [17]
Schein: *Cantional*, Leipzig, 1627
Crüger: *Praxis Pietatis melica*, 1647 ff.
Scheidt: *Tabulaturbuch*, 1650 [18]
Briegel, Darmstadt, 1687
Speer, 1692
Freylinghausen: *Geistreiches Gesangbuch*, Halle, 1704 ff.
Bachofen, Zürich, 1727
Schemelli, 1736
König, Frankfurt, 1738

These publications clearly demonstrate the internal history of the chorale, namely the development from modal to tonal harmonization and from the original free rhythm to an accentual isometric rhythm. In their original form the chorales showed the flexible mensural rhythm and the durational accent of renaissance song, to which they were indebted by numerous *contrafacta*. With the turn to the sacred aria, to an accentual rhythm, and to tonal harmony toward the end of the century a rhythmic decline made itself felt in the course of which the rhythm was smoothed out to the even pace of one syllable to one beat, as we know it in Bach's harmonizations. The process of rhythmic equalization was well advanced in Briegel's chorale collection and was completed in Freylinghausen's *Gesangbuch*, the most influential collection of the eighteenth century, in which relatively few liturgical chorales were buried under a mass of pietistic songs. The innumerable *contrafacta* of operatic arias in the late chorale books marked the end of chorale composition.

Chorale harmonizations were functional music or *Gebrauchsmusik* without higher ambition and derived their strength from this very fact. The wide musical range within the small frame can be seen in Ex. 19 in which five settings of *Ein feste Burg*, Luther's paraphrase of *Deus noster refugium*, by the leading masters Schütz, Schein, Scheidt, König, and Bach are juxtaposed.[19] The first three preserve in their free distribution of durational accents the old flexibility of rhythm, while the last two belong to the isometric type. Recently attempts have been made to restore the old "polymetric" rhythm of the chorales in the congregational singing of our

---

[16] See CE.
[17] Reprinted Bärenreiter edition no. 53.
[18] See CE, also reprinted 1940, Bärenreiter ed. by Dietrich.
[19] For nine earlier settings of the same chorale see Blume *Evangelische Kirchenmusik*, 76.

day. It must be realized, however, that the original mensural rhythm can be revived only at the expense of the tonal harmony which characterizes our modern usage. While the modal settings readily allow of polymetric flexibility, Bach's harmonies would lose much of their directed drive if forced on the original rhythm.

Ex. 19. Chorale harmonizations *Ein feste Burg.*

The music of the Reformed Church was restricted to the Huguenot Psalter in the German translation of Lobwasser. Goudimel's settings of the traditional melodies, most commonly used, were expanded by Moritz, Landgrave of Hessen (1612). The simple settings of the Basle organist Mareschall (1606) carried the melody in the highest voice. Schütz also composed a book of metrical psalms after the translation of Cornelius Becker, mostly with new melodies of his own. The psalms were sometimes presented in amusing editions for edification, with flower pictures and emblems—for example in the *Lust und Artzeney-Garten* (1675) (see plate 8).

The great fashion of spiritual continuo songs in the vernacular prompted also a number of important Catholic collections espoused especially by the Jesuits. They included publications by the Austrian Prior Corner (*Grosscatholisch Gesangbuch*, 1625), Kuen, Glettle, Laurentius von Schnüffis (*Mirantisches Flötlein*, 1682) and, above all, the *Trutznachtigall* (1629, published posthumously in 1649) by the Jesuit Friedrich von Spee. The latter overcame the generally mawkish tone of the words in a few inspired, yet simple, songs of which *In stiller Nacht* has actually remained alive to the present day in a famous setting by Brahms which he passed off as a "German folksong." Occasionally German songs were even used as substitutes for the Mass music in the Catholic service (*Singmesse*), if no other music was available.

CHORALE MOTET AND CHORALE *Concertato*: SCHEIN

The two methods of exegesis, the objective presentation and the subjective interpretation of the "word" divided the figural music of the Protestant church into two equally important fields. They had the *concertato* style in common, but the first was bound by a chorale *cantus firmus*, the second only by the subjective imagination of the composer. Most German composers were active in both fields; only in the orbit of Schütz was the interest in the chorale subordinated to free composition. The greatest German masters of the early baroque, Hans Leo Hassler (1565-1612), Michael Praetorius (1571-1621), Heinrich Schütz, (1585-1672), Johann Hermann Schein (1586-1630), and Samuel Scheidt (1587-1654), were surrounded by a host of lesser lights whose music is comparatively well known thanks to the various *Denkmäler* editions. Hassler was the first great German composer to undertake an "Italian Journey" which must be regarded as a symptom of the Italian domination over German music. Like his friend Giovanni Gabrieli he studied with Andrea Gabrieli, and from the time of Hassler to that of Handel and Mozart German composers traditionally sought their final education in Italy.

The most conservative of the *cantus firmus* compositions was the chorale motet which continued the polyphonic chorale settings of the renaissance. Although the chorales were not strictly biblical in their texts they were regarded as the pillars of the liturgy and thus paralleled the liturgical function of the Gregorian chant in the Catholic church. Music with a chorale *cantus firmus* showed generally a retrospective style. The task of adapting the chorale to the Italian innovations, the affective interpretation of the word, the continuo, and the *concertato* style could not be solved at one stroke. Hints at the future can be observed first in the penetration of counterpoint by an advanced harmonic vocabulary and in the migrant *cantus firmus,* that is a chorale that shifted in the course of the composition to any one of the voices in alternation. The famous chorale motets (1597), and the *Preussische Festlieder* by Eccard (d. 1611), posthumously published and expanded by his pupil Stobäus (1642), established the type for the baroque period. Michael Praetorius presented in his *Musae Sioniae* (I–IX, 1601 ff.) a veritable encyclopedia of chorale arrangements. The collection comprised more than 1200 compositions ranging from simple chorale harmonizations to overwhelming polychoral settings in the Venetian manner. In Part IX of the work Praetorius discriminated between three manners of chorale arrangement, "motet-wise," "madrigal-wise," and "*cantus-firmus*-wise." In the first manner the chorale pervaded the contrapuntal interplay of all the voices; in the second, the chorale was broken up into small fragments and motives set in a *concertato* dialogue; in the third, the *cantus firmus* was left intact and led against ostinato motives also derived from the chorale—a procedure obviously borrowed from the technique of the organ chorale. Only the first and last manners belonged to the chorale motet, the second showed Praetorius on the way to the chorale *concertato,* but all three were to become important for the elaborate chorale treatment in the future. Occasionally also instruments participated in the chorale motet, as can be seen in the works of Praetorius and Johann Staden.[20]

The *Psalmen und christliche Gesäng* (1607) by Hassler were, according to the author "composed fugue-wise," that is, they corresponded to the motet manner of Praetorius. Equally important in musical and liturgical respect, this collection belongs to the small group of compositions that were revived as early as the eighteenth century. It has been re-edited by Kirnberger, the pupil of Bach.[21] Hassler gave in his *Psalmen* classic examples of the chorale motet in which all voices participated in the melodic contours of the chorale. The organ master Scheidt also made, in his *Cantiones sacrae* (1620), a significant contribution to the chorale motet. In imitation of his organ variations he cast each verse of the chorale into a different

[20] See DTB 7:1, and 8:1.
[21] Reprinted by Saalfeld, Bärenreiter edition.

setting and thus arrived at a chain of contrapuntal variations which forms one of the roots of the chorale cantata.

Unlike the conservative motet the chorale *concertato* was written in a progressive style, clearly manifested in the use of the continuo. Whereas the continuo formed only an optional part of the motet, it was indispensable in the *concertato*. The continuo found a staunch supporter in Praetorius whose *Syntagma musicum* (I–III, 1615 ff.) is an invaluable source of information for early baroque music. Praetorius translated the rules of Viadana and naturally adhered to Viadana's conservative conception of continuo practice. Praetorius's first experiments with the continuo in the *Musae Sioniae* were feeble and insignificant. However, in his *Polyhymnia caduceatrix* (1619) he applied it to the resplendent Venetian style. This collection contains many-voiced *concertato* compositions with brilliant instrumental and vocal choruses and lively *gorgia* passages for the soloists which clearly bespeak a modern spirit. It should be noted that Praetorius was cautious enough to print the ornamented version above the unembellished parts in case the German singers were not able to cope with the *gorgia*. Even though Praetorius could not compete with the harmonic ventures and the magic sonorities of Gabrieli, he handled the polychoral style most skilfully and brought to it the elements of the chorale, which Gabrieli did not know; at the same time the chorale restrained him from going far into the affective representation of the words.

The affective spirit remained, as in Italy, the domain of the few-voiced *concertato*. It found its first clear expression in Schein's *Opella nova* or *Geistliche Konzerte* (I, 1618; II, 1626) which must be considered as a milestone in the development of the chorale *concertato*. The title *Geistliche Konzerte* appeared here for the first time in German music. Schein, the successor of Calvisius at St. Thomas' in Leipzig and, like Kuhnau, one of the outstanding predecessors of Bach, combined a restless and excitable harmonic sense with a pronounced talent for affective melody. All pieces of Part I of the *Opella nova*, except one, are based on chorale texts for the liturgical year, and nearly always, also, the melody is retained. Not content with the presentation of the chorale Schein strove at the same time for a highly subjective interpretation. In his desire to interpret the affection of the words he distorted the chorale tunes, broke them up into fragments, vivified the rhythm, and infused them with extraneous chromaticism or exuberant *gorgia* (Ex. 20). As a rule, the single phrases of the chorale are stated at intervals in *cantus firmus* fashion [22] and the concerting voices emphasize the verbal interpretation by an almost manneristic repetition of single words. Sometimes, however, the chorale is completely absorbed into the intricate rhythmic dialogue of the voices and appears only in motivic,

Ex. 20. Schein: Chorale *Concertato, Aus tiefer Not* from *Opella nova.*

not in integral form. The style of Schein was heavily indebted to Italian models, especially to Monteverdi's duet style with concerting instruments. While the contrast motives and the lofty interplay of the instrumental and vocal parts were obviously due to Italian influence, the fast pace of the changing harmony and the affective *cantus firmus* treatment were German characteristics.

Schein proceeded even more radically in the chorale monody which laid the ground for the future solo cantata. In the few monodic compositions of the *Opella nova* the solo voice was forced to give both the chorale and its interpretation simultaneously. While the vocal part retained the remarkable rhythmic and melodic flexibility of the monodic style, the vague bass line that was customary in the Italian monody was disciplined by the rigidly progressive beat of the instrumental accompaniment. Schein achieved here a unique fusion of the mechanical instrumental style of the north with the Italian monody.

With the rising trend toward subjective interpretation composers tended to ignore the dogmatic significance of the chorale melody and to set the chorale texts as a free chorale *concertato* without reference to the melody. Schein took this last step also. In Part II of the *Opella nova* the relations between chorale text and melody are sometimes completely severed. The memorable monody *O Jesu Christe* of Part I may be mentioned, too, as an example of the free chorale *concertato*. Its musical intensity testifies to the powerful personality of its composer.

Schein's works stand at the beginning of the long and devious development from the chorale *concertato* to the chorale cantata. Many organists and cantors pursued the course of Schein, notably Scheidt in his *Geistliche Conzerten* (1631 ff.). The smaller masters of the chorale *concertato* in the early and middle baroque period can be grouped into three regional schools.

[22] GMB no. 188.

The north German school included Thomas Selle (d. 1663) in Hamburg; Matthias Weckmann (d. 1674), a pupil of Schütz; the important Franz Tunder (1614-1667) of Lübeck, predecessor and father-in-law of Buxtehude; and finally Christoph Bernhard who transmitted to us a valuable treatise on composition, based on the precepts of his teacher Schütz. The south German school which had its center in Nuremberg comprised Johann Staden (d. 1634), and Erasmus Kindermann (d. 1655), a pupil of Staden and Cavalli. The central German school of Saxony and Thuringia centered round Andreas Hammerschmidt (1639-1675), a most prolific and popular composer who watered down the achievements of Schütz for the multitude. It included also the three Thomas cantors between Schein and Kuhnau: Michael, Knüpfer, and Schelle.

All these masters contributed to the expansion of the chorale *concertato* into the chorale cantata. The various media of the chorale *concertato*, the many-voiced, the few-voiced, and the monodic, were no longer kept apart but were combined in large multipartite compositions in which solo, choral, and instrumental sections alternated. Here lie the beginnings of the chorale cantata. The organ chorale variation which Scheidt had already transferred to the chorale motet was also applied to the chorale *concertato* so that the composer had a great variety of styles at his disposal. The single verses could now be composed alternately as duets, monodies, choruses, and ensembles with or without instrumental accompaniment. One of the earliest attempts in this direction was Scheidt's *Nun komm der Heiden Heiland* from the *Geistliche Conzerten,* in which the eight verses were set in strictly organistic manner with *cantus firmus* and a simple chorale harmonization at the end, as customary in the later cantata. Selle was active primarily in the few-voiced medium, Weckmann [23] in the many-voiced *concertato.* Tunder's chorale variations are remarkable for the extensive use they make of the *concertato* style and the inner expansion of the form. He more nearly approached the cantata than any other composer of the time. Tunder and Hammerschmidt both cultivated the chorale monody, the latter also the free composition of chorale texts. The chorale *concertato per omnes versus,* that is with a varied setting for each stanza, can actually be called a cantata although we find as yet only very sporadically the distinguishing feature of the late baroque cantata, namely a freely inserted poetic passage that interrupts the liturgical text by moralizing reflections. However, the strict chorale cantata in form of variations like Bach's *Christ lag in Todesbanden* grew directly out of the cantatas of Franz Tunder.

[23] EL II, 4.

THE DRAMATIC *Concertato*: SCHÜTZ

Compositions bound by a chorale represented in spite of their liturgical prominence only the smaller portion of Protestant church music. The larger portion consisted of freely composed "church concerts" which interpreted the word subjectively with all the dramatic resources of the *concertato* style. In keeping with the orthodox attitude of the time the composers used as the main textual source the psalms and the gospel in either Latin or German.

The dramatic *concertato* was cultivated by nearly all composers referred to above in connection with the chorale motet and the chorale *concertato*. However, while it was only a side issue with them, it held a central position in the works of composers who were dazzled by the Italian style in general and by the Venetian polychoral style in particular. They shared with the Italian composers the belief that *cantus firmus* composition was a thing of the past. The earlier generation of German composers still managed to do without the continuo and betrayed its conservatism also in adhering to Latin text. It included masters like Demantius (d. 1643), Dulichius (d. 1623), Staden, Melchior Franck, Friderici,[24] Hassler, Michael Praetorius, and Hieronymus Praetorius (d. 1629). The latter Praetorius, who was active as organist in Hamburg, wrote for a combination of four five-voice choruses with considerable ease. Schein paid his tribute to Venice in the *Cymbalum Sionium* (1615), and Scheidt in the *Concertus sacri* (1622) which contained colorful settings for solo ensembles, echo choruses, and instrumental sinfonie. The harmonic language of these compositions was conservative and did not venture much beyond the cadential frictions that can be found in the music of Gabrieli.

More influential than the grand *concertato* works were the few-voiced or monodic compositions. They were usually set to German texts and always called for an obligatory continuo, as for example the *Geistliche Concertlein* by Selle, several works of Johann Staden, and the little-known, but charming, *Liebliche Krafftblümlein* (1635) by Scheidt. The free compositions in Schein's *Opella nova* represented the most serious attempt at assimilating the monodic principle into German music. Tobias Michael gave in his *Seelenlust*, like Praetorius, an optional *gorgia* interpretation of his solo parts.[25]

The rich instrumental accompaniment that Schein and others added

[24] EL II, 2.
[25] Example in Adler HMG, 458.

to their monodies reveals a certain hesitancy on the part of the German composers in appropriating the monody in its pure form. Praetorius succinctly expressed this attitude in his *Syntagma* by the remark that one or more *concertato* voices by themselves were "too naked." He advised supplementing them by what he called a *capella fidicinia,* a string ensemble, the favorite medium of dance music. Scheidt composed seventy *Symphonien auf Conzerten-Manier* (1644) expressly for this purpose.

German music soared to unprecedented heights in the works of the undisputed master of the dramatic *concertato:* Heinrich Schütz (1585–1672), the greatest of the quartet of S's. Schütz belonged to the few German baroque composers who combined a wide European perspective with the aristocratic attitude of an highly individual artist. Reared in a Calvinist milieu, but an orthodox Lutheran himself, he showed remarkable tolerance in religious matters. He approached, at times, a Catholic spirit in his music. Schütz and Handel were the only great Protestant composers of the time who took little interest in the chorale as such. Although his official duties brought him in constant contact with the chorale, Schütz made it subservient to his personal artistic expression. The composer-prince Moritz of Hessen discovered the young Schütz among the promising choir-boys and decided to provide for his musical education. It was completed by an apprentice period in Venice with Gabrieli, who recognized in him a worthy successor. Schütz served for fifty-five years (1617–72) as music director to the elector of Saxony, but was permitted to take several long leaves during the Thirty Years' War which he spent at the court in Copenhagen.

Schütz's apprentice piece, his op.1, was a book of Italian madrigals (1611) in which he carried the affective pictorialism of the madrigal style to its last possible extreme. The consistent use of contrast motives, the adventurous dissonance treatment, the realistic and intellectual representation of words, which could successfully rival the mature madrigals of Gesualdo and Monteverdi, appeared here for the first time. They remained the fundamental elements of his style. Schütz's fertile imagination drew ever new plastic ideas and inspiration from these devices.

In his first great work of German church music, the polychoral *Psalmen Davids* (1619), Schütz adopted the grand manner of Gabrieli in compositions for two, three, and four choruses with instruments. Like Gabrieli, he allowed a wide margin for the arranger since he did not always specify the orchestration. As described in the *Syntagma* by Praetorius, the clefs of the individual parts hinted at almost unlimited vocal and instrumental combinations. Schütz distinguished in the preface between *cori favoriti* (vocal and instrumental solo ensembles) and the full *cappella,* one or two of which could be added "for splendor" at the higher or lower octaves. He clearly evolved a stylistic differentiation between solo and choral ensemble, only tentatively suggested in Gabrieli's music. A continuo for one or more organs held the compositions together, but it was frequently as superfluous as in the grand *concertato* of his teacher. Schütz claimed in his preface that he had composed the psalms in *"stylo recitativo,* hitherto almost unknown in Germany." He referred here not to the monodic style, but merely to the rigid declamatory principle that governed his choral settings. Imaginatively utilizing speech rhythm, he arrived at a discontinuous, yet rapidly flowing, musical rhythm that was frequently interrupted by cadences and echo effects. His plastic pictorial imagination manifested itself in the characteristic contours of his motives; sometimes, however, he overreached himself, for example when he depicted the words "he slumbers not" by a rocking slumber motive in exact inversion of the sense. Schütz's urge to write the meaning of the words into the hearts of his hearers at any cost led to curious examples of negative interpretation, which can be found not only with the masters of the Italian madrigal, but also with Bach. Schütz warned in his preface against an overhasty performance and pleaded for a moderate tempo so that "the words of the singers may be intelligibly recited and understood." The omnipresent contrast motives indicated that Schütz, like Gabrieli and Monteverdi, transposed the madrigal style to sacred music. The point is confirmed by the musical monument that Schütz raised to his teacher. He turned Gabrieli's madrigal *Lieto godea* into a German *contrafactum* without essential changes. It is significant that the disguised madrigal did not differ stylistically from the other psalm compositions. Praetorius praised the madrigalian alternation of very slow and very fast sections for its "charm and grace" though he conceded that the conservatives objected to this "levity."

Schütz accomplished in the *Psalmen Davids* and his subsequent works as perfect a union of words and music in the German language as Purcell did in the English language. It is true that certain passages seem to run counter to the natural speech rhythm, but many of them (though not all) do so only if sung in the modern accentual interpretation, not yet applicable to Schütz. Perhaps no other German composer ever derived so much purely musical inspiration from the German speech rhythm. Masterpieces of the collection, like *Ist nicht Ephraim* for two solo voices with *cornetti* and trombones, or the monumental polychoral *Zion spricht* demonstrate how consciously and often intellectually Schütz arrived at his inspired pictorial motives. Significantly enough, Christoph Bernhard, the author of one of the best treatises on the doctrine of figures, was a pupil of Schütz.

The formal structure of the expansive *concertato* compositions was made clear by *Alleluia* refrains in Gabrieli's manner, or by other recurrent sections which served to heighten the rondo character of the form. Rhythmic transformations of sections from duple to triple meter, and the use of identical musical material for psalm verses and the concluding doxology further unified the highly flexible form.

The *Cantiones sacrae* (1625) were based on mystic Latin texts, more appropriate for the Catholic than the orthodox Lutheran service. In their extremism they form a sacred pendant to the madrigal book. Schütz composed them in a radical *concertato* motet style for four voices and continuo which he added only reluctantly at the entreaties of his publisher. The subjective attitude of the texts very closely corresponds to that of the music which goes to the very limits of pictorial dissonance treatment. The severely contrapuntal texture is shot through with simultaneous cross-relations, melodic dissonances, and augmented triads, characteristically set to the word *dulcis* (Ex. 21).

Ex. 21. Schütz: *O bone* from *Cantiones sacrae.*

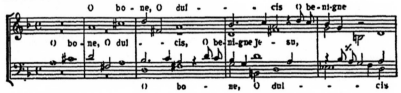

Although Schütz continued to write music of remarkable austerity he never returned in his later works to this overemphatic style. Very few other German composers could equal it. A work of similar intensity was the *Fontana d'Israel* or *Israel's Brünnlein* (1623) by Schein in which the author exhausted the pictorial possibilities of the German words, as he put it, "in the manner of the Italian madrigal." Also the profound *Kernsprüche* (1648 ff.) by Rosenmüller belong to this category.

In the *Symphoniae sacrae,* published in three parts (1629, 1647, and 1650), Schütz reaped the fruits of his second journey to Italy. They hold as important a position in his creative career as the works of the same title do in that of Gabrieli. The fact that Schütz in his full maturity went a second time to Italy to learn from the "sagacious" Monteverdi, as he called him, bespeaks not only his personal humility but also his great respect for the Italian style. In Part I of the *Symphoniae sacrae* the *concertato* style appears fully stabilized and the three vocal parts form, with the exactly specified instrumental ensembles, a highly coloristic yet thoroughly unified whole. Several of Schütz's pieces were only German adaptations of Italian compositions by Monteverdi and Grandi.[26] In the medium of the small *concertato* Schütz created scenes of great vision, like the somber plaint of David for Absalom, for bass voice and four trombones, which must be singled out as an incomparable masterpiece. At the beginning the trombone quartet intones a sinfonia that anticipates the motive of the voice, and then the bass comes in with a bold idea of successive major thirds, a typically Schützian theme of a sophisticated simplicity (Ex. 22).

Ex. 22. Schütz: *Fili mi, Absalon* from *Symphoniae sacrae I.*

In Parts II and III of the *Symphoniae sacrae* Schütz acknowledged his debt to Monteverdi not only in his interesting revisions of Monteverdi's compositions, but especially in the adoption of the *stile concitato*. While he adhered in Part II to the few-voiced *concertato* he resuscitated in Part III the splendor of his earlier polychoral compositions. The vast combinations reflect the reassembling of the Saxonian court chapel after its dispersal during the Thirty Years' War. Part III contains works on the largest scale which approach the dramatic church cantata. One of these, the deeply stirring Pauline conversion (Acts 9, 4 ff.) *Saul, Saul, was verfolgst Du mich?*, is perhaps the most impressive of all of Schütz's compositions. This dramatic *concertato* was rediscovered by Winterfeld[27] more than a century ago. It is scored for an ensemble of six *favoriti* (solo sextet), two four-voice choruses or "complements," two violins, and organ continuo. At

[26] Monteverdi's *Chiome d'oro* (seventh book of madrigals) appears in the works of Schütz as the canzonetta *Güldene Haare* (CE XV, 91). Monteverdi's *Armato il cor* and *Zeffiro torna* (CE IX) have been used in *Es steh Gott auf* (*Symphoniae sacrae* II, 16), and Grandi's *Lilia convallium* reappears as *O Jesu süss* (*Symphoniae sacrae* III, 9).

[27] Winterfeld, *Gabrieli und sein Zeitalter*, II, 197. In spite of its early date this book still is one of the finest pieces of musical research. The lucid style of presentation stands in marked contrast with the studied profundity of many later books on musicology.

the beginning the solo voices give out the insistent calls "Saul, Saul" in an impetuously accelerated rhythm and come to an uncompromising cadence with stern parallel seconds, of which Schütz was as fond as Monteverdi (Ex. 23). The calls are answered by the complementary choruses and lead

Ex. 23. Schütz: *Saul, Saul* from *Symphoniae sacrae III.*

to a *fortissimo* climax which tapers off in a staggered echo effect, expressly prescribed by the composer. In the course of the composition Schütz uses the motives of the calls in contrapuntal combination with the graphic idea of "kicking against the pricks" and achieves a dramatic grandeur un-matched by any of his contemporaries.

The *Kleine geistliche Konzerte* (1636-39) were composed for very modest combinations as strict monodies or small solo ensembles. They call only for a continuo but no other instruments because, as Schütz remarks in the preface, the ruinous effect of the war had completely paralyzed musical life. In this collection Schütz gave his version of monody or, as he called it, the *stylo oratorio;* it was more flexible in style and more highly integrated by bass imitations than the early Italian parallels. Some of the sacred concerts are based on the words of chorales or Latin hymns. It is highly characteristic of Schütz's undogmatic and highly personal approach that he retained the traditional tunes only occasionally. He preferred to ignore them in favor of a free *concertato* interpretation. Two chorale set-tings (I, 24 and II, 22) even coupled the idea of chorale variation to a strict ostinato of the Italian *ruggiero* type. In this curious combination of sacred and secular techniques it was the ostinato that dominated the *cantus firmus.* The "aria" *Ich hab mein Sach* quotes the chorale in strict form only in the first and last (eighteenth) variation, while the other statements are more or less free variations on a ground bass. The *Musikalische Exe-quien* (1636), an important forerunner of Brahms's German Requiem, also made free use of chorale melodies, this time however in the polychoral medium.

The *Geistliche Chormusik* or *Musicalia ad Chorum Sacrum* (1648), dedicated to the city of Leipzig and the Thomas choir, brought the con-servative side of Schütz's genius to the fore. In the preface the aging Schütz expressed his concern about the steadily progressing decline in technical proficiency that he thought to observe in the younger generation, brought up only on the continuo, and advocated the return to the thorough training that he had himself received in Italy. He admonished the budding German composers to perfect themselves properly in the style without continuo before they proceeded to the *concertato* style, to learn the requisites of a "regulated composition," [28] and to "crack the hard nut in which one has to seek the kernel and the proper foundation of a good counterpoint." Schütz called in the *Chormusik* for a mixed vocal and instrumental performance and discriminated between two possibilities: one in which the solo or choral ensemble could be doubled by instruments, another in which vocal and instrumental parts were deliberately kept apart. For neither one was the continuo obligatory; both stood halfway between a-cappella and *concertato* styles. The *Chormusik* is written in a remarkably archaic contrapuntal style. The affective intensity of the music is subdued by the graphic terseness of the melody and the austere asceticism of the counterpoint that seems to hark back to the old motet. Only the restive contrast motives and the relentlessly dissonant harmonic vocabulary betray a modern spirit. In the *Geistliche Chormusik* Schütz succeeded in doing the impossible: he fused *stile antico* and *stile moderno* into a higher unity. It is symbolic of the whole collection that Schütz inadvertently slipped into the collection a motet by Andrea Gabrieli that he had provided with a German text, probably during his student years in Italy.

The oratorical compositions of Schütz which accompany his entire career form a group by themselves. They consist of the *Auferstehungs Historie* (1623), the *Sieben Worte am Kreuz*, the *Historia von der Geburth Gottes* (1664), and three Passions according to St. Luke, St. John, and St. Matthew (1666). The Passion according to St. Mark is probably spurious. Some of these have come down to us only in strongly revised versions. The first of the so-called "histories," the Easter Oratorio, is a freely modernized variant of an earlier work by Scandello (d. 1580). Schütz used here an old-fashioned type of recitative that combined the elements of the Gregorian *tonus lectionis* and the operatic recitation. The archaic style appears also in the fact that text passages of single persons are set for more than one voice, an indication of how far removed the "history" still was from the opera. The Seven Words at the Cross and the Christmas Oratorio are much more complex works written in the modern dramatic style and involving a great many instrumental and vocal en-

---

[28] Compare the use of the same term with Bach, p. 272.

sembles in the presentation of the story. Both compositions are framed by powerful instrumental and choral movements between which the story unfolds in form of recitatives and ensembles. The choral introduction and conclusion of the Seven Words are based on the text of a chorale, but, significantly, its melody is not used. The words of Christ are often accompanied, as in Bach's Matthew Passion, by the halo of a string ensemble. The colorfully orchestrated Christmas Oratorio consists of single scenes or *intermedii,* bound together by the same key. In the preface Schütz draws attention to the novel recitative of the Evangelist which is far advanced over that of the Easter Oratorio. It lacks the affective tone we find in Schütz's monodies and points in its neutral parlando toward the *secco* recitative of the bel-canto opera.

In the Passions,[29] which belong to the latest works of the composer, Schütz dispensed with instruments altogether, including even the continuo. Written in a strict a-cappella style they employ with extreme economy only an unaccompanied (!) solo recitative and *turbae* or choruses. The recitatives are freely composed in the fashion of a "neo-Gregorian" *tonus lectionis.* In continuation of the ascetic trend, already manifested in the *Chormusik,* Schütz resuscitated the old Gregorian Passion in so rarified an atmosphere that it had little effect on any of his contemporaries or pupils. These works, in which liturgical severity and highly personal artistry strangely intermingle, are symbols of the creative solitude in which the aged master was to outlive his own fame.

Schütz never wrote any instrumental music independent of vocal compositions; all his efforts were directed toward the vocal pole. This fact marks the abyss that separates him from Bach who probably knew not a note of his, except perhaps his music for the Calvinist Psalter. Deeply concerned over the spreading of facile and shallow compositions prompted by the German vogue for the Italian style—the very style Schütz had brought home and Germanized in his own fashion—Schütz staunchly upheld throughout his life the supremacy of the Italian style even when it was challenged by such conservatives as the organist Siefert.

It is difficult to summarize the oratorical music and the dramatic *concertato* of Schütz's contemporaries and successors, not so much because of its immense quantity, but because it seems much less alive by comparison, though it is music of excellent workmanship. The scriptural cantatas,

[29] GMB no. 192.

dialogues, and Passions ranged from the old-fashioned motet Passion (Demantius) and the Gregorian Passion with *turbae* (Mancinus, Besler, Vulpius, Christoph Schultze), over dramatic and allegorical dialogues (Hammerschmidt, Kindermann, Rudolph Ahle), to Passions with arias and other textual insertions of contemplative character. Of the many church concerts in dramatic *concertato* style the Gospel dialogues *Musicalische Andachten* (1638–52), and *Gespraeche über die Evangelia* (1655) by Hammerschmidt [80] must be mentioned, which were widely imitated by the parochial musicians of central Germany. The light but not superficial style of his music was referred to in affectionate irony as "Hammerschmidt's foot" (Fuhrmann, 1706). The dramatic type of Passion with non-liturgical insertions appeared first with Thomas Selle (St. John Passion, 1643), Christian Flor, Sebastiani, and the Schütz pupil Johann Theile, and was further developed by Pfleger, Briegel, Meder, and Kühnhausen.[81] As early as the Passions of Sebastiani (1672) and of Theile (1673) chorales appeared at strategic places in alternation with contemplative arias, a practice that laid the ground for the Passion of the Bach type.

The Catholic church music of southern Germany stood in the shadow of Rome and, to a smaller degree, of Venice. For internal and external reasons a specifically German style did not develop in Catholic church music. The internal and decisive reason was that composers looked upon Rome as their spiritual center and therefore emulated the Italian style. The external reason was that the key positions in Munich, Salzburg, and Vienna were occupied by Italians such as Giovanni Valentini, Bertali, the two Bernabeis, and Bernardi. The influence of Lasso, greater in Germany than in any other country, lingered on well into the seventeenth century and was only slowly displaced by that of Palestrina. The conservative Aichinger,[32] an outstanding master of the transition period, was indebted to the style of Palestrina rather than to that of his teacher Gabrieli. His highly polished music in *stile antico* is noteworthy for its harmonic richness. Aichinger did not yet write monodies though he was the first to publish a printed continuo score (1607), the description of which he drew directly from Viadana whose pseudo-monodies were widely disseminated in Germany. Sacred monodies of German composers were few and far

[80] DDT 40.
[81] Reprints: Selle in CW 26, Sebastiani in DDT 17, Theile in DDT 17, Pfleger in CW 52, Kühnhausen in CW 50.
[32] DTB 10:1.

between; Klingenstein (1607) was the first to imitate the conservative continuo writing of Viadana.

The *concertato* style with instruments assumed importance with local Austrian masters such as Stadlmayr (d. Innsbruck 1648), Emperor Ferdinand III, Christoph Strauss, and, in the middle baroque generation, Johann Schmelzer, Biber, Kerll, and Emperor Leopold I. They wrote their Masses, requiems, and magnificats for great choral combinations, two or three choruses (Kerll), and impressive orchestral accompaniments with massed brass ensembles and timpani which were popularly used in the seventeenth century to lend pomp and splendor to important sections of the Mass. Like Schütz, the Catholic masters paid particular attention to the stylistic difference between solo and choral ensemble, and to the declamation of the text. Kerll set his choruses in the manner of his teacher Carissimi with imitative, though harmonically conceived, texture. The Austrian composers did not hesitate to employ in the orchestral accompaniment of their Masses such operatic devices as the tremolo which occurs in Kerll's Requiem,[33] or the programmatic imitation of bells, which can be found in the sinfonia to a Kyrie by Strauss.[34] The Mass was internally organized as a unified whole by means of repeats of the same music to different words, rhythmic transformation of the same motives (Kerll's Requiem) and the alternation of florid solo ensembles and concise chordal choruses in church cantata fashion. The plainsong Mass was definitively supplanted by the *concertato* Mass or cantata Mass, designated by such general titles as *Missa S. Henrici* (Biber) or *Missa solemnis* which have survived to the present day.

CONTINUO LIED, OPERA, AND ORATORIO

Although secular German music of the early baroque was heavily indebted to Italian innovations, it preserved an individual tone because of its conservatism and its traditional penchant for contrapuntal texture. As in sacred music, German composers were slow in assimilating monody. The point of departure for the secular song literature was the Italian partsong "to sing, dance and play" which Hassler had brought back from his Italian apprentice period. In his German songs "in the manner of foreign madrigals and canzonets," and especially in his valuable *Lustgarten* (1601) [35] Hassler transplanted to German soil the villanelle, canzonette,

[33] DTOe XXX:1 (vol. 59).
[34] *ib.*
[35] Eitner PAM 15.

and dance songs of Gastoldi and Vecchi. The charming sentiment and freshness of his melodies was not yet tinged by the modern affective tone. Like the dance-song collections for voices or instruments by Melchior Franck, Haussmann, Widmann, and Johann Staden, Hassler's songs represented a hybrid vocal-instrumental literature in which the continuo was either optional or altogether lacking, as was characteristic of the transition period.

The few-voiced *concertato* style with obligatory continuo made its entry in the three-voice *Musica boscareccia* (1621–28) by Schein. In the preface the author suggested various manners of performance, ranging from a-cappella singing to solo song with continuo for either soprano or tenor. It is symptomatic of Schein's modern attitude that he left the choice of voice register to the performer as many Italian monodists had done before him. Written in what Schein called the "Italo-Villanellian invention" the *Musica boscareccia* consisted of strophic songs with slight *gorgia* passages. Schein adopted here the airy dialogue of the Monteverdian continuo canzonetta and not by coincidence did he supply dynamic and tempo marks in Italian. The adroit pictorial open-work of his gay and concise motives was far removed from the self-contained melodies of Hassler's songs. Schein frequently wrote his own lyrics, which disclose a respectable poetic talent though the trifling pastoral subjects are presented with a mannered emphasis on diminutives. The *Diletti pastorali* (1624), composed in the "madrigalian manner," pay tribute to the Italian continuo madrigal. Here Schein, in obvious emulation of Monteverdi, gave most valuable German madrigals for five voices and instruments in through-composed form.

Schein was one of the first German musicians to adopt the poetic form of the madrigal in music. Schütz followed suit in a few madrigalian *concertato* compositions with instrumental sinfonie to words by Opitz; Selle also wrote in a similar vein. In spite of Schein's very successful madrigals, madrigalian poetry was slow to gain a foothold in Germany. As late as 1653 the poet Caspar Ziegler, with the aid of Schütz, made a strong effort to introduce the madrigal into German poetry, praising it as "a beautiful kind of verse, most suitable for music." His plea found an echo with Knüpfer whose *Lustige Madrigale* (1663) [36] brought a belated vogue for the German continuo madrigal.

Strict monodies, apparently, did not appeal very strongly to German

[36] H. J. Moser, *Corydon* II.

musicians. The first monodic collection in Germany, the *Arie passegiate* [37] by Nauwach, appeared as late as 1623. The author acknowledged his debt to Italy not only by the title and the texts, but also by including Caccini's well-known monody *Amarilli* which he paraphrased with flamboyant *gorgia* passages. Nauwach's *Teutsche Villanellen* (1627) assume, except for an ambitious *romanesca* variation, a very popular tone, characteristic of the entire German literature. The static basses and the discontinuous rhythms of the Florentine recitative had on the whole only a negligible effect on German monodies. The *Arien und Kantaten* (1638) by Kittel, a pupil of Schütz, represent the rather naïve attempt to turn the virtuoso technique of castrato singing into a vocal drill for German choir boys. Following the practice of Grandi, Nauwach and Kittel composed their "cantatas" in the form of strophic variations. It is therefore hardly surprising that they are based in part on the *ruggiero* [38] and the *romanesca*. Kittel advised beginners to sing all stanzas to the music of the first and simple variation before they tried the subsequent ones which became progressively more ornate. The German text by Opitz that Kittel used for the *ruggiero* variations was also set by Nauwach, but without ostinato.[39]

The main stream of secular music took the course of the strophic continuo lied which paralleled in scope and perfection of style the song literature of the English lutenists. The continuo lied represented the second great flowering in the history of the German song, its first peak being the tenor lied of the renaissance and its third the piano lied of the classic and romantic periods. Consistent with their conservative proclivities the German composers did not cultivate exclusively the modern monodic style but included in their collections polyphonic songs, even suggesting that in monodic songs a second voice might be improvised. They frequently provided ritornelli for as many as five voices, to be played between the stanzas.

The continuo lied flourished in the three regional schools. The leader of the north German school was Heinrich Albert (1604-1651), the cousin of Schütz, whose inspired *Arien* (1638-1650) [40] were sung all over Ger-

---

[37] Einstein, SIMG XIII, 286 ff.
[38] Riemann HMG 2:2, 352; compare the similarities between Kittel's and Frescobaldi's *ruggiero* variations (TAM IV).
[39] Haas B, 100.
[40] GMB no. 193.

many. Albert set to music not only the lyrics of Simon Dach but also his own. The north German school comprised in addition Thomas Selle, notable for his monodic collection *Monophonetica* (1636),[41] Rubert, Loewe, Delphin Strungk (the father of Nikolaus), Caldenbach, Gre'fflinger,[42] and the poet-musician Rist.[43] With the musical aid of Schop and others Rist published *Galathea, Sabbathische Seelenlust, Florabella* (1644), and many other collections containing sacred and secular miniature songs in very popular style. The trumpeter Gabriel Voigtländer contributed, in his *Allerhand Oden* (1642),[44] to the lowest stratum of German songs. They were exclusively parodies of *airs de cour* and other songs drawn from Italian, English, and French authors whose names were never disclosed. Rist's and Voigtländer's collections included among other English songs also Dowland's *Can she excuse* (which appears in the Fitzwilliam Virginal Book in an anonymous arrangement)—an indication that English songs remained popular in Germany even longer than in England. The south German school included Johann Staden (*Venus Kräntzlein* and *Hertzenstrost-Musica*), Sigmund Staden (the son of Johann), Kindermann, and Capricornus (Bockshorn). The most fertile center was the central German school with Schein, Nauwach, Kittel, Rudolf Ahle, Hammerschmidt (*Weltliche Oden*, 1642),[45] Neumark, Dedekind (*Aelbianische Musenlust*, 1657), and Adam Krieger (1634–1666), the pupil of Scheidt.

In Krieger's *Arien* (1657–1667) for solo voice or small solo ensembles and sonorous five-part ritornelli, the continuo lied achieved its perfection. He combined in his melodies the clarity of the Italian bel canto with the strong and concise rhythms of the German song style, obviously derived from the dance. The influence of the dance on song style can be seen in occasional rhythmic transformations, in the manner of the varied couple, that occur in Albert's songs. The homespun humor and the delicate gravity of the texts was matched by the profound sentiment of the music. Although popular in tone these songs were not folksongs, but were intended for "civil" use, to revive a term of the English theorist Butler. The civil songs served as popular entertainment and were sung in the homes of the middle class in the cities and at the gatherings of students in the *collegia musica* of the universities.

[41] Haas B, 100.
[42] GMB no. 206, Müller *Geschichte des deutschen Liedes*, App. 18.
[43] Müller, *l.c.* p. 14.
[44] See Fischer, SIMG XII, 17 ff.
[45] GMB no. 194, H. J. Moser. *Alte Meister des deutschen Liedes.*

Albert and Krieger were great only in the medium of the small forms; they represent respectively the early and the mature phase of the continuo lied. It is characteristic of Albert's German background that his collections make no clear distinction between secular and sacred literature and present dance songs, chorales, short recitatives, and choral songs indiscriminately mixed together. Both composers expanded the strophic form to larger units by joining different strophes together, to be sung in alternation. Although Albert admitted in the preface to his arias that only the through-composed song did justice to the words, he wrote in this form only occasionally. The influence of Schütz on Albert's style may account for Albert's marked leanings toward the Italian recitative; recitative sections frequently interrupt the continuity of the song, and Albert expressly pointed out that these should be sung "without measure" in the manner of "a clear narration." The rhapsodic elements in Albert's melodies give his songs a peculiar charm. Krieger on the other hand kept aloof from the recitative and designed his bel-canto melodies against a very active bass in close adherence to dance patterns (Ex. 24). He approached

Ex. 24. Adam Krieger: Continuo Lied.

at times the Italian chamber cantata with ritornelli in which aria and arioso were consciously differentiated. After Krieger, the continuo song rapidly declined under the impact of the oncoming German opera. It was assimilated by the operatic aria or survived only in modest songs derived from French à-la-mode dances.

The origins of the German opera and oratorio cannot easily be traced because of lack of sources. The low comedy plays of the English comedians, who swarmed all over the Netherlands and Germany after 1600, can hardly be called operas since the numerous stanzas were sung to a few popular ballad tunes, among which the *English Roland* or *Lord Willoughby, Fortune my foe,* and *Pickelherring* were the most famous. Some of them appeared in keyboard arrangements in the Fitzwilliam Virginal Book. The farce *The Singing Simpkin* was translated into German (*Pickelherring in the Box,* 1620) [46] and similar farces were contained in Ayrer's collection (1618) and the *Liebeskampf* (1630), which transmitted a large repertory of popular theatre on English models.

The decisive stimulus for the opera in Germany came, of course, from Italy. It can be traced as early as 1618 (Salzburg). The first German opera *Dafne* was composed by Schütz (Torgau, 1627). It was based on the translation of Rinuccini's first libretto by Martin Opitz, the leading German baroque poet whose treatise *Von der Teutschen Poeterey* was a milestone in the development of German literature. Schütz's music is not extant, and from the libretto it can only be gathered that Opitz stressed the idyllic rather than the dramatic side of the pastoral. Schütz composed during his stay in Venice (1629) another opera, an Italian "comedy" that could be "acted singing," of which we know only through one of his letters. [47] His casual remark in this letter that the *stile rappresentativo* was "as yet totally unknown in Germany," seems to imply that *Dafne* contained little if any recitative. Schütz's ballet *Orfeo e Euridice* (1638) is also lost. The first German opera to survive was *Seelewig*, [48] a rather wooden allegorical play from the *Frauenzimmer-Gesprächsspiele* (1644) of Harsdörffer with music by Sigmund Staden. In the music chorale quotations, continuo songs, and Florentine recitatives form a strange mixture of styles.

The school dramas and the Jesuit morality plays also furnished a small basis for semi-operatic spectacles. The first group is represented by the *Actus oratoricus* with incidental music by Melchior Franck. [49] In Munich, one of the centers of the Jesuit drama, the anonymous *comedia sacra Philatea* [50] was performed in 1643. It was followed by the sacred play *Pia et fortis mulier* (1677) by Kerll, the music of which was through-composed in operatic fashion.

The main activity in the field of opera lay, however, in the hands of Italian musicians employed at the German and Austrian courts, such as Maccioni, Ercole and Giuseppe Bernabei in Munich, and Bontempi in

[46] See Bolte in *Theatergeschichtliche Forschungen,* 7 (1893).
[47] Moser, *Schütz,* 122.
[48] Reprinted in MfM 13, 1881. Excerpt in GMB no. 195.
[49] Haas B, 170.
[50] Lavignac E I:2, 912.

Dresden. The latter also composed (with Peranda) two German operas, *Daphne* (1672) and *Jupiter und Io* (1673). Vienna must be regarded as the main outpost of Italian opera. The Italian tradition began with the performance of Monteverdi's *Ritorno* and Cavalli's *Egisto* and persisted throughout the baroque period with Bertali, Cesti, Pietro Ziani, and Draghi whose works are discussed in Chapter IV. The Austrian emperors Ferdinand III and Leopold I were both active in the field of opera; Ferdinand disclosed his respectable musical proficiency in the *Drama musicum* (1649) composed in strictly Venetian style, and Leopold wrote arias and many *feste teatrale* that were inserted in operas and school dramas. Biber's only extant opera *Chi la dura la vince* [50a] (Salzburg, 1687) shows in spite of its dependence on the Italian bel-canto style a remarkably independent attitude.

The German oratorio literature of the middle baroque was at first insignificant. It developed out of modest school dramas such as the sacred *Nuremberg Acts* (c. 1650) in which chorales, choruses, and songs alternated with spoken narration. The decisive influence came again from Italy after Carissimi had established the oratorio. The first attempt to transplant the originally Catholic form into the Protestant milieu was made by Fromm in the *Actus musicus: De Divite et Lazaro* [50b] (Stettin, 1649). He closely adhered to Carissimi's oratorios, but Germanized them by means of chorale melodies. The oratorical dialogue in Latin was extensively cultivated by Kaspar Foerster who had received his training in Italy and was active in Copenhagen and northern Germany. His Latin dialogues *David, De Divite, Holofernes* (c. 1660),[51] are strongly influenced by Carissimi's plastic and concise choral style. The Austrian oratorios, too, were predominantly Italian, not only in their style but also in their texts. Emperor Leopold's oratorio *Die Erlösung des menschlichen Geschlechts* (1679),[52] one of the few oratorios in German, is noteworthy for the individual tone of the music. The Viennese evolved a special type of oratorio in the so-called *sepolcro* performed during Holy Week in semi-operatic manner. The brief allegorical action of the *sepolcro* took place before a representation of the Holy Sepulchre in the church. The *Sacrificio d'Abramo* (1660) by Emperor Leopold established the form, and later the Austrian Schmelzer and Richter contributed to the *sepolcro* composition, not to mention Sances, Draghi, and the other Italians. Except for

[50a] See Schneider, AMW, VIII, 281.
[50b] *Denkmäler der Musik in Pommern, 5.*
[51] Schering, *Oratorium*, 160.
[52] GMB no. 225.

the occasional use of naïve popular songs of Viennese local color the Austrian operas and oratorios depended on the Italian middle baroque style.

INSTRUMENTAL MUSIC: SCHEIDT, FROBERGER, BIBER

In German keyboard literature of the early baroque period the organ held the central position and most of the music was composed for this instrument, even if the titles left the choice between organ or harpsichord. The distinction between the idioms of the two instruments was in its incipient stage, since very little use was as yet made of the pedal, and when it occurred at all the composer took pains to indicate the fact in the title.

Three influences converged in the German tradition of keyboard music, all of which contributed to the great achievements of the future. The first was the German tradition of the colorists who embellished vocal settings with a highly intricate embroidery of idiomatic keyboard figuration which completely obscured the vocal origin of the model. The second came from Italy, especially from the Venetian and Roman schools (Merulo, Gabrieli, and Frescobaldi). The third and most potent was the Dutch influence of Sweelinck, the maker of German organists, who transmitted the Anglo-Italian style to the schools of northern and central Germany.

Of the three regional schools, the south German school was directly dependent on Gabrieli and Merulo. Hans Leo Hassler and his brothers, Christian Erbach (d. 1635),[53] Holtzner, Steigleder (d. 1635), and Kindermann (d. 1655) preserved the tradition of the colorists and in their toccatas and canzonas leaned heavily on the Italian models. The *Tabulatura italica,* a set of fugues by the organist Klemme (a pupil of Erbach and Schütz), followed the order of the twelve modes, a favorite pedagogical arrangement that persisted not only in the works of Pachelbel and Ferdinand Fischer, but also in the Inventions and the Well-Tempered Clavier of Bach. The *Harmonica organica* (1645) of the Nuremberg organist Kindermann is noteworthy for the obligatory use of pedals. Steigleder's forty variations on the chorale *Vater unser*[54] are concluded by a toccata. The complete interpenetration of secular and sacred techniques of variation in Steigleder's music shows the influence of the north German school, but no north German organist would have thought of making a toccata an integral part of a set of variations.

---

[53] DTB 4:2.
[54] Reprinted by Emsheimer, Bärenreiter ed. 1928, see also HAM no. 190b.

The north German school, being almost exclusively a Sweelinck product, was the bulwark of the patterned chorale variation. It could pride itself on such masters as Melchior Schildt (Hanover), Paul Siefert (Danzig), Delphin Strungk, Jacob Praetorius (the son of Hieronymus), and Heinrich Scheidemann (d. 1663). The last two were active in Hamburg, the prominent center of the school. The middle baroque generation included Franz Tunder (d. 1667), Matthias Weckmann (a disciple of Jacob Praetorius), Nikolaus Hanff (d. 1706), and Jan Reinken (1623–1722) who lived to hear Bach improvise on the organ in Hamburg.

The central German school centered round Samuel Scheidt in Halle, the most distinguished of the Sweelinck pupils, and comprised Rudolph Ahle, Briegel, and Johann Christoph Bach (1642–1703), the greatest musical ancestor of Johann Sebastian.

With Scheidt German organ music came into its own. His epoch-making *Tabulatura nova* (1624 ff.) [55] was "new" because it abandoned the traditional German organ tablature in favor of the Italian keyboard partitura which reserved for each voice a separate staff. Scheidt applied the patterned variation technique of Sweelinck with a thoroughness and severity that would touch pedantry were it not for his abstract combinative imagination. Brahms confessed that he "revelled in admiration" of it. Scheidt's chorale variations are literally "elaborations" since ceaseless "labor" in the service of God was regarded as the measure of devotion. The first two parts of the *Tabulatura nova* include, besides fugues and echoes, German chorales and secular songs; the third contains, with one exception, strictly liturgical hymns and chorales that serving as *cantus firmi* are not touched by the variational patterns. The preface expressly designates these variations as *absque ullo colore*. In his extended variations Scheidt sharpened the contrast between chorale melody and the abstract patterns of the other voices in order to emphasize the structural function of the *cantus firmus* and to make it as prominent as possible. This musical style was directly bound up with the baroque organ, minutely described by Praetorius in the *Syntagma musicum*. It provided the pedal with independent four-foot and two-foot ranks for the *cantus firmus* and made the rhythmic patterns of the voices easily audible by virtue of its brilliant, penetrating, and nasal timbres and mixture stops.[56]

[55] DDT I.
[56] In recent years organ builders have returned more and more to the baroque organ. At the suggestion of Professor Gurlitt a Praetorius organ has been reconstructed by Walker at the University of Freiburg. The reform movement was inaugurated in this country by Walter Holtkamp who has built several splendid organs in Cleveland. Also Donald Harrison's organs in the Germanic Museum at Harvard University and at the Westminster Choir School in Princeton should be mentioned.

Scheidt shared with Sweelinck the strong emphasis on rhythmic variety. His chief contribution was to show the infinite possibilities of combining abstract patterns with the *cantus firmus*. It easily escapes attention that often each phrase of the chorale melody is set off by a different rhythmic idea. The seventh verse of the chorale variation *Warum betrübst Du Dich mein Herz* (Ex. 25) [57] begins with one of the typical upbeat patterns,

Ex. 25. Scheidt: Chorale Variation from *Tabulatura nova.*

7. *Versus, Choralis in cantu*

which Scheidt liked as much as Sweelinck did, and then introduces for the second line of the melody an eighth-note pattern of similar phrasing. The variations include *bicinia* and *tricinia,* often in double counterpoint, chromatic variations *per semitonia,* and sections in *imitatio violistica* which prove that the measured string tremolo was also transferred to the organ.

The fugues of the *Tabulatura nova* are wrought in a solid contrapuntal texture and correspond exactly to what Sweelinck would have called fantasia. Scheidt expanded them to grand tripartite forms by lengthening the sections in which the theme appears in augmentation and diminution. The fantasias in echo do not transcend the limits of Sweelincks's form.

The various sets of secular variations were based on French and Flemish songs or on dances like allemandes or the *passamezzo antico.* In contrast with the chorale variation Scheidt restricted himself in the secular variation to the elaboration of a single pattern for each statement of the melody. The sequence of variations was conceived as leading up to a rhythmic climax, brought about by a consistently accelerated pace of the elaboration in ever shorter note values. The set was rounded off by a swift conclusion in triple meter. In the fugues also the drive toward a rhythmic climax is very noticeable.

Scheidt significantly distinguished between secular and sacred variation

[57] The articulation has been added in order to show the phrase structure. Compare Bach's harmonizations of the same chorale (nos. 331–333).

by calling the single statements *variatio* or *versus* respectively. The different "verses" of the chorale could be used, like the Catholic versets, for the *alternatim* practice in the service. Since the chorale had a dozen or even more stanzas, it was performed alternately either by the congregation in unison, by the *Kantorei* in a polyphonic setting, or by the organist in an organ variation. It should be noted that the number of variations did not necessarily coincide with the number of stanzas, nor was there any palpable relation between the musical patterns and the words of any particular stanza. The subjective musical interpretation of the chorale text was foreign to the early baroque organist. He merely "presented" the chorale in a purely abstract elaboration which no longer held a secular connotation but was hallowed by its liturgical purpose.

Aside from the chorale variation Scheidt cultivated also the chorale fantasy, *e.g. Ich ruf zu Dir* from the *Tabulatura nova*. In structure the chorale fantasy did not differ from the chorale motet; it consisted of a chain of strictly fugal expositions based on the successive phrases of the chorale melody. Fantasy and variation were the only forms of the organ chorale known in the early baroque period. The chorale prelude proper did not yet exist.

After Scheidt both the variation and the fantasy lost much of their liturgical severity. In the hands of the middle baroque composers the organ fantasy became a fantasy in the modern sense, namely a rhapsodic composition of demanding technical difficulty, characterized by virtuoso writing, echo effects, and an exuberant ornamentation of the chorale melody. Scheidemann, Tunder, and Reinken were the main contributors to the development of the form. Weckmann remained faithful to the figural chorale variation. It is significant that with all these composers the chorale melody was often drawn into the process of ornamentation and thus subjected to an imaginative and personal interpretation. Some late sources transmit the works of Scheidt with posthumously added embellishments of the melody.

The increasingly subjective approach to the chorale and the gradual weakening of its liturgical objectivity brought a growing rapprochement between chorale and devotional song. The origins of the chorale prelude proper were closely related with these tendencies. The prelude presented the melody only once in a contrapuntal or figurative statement, treated either as a concise fantasy or as a single variation. In fact certain manuscripts prove that single variations were selected from the set and copied down separately to serve as preludes. The chorale prelude proper arose in the north German school of the middle baroque with Nicolaus Hanff [58] and flowered with Buxtehude, Pachelbel, and Böhm. With the last three composers we have reached the transition from the middle baroque to the late baroque period. Since their works form the background to those of Bach, they will be discussed in Chapter VIII.

German harpsichord and clavichord music assumed distinctive features only in the middle baroque period. It developed an idiomatic style after the suite had been transferred from the chamber ensemble and the lute to the keyboard. This transfer originated in France and quickly spread over Europe. The first important composer for the harpsichord was Johann Jacob Froberger (1616-1667), a pupil of Frescobaldi, who served as organist at the Austrian court. He travelled extensively and came in intimate contact with the Italian, English, and French lute and harpsichord masters. The assimilation of so many diversified styles would have been a serious challenge to a less creative mind, but Froberger was able to fuse the free-voiced style and the delicate *agréments* of the French dance music with the bold harmonic language of the Italians. His facility in the various styles is reflected even in the notation of his autographs: he wrote his toccatas in the Italian keyboard score with two staves of six or more lines each; his canzonas in the polyphonic keyboard partitura with as many staves as there were parts; and his suites in the French manner on two staves with five lines each, that is the piano score as we know it today.

Froberger's powerful toccatas are written in a scintillating clavieristic style which remained exemplary for a long time. Even Bach is known to have been especially fond of Froberger's toccatas. Although very obviously tinged by the idiom of Frescobaldi the toccatas easily surpass their model in their expansive structure, their imaginative chromaticism, and their fantastic angular runs and passage work. Froberger's short toccatas *"alla levatione"* are liturgical music for the organ. They do not have the fugal sections that usually conclude the toccatas for harpsichord.

Froberger excelled in canzonas and ricercars for harpsichord and organ which are noteworthy for their clear formal organization. He brought the two main currents, represented respectively by Frescobaldi and Sweelinck, together on a higher level by directing the rhapsodic flow of Frescobaldi's variation canzona into the large form of three, four, or five parts that Sweelinck had established. The restless discontinuity of the early baroque

[58] Straube, *Alte Meister des Orgelspiels. Neue Folge*

canzona and ricercar gave way to a noble and evenly flowing polyphony which unified the individually contrasted parts. The themes, imbued with bel-canto style, assumed a characteristic shape that remained valid for the entire part. Although usually differentiated by contrasting meters, the parts were bound together by the idea of variation (Ex. 26). Froberger's

Ex. 26. Froberger: Variation canzona.

fugal forms can be regarded as the classic examples of the middle baroque variation ricercar and variation canzona. He was still very conscious of the distinction between canzona and capriccio on the one hand, and the ricercar and fantasia on the other, as can be seen in the vivacious themes of the first group and the vocal or abstract (hexachord) themes of the second group.

In his dance music for harpsichord and clavichord Froberger adopted the flexible pattern of the French suite as he found it in Chambonnières. The French suite was not yet fixed as to number and types of the dances, and the gigue, especially, did not yet form an integral part of it. Froberger's suites consisted of three basic movements: allemande, courante, and saraband. Although some of his suites foreshadow the four-movement form of the late baroque suite they differed from it in their order. In Froberger's autographs the gigue appeared, if it was present at all, as an insertion in the middle; only in the posthumously printed edition (1693) did it become the final dance. We find in the music of Froberger occasional survivals of the variation suite, but the rhythmic transformations are usually restricted to the allemande and courante.

The texture of the harpsichord suites reflects the *style brisé* and the free-voiced idioms of French lute music, discussed in Chapter V. Froberger's famous *Lamento* [59] on the death of emperor Ferdinand IV which ends with an ascending scale symbolizing the ascent to heaven, is a subtly programmatic piece in allemande rhythm which serves like an ordinary allemande as the first movement of a suite. It parallels the French *tombeau* and similarly free preludes in *tempo rubato* of the French lutenists and clavecinists; symptomatically, Froberger prescribed in one of his *tombeaux* that it should be played *sans observer aucune mesure*. The famous variation suite on the *Mayerin* [60] discloses the fusion of styles that Froberger so brilliantly effected. He treated the famous and popular allemande tune first in six patterned variations and then as varied dances with highly ornamented *doubles*. Such mixture of dance patterns and formal variations had already occurred in Frescobaldi's partitas. If the *Mayerin* suite is analyzed according to national influences the result is truly amazing: the order of the dance movements is French, the idea of the variation suite German, the mechanical patterns of the variation English, the inclusion of the dance in the variation Italian. The *Mayerin* suite thus represents a veritable inventory of national styles. The *double* of the courante from the *Mayerin* suite demonstrates that in the transfer of the lute style to the keyboard medium Froberger was perhaps more subtle than any of his German contemporaries (Ex. 27). He made of the technical limitations of

Ex. 27. Froberger: *Courante* (*Double*) from the *Mayerin* suite.

the lute a virtue by distributing the notes so as to form a composite rhythm of continuous quarter beats. Chords appeared only on important beats, so that the structure remained clear even if the music was plucked or played *staccato* in lute fashion.

[59] HAM no. 216, TAM VI.
[60] TAM VI.

If Froberger's *Mayerin* variations are compared with Jan Reinken's variations of the same tune [61] the difference between the north German and south German schools becomes very clear: Froberger's diversified elegance is the very opposite of Reinken's rigidly patterned but highly imaginative style. Among the lesser keyboard composers of the Austrian school Wolfgang Ebner stands out for a set of thirty-six variations on a theme by emperor Ferdinand III (1648) [62] in which the number of variations corresponds to the age of the composer. The entire set is organized as a variation suite; each of the three basic dance movements is varied a dozen times. Johann Kaspar Kerll (1627–1693), a pupil of Frescobaldi (and Carissimi), was the only peer of Froberger in the Austrian group. His canzonas, toccatas, and versets to the *magnificat*, are more strongly influenced by Italian style and less imaginative than those of Froberger. The Italian harpsichord virtuoso Poglietti, who was employed at the court in Vienna, gave in his suites jocular genre pieces on bird calls and other animal sounds. Kerll also used bird calls in his music, but merely as themes; Poglietti carried his programmatic tendencies much further in an *Aria* of an allemande type with twenty-three variations,[63] each of which is a picturesque caricature of various national customs. He depicted in a suite of abstract dance movements the history of the Hungarian rebellion (1672); [64] it included the trial, the decapitation of the rebels, and the final requiem in which the composer adroitly imitated the tolling of the bells. Both Ebner and Poglietti were given to resourceful, if shallow, virtuoso effects.

The German lute music of the middle baroque is best represented by Esajas Reusner (1636–1679) who, trained in the French school, brought the refined French lute technique to Germany. Symptomatically, he applied it not only in the suite but even in chorale arrangements. His imaginative suites *Deliciae testudinis* (1667),[65] which leave the sphere of ordinary dance music far behind, often begin with a stylized prelude or sonatina. His dignified style was consummated in the late baroque period by the Saxon lute master Silvius Weiss (1686–1750) who strikes in his serious music [66] a note of Bachian gravity.

[61] TAM VII.
[62] TAM VII.
[63] TAM VIII, HAM no. 236.
[64] TAM VIII.
[65] GMB no. 216, HAM no. 233.
[66] Neemann, *Alte Meister der Laute*, IV (Vieweg), and ER 12.

The steady influx of English comedians and violists into Germany at the beginning of the seventeenth century brought orchestral dance music to the Continent where it developed at a very fast pace. The preferred ensembles of the dance were quartets or quintets of viols, which should not be regarded as orchestras in the modern sense. It is significant that in Füllsack's *Auserlesene Paduanen* (Hamburg, 1607), one of the most popular dance collections of the time, English, Dutch, and Danish composers were by far in the majority. We meet here with names like Grep, Borchgreving,[67] Brade, Dowland, Harding, Edward Johnson, Peter Philips, and Thomas Simpson. The works of Simpson, the most influential English violist in Germany, were printed in Hamburg and Frankfort. Similar dance collections for four, five, or six string or wind instruments without continuo were published by Hassler in his vocal and instrumental *Lustgarten* (1601), as well as by Melchior Franck (numerous collections, 1603 ff.), Valentin Haussmann (1602 ff.), Johann Staden, Johann Moeller, Erasmus Widmann (1618), Demantius, Scheidt (*Ludi musici,* 1621), and Johannes Schultz.[68] In these sets, dances of the same type were as a rule lumped together as they were in the contemporary Italian collections. Michael Altenburg attempted, in typically German fashion, to bridge the gap between the dance and the chorale. In his chorale intradas (1620) he added a chorale melody to the instrumental ensembles "so that everybody could join in." A rather exceptional instrument chorale setting by William Brade proves that English composers also recognized the importance of the chorale for German music.

The preferred dance types included the by now old-fashioned pair of pavane and galliarde, the allemande, the courante, and the intrada. The latter was a festive processional piece which Wagner revived in the prelude to the *Meistersinger.* The pattern of the intrada was not rigidly stereotyped, but occurred in duple or triple meter, the pompous duple meter being more frequent. The dances were sometimes grouped in pairs as varied couples, but often only a single dance was printed and its rhythmic transformation to triple time (*tripla* or *proporz*) was left to improvisation. In the preface to the *Venusgarten* (1602), Haussmann expressly called for the improvisation of a *tripla* in the "Polish manner."

The most important German contribution to the development of the suite was the expansion of the form by progressive variation—a procedure that closely corresponds to the variation canzona. The varied couple

---

[67] For Grep and Borchgreving see VNM 34.
[68] See the highly variegated collection *Musikalischer Lüstgarte* (1622) in EL.

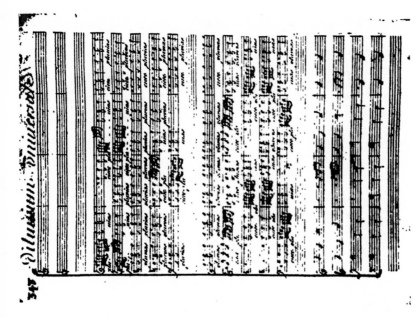

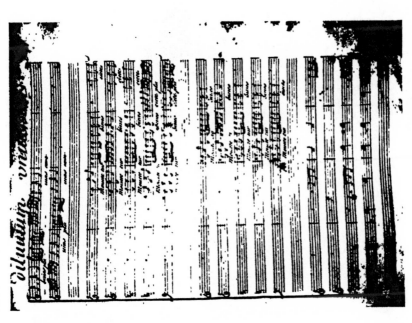

From the manuscript of Carissimi's Oratorio "The Deluge"

PLATE 3

The Palace of Paris from Cesti's "Il Pomo d'Oro"

could not yet be regarded as a cyclic form, but the combination of two varied couples led to the organization of the variation suite. This truly cyclic form was unified not only by the same key but especially by the use of the same thematic material for all the dances of the suite. The first variation suites were contained in the *Neue Paduan* (1611) [69] of the Styrian organist Paul Peurl. In Schein's famous *Banchetto musicale* (1617) the variation suite assumed its classic form. Schein made a sharp distinction between stylized dances and straight dance music by scoring the pavanes, galliardes, and courantes for a five-voice ensemble in subtly polyphonic texture, the allemande and *tripla* for only four instruments in a simple chordal texture. While the last pair was always very clearly a varied couple the first three dances were not exactly variations of an entire piece but more or less closely related transformations of the same initial motive and a free continuation (Ex. 28). That Schein consciously applied

Ex. 28. Schein: Variation suite from *Banchetto Musicale*.

the variation to the entire suite clearly transpires from the preface which asserts that the dances "well correspond to each other in *tono* and *inventione*." Other composers of variation suites, notably Isaac Posch (1617), Hammerschmidt (1636), and Neubauer (1649), observed thematic unity less consistently than Schein. It can still be discerned in their works that the variation suite originated in the joining together of two different varied couples.

The suite of the early baroque did not observe any stereotyped order and practically any combination of dances was possible.[70] Pavanes and galliardes usually opened the suite as the leading pair. Formal variations of

[69] DTOe XXXVI:2 (vol. 70).
[70] See Norlind, SIMG VII, 172, and Nef, *Geschichte der Sinfonie und Suite.*

the *passamezzo* stood, because of their length, outside of the suite. They were incorporated in the collections as an independent set of variations, as the *passamezzi* of Thomas Simpson and Haussmann show.[71] Schein adopted in his courantes the French type, characterized by a slow tempo and a sophisticated hemiola rhythm. The variation suite formed only a small, if important, part of the entire suite literature. Its technique gradually fell into oblivion in the middle baroque period and survived only very sporadically in the late baroque.

In the middle baroque phase of the ensemble suite, pavanes and galliardes all but disappeared and other dances took their places. After the model of the French suite, allemande and courante became the leading pair, often still loosely treated as a varied couple. They were followed by gigues, sarabands, and other dances most of which were taken over from French lute and harpsichord music. Stylized introductory movements began to precede the dances proper. In one of the earliest German instances of this practice, the suites of Johann Jakob Loewe (1658), the introductions were designated as sinfonie. In other collections they were called prelude, sonata, toccata, or even pavane which by this time had completely renounced its dance character. These independent introductions paved the way for the overture in the late baroque suite.

In spite of the German reserve toward the continuo the harmonic language of the suites was fairly advanced. Seventh chords were frequent at cadences and the melodies were conceived on the basis of the polarity between bass and soprano. The deeply ingrained German predilection for polyphony came to light especially in the stylized movements which contain very closely spaced imitations and a great deal of open-work within static chords. The modern trio setting with continuo was only slowly absorbed into the suite. It can be found in Peuerl (1625), Vierdank (1641), and Rosenmüller (1645).

The ensemble suites of the middle baroque comprise the collections of Loewe,[72] Diedrich Becker (1668), Furchheim[73] (who wrote the five-voice ritornelli to Krieger's *Arien*), Schmelzer (1662), the charming wind ensembles of the clarino virtuoso Pezel (d. 1694), and the *Sonate da camera* (1667)[74] by Rosenmüller. In the last collection inspired sinfonie serve as introductory movements. Johann Rosenmüller (c. 1620–1684), a composer of unquestionable genius, wrecked his promising career by

[71] See Simpson in OCM, 50, and Haussmann DDT 16, 141.
[72] Two suites in *Nagels Musikarchiv*.
[73] See the suite in *Organum*.
[74] DDT 18, GMB no. 220.

questionable morals, which made it necessary for him to flee Leipzig and live in Venice. The Venetian background of his music is apparent in his sinfonie which resemble in their variegated structure Venetian opera overtures. Hints of thematic unity between the various movements betray, on the other hand, the German background.

In the field of the ensemble canzona, less common in Germany than in Italy, Rosenmüller and Weckmann were the leading masters. The latter wrote a number of canzonas for wind instruments. The restless temperament of Schein was congenial to the quilt canzona which he adopted after the Italian precedent, but his example found no echo with other composers. The long list of canzona composers includes Vierdank, Peuerl, Hammerschmidt, Johannes Schultz, Kirchhoff, Foerster, Furchheim, Capricornus, Schmelzer, Nikolaus Strungk, and Loewe. Johann Theile's rather dry but learnedly contrapuntal sonatas of the *Musicalisches Kunstbuch* turned the technique of the variation canzona to didactic purposes. The canzonas paralleled the development in Italy: the single sections became less numerous as their dimensions grew, and as a rule the final return to the beginning was retained. This return was sometimes expanded to a true da-capo part, which occurs in the sonatas of Weckmann and Philipp Krieger.

It is symptomatic that the viol maintained a relatively important position in the polyphonic ensemble canzona, next to the wind instruments of which the German composers were especially fond. In the solo and trio sonata, however, the violin was unquestionably the leading instrument. Violin music received a powerful stimulus from such remarkable virtuosi as Johann Schmelzer of Vienna (d. 1680), his pupil (?) Heinrich Biber of Salzburg, Johann Jakob Walther, Westhoff, Thomas Baltzar,[75] and Nikolaus Strungk. They perfected the technical resources of the instrument not only with regard to range, high positions, and bowing, but especially with regard to multiple stopping, another symptom of the German penchant for polyphony. In order to facilitate polyphonic playing they most ingeniously exhausted the possibilities of the scordatura. This "mistuning" of the conventional accordatura in fifths permitted greater simultaneous use of the open strings. The solo sonatas did not observe the distinction between chamber and church sonata and indiscriminately mixed rhapsodic preludes, arias with figurative variations, dances, and

[75] GMB 237.

programmatic pieces. Walther [76] was given to fanciful programs which served, as with Farina, as a pretext for the display of stupendous virtuosity. The last piece of his *Hortulus chelicus* (1688) is a *serenata* for solo violin without continuo in which a score of instruments, including the organ, guitar, flutes, trumpets, and timpani (!), are imitated. The chamber music of Schmelzer includes a set of twelve trio sonatas (1659), another set for violins, viols, and trombones, and *Sonatae unarum fidium* (1664) which exerted a strong influence on Biber.

The violin music of the middle baroque found its consummation in Heinrich Biber (1644–1704) whose trio sonatas for viola d'amore or gamba pose many technical problems, but never allow virtuosity to become an end in itself. His valuable solo sonatas include the famous fifteen *Mystery Sonatas* (c. 1675),[77] noteworthy not only for their artistic utilization of the scordatura but also for the visionary power of their preludes. They are not programmatic in the sense of Walther's sonatas, but represent only the general affection in abstract commentaries on biblical incidents, each of which is illustrated in the autograph by a picture. Biber's eight solo sonatas (1681) combine, like the music of Froberger, a variety of national influences: French are the highly embellished doubles of the dance movements, Italian the numerous arias with variations and the frequent ostinati, English or German the consistent patterns of his variations. His monumental passacaglia in *g* for unaccompanied solo violin (Ex. 29) is built on the first type of chaconne bass (see Ex. 8). This model of systematic yet imaginative use of the patterned variation was surpassed only by the solo

Ex. 29. Biber: *Passacaglia* for unaccompanied violin.

[76] ER 17, *Scherzi da Violino solo* (1676); see also Beckmann, *Das Violinspiel in Deutschland, Beispielsammlung*, 1921.
[77] GMB no. 238, HAM no. 238.

violin sonatas of Bach. Biber fully absorbed the diversified national styles, but merged them in a highly personal stylistic unity. His music is equally far removed from the experimental harmonies of early baroque and the fully developed tonality of the late baroque style.

CHAPTER FOUR

Italian Music of the Middle Baroque

THE BEL-CANTO STYLE

THE COMPOSER Bonini to whom we owe one of the earliest histories of monody closes his report (1641) with a reference to two "new swans": Luigi Rossi in Rome and Cavalli in Venice. These names mark a new period in Italian music which coincides with the emergence of the bel-canto style between 1630 and 1640. The bel-canto style, one of the most significant contributions to the stylistic development of baroque music, has left its indelible stamp not only on the late baroque, but even on the classic period. Although it did not create many new forms it transformed the existing ones by a new concept of melody and harmony. The bel-canto style represents the reaction of musicians against the dictates of the poets. The immanent musical laws were restored, and the music was now coordinated with, rather than subordinated to, the words. As the name implies, the bel canto was essentially vocal music as found in the cantata, the oratorio, and the opera. From here its influence spread also to instrumental music.

The simplicity of bel-canto style which may appear almost trite today must be seen in the perspective of the monodic style. The melody assumed a lilting flow, nòt impeded by the exuberant coloraturas of the singer although florid sections continued to be employed for certain words. Garish virtuosity was abandoned in favor of a more restrained vocal idiom, essentially based on the penetrating and sustaining power of the castrato voice. Bel-canto melodies were more highly polished and less ostentatiously affective than those in the monody. The melodic flow was caused by a rhythmic treatment that discarded the nervous contrast motives for a continuous ternary rhythm. So often did this rhythm appear that the bel canto can actually be called the apotheosis of triple meter.

The melody was organized by stylized dance patterns, especially those of the saraband and courante, the uniformity of which was broken by the declamation of the words. The melodic ideas themselves were short and were delimited by cadences with stereotyped anticipations of the final note. Another important feature of the bel canto lies in the integration of bass and melody. The bass moved likewise in stylized dance rhythm and was often also melodically dependent on the contour of the voice line. This contrapuntal equivalence of parts increasingly asserted itself and led finally to the anticipatory imitation of the melody by the continuo at the beginning of the aria.

The harmony of the bel-canto style differed from that of the early baroque in its striking simplicity. In contrast to the empirical and not yet tonally directed progressions of the early baroque, the chords of the new style outlined a rudimentary tonality by an annoying insistence on the IV-V-I or II_6-V-I cadence in closely related keys. The frequent cadences reduced the phrase lengths of the melody and necessarily brought about a characteristic, short-winded effect which abated only in the second half of the century. The insistence on simple triadic harmony can also be felt in the melodic design, not only in the innumerable operatic "alarum" choruses but also in the bel-canto melody in general. The affective "false" intervals of the melody, usually appearing shortly before the cadence were integrated into the harmony. The directive power of the harmonically conceived cadence arose for the first time in the bel-canto style.

Hand in hand with the harmonic simplification went an important formal development: the gradual differentiation between recitative and aria. The characteristics discussed so far apply primarily to the aria or arietta. But the recitative also was reduced to triadic harmony, became more restrained and less affective, and developed the rapid parlando of the secco or "dry" recitative. For the highly affective passages a new category emerged, the arioso for which gorgia effects, static basses, and harmonic experiments were reserved. As can easily be seen, the arioso is actually nothing but a new name for the old Florentine recitative which embraced both aria and secco recitative as two possible extremes. It is symptomatic that Doni, the theorist of the bel-canto period, criticized the early recitative because it was, in his opinion, neither fish nor fowl, neither a secco recitative nor an "artificial" aria; he praised the latter as the best means to dispel tediousness.[1] The differentiation of recitative, arioso, and aria enabled the

[1] Solerti, Le origini del melodramma, 217.

composer to use three styles for narrative, dramatic, and lyrical or purely ornamental purposes.

THE CHAMBER CANTATA: LUIGI ROSSI AND CARISSIMI

In the early baroque Venetian school the term cantata denoted a vocal composition in form of strophic variations on a recurrent bass. These cantatas naturally lack the division of recitative and aria although hints of the incipient differentiation do occur as early as in the *Musiche* of the remarkable Neapolitan Falconieri.[2] Also the numerous dialogues and monodic cantatas by Berti, Sances, and Rasi can be considered forerunners of the chamber cantata. The form was definitively established coincident with the bel-canto style in the sophisticated literary and musical circles in Rome. It was based on a pastoral or dramatic story, narrated in an alternation of recitative and arioso, and punctuated by strophic arias at lyrical or dramatic points. Formally, it was closely allied with the opera, as implied in the term "dialogue without stage" that Doni used for this type. The strophic variation persisted as the major means of creating unity in the works of the two leading Roman composers: the singer-composer Luigi Rossi (1598–1653) and Giacomo Carissimi (1605–1674). Also Manelli and Ferrari, who developed the bel-canto style in Venice, Orazio (Michi) dell'Arpa, and Caprioli [3] belong to the first generation of bel-canto composers.

Rossi was pre-eminently a composer of cantatas of which about two hundred and fifty are extant.[4] In his hands the cantata assumed the expansive composite form in which recitative, arioso, and aria freely alternated to form as many as fourteen sections. A primitive type of cantata, the aria cantata, consists of only one aria [5] repeated for every stanza of the text. In the refrain cantata only the middle part of the aria changes while the first section serves as refrain. This type is exemplified by *Difenditi Amore.*[6] The most complex type is, however, the rondo cantata in which the various recitative and arioso sections are held together by a short aria, repeated at intervals in rondo fashion. The formal division between *secco* recitative and aria is unmistakable in Rossi (Ex. 30) and is further empha-

---

[2] Adler HMG, 438.
[3] Prunières, *L'Opéra Italien*, Appendix, 13.
[4] See the bibliographical notes of Prunières, ZIMG XIV, 109; Riemann HMG 2:2, 372, and Landshoff, *Alte Meister des Bel Canto.*
[5] Torchi AM V, 190, see also HAM no. 203.
[6] Riemann HMG 2:2, 381.

sized by instrumental ritornellos, mostly for the continuo, but sometimes also for a violin solo or duet. While the majority of Rossi's works belong to the category of solo cantatas in which the same singer both narrates and "acts," there are also about three dozen chamber duets and trios in which

Ex. 30. Luigi Rossi: Chamber cantata.

ensembles in a noble imitative style alternate with solo arias. The solo cantata *Gelosia* [7] is subdivided into an arioso, a short aria, and a recitative; this entire sequence is then twice repeated to new words and with some melodic variation in the voice part, but not in the bass. Here the idea of strophic variation is retained in principle, but the strophe itself has gained flexibility by the juxtaposition of recitative, arioso, and aria. Exactly the same form can be found in Manelli's *Bella tu*.[8] The arias of Rossi are generally brief and gain length only by varied repeats that are always fully written out. These repeats characterize the favorite bipartite form of the bel-canto aria: A A′B B′, or A B B′. Sometimes the first section returns at the end (A B [B′] A′) to form the first clear manifestation of the da-capo aria, on a diminutive scale, however. This brief da-capo aria which becomes quite frequent in cantata and opera after 1650 should not be confused with the grand da-capo form of the late baroque. In the brief da capo the return is written out because of the variation of the melody and because the sections do not yet form self-contained and almost independent movements, but consist merely of groups of phrases. Rossi shows his outstanding melodic inventiveness in his ability to spin a bel-canto line out of a single rhythmic motive, and sudden shifts from triple to duple meter bespeak his subtle rhythmic sense.

Carissimi's importance for the cantata has been too frequently minimized in favor of his oratorios. In the cantata, however, Carissimi reveals sophisti-

[7] Gevaert, *Les Gloires de l'Italie*, no. 9; see also OHM III, 153.
[8] Riemann, *Kantatenfrühling* no. 3.

cated and experimental traits conspicuously absent in the oratorio. Like Rossi he excelled in rondo cantatas,[9] strophic variations, and chamber duets in concerted counterpoint.[10] His sparkling cantatas on humorous subjects like the "Charlatan," [11] the *Testamentum Asini, Requiem Jocosum*,[12] form a class by themselves. In the famous *I Filosofi* [13] he depicts the good and the ill "humors" of Heraclit and Democrit by a drastic turn from major to minor which demonstrates that the rudiments of modern key feeling are clearly established; not by accident does Carissimi in his theoretical treatise reduce the multitude of modes to only major and minor.

The ostinato bass, especially the descending tetrachord, appears in Carissimi as well as in Rossi. However, the *obbligo* of a strophic bass and the rigid chaconne bass yielded in the bel-canto style to the freer device of the patterned bass or quasi-ostinato in which only the rhythm persisted in ostinato fashion while the melody was not strictly, but only sequentially repeated. The element of variation became less prominent in the measure in which the single sections gained in internal organization by means of patterned basses, sequential melodies, and contrapuntal integration of continuo and voice. By virtue of his concise and formal melodic design Carissimi achieved a flowing continuity of line unimpeded by the affection of single words. His coloraturas have a neutral flavor by dint of their rhythmic drive, as for example in the well-known *Vittoria*.[14] In their harmonic complexity his cantatas and chamber duets differ noticeably from his oratorios. The affective intervals of the melody were made an integral part of the harmony, notably by the use of the Neapolitan-sixth chord. This chord received its misleading name because it was erroneously thought to have originated in the Neapolitan opera. Actually, however, it was established as a cadential idiom in the bel-canto style and can be found in nearly all middle baroque composers. In Carissimi's chamber duet *Il mio cor* (Ex. 31) it appears on an affective word to reinforce the cadential drive

Ex. 31. Carissimi: Chamber duet.

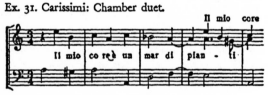

Il mio | co re è un | mar di | pian - ti

[9] Haas B, 127.
[10] Landshoff, *Alte Meister des Bel Canto* (several examples).
[11] Torchi AM V, 239.
[12] Haas B, 131.
[13] Landshoff, *Alte Meister;* also in Burney's *General History.*
[14] Gevaert, *Gloires de l'Italie* no. 2; Parisotti, *Anthology of Italian Songs (Arie antiche)* no. 1.

of the harmony. The cadence is also rhythmically emphasized by the broadening effect of the hemiola, very typical of the bel-canto style.

The second generation of cantata composers comprises Cesti (the pupil of Carissimi), Mazzaferrata, Savioni, Tenaglia, Legrenzi, and Stradella, the last two better known for their operas and oratorios. The painter-composer Salvatore Rosa, whose bitter satire against music aroused the belated protests of Mattheson, must also be mentioned here.

Cesti's cantatas are distinguished for their expansive ariosi and the pronounced lyrical quality of his melodies. Written in triple meter with supple syncopations, they abound in such melodic dissonances as diminished thirds and fourths although the underlying harmonies are essentially simple.[15] With Savioni, Legrenzi, and Stradella the cantata grew to major proportions and showed in its increased use of imitation the definite resurgence of counterpoint. The anticipatory statements of the melody by the continuo have now become the stereotyped form of aria beginning, as for example in Pasquini's *Al tramontar*.[16] Instrumental ritornelli and arias with obbligato instruments are characteristic for Legrenzi and Stradella, a feature that again discloses the parallelism of the opera and cantata. Stradella's *serenate,* as he called them, served as model for Handel who paid the older composer the highest form of compliment by actually using some of his music.[17] Of the nearly two-hundred cantatas of Stradella only a few are available in modern editions [18] which hardly do justice to the forceful curves of his flowing melodies, in which Cesti's melodic dissonance technique is brought to perfection. Occasionally, Stradella's rich harmonies, like those of Legrenzi, even point to the expanded tonality of late baroque music.

THE ORATORIO: CARISSIMI AND STRADELLA

The oratorio was a sacred, but non-liturgical dramatic composition in which a biblical subject was presented in the form of recitative, arioso, aria, ensemble, and chorus, usually with the aid of a narrator or *testo*. According to Spagna, the outstanding oratorio poet of the period, the presence of the *testo* formed the distinguishing characteristic between opera and oratorio.

[15] Adler HMG, 439.
[16] Vatielli *Antiche Cantate d'Amore*. The piece has also been printed in Riemann *Kantatenfrühling*, here erroneously ascribed to Carissimi.
[17] One serenata has been printed in the *Handel Gesellschaft*, Suppl. 3. It should be noted, however, that Stradella's authorship has been questioned on stylistic grounds; see Robinson, ML XVI.
[18] Parisotti, *Anthology;* Riemann HMG 2:2, 397; Lavignac E I:2, 733; Zanon, *Raccolta di 24 arie*, no. 22.

In the presentation of the action and the general dramatic spirit akin to the opera, the oratorio appealed to the imagination of the audience and dispensed in principle, though not always in practice, with the stage. This feature it had in common with the chamber cantata; Spagna, indeed, called the early oratorical dialogues "cantatas." The form was contrived by the Jesuits to stem the tide of secularization. Capitalizing on the vogue of the opera they made the oratorio a pliant tool of their propagandistic endeavor. The name *oratorio* (= prayer hall) was derived from the meeting place of a devout congregation of laymen, the *Congregazione dell'Oratorio,* where the members met for prayer and the singing of devotional songs such as the lauda. Palestrina and other composers connected with the counter-reformation composed laude in a simple polyphonic style; the dialogue laude by Giovanni Anerio (*Teatro Armonico Spirituale,* 1619) have even a polyphonic *testo.* In spite of their title these laude are, however, not really dramatic. Cavalieri's *Anima e Corpo,* since Burney often regarded as the "first" oratorio, is actually a cross between oratorio and sacred opera, but purists have gone too far in ruling the work out from the history of the oratorio altogether. *Anima e Corpo* shares at least some features of the oratorio form. Moreover, it was performed in the hall of the *Oratorio* and even contains some of the familiar lauda texts. It was not called oratorio, because this name, around 1600, designated merely a locality, as the term *da camera* and *da chiesa* did in instrumental music.

The stylistic premise of the oratorio was monody, and in this respect Cavalieri set a model that was followed by Ottavio Durante, Vittori, and the brothers Mazzocchi who composed laude in monodic style. Certain Latin dialogues for solo and chorus, preserved in motet collections of Venetians like Romano, Tommasi,[19] Capello,[20] and Pace, have been claimed to be forerunners of the Latin oratorio. They are strictly liturgical, if dramatic, music, composed in the conservative pseudo-monodic style of Viadana. Neither the polyphonic lauda nor the Latin dialogue belong stylistically to the history of the oratorio. The form does not crystallize before 1630, its beginnings coinciding with the beginnings of the bel-canto style.

Two types of oratorio can be distinguished: the *oratorio volgare* in Italian, and the more aristocratic Latin oratorio, both equally dramatic and popular in their appeal. The center of the Latin oratorio was, according

[19] Schering, *Geschichte des Oratoriums,* Appendix XVI.
[20] GMB no. 180.

to a highly informative report of Maugars (1639), S. Marcello in Rome where Carissimi was employed after 1649. Carissimi's works are the first extant oratorios proper, and though he did not invent the form, it is he who established it artistically.

The sixteen extant oratorios of Carissimi all belong to the Latin type, except *Daniele*, thus far unpublished, and not identical with the *oratorio volgare* of the same title that is sometimes hypothetically ascribed to him.[21] The most impressive works include *Jephte* (his masterpiece), *Jonas*, the *Judicium Salomonis*, *Balthazar*, the *Diluvium Universale*, the *Judicium Extremum*, and the *Historia Divitis*.[22] Nearly all of the subjects are taken from the Old Testament and are presented by an unknown librettist in tersely dramatic scenes of great economy. Carissimi who was known in his day as "the musical rhetor" fully deserves his honorary title in view of his powerfully rhythmic recitatives and sweeping declamatory choruses. The main pillars of the oratorio structure are the choral sections which call sometimes for large combinations such as a double chorus and soloists, as in the *Diluvium;* or even a triple chorus with orchestra, as in the *Judicium Extremum*. The chorus which sometimes serves as a moralizing spectator, but more often takes part in the action, is written in a strictly chordal and extremely rhythmic style, inspired by the fiery anapaests and the relentlessly hammering dactyls of the Latin language. The sea storm in *Jonas* and the tumultuous gathering of the elements during the Deluge in the *Diluvium* are depicted in superb rhythmic stylization. Other memorable scenes are the sudden calm of the sea after Jonah has been sacrificed to the waves, where the chorus comes in after an uncannily eloquent rest on a single sustained chord; or the battle chorus in *Jephte* in which alternating choral and soloistic snatches conjure up a sharply profiled picture of strife.

Concentration on rhythm in the choral writing makes up for the lack of harmonic interest. The astonishing simplicity of harmony comes out not only in the emphatic use of triadic melodies in the recitative, but also in the almost childish insistence on a few simple chords. Since this harmonic restriction does not obtain in Carissimi's cantatas, it must be due to the popular and propagandistic function of oratorio music which allowed of only the most obvious effects. The choruses by themselves seem primitive and take on significance only in their dramatic context. What

[21] Torchi AM V, 117.
[22] The first four oratorios have been printed in Chrysander, D, II, the first three in excerpts in ICMI 5. Single scenes in GMB no. 198, HAM no. 207.

Handel admired in Carissimi's choral oratorio was primarily, as his musical borrowings prove, the structural dramatic function of the chorus, and whoever hopes to find Handelian grandeur in Carissimi will be disappointed. The oratorios are a mosaic of short-winded phrases, typical of the bel-canto style, and are organized in free rondo-like structures by recurrent arioso, choral, and instrumental sections. The formal differentiation of recitative, arioso, and aria is less conspicuous than in the cantata, but the bel-canto style of the aria is always clearly recognizable, as for example in *Ite angeli* (Ex. 32) in which the hemiola cadence retards the flow of the simple line in characteristic fashion. The example is taken from *Lucifer,* one of the rare solo oratorios without chorus.

Ex. 32. Carissimi: Bel-canto aria from *Lucifer.*

Only in a few significant ariosi does Carissimi venture into affective harmonies, written either on chromatically descending tetrachords, as in the *Judicium Salomonis* and *Jephte,* or on diminished steps, as in *Jephte.* Contrapuntal texture appears in the oratorios only in neatly chiselled solo duets or, occasionally, in final choruses, but even here the consideration of a lucid speech rhythm restrains Carissimi from showing the contrapuntal skill which he did not hesitate to apply in his church music and cantatas.

The instrumental accompaniment comprises besides the continuo only a scanty combination of two violins. These trios, if present at all, provide the modest introductory music and serve otherwise in a rather subordinate function. Carissimi's choral oratorio did not find many successors in Italy, except among his personal followers and lesser men like Graziani, Foggia, and Marcorelli; only in France (Charpentier), where the sober brilliance of his music was especially appreciated, and in Germany (Foerster, Capricornus, and Meder) did his model stimulate imitations. In Italy, the emphasis shifted after Carissimi from the Latin oratorio to the *oratorio volgare,* in which the chorus lost its central position and served as a theatrical or decorative prop, setting the scene with short interjections, wails, and battle cries, or giving a sententious moral at the end. In exact parallel to both cantata and opera, the interest was now focussed on the soloist, the castrato singer; and the formal aria, which does not yet stand out in Carissimi's oratorios as an independent form, monopolized the attention of composer and audience. The solo oratorio became a courtly, aristocratic form that served as a substitute opera. During the Lenten season opera houses were traditionally closed, but this regulation could be circumvented by the presentation of oratorios so the nobility did not have to forego the pleasure of hearing their favorite castrato.

The sensuous mysticism of the Jesuit baroque found its congenial expression in the so-called *oratorio erotico*. Only by dint of the sacred subjects and the lack of stage action do these oratorios differ from the opera, in their brilliant concerting style, their luscious bel canto, and their sensuous, if not voluptuous, tone they surpass even the opera in which such effects could be left to the stage presentation. It is not surprising that most of the opera composers of the period were also the leading oratorio composers. The oratorio composition was centered in the states of northern Italy, especially Modena and Bologna, beside which Florence and Rome took second place. Since the oratorio flourished mostly at courts, Venice did not directly participate, but Venetian opera composers did write oratorios for the Italianized Austrian or German courts, such as Vienna and Munich. The Italian school included Ferrari, the founder of the Venetian opera, and masters better known for their instrumental music, such as Cazzati, the elder Vitali, Arresti, degli Antonii, and, most important of all, Legrenzi (d. 1690) and Stradella (d. 1682).

Ferrari surprises in his *Sansone* (c. 1660) by a keen dramatic characterization in aria and recitative.[23] Vitali's *Giona* (1689) deserves special attention for the polyphonic *testo*, which in form of a five-part chorus narrates the story while the passages of direct action are sung by soloists. It is one of the few links that connect the choral narrations of Carissimi with the choral recitatives in Handel's oratorios. Legrenzi and Stradella, who both wrote six oratorios, represent the peak of middle baroque oratorio composition. The lofty aim of these composers is evidenced in ponderous contrapuntal choruses, as, for example, in Legrenzi's *La Morte del Cor Penitente*. According to the Roman composer Pitoni, chapel master at St. Peter's, Stradella considered as his best work not one of his operas, but the oratorio *S. Giovanni Battista* (1676). It is indeed a masterpiece of characterization, endowed with a "Handelian" breadth of melody and a wealth of harmonic ideas that indicate his advanced stylistic position. It is furthermore symptomatic that Stradella experimented with the concerto and prescribed in an *aria concertata* the accompaniment of a *concerto grosso* and a *concertino* which were, however, not yet written in the late baroque con-

23 Schering, *Geschichte des Oratoriums*, Appendix XXVII.

certo style. The ostinato appears often in modulatory form, as for example in *Susanna*.[24] In the last scene of *S. Giovanni Battista* Stradella combines the joy of Herod's daughter over the death of St. John with the remorse of the father in a remarkable duet on a chaconne bass,[25] in which he represents simultaneously two mutually opposing affections in a contrapuntal contrast. This occurs so rarely in baroque music that the use of the same device with Handel, who was familiar with Stradella's music, does not seem coincidental.

The Roman oratorios, furthered by Vittori, Luigi Rossi, Pasquini, and Foggia, did not rise to the high level of the northern school and only in the late baroque period did Rome recapture its leading role. Italian oratorio in Germany was an offshoot dependent on the Venetian masters and the numerous Italians who held permanent court positions in Vienna and Munich. The Italian domination of the Viennese court began with Bertali (d. 1669), Sances, Pietro Ziani (d. 1711), Pederzuoli, and especially Antonio Draghi (d. 1700), who, for the second half of the century, held the position of music director at the court. Draghi's amazingly prolific output (forty-three oratorios) did not leave him time to complete the scores, which are often only sketched out in a shorthand continuo. We find here all the operatic forms of the day, including the heavily orchestrated accompanied recitatives and thickly scored choruses which were a Viennese specialty reflecting the conservative taste of the court. In spite of the full differentiation of recitative and aria, the arias themselves were singularly short, often overladen with mechanical coloraturas, and not exactly distinguished by inspiration.

THE VENETIAN OPERA SCHOOL

It is difficult to ascertain whether the bel-canto style originated in the cantata or in the opera since it appeared in both forms simultaneously. According to a report by Meder in Mattheson's *Ehrenpforte* it was Cesti who transposed the cantata style to the opera. The pronounced bel-canto idiom of Cesti's cantatas was at the time associated primarily with the cantata, although it was also distinctly tried out in the operas of the first bel-canto composers. Since these operas, however, had not yet definitely abandoned the supremacy of the continuous recitative, the priority of the cantata in the evolution of the bel canto seems at least plausible, even though the style ultimately triumphed in the opera.

[24] GMB no. 230.
[25] Lavignac E I:2, 735, and Burney *History*, 588.

The tendency to emphasize the aria at the expense of the recitative and to make the latter less affective had already been suggested in the early Roman operas of Landi, Vittori, and Domenico Mazzocchi; but this emphasis became obvious only in the operas of Luigi Rossi, notably in *Il Palazzo incantato* (1642), based on a libretto by Rospigliosi, and *L'Orfeo* (Paris, 1647) in which arias and ensembles hold the main musical interest.[26] In these works recitative and aria are clearly differentiated although recitative and arioso are not yet as clearly distinguished.

While Rossi's contributions to opera cannot compare with those to the cantata the reverse is true of Cavalli (1602–1676), organist at S. Marco and later successor to Monteverdi's position in Venice, whose exceptional melodic gift predestined him for the opera. His works in the field of instrumental and church music are far outweighed by his forty-two operas. Even his early *Nozze di Teti* contains a few strophic arias in the lilting rhythm of a stylized dance which may have set a model to Monteverdi. The profuse madrigal choruses and ensembles of the score attest to his contrapuntal skill. The bel-canto aria appears fully established in *Didone* (1641), the unprecedented success of which eclipsed Monteverdi's fame, and it is further solidified in *Egisto* (Vienna, 1642), and *Giasone* (1649). His later works include *Pompeo* (1666), and *Ercole amante* (Paris, 1662) composed for the marriage of Louis XIV, with interludes by Lully.

Of the progressive aria forms, the brief da capo comes to the fore only in the later operas, nowhere as clearly demonstrated as in the lullaby from *Ercole*,[27] the murmuring sounds of which were closely imitated in Cesti's *Pomo d'Oro*.[28] The differentiation of *secco* recitative and arioso, also, is definitely established only in the late works, in which the ariosi are reserved for the pathetic passages while the *secco* prevails in the neutral dialogue. In his early phase Cavalli showed his indebtedness to Monteverdi in affective recitatives, the frequent use of the *stile concitato,* and composite strophic arias. These arias are suddenly interrupted by recitative or arioso sections, after which the aria is resumed; the composite form is then repeated in its entirety with different words.[29] This integration of recitative and aria persisted even in Cavalli's later operas. Cavalli was pre-eminently a master of dramatic characterization by means of terse and gestic melodic ideas and simple triadic harmonies, as can be seen in Me-

---

[26] Examples in Goldschmidt, *Studien,* I, 295, 385. GMB no. 199.
[27] Prunières, *L'Opéra Italien,* App. 27; compare HAM no. 206.
[28] DTOe III:2 (vol. 6), 106.
[29] See *Giasone* in Eitner PAM 12, 73.

dea's impelling invocation of the furies [80] which provoked innumerable supernatural incantation scenes in later operas. The constant triple rhythm, which the Venetians may well have liked best in Cavalli's music, would be monotonous were it not for the melodic charm of the arias. Especially the laments on chromatic chaconne basses, since Cavalli an indispensable ingredient of the opera, demonstrate his art of characterization in their affective melodic steps, best illustrated by the famous plaint of Climene from *Egisto* (Ex. 33). The subtly overlapping phrases of melody and bass

Ex. 33. Cavalli: Lamento on a ground from *Egisto*.

and the shifting chromatic harmonies of this masterpiece of variation remained exemplary for middle baroque composers like Cesti, Legrenzi, and even Purcell.

The exact opposite of the pathetic chaconnes were comic arias which by their amusing exploitation of the parlando established a new type, illustrated by the spirited aria of the bragging stutterer Momo in *Giasone* (I, 7). It is built on a modulatory ground bass and accompanied by two violins. Cavalli was very fond of ensembles, especially duets, but the duet technique went hardly beyond that of Monteverdi since the soloists sang more often in alternation than together.[81] The exuberant choral ensembles, typical of his first opera, were reduced later to brief decorative or dramatic choruses, such as battle cries and alarm signals. While at times he dispensed completely with choruses (*Egisto*), he emphatically returned to them in the court opera *Ercole,* which calls for combinations of instruments and voices far greater than usual.

The instrumental sinfonies are generally short, but in spite of their brevity they significantly set the mood in a few bold, evocative lines over

[80] GMB no. 201.
[81] Wolff, *Venezianische Oper,* App. 3.

triadic harmonies; the overtures, too, in which the rhythmic transformation of the varied couple is still sometimes discernible, serve that purpose. Instruments and voice usually alternate in the arias, but the trend toward a greater prominence of the instruments is disclosed in occasional obbligatos and *accompagnato* recitatives which appear in *Ercole* purposefully contrasted with the *secco* passages.

When Cavalli returned from Paris after the rather disappointing *succès d'estime* of *Ercole* he was resolved to forswear opera altogether. He did not keep this resolution because a new rival had arisen in Cesti who overshadowed the later years of Cavalli as much as Cavalli did those of Monteverdi. Marc'Antonio Cesti (1623–1669) received his training in Rome, the cradle of the cantata, and, although ordained to the lower orders, devoted himself primarily to the opera. He scored his first successes in Venice with *Orontea* and *Cesare amante* (1651). His eminently successful masterpiece *La Dori* (1661 Florence) was performed all over Italy. For the *Pomo d'Oro* (1666) he went to Vienna, glad to leave Venice where his licentious conduct had irritated even the broad-minded Venetians. A lyrical rather than a dramatic talent, Cesti endowed his arias with a solemn, hymnic tone that ever since has been associated with the bel canto. The feminine chromaticism of his melodies led to striking harmonic complexities which explain why augmented sixth chords and "Neapolitan" sixths hold so conspicuous a place in his music. As with Carissimi, the latter chord (see Ex. 34 below) was adduced by melodic means and served to strengthen the cadence by the integration of the flat second of the Phrygian mode into the major or minor key—a clear indication of the growing tonal consciousness in middle baroque harmony. As to the aria forms, strophic variations and strophic arias, often in an ostentatiously popular style, are in the majority, and continuo arias still heavily outnumber arias with obbligato accompaniment. Brief da-capo and rondo forms occur sparingly but significantly, as for example in the very impressive rondo aria *Rendete mi il mio bene* from *Dori*.[32] The favorite ABB' form of the bel-canto cantata appears very frequently with Cesti. Proserpina's first aria in the *Pomo d'Oro*,[33] one of Cesti's most extended pieces with written-out variations, is cast in this form, and is preceded by an "infernal" ritornello for a regal with two *cornetti* and two trombones. Most arias are, however, composed on a more modest scale.

The grand festival show piece *Il Pomo d'Oro*, dramatically inferior to

[32] Eitner PAM 12, 129.
[33] DTOe III:2 (vol. 6), 48.

Dori, suffers from the labyrinthic accumulation of sixty-seven scenes. The
rich choral ensembles of the prologue, written in the brittle chordal style
of Carissimi, indicate the courtly background of the work, the sumptuous
scenery of which was designed by Burnacini who was, next to Giacomo
Torelli, the most famous theatre architect of the day. Cesti adhered in his
ensembles to alternate singing, as exemplified by the trio (Ex. 34) from

Ex. 34. Cesti: Terzetto from *Semiramide.*

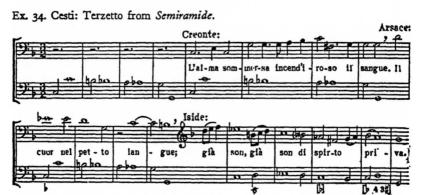

Semiramide (1667). Freely built on a chromatic chaconne bass it illustrates
the typical dissonant progressions in Cesti's melodies. Characteristically,
Cesti did not fill in the skip from *a*-flat to *f*-sharp as Cavalli would
have done, but relished the poignant effect of the diminished third.

In his recitatives Cesti juxtaposed short *secco* passages with ariosos and
accompagnato sections. Like Cavalli, he reserved the latter for solemn or
affective occasions, such as the so-called *ombra* scenes, in which the spirit
of one departed was invoked. These solemn scenes became later the indispensable equipment of the *opera seria* and their influence can be traced
as far as Gluck and Mozart.

Many arias of Cesti begin in a peculiar manner with a fragmentary
statement that, after a brief rest, is once more resumed and continued
without interruption. The initial presentation of a plastic motive that
sums up the basic affection of the aria, like a musical motto, can occasionally be found in the cantatas of Rossi and in Cavalli, but not before Cesti
was it on the way to becoming a mannerism.[34] The motto beginning had
not only the formal function of setting a rhythmic and melodic pattern
in motion, but it had also a dramatic significance because the first words
emphatically summarized the whole aria text. A comic aria from *Le
Disgrazie* (1667) illustrates the typical motto beginning and at the same

[34] GMB no. 203.

time the brisk rhythms of Cesti's comic and popular style (Ex. 35).
The achievements of Cavalli and Cesti were solidified and expanded
by a later generation of Venetian composers, comprising besides the
brothers Ziani, Pier Agostini, Boretti, and Sartorio, three outstanding masters: Legrenzi, Stradella, and Pallavicino (d. 1688). In their music the
return of counterpoint became increasingly more apparent, especially in

Ex. 35. Cesti: Comic aria with motto beginning.

the carefully wrought texture of the ensembles and in the anticipatory
statement of the vocal line by the continuo, which can be regarded as a
contrapuntal extension of the motto beginning. Like the motto beginning
itself, its contrapuntal extension was established as a stereotyped device
only with Legrenzi, Stradella, and Pallavicino. In their operas the contours of melody and bass underwent a process of mutual assimilation and
differentiation in which the bass either assimilated the bel-canto style, or
else developed a strictly instrumental idiom the angular pattern of which
gave more relief to the bel-canto melody than ever before. The first alternative, that of assimilation, can be found in the brief da-capo aria *Ti
lascio* [85] from Legrenzi's *Giustino*, the libretto of which was later also
composed by Handel. The ground bass of the aria appears in several keys
in keeping with the gradual widening of tonality. The second alternative,
that of differentiation, is illustrated by the aria *Resta il core* from Legrenzi's
Totila (1677) in which the constancy of the heart, represented in the motto
beginning of the voice, is emphatically contrasted with the running of the
feet, depicted by a rushing quasi-ostinato bass (Ex. 36). This bass demonstrates a high degree of instrumentalization and mechanical stylization,
not found in the earlier opera. The example given comprises the complete
da-capo section—an indication how far removed the brief da-capo aria still
was from the grand da capo of the late baroque period.
    In his recitatives Legrenzi showed himself considerably advanced over
his predecessors. He supplanted the sustained cadences of the Florentine

[85] The aria has been reprinted by Wolff, *Venezianische Oper*, App. 32, and also by
Schering GMB no. 231. The latter version is, however, faulty because the two sharps
of the key signature have been erroneously omitted.

recitative which prevailed as late as Cesti, by the typical *secco* cadences which snap abruptly off on an unaccompanied fourth, confirmed by the stereotyped V-I cadence of the continuo.[36]

Ex. 36. Legrenzi: Aria from *Totila*.

Stradella's works, which include among many others *La Forza del Amore paterno* (1681) [37] and the comic opera *Il Trespolo Tutore*, contain many arias with obbligato accompaniment in which the dimensions of the form are noticeably expanded. Like his fellow composers Stradella was partial to trumpet obbligatos in the conventional martial or revenge arias which occurred only exceptionally in Cavalli. His impassioned melodies point, in their pathos and their bold and widely spaced curves, toward the pompous Handelian style. His thoroughly instrumental ostinati give, by their modulations, ample range to the harmony.

The trend toward expansion can also be seen in Pallavicino's operas, especially in his most mature work, *Gerusalemme liberata* (Dresden 1687).[38] In his operas quasi-ostinato and real ground basses tended to become indistinguishable because of the melodic consistency of the former and the modulatory freedom of the latter. In the *ombra* aria *Ombre care* from *Le Amazzoni* [39] the modulatory chaconne bass is ingeniously elaborated by constantly running arpeggios. How strongly this bass gained a hold on the design of the melody can be seen in an excerpt from *Demetrio* in which joy and torment are juxtaposed in a keen dramatic characterization (Ex. 37). The occasional use of the instrumental concerto style, as, for example, in *Messalina* (1680) [40] marks the most advanced phase of Pal-

---

[36] See Legrenzi's *Totila* in Wolff, *Venezianische Oper*, App. 19.
[37] Vocal score 1931 (Ricordi). For another aria see HAM no. 241.
[38] DDT 55; see also GMB no. 224, and Goldschmidt, *Studien*, I, 403.
[39] DDT 55, XIX.
[40] See the aria *Lascia mi gelosia* (Wolff, *Venezianische Oper*, App. 69). For the discussion of the concerto style see Chapter VII.

lavicino's development, clearly signalling the transition to the late baroque style. While he adhered in his earlier operas to the bipartite aria form, he favored in *Gerusalemme* the brief da-capo aria, which is here no longer

Ex. 37. Pallavicino: Excerpt from *Demetrio.*

strophic but has only a single stanza. His strong talent for the popular found an outlet in very numerous songs, popular in tone and diminutive in form. The Venetian opera supplied for city audiences the "song hits" of the day, which combined in their chatty rhythm, lively bass, and melodic appeal elements of both the canzonetta and *air de cour.* These modest tunes correspond so much to our commonly accepted idea of folksong that they have sometimes been designated as such. Far from being folksongs, they are composed civil songs which were as short-lived as they were successful. A typical example from *Gerusalemme* begins strikingly like one of the "synthetic" folksongs in Rousseau's *Devin de Village* (Ex. 38).

Ex. 38. Pallavicino: Popular song from *Gerusalemme liberata.*

The popular song style which held a firm place in the serious opera was cultivated even more in the comic opera, in which the middle class of the time appeared on the stage. The historically important experiments with opera comedy began in Rome with *Chi soffre speri* (1639) [41] by Virgilio Mazzocchi and Marazzoli, and continued with *Dal mal il bene* (1654) [42] by Abbatini and Marazzoli (based on a libretto by Rospigliosi after Calderon), Sacrati's *Finta pazza* (1641), Melani's *La Tancia* (Flor-

[41] Examples in Goldschmidt, *Studien,* I, 312 ff.
[42] *ib.* 325 ff., also GMB no. 204.

ence, 1657),[43] and Stradella's *Trespolo Tutore*. We find in these operas the typical comic parlando passages, lively canzonette, and formal arias. Even the favorite devices of the future *opera buffa* make an occasional appearance: *La Tancia* contains a parody of the serious opera and *Dal mal il bene* early examples of the ensemble finale, one of the most significant innovations of operatic history.

The Italians in the northern countries such as Zamponi in Brussels (*Ulisse*, 1650),[44] Bontempi in Dresden (*Il Paride*, 1662),[45] Scacchi in Poland, Bertali and his successor Draghi in Vienna, did not rise above the average level of Italian opera production. The prolific Draghi who could boast of more than a hundred operas in addition to all his other works, lavished a great variety of solo and choral ensembles on his works, but he was able to relieve the prevailing monotony of his music only by virtue of his pronounced talent for comic scenes.[46] The stiff and heavy armor of his orchestration reflects the German proclivity for thickly scored, five-voice ritornelli, which are as apparent in Pallavicino's operas as in the continuo songs of Krieger.

INSTRUMENTAL MUSIC: THE BOLOGNA SCHOOL

After the great flowering of keyboard music in the early baroque period, organ and harpsichord music in the middle baroque went through a phase of quiet and somewhat eclectic development. Michelangelo Rossi, the most gifted pupil of Frescobaldi, Storace, Strozzi, and the Roman organist Pasquini (the pupil of Vittori and Cesti) all lived mainly on the heritage of Frescobaldi, whose harmonic style had its after-effects in Rossi [47] and whose keyboard technique was given a turn to virtuoso dexterity in the toccatas of Pasquini.

Of far greater musical importance was the instrumental chamber music [48] that flourished in three centers of northern Italy: Modena, Venice, and Bologna. In the works of these schools the difference between dance music and the stylized and representative chamber music of more or less con-

---

[43] Riemann HMG 2:2, 242; Goldschmidt, *op. cit.*, 349 ff.

[44] Haas B, 195.

[45] Lavignac E I:2, 914.

[46] Neuhaus, *Draghi*, 191, GMB no. 226.

[47] Examples in Torchi AM III, TAM VI, ICMI, 26. The sonata, printed in many popular editions (*e.g.* Oesterle, *Early Keyboard Music*) under the name of Michelangelo Rossi, proves by its style that the editors confused Michelangelo with another Rossi, a composer of the classic period.

[48] See the bibliographical list in Schlossberg, *Die italienische Sonate*. Examples in Wasielewski, *Instrumentalsätze;* for Legrenzi see also HAM no. 220.

trapuntal texture was consciously developed. This is seen in the fact that the distinction between *sonata da camera* (or suite) and *sonata da chiesa* took on a formal significance, as important as the distinction between recitative and aria in the bel-canto style.

The Modenese school, characterized by an aristocratic attitude, comprised Uccelini, chapel master in Modena from 1654 on, Colombi, Reina, Stradella, and the theorist and composer Giovanni Maria Bononcini (d. 1679). A leaning toward violinistic virtuosity is noticeable especially with Uccelini who widened the range of the instruments to the sixth position. At the expense of the many-voiced canzona Colombi favored the solo and trio sonata, cast in the form of the church sonata with four movements. The laxly-handled counterpoint of his fugal movements was written for external display and only in Reina's sonatas did the counterpoint maintain a solid texture. The numerous chamber sonatas of Bononcini were less pretentious in style, and Stradella's few sonatas [49] also, combined moderate technical demands with good contrapuntal workmanship.

Chamber music in Venice received fresh impulses from the flourishing opera. The favorite type of middle baroque opera overture consisted of several short and sharply contrasted parts with little polyphony and was written for three violins in constant voice-crossings. Whereas in the overture the polyphonic texture was subordinated to the display of sonorities, it was considerably strengthened in the field of chamber music. Besides the sonata collections of Guerreri (Milan), the trio and quartet sonatas of Legrenzi and Pietro Ziani stand out as the major works of the period. Even in the rather retrospective ensemble canzonas of Cavalli (1656) it can be observed how composers broke away from the even and inarticulate flow of the old canzona themes to evolve a new motivic type in which the strong beats were articulated and rhythmically emphasized by characteristic long upbeat patterns. A canzona theme by Cavalli symptomatically combines both the old and the new type; it starts in the old manner, and gathers momentum and rhythmic emphasis in the second half (Ex. 39).

Ex. 39. Cavalli: Canzona theme.

In the church sonatas of Ziani and Legrenzi the multisectional structure of the canzona was reduced generally to five or even fewer parts, each of

[49] GMB no. 229.

which was however gradually expanded into a concise independent movement. Although their order was not yet rigidly fixed, the first and last
movements were as a rule fugal and flanked a variety of chordal or slightly
contrapuntal movements, of which at least one was written in triple meter.
Legrenzi liked to emphasize the independence of the single movements by
abrupt harmonic turns to third-related keys. In spite of these contrasts,
however, the outermost movements were frequently bound together by
the same thematic material—an obvious survival of the variation canzona.
Legrenzi's numerous collections, published between 1655 and 1682, can
hardly be overrated for their importance in the development of the church
sonata. He impresses the musician of today by his assuredness in the
handling of a harmonically saturated counterpoint, by the plastic contours of his themes, and the driving rhythm of his countersubjects. In his
op. 2 (1655) these features are already remarkably clear (Ex. 40).

Ex. 40. Legrenzi: Trio sonata *La Cornara*.

The thoroughly instrumental character of the quoted theme—notice the
typical tone repetitions—is unmistakable, as is also the assimilation of the
melody with the chaconne bass, which is, however, yet as richly harmonized
as in the case of Pallavicino (see Ex. 37 above). In his instrumental style
Legrenzi anticipated the vigor of certain themes by Bach; and Bach did,
indeed, study him carefully basing the organ fugue in *c* on one of his
themes. The slow movements were powerfully influenced by the bel-
canto style, as can be seen in the numerous stylized sarabands [50] in which
both the upper parts and the bass were integrated in a solemnly flowing
counterpoint.

[50] Riemann HMG 2:2, 161.

The third and greatest center of violin music was constituted by the musicians employed at S. Petronio in Bologna. This church, famed for the adornment of its services by instrumental music, needed a great repertory of church sonatas. Cazzati (d. 1677), from 1657 music director of the church, established the Bologna school. It reached its first flowering in his pupil Giovanni Battista Vitali (d. 1692), who was followed by Mazzaferrata (Ferrara), Grossi (Mantua), the cellist Gabrielli, degli Antonii, and Arresti. The conservative Cazzati differentiated the canzona movements less distinctly than did his Venetian contemporaries, and though his themes were longer and more characteristic than those of the traditional canzona,[51] he made little use of the long upbeat patterns. Contrapuntal texture predominated, especially in the first movements.' With Gabrielli, the literature for unaccompanied cello took its first strides in some remarkable compositions [52] which stand stylistically, like those of Antonii, on the borderline of middle and late baroque periods.

Like all works of the Bologna school the sonatas of Vitali also are distinguished by a triumphant return of instrumental counterpoint. Preoccupation with contrapuntal problems characterizes the *Artificii musicali* (1689) in which Vitali delved into the mysteries of counterpoint and canon, and indulged in exploits like the combination of three different time signatures.[53] Published for purposes of instruction and edification, collections of this sort witness the intense interest baroque composers took in the recondite technical problems of a mystic *ars combinatoria,* the tradition of which culminated in Bach's *Art of the Fugue.* Vitali made the distinction between church and chamber sonata on the title-pages of his publications, sometimes using the term sonata without further qualification to mean church sonata.

While chamber sonatas contained a freely ordered series of dances in the usual bipartite form, church sonatas presented four or five slow and fast movements in alternation. Since the first movement was not governed by a convention with regard to tempo, it could be either slow or fast, but in either case it was usually fugal. Vitali's intimate knowledge of the string technique is unmistakably proven by his themes which, directly inspired by violinistic idioms, were admirably designed, like broad evocative gestures. With remarkable consistency Vitali employed, except in his

---

[51] See Schlossberg, *op. cit.* 65; HAM no. 219.
[52] GMB no. 228.
[53] Torchi AM VII, 174, 176. Other sonatas in Wasielewski, *op. cit.,* XXV–XXVIII, HAM no. 245.

dance music, long upbeat patterns by which he increased the rhythmic drive. Of the three beginnings (Ex. 41) from a violin sonata (1689) the first and last show the complete contrapuntal equivalence of melody and

Ex. 41. Giovanni Battista Vitali: Violin sonata.

bass whereas the second demonstrates the characteristic broken line resulting from the skilful use of open strings. All three beginnings are unified by the transformation technique of the variation canzona, which obtains in many, but not all of Vitali's sonatas.

Vitali's themes lent themselves thus readily to contrapuntal treatment because they were conceived from the outset for what they could do with regard to counterpoint. He supported the contrapuntal flow of the parts with the impelling force of his directed, if simple, harmonies and, consequently, could sustain the movements more firmly than could his predecessors. The peculiarly energetic and austere character of his music was destined to take on a new significance in the concerto style which the late baroque masters of the Bologna school originated.

CHAPTER FIVE

French Music Under The Absolutism

THE *Ballet de Cour*

AS IN England and Germany, the turn to baroque music took place in France only slowly and by degrees. Bound by their respect for tradition the French musicians were among the last to accept wholeheartedly the innovations of the baroque style and among the first to mitigate its severity. French baroque music reached in Lully a sudden, yet short-lived efflorescence. After his death the French composers were quick to transform the late baroque into the rococo style, more congenial to their artistic convictions.

The lucid rationalism of the French classical tradition prevented French music from succumbing to the turbulent affections unleashed by the Italian baroque. The seventeenth century was for the French drama the *grand siècle* of the "classics" in the strict sense of the word. Although Corneille, Racine, and Molière belonged essentially to the baroque era, they showed in their observance of the Aristotelian unities, the courtly elegance of language, and the strict reglementation of the "passions" how deeply they were impressed by the purportedly "classical" concepts of the ancient drama. The French attitude toward music in this period was characterized by a similar reserve: music was regarded as a sonorous decoration rather than as the vehicle of unruly affections. This was made quite explicit in Mersenne's *Harmonie Universelle* (1636/37), the most valuable source for the musical thought of the French early baroque. Commenting on the fundamental difference between Italian and French music Mersenne contrasted the "extraordinary violence" of the former with the "perpetual sweetness" of the latter. He reproached his countrymen for their desire to please the senses and their neglect of stirring the emotions. They were, in his opinion, content with "flattering the ear" and far too timid in their attempts to adapt the strong accents of Italian music to the *douceur fran-*

çoise. The monody, the dramatic recitative, seemed unnatural to those accustomed to the *raisonnements* of the French tragedy; it does not lack symbolic significance that the two great innovators of the French opera, Lully and Gluck, were not Frenchmen.

The polarity of the Italian and the French attitudes toward music can hardly be more emphatically shown than in the manner in which each nation effected its musical reform. While the *Camerata* "imitated" the "Ancients" by developing monody, the continuo, and the new dissonance treatment, the *Académie de musique* (1571) of the French humanists attacked the problem, in typically French fashion, by imitating the ancient quantitative meters. The result of these experiments, the French *vers mesuré*, was a creation of the renaissance and concerns us only because it exerted a far-reaching influence not only on French baroque music but even on the Italian canzonette of Monteverdi (cf. p. 39). The peculiarities and the slow development of the French recitative were due precisely to the difficulty of fusing the affective Italian declamation with the quantitative meters of French poetry.

The musical baroque began in France after the death of Henri IV (1610) with the succession to the throne of Louis XIII, who was himself a composer, and reached its apex under the *Roi Soleil,* Louis XIV (1643–1715). In the hands of such astute statesmen as Richelieu, Mazarin, and Colbert music was a pliable political tool; rarely in history have the relations between politics and music lain more openly on the surface than during the French absolutism.

Dramatic music in France entertained close relations with the dance, especially the stage dance or ballet, a feature that French music has not surrendered to the present day. The courtly renaissance entertainments were established in France after Italian models and with the help of Italian artists by the performance of *Circé* (1581), the *Ballet comique de la Reine.*[1] These musico-dramatic *ballets de cour* influenced, in turn, Rinuccini who introduced them in Italy. In strict accordance with humanistic ideas even the dance steps of the *ballet de cour* were sometimes governed by the ancient meters in the so-called *ballet mesuré.* The *ballet de cour* consisted of an optional number of *entrées,* acted in dumb show, and explanatory verses or *récits* that were either spoken or sung. Choral ensembles for four or five voices, solo songs with lute accompaniment, and music for lute or string ensembles accompanied the *entrées.* As in early

---

[1] Reprinted in COF. It should be noted that *comique* did not mean comical, but was the generic term for dramatic.

opera, the professional musicians were at first hidden from the audience unless they appeared in costume as integral part of the *décor*. The strictly courtly nature of the ballet is confirmed by the fact that they were danced by the courtiers themselves, the final *grand ballet* even by royalty.

In the course of the seventeenth century the *ballet de cour* went rapidly through several stages that were closely paralleled in the development of the English court masque. Originally a renaissance form, the *ballet de cour* gradually assumed baroque characteristics. The first step toward baroque style was taken after 1605 when the *récits* were as a rule no longer spoken but sung. Thus the *ballet de cour* lost its distinctive renaissance feature: the equivalence of poetry and music, and became a stylized form, unified by the medium of sung and danced music. This important innovation was possibly prompted by the presence at the court of Henri IV in 1604–05 of Caccini, whose dramatic manner of singing impressed Guédron, music master to the Queen and composer of numerous ballets. After 1620 the baroque style was fully established. In this phase of its development the connection between drama and ballet became so loose that the *ballet de cour* consisted of no more than an almost incoherent series of danced *tableaux*. This type, the so-called *ballet à entrées*, had no longer a dramatic, but merely a decorative and entertaining function; but coincident with the decrease in dramatic interest the importance of music increased.

A new phase of the ballet began about 1650 with the appearance of Benserade whose elegant poetry raised the *ballet de cour* to a refined literary art-form. He reinstated a unified dramatic plot that was later continued in the *comédie-ballets* of Molière. The ballet librettists indulged in fantastic and exotic subjects which gave a welcome pretext for costumes and strange stage architecture. The ballet *La Douairière de Billebahaut* is noteworthy for an amusing entry of "American" music in which four Indian bagpipe players lead onto the stage a truly exotic lama pulling a Chinese gong chime which no Indian of the time could possibly have seen!

The composers of the *ballet de cour* all held important positions at court. The first baroque generation included Pierre Guédron (d. 1621), the successor of Claude Le Jeune; Henry Le Jeune; Antoine Boesset (d. 1643), the son-in-law of Guédron; Vincent, Bataille, Auger, and Moulinié. The next generation comprised Jean-Baptist Boesset (d. 1685), the son of Antoine; the brilliant Jean de Cambefort (1605-1661) who set the music to many ballets of Benserade; and Guillaume Dumanoir, the chief of the *Vingt-Quatre Violons du Roi* who held the coveted title *roi des violons,* bestowed on the worthiest member of the medieval guild of musicians, the *Confrérie de St.-Julien.* To the same group belonged, finally, Michel Lambert, the father-in-law of Lully, and Lully himself.

The ballet music has come down to us only in fragmentary form. Since it was restricted to court use, very little was printed; only that part of the music was published that had a wider appeal, namely the *airs de cour.* The choral music and the extensive instrumental music has survived, if at all, only in manuscript collections of which the *Collection Philidor* [2] is the most famous. It transmits the ballets in reduced form for melody and bass only. The ballet music, making little use of the conventional rhythmic patterns of the social dance, was freely composed with occasional programmatic hints relating to the story. The earliest ballets retained the massed ensembles of singers and instruments (lutes and strings), characteristic of the renaissance ballet, but they were soon supplanted by the regular five-part string ensemble of French stage music. The music is not very interesting intrinsically since it was composed not to be heard, but as incidental music to the ballet; it ought not to be judged by the standards of "absolute" music.

The early dramatic type of *ballet de cour* is illustrated by *La Délivrance de Renaud* (1617) [3] the music of which was composed jointly by several musicians, notably Antoine Boesset and Guédron. The custom of collective composition in the *ballet de cour* was broken only by Lully, whose dictatorial talent did not tolerate rivals. The ballet begins with a *grand concert* for accompanied chorus and contains in addition ensembles calling for more than a hundred performers. The solo *récits* are the most interesting compositions of the ballet because they disclose how tentative were the attempts of the French composers to assimilate the Italian recitative style. The *récits* by Guédron, completely devoid of an affective tone, are most conservative in style, as can be seen in his basses which are often more active than the voice; they are in fact the exact opposite of the affective Italian recitative.

Cambefort's *récits* in the *Ballet de la Nuit* (1653) and the *Ballet du Temps* (1654) were more advanced. Cambefort made great use of the

[2] Compiled by André Philidor, a member of the Philidor dynasty of musicians. Parts of the collection are now in the *Conservatoire* (Paris), and in St. Michael's College, Tenbury. For a similar collection in Cassel see Ecorcheville: *Vingt Suites d'Orchestre,* 1906.

[3] See Prunières: *Le Ballet de Cour,* App. 49.

typical anapaestic patterns that the French language so obviously suggested, patterns that Lully was apt to run into the ground. The chorus had an important function in the ballet: it served as an introductory piece, as interlude, or even as accompaniment of the dance. This practice, known as *ballet aux chansons*, was also taken over by Lully into the opera.

Aside from the chorus and the *récits* the vocal music of the *ballet de cour* included the *air de cour*, the best known and most influential component of ballet music. The *air de cour* represents a huge literature which was published by the famous presses of Le Roy and Ballard. It swept the whole of Europe in the seventeenth century; it prompted in England the short vogue of the English ayre and provoked innumerable imitations in Germany. Its influence can be seen even with Heinrich Albert who incorporated airs by Moulinié and Antoine Boesset into his *Arien*. The *air de cour* was originally not so courtly as its name seems to imply. In the first printed collection (1571) the publisher and lutenist Le Roy reports that the *air de cour* was formerly called *voix de ville*, a term from which the French *vaudeville* is probably derived. These courtly and civil songs for solo voice and lute constituted the French parallel to the Italian and Spanish renaissance song. At the beginning of the baroque period the airs lost their popular features, notably square rhythm and melodic simplicity. Merged with the sophisticated tradition of the *vers mesuré* they were stylized to what Parran called in his *Traité de la musique* (1646) *le style d'air*. The stylization was enhanced by very ornate improvised diminutions the subtlety of which matched the precious pastoral tone of the lyrics. The airs were always strophic and almost invariably accompanied by the lute. The composers often made the lute arrangements themselves, as can be seen in the typical title *Airs de différents auteurs mis en tablature de luth par eux-mesmes* (Ballard, 1617). Even if published in four parts, the setting showed predominantly chordal texture with definite emphasis on the soprano as the leading voice.

The French ornamentations, the so-called *broderies,* varied greatly by virtue of their rhythmical intricacy and melodic delicacy from the more robust and sensuous embellishments of the Italian singers. The unadorned type can be illustrated by an *air de cour* by Antoine Boesset (Ex. 42a) for which Mersenne fortunately recorded the elaborate *broderies* as sung by Moulinié (Ex. 42b). The numerous slurs of the original indicate that the syllable-change did not coincide with the bar line and that many words began in the archaic manner on the weak part of the beat.

The instrumental music of the *ballet de cour* was performed by the

Vingt-Quatre Violons du Roi who rose to international fame during the reign of Louis XIII. The importance of this orchestra for the evolution of baroque music can hardly be overestimated because it represents the first permanent orchestra of the period. Whereas the orchestras in Italy and in

Ex. 42. Mersenne: *Air de cour* with embellishments.

other countries were as a rule only solo ensembles, the *grande bande* consistently reinforced all five parts and thus established the practice of the modern orchestral doubling, celebrated at the time as an amazing innovation. It is significant that all the doubling instruments belonged to the violin family which, as Mersenne pointed out, surpassed the old-fashioned viol ensembles by its penetrating sound. The *Vingt-Quatre Violons* were conservative with regard to the continuo since the full five-part scoring in conjunction with the doubling made a supplementary harmony unnecessary. The thorough-bass in fact appeared in France very late; only after 1650 did it become common. In spite of the conservatism of the *grande bande* the music showed the structural contour typical of baroque music in general: the outermost voices were more heavily reinforced than the middle voices. The first violins and the basses had six players each, the two other violin sections and the viola only four.

The dances in the ballets were unpretentious compositions of small musical interest, each section of which was frequently repeated with ever changing *broderies*. The manuscripts do not record those diminutions on which the *grande bande* prided itself, but Mersenne comes again to our rescue.[4] The technical demands on the orchestra were surprisingly small—the players hardly ever went beyond the first position—but they required great agility of the left hand and the bow.

Of greater musical interest were the orchestral overtures which can be traced back to about 1640. It is in the *ballet de cour* that the orchestral introductions, called *sinfonie* by the Italians, received the name *ouverture*, and from here the term passed to the opera. In the ballet *Mademoiselle* (1640) the overture assumed a bipartite form of which the first part was slow, the second fast—a first foreshadowing of the French overture. In the ballets *Les Rues de Paris* (1647) and *Feste de Bacchus* (1651) the slow part even displayed a ponderous dotted rhythm, the *rhythme saccadé* of the Lullian overture, but the fast movement did not yet have the fugal texture that became typical later on.

Many literary and musical threads of the *ballet de cour* were woven into the fabric of the French opera, which has, down to the present, remained partial to ballets. Choral dance music, recitative, and programmatic orchestral music were first established in the *ballet de cour* before their integration into the opera. Certain literary motives also confirm the relations: Lully returned in his *Armide* to the subject of the *Délivrance de Renaud*, and Campra (*Tancrède*) made use of the plot to the ballet *Tancrède en la forest enchantée* (1619).

FRENCH REACTIONS TO ITALIAN OPERA

The *ballet de cour* by itself would never have led to the creation of the French opera had it not been for the Italian opera which the French musicians had watched with keen interest ever since Caccini's visit to France. The personal taste and the shrewd politics of Mazarin were largely responsible for the visits of Italian artists at the French court. Italian by birth, he had acquired his fondness for opera during his youth. He had been associated with the sumptuous patronage of the opera by the Barberinis in Rome and had personally taken part in the staging of Landi's *Sant' Alessio*. Convinced that the opera was the most aristocratic of spectacles he supported it to keep the court entertained and to divert attention from his machinations. At his instigation a group of Italian artists was invited to acquaint the court with Italian opera. The group included the Roman composer Marazzoli, Melani, and the celebrated singer Leo-

---

[4] Excerpts in Lavignac E, I:3, 1254; see the dances by Henry Le Jeune in Ecorcheville, *op. cit.* App.

nora Baroni, Mazarin's former mistress. Baroni's voice aroused admiration, but also the typically French complaint about the "rudeness" of her singing. In 1645 Sacrati's *Finta pazza* was performed in a revised version in which, characteristically, the recitatives were partly replaced by spoken dialogue. The work was successful mainly for the machine effects of the *grand sorcier* Giacomo Torelli. Operatic events of outstanding importance were the performances of Cavalli's *Egisto* (1646) and Luigi Rossi's *Orfeo* (1647). The latter was expressly written for Paris at the command of Mazarin and the Roman nobleman Barberini, now living in exile in Paris because of his dubious financial operations. The resounding success of Rossi's opera was due less to the sterling qualities of his bel-canto style, too strange to the French to be at once fully appreciated, than to the lavish sets and the ingenious machines of Torelli. While the Italian faction, led by Queen Anne of Austria and Mazarin, was enthusiastic, the French faction again criticized the violence of the singing and ridiculed the realistic accents as "convulsions."

The exorbitant costs of the *Orfeo*—more than 300,000 *écus*—which were pressed out of the people by stringent taxation gave a welcome target to the opposition party. In the subsequent upheaval of the *Fronde* the court and Rossi were forced to flee Paris, Torelli was imprisoned, and some of the Italian singers had a narrow escape. The political songs against Mazarin, the so-called *Mazarinades,* bitterly attacked the *Orfeo,* its expenses, and naturally also the castrati to whom the French taste never got accustomed.

Caprioli's *Nozze di Peleo e di Teti* (1654) incorporated numerous ballets, written by Benserade in an effort to meet the French taste half way, but Italian opera won only a Pyrrhic victory. In a desperate move to bolster the Italian faction at the court Mazarin invited Cavalli, the greatest celebrity of the day, to compose a festival opera for the imminent marriage of Louis XIV. After some hesitation, which was overcome by a better offer, Cavalli finally accepted the invitation. For the preliminary festivities Cavalli's *Serse* was performed in a revised version in which, symptomatically, the choruses were replaced by ballets that had no relation to the plot. Composed and danced by Lully, the inserted ballets were more successful than the opera itself. The marriage of Louis XIV was finally celebrated with Cavalli's *Ercole amante* (1662), for which Buti, the librettist of Rossi's *Orfeo,* supplied the libretto. The splendor of this spectacle which assumed truly Wagnerian proportions—it lasted six hours—outshone all previous operas. Each act was concluded by huge ballets for which Lully wrote the music, the last one having twenty-one *entrées.* The

French reaction to the spectacle is revealing: it was taken not as a musical drama with inserted ballets, but as a gigantic ballet with inserted dramatic interludes—so much had Lully pushed himself into the foreground. The infuriated Cavalli vowed that he would never write another opera. Mazarin did not live to see *Ercole* performed. With the head of the Italian faction gone, the French faction under the leadership of Colbert quickly won complete control of the court, and what had been conceived as the final victory of Italian opera eventually prepared its external and internal downfall. In reaction to Venetian opera the French musicians forged their weapons for their own national opera. The performance in Versailles of the Italian pastoral *Nicandro e Fileno* (1681) by the Roman composer Lorenzani (a pupil of Benevoli) constituted the last, though futile, attempt to upset the French opera, by now firmly entrenched at the court.

The French experiments with the musical drama were at first feeble and undistinguished. Corneille wrote a *tragédie à machines* entitled *Andromède* with the express purpose of using again Torelli's machines, which had been constructed at great expense for Luigi Rossi's *Orfeo*. The music was supplied by the poet-musician Dassoucy. Machine plays were very popular in the *Théatre du Marais* in Paris, but their musical importance was slight. Corneille made it very clear that music had for him no dramatic, but merely a subsidiary ornamental function: "I have employed music only to satisfy the ear while the eyes are occupied with looking at the machines . . . but I have been careful to have nothing sung that is essential to the understanding of the play because the words are generally badly understood in music."

The pastorals, in vogue since the renaissance after the Italian models of Tasso and Guarini, were also important forerunners of French opera. Their influence persisted even in Lully's operas, e.g. *Cadmus* and *Acis et Galathée*. In Dassoucy's *Amours d'Apollon et de Daphné* (1650)—another one of the numerous Daphne plays—spoken verses and sung airs alternated in the manner of the oldest type of *ballet de cour*. The pastoral *Triomphe de l'Amour* (1655) by de Beys with music by de la Guerre is interesting only for its ingenious, if primitive, circumvention of the recitative. The composer simply strung together a great number of chansons, as was done later in the prison scene of *The Beggar's Opera*.

The most serious attempts to create a national opera were made by the poet Perrin and his musical collaborator, Robert Cambert (c. 1628–1677) who had learned his craft with Chambonnières and served as organist, and later as composer to the Dowager Queen Anne of Austria. In the *Pastorale d'Issy* (1659), presumptuously called the "first French comedy in music" Perrin and Cambert strove for a compromise between the Italian and the French approach. This aim clearly transpires from the preface: "Our language is capable of expressing the most beautiful passions and the most tender sentiments, and if one mixes the Italian style of music a little with our manner of singing one may achieve something in between the two, more agreeable than either." The *Pastorale d'Issy* was followed by *La Mort d'Adonis* by Jean Baptiste Boesset and *Ariane* by Cambert, but both operas were not performed. If the judgment of the opera-hater St-Evremond can be trusted, *Ariane* must be regarded as Cambert's masterpiece. It contained a lament of the heroine that, obviously fashioned after Monteverdi, was said to have surpassed anything that Lully ever wrote.

The favorable reception of the *Pastorale d'Issy* was, according to Perrin's own admission, due to the rising French chauvinism, namely "to the passion to see our language, our poetry, and our music triumph over a foreign poetry and language." These vainglorious nationalistic feelings were nurtured by Colbert who, in keeping with his theories of mercantilism and national self-sufficiency, also promoted the idea of spiritual autarchy. He backed Perrin's efforts to create a national opera, and procured for him in 1669 a royal patent that gave him the exclusive right to operatic performances. In 1671 *Pomone* [5] by Perrin and Cambert, the first French opera really deserving this name, opened the newly founded *Académie Royale de Musique* and was greeted with enthusiasm. Of the music only the prologue and fragments of the first two acts are extant.

Cambert's style compares on the whole not too favorably with the music Lully wrote at about the same time. Like his predecessors, Cambert prescribed in his recitatives frequent meter changes, dictated by the close adherence of the music to the French verse. The recitatives are distinguished for short affective sections and typically French rhythmic intricacies. *Pomone* opens with an overture in four parts of which only the first three resemble the Lullian type. The scene of the prologue is laid in the Louvre which gives ample occasion to apostrophize Louis XIV in the fawning and pompous manner that characterizes all prologues to ballets and operas of the time. A bipartite second overture leads to the opera proper. The airs which are sometimes preceded by ritornelli are written on a very small

---

[5] Reprinted in COF; see also HAM no. 223.

scale in a graceful, if unpretentious, style, familiar from the *ballet de cour.*
It is significant of the French conception of opera that they have no dramatic significance, the libretto, too, being idyllic rather than dramatic.
Aside from short ensembles for soloists, Cambert made use of bass arias
with "doubled continuo," in which the bass sang the same line as the
continuo while two instruments furnished the harmony above—a rather
primitive type of aria, frequently found also in Lully. Cambert was conservative in his harmonic vocabulary and rarely even hinted at the rich
resources of the Italian style. It is difficult to determine to what extent
Cambert was an original composer because the music for his first opera,
the *Pastorale d'Issy,* is lost, and his *Pomone* may already have been written
under the influence of Lully, who by that time had established himself as a
domineering composer.

In 1672 Cambert followed up his first operatic success with the *Pastorale
héroique des Peines et des Plaisirs de l'Amour,*[6] also only fragmentarily
preserved. Here the ballet is given a more prominent place and some
progress is made in dramatic intensification. Some comic sections, for
which Cambert had shown aptitude in the trio *Cariselli* [7] (an insertion in
a spoken play), also deserve notice.

Lully's machinations set an abrupt end to the promising career of Cambert and the embittered composer turned to England where he appeared
for a time at the court of Charles II before he found a violent death.

Comédie-Ballet AND Tragédie Lyrique: LULLY

With the steady rise of Lully at the French court all other musicians
were slowly but surely pushed into the background. The Florentine
Gianbattista Lulli (1632-1687), later known as Jean Baptiste Lully, came
to France in 1646 and entered the service of the young Louis XIV in 1652.
He was taught by the organists Métru, Roberday, and Gigault; his musical
training was therefore primarily French, not Italian. He distinguished
himself as violinist, dancer, and Italian comedian, and as early as 1653 he
became composer of the royal chamber music, succeeding Lazarin, a composer of the *Vingt-Quatre Violons,* who was likewise of Italian descent.
Lully broke with the time-honored custom of embellishments, practiced
by the *grande bande,* and pressed the king for permission to have an orchestra of his own, the sixteen (later twenty-one) *petits violons* (1656). He

[6] Reprinted in COF.
[7] Pougin, *Les vrais créateurs,* 282.

drilled this group in a dry and pointed style of utmost rhythmical precision which was later admired and imitated by all European composers. Lully's reform of orchestral technique, which passes as a typically French achievement, was actually undertaken in opposition to the traditional French style the perpetual diminutions of which were too imprecise for Lully's taste. He combined the unornamented, straight playing of the Venetian opera orchestra with the emphatically rhythmic style of French music and thus evolved the famous Lullian orchestral discipline by which he established his superiority in the field of ballet composition. The reviews of the time never fail to mention the brilliant precision of his orchestral "concerts."

Endowed with a calculating temperament and spurred by boundless ambition Lully systematically took advantage of his privileged position with the king. As successor of Cambefort he became superintendent of the king's music (1661) and gained complete control of the *grande bande*. When the success of Perrin and Cambert in the opera threatened to eclipse his own he took quick action: he wrested the royal patent from Perrin who, being in prison at the time, was hardly in a position to bargain. The new patent (1672) gave Lully complete monopoly over the opera; it strikingly restricted the use of music in theatrical productions other than his own, and granted all proceeds from his music to himself and his heirs.[8] He enforced the closure of a rival opera house, expelled Molière's troupe from the royal palace, and established his own *Académie Royale de Musique*. Thus Lully became as absolute a sovereign in music as Louis XIV was in state affairs. Lully died with one of the greatest fortunes ever amassed by a musician, derived partly from shrewd real estate speculation, partly from the income of his music. Lully's tyrannical egotism and unscrupulous exploitation of friends can only be compared with that of Wagner; but both bent the whole musical world into submission to their artistic achievements.

Lully's musical career falls into two major periods, that of ballet composition (1653–1672), and that of opera composition (1673–1687). At first his position at the court was ambiguous. On the one hand, he adopted in his instrumental ballet music the rhythmic style of the French dance, but on the other hand, he adhered in his *récits* and *airs* to the Italian bel-canto style. Not by accident were most of these *récits* set to Italian words. The ballets show therefore a Janus face, they are French in their instrumental, but Italian in their vocal portions. Lully gradually strengthened the role

---

[8] For the full text of this astonishing document see Nuitter-Thoinan, *Les origines,* 237.

of vocal music by inserting interludes for solo and choral ensembles in the *ballet de cour*.

The dances were in part freely composed in correspondence with the choreography of the ballets, but we find besides the older ball-room dances like the galliarde and courante several important dance patterns of a more recent origin. Although they appeared in the *ballet de cour* sometime before Lully, it was he who gave them the stamp that made them famous. They include the *passepied* in lively 3/8 time, the *rigaudon* and *bourrée* in vigorous duple time, the *loure* in dotted rhythm and moderate 6/4 time, the *gavotte* in graceful duple time, and above all, the minuet in stately 3/4 time with typical soft syncopations and hemiolas. Also the march must be mentioned here, which Lully elevated to the level of art music. Originally designed for the display of military might in pompous entries, the march was derived melodically from the stylized fanfare of the trumpet as is clearly discernible in many of Lully's march melodies. Like the military uniform, the march step, *i.e.* the movement of troops in a uniform motion, was essentially an achievement of the baroque era, prompted by the growing rationalization of warfare to which the standing armies of the baroque states testify.

None of Lully's fellow composers could compare with the caustic wit of his Italian vocal compositions which established his fame not only as a composer but also as a comedian and dancer. For the Italian play *Amore malato* (1657) by Buti he composed the ballets and also played the part of Scaramouche. He deliberately set the Italian style against the French in the prologue to the ballet *Alcidiane* (1658), and, similarly, in the *Ballet de la Raillerie* (1659) he composed an amusing dialogue between Italian and French music [9] in which he cleverly contrasted the simple syllabic style of the Italian canzonetta with the subtle turns of the French air. The *Ballet de l'Impatience* (1661) contained a grotesque *récit* of the "snuff takers" for a three-part choral ensemble in canzonetta style. The same work introduced also the air *Sommes-nous pas trop heureux?* (words by Benserade) which became later one of the most popular civil songs, known at the time as *brunettes* (Ex. 43).

Ex. 43. Lully: *Brunette.*

Som-mes -nous pas trop heu - reux Belle I - ris, que vous en sem-ble?

[9] Prunières, *L'Opéra Italien*, App. 16

The ballet *Alcidiane* is noteworthy for the first distinct example of the French overture. It begins with ponderous dotted rhythms and then turns to a fugal second part, written in duple time, not yet in the triple meter that was to become standard practice. The substitution of fugal for chordal texture was probably due to the Italian canzona overtures with which Lully was familiar. Thus even the French overture was the product of a mixture of styles. Lully's overture to the ballet insertions in Cavalli's *Serse* (1660) is perhaps the first example of the fully developed French overture with the second part in fugal texture and triple meter.

In spite of the assimilation of Italian and French features Lully passed at court as the representative of Italian music—a wise policy so long as Mazarin was alive and the Italian faction dominant. After the death of Mazarin (1661) Lully made a complete about-face, joined the ascendent French faction, and became an ardent advocate of French music. Precisely at this time he was appointed superintendent, hastened his French naturalization, and married the daughter of Michel Lambert. The second phase of Lully's ballet composition began with the *comédies-ballets,* a genre that Molière invented to enhance the play by the diversion of the ballet and to restore the original dramatic significance of the ballet. In 1664 the glorious cooperation of the two Baptistes began with the *Mariage Forcé;* it continued with *Princesse d'Elide, Amour médecin, Pastorale comique, Monsieur de Pourceaugnac, Bourgeois Gentilhomme* (1670), and the *tragédie-ballet Psyché* (1671) for which Corneille and Molière wrote the spoken verses, Quinault and Lully himself the lyrics for the *récits.*

In the comedy-ballets Lully expanded his music in two directions: he made the French recitative more dramatic and developed large choral and orchestral forms; both were to become important components of his operas. While the French *récits* of the *ballet de cour* were written mostly in the fixed forms of the *air,* the single scenes of the *comédie-ballets* were connected by *secco* recitatives, as in the contemporary Italian opera. The closeness to opera appears also in the beginning of the *Pastorale comique* which is a persiflage of a magic incantation scene, so popular in Venetian opera. The *buffo* style that Lully had formerly reserved for the Italian scenes appeared now also in the French scenes, as for example in *Pourceaugnac* or *Bourgeois Gentilhomme.* The latter contains a highly entertaining scene in which a composer is shown in the process of composing a *récit.* With the French recitative made more flexible, Lully did not hesitate to avail himself in earnest of the affective Italian style which he had ridiculed in the parodistic plaint of Tirsis *Ah quelle douceur* from *Elide*

(IV, 2). The entry of the Italians in the *Ballet des Nations* (*Bourgeois Gentilhomme*) contains strophic variations with Italian words that could almost be mistaken for the music of Luigi Rossi; a similarly affective style prevails in the famous Italian plaint *Deh piangete* from *Psyché*, a work that Lully later transformed into an opera. He finally took the decisive step by transferring the affective pathos and the melodic dissonances of the Italian *lamento* style to the French air and recitative. The plaint of Venus [10] in the *Ballet de Flore* (1667) or the plaint of Cloris *Ah mortelles douleurs* (Ex. 44) from the *Fêtes de Versailles* eloquently bespeak the

Ex. 44. Lully: Plaint from *Fêtes de Versailles*.

artistic result of this fusion of styles without which the French opera would not have been possible.

In the music of the comedy-ballet solo and choral ensembles overshadowed all other elements. The riotous Turkish ceremony in the finale of *Le Bourgeois Gentilhomme,* and the double chorus at the end of *George Dandin* are extended choral cantatas with interspersed solo sections. The solo trio *Dormez beaux yeux* from the *Amant magnifique* (1670) is written in obvious imitation of Rossi's slumber trio *Dormite begli occhi* from the *Orfeo.*[11] It begins with a bass ritornello very similar to the bass of Ex. 44 and corresponds to Rossi's composition in numerous details. In his choral writing also Lully was dependent on Luigi Rossi and Carissimi. From the latter he borrowed the rhythmic declamation in chordal texture which pervades all his choruses. In the exceptionally wellwrought chorus of the "distributors of ballet-books" from the *Bourgeois Gentilhomme* he represented the tumultuous throng before the beginning of a ballet performance by a perspicuous rhythmic counterpoint.

The beginnings of Lully's opera period were clouded by crafty intrigues. Lully had thus far maintained that opera was "impossible to execute in our language," but his professional jealousy made him change his mind. Although he was growing ever closer to the opera in his *comédie-ballets* he would hardly have taken the final step had it not been for the success of Perrin-Cambert and the *Triomphe de l'Amour* by Sablières. Unable to stand success except his own, Lully secretly snatched Perrin's patent for himself in violation of an agreement with Molière. But for Lully's personal ambition, Molière, and not Quinault, would have become the official librettist of the French opera.

From 1673 on, Lully produced an opera almost yearly, or, as he called it, a *tragédie lyrique*. The transition from the *comédie-ballet* to the opera can be seen in the pastoral *Amour et Bacchus*, an insignificant pasticchio of earlier stage works. The *tragédie lyrique* was established with *Cadmus et Hermione* (1673) and then followed in quick succession masterpieces such as *Alceste* (1674), *Thésée* (1675), *Isis* (1677), *Persée* (1682), *Amadis* (1684), *Roland* (1685), and *Armide* (1686). The librettist Quinault provided Lully with tragedies in the manner of Corneille and Racine whose works had received universal acclaim some years before Lully turned to the opera. Quinault at first retained the comic scenes of the Venetian libretto, but abandoned them after *Alceste*. Unlike the dramatists he mixed in his libretti the traditional French Alexandrines with shorter rhymed verses and did not observe the three unities. The plot revolved round the eternal conflict between *gloire et amour*.

Lully studied in the *Comédie française* the quasi-musical accents and emphatic inflections of the celebrated actress Champmeslé whose dramatic rendition of Racine became exemplary for him. He projected the wide range of spoken accents into his recitatives and heightened the rolling and eloquent rhetoric of the verses by means of a stylized music, characterized by great reserve toward affective dissonances and persistent use of anapaestic patterns. The danger of monotony was obviated by the lively and intense delivery of the singer. The meter signatures of the recitative freely alternated in strict accordance with the verse between 4/4, 2/2 (twice as fast as the preceding time), 3/2, etc. The meter changes were not supposed to be heard as such, but merely made the music flow vivaciously "like champagne," as Telemann put it.

The French conceived the recitative in rhetorical rather than musical terms. While the Italians traced the words primarily by the melodic curve, leaving the rhythm to the singer, the French directed their main attention to the rhythmic patterns giving only small attention to the melody. Lully remained in his recitatives essentially faithful to the French tradition and infused them with just enough of an affective tone to make them suitable for the pathetic passages of the tragedy. With regard to the differentiation of recitative, arioso, and aria Lully held a most conservative position. Although certain sections may be said to display *secco* style the recitative was generally so undeveloped that no clear distinction can be made. Lully moved imperceptibly from recitative to arioso, and from arioso to air, and did not go beyond the fluid stage of differentiation he found in Cavalli. His conservatism is further confirmed by the unwieldy slow cadences that separated the verses. The recitatives were as a rule through-composed but often adroitly unified by pregnant refrains which gave them a rondo character.[12] The wavering between recitative and arioso can also be seen in ensemble recitatives and short duet sections, as for example in *Cadmus* (I, 1).

Accompanied recitatives and ariosi were even more prominent than arias. Reserved for points of highest dramatic tension, they demonstrate his superb art of orchestration and his ability to make it subservient to the musical drama (*Amadis* III, 2, and *Roland* IV, 2). The memorable dream narration from *Armide* (Ex. 45) is accompanied by an ensemble of

Ex. 45. Lully: Accompanied *Récit* from *Armide*.

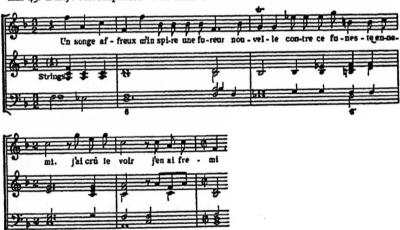

low strings which give a somber background to the impassioned accents of the voice.

In his arias, too, Lully took a conservative attitude. He restricted him-

12 See *Cadmus* V, 1, and *Persée* (GMB no. 232).

self to the short forms of the early Venetian opera and of the *ballet de cour*. Most commonly they were composed in bipartite AABB′ form, in which B and B′ differed in the cadence and some melodic variants (*Amadis* II, 4; *Cadmus* I, 3; *Armide* I, 2). Brief da-capo forms appeared only in the most significant arias with a heavy five-voice accompaniment, either as solo aria (*Armide* I, 3) or as duet (*Armide* II, 2). Lully was partial to arias with doubled continuo which gave a curious lopsided effect because the bass voice served here in two functions: as melody and as support of the instrumental accompaniment. As the aria *Bornez vous* from *Armide* (Ex. 46) shows however they differed markedly from the primitive type of

Ex. 46. Lully: Accompanied Air from *Armide*.

Violins

Cont &
Voice

Bor-nez   vous vos   dé-sirs   à   la   gloi-re   cru-el-le   des   maux

Cavalli and Cesti by virtue of the emphatic rhythmic declamation of the voice.

Many important arias were through-composed, as for example the celebrated air of Renaud (*Armide* II, 3) in the magic garden of the sorceress. Here a ritornello precedes and concludes the aria in which the muted strings depict with their softly undulating figures the murmuring of a brook. Modern devices, such as the motto beginning and the announcement of the melody in the continuo, hardly ever occur with Lully, and the long coloraturas of Italian opera are reduced to modest flourishes on important words. Likewise, little use is made of strophic variations and ground basses. In *Atys* (I, 4) a section of the aria is exceptionally built on type I of the chaconne bass.

The shortness of the arias explains why extended forms appeared only in conjunction with the chorus. The chorus assumed in Lully's operas an unprecedented prominence. It served as the main means of organization since the aria was not weighty enough for this purpose. Only in the oratorios of Carissimi did the chorus hold a comparable position. Even though the rhythmic precision of Lully's choral writing was inspired by Carissimi, Lully left his Italian model far behind. His prologues represent independent choral cantatas on a scale not previously realized by any composer. Throughout the five acts of the opera, sung and danced choruses created points of rest in the dramatic action and nearly all acts were rounded off by them. Lully combined solo ensembles and choral sections in large rondo forms, as for example in *Armide* (I, 3). The choral ensembles often appeared in the form of gigantic chaconnes, perhaps the greatest monuments of Lully's art. They had already occurred in the ballet *Alcidiane* in instrumental form, and in the comedy-ballet *Pastorale comique* in choral form. Lully treated the chaconne with considerable freedom as variations of a rhythmic pattern—saraband rhythm with emphasis on the second beat—rather than as strict ground basses. The stereotyped descending tetrachord appeared at times only in the course of the composition, as in *Roland*,[13] and, especially in choral chaconnes, the bass was even more freely varied by modulations and melodic inversions. The chaconnes of the operas developed into huge choral and instrumental rondos which were punctuated by trio episodes for woodwinds—a practice that anticipates an essential element of the concerto grosso.[14] The rondo form was further strengthened by the juxtaposition of large key areas which made the chaconne a tripartite form: the first and third parts enclosed a middle part in the tonic minor or the relative major.[15] The monumental chaconne in *Amadis* (V, 5) illustrates with its heavy-footed pomp and its inexorable drive a power to sustain an extended movement paralleled only in the music of late baroque composers such as Vivaldi, Bach, and Handel.

A thickly scored five-part ensemble of strings formed the nucleus of the orchestra which could be expanded for coloristic reasons by a trio of woodwinds. Lully's keen sense of color is proved by his effective, if essentially simple, orchestration. Wind instruments appeared preferably in the ritornelli and accompaniments for battle arias and magic scenes. His evocative descriptions of nature conform in their stylized rationalism to the grand manner of the heroic landscapes by Claude Lorrain.

Next to the orchestral chaconnes, the overtures constituted the weightiest instrumental form in the opera. They were usually played twice, before and after the prologue. The French overture as shaped by Lully became with its austere pathos and its pretentious and rather superficial counterpoint the symbol of courtly ceremonial. They call for the dry, precise and brilliant orchestral technique on which Lully's European fame was primarily based. Formally, the overture was bipartite: a cadence on the dominant separated the slow and the fast section, both of which were repeated. The coda-like return to the slow part at the end was not typical

[13] GMB no. 233.
[14] The trio of the minuet in the classic symphony is a direct descendent of the Lullian trio.
[15] See GMB no. 233.

of Lully himself; it became the rule only with his late baroque imitators.

In Lully's part-writing the outermost voices always show unmistakable character while the inner voices, especially the fifth part, move awkwardly, often in parallel fifths and octaves. It seems that Lully sketched out only the structural contour of the composition leaving the filling-in to his underlings, who may also have been responsible for the frequent cadential clashes. Even the structural parts, however, have an angular, if not erratic, quality. They move not according to their inherent melodic logic but according to rhythmic patterns which cause a striking asymmetrical phrase structure, highly characteristic of Lully's instrumental style. When Lully set words, their rhythm dictated that of the music. But even in the airs the influence of dance patterns is always perceptible and often dominant. Many of Lully's instrumental dance tunes do not differ in style from his airs; in fact, many of them became famous as *vaudevilles* through the addition of text, a procedure that was called *canevas* at the time.

The harmonic vocabulary was conservative, hardly richer than that of Luigi Rossi, and as free from the pre-tonal ventures of early baroque style as from the rich tonal resources of late baroque style. His frequent use of cross-relations is typical of middle baroque harmony. Major and minor keys are clearly established at the cadences, but the harmonies between the cadences do not progress in a logical drive, and are, like his melodies, dependent on rhythm. Also his more suggestive than real counterpoint produces rhythmic rather than harmonic interest. This conspicuous dependence on rhythm adduces homogeneous, if not monotonous, progressions; only the V_3^4 chord stands out as a powerful harmonic resource, especially at the beginning of the overture. Chromatic sections occur in the opera only in laments, written in deliberate imitation of the Italian style; otherwise the harmony is essentially diatonic. Lully handled his keys with striking monotony. Most of the ballet *entrées* are restricted to one key which may at best be changed to the opposite mode or the related key; the single scenes of the operas usually observe the same restriction.

In spite of all traceable influences on Lully's music it bears an unmistakably personal stamp. Lully was not a spontaneous composer. His musical imagination was stimulated neither by the sensuous appeal of the bel-canto melody nor by the expressive possibilities of harmony, but by the idea of abstract rhythm and motion. Within these restrictions he was an incomparable stylist. His highly rational sobriety showed to best advantage in the rigidly reglemented forms of the chaconne and the French overture which attest to his boundless rhythmic imagination. The paradoxical fact that Lully drew strength from the very restrictions of the form made him the true representative of the precious artificiality which obtained in music, as well as in the other arts, at the French court. He brought baroque music in France to an acme of stylization which none of his successors was able to surpass. After Lully the heavy orchestral armor, the contrapuntal pretense, and the stiff dignity of the music were no longer maintained. Music was reduced to a less austere tone and to a smaller scale. While other countries rose to the heights of late baroque style, France evolved in the rococo style an idiom that, although an outgrowth of baroque style, was destined to overthrow baroque music altogether.

CANTATA, ORATORIO, AND CHURCH MUSIC

The opera at the French court held such a dominating position that other forms of vocal music did not develop very vigorously. From the beginning of the seventeenth century Italian precedents were and remained decisive. The sacred compositions of Formé (d. 1633) and Bouzignac, honorably mentioned by Mersenne, were works of transition, written in a conservative idiom. The unaccompanied sections in Bouzignac's motets clearly display renaissance style, but his Latin gospel dialogues are remarkable for their terse declamation and dramatic choral interjections which actually anticipate the choral style of Carissimi. The striking pictorial chromaticism in the polyphonic chansons of Bouzignac is strangely reminiscent of certain passages in the works of the English madrigalists.[16] Pierre de la Barre, organist and lutenist to Louis XIII, deliberately composed in the Italian manner, so successfully in fact that when a trio of his was posthumously printed in the *Mercure Galant* (1678) it was mistaken for a composition by Luigi Rossi.

The two outstanding cantata composers of the French middle baroque, Jean de Cambefort and Marc-Antoine Charpentier (1634-1704), have received very little attention and only a few of their works are at present accessible. Charpentier was, next to Lully, the most remarkable figure in French music. As a pupil of Carissimi he was well grounded in the Italian style and therefore never succumbed to the influence of Lully. In a curious reversal of national attitudes Charpentier, the native French composer, upheld in France the Italian style against the French style of Lully, the native Italian. Charpentier distinguished himself by his superb melodic

---

[16] Compare the second part of *Heureux séjour* (SIMG VI, 377) with the last section of Weelke's *Cease sorrows now* (in vol. IX of *The English Madrigal School*).

invention, far superior to that of Lully. His cantata *Coulez*[17] for solo voice
and three instruments, written in the pathetic style of a plaintive pastoral,
discloses how he adapted a noble bel-canto melody to the French style by
the use of the French type of embellishments. His obligation to Italian
style appears also in the use of chaconne basses, as for example in the
gentle air *Sans frayeur* (Ex. 47), based on the fourth type of chaconne bass

Ex. 47. Charpentier: Air on a ground.

(see Ex. 8). The angular squareness of the bass is softened here by the
overlapping asymmetrical phrases of the voice. Charpentier became the
musical collaborator of Molière after the latter had broken with Lully. It
was he who wrote the music for Molière's *Malade Imaginaire* (1673) and
for the revival of the *Mariage Forcé* for which the original music by Lully
was discarded. In the comic intermezzi of the *Malade Imaginaire* and,
especially, in the important opera *Médée* (1693, libretto by Thomas Corneille) Charpentier achieved a vigorous personal style, which, although less
austere than that of Lully, was well suited for the stage because of its
melodic appeal.

His most original contribution was, however, the establishment of the
oratorio in France. He wrote the music for the sacred tragedies that the
Jesuits performed in Paris. His Latin and French oratorios include *Judicium Salomonis, Extremum Judicium, Josué, Quatre Saison,* and *Le Reniement de St-Pierre*,[18] his masterpiece. As the Latin titles indicate,

---

[17] Gastoué, in *Mélanges Laurencie*, 153; see also the cantata *Orphée*, repr. by Quittard, RM, 1904, App. 136.

[18] Reprinted in *Concerts spirituels, Schola Cantorum, sér. anc.* III, ed. by Charles
Bordes. See also HAM no. 226.

Charpentier dealt with subjects on which his teacher also had composed, and it cannot surprise us that he leaned heavily on Carissimi's model. Likewise the significant dramatic function of the chorus and the concise and lucidly profiled coloraturas of the soloists were borrowed from Carissimi. However, Charpentier paid greater attention to the instruments and did not artificially restrict his harmonies to the popular style of Carissimi's oratorios. The final plaint of St. Peter after the third denial in *Le Reniement* discloses his special talent for poignant affections.

With the concentration of cultural life at the French court, the church did not hold as independent a position as it did in Italy and Germany. For this reason church music took second place beside court music. Compositions of the ordinary of the Mass on the large scale, very common in Italy and in Vienna, were hardly cultivated in France because the king more often attended the short low Mass than the lengthy high Mass. In order to give royal dignity to the recited service of the low Mass, it was transformed into the so-called *messe basse solennelle* by means of inserted motets with elaborate instrumental accompaniment. Such stately motets were composed not only by minor masters like Gobert and Villot, but also by such shining lights as Henri Dumont (d. 1684), Lully, and Charpentier. The *Cantica sacra* (1652) by Dumont were one of the first printed motet collections to prescribe the *basse continue*. In his *Messes Royales* Dumont experimented with the plainchant, not only by putting it into measured form, but "enhancing" it with modern accidentals that forced the modal melodies into modern keys. The French modernization of the chant to what was called the *plainchant musical* formed part of the national reform movement which stressed the independence of the French church from Rome.

The solemn motets of Lully and Charpentier were expansive cantatas for solo, chorus, and orchestra, similar in form to the English anthem. Lully transplanted the musical pomp of the court theatre to the motet by levying gigantic combinations of soloists, double chorus, and a full orchestra with trumpets and kettledrums, such as we find in the motet *Miserere* (1664), universally admired for its splendor. Neither here nor in the *Te Deum* and *Dies Irae* did Lully set a Gregorian melody, only in the *Dies Irae* did he quote the initial phrase as *plainchant musical* with a distorting accidental. The hammering and fiery declamation of the choruses, the massive sonorities of the orchestral symphonies, the *récits* for the soloists. and the rhythmic counterpoint of the part-writing produced an overwhelming effect of ceremonial brilliance. Of all Lully's compositions these motets were the most contrapuntal, but even here frequent cadences interrupted the flow so that the whole formed a rhythmic procession of short-winded contrapuntal sections. The church works of Charpentier far exceed those of Lully in quantity. They include a number of Masses, *Te Deum, Magnificats, Leçons de Ténèbre,* and more than thirty psalms, all of which remained in manuscript. Only the *Motets meslez de Symphonies* appeared in print. Although Charpentier did not lavish so much splendor on his church compositions as Lully, he favorably compares in his vivid themes and his melodious counterpoint with the music of his rival.

LUTE MINIATURES AND KEYBOARD MUSIC: GAULTIER AND CHAMBONNIÈRES

At the beginning of the baroque period the French composers of instrumental solo music, notably the lutenists and the clavecinists, developed idioms that became exemplary for the rest of Europe. The art of the lutenists, which flourished mainly in the early and middle baroque, laid the basis for that of the clavecinists which flourished mainly in the middle and late baroque periods. The school of organists, more conservative than the other two schools, remained of only local significance throughout the period. Instrumental ensemble music was restricted in France to the dance, especially the *ballet de cour;* the only exception was the polyphonic fantasy for viols which experienced a short vogue in the early decades of the seventeenth century, obviously prompted by the flowering of the fancy in England.

The high development of French lute music can only be understood from a sociological point of view. According to Mersenne the lute was considered the noblest of all instruments,—quite literally the instrument of nobility since the king and his noblemen were more or less competent lute players themselves. Lute music served in the *ballet de cour* not only as accompaniment of the *airs de cour,* but also as independent instrumental introduction, performed usually in massed ensembles. The abundance of printed lute collections amply attests to the wide dissemination and the high standard of lute playing in France. The *Trésor d'Orphée* (1600) [19] by Francisque and the *Thesaurus* (1603) by Besard gave a comprehensive survey of all forms of the transition period: *airs de cour,* dances, and transcriptions of vocal models. The dances at this time were not yet ar-

[19] Reprinted by Quittard, 1907.

ranged according to suites but according to types. Besard's *Novus partus sive concertationes musicae* (1617) contained, among other pieces for concerting lutes, a version of Dowland's *Lachrimae* for the exceptional ensemble of three lutes. Nearly all the composers of the *ballet de cour* contributed to these collections, notably Antoine Boesset, Bataille, Vincent, Guédron, and Chancy.

In the printed lute pieces each part of the air was often stated twice, first without embellishments, then with figurate variations that corresponded to the improvised *broderies* of the sung *air de cour*.[20] Both the varied repeats and the patterns of the variations stemmed from the English virginalists. While the earlier lute books contained primarily transcriptions of vocal works, adapted to the lute by idiomatic embellishments, the later ones shifted to a completely instrumental repertory. Lute music gained its final independence in the works of the Gaultier dynasty, a family of lute virtuosi. It rose to fame with Jacques Gaultier, known as *le vieux*, who served since 1619 at the English court, and his even more famous cousin Denis Gaultier (c. 1603–1672), called *l'illustre*. The works of Denis comprise the *Pièces de luth* (1669) and the famous *Rhétorique des Dieux*, not printed during his lifetime, but preserved in a sumptuous manuscript.[21]

The most striking stylistic trait of Gaultier's music was the imaginative utilization of such lute idioms as free-voiced texture, intricate ornaments, and what was known as the *style brisé*. The quickly fading sound of the lute did not lend itself to polyphonic voice-leading and called for specific techniques that compensated for the technical limitations of the instrument. The "broken style" of lute music, a most ingenious and consistent application of such a technique, may be called the glorification of the simplest lute figure: the arpeggio. The broken style is characterized by rapidly alternating notes in different registers that supply, in turn, melody and harmony. Seemingly distributed in arbitrary fashion over the various registers, the notes produced in their composite rhythm a continuous strand of sound. The lute composer was able to articulate the even flow by means of double and triple stops which suggested the rhythmic patterns, essential to the dance. The texture of lute music was of necessity free-voiced since no voice could be carried through and since notes that hinted at one voice at the beginning of the measure dropped out as soon as they had appeared. The intricate texture will become clear if two versions of a *Pavane*

---

[20] Lavignac E, I:3, 1230.
[21] See Tessier in *Publications, Société française de musicologie*, 6–7, also Fleischer VfM II, 1886; GMB no. 215, HAM no. 211.

by Gaultier are compared. The first version (Ex. 48a) gives the literal transcription of the tablature notation which indicated, not the absolute duration of each note, but only its duration in relation to the next one. It contained therefore no hint with regard to voice-leading. The second version (Ex. 48b) reproduces the transcription into ordinary keyboard

Ex. 48. Gaultier: *Pavane.*

notation by Perrine, a lutenist of the period, who realized the chordal and melodic structure, merely implied in the free-voiced version. It should be noted that both versions contain the "identical" music. The peculiar charm of free-voiced texture cannot be felt if lute transcriptions are played on the piano. Its texture, more suggestive than real, is definitely bound up with the instrument. Lute music represents perhaps the cleverest example of making a virtue of necessity—a veritable triumph of mind over matter.

More than any other instrument, the lute called for sustaining ornaments in all voices. While in the lute music of the renaissance the florid sections of the melody were carefully written out in the tablature, they were indicated in baroque tablatures by means of newly invented symbols. The use of ornamental symbols was again derived from the virginalists. Instrumental ornaments were as essential a factor in the chordally conceived lute music as vocal ornaments were in the monody. In spite of the full accounts of lute ornamentation in Mersenne and Mace, its variety and subtlety is hard to describe. Aside from various symbols for appoggiature, ascending and descending arpeggios, sudden dampening of the string, and other niceties, the *tremblements* formed a specially refined group of ornaments. The two main trills, called by Mace the "hard" and the "soft" shake were both executed by the left hand while the right hand plucked the string only once. The hard trills prolonged the sound by a rapid scratching of the string producing a tremolo of even pitch. The soft shake, called *battement* by Mersenne, was a real trill of two notes in the modern sense, but a most delicate ornament, always coupled with a decrescendo because of the quick fading of the sound. According to Mersenne, the *battement* was typical of violin music rather than of lute music. Other refinements included the vibrato or *verre cassé,* and several forms of legato playing of the left hand. The extreme delicacy of the ornaments bespeaks the highly intimate character of lute music; it was destined for a solo virtuoso and a very small audience.

True to the French tradition, Gaultier gathered in his lute collections mainly dances, but dances in highly stylized form. They were arranged in groups or suites with no rigidly established order. Only allemande, courante, and saraband formed the kernel of the suite, the gigue being at this time still an optional movement. This stage is reflected in the autograph version of the harpsichord suites by Froberger; they were cycles of three or four movements, sometimes unified by variation, in which no dance of the same type occurred more than once, except for the *double.* To the French the suite was an anthology rather than a strict sequence of dances. This can be seen not only in the fact that the basic movements were freely interspersed with other dance types (pavane, chaconne, canarie, gigue) but, particularly, in the practice of including in a single suite several courantes with their *doubles.* The French lutenists and clavecinists both were more partial to the courante than were the composers of any other nation. It was naturally the French type that appeared with Gaultier in highly developed form. In contrast with the quick 3/4 time and the straightforward melodic style of the Italian *corrente,* the French courante was characterized by sophistication. Written in 6/4 and 3/2 time it favored hemiola rhythms, subtle syncopations, and intricate melodic patterns, all of which made a comparatively slow tempo necessary without which the subtleties would pass unnoticed. The high degree of stylization indicates that the courante had ceased to be a ballroom dance.

The great variety and the frequent duplication of dance types almost obliterated the cyclic unity of the suite. The only principle of unification was the unity of key, and this unity was indeed strictly observed. The *Rhétorique des Dieux* is arranged strictly in the order of the twelve modes, each of which is represented not only aurally by a suite, but also visually by an allegorical picture describing the affection of the mode.

The individual dance movements in Gaultier's suites were stylized genre pieces carrying suggestive titles such as "The Virtuous Coquette," "The Homicide," or names of mythological or real persons to whom the piece was dedicated. These intimate titles, which had been taken over from the English virginalists, did not convey any definite program, but reflected

the French penchant for literary allusions in music; they frequently referred to the mythological subjects of the *ballet de cour*. Gaultier set a
precedent to future lutenists and harpsichordists by the creation of the
tombeau, a gentle miniature composed in memory of noble persons, rela-
tives, or friends. Gaultier is known to have written *tombeaux* for several
aristocrats, for Mlle. Gaultier, and for the lutenist M. de Lenclos,[22] the
father of Ninon de Lenclos who received lute instruction from Denis
Gaultier himself. How strongly the dance dominated French music can be
seen in the fact that even the *tombeau* was based, in spite of its grave
character, on the stylized pattern of the allemande. Of all the movements
of the suite only the prelude was not dependent on the dance. This dignified introduction was composed in a most peculiar manner without fixed
note values like a rhapsodic toccata. The lute player was supposed to bring
the freely hovering lines into a rhythmical order according to his own
conceit so that no two performances of the same prelude were identical.
Tombeau and prelude can be considered as the most significant manifestations of Gaultier's at once profound and playful imagination.

Gaultier was widely imitated by a host of French lute composers many
of whom counted among his personal pupils. They included Ennemond
Gaultier (the son of Denis), Mouton, Du Faut, Pinel, and Gallot, a member of the Gallot dynasty who liked to "portray" persons in his lute pieces.
Mouton transcribed a number of Lully's airs for the lute and associated
definite affections with certain dance patterns, *e.g.* the gigue with the
comic. The music of the second generation of lute masters was so overladen
with ornaments that the tablatures became almost illegible. The exuberance
of ornaments was symptomatic of the inner decline of lute music. With the
increasing importance of the thorough-bass the theorboe and the chitar-
rone, far better suited to chordal playing than the lute, slowly pushed the
solo literature into the background. Fleury published a theorboe method
of continuo accompaniment (1660). The lute tablature became too difficult
for the average musician and fell into disuse. In 1680, the lutenist Perrine
arranged the lute music of Gaultier *en musique,* that is, in ordinary keyboard notation, designed for both lute and harpsichord performance (see
Ex. 48b). This telling change in notation marks the end of soloistic lute
music. The vulgar guitar with its simple technique of chord strumming
took over. Supported by Spanish guitar virtuosos, Robert de Visée, guitarist
of Louis XIV, inaugurated the rage for the guitar at the court. He ad-

[22] GMB no. 215.

mittedly imitated in his *Livre de Guitarre* (1682) the brittle rhythmic
dance style of Lully. The end of the development is clearly reflected in the
rococo paintings of Watteau. His shepherds and courtesans do not play
the lute but pluck the fashionable guitar.

Although French lute music declined after the death of Gaultier its
musical achievements were not dissipated. They survived in the music for
the harpsichord or clavecin. The clavecinists studiously imitated nearly all
the lute idioms on their instrument. This astonishing and unique transfer
of idioms had no technical justification because the clavecin did not have
the technical limitations of the lute. Here again sociological factors proved
decisive. Since lute music enjoyed the highest social prestige it naturally
invited imitation. As the keyboard composers in the northern countries
had done, the clavecinists of the middle baroque likewise built on the
idiomatic keyboard style of the virginalists, but the lutenists served as in-
termediaries and transmitted the English heritage in modified form. The
three features that French lute music shared with virginal music—the patterned variation, the fanciful titles, and the adoption of symbols for ornaments—were retained also in the clavecin music. The manner in which
the clavecinists transformed the English influence strikingly demonstrates
the fundamental difference between the French and the German conception of music. While Sweelinck and the German harpsichordists were attracted primarily by the idea of mechanical severity, the clavecinists seized
on the idea of playful imagination. Both ideas had lain as yet undivided
and undeveloped in English virginal music; they now developed independently in the two national branches of keyboard music.

Through the mediation of the lutenists the harpsichord composers discovered their own idiom, which had thus far hardly differed from that
of the organ. Not bound by the technical handicaps of the lute they were
able to bring the broken style to a perfection not dreamed of by the lutenists.
In clavecin music the free-voiced texture was no longer a necessity but a
calculated stylistic feature. They substituted for ornaments that could only
be executed on the lute a great number of new keyboard *agréments* which
gave the melody not only an unprecedented flexibility but also a brilliant
rhythmic sparkle. The free-voiced style of the clavecinists differed from
that of the virginalists by its highly developed "suggestive" part-writing
that hinted at the various voices without actually realizing them, and by

the dualistic nature of the music, clearly brought out in the contrast of the extremely florid melody and the constantly arpeggiated chords of the accompaniment.

The French school had its first great representative in Jacques de Chambonnières (c. 1602-1672), clavecinist to the French court, whose personal style left its mark on the subsequent members of the school, notably Louis Couperin (d. 1661), Hardelle, Le Bègue (1630-1702), Nivers, and Jean Henri D'Anglebert (1635-1691). Chambonnières exerted also a strong influence on Froberger—the latter visited Paris in 1652—and thus indirectly on the south German school of keyboard composers. His *Pièces de Clavessin* [23] (written c. 1640, printed 1670) which faithfully follow the model of Gaultier's lute suites contain delicate miniatures or genre pieces and stylized dances with imaginative titles. As with Gaultier, Chambonnières' suites consist of three main types, the allemande, courante, and saraband, and an optional gigue. The great number of courantes with their ornamental *doubles* and other freely inserted dance types in a single suite showed that each dance movement was more important than the order of the cycle as a whole. Neither Chambonnières nor his successors unified their dances in the German manner by means of common thematic material; they strove on the contrary for as much contrast between the single movements as possible, observing, however, the unity of key. Except for the tripartite pavane all dances fell into the common bipartite form with repeats for each section. Chambonnières's judicious utilization of the free-voiced broken style prompted at times a highly intricate rhythm, especially appropriate for the courante (Ex. 49). In the quoted example the typical hemiola rhythm of the bass is overlaid with a network of measured ar-

Ex. 49. Chambonnières: *Courante.*

[23] CE by Quittard 1911, Brunold-Tessier 1926. See also TAM VII, 30 ff; HAM no. 212.

peggios that suggest four or even five independent voices. The composite rhythm of all voices produces at the beginning a ceaseless eight-note movement. The great importance that Chambonnières attached to the ornaments can be seen in the fact that he printed an explanatory table of symbols in his publication—a practice that became exemplary for his followers.

The next generation of clavecinists, especially D'Anglebert, substituted a symbol (a slanted stroke) for the measured arpeggio which Chambonnières was careful to write out in his music. Louis Couperin, the uncle of François and the first important master of the famous dynasty of Couperins, deployed in his few, but remarkable, suites all the keys that the meantone tuning made accessible, including such remote ones as *f*-sharp and *b*. His preludes were so closely fashioned after the rhapsodic type of Gaultier that they even retained a feature of the lute notation. The rhapsodic parts were nothing more than a series of unmeasured semibreves, some of which were connected by slurs, indicating here, as in lute notation, sustained notes.[24] Their rhythmic interpretation was again the responsibility of the performer. Couperin's preludes, formally more highly developed than those of Gaultier, were tripartite toccatas in which two rhapsodic sections enclosed a fugal middle part. Couperin differed from his fellow composers by his very serious temperament and gravity, manifested not only in the poignant modulations of his *tombeaux*, but also in his tendency to combine the dance with contrapuntal artifices, *e.g.* the saraband with the canon. His chaconne in *g* [25] built on a descending tetrachord consists of three parts, set off by an abrupt turn to the major mode—a device that Lully frequently imitated in his chaconnes.

The clavieristic technique of D'Anglebert surpassed that of his predecessors by the richness of its texture and the full utilization of the high and low range of the clavecin. He expanded the suite by lengthening the single dances without however sacrificing the bipartite form. His *tombeau* in memory of Chambonnières and the twenty-two variations on the *folia* bass [26] are impressive documents of his resourceful keyboard style, which betrays the influence of Lully. D'Anglebert in fact transferred the sonorities of the Lullian orchestra to the clavecin—a striking early parallel to the orchestral expansion of piano technique by Liszt. It is noteworthy that D'Anglebert included in his *Pièces de Clavecin* (1689) numerous tran-

[24] TAM VIII, 40. CE ed. by Cauchie (*Oiseau Lyre* Edition); see also HAM no. 229.
[25] TAM VIII, 35.
[26] TAM VII, 122, 148. CE in *Publications, Société française de Musicologie*, 8.

scriptions of airs and even overtures by Lully. The clavecin arrangement of the overture to *Cadmus et Hermione* [27] represented the first step toward the independent keyboard overture which served in late baroque suites as the opening movement.

The suites of the organist and harpsichordist Le Bègue foreshadow in their rich chromaticism certain features of the late baroque harmony. Le Bègue broke the unity of key and admitted to his suites not only the opposite mode (which can be found even with Chambonnières), but also relative major or minor keys such as occurred in the ballet *entrées* of Lully. He eliminated the fugal section from the rhapsodic preludes and, like D'Anglebert, gave in his notation more precise rhythmic indications than Louis Couperin had done, though they still preserved a good measure of freedom. Le Bègue also broke with the habit of giving titles to the dances; he substituted for the literary means of characterization a purely musical one by juxtaposing a *courante grave* with a *courante gaie*.[28]

Although French organ music [29] could not rival the brilliant development of clavecin music, it maintained its independence beside the German and Italian schools. Three traits characterized the French organists. Firstly, they were conservatives by profession and adhered to the traditional polyphonic texture, especially in the fantasies and the versets, in which fragments of the *plainchant musical* appeared in the pedal in evenly sustained notes. Secondly, they devoted a great deal of attention to the coloristic possibilities of the organ, as can be seen in the consistent use of carefully specified registrations; in French organ music coloristic considerations were so pronounced that they sometimes took precedence over those of structure. Thirdly, they assimilated those elements of clavecin music that lent themselves more or less happily to the organ idiom. Not only were numerous ornaments bodily transferred to the organ, but even the *style brisé*, the very opposite of true organ idiom. The transfer to the organ of a lute idiom demonstrates in spectacular fashion that whenever in baroque music there was a conflict between the idiom of a style and that of an instrument, stylistic considerations prevailed. Disregard for the medium is a prominent feature of baroque art in general. But for the polyphonic texture, there was little difference between organ and clavecin

[27] TAM VII, 146.
[28] TAM VIII, 30.
[29] Guilmant, *Archives des maîtres de l'orgue;* HAM no. 231.

style; the harpsichord thus played the same role with regard to the organ as the lute did with regard to the harpsichord. It is not surprising that music for both clavecin and organ appeared indiscriminately in the organ collections. The national characteristics of the florid organ style were later taken over by the German organists, notably Böhm.

The organ works of Titelouze (d. 1633) belong in dissonance treatment and texture to the last flowering of renaissance style, except for scattered hints of modern *concertato* motives in complementary rhythms.[30] The early baroque organ music was represented by Racquet of whose music we know mainly through Mersenne. One of the Gaultiers composed a *tombeau* in his honor. The middle baroque generation comprised the three teachers of Lully: Roberday, Métru, and Gigault (d. 1707), and, in addition, Dumont, Louis Couperin, Le Bègue, and Nivers, the last three of whom were pupils of Chambonnières. Roberday made in his *Fugues et Caprices* (1660) an interesting experiment by grouping variation ricercars and capriccios in pairs that were bound together by thematic unity. The idea of deriving a sprightly capriccio theme from the placid ricercar theme by means of rhythmic transformation was obviously inspired by Frescobaldi and Froberger, but the contrasting arrangement in pairs was a novelty. Roberday borrowed the themes of his variation fugues from other composers, notably Louis Couperin, Cambert, Froberger, and Cavalli. The five fugues that D'Anglebert added to his clavecin collection were also variation ricercars on a single theme.

The coloristic bent of French organ music is attested by numerous solo recitations and echoes for specified stops or the pedal, found especially in the works of Nivers and Le Bègue. The latter made it in his *Livre d'Orgue* (1667) a special point to play *sur tous les jeux*. Le Bègue and Gigault were noteworthy not only for their bold chromaticism but also for their charming and popular *noëls,* published side by side with the weighty liturgical music. The rising influence of secular music made itself felt in the increased use of *agréments* and typical dance patterns. In the organ works of André Raison the dances actually intruded into the liturgical versets; the composer naïvely remarked that the dances should be played on the organ more slowly than on the harpsichord in keeping with "the sanctity of the place." Raison gained some notoriety for the fact that an idea of his passacaglia in *g* (*Livre d'Orgue,* 1688) was immortalized in Bach's organ passacaglia in *c.* Gigault carried the idea of "functional music" to so fine a point that the result became questionable. His compositions could be

[30] HAM no. 180.

broken off at several specified places in order to allow the organist perfect timing with the exigencies of the ritual.

MUSIC IN THE IBERIAN PENINSULA, NEW SPAIN, AND COLONIAL AMERICA

Throughout the baroque period music in Spain maintained a distinctly local color in spite of Italian influence which made itself increasingly felt as the century progressed. Spanish masters were active all over Europe, notably the guitar virtuosi Doisi in Italy and Brizeño in France, and the bassoon virtuoso Bartolomeo de Selma at the Austrian court. De Selma's flamboyant solo and trio sonatas for bassoon, printed in Venice (1638),[81] are written in early baroque virtuoso style in the vein of Castello and other Venetian composers. The Catalan harpsichordists Romaña and Marqués, who also belonged to the early baroque, deserve mention for their variations on secular dance tunes.

Organ music[82] was represented by Aguilera de Heredia, from 1603 organist at Saragossa, the Portuguese organist Coelho (*Flores de musica,* 1620), and Correa de Araujo (d. 1663). Correa's *Facultad orgánica* (1626), the most representative Spanish collection of early baroque organ music, displays a strange mixture of archaic and progressive features. Correa combined the traditional polyphonic texture with strikingly erratic melodic contours and somber colors, highly reminiscent of the contemporary paintings of El Greco. The bizarre melodic turns to be found in his ricercars or *tientos* had already occurred, if rarely, in the works of Cabezon, but with Correa they became common practice. He shared with Frescobaldi the frequent use of pre-tonal chromaticism or *falsas,* but the music of the Spaniard was more chaotic and restless. The strongly affective character of Correa's subjects stands in striking contrast to the rigid and mechanical figures that he borrowed from the English and Dutch organ style. The fusion of these conflicting elements characterizes all the Spanish artists of the time: it betrays powerful affections that are, however, ascetically controlled by equally powerful inhibitions. In his turbulent *tiento a modo di cancion,* Correa paradoxically combined the variation ricercar with the form of a quilt canzona, moving restlessly in fits and starts as if driven by the ascetic lust for painful affections.

[81] Lavignac E, I:4, 2086.
[82] See the collections of Pedrell and Villalba (*Antología de organistas*), and Bonnet's *Historical Organ Recitals,* VI. Coelho's *Tentos* have been edited by Kastner (1936); see also HAM no. 200.

The ascetic spirit abated in the music of Juan Cabanilles (1644-1712), the greatest organist of the Spanish middle baroque. Of his voluminous works only his organ music is at present accessible. Cabanilles proved his keen coloristic and harmonic sense by his *tientos de falsas;* his temperate and energetic counterpoint, characterized by upbeat patterns and repeated notes, was harmonically stable enough to sustain large multipartite forms. His extended *tientos* are often reduced to three major parts; combining the features of the polythematic ricercar and the variation ricercar, they include long pedal points on different degrees of the scale in which the same melodic material recurs in various keys.[33] His formal variations on secular themes, national dances, and ostinati, such as the *passacalles* and the *folia,* bespeak a happy imagination, no longer under the spell of self-denial and inhibition.

Spanish church music [34] reflected in its hyper-conservative attitude the spirit of severe orthodoxy that prevailed in Spain. The innovations of baroque style were shunned. The music of Victoria, more advanced with respect to harmony than that of Palestrina, but otherwise equally conservative, became the prototype of the Spanish church composers who studiously preserved the *stile antico* well into the eighteenth century. The conservative school included the Catalan masters Juan Comes, Juan Pujol,[35] and Cererols [36] of Montserrat; Romero, known as "El Maestro Capitán," and the Portuguese composers Rebello, Magalhães and Melgaço. The late baroque church music was represented by Francisco Valls (d. 1747) who no longer adhered to the *stile antico.* He composed an *auto-sacramental* or oratorio in Italian style. The unprepared (though very innocuous) dissonances in his Mass *Scala Aretina* aroused a lengthy controversy among the Spanish musicians, comparable to that between Monteverdi and Artusi.

The secular music of Spain was more thoroughly tinged with national color than any other field of music. The *villancicos, ensaladas, tonadas* (songs), and other secular Spanish forms displayed unique rhythmic patterns that bore the traits of a nationally restricted literature. Here we have one of the very few examples of baroque music in which the influence of folk music on art music is more than mere wishful thinking. Some of the syncopated patterns of Spanish folk music that are to be found even in the renaissance *villancico* are as striking today as they were several hundred years ago. The *villancico,* the favorite form of secular polyphonic music,

[33] See CE III, no. 38, ed. by Anglès.
[34] Eslava, *Lira sacro-hispana.*
[35] CE ed. by Anglès; see also GMB no. 179.
[36] *Mestres de l'Escolania de Montserrat* I-III; HAM no. 227.

appeared sometimes also in sacred music. It corresponded formally to the *frottola* which had long since fallen into oblivion in Italy. Written sometimes in a slightly polyphonic but always in an extremely rhythmic style, it consisted of a couplet or *copla* for solo voices and a choral refrain or *estribillo*. It was frequently inserted into spoken plays, ballets, and other stage productions. The *Cancionero de Sablonara* [87] contains many examples of the form by Romero and Juan Blas who set to music the lyrics of Lope de Vega, the leading Spanish poet of the time.

The few but illustrious attempts to establish a national Spanish opera were overshadowed from the very beginning by Italian influence. The music of the first Spanish opera is not extant, a fate that it shares with the first opera of nearly every country. It was set to Lope de Vega's *La Selva sin amor* (1629). From the preface it can be inferred that the opera was through-composed, probably with recitatives. Not before the middle baroque period did the music of a Spanish opera survive, at least in fragmentary form: *Celos aun del aire matan* (1660) [88] by Juan Hidalgo (d. 1685). It was based on a libretto by Calderon, who had already written a libretto for another opera, the music of which is also not extant. Although Hidalgo's music faithfully reflects in its short arias and its flexible recitative refrains the middle baroque stage of the Italian opera, it has nevertheless an unmistakable Spanish flavor. His arias include modest variations on simple dance-like basses in hemiola rhythm (Ex. 50). These basses fell into

Ex. 50. Hidalgo: Bass from *Celos*.

two parts, the second of which was merely a literal transposition of the first—a device that frequently recurs in folk music.

The opera in Spain held second place beside the *zarzuela,* a courtly stage entertainment which derived its name from the royal mansion where it was first performed. The *zarzuela* occupied the best composers and poets of the time, including Calderon. It can be described as the Spanish parallel to the French *ballet de cour* and the English court masque. The three courtly forms had in common the alternation of spoken and concerted sections and the emphasis on stage sets, costumes, and ballets. Spanish dances with guitar accompaniment gave the music of the *zarzuela* its national character. The dialogue, choruses, *villancicos,* and *seguidillas* that

[87] Ed. by Aroca, 1916.
[88] Ed. by Subira, 1933.

freely alternated with occasional recitatives were written in an unassuming style, only the more pretentious *cuatro de empezar*, the introductory quartet, mustered polyphonic resources. Of the middle baroque *zarzuela* only very little music has come down to us. Its leading masters were Juan de Navas, Marin, and Berés whose burlesque *tonada* of an enamored old man deserves mention for its harmonic and rhythmic characterization.[39] The late baroque *zarzuela* is represented by such shining lights as Duron, Literes, and the prolific José de Nebra who wrote the music to Calderon's *La Vida es Sueño*. Literes adopted in his *zarzuela Acis y Galatea* (1708),[40] a subject that Handel also treated in a masque, the airy tone of the Neapolitan opera. Although the late baroque *zarzuelas* were dominated by Italian, especially Neapolitan, influence they preserved in their dances at least a rest of their former independence.

Music theory in Spain and Portugal was essentially eclectic except for thorough treatises on guitar and organ playing. The lengthy theory books usually expatiated on material borrowed from Italian sources. The list of theorists included, aside from the ultra-conservative Italian Cerone, who published his work in Spanish, Frovo, da Cruz, the organist José de Torres, Lorente, Nasarre, and King John IV of Portugal. The last was notable not only as author of the *Defensa de la musica moderna,* but also as collector of one of the most valuable music libraries of the seventeenth century which unfortunately was later destroyed by fire.

The music in the Western Hemisphere, New Spain and Colonial America, naturally depended wholly on musical imports from the mother countries. The Spanish missionaries who regarded music as an important tool in the conversion of natives were the first on the American continent to print music though it was exclusively Gregorian chant. The part-music imported to Mexico consisted of conservative Spanish church music. In the second part of the seventeenth century Lima was an important center of musical activity. Here José Diaz composed on American soil the music to the stage works of Calderon. A Peruvian codex of the seventeenth century,[41] one of the very few musical documents of the seventeenth century that have survived in the Western Hemisphere, contain some part-music written in a popular Spanish style.

[39] Lavignac E, I:4, 2077.
[40] Lavignac E, I:4, 2111.
[41] Vega, *La Musica de un códice colonial,* 1931.

The music of the early settlers in North America was restricted mainly to psalm singing. The immigrants had brought over from England the traditional psalters of which only those of Ainsworth and Ravenscroft belong to the baroque period. Secular music, especially instrumental music, was a hotly contested issue among the Puritans. That some secular music was cultivated can be proved by implication, namely by the numerous prohibitions of the use of instruments and of dancing. However, practically no music of the seventeenth century has survived save the psalms. The psalm singing was done from memory and was later aided by the practice of "lining out" the psalm line by line. The oral tradition distorted the tunes more and more by "graces" so that by the end of the century a unification became necessary because the singing had deteriorated into "a horrid medley of confused and disorderly sounds," as Thomas Walter described it. The *Bay Psalm Book* (1640), published originally without music, contained in its ninth edition (1698) a two-part version of twelve metrical psalms; it represents the first part-music ever printed on the American continent. In spite of Puritan opposition the teaching and reading of music made progress. The first American singing-books, based on English models (Ravenscroft and Playford) were John Tuft's *Introduction to the whole Art of Singing Psalms* (c. 1714), and Thomas Walter's *Grounds and Rules of Musick* (1721) which included several three-part settings, copied from Playford's psalter.

The German and Swedish immigrants who settled in Pennsylvania introduced polyphonic chorale singing into America. Not restricted by the Puritan caution against instrumental music, they freely employed organs in their services, the novelty of which served "to attract many of the young people away from the Quakers," as a contemporary report puts it. The German Pietist Conrad Beissel founded a mystic sect in Ephrata and composed a great number of hymns and chorales for its services. A reflection of this literature can be found in the Ephrata hymn collection, published without music by Benjamin Franklin in 1730. The highest musical level was attained by the Moravians in Bethlehem who in 1741 organized a musical life in their secluded community that surpassed all other musical centers of the time. The music they brought over was naturally dependent on the German late baroque style. However, the greatest period of Moravian music falls into the classic era.

Carl Pachelbel, a son of the famous German organist, was perhaps the most distinguished professional musician in America before 1750. He gave a public concert in New York (1736) and served as organist, first in Newport, Rhode Island, and then, until his death (1750), in Charleston. An impressive *Magnificat* [42] for soli and chorus, written in a vigorous late baroque style, attests to his attainment as composer, but the piece was not performed in this country during his lifetime. In Charleston, Pachelbel came in contact with John Wesley. It is significant in view of the close relations between Methodist hymnody and Protestant chorale that Wesley was well acquainted with the German chorale and that he owned a copy of the Pietistic hymn and chorale book by Freylinghausen. Wesley's first hymn book was published in Charleston (1737), but it contains no music. The numerous concerts in the cities, around 1750, and the performances of the ballad opera *Flora* in Charleston (1735) and of *The Beggar's Opera* in Maryland (1752) show how quickly the stylistic trends of the mother country found their repercussions in the colonies.

[42] Score edition of the New York Public Library.

CHAPTER SIX

English Music During the Commonwealth and Restoration

THE MASQUE AND THE ENGLISH OPERA: LAWES AND BLOW

THE IMPARTIAL evaluation of English music of the seventeenth century has suffered for two centuries from the double handicap of political and aesthetic prejudices. On the one hand, the effect of Cromwell's political revolution on music, and its purported uprooting of the English musical tradition has been overemphasized in disregard of the facts; on the other hand, the turn to baroque style has been judged by the standards of "Elizabethan" music with the inevitable result that English baroque music has appeared as a deplorable degeneration of the high achievements of renaissance music. In consequence even the term "Restoration music" used to carry a rather odious connotation. Actually the Restoration does not usher in a new stylistic period, because the salient features of what has been called "Restoration style" are already clearly apparent before the Commonwealth. The ascendancy of the Stuarts coincides with the transition from renaissance to baroque. The formative period of English baroque music falls into the reign of Charles I (1625-1649).

The new style did not make its entry in England with the suddenness of a revolution; this is typical of all countries that imported the baroque style from without. The ties with the past were not severed at once, and in works of the transition period a disconcerting wavering between old and new concepts can be often observed. At the same time, the daring experimental features of the Italian early baroque are not very pronounced in England so that it becomes at times difficult to draw a line between early and middle baroque styles.

The first drastic signs of change appeared, naturally enough, in the music for the stage for which the adoption of the recitative had become a burning question. In England the main theatrical form to rely heavily on the musician was the court masque, not the opera, as in Italy. The masque, this exclusive and costly court entertainment, corresponds in scope, social significance, and to some extent in form to the *ballet de cour*. The typical masque hinged round three specially designed ballets or stage dances of the masquers: "entry," "main dance," and "going-off," and was supplied with an allegorical and spectacular plot or "device" which justified the sudden appearance of the masquers who performed in dumb show. The going-off was followed by the revels, in which the masquers took out the noble ladies of the audience for a series of ballroom dances. Although allowing of many exceptions, the form of the masque was stereotyped by its three dances. The main office of the music consisted in supplying the musical introduction, filling in the transitions, accompanying the dances, and setting such sections of the words as were sung. The acting of the prologues, the stage dialogue, and the singing was done, as a rule, by professionals whereas the masquers were, as in the French model, the nobility of the court. The features the masque had in common with the *ballet de cour* bespeak the close relation between the two forms: both were centered round stage, not ballroom dances; both followed an allegorical plot; both were performed in their essential parts by members of the nobility; both transcended the framework of a mere spectacle by the taking-out of the ladies; both set great store by staging, costumes, and, before all, elaborate machines.

In spite of the obvious dependence of the masque on plots taken from the *ballet de cour* and the Italian *intermezzo* the English masque became a distinctive art form of its own because of the literary genius of Ben Jonson, Milton, and others, and the formalism of its tripartite structure. The baroque masque had crystallized after manifold renaissance antecedents in the masque *Proteus*, and Daniel's *Vision of Twelve Goddesses* (1604). In the next year began the famous collaboration of Ben Jonson with the architect Inigo Jones (*Masque of Blackness*, 1605). Jones brought to the English stage the Italian innovations of the movable set, and the change of scenery before the eyes of the audience by means of machines, thus setting an end to the static scenery of renaissance "mansions." With Jonson's *Masque of Queens* (1609) the antimasques which emphasized the comic and burlesque appeared for the first time. They very soon spread to such an extent that continuity and unity of the argument were well-nigh lost. These developments correspond to the effusion of unrelated entries in the *ballet à entrées*.

The masque as a literary form influenced in turn the drama, in which music found an increasingly important place, as the plays of Beaumont and Fletcher show. Besides Jonson and Milton, whose *Comus* cannot be considered as a typical masque, the outstanding poets of the masque were the poet-musician Campion, Shirley, Carew, and Davenant who succeeded Ben Jonson as poet laureate at the court.

The music to the early masques was written on an unpretentious scale with the resources available at the beginning of the century. The dance music proper consisted, like that of the *ballet de cour*, of simple, if somewhat dry, melodies in bipartite form that stood outside of the stereotyped rhythmic patterns of ballroom dances. Most of the dances have come down to us only in outline form as melody and bass, and rarely suggest the very elaborate orchestration and doubling to which the stage directions sometimes refer. The *passamezzi*, galliardes, corantos, and other ballroom dances of the revels were unfortunately almost never recorded with the other extant music.

Since much of the music for the masque has been lost, occasional references in the stage directions are often our only source of information about the character of the music. The extant songs of the early masques did not differ in style from the lutenists' songs discussed in Chapter II. Campion's *Masque of Lord Hayes* (1607) [1] of which only two songs and three dances are known proves that the music of the Jacobean masque showed at first no sign of operatic influence, and not by coincidence did masquing songs appear in the printed lute books of the time. The traditional lute song and instrumental dances and consorts provided at first enough variety. In the *Lord's Masque* Campion combined spoken words and music in the manner of the eighteenth-century melodrama, an innovation that occurred also in contemporary French music (Bouzignac), but that remained without consequence at the time.

The first mention of recitative can be found in Ben Jonson's *Vision of Delight* (1617), one of his most charming masques, in which the introductory speech "Let your shows be new and strange" was sung, fittingly enough, in *"stylo recitativo."* In Jonson's *Lovers Made Men* of the same year the poet asserted that "the whole masque was sung after the Italian manner, *stylo recitativo,* by Master Nicholas Lanier, who ordered and made both the scene and the music." A later reference to recitative occurs

---

[1] Arkwright, *Old English Edition*, 1.

in Townshend's *Albion's Triumph*. It is difficult to determine how much recitative was actually used in the masques, but it is certain that masques sung throughout were exceptional.

The first generation of masque composers comprising Campion, Coperario, Alfonso Ferrabosco, Giles, and Robert Johnson was on the whole obligated to the late renaissance style. Of these masters Ferrabosco was exalted by Ben Jonson as "mastering all the spirits of music." In the music of the second generation the early baroque style is clearly apparent in the adaptations of the *stile rappresentativo* to the English language, and the monodic conception of melody. The masters to be mentioned here are Nicholas Lanier (d. 1666), William Lawes (d. 1645), Henry Lawes (d. 1662), Simon Ives, and Wilson, who were followed by a slightly later group of the declining phase of the masque like Coleman (d. 1664), Captain Cooke (d. 1672), Christopher Gibbons (the son of Orlando), and Matthew Locke.

The adoption of speech rhythm in the recitative, and the dualism of melody and merely supporting bass have cast a shadow of low esteem on the music of Lanier and the brothers Lawes. Lanier's cantata *Hero and Leander,* composed "in recitative musick" for solo voice and thoroughbass, gives us an idea of the Englished form of recitative (Ex. 51). This

Ex. 51. Lanier: Monody *Hero and Leander.*

piece, composed upon Lanier's return from Italy, was at the time a famous composition which "for many years went around from hand to hand," as Roger North asserts in his *Musicall Gramarian.* The plaint of Hero, "altho it comes not up to the spirit of the Italian compositions of the time" (North), was the only English monody that more nearly approached an affective recitative than any other by his contemporaries. It was obviously composed in imitation of the *Lamento d'Arianna,* even more closely imitated in Henry Lawes' lament *Ariadne deserted* (c. 1640).[2] The difference between Monteverdi's and Lawes's compositions strikes the ear at once and indicates the wide gap between Italian and English conceptions of musical declamation.

The English composers of the early baroque were unable to grasp the essence of the recitative, the affective intensification of the word, and had to find a substitute for it. Like the French, they emphasized the rhythmic factor in the recitative at the expense of melodic contour and harmonic interest. Although similar with regard to rhythm, the French and English recitatives differed with regard to prosody; whereas French composers preferred dactylic and anapaestic patterns, the English favored dotted rhythms on the upbeat and such syncopations as occur naturally in "never" (♪♪♪). Compared with the Italian recitative those of the early French and English were lacking in pathos and flexibility; they stood on the borderline between song and recitative, with too arid and stiff a melody for song and too active a bass for recitative. Not touched by the affective intensity of Peri and Monteverdi they had also little of the spectacular virtuosity of Caccini. What the English composers shared with the Italians was merely the declamatory principle, not its affective application. Only in the middle baroque did composers like Humfrey, Blow, and Purcell infuse sufficient pathos into the melody to achieve affective declamation in music.

The "songs" of the masque were usually written for voice and unfigured bass, and were interspersed with small chordal choruses. The artful manner in which Henry Lawes set words to music has been extolled by many poets of the time, especially by Milton in his sonnet:

> Harry, whose tuneful and well measur'd Song
> First taught our English Music how to span
> Words with just note and accent . . .

This praise is undeserved insofar as it raises one individual out of a group of composers of equal merit. Milton's enthusiasm is all the more exaggerated because the poet had the opportunity during his stay in Rome to

[2] OHM III, 211.

hear the genuinely operatic performance of Leonora Baroni (see Chapter V), whose praise he sang in his Latin verses. The songs of William Lawes betray a less vigorous temperament than that of Henry, but are hardly inferior in "just note and accent." The five extant songs from Milton's *Comus* (1634) [3] by Henry Lawes are typical examples of the early baroque continuo song. They are quasi-recitatives characterized by incisive marking of the rhyme, frequent and sudden cadences, discontinuous rhythm, and an erratically moving bass. The melody is carried forward mainly by the prosody of verse fragments. The musical rhythm is, however, not derived from the regular meter of the verse, but is achieved by emphatic repeats of single words or phrases. The tension between the regularity of the poetic meter and the discontinuous cadential falls of the music makes for the strong rhythmic interest of these songs, as can be seen in Lawes's music to the Eighth Sonnet of Spenser's *Amoretti* [4] (Ex. 52). Lawes introduces

Ex. 52. Henry Lawes: *More than most fair.*

here three cadences in the first two lines and forcefully shifts the accent at the words "unto thy maker." The angular melody, the rhythmic vigor, and the absence of affective skips distinguish this style from the Italian. Burney's harsh censure of Lawes's songs—he speaks of "a series of unmeaning sounds" characterized by "insipid simplicity"—misses the point of the music and amusingly illustrates the prejudice of eighteenth-century judgment, though a few of Burney's remarks on faulty accentuation are still valid today. But Burney could not comprehend the peculiar rhythmic vitality of the songs derived from the close interdependence of poetry and music.

Music for masques was often composed collectively by several composers. For Milton's *Comus* and Carew's *Coelum Britannicum* [5] Henry Lawes alone wrote the music, but for Davenant's *Triumph of the Prince d'Amour* [6] (1636) the brothers Lawes collaborated, as did William Lawes and Ives in the music for Shirley's *Triumph of Peace*. After 1630 the masque

[3] Ed. by Foss, 1938; HAM no. 204.
[4] See Evans, *Henry Lawes*, 67.
[5] Evans, *op. cit.* 96, points out certain resemblances between these atypical masques.
[6] Dent, *Foundations*, 30.

entered its phase of decline. In the measure in which splendor and costs mounted, the plot of the masque grew more and more chaotic. *Luminalia* [7] by Davenant and Inigo Jones with music by Lanier illustrates the decline; it is slavishly based on an Italian model. The inner disintegration could not be stopped by a concentration on the musical elements of the masque. Attacks from without hastened its downfall, especially the *Histriomastix* (1633) by Prynne, whose abusive denunciation of the masque, the theater in general, and the depraved use of "lust-provoking songs" epitomizes earlier and later Puritan criticism.

When the masque as a regular court institution fell with Cromwell's rise to power, it was an overripe and doomed form. The Commonwealth did not interrupt the musical life as severely as Burney and others have claimed. Although stage plays were forbidden, musical shows passed the censorship and music in the homes of the urban middle classes flourished more than ever. Shirley's masque *Cupid and Death* (1653) was privately performed with music by Christopher Gibbons and Locke.[8] In 1656 Davenant received permission to perform publicly an "Entertainment at Rutland House by Declamations and Musick, after the manner of the Ancients" with music by Henry Lawes, Captain Cooke, and Hudson. In the introduction the sullen and cheerful dispositions of Diogenes and Aristophanes were contrasted in music, an idea obviously suggested by Carissimi's cantata *I Filosofi* (see p. 122).

The performance of the first English opera, *The Siege of Rhodes* (1656) by Davenant with music by Henry Lawes, Captain Cooke, and Locke, falls under Puritan rule. Davenant cautiously called his work "representation," not opera, a term that might have aroused the suspicion of the Puritans, and designated the five acts as "entries" in the manner of the masque. The plot was historical, not mythological like the majority of Italian operas of the day. Davenant informs us that the story was "sung in recitative musick" and that he varied the length of the verses because "alterations of measure . . . are necessary to recitative musick for variation of ayres." Whether or not this remark implies a distinction between recitative and aria, just becoming fashionable in Italy, cannot be determined since the music is unfortunately not extant However, the appearance of stanzaic songs in the libretto suggests an affirmative answer.

[7] OHM III, 200.
[8] Example in Dent, *op. cit.*, 89.

That the first effort toward English opera has remained without consequence, and that also subsequent attempts by Blow and Purcell must be considered isolated, if successful, experiments, has been explained by the theory of an English aversion to opera in principle and by temperament. While it is true that the recitative had to overcome in the process of its nationalization the same kind of resistance as in France, its refined and truly affective handling by typical English composers like Blow and Purcell refutes the theory. Actually, the opera lacked in England the social foundation on which it flourished in Italy, France, and Germany, namely the spiritual center of a representative court. The restored English court was politically weak and in spite of its aping of French manners had nothing of the austere, if pompous, spirit of the French court. Had the Commonwealth continued, a commercial public opera like that in Venice or Hamburg might possibly have developed out of the tentative beginnings. After the Restoration the court masque was revived as a main form of entertainment, and it is symbolic that Purcell's *Dido and Aeneas* was not written for the court but for amateurs.

After his only and very successful opera Davenant wrote two stage works that he called "operas" though they were really masques. The music of these is also lost. They were later condensed and combined in his *Playhouse to be Let* (1663) in which he answered those who found the recitative not "natural" with the following very apt definition:

> Recitative Musick is not compos'd
> Of matter so familiar, as may serve
> For every low occasion of discourse.
> In Tragedy, the language of the Stage
> Is rais'd above the common dialect.

The masques and theatrical plays of the Restoration brought new composers to the fore, notably Matthew Locke (1633?–1677) and John Blow (c. 1648–1708) who both held court positions under Charles II. In the works of these masters the middle baroque style is firmly established. Also the French musician Grabu, a pupil of Lully and court composer to Charles II, must be mentioned, whose wretched English declamation makes that of Handel's early English works appear flawless by comparison. Grabu wrote the music for Perrin's *Ariane* (originally composed by Cambert), performed in London by the newly founded Royal Academy of Music (1674), and also for Dryden's unsuccessful opera *Albion and Albanus* (1685). The latter work is historically important as another attempt at developing the masque into a real opera, but musically hardly absorbing.[9] The distinction between recitative and aria or, as Dryden translates, "the songish part," is openly acknowledged and observed. The allegorical nature of the plot and the frequent dances are obvious survivals of the masque.

Matthew Locke, indubitably the greatest theatrical talent before Purcell, wrote music for numerous stage productions, notably *Cupid and Death*, the masque *Orpheus and Euridice* (an intermezzo in Settle's *Empress of Morocco*, 1673), Shadwell's adaptation of the comedy-ballet *Psyche* (1675) by Molière-Lully, *The Tempest*, and *Macbeth*. The two latter works belong to the group of bowdlerized Shakespeare arrangements which became the Restoration fashion.[10] The music to *The Tempest* and *Psyche* was published in 1675 under the title *The English Opera*.

Locke's affective vein is already clearly manifested in his youthful *Cupid and Death*.[11] Although the style of this work can hardly conceal its indebtedness to Italy, there are also some definitely non-Italian features, especially uncouth progressions, that seem to mar the curves of the bel canto. These progressions have, in the case of Blow, become famous as "crudities" (Burney); they can, however, be found in at least equal measure in Locke. Awkward harmonic progressions, odd melodic turns, and many simultaneous or closely spaced cross-relations are characteristics of the English middle baroque style, which have incorrectly been interpreted as symptoms of a deficient artistic training. Actually, however, they reflect the peculiarly "late" historical position of the English musicians. Only toward 1650 did Locke and his contemporaries discover the possibilities inherent in the experimental harmonies of the early baroque recitative, at a time when they had already developed the elementary tonality of the middle baroque. The belated fusion of early and middle baroque concepts created this unique English idiom in which "crudities" were sought after as an end in themselves for the sake of harmonic richness and sheer sonority, not, as in Byrd's music, for the sake of contrapuntal part-writing. In spite of strong tonal progressions an overall direction of harmony was lacking in the English style. The augmented and diminished steps of the melody with their erratic and vigorous rhythm seemed to contradict the full tonal cadences. The peculiar effect of the English idiom can be described as the clash between the chromatic, or rather non-tonal

<hr />

[9] Example in Dent, *op. cit.*, 166.
[10] The music for *Macbeath* has been ascribed to Leveridge and also to Purcell, but the latter ascription is highly improbable on stylistic grounds.
[11] Dent, *op. cit.*, 89.

melody and an essentially diatonic harmony. To put it paradoxically, the chromaticism of the English style was diatonically conceived.

Locke, one of the first important composers in the English idiom, did not consistently adhere to it. In the vocal sections to *Psyche* [12] he did not always show himself venturesome, because his growing tonal consciousness barred unorthodox turns. The English idiom triumphed in John Blow's *Venus and Adonis* (c. 1682),[18] written for one of the mistresses of Charles II. Blow called his work, the only court opera composed by an English musician, "masque" in conformity with the titles of the other court entertainments, but in spite of its title and its diminutive dimensions it was a full-fledged opera.

Venus and Adonis begins with a French overture and the French model obtains also in the pastoral prologue. At this point, however, the French influence ends. The music of the subsequent three short acts shows a strong Italian cast. Blow has little regard for tonal unity, and the affective style of his recitatives goes often far beyond what any other English master has ever dared to write. Especially the last act, consisting of a passionate dialogue between Venus and Adonis (Ex. 53) and a final chorus, sets the

Ex. 53. Blow: Recitative of Venus from *Venus and Adonis*.

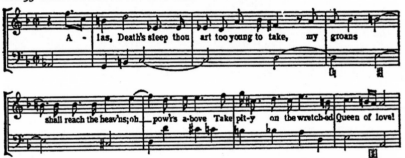

violence of affections above any other consideration. The stereotyped tonal cadence at the end of the quoted excerpt strangely conflicts with the powerful melodic design at the beginning. Blow's inability to master this inconsistency inherent in the English idiom appears in his music as wavering, and is much more disturbing than the actual "crudities," such as the scarcely disguised parallel fifths on the word "groan," which may have been written for descriptive purposes.

[12] Examples in OHM, III, 291 and Dent, *op. cit.*, 117.
[18] Ed. by Lewis (*Oiseau Lyre*), 1939; a less complete edition in Arkwright, *op. cit.*, 25; also HAM no. 243.

The arias which are clearly set off from the recitatives give testimony
of Blow's influence on his pupil Purcell. The characteristic gracing figure,
the written-out "slide" on the strong beat, has wrongly been regarded
as a personal characteristic of Purcell; actually, it is typical of the period and
can frequently be found in Blow's music (Ex. 54).

Ex. 54. Blow: Excerpt from *Venus and Adonis.*

And a great rea - der   of____   ro man-ces

The important function of the chorus and instrumental music in *Venus
and Adonis* represents, of course, a heritage of the masque. The first two
acts end with dances, including the inevitable ground on a descending
fourth, indebted in its formal rhythmic patterns to the chaconnes of Lully.

That Purcell must have carefully studied Blow's score when he wrote
Dido and Aeneas becomes evident not only from occasional melodic similarities but especially from resemblances in structure, such as the distribution of the dances and of choral and solo passages. Both works end with
a chorus in g of similar texture and character, and the delightful interlude
or "spelling lesson" in *Venus* very closely corresponds to the intermezzo
Oft she visits in *Dido.* It seems more than coincidental that the basses of
the two pieces resemble each other in contour and rhythm.

CONSORT MUSIC: JENKINS AND SIMPSON

In the field of instrumental music the Commonwealth régime acted
indirectly as a strong furthering factor so that the line of tradition has in
no other field been better maintained than here. In the absence of courtly
patronage, private music of the middle class and the nobility flourished in
unprecedented manner, and as a result more music was printed for the
public than ever before. Significantly, John Playford's career as music
publisher began with the Commonwealth. Even North, whose testimony
can readily be trusted because of his anti-Cromwell bias, attests to the great
spurt of music "in private society, for many chose rather to fidle at home,
then to goe out and be knockt on the head abroad."

English music for keyboard instruments in the seventeenth century does
not measure up to the great tradition of the virginalists. Surrendering its

leading position in Europe, this music assimilated first Italian, later French influences. Organ music did not develop because the art of organ building lagged behind the times. Under the Commonwealth, church organs were destroyed by official order, though chamber organs were not affected. After the Restoration Harris and the German organ builder Father Smith inaugurated a period of fine organ construction.

It is characteristic that English organ pieces for two manuals were often specially designated as "for the double organ" because two manuals were considered an exceptional resource. The organ music of Tomkins (d. 1656) was the belated product of the old school. The new school arose with Christopher Gibbons, Rogers, Cromwell's organist Hingeston, Locke, and Blow,[14] and was continued by Purcell, Croft, Roseingrave, Greene, and Handel. One of the main forms of organ music, beside the verset, was the voluntary, roughly corresponding in its imitative texture and scope to the fancy of viol music and to the Continental organ fantasia. Like the fancy, the voluntary became toward the middle of the century more sectional and fell into restless, contrasted passages; it absorbed, in addition, improvisatory elements of the toccata. According to Mace the improvising lutenist or organist could "Plainly shew his Excellency and Ability" in "Voluntary, or Fansical Play." The curious overlapping of early and middle baroque styles can be studied in a verse by Blow,[15] one section of which is borrowed *verbatim*, without acknowledgment, from a toccata by Frescobaldi.

The harpsichord music consisted chiefly of single dance movements, grounds, freely combined suites, or arrangements of songs and instrumental chamber music. Locke's *Melothesia* (1673) gives besides "Certain Rules for Playing upon a continued-Bass" a number of lessons and suites by Locke himself, Gregory, Banister, and others. They contain in varying order the familiar almains, corants, gavots, but also such titles as "country dance" and "Round O" appear. The latter term, an English interpretation of the French *rondeau*, belongs to the large group of more or less happily Englished expressions, as for example: consort (*concerto*), tucket (*toccata*), passing measures (*passamezzo*), kickshaw (*quelque chose*), and chacony. Playford's collection *Musick's Handmaid* (1678 ff.) presents the outstanding harpsichord music of the period, including that of Purcell. In this collection the French influence manifests itself especially in the partial adoption of the French symbols for graces and ornaments, whereas Locke's *Melo-*

---

14 See West, *Old English Organ Music*.
15 West, *op. cit.*, no. 35.

thesia is restricted to the old method of single and double dashes. Blow ranks highest among the pre-Purcellian harpsichord composers. In his keyboard works he displays less harmonic wilfulness than in his vocal music, but much rhythmic imagination. Some of his grounds and chaconnes break the harmonic monotony by sudden changes to the opposite mode in the manner of Louis Couperin and Lully, a device that Purcell was to adopt with such success.

The consort music for viols and violins held among all other instrumental combinations the most significant position in the Caroline and Commonwealth periods. During the Restoration the popular, though formerly rather lowly, violins supplanted the viols, which had nevertheless staunch supporters well into the eighteenth century. The excellence of English viol music in the middle baroque is attested not only by the remarks of Christopher Simpson, North, Mace, and others, who could be suspected of speaking with nationalist's pride rather than modesty, but also by Continental authors like Mersenne, Rousseau (*Traité de la Viole*), and Eisel. The latter goes so far as to claim that the viol was an instrument of English invention, a symptomatic error indicating that viol music had become associated with England.

In consort music "fancies are the chief," as Simpson rightly asserted. Instrumental elaborations on Gregorian or abstract *cantus firmi* became more and more obsolete. William Lawes, who unlike his brother was active mainly in the instrumental field, wavered in his fancies between the retrospective style of his teacher Coperario and a highly personal, if not eccentric one in which harmonic experiments, wide skips, and erratic rhythms heralded the new era.[16] Lawes' conservative *Royal Consort*[17] is written for two violins, two bass viols, and two theorboes which fill in the harmony in the old manner. The same work exists, however, also in a "modernized" version as trio sonata with continuo. A number of Lawes' dances were posthumously printed for violins (or viols) and thoroughbass in Playford's *Courtly Masquing Ayres* (1662).

The stylistic change that took place in the fancy can best be studied in the works of the leading composer of fancies, John Jenkins (1592–1678)

[16] See the amazing fancy in *c* in Meyer, *English Chamber Music*, 265.
[17] See the *Pavan* in *King's Music*, 50, and the *Almand* in Meyer, *op. cit.*, 181. The oft-quoted statement that Charles I referred to William Lawes as "the Father of Music" confuses William Lawes with an older musician of the same name; see Evans, *op. cit.*, XVI.

who started in the old style, "but afterwards turned reformer and with great success" (North). Jenkins' early fantasias for four to six viols still adhered to the precepts of the old fancy in their austere, ricercar-like themes, their consistently polyphonic texture, their complex rhythmic continuity, and their cautious handling of chromatic progressions. In his later works Jenkins obviously succumbed to the spell of the Italian trio sonata, especially in his three-part fancies [18] in which the viols were, significantly, replaced by violins. A modern and somewhat popular style obtains in his three-part suites, and the suites for solo violin and organ continuo. Under the Italian impact the fancies broke up into dramatically contrasted and discontinuous sections of different tempo and varied texture in the manner of the quilt canzona. Chordal triplas alternated with fugal passages. The themes already featured at times the typical upbeat patterns with their energetic, swift rhythms, and also idiomatic violin figures, such as rapid skips and double stops. The fancy often served in the suites as opening movement, thus giving the form an English stamp. The pavane also survived as an opening movement in England longer than in Italy. Jenkins liked to conclude the suite with a slow "drag" or coda which emphasized the cyclic unity of the form although there were no thematic relations between the single movements.

In his combination of Italian and English styles Jenkins did not stand alone, as the fancies by his contemporaries [19] prove, notably those by Christopher Gibbons, John Hilton, Coleman, Hingeston, Rogers, and Locke. In Locke's instrumental music Italian influence can be as clearly discerned as in his vocal music. Locke turned to the fancy even where it was not expressly thus designated, as in the "curtain tune" to The Tempest.[20] He made abundant use of the upbeat patterns of the middle baroque. In his consort for four viols (c. 1672) [21] he combined three dances with an opening fantasia, in which he pushed the nervous discontinuity of the fancy even farther than Jenkins. None of Locke's instrumental music, not even his stage music, shows the harmonic daring of his vocal music, but in The Tempest the startling dynamics ("soft," "louder by degrees," and even "violent"), tremolo sections, and occasional strong dissonances sufficiently indicate the stormy temperament of the composer. The Little Consort of Three Parts (1656) is a collection of suites, each consisting of four dances in a remarkably constant order, and the usual bipartite form.

[18] See Meyer, op. cit., 288.
[19] Examples in Meyer, op. cit., 225 ff., 294.
[20] OHM III, 289; Meyer, op. cit., 237.
[21] Ed. by Warlock and Mangeot, 1932; see also the fancy in HAM no. 230.

In the eight suites of four parts [22] the sequence of dances is quite fanciful. As a rule, the English composers followed the French in their disregard for a fixed order of the suite movements. The huge collection of *Court Ayres* published by Playford (1655 and 1662) amasses a repertory of more than five-hundred dances in varied order to which almost every composer of the time contributed. Rogers' collection, *The Nine Muses*,[23] also strings together an arbitrary number of dances and airs. Rogers enjoyed some popularity in England and, while it is true that he spent some time on the Continent and presented the queen of Sweden with his music, his alleged fame abroad seems to have been largely a figment of his own imagination.

"Lessons" for viols were printed in several of Playford's publications, notably the *Banquet of Musick* (1652) and *Musick's Recreation on the Lyra Viol* (1652 ff.) The latter contains short remarks on viol playing and works by Coleman, Gregory, Hudson, Ives, Jenkins, Porter, Young, and others in tablature form. However, the most illuminating printed source of viol music is the *Division Violist* (1659) by Christopher Simpson.

The so-called division viol was used for purposes of improvisation, the "applied art" that forms one of the cornerstones of baroque music. Improvisations on grounds and *cantus firmi* had been discussed, more than a hundred years before Simpson, by Ortiz and other Continental authors; by the middle of the seventeenth century this practice had declined on the Continent, but had survived among the English violists. Simpson's grounds could be either a short bass melody in simple, dance-like rhythm, or a "continued ground . . . , the thorough-bass of some motett or madrigal." The second, quite common form implies that the term "ground" denoted here the foundation of a composition in general, not merely *basso ostinato*. Simpson's two types of "grounds" were played by the organ, and the violist improvised upon them in three manners: by "breaking" the ground, that is by duplicating the bass in a highly florid form; by "descant divisions" in which the bass merely served as support for a new florid counterpoint of the viol; or by a mixture of the two. In any case the result was essentially a patterned variation. The frequent shifts to higher positions, double stops, and the swiftness of the divisions bear witness to the high technical attainment of soloistic viol playing. It is interesting that among the real ostinati of the *Division Violist* some were descendents of the old *romanesca* and *passamezzo* family, although Simpson did not use these names and possibly was no longer conscious of the Italian roots of the

---

[22] Ed. by Beck, New York Public Library, 1942.
[23] OHM III, 330.

tradition. The improvised divisions furnished complements to the formal compositions of the time which often were nothing more than "frozen improvisations." A division on a ground resulted, if written down, in a passacaglia or chaconne; a division on a thorough-bass became a solo sonata or, when two players improvised, even a trio sonata.

The polyphonic ideal of viol music, characterized by Mace's remark that "our great care was, to have all the parts equally heard," was doomed by the advent of the continuo and the dualistic conception of the sonata. In spite of the opposition of many amateurs who remained faithful to viol music, the ascent of the violin could not be stopped. Mace bitterly complains of the "High-Priz'd Noise" of the violins, "fit to make a man's Ear Glow, and fill his brains full of frisks." Violins were extensively used first in masque music where a penetrating sound was desirable. They also appeared early in the chamber music of Coperario, William Lawes, Jenkins, and Porter. When Charles II established at his court a band of twenty-four violinists after the French model, he merely followed the trend of favoring the violins over the viols; he was, however, not responsible for the introduction of violins into England, as legend has it. Charles had an "utter aversion to fancies" and "could bear no music to which he could not beat time. Of songs he only approved the soft vein, in triple time" (North). Apparently, the prince absorbed only one aspect of the French taste at the French court, the pointed and "airy" style, but not the pompous manner of Lully which came to its height only after Charles' departure from France.

As early as the Commonwealth period Continental violin virtuosos came to England. The English violinist Mell was outplayed by Baltzar, "the Swede," [24] whose stupendous double stops in the German manner and frequent use of high positions have been described by Evelyn, North, and Wood. Later Nicola Matteis brought the Italian virtuoso style to England. In his popular *Brief Introduction to the Skill of Musick* (1658 ff.) Playford gives a few instructions for the violin, "a sprightly instrument and much practised of late," though he is mainly concerned with the viol. His *Division Violin* (2nd ed. 1685), obviously a complement to Simpson's book, contains grounds and other compositions by Baltzar, Mell, Banister, Simpson, and Farinel whose name became famous through "Farinel's ground." This much-discussed and misleading title is actually just another

[24] He was German born, but had served in Sweden before he came to England.

name for the *folia.* That the chamber sonatas (1653) by William Young call for two or three violins is hardly surprising since they were composed on the Continent. Two trio sonatas by Blow [25] betray, on the other hand, a strikingly English idiom.

The violin also appears in Playford's *English Dancing Master* (1650) [26] as the use of the French violin clef implies. With this collection we approach the large body of popular music and civil songs for the middle class of the city. Playford's country dances preserve a motley repertory of traditional ballad tunes and instrumental dance melodies of varied and often obscure origin. Some of the "common tunes," as Mace calls them, can be traced back to Elizabethan and Jacobean composers or to famous Italian grounds.[27] Tunes like *Pauls Steeple* and *Goddesses* are clearly dependent on the *passamezzo antico* for their "harmonization." That the tradition of these grounds was, not yet quite forgotten can be seen in a setting of *Greensleeves,* found in a seventeenth-century virginal manuscript.[28] Here the tune appears as a variation upon the *romanesca* bass, strictly preserved in *cantus-firmus* manner (Ex. 55).

Ex. 55. *Greensleeves* for harpsichord.

[25] Ed. by Whittaker (*Oiseau Lyre*).
[26] Facsimile edition, London, 1933.
[27] See Newton, PMA 65, 72, and Gombosi, PAMS 1940, 88.
[28] New York Public Library, MS Drexel 5609.

The civil songs of the time, many of which were inserted in stage plays, moved preferably in triple time and observed the symmetrical melodic structure of dance music. Nearly all composers of the period, including Purcell, have written songs of a very popular nature, often in imitation of Scotch and Irish tunes, though these melodies cannot claim to be folksongs. A great variety of such songs was printed in Playford's collections which drew, in spite of their later date, in part on the vocal music of the Caroline masque. As another important anthology of English continuo songs in popular and often also more elevated style, John Gamble's commonplace book should be mentioned which now forms one of the treasures of the New York Public Library. The tunes of country dances and civil songs were often supplied with new and sometimes topical words, especially by Durfey whose *Wit and Mirth, or Pills to Purge Melancholy* (1719-20) represents one of the main musical and literary sources of *The Beggar's Opera* in which Gay adopted the same principle of parody. The catches and glees of the period provided musical entertainment, especially for gatherings of men in chambers and ale-houses, as the words, often unprintable, indicate. Hilton's *Catch that Catch Can* (1652 ff.) which contained contributions by the leading musicians, ran through many editions. In the only superficially polyphonic catches and the openly chordal glees, the convivial singing of the madrigal period found its rather lowly continuation.

The only significant attempt at fusing the thorough-bass with the madrigal was made by Walter Porter (1595-1659), a little-known pupil of Monteverdi. His set of *Madrigals and Ayres* (1632) [29] for from two to five voices, two violins (or viols), and thorough-bass, is modelled in its variety after his master's seventh madrigal book. It contains one of the first references to "continued Base" in printed English music. Porter carefully explained the new device to the "practitioner" and, putting little trust in the performer's improvisatory ability, advised him to write out the continuo in advance. He also gave English translations of some Italian terms, as Purcell did in his trio sonatas half a century later, and clarified the performance of the tremolo or *trillo*, an ornament of frequent occurrence that he always notated "with division." The compositions of Porter's collection include quite effective continuo madrigals in Italian style with very florid solo passages on affective or pictorial words. Links with the old madrigal school can be discovered only sporadically; usually

[29] Examples in Arkwright, *Musical Antiquary* 4 (1913), 236, and Hughes, MQ 20 (1934), 278.

the style of the melodies presupposes a continuo. The instruments merely double the voices and are independently employed only in ritornelli or in introductory "toccatas," a term reminiscent of Quagliati.

ANGLICAN CHURCH MUSIC: PORTER, HUMFREY, BLOW

The sacred music of the Anglican church falls into two main categories. The first consists of the traditional Anglican chant and the metrical psalms, corresponding respectively to the Gregorian chant of the Catholic church and the chorales of the Protestant church. The second comprises "figural music," the anthems and the services. A group apart is the sacred music for private devotion with freely invented, not necessarily scriptural words.

The metrical psalms were the only church music to which the Puritans did not object. They were sung to the so-called "church tunes" or "proper tunes," distinguished by proper names. The psalms could be performed unaccompanied, as the Puritans preferred; with instrumental accompaniment; or, finally, in simple note-against-note harmonizations. Among the metrical psalm books of the seventeenth century Ainsworth (1612), Ravenscroft (1621), Playford (1677), and Tate and Brady (1696) were the most famous. Metrical psalms served also as devotional house music, and even as a musical pastime; it is therefore hardly surprising that Cromwell regaled a party with "wine, and a psalm." Settings of versified psalms, more pretentious than those of the psalm books, appeared in Henry Lawes' music to Sandy's paraphrases for one voice "set to new tunes for private devotion" (1638), the *Choice Psalms* (1648) of the brothers Lawes, John Wilson's *Psalterium Carolinum* (1656), and Porter's *Motets* (1657), of which the last two were also based on words by Sandy. All these works had a thorough-bass though the style of some of them, *e.g.* the *Choice Psalms,* did not really make it obligatory.

In the second category of church music, the anthems partook more vigorously of the change of style than the services, which ranked second also with regard to the quantitative output of the composers. The services contained, among other texts, the invariable canticles of the liturgy, notably the *Te Deum* and *Jubilate* of the Morning Service, and the *Magnificat* and *Nunc dimittis* of the Evening Service. The first two were also composed for special festive occasions, such as the famous examples by Purcell and Handel. The anthems corresponded to the motet in the Catholic and Protestant rites, and, after the introduction of the continuo and the *concertato* style, to the church *concertato* and cantata. In contrast with the free textual insertions permissible in the cantata, the words of the anthems were restricted to the psalms, but both cantata and anthem belonged to the variable, or *de tempore* compositions of the liturgical year.

By the beginning of the seventeenth century the verse anthems, *i.e.* anthems with solo sections, far outnumbered the full anthems, as can be gleaned from a Chapel Royal Anthem Book (1635) of the Caroline period. This book also discloses that the majority of church composers performed at the time belonged to the old school, a fact also borne out by Barnard's important church-music collection of 1641.

On the authority of Burney and Tudway [30] it has frequently been claimed that the new style of anthem writing originated with the Restoration and was brought about largely by the personal taste of Charles II. It is true that in 1662 the newly established band of violins invaded the Chapel Royal by playing ritornélli "between every pause after the French fantastical light way, better suiting a tavern or playhouse than a church," as the shocked Evelyn reports. Yet the features of the "Restoration anthem" with their admixture of theatrical style crop up as early as Porter's *Madrigals,* which contain the verse anthem *O praise the Lord,* and William Child's *First set of Psalms* (1639). Child's collection, written for three voices and continuo, is the first important document of the Italian influence on English church music, and its style and its importance can be compared with that of the *Kleine geistliche Konzerte* by Schütz. Child tells us himself that his psalms had been "newly composed after the Italian way," though his efforts in this direction cannot be called entirely successful. [81]

In the development of the baroque anthem [32] four groups of composers can be distinguished. The first, consisting of Porter, Child (1606–1697), Portman, and the brothers Lawes, already occurs in the Anthem Book of 1635. To the second group belong composers of a somewhat later date, notably Captain Cooke (d. 1672), Gibbons, Locke, and Rogers (d. 1698). The Italian leanings of Locke have been pointed out above, and of Captain Cooke it is known that he was the best English singer in the "Italian manner" (Evelyn). The masters of the second group who were active during the Commonwealth period and resumed or assumed important court positions after the Restoration, were the immediate model for the next generation of composers whose activity began with the Restoration:

[30] See the vividly written passage in Burney, 348.
[81] OHM III, 206.
[32] For examples see Boyce's *Cathedral Music.*

Pelham Humfrey (1647–1674), John Blow, Michael Wise (d. 1687), William Turner (d. 1740), and Henry Aldrich (d. 1710). The fourth and last group is formed primarily by Henry Purcell, together with lesser composers like Jeremiah Clark (1659–1707), Croft, Weldon, and Greene, the last three of whom bridge over to the period of Handel.

The works of these composers are far from being stylistically homogeneous because of the coexistence of conservative and progressive tendencies. However, a continuous progressive line runs from Porter and Child, over Cooke and Locke, to Humfrey and Blow, culminating and ending with Purcell. The anthems of Aldrich stand somewhat apart; they are influenced by Carissimi, whose works he admired and diligently collected.[88] The anthems of Wise greatly appealed in their uneventful simplicity to Burney's orthodox taste. The progressive style manifests itself less in the instrumental accompaniment by strings and the organ, which was familiar even to the composers of the old school, than in the new affective conception of melody and the abandonment of polyphonic texture. The *concertato* style with frequent alternations of solo voices and full choral sections in rapid syllabic declamation characterizes the modern trend in English church music from Child to Purcell.

Pelham Humfrey, Cooke's successor as master of the children in the Chapel Royal, received part of his training in France and Italy. Much has been made of an alleged influence of Lullian dance rhythms on his church music. While dotted rhythms in triple time do appear in his anthems and even more frequently in his secular music, the Italian and not the French influence must be regarded as the decisive factor in his sacred music. Pepys refers to a certain anthem as "a good piece of musique," but criticizes it by the remark: "but still I cannot call the Anthem anything but instrumental musique with the voice, for nothing is made of the words at all" (Diary, Nov. 1, 1667). Yet in works like the sacred songs, published in Henry Playford's *Harmonia Sacra,* Humfrey surprises by his profound sincerity and affective intensity of which it may be said that everything is made of the words (Ex. 56). The delight in "false" intervals and the violence of pictorial representation in the quoted passage indicate Humfrey's obligation to the English idiom. In comparison with Locke, however, his harmonic progressions show less awkwardness, firmer direction, and a wider sweep. The scrupulous observance of verbal inflections in the musical rhythm must be regarded as one of Humfrey's greatest virtues. It set an

---

[88] His collections containing important source material for the works of Carissimi are preserved in the library of Christ Church College, Oxford.

exemplary standard for Purcell, his pupil, whose excellence in matters of setting English words to music has too often been praised at the expense of earlier masters.[84]

Ex. 56. Humfrey: Sacred solo cantata.

As successor of Humfrey, John Blow also became the teacher of Purcell. Blow wrote more than a hundred anthems, services, and motets, and about thirty odes (for soli, chorus, and orchestra) for royal birthdays, St. Cecilia's Day, New Year, and similar occasions. Much of his vocal music was published in the *Amphion Anglicus* (1700), a collection prompted by the success of the *Orpheus Britannicus*.

The choral works of Blow are written either in simple chordal style or in a contrapuntal manner that shows at times an unrequited love for

[84] This point is indirectly confirmed by the fact that Humfrey's anthem *By the waters of Babylon* was erroneously included in the Novello edition of Purcell's sacred music (1832) and for a long time mistaken for a Purcellian composition.

polyphony. In contrast to Humfrey's pronounced harmonic gift, Blow excelled in the forceful invention and affective design of melodies which he unfolded over stiffly managed basses. His great melodic imagination may be the reason for his penchant for the ground bass, which he implanted also in his distinguished pupil. Striking use of the ostinato technique is made in Blow's elegy on the death of Queen Mary, published together with Purcell's elegies in 1695. The first part (Ex. 57a) is constructed in slow triple meter on a modulating ground. In the second part (Ex. 57b),

Ex. 57. Blow: Elegy on Queen Mary.

the same ground is presented in rhythmic, but not melodic transformation. It appears now in fast duple meter as a figure of running eighth-notes. After a third, affective section in recitative style, the original form of the ground returns and concludes the elegy. Aside from the fact that such radical rhythmic variation is very rare in ground basses the piece is of considerable interest because it throws light on the latest phase of Blow's development which reveals a definite clarification of style. The violent melodic strides, now disciplined, were smoothed out in unusually perspicuous lines. It is possible that the new firmness of melody was due to the converse influence of the pupil on the teacher. If so, Blow's succession to Purcell's post at the Westminster organ would be only the outward symbol of a more significant, artistic succession.

HENRY PURCELL, THE RESTORATION GENIUS

Henry Purcell (1659-1695) not only had "the advantage of greater genius," as has been justly if naïvely stated, but appeared at a time when he could bring to consummation the divergent tendencies of the English middle baroque, just before the wave of Italian late baroque style rolled over England. Nothing could be farther from the truth than the oft-repeated statement that Purcell was the only musician who rekindled the fire of English music after the Golden Age of the madrigalists. Purcell came to fulfill, not to begin anew. Reared in an atmosphere of court life and throughout his all-too-short career intimately connected with the court, Purcell accepted the conventions and mannerisms of Restoration society without questioning. Within these limitations he made of the superficialities of his age a profound work of art; as the true genius of the Restoration, he shared the defects of its virtues and the virtues of its defects. The often criticised superficial and secular traits in his music, especially his church music, merely reflect the curious function of music in Restoration society. English music of the time lacked the human pathos of Italian music, the fervor and rigid liturgical observance of German Protestant music, and the austere spirit of courtly representation of French music. The prime object of the court music in England was to provide sensuous entertainment and to serve as a sonorous ornament. Purcell's preoccupation with sensuous effects is evinced equally in his choral writing, his orchestration, his dissonance treatment, and the premeditated grace of his melodic style. Although he absorbed the human pathos of Italian music and the pompous spirit of French music, these elements took a more sensuous, less demanding, almost boyish turn in Purcell, and in their adoption he always remained his own inimitable self.

The various streams of musical tradition that flowed together in Purcell cannot easily be separated. As chorister of the Chapel Royal (since 1669) Purcell sang the traditional anthems of Tallis and Byrd. His autograph copies of works by the older masters from 1681/2 prove that he studied them even after he had begun to compose. The majority of anthems sung at Purcell's time in the Chapel Royal were those by Child, Blow, and Humfrey, which the boy naturally accepted as models. The influence of his teachers, Cooke, Humfrey, and Blow, tended toward the Italian style. However, the Lullian style of the twenty-four violins must have impressed the young Purcell very strongly because the French "levity," as Purcell called it himself, appeared rather early in his anthems, and because, when only eighteen, he succeeded Locke as composer in ordinary for the violins. This was one of the most "progressive" posts of the musical hierarchy. Purcell amassed a number of important positions held simultaneously throughout his life which bespeak the recognition he was readily accorded: organist at Westminster Abbey (1679), organist to the Chapel Royal (1682), and composer to the court under Charles II (1683), James II, and William III after the Glorious Revolution.

The works of Purcell can be divided into four groups: anthems and other sacred music, odes and welcome songs, compositions for the stage, and instrumental music. Of these only the odes and welcome songs run almost continuously from the beginning to the end of his creative career. The anthems belong primarily to the early period from the late seventies to about 1685 whereas the bulk of his stage works falls into the last six years of his life.

That most of Purcell's anthems must be classed as verse anthems is indicative of the trend of the time away from the full anthem. In his relatively few full anthems, the composer experimented with the traditional motet style and ventured into settings for five, six, and even eight voices without resorting to the facile device of double chorus. He was grappling with contrapuntal technique, and in the thick spacing of the voices he resuscitated the rich sonorities of the polyphonic era. However, Purcell vigorously transformed rather than revived the Elizabethan tradition. The difference between the early and the Restoration motet lay above all in the character of the themes. Purcell's declamatory themes no longer had the abstract continuity of Byrd's motives. Though Purcell tried at times to recapture the even flow of themes, typical of the Elizabethan era, for example in the eight-voiced *Hear my prayer, O Lord*, the attempt was stifled by the underlying declamation of the words and the unorthodox shape of the melody. Polyphonic devices abound in the full anthems, but the imitations are often so closely spaced that they appeal, significantly, to the eye rather than the ear.

The harmony of the full anthems turned to new effect the harmonic licenses of the English idiom to which Byrd had already drawn attention in the preface to his *Psalms and Sonnets*. In the hands of Purcell simultaneous cross-relations and other dissonances were deployed as ends in themselves for the sake of increased sonority, not merely, as with Byrd, as the result of independent part-writing. An excerpt from one of Purcell's earliest anthems, *In the Midst of Life,* makes the harmonic conception of his dissonances abundantly clear (Ex. 58). In the same composition a strongly chromatic

Ex. 58. Purcell: Excerpt from a full anthem.

passage occurs on the affective words "the bitter pains," depicted by a succession of augmented triads in first inversion. They belong to the experimental harmonies of the early baroque which, in Purcell's time, were a thing of the past. That Purcell was aware of the oncoming tonality can be shown by his most arresting revisions of earlier works. The two states of the anthem *Hear me, O Lord* are a case in point.[35] Whereas the first version turns twice to a colorful, if repetitious, deceptive cadence, the second version replaces it by modern harmonic progressions that move logically through the circle of fifths. Revisions of this kind indicate how Purcell gradually abandoned experimental progressions in favor of tonally directed harmony, however disguised by dissonant and independent voice-leading. In their mixture of archaic and modern features Purcell's full anthems figure as the complement to the *Musicalia ad chorum sacrum* by Schütz. Both composers brought polyphonic principles to bear on affective motives that had obviously gone through the phase of declamatory melody-writing, both arrived at highly dissonant combinations, and both created in their own way a unique fusion of polyphonic and harmonic concepts.

The emphasis of Purcell's church music lies, however, on his verse anthems. In the early works of this category instrumental accompaniment, save for the organ, was still lacking, but it became the rule in the later anthems. The string accompaniment took the form of a French overture which was sometimes repeated as symphony between the verses. Other instrumental ritornelli often anticipated or repeated the melodic material of the choral sections. The fast section of the French overture, usually in triple time, likewise served as a springboard for the subsequent chorus, quite in contrast with Lully to whom the overture usually remained an independent introduction. The participation of the instruments ranges from mere duplications in the heavy choral sections to a completely independent *concertato*, linked by imitation to the voices, as, for example, in the resplendent ending of the ten-voice anthem *Behold now, praise the Lord*. In the solo verses, melody instruments enter only for special occasions, either singly in form of a solo obbligato or even jointly in the manner of an accompanied recitative of the opera. *My beloved spake* illustrates the first, *O sing unto the Lord* the second, quite rare alternative.

How faithfully Purcell followed the path of Humfrey and Blow is nowhere more clearly apparent than in the recitative and arioso verses of the anthems. The dramatic and affective power of wide skips, "false" intervals, and wilfully ruffled rhythms could hardly be pushed any further. Purcell avidly seized every possibility for pictorial representation. Great demands are made on the agility of the voice, especially in bass solos, intended for the extraordinary singer John Gostling of the Chapel Royal. Other solo verses are set in aria fashion with symmetrical melody, preferably in triple time. Here is the place where the overused dotted rhythms invariably appear to such words as joy, praise, triumph, and alleluia. The excerpt from *I will give thanks unto thee* (Ex. 59) illustrates not only the

Ex. 59. Purcell: Excerpt from *I will give thanks.*

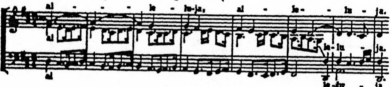

mannerism of dotted rhythms in its favorite form, namely parallel thirds, but also the use of unprepared sevenths which belongs to the English contrapuntal equipment of the time. Dotted rhythms should not be regarded as an exclusively French trait. They were inherent characteristics of fanfares and trumpet melodies of the Italian opera. For example, the trumpet aria from Sartorio's *Adelaide* (1672) [26] might very well be mistaken for a "French" beginning by Purcell.

The chorus sections of the verse anthems differed from the verses for more than one solo voice by a simpler, less exacting melodic line. Purcell observed, on the whole, the subtle idiomatic contrast between solo ensemble and full choral setting, unfortunately often obscured by modern mass performances. For the full chorus Purcell had two styles at his disposal: massive chordal declamation, and the thick archaic polyphony of his own making. This latter manner persisted even in mature works like *My heart is inditing* (1685), written for the coronation of James II. The imposing chorus for eight voices with doubling instruments seems to revive the many-voiced *concertato* of the Venetian school; the harmony is archaic and remarkably free from the strong pull of dominant relationships. The choral endings on the word "alleluia" range from heavy hammerblow style to rapid declamatory style in eighth-notes. They have been censured as one of the worst mannerisms of the Restoration anthem, but they must be recognized as a general mannerism of the middle baroque period and by no means a specifically English one, as Carissimi and all composers dependent on him demonstrate.

There are many indications in Purcell's choruses that his imagination was vividly stimulated by the possibilities inherent in the choral medium and the sonorities it suggested. The celebrated *Te Deum* and *Jubilate* for St. Cecilia's Day (1694) gives full vent to the display of choral sonorities and many of its striking dissonances can be explained as byproducts of idiomatic choral scoring. Written on a grand scale with a somewhat annoying overemphasis on the trumpet key of *D*, it anticipated the Handel style, or, more correctly, Handel paid it the highest form of compliment in his *Utrecht Te Deum*. The anthem *O sing unto the Lord* (1688) is noteworthy for a verse on a slightly varied ground bass, a comparatively rare procedure in Purcell's anthems. It seems that the ground bass held for Purcell a secular connotation; and if any distinction between his chamber and church style can be made at all, it would lie in the sparing use of grounds in his church music. The same anthem is distinguished by an overture that does not observe the French pattern. Purcell adopted here the Italian overture consisting of a full chordal section, later taken up in the first verse, and a short canzona.

Two classes of works other than anthems must be mentioned here though they do not belong to church music proper: the sacred songs, and the elegies on the death of Queen Mary (1695). The sacred songs, published in Playford's *Harmonia Sacra* with a score of similar works by Purcell's contemporaries, are solo cantatas for private devotion, mostly through-composed in a recitative style that surprises by its unique and extreme subjectivism in the treatment of the words. Here Purcell raised the rhapsodic type of cantata to its highest level, at a time when it had already run its course in other countries. Only in a few of the sacred songs did he make the by now customary distinction between recitative and aria. The elegies with their rich chromaticism and bold appoggiature show the pathetic style of Purcell at its best. They are steeped in a somber pathos as if the composer had, when he wrote them, a premonition of his own premature death.

The two dozen odes and welcome songs, written for courtly occasions, welcomes, and St. Cecilia's Days, show traces of routine and haste, although they contain some of Purcell's most exquisite music. The fatuous texts contrast in their artlessness with the adroit, if fawning, prologues of French operas and reveal the spiritual distance between the French and the English court. The odes can be described as cantatas for chorus, soloists, and a string orchestra, frequently reinforced by trumpets, recorders, and oboes. The orchestration follows at times the thick five-part setting of Lully. The solos are designated as "verses," a term that implies close relations with the anthem. The unity of key is strictly observed in the first and last movements of the odes, while middle sections are set in related keys. The often superficial splendor of the trumpet keys D and C, and the perfunctory triumphal sections in dotted rhythms should not prejudice us against the wealth of imagination displayed in the arias and solo ensembles, especially in the very numerous ground basses. The odes for Queen Mary and St. Cecilia's Day from Purcell's late period contain passages of supreme mastery, such as the lament *But ah, I see Eusebia drown'd in tears* from *Arise my Muse* (1690) with its highly resourceful handling of the Phrygian cadence (Ex. 60). *Love's Goddess* (1692) con-

Ex. 60. Purcell: Excerpt from *Arise my Muse.*

tains a fugal chorus on a sturdy sequential theme in simple tonal harmony, characteristic of the grand oratorio style of the late baroque. In choral fugues of this type Purcell set the direct model for Handel. However, not all choruses of the odes and welcome songs are on this level; they are

The Concert

An engraving by Etienne Picart after Zampieri

PLATE 5

Entrance of American Music
from the ballet "La Douairière de Billebahaut"

PLATE 6

Aeolian Mode
from Denis Gaultier, *Rhetorique des Dieux*

usually less consistently polyphonic and move in chordal blocks. In the
ode *Hail bright Cecilia* (1692), the famous *'Tis Nature's voice* was sung
by Purcell himself with "incredable graces" which, fortunately, have come
down to us (Ex. 61). The words of the arioso deal with the power of music

Ex. 61. Purcell: Excerpt from *'Tis natures voice.*

to "express the passions" of which Purcell gives, as it were, an object lesson. The affective, pictorial delineation of the words needs no comment;
the drastic juxtaposition of major and minor modes on "we hear, and
straight we grieve" was a favorite device of Purcell's, also found in dramatic places of his anthems. A similar arioso occurs in *Celebrate this Festival* (1693) to the words *Let sullen discords smile*. The ode *Hail bright
Cecilia* stands out for a fine fugal chorus in the Handel manner and the
splendid da-capo aria *Wondrous machine* which, written on a mechanical
ground, starts in the Italian way with a motto beginning. In this aria
Purcell pays high tribute to the power of organ music.

In the discussion of Purcell's dramatic works *Dido and Aeneas* (1689?)
comes first not only because of its chronology, but primarily because it
is the only real opera by the composer and, at the same time, the only
enduring English opera of the period. When Purcell was called upon to
write the opera, his only works for the stage consisted of some incidental

music and songs to stage plays. However, he had had ample opportunity
to familiarize himself with the dramatic style in his odes and anthems.
Since *Dido and Aeneas* was written, like many other masques, for amateurs—in this case a boarding school for girls—its scope and resources
were necessarily limited, and fortunately so, because the result was a
chamber opera of which there are so few.

The chorus in *Dido and Aeneas* comments on and participates in the
action in the manner of a Greek tragedy. This significant emphasis on
choral drama, which is not paralleled even in the French chorus opera,
proves how strongly the imaginations of Purcell and his librettist Tate were
conditioned by the choral traditions of the masque. The arias and recitatives are clearly differentiated in the Italian manner. Most of the solos and
duets are continuo arias without further accompaniment, save Dido's farewell, and *Pursue thy conquest love*. The latter parades an orchestral garb
in fanfare style and differs from the other concise arias by its brief da-capo
form. For some important recitatives, such as that of the sorceress, Purcell
resorts to an uncanny *accompagnato*, in which he depicts supernatural
fright in the horror key of *f*. The strings come in for emphasis at the end
of the three arias on ground basses, the last of which, Dido's farewell *When
I am laid*, has justly become one of Purcell's most celebrated compositions.
In its deceptive simplicity this lament stands out as a monument to his
dramatic genius. The disregard of the melody for the periodic returns of
the chaconne bass (third type) and the shift of phrase structure and harmony bespeak his supreme mastery. Neither the bass of the lament nor
the asymmetrical structure of the voice part were original with Purcell,
who used similar basses, though less successfully, on several other occasions,
for example in the *Fairy Queen* and the St. Cecilia's ode of 1692 (compare
Ex. 65). The fourth ground bass in *Dido* is the short chacony or "Triumph-
ing Dance" which concludes the first scene in Lullian rhythms and manner.
In each of the scenes tonal unity prevails as strictly as in the odes. At first
glance the third scene seems to deviate from the rule, but its instrumental
introduction must probably be repeated at the end for the dance of the
witches that the libretto prescribes. This repeat, suggested also by the
designation "ritornelle" restores the tonal unity. The features that *Dido
and Aeneas* has in common with Blow's *Venus and Adonis* have already
been discussed. It goes without saying that *Dido* is a more mature work,
and that the differences between the two operas are more decisive than
their similarities.

The other dramatic works of importance include masques, operatic scenes, and songs inserted in plays by Dryden, Betterton, Congreve, and others, notably *King Arthur, The Indian Queen,* and *Dioclesian.* To the same group belong the oft-abused adaptations of Shakespeare: *Timon of Athens, The Fairy Queen* (after *A Midsummer Night's Dream*), and *The Tempest.* In comparison with French and Italian hack writers for the opera, the libretti of Shadwell rank rather high for sheer fantasy, however base a distortion of the Shakespearean spirit they may be. Regrettably enough, the arrangements give Purcell hardly a chance to set an original line by Shakespeare, except for such songs as *Come unto these yellow sands* and *Full fathom five* from *The Tempest.*

What is striking in Purcell's most mature music is, above all, the vast scale on which it is conceived. Imposing recitatives and long arias, either in full orchestral setting or with brilliant obbligatos, have now become the rule. Purcell worked with large units, and combined chorus and solos in extended rondo structures, one of his favorite forms which occurs also in the odes and anthems. The vocal terzetto at the end of *Dioclesian* presents a chaconne bass (fourth type) in a varied da-capo form. In the middle section the bass is suddenly given out in the tonic minor in the manner of a Lullian chaconne, and the return to major has the effect of a da capo. The same ground bass was used not only by Italian composers (Monteverdi) but also by Blow who called it *Morlake's Ground* in one of his harpsichord pieces.

As the single movements expanded, Purcell carried the musical organization to a higher plane. In the gigantic passacaglia *How happy the lover* from *King Arthur* he vied with Lully's most pretentious and ponderous works; its interspersed trio episodes for voices or instruments enhanced the rondo effect of the whole. Sometimes Purcell elaborated a chaconne twice with such ingenuity that the connection between the two related versions escaped attention, as, for example, in the *Chinese chaconne* and air of the *Fairy Queen,* printed in the edition of the Purcell Society as two independent pieces. In the famous frost scene of *King Arthur* Purcell depicted the shivering cold by an instrumental and vocal tremolo, an idea that can again claim Lully as its godfather. Lully introduced the same effect in the frost scene of *Isis* (1677) for the chorus of the *Trembleurs.* The imitation surpasses the model, however, in harmonic interest. Chromatic progressions lend a curiously eerie quality to the whole scene, especially the Neapolitan-sixth chord, otherwise quite rare in Purcell. The music for the airy and fairy realm of the *Fairy Queen* assumes a sprightly tone and a gossamer clarity that almost approach the romantic conception of "characterization." However, only such qualities could be represented in baroque music as could be characterized by the appropriate affections. As a matter of course, Chinese, Indian, or other "exotic characterizations," which modern musicians would strive for if they were to set the *Indian Queen* or the *Fairy Queen*, cannot be found in Purcell's music.

In a single case Purcell is known to have borrowed a melody from Lully, namely from the opera *Cadmus et Hermione* which he probably heard at its London performance in 1686.[37] He adopted Lully's melody of the "dancing winds" from the *Entrée de l'envie* for his dance of the subterranean winds in the *Tempest*, using however a bass of his own instead of Lully's. The comparison of the two harmonizations is illuminating though the melody itself can hardly be called distinctive. Purcell seems to have borrowed it only because he readily found in Lully what was called for at this particular place in the *Tempest:* a music suggesting the dancing of the winds by bustling string passages. French influence could be proved in Purcell's music without this conclusive bit of evidence. The style of the chaconnes and overtures, the ever-present upbeat patterns in his vocal and instrumental music, the bass arias with doubled continuo of his middle period, and the frost scene speak an unmistakable language. Yet toward the end of his career Italian influence came strongly to the fore again, this time the late baroque style just being developed in Italy.

The stylistic change manifests itself most clearly in the works of the last three years. The prominent traits of this change are the adoption of the da-capo aria, the sudden sparseness of the English idiom, and the tentative use of the concerto style.[38] In the *Fairy Queen* da-capo arias on the grand scale appear several times in combination with a ground, a combination that also occurs in *Wondrous machine* from St. Cecilia's Ode. *Fair and serene* from the *Tempest* is an experiment with the modern rondo aria, and the delightful song *I attempt from love's sickness to fly* from the *Indian Queen* is also written in rondo form. Extraordinary da-capo arias with a subdivided first part and a tonally contrasting middle section can be found in the *Tempest* (*Halcyon Days*). The energetic concerto style, described by North as "the fire and fury of the Italian style," prevails in the outstanding arias of the *Tempest: Arise ye subterranean winds, While these pass*, and *See the heavens smile*. The first two of these are written in the large bipartite aria form with repeated second part, the favorite Italian aria form of the time. It should also be noted that they make use of the

Italian motto beginning which cannot be found in Purcell's earlier works. The manner in which Purcell seized upon the continuo homophony of the concerto style can be illustrated by the ritornello to *While these pass* which, like the very similar ritornello to *See the heavens smile*, is characterized by aggressive rhythm, a steady bass line, and clearly directed harmony (Ex. 62). Characteristically, Purcell also adopted, along with the concerto

Ex. 62. Purcell: Ritornello from *The Tempest.*

style, the language of fully established tonality and nearly abandoned the harmonic archaisms and tonal ambiguities of the English idiom, not compatible with the late baroque conception of harmony.

It has not yet been determined exactly which Italian operas were known to Purcell, but his familiarity with them cannot be questioned. The visit of the famous castrato Siface to the English court may have been instrumental in acquainting him with the latest Italian developments, especially the early operas of Scarlatti, in which Siface had sung himself to fame. Purcell commemorated the singer's departure from England in a "farewell" for harpsichord.

Among Purcell's instrumental works the harpsichord pieces are least representative of the composer, several of them being merely arrangements of other compositions. The suites or lessons for harpsichord, written in the French manner, are more distinguished than the few organ pieces that have come down to us. The exceptionally fine organ toccata in *A*, written in the Italian vein, was erroneously included in the volumes of the *Bach Gesellschaft.*[39]

The chamber music for strings can be classed into an archaic and modern group, depending on the absence or presence of the continuo. To the first group belong the fantasias for from three to seven parts, and the chacony in *g*. These works show that Purcell at the age of twenty-one had already fully mastered the polyphonic art of the fancy for viols. They are the last examples of the kind and include even the *In nomine*, by now almost ex-

[39] The work has also been ascribed to Michelangelo Rossi; see Westrup, *op. cit.*, 238.

tinct. Purcell carried the sectional fancy of Jenkins to its point of perfection with sudden "drags" and other contrasts of tempo, and a restless harmony, distinguished by the boldest and most radical utilization of the English idiom.

The two sets of trio sonatas [40] for violins (1683 and 1697) form the second and modern group. Written in "just imitation of the most fam'd Italian masters" they were supposed to bring the "gravity" of Italian music into vogue and combat the "levity" of the French neighbor. It may seem strange to hear levity smugly denounced by a composer whose anthems openly belie his own words. However, Purcell referred here solely to instrumental music, associated in France mainly with the dance. The question as to Purcell's models can be answered by North's assertion that the works of Cazzati and Vitali were known in England; Matteis also may have made Purcell familiar with the Italian literature then current. The trio sonatas are divided into four or five contrasting movements and fall into the pattern of the church sonata of the Vitali type. On the other hand, the close bonds with the English fancy, which come to light in highly imitative movements, belatedly called canzonas, should not be overlooked. What distinguishes Purcell from Vitali are such features as the length of the single movements, the skilful use of contrast motives, the English harmonic idiom (especially noticeable in the second set), and the absence of thematic relations between the movements. Purcell gained considerable length by adroitly postponing cadences with suspensions and sequential devices. It should be noted that the church sonata appears at times also in the guise of orchestral overtures; the symphony to the second act of the *Indian Queen*, for example, is a church sonata designed on a large orchestral scale.

If Purcell's artistic achievements are surveyed as a whole, the intimate ties with insular tradition appear to be the outstanding single factor. His dissonance treatment especially can only be understood as an English characteristic. It differs from continental practice less in the nature of the harmonies involved than in the reason for their application.[41] Purcell

---

[40] The second set is called "in four parts," a designation Purcell himself would not have chosen. In both sets the bass and the continuo do not always coincide, as was common in many trio sonatas.

[41] It seems hardly necessary to point out that no single feature in music can be regarded as the monopoly of any one nation. The attempt of Sir Walford Davies (*King's Music*, 1937) to arrive at absolute criteria of what is "English" in music is as naïve as it is amateurish. If Purcell's simultaneous cross-relations are compared with the Italian examples of the early baroque (Exs. 3, 15, 21) it will become clear that all "national" criteria are relative and subject to very distinct historical changes.

brought to perfection what Locke, Humfrey, and Blow had begun: they all sought dissonances not merely for pictorial reasons (as the continental composers did), but for the sake of thick sonority. In the remarkably dissonant overture to the anthem *I will give thanks unto thee, O Lord,* there is no pictorial justification for the constant frictions between the parts. The clashes are achieved by two favorite devices of Purcell's: the simultaneous use of suspensions and retardations, and the resolution of a suspension in a new harmony. Another harmonic peculiarity, the insistence on cross-relations, especially in cadences, represents an attempt to unite modal and tonal concepts. In its typical form the cadence combines major and Mixolydian, or minor and Dorian respectively. From countless examples of this practice a chorus from the *Tempest* has been selected in which the tolling of the bell is depicted (Ex. 63). This ambiguous cadence, expressly

Ex. 63. Purcell: Bell chorus from *The Tempest.*

codified by Purcell in Playford's *Introduction to the Skill of Musick* as "half cadence," presupposes for its cadential effect the distinct, if elementary, feeling for tonality of the middle baroque. In its most condensed form the cadence entails a simultaneous cross-relation, as in the anthem *My heart is inditing* (Ex. 64). In this example, which, incidentally, has been "im-

Ex. 64. Purcell: *Alleluja* from *My heart is inditing.*

proved" in older editions by the elimination of the b-flat, the dissonant notes of the middle parts do not essentially alter the underlying harmony, but they do substantially increase the sonority. In contrast with the narrow spacing of the simultaneous cross-relation found in Ex. 58, it is spaced here an octave apart. This far more satisfactory spacing, which, in the late works, supplants the cruder archaic method, illustrates Purcell's growing tonal consciousness. The difference between Continental and English contrapuntal practice is born out not only by the above examples, but also by the theoretical recognition of unprepared consecutive sevenths, to which Purcell devoted a whole paragraph in his contribution to Playford's theory book.

Purcell's melodic fecundity, which stands directly opposed to Lully's rhythmic approach to melody, brightens even his weaker works. However uniform his melodies may be, they always have personal distinction. Tunes like *If Love's a sweet passion* from the *Fairy Queen* have never been forgotten, thanks to broadsides, Durfey's *Pills,* and *The Beggar's Opera.* The almost mannered partiality to augmented and diminished steps, and to softly syncopated minuet rhythms represents an external, if characteristic, feature of his melodies. More significant are certain angular qualities to which the Purcellian grace owes, paradoxically, much of its peculiar charm. Especially in tunes that approach the sphere of folksong and morris dance, unvocal progressions can be found which sharply contrast with the smoothness of the Italian bel-canto style. In their angularity they recall fiddle tunes, as for example the studiously naïve dialogue of Corydon and Mopsa from the *Fairy Queen.* Purcell's relation to folksong, which wishful thinking is apt to aggrandize, is actually a very loose one. Only on two occasions did he actually quote ballad tunes: *Cold and raw,* and *Hey boys, up we go,* and here they were, significantly enough, merely foils for his own music.

The discussion of Purcell's compositions cannot be closed without a word about his *obbligo* forms. His resourcefulness in inventing canons and grounds was without limits though he rarely attempted such artifices as the canon for two recorders on a ground bass (*Dioclesian*). In the *Skill of Musick* Purcell asserted that composing upon a ground was "a very easy thing to do," a remark that bears witness of his great facility in these matters. His ground basses show a wide variety of types (Ex. 65). The most frequently used basses include the chromatic type (nos. 1-3), the triadic type (nos. 5 and 7), the running or patterned type (no. 9), and the widely spaced type, obviously derived from the idiom of the string instrument (nos. 7 and 8). One feature that all the quoted basses have in common may be easily overlooked: they all elaborate the melodic pattern of the descending fourth, though it is often disguised by broken "divisions." The quasi-ostinato basses form a group by themselves; since the rhythmic pattern, not the melody, is the fixed element here, they allow of more harmonic freedom than the strict ostinato. Purcell's grounds frequently appear in transpositions to related keys or the opposite mode so that contrasting tonalities are brought into play in the manner of a rondo. The occasional disregard, in the upper parts, for the recurring pattern of the ground produces sophisticated overlaps of phrases, so smoothly effected that the hearer is scarcely aware of the constraint at all. Much of Purcell's elaboration on grounds is purely musician's music which may have been lost on his courtly audience.

Ex. 65. Purcell: Ground basses.

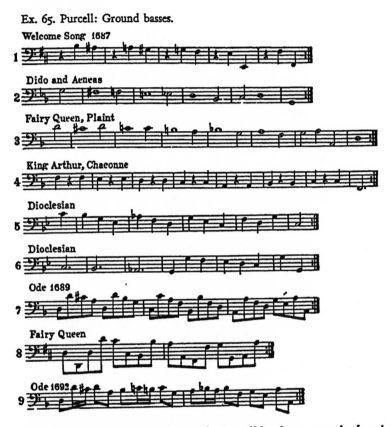

From the days of Burney until recently Purcell has been appraised mainly in the light of what has come after him. Only the latest phase of his stylistic development, characterized by the tentative turn to late baroque style, has been taken to represent the "real" Purcell. Since the works of the early and middle periods do not conform to this distorted picture of Purcell's style, they had to be forced into line by the notorious Victorian "revisions." Today a reversal of opinion has occurred. Works that seem to anticipate Handel hold less interest for us than the earlier ones in which the English idiom of the middle baroque reaches its consummation. The "Handelian" compositions strike us today as works of transition, the others more nearly as works of perfection, not in spite of, but because of their being "clog'd with somewhat of the English vein" (North). The stylistic position of Purcell has been succinctly summarized by North who refers to him as one who "began to shew his Great skill before the reforme of musick, *al Italliana,* and while he was warm in pursuit of it, Dyed, but a greater musical genius England never had." The last clause of this quotation merely paraphrases the title of the most famous seventeenth-century collection of Purcell's music, which has justly become his honorary title: *Orpheus Britannicus.*

CHAPTER SEVEN

Late Baroque: Luxuriant Counterpoint and Concerto Style

THE CULMINATION OF LATE BAROQUE MUSIC IN ITALY

IT IS a strange though incontestable fact that of the immense treasure of baroque music only certain compositions in late baroque style have succeeded in finding a permanent, if subordinate, place in the present-day musical repertory and that, as a consequence, the characteristics of late baroque style are commonly mistaken for those of the baroque as a whole. It would be wrong to explain this preference by contending that the late baroque masters were "greater" than their predecessors; this interpretation would only confirm the lack of familiarity with the previous periods of baroque music. The reason lies deeper than that. Late baroque music does indeed differ from that of the earlier phases of baroque style in one important respect: it is written in the idiom of fully established tonality. After the pre-tonal experimentations of the early baroque and the use of a rudimentary tonality in the middle baroque period, the definitive realization of tonality in Italy about 1680 marks the decisive turning point in the history of harmony which coincides with the beginning of the late baroque period. It is precisely the use of tonality in the late baroque that connects this period more closely than any other with the living musical repertory of today.

THE RISE OF TONALITY

Tonality was not "invented" by a single composer or a single school. It emerged at approximately the same time in the Neapolitan opera and in the instrumental music of the Bologna school and was codified by Rameau more than a generation after its first appearance in music. Tonality established a gradated system of chordal relations between a tonal center (the tonic triad in major or minor) and the other triads (or seventh chords) of the diatonic scale. None of these chords was in itself new, but they now served a new function, namely that of circumscribing the key. While in middle baroque harmony this function had been performed chiefly by the two dominants, it was now extended to all chords. Significantly, this inclusive system of chordal functions is known as functional harmony.

The functional or tonal chord progressions are governed by the drive to the cadence which releases the tension that the movement away from the tonic produces. The technical means of achieving key-feeling were, aside from the cadence itself, diatonic sequences of chords that gravitated toward the tonal center. The degree of attraction depended on the distance of the chords from the tonic, and this distance was measured and determined by the circle of fifths. The sequence in fifths crystallized as the most common and conspicuous harmonic formula that underlay the harmonic structure of an extended piece. The diatonic circle always included a diminished fifth and precisely this irregularity gave it its defining power with regard to key. The logic of chord progressions was heightened by melodic means, such as dovetailing suspensions of the seventh (compare Ex. 68 below). Seventh chords on every degree of the scale, one of the most characteristic earmarks of late baroque music, were uncommon in early and middle baroque harmony. Also the seventh chord on the leading tone in minor (diminished-seventh chord) became an important resource of tonality. It was considered not as a chromatically altered chord but as a member of the diatonic family. It had already occurred in early baroque harmony, though only sporadically and not in the strictly tonal function it acquired now. Its dissonant quality made it the favorite chord at climactic points placed directly before the release of the accumulated tension in the final cadence.

Among the various harmonic formulas and sequences that tonality employed, the descending series of sixth chords stands out as another important resource. Tonally less conclusive than the circle of fifths and still subservient to contrapuntal part-writing, it harmonized the steps of the scale in diatonic fashion and thus also served as a means of circumscribing the key. This formula occurred in its barest form with Corelli (Ex. 66) who was the first to put the tonal formulas to systematic use.

Both formulas appear so often in late baroque style that it can be categorically stated that there is hardly a composition in late baroque style in which they are not present. The formulas presented the tones of the diatonic scale in systematic form, preferably in descending order, and defined the key; however, since they could be interrupted at any point they served at the same time as the main means of modulation. Simple as they may seem today, they were elaborated time and again with astonishing resourcefulness.

Ex. 66. Corelli: Excerpt from violin sonata op. 5, 7.

The establishment of tonality naturally affected all aspects of composition. Above all, it permeated the contrapuntal writing. The absorption of tonality into counterpoint gave the melodic design and the contrapuntal texture unprecedented harmonic support. The poignant melodic dissonances or "false" intervals could now be integrated into the tonal system. The interpenetration of harmony and counterpoint resulted in the harmonically saturated or "luxuriant" counterpoint of the late baroque period, which began with Corelli and culminated in the works of Bach. Tonality provided also a framework of harmony able to sustain large forms. It set up harmonic goals without which the extended forms of late baroque music would not have been possible. It gave a new perspective to the two structural voices of the composition. In the relation between melody and chord progression the consideration of the latter began to weigh more heavily than the former. The melodies were increasingly conditioned by and dependent on the harmonic accompaniment—a process that led finally to the homophony of the Mannheim school. However, in late baroque music the homophony was held in check by the continuo which preserved the dualistic conception of musical structure. The harmonic orientation was thus counterbalanced by the melodic orientation of the bass. This most characteristic idiom may be designated as continuo-homophony after its two constituent elements. Luxuriant counterpoint and continuo-homophony represent opposite poles in the texture of late baroque music. Continuo-homophony differed from the plain homophony of the Mannheim school in its fast harmonic rhythm and its energetic and sweeping rhythmic patterns that prevailed in both melody and bass.

Continuo-homophony originated in the concerto style which must be regarded as the most significant stylistic innovation of the late baroque period because it pervaded not only the concerto but also all other forms of music, both instrumental and vocal. The concerto style realized a strictly instrumental ideal of abstract or "absolute" music. It was characterized by its consistent adoption of continuo-homophony, frequent unison passages in all voices, fast harmonic rhythm, and themes that emphatically circumscribed the key by stressing the fundamental triads and the diatonic scale. Contrapuntal writing disintegrated in the concerto style under the impact of continuo-homophony and remained essential only to the outermost voices. In the *allegro* movements the instrumental nature of the concerto style became particularly obvious in such features as rapid tone repetitions, fast scale passages, and the wide range of the themes. The rhythmic energy manifested by the mechanical and ceaselessly progressing beats was aptly described by North as the "fire and fury of the Italian style."

CONCERTO GROSSO AND SOLO CONCERTO

Although the concerto was essentially a creation of the late baroque some of its elements can be found in isolated form much earlier. Suffice it to recall the widespread use of the tutti-solo contrast in the *concertato* style, especially in the ensemble canzonas of Gabrieli and the Venetian school (Usper and Neri). Important factors in the genesis of the concerto were the French orchestra discipline and the trio episodes in the Lullian chaconnes. Furthermore, the trumpet sonatas of the early Bologna school must be mentioned, notably those of Cazzati, Stradella, and Giovanni Vitali, which led directly up to the concerto proper. In these sonatas, so far little known, the trumpet was accompanied not by a solo ensemble, but by a full string orchestra. Stradella, finally, clearly distinguished in his operas and oratorios and in his *Sinfonie a più instrumenti* (c. 1680) between a concertino and a concerto grosso. In spite of the use of contrasting sonorities none of these incipient concertos was written in concerto style. It is this style that distinguishes the late baroque concerto from its forerunners.

The decisive step in the development of the concerto proper was taken by Corelli and Torelli, both closely associated with the late Bologna school. Arcangelo Corelli (1653–1713) can take the credit for the full realization of tonality in the field of instrumental music. His works auspiciously inaugurate the period of late baroque music. The title pages of his first publications refer to him as "il Bolognese." He actually belonged to the Bologna school only by virtue of the musical training he received there; the place of his main activity was Rome. His visits to Germany and France have not yet been conclusively documented. Although closely bound to the contrapuntal tradition of the early Bologna school, Corelli handled the new idiom with amazing assuredness. Of his comparatively few printed works only twelve concerti grossi (op. 6, 1714?) belong to the concerto literature. The date of publication is misleading: according to the testimony of his pupil Georg Muffat the concertos were played in Rome as early as 1682; they represent in fact the earliest known examples of the concerto grosso.[1] The innovation was instantly successful and widely imitated.

Corelli divided the orchestra into two groups, the tutti or concerto grosso in the strict sense, and the solo or concertino, both of which were supplied with a continuo of their own so that they could also be spatially separated. He selected for his concertino a string trio, thus projecting the idiom of the trio sonata against the background of the orchestra. Even if we did not have external evidence for the early date of Corelli's concertos, their very conception in terms of the trio sonata represents so conservative a feature that it could serve as internal evidence on stylistic grounds. This point is borne out by the formal aspects of the concertos, which seem in the light of the later development, primitive and tentative. The first of these relates to the form as a whole. Corelli did not evolve a new formal scheme for the newly created medium in any of his concertos, but merely transferred to them the two traditional types of chamber music: the church and the chamber sonata. He thus established the church and chamber concerto, specifically distinguished as *concerto da chiesa* and *concerto da camera* on many title pages of the time. The first eight concertos belong to the first type and are formally even less advanced than Corelli's own trio sonatas. He cast them not into the four-movement form that he himself stereotyped in his chamber music, but into the more conservative form of five or more movements. However, the diminutive *adagio* sections often merely veil an underlying four-movement structure since they serve only as transitions between the main movements. That the church concertos of the collection are in the majority cannot surprise because this form corresponded to the function of the music: it was played before, after, or even during High Mass. Only the last four concertos of op. 6 are chamber con-

---

[1] Fischer's categorical statement (Adler HMG, 555) that Giovanni Maria Bononcini published the first concerti grossi in 1677 must be questioned. The list of printed works by Bononcini does not include a set of concerti grossi.

certos containing a prelude and the suite proper. Here also we find at times brief transitional sections between the movements.

The second primitive trait relates to the musical texture, especially the distribution of solo and tutti. Significantly enough, hardly ever is a structural distinction between the two bodies of sound made. The extreme brevity of the contrasted sections and the lack of thematic differentiation clearly indicate that the mere alternation between concerto grosso and concertino, the contrast between loud and soft as such, was as yet more important than a musically well-defined tutti and solo. The two ensembles frequently merely echo one another on a small space, or play one continuous phrase in quick alternation, as, for example, in the first *allegro* of the *Christmas Concerto* (no. 8). Also in technical respect Corelli put the tutti and solo on almost equal footing, as shown by the indiscriminate distribution of violinistic figuration. It seems significant in this connection that Corelli did not actually prescribe the orchestral doubling of the concerto grosso, but merely suggested it as optional.

The third primitive feature relates to the internal organization of the concertos. The chains of brief, almost fragmentary parts vividly recall the Venetian overture, which has obviously left its mark on the first movements of the concertos nos. 2 and 7. The latter example consists of six sharply contrasted units which would fall completely apart had Corelli not obviated this danger by making the first three sections correspond to the last three. He thus produced a large bipartite form, which obtains in many of his movements. In the *Christmas Concerto*, both the first *allegro* in fugal style and the last one (a stylized gavotte without dance title) are dependent on the bipartite scheme of the suite. Occasionally, Corelli employed the da-capo form with a clearly set-off middle part, as for example in the first *allegro* movements of concertos nos. 6 and 12, very similar also with regard to harmony.

However undeveloped in respect to form, the concertos are progressive in respect to the idiom of continuo-homophony. Long passages amount to nothing more than meager elaborations of the typical formulas which make different concertos almost identical as to harmonic progressions, as we can see by comparing the sequential treatment in the first *allegro* movements of nos. 6, and 12, and the allemande of no. 11. Harmonic sequences also dominate the violinistic figuration. Corelli's music is perhaps more idiomatic for the violin than anything written before his time. The figuration rests entirely on a few broken-chord patterns. Although nothing new in themselves they acquired new musical interest by means of sequences that carried them through the keys. The contrapuntal movements, however, present a sharp contrast to the movements with figurative harmony. The church concertos contain at least one fugal movement, and the prelude of the chamber concertos is more contrapuntal as a rule than the subsequent dances. The luxuriant counterpoint of the fugal movements faithfully guards the heritage of the Bologna school. Ponderous and solemn beginnings like that of concerto no. 11 (Ex. 67), in which a contrapuntal duet

Ex. 67. Corelli: Excerpt from Concerto grosso XI.

unfolds over a steadily moving bass, have been imitated time and again by late baroque composers. Late baroque polyphony derived its vigorous and heavy pathos from the clearly defined tonality of the chord progressions that allowed the voices to move more independently than ever before. Continual suspensions and retardations constantly deferred the cadence and produced a weft of great complexity and sustaining power, hitherto unknown. In the first *grave* of the *Christmas Concerto* the endlessly intertwining parts move from beginning to end without ever arriving at a single intermediary cadence. It should be noted that Corelli wanted this particular movement played without embellishments *come stà*. The customary improvised ornaments of the soloist would have ruined the hymnic and broad *adagio* cantilena which Corelli was striving for. The last movement of the *Christmas Concerto,* the famous *Pastorale* for Christmas that has given the concerto its name, is only an optional addition. A favorite form of the time, it occurs also in the concertos of Torelli and Locatelli.

The orchestral *adagio* cantilena of the slow movements had its complement in the orchestral *allegro* style in which Corelli adapted the French orchestral discipline to Italian music. The influence of Lully on Corelli is confirmed not only by the testimony of Geminiani, but also by the first movement of concerto no. 3 which, though not thus designated, is a French overture seen through the eyes of an Italian. The concerto style appears with Corelli only in tentative and melodically undeveloped form. He came closest to it in the first *allegro* of concerto no. 12 (Ex. 68) which may well have been composed somewhat later than the other concertos. The quoted excerpt also illustrates the use of the sequential circle of fifths in inter-locking suspensions. It should not be overlooked that the first violin part receives more emphasis than the rest of the concertino—an indication that Corelli stood at the very beginning of the road that led to the solo concerto.

Ex. 68. Corelli: From Concerto grosso XII.

Corelli's innovations in Rome had their counterpart in the revolutionary works of the guiding spirit of the late Bologna school, Giuseppe Torelli (d. 1708), since 1686 active at San Petronio and later for some time also in Germany and Austria. His outstanding contribution to the concerto was the convincing realization of the concerto style and the establishment of the baroque concerto form. In his *Sinfonie a tre e Concerti a quattro* (op. 5, 1692) Torelli clearly distinguished between sinfonie and concertos. This distinction is puzzling because the concertos completely lack the tutti-solo contrast and thus seem to contradict the meaning of the term. They must be classified as "orchestral concertos," a type of baroque concerto that has been minimized in favor of the concerto grosso and the solo concerto. This type is characterized not by opposed groups or contrasted sections, but by melodic emphasis on a uniformly reinforced violin part and the bass. This feature, typical of continuo-homophony, explains the mystery why the pieces are called concertos: they are without exception written in concerto style, quite in contrast with the luxuriant counterpoint of the sinfonie. It is a vital point for the correct understanding of the concerto that the dis-tinction between sinfonia and concerto was originally one of style, not one of form or orchestration. The use of the term concerto in the orchestral compositions of Torelli was justified only because of stylistic reasons.[2] The

[2] In his *Geschichte des Instrumentalkonzerts* Schering introduces the term concerto-sinfonia for this form. The term orchestral concerto, proposed here, seems preferable because it does not confuse the concerto with the sinfonia which Torelli took pains to distinguish.

same stylistic distinction obtains also in the collections of Taglietti, Albinoni, dall'Abaco, and others, who all contributed to the orchestral concerto. It was cultivated alongside of the other concerto types throughout the late baroque period and finally reached its consummation in the works of Handel.

Torelli cast his concertos at first in the mold of the church and chamber sonata but soon threw off the shackles of the sonata forms and established the typical concerto form, consisting of three movements in the order of *allegro-adagio-allegro*. This form obviously stressed the favorite tempo of the concerto style, the *allegro*, often even to a point where the intermediate slow movement was reduced to a few chords. The new formal scheme was closely bound up with the evolution of the solo concerto, the first examples of which fall into the early eighteenth century. The manner in which the first violin took the lead in Corelli's concerti grossi (see Ex. 68) shows how imperceptibly the one form could approach the other. Similarly, Torelli's orchestral concertos op. 6 (1698) contained short interludes for the violin for which the composer explicitly prescribed solo performance. Thus both the concerto grosso and the orchestral concerto laid the ground for the solo concerto, the most fertile of the three types of baroque concerto.

Torelli's collection of concertos op. 8 (1709) contrasts six concerti grossi with six full-fledged solo concertos. Since the collection was published posthumously, it is difficult to decide whether Torelli's solo concertos actually antedated the first printed violin concertos by Albinoni (1700) and the first cello concerto by Jacchini (1701). Since both Albinoni and Jacchini were presumably younger—both began to publish after Torelli—the latter may well have the priority in the establishment of the form. However this may be, Torelli established, possibly even before Albinoni, a distinct balance between tutti and solo; the solo ceased to be merely a transitional interlude so that orchestra and soloist became rivals of equal importance. For the first time the tutti-solo contrast was also musically defined by means of virtuoso figuration in the solo and a pregnant idea in the tutti. This thematic differentiation, which obtains also in Torelli's concerti grossi, represents the great advance over the primitive organization of Corelli's concertos.

The musical differentiation of orchestra and solo was also decisive for the form of the single concerto movement, the ritornello form,[3] so called

[3] The term concerto form presents the same difficulty as the term sonata form. Both are ambiguous because they are used to designate the form as a whole (three of four movements) and the form of a single movement.

because the writers of the time referred to the periodic returns of the tutti idea as ritornello. The ritornello recurred throughout the movement in rondo fashion, however, not in the tonic (as the rondo refrains did) but each time in a different key except for the first and last ritornello. The concerto had a much wider formal and tonal scope than the rondo, since the various keys of the ritornello served as the pillars of the formal architecture and circumscribed at the same time the main key of the whole movement. Once established, the ritornello form was transferred from the solo concerto back to the concerto grosso although here the tradition of the church sonata could never be completely uprooted.

With Torelli the concerto style assumed its classic features and crystallized in typical mannerisms, such as consistent use of extremely prolonged upbeat patterns, impetuously driving rhythms, triadic themes that clearly set the key, and three chordal "hammerstrokes" on the tonic or I-V-I which drastically signalled the beginning of the ritornello. The last two features were derived from the fanfare style of the trumpet sonata. A trumpet sonata (1682) by Grossi, a little-known composer of the Bologna school, discloses how early the concerto style appeared in works of this category (Ex. 69).

Ex. 69. Grossi: Trumpet sonata.

The tradition of such stereotyped beginnings on a broken triad can be traced from the trumpet sonata to Torelli and his contemporaries, and from here to Vivaldi and Bach (violin concerto in *E*). It was taken over into the opera overture and thence transmitted to the symphonies of the classic school. Torelli's double concerto for two violins (op. 8),[4] for example, begins with three chordal "hammerstrokes" that sound like an anticipation of the first measures of Bach's fourth *Brandenburg Concerto*, which stands moreover in the same key.

Torelli did not entirely abandon the contrapuntal texture of the church sonata. In his remarkable violin concerto in *d* (op. 8),[5] one of his most

[4] See Jensen, *Klassische Violinmusik*, Augener Edition; and Wasielewski, *Instrumentalsätze*.
[5] Score edition by the New York Public Library, GMB no. 257, see also the organ arrangement by Johann Gottfried Walther, DDT 26-27, 343. For another example see HAM no. 246.

mature works, he presents his tutti theme in fugal fashion. It is based on the third type of chaconne bass, here tonally interpreted with a sequential violin figure. Its mechanical and precise rhythms and its driving harmonies aptly illustrate his highly energetic concerto style.

After the death of Torelli the center of concerto composition shifted from Bologna to Venice where Antonio Vivaldi (c. 1676–1741), a pupil of Legrenzi, brought the trend toward the solo concerto to its height. The concerti grossi of the "Red Priest" were so closely fashioned after the solo concerto that the line between the two forms cannot always be drawn. He treated the concertino not only as a self-contained group in concerto-grosso manner, but preferably as a flexible ensemble of several independent soloists. His double, triple or quadruple concertos stand midway between concerto grosso and solo concerto. Vivaldi's keen and often capricious imagination finds its external expression in the variety of instrumental combinations which clearly reflect the Venetian fondness for coloristic effects. His concertos range from solo concertos for violin or flute to concerti grossi with wind ensembles.

Only a small part of Vivaldi's incredibly prolific production has ever been published. More than any other composer of the time he devoted himself to the writing of concertos almost to the exclusion of other instrumental music. In his concerto collections he was given to using fanciful titles, such as *Estro armonico* (Harmonical Whim), *La Stravaganza*, or *Il Cimento dell'Armonia e dell'Inventione* (The Contest between Harmony and Invention). The *Cimento* contains several programmatic concertos (The Tempest, The Hunt, The Pleasure) and a group of four concerti grossi, entitled *Le Stagioni*,[6] which represent an important baroque parallel to Haydn's oratorio *The Seasons*. Each season is described in a sonnet that furnishes the program for the concerto. Although Vivaldi revelled in naïve, if delightful, imitations of bird calls, the murmuring of the brook, or the unsteady gait of a drunk, he did not become the slave of the programs; he strictly maintained the formal structure of the ritornello form and indulged in playful descriptions only in the solo sections. The program served at the same time as a welcome pretext for virtuosity which Vivaldi expanded far above the level of his predecessors, notably by the resourceful use of arpeggios in the highest and lowest registers, *bariolage*, and extended scale passages. More than Torelli he exploited the relentless

[6] ICMI 35

mechanical beat of the concerto style. The insistence on running basses and on even subdivisions of the beat in the violin part lent his concerto movements not only the characteristic breathless drive but also a uniform continuity.

Vivaldi owed his European fame to the gestic simplicity and precision of his themes (Ex. 70) which all progressive concerto composers of his time

Ex. 70. Vivaldi: Concerto themes.

imitated. With a few bold strokes he designed pregnant and vivid ideas which, though all built on only a few patterns, set the characteristic seal to each one of his innumerable concertos. They served as the easily remembered motto of the ritornello.

In the works of Vivaldi the concerto form is definitely standardized as a cycle of three movements that may be exceptionally extended by a slow introduction. As the length of the single movements increased, the tutti ritornellos took on greater importance for the formal design. Vivaldi raised the number of tuttis to as many as five and further emphasized the tutti idea by breaking it up into fractions that were thrown into the solo sections—a technique that Bach perfected after Vivaldi's model. Of particular interest is his manner of presenting the thematic material of the solo. Three methods can be distinguished: (1) virtuoso figuration, not related to the tutti theme, (2) soloistic figuration and expansion of the tutti idea, and (3) a solo idea distinct from that of the ritornello. While Albinoni and Torelli favored the first, most primitive method and made occasional use of the second, Vivaldi favored the second method and made occasional use of the third. The last one, the most arresting of the three, seems to anticipate the idea of thematic contrast that prevails in the classic period. However, an examination of Vivaldi's tutti and solo themes reveals that, while the two ideas are distinctly independent of each other, they are not dramatically contrasted but actually unified by key and the uniform rhythms of the concerto style. The concerto in *a* from the *Estro armonico* (op. 3, 8) [7] presents the two themes in this manner; it is significant that

---

[7] See *Chamber Suites and Concerti Grossi* (Longmans Miniature Score Library), 290; compare also HAM no. 270.

the solo idea is succeeded by a motive derived from the tutti and thus serves to unify the two sections. Bach transcribed this concerto, like many others, for organ. As one of the best of its kind it gives the essence of Vivaldi's style. The first movement begins with the stereotyped three hammerstrokes, and then proceeds with bustling scale passages and the typical diatonic sequence in fifths, touching on all degrees of the scale. The second movement is built on the first type of chaconne bass, stated in *unisono* by the whole orchestra in a powerfully rhythmized form; also the last movement displays the characteristic unison passages of the concerto style.

The three central figures of the concerto: Corelli, Torelli, and Vivaldi were surrounded by a host of brilliant composers whose works cannot even be outlined here. They fall roughly into a conservative and a progressive group though many composers cannot be categorically classified. The conservatives continued the tradition of the church concerto in the polyphonic style of Corelli, notably Albicastro, Albinoni, Bonporti, Gregori, Mascitti, and also Alessandro Scarlatti whose retrospective concertos and sinfonie contrast with the progressive style of his operas. The progressive group comprised mainly Venetian composers who emulated the concerto style of Vivaldi, notably the Germanized Italian dall'Abaco, Gasparini, Manfredini, Marcello, Montanari, Taglietti, Tessarini, and Giuseppe Valentini.

The younger generation was represented by Geminiani (d. 1762) and Locatelli (d. 1764). Geminiani, a pupil of Corelli and Scarlatti, belonged to the conservative camp. He enlarged the traditional trio of the concertino to a full string quartet by the addition of the viola and arranged in this heavy medium the trio sonatas of Corelli as concerti grossi—a clear indication that for the conservatives the trio sonata still dominated the conception of the concerto grosso. Geminiani's leanings toward strict counterpoint come to light in his use of canonic writing [8] and such significant titles as *Arte della Fuga*. In spite of its contrapuntal complexity, however, his style seems pallid and lacks individual distinction. Locatelli; on the other hand, also a pupil of Corelli, turned the modern concerto in a highly personal manner into a vehicle of stupendous virtuosity. The technical demands of his *Capricci*—optional cadenzas for the solo concertos—have

---

[8] See the last movement of concerto grosso op. 2, 3, in *Chamber Suites and Concerti Grossi*, 315.

hardly been surpassed even by composers of the classic period. In his concerti grossi Locatelli adhered, like Geminiani, to Corelli's solid contrapuntal style, but his harmonic imagination was far superior to that of Geminiani. The powerful influence of the opera can be seen in the *Pianto d'Arianna* in which the late baroque recitative is transferred to instrumental music. The numerous solo concertos of Tartini (d. 1770) are already indebted to the *style galant* which set an end to the music of the baroque era.

ENSEMBLE SONATA AND SOLO SONATA

The composers of the Bologna school held the key position in the field of chamber music. Next to Corelli, Giovanni Battista Bassani (1657-1716) stood out as the leading composer of sonatas. He was seconded by Aldrovandini, Giuseppe Alberti, Pietro degli Antonii, and Tommaso Vitali (the son of Giovanni Battista) [9] who brought the brilliant history of the school to a close. A large group of composers who did not belong to the Bologna school likewise cultivated sonata composition, notably dall'Abaco, Albinoni, Bonporti, Caldara, Carlo Marini, Taglietti, Antonio Veracini, and Vivaldi.

The works of Corelli are as fundamental to the development of chamber music as to that of orchestral music. They include four sets of trio sonatas, equally divided into church sonatas (op. 1, 1681, and op. 3, 1689) and chamber sonatas (op. 2 and op. 4), and one set of solo sonatas (op. 5, 1707), each set containing a dozen sonatas. In his church sonatas (with organ continuo) Corelli established the standard four-movement form (slow-fast-slow-fast) though he occasionally reverted to the old practice of combining more than four movements and even to the transformation technique of the variation canzona which survives in the trio sonata op. 1, 10. In the first movements he usually projects two imitative voices against a steadily running bass (compare Ex. 67 above). The complete integration of the bass into the imitative texture of the upper voices accounts for the complex harmonic idiom that characterizes Corelli's chamber music. The second movements begin with a fugue subject, frequently coupled to a brief countersubject in double counterpoint. The combined subjects serve as concise contrapuntal cells that often prevail throughout the movement in repeated or modified form. It is worth noting that the fugal movements often sound more polyphonic than they actually are because of numerous redundant entries which merely pretend to introduce a new voice—a favorite Italian device

[9] GMB no. 241, HAM no. 263.

that can be found as early as Frescobaldi. Melodically little developed, the fugal movements can hardly be considered as real fugues, especially those in which the subject drops out in the course of the composition to be replaced by a continuous expansion of thematically free, though similar, material.

The two last movements both depend on the dance; the third movement is usually a broad and chordal *adagio* cantilena in the stylized triple time of the saraband, the last one a lively gigue. This inclusion of dance patterns in the church sonata marks the beginning of the internal disintegration of the form which coincides in the works of Corelli with its external stabilization in four stereotyped movements. The chamber sonatas (with harpsichord continuo) open with a prelude in strict style, which in turn betrays the influence of the church sonata, and then present two or three dances written in continuo-homophony but not without slight contrapuntal touches.

The twelve solo sonatas are equally divided, like the trio sonatas, into church and chamber sonatas. In spite of their later date of publication the church sonatas for solo violin seem formally less stereotyped than the trio sonatas. Here also Corelli availed himself of dance patterns although he suppressed dance titles. Like all composers of the Bologna school he did not indulge in virtuosity for its own sake. The greatest demands on violinistic technique are made in *perpetuum mobile* movements (see Ex. 66), which set the model for the technical "study" of later times. The printed form of the solo sonatas does not faithfully reproduce the intentions of the composer. According to the Italian tradition the performer was expected to ornament the slow movements by improvised virtuoso embellishments. One edition of the time, significantly a non-Italian publication, actually records the ornaments in full (Ex. 71). However, the strangely rhapsodic

Ex. 71. Corelli: Violin sonata with embellishments.

taste they reveal throws some suspicion on the publisher's claim that they represent Corelli's own graces *comme il les joue.*

In view of the contrapuntal organization of his music it is not surprising that Corelli made only little use of *obbligo* forms. His chaconne on a descending fourth (op. 2, 12) forms a worthy complement to his celebrated variations on the *folia* bass for violin and continuo. The rich tonal idiom of his harmonies, his noble counterpoint, the hymnic pathos of his *adagio* melodies, and the classic simplicity of his lines aroused the enthusiasm of the time and became a symbol of baroque chamber music.

What has been said about Corelli applies on the whole also to the other composers of the late Bologna school. The chamber works of dall'Abaco, Albinoni, and Bonporti were highly esteemed by Bach, as his borrowings and manuscript copies show. Four of Bonporti's valuable *Invenzioni* (1712) for violin and continuo exist in Bach's handwriting—he copied them without adding the author's name—and have been included in the *Bach Gesellschaft* edition [10] as genuine works. The error is easily understandable since they anticipate the characteristic melodic turns and the profuse harmonies of Bach's style. Bonporti's dignified and solid workmanship strongly contrasts with the purely melodic gift of Ariosti. His *Lezioni* [11] for the viola d'amore inaugurated the special literature for this instrument which later became a favorite in eighteenth-century chamber music. The lessons were written in a peculiar tablature notation that also enabled the violinist to play the instrument without knowledge of the viola d'amore fingering.

The last phase of baroque chamber music was characterized by a conspicuous shift of emphasis from the trio sonata to the solo sonata which was also to remain the leading form in the classic period. The generation after Corelli comprised Geminiani, Locatelli, Meneghetti, Somis (a pupil of Corelli), Tessarini (a pupil of Vivaldi), and Francesco Veracini (1690–1750), the nephew of Antonio. Of these the first was the most conservative, and the last the most important violinist.

Like Geminiani, Veracini spent much of his life outside of Italy. Although he was the leading and most brilliant virtuoso of his day he kept his thoroughly idiomatic solo sonatas (op. 1, 1721; op. 4, 1744) free from the passage work of empty virtuosity. His individual, if not subjective, style has no precedent in baroque music and clearly heralds the end of the entire era. The capriciously ruffled contours of his melodies and his farfetched harmonies form only one aspect of his style. We also find sudden passages in a simple *style galant*. Veracini's international audiences in Lon-

[10] Volume 45: I, 172.
[11] Boyden, MQ 32 (1946) 562.

don and Dresden were quick to appreciate the virtuoso but found little pleasure in his compositions.

The sonatas of Veracini and his contemporaries are interesting particularly with regard to form. In the latest phase of sonata development the classification into church and chamber sonata became almost meaningless because the forms merged and because the formal innovations of the opera and the concerto intruded into the sonata, the universal meeting ground of all styles. Taglietti had already fashioned his sonatas (*Pensieri musicali*) deliberately after the grand da-capo aria. Veracini frequently began the sonata with an Italianized French overture and adopted the ritornello form of the concerto in subsequent movements, for example in op. 1, 8.[12] The da capo of the opera aria and the ritornello of the concerto form introduced a new formal element: the return to the beginning in the tonic key. In the sonatas of Somis the bipartite form of the chamber sonata was regularly extended by such a return. Retaining its bipartite division and key structure Somis expanded the second part by a rudimentary recapitulation in the original key.[13] This scheme, around 1720, became the standard form of the monothematic, late baroque sonata. The trio sonatas of Pergolesi and the solo sonatas of Tartini solidified the form, but the pronounced *goût galant* in their music marks the end of the baroque sonata in Italy.

After the ebb of keyboard composition in the middle baroque Italian keyboard music of the late baroque rose to prominence again with Pasquini who stood on the borderline between middle and late baroque styles. The first generation of the late baroque keyboard composers included Bencini, della Ciaja (a pupil of Pasquini), Casini, Grieco, Alessandro Scarlatti, and Zipoli.[14] Only the late works of Pasquini betray, in their rich tonal idiom, the advent of the late baroque style. His main contribution was the transfer of the violin sonata to the harpsichord, but it should be noted that not all compositions he designated as sonatas belong to this class. The "sonatas" in Gregorio Strozzi's *Capricci* (1687) still belong to the conservative canzona type. While Pasquini cultivated the then old-fashioned variation technique of Frescobaldi in his canzonas, he wrote his ricercars as monothematic fugues with distinctive themes, giving full

---

[12] ICMI 34.
[13] Einstein, *A Short History*, Ex. 32.
[14] For various examples of this group of composers see Farrenc, *Trésor;* Torchi AM III; TAM VIII–X.

range to tonal harmones. His *partite* on the *folia* and the *bergamasca* [15] attest to his thoroughly idiomatic handling of a rippling harpsichord style and his enriched harmonic vocabulary. The sonatas for the unusual combination of two harpsichords are stenographically sketched out as two thorough-basses leaving the realization to the skill of the performers.

The strictly polyphonic *Pensieri* for organ (1714) by Casini are extremely interesting compositions which carry the idea of the variation ricercar to its very limits. Casini wrote a cycle of three independent fugues on a single subject that appears in each fugue in rhythmic and melodic transformation. He thus anticipated a technique Bach put to systematic use in the *Art of the Fugue*. Italian fugue writing culminated with Bencini [16] whose music is noteworthy equally for his audacious and profiled themes and the lucid distinction between thematic and episodic sections. The keyboard works of Alessandro Scarlatti,[17] especially the toccatas, are curiously conservative, like his orchestral music, although the dazzling variations of the *folia* bass show his full command of the keyboard style.

While the harpsichord compositions do not represent Alessandro Scarlatti from his most significant side, the contrary is true of his son Domenico, the undisputed leader of the latest generation of harpsichord composers. The younger Scarlatti (1685-1757) was so eminently the overtowering virtuoso of the harpsichord that his works in other media seem insignificant by comparison. Scarlatti and Handel were united by a cordial friendship that rested on the mutual admiration they felt for each other; in the famous, though perhaps legendary, contest in Rome Scarlatti frankly conceded Handel's supremacy on the organ, but held his own on the harpsichord. Scarlatti's teeming imagination was directly inspired by and inseparably bound up with the harpsichord idiom. Much of his music looks inconsequential on paper and comes to life only through the sparkling sonorities of the instrument. About six-hundred sonatas have survived [18] of which only thirty were published by the composer himself under the modest title *Esercizi* (1729?, Madrid). Like Pasquini, Scarlatti associated with the sonata no definite type of composition; his sonatas consist of only one movement, many of which must indeed be classified as "exercise" or study because they consistently utilize a single technical device at a time, such as trills, arpeggios, crossing of the hands, wide skips, repeated

[15] TAM VIII.
[16] Torchi AM III, 412. The piece is erroneously called sonata.
[17] ICMIB 12, TAM IX.
[18] The sonatas are quoted here according to the numbers of the Longo edition (Ricordi). The editor grouped the sonatas arbitrarily in "suites." See HAM no. 274.

notes (in toccata manner), scales, and measured tremolos produced by the rapid alternation of the left and right hand in the same register.

Like all members of the Neapolitan school Scarlatti showed little interest in genuine polyphony. The free-voiced texture of his keyboard style aided much in the disintegration of contrapuntal devices. His works actually mark the turn of Italian keyboard music from the baroque to the early classic period. Only his presumably early sonatas can be said to belong fully to the baroque era; they elaborate a single idea and maintain the polyphonic texture and the ceaselessly running rhythmic patterns of the invention (no. 27 in *f*, no. 32 in *f*-sharp). His fugues, among which the so-called "cat fugue" is best known, give with their continual parallel thirds and octave doublings only the semblance of really independent part-writing. The cat fugue which has received its sobriquet only after the death of the composer is only one of the many examples of studiously bizarre themes, very common in the Neapolitan school. The oncoming classic style manifests itself openly in homophonic types of melody, Alberti basses (no. 358 in *C*), and especially in dramatically contrasted themes and key areas. In his polythematic sonatas Scarlatti liked to present a distinct second theme in the minor dominant (no. 461 in *D*) as became the custom with Emanuel Bach. While the first themes often retain polyphonic texture the second themes are as a rule plainly homophonic. The use of polyphony and homophony as a means of underscoring the contrast of themes and keys is a striking symptom of the new stylistic situation: polyphony obviously represents no longer an obligatory style but merely an optional technical device.

It is characteristic of Scarlatti's typical Italian conservatism in respect to form that he expressed his stylistic innovations regularly in the traditional bipartite sonata form, thus turning a most pliable formal scheme to new use. Fundamentally, the form was based on the modulation from tonic to dominant in the first part, and the reversed modulation in the second part. The end of the second part usually repeated that of the first in the tonic key. Within the bipartite division Scarlatti moved with complete freedom. In his most regular polythematic sonatas he emphatically identified the two key areas of the first part by their respective themes and exactly mirrored this structure in the second part so that a completely symmetrical sonata form resulted that was fraught with possibilities for the future. But this type is only one among a great number of other types: the second part often begins with a sudden assumption of a third-related key, or with an entirely new idea which supplants either the first or the second theme. The second part sometimes also brings an incipient harmonic development of the themes which leaves the baroque concept of sequential and continuous expansion far behind. Scarlatti carried the transfer of forms to the keyboard medium even further than Pasquini: he adopted not only the violin sonata, the idiom of which exerted a strong influence on his music (no. 93 in *a*), but also the orchestral *unisono* style of the Neapolitan overture (no. 406 in *c*), and the concerto style (Ex. 72).[19] In spite of the

Ex. 72. Domenico Scarlatti: Sonata.

deliberate use of virtuoso devices, especially the crossing of hands at lightning speed on which he drew invariably in his most dazzling sonatas (no. 215 in *d*), his compositions, because of their purely musical interest, never became mere showpieces.

The harmonic vocabulary of Scarlatti is steeped in the rich harmonic idiom of the Neapolitan opera school. Some of his most startling chords are due to the so-called *acciaccatura* or "crush"—a practice that can also be found in the works of his father and his contemporaries. The *acciaccatura*, minutely described in the *Armonico pratico* by Gasparini (the teacher of Domenico), was a harmonic embellishment consisting of a sharply dissonant attack to a full chord that was instantly released while the consonant members of the chord were held. Scarlatti, little concerned with the release of the dissonance, uses biting "crush chords" in a highly individual manner transforming the dissonances to inner pedals that underlie the harmony and thus achieving combinations of unmatched harmonic punch (Ex. 73).

Ex. 73. Domenico Scarlatti: *Acciaccature.*

The strumming effect of these passages suggests the technique of Spanish guitar music. Since Scarlatti spent the greatest part of his life in Spain, he was obviously influenced by the guitar accompaniment of Spanish popular

[19] This sonata does not appear in the Longo edition. Since the completion of this edition several new works have been discovered, see Newton, *Four Sonatas by Dome-*

music (no. 449 in *b*) and by the harmonic and rhythmic patterns of Spanish dances (no. 338 in *g*). These Spanish sonatas represent significant excursions into "exotic" regions, rarely considered by the composers of the time, but they do not touch Scarlatti's essentially Italian attitude. It would therefore be an exaggeration to call Scarlatti a Spanish composer. His works are too similar in style to those of his fellow Neapolitan Francesco Durante [20] whose *Studii e Divertimenti* pursue a similar trend though they cannot rival the dazzling brilliance and coloristic astuteness of Scarlatti.

Opera Seria AND *Opera Buffa*

CANTATA AND SACRED MUSIC

The vocal music of the late baroque period received its decisive impulse from instrumental music. This preponderance of the instrumental style brought the exact reversal of the situation we saw in the early baroque period. The increasing instrumentalization of the vocal idiom, the beginnings of which are noticeable even in the late phase of middle baroque music, is one of the most fascinating processes of music history. The instrumental stylization of the bel-canto deeply affected the virtuoso singing which at the height of its development could successfully compete with virtuoso playing.

The most conspicuous innovation in the field of opera was the differentiation between *opera seria* and *opera buffa*. The *opera seria* originated in the reform of the Italian librettist Zeno (d. 1750), who purged the libretto of comic characters and rigidly divided the action according to the musical contrast of recitative and aria. Since the dramatic action was reserved for the recitative, the aria became a static and contemplative point of rest of the "inner action." The "simile aria" comparing the affection of the hero to a state of nature crystallized as a literary type; it reigned supreme in the librettos of Metastasio, the successor of Zeno in Vienna. The librettos of these two poets, set to music time and again by all major composers of the

nico Scarlatti (Oxford University Press), and Gerstenberg, *Die Klavierkompositionen Domenico Scarlattis*. Whether all of these are genuine works is, however, an open question. Gerstenberg's thematic catalogue of the newly found sonatas contains at least one item (no. 8 b) that is definitely not by Domenico. It turned out to be identical with the aria *Le Violette* (*Rugiadose odorose*) from Alessandro Scarlatti's opera *Pirro e Demetrio* (1694). There is reason to believe that more arias were arranged for harpsichord and passed off by the publishers as works of Domenico.

[20] ICMI 19.

period, influenced even the spoken court drama of the time. After the model of Racine, Zeno bestowed on the *opera seria* its classic dignity and heroic grandiloquence which dominated the scene till the day of Gluck and Mozart. The arias of the *opera seria* were written in polished and terse, if sententious and abstract, poetry. They provided the composer with only one basic affection and ruled out the detailed description of single words. The affection was musically represented by a suggestive motto beginning the sequential expansion of which dominated the entire form. The second part of the aria text which usually formulated a slightly contrasting aspect of the affection furnished the words for the middle part of the aria, after which the first part was repeated. The form of the aria text was conceived in musical terms and was therefore the ideal vehicle for the grand da-capo aria, the leading vocal form of the time.

The change to late baroque style in the opera coincides with the rise of the Neapolitan opera school. The opera in Naples had so far been supported mainly by the Venetian opera. Monteverdi's *Poppea* was performed there after the composer's death in a revised and enlarged version, but except for the performance of Cirillo's *Orontea* (1654) little is known about the Neapolitan opera of the middle baroque. The Neapolitan school can be said to begin with Francesco Provenzale (d. 1704), perhaps the most neglected of the great composers of baroque opera. His numerous stage works include the humorous opera *Il Schiavo della sua moglie* (1671), *La Stellidaura vendicata* (1678) and *Candaule* (1679). The melodic inventiveness, harmonic imagination, and fiery pathos of the operas bespeak a musical dramatist of the first water. The aria *Fra tanti martiri* from *Stellidaura* (Ex. 74) shows one of his favorite aria types, a stylized saraband in which the background of the chromatic chaconne bass is still faintly recognizable.[21] The intensely dramatic "false" intervals are harmonized in the idiom of tonality which Provenzale established in the field of vocal music. Although his profuse harmonies were indicative of late baroque style he did not yet observe Zeno's opera reform and mixed tragic and comic scenes as Cirillo did in *Orontea*.

The Neapolitan school moved into the limelight with Alessandro Scarlatti (1660–1725). Commonly regarded as the main representative of the school, he was actually a descendant of the Roman and Venetian opera and only gradually developed the typical traits of the Neapolitan opera. There is no evidence for the oft-repeated claim that Provenzale was his

---

[21] An aria of the same type can be found in Rolland, *Histoire de l'Opéra*, App; see also HAM no. 222.

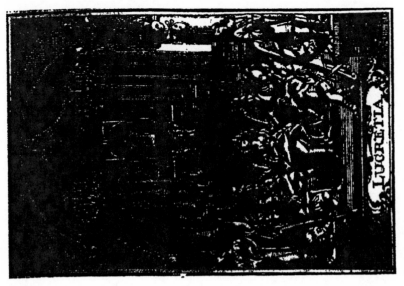

Frontispiece to the libretto of Reinhold Keiser's "Lucretia"

From Christopher Simpson's *The Division Violist*

PLATE 7

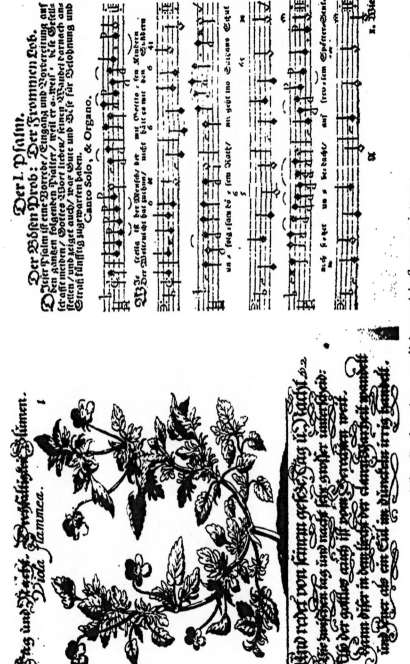

The Psalms in an edition with flower pictures

from *Lust und Artzeney-Garten des Propheten Davids, 1675*

teacher; on the contrary, the claim is suspect for stylistic reasons. Of the 115 operas that Scarlatti listed himself not a single one has been completely reprinted—a fate that he shares with many other great baroque masters.

Scarlatti's opera style brought two important innovations: the vigorous

Ex. 74. Provenzale: Aria from *La Stellidaura.*

development of continuo-homophony and the transfer of the concerto style to the aria. The clear-cut separation between *secco* recitative and aria became definitive and absolute; the resources of tonality endowed the recitative with the luxuriant harmonies that distinguish the late baroque recitative from the earlier one. The downward skip of the fourth was formalized as the obligatory cliché of the recitative cadence. It must be noted, however, that Scarlatti's formal and harmonic innovations appear distinctly only in the works of his late period.

The early period (1678–c. 1696) which began with *Gli equivoci* and ended with *Pirro e Demetrio* is characterized by concise aria forms. The continuo aria with motto beginning still predominates, the extended bipartite form ABB′ still holds its own against the da-capo aria, and modulatory ostinato basses still supply the framework for the aria. The already old-fashioned strophic aria has not yet fallen into disuse, and sometimes the middle section of a strophic da-capo aria appears in varied form, as it does for example in *La Rosaura* (II, 6 and 7).[22]

The period of maturity which began with Scarlatti's employment in

[22] Eitner PAM, 14. See also the numerous examples in Lorenz, *Die Jugendopern Alessandro Scarlattis*, II.

Rome (1703-1706) includes his most famous and significant operas: *Mitridate* (1707), *Tigrane* (1715), and *Griselda* (1721),[23] based on a libretto by Zeno. The last two must be regarded as his masterworks. In the late operas the da-capo aria leads; the continuo accompaniment is frequently expanded by a small string orchestra that may be reinforced in extraordinary scenes by trumpets, woodwinds, or horns. The ostinato bass is supplanted by the patterned quasi-ostinato bass. The harmonic vocabulary includes Neapolitan-sixth chords and diminished-seventh chords, quite rare in the early period. With his essentially melodic gift Scarlatti adopted the concerto style in his arias but transformed it by *cantabile* elements without obscuring its instrumental origin. Ottone's aria *Mi dimostra* from *Griselda* (Ex. 75) clearly shows the typical running basses and the mechanical

Ex. 75. Alessandro Scarlatti: Aria from *Griselda*.

rhythms of the concerto style and the use of instrumental coloratura (on the word *grandezza*). It should be noted, however, that his coloraturas are never as excessive as in the later Neapolitan school. The unique appeal of Scarlatti's music is due to the clear tonal direction of his melodies and to the spell-binding power of his rhythms, especially the siciliano.

Ensembles are comparatively rare even in the latest works and often still adhere to the primitive technique of alternate singing. Accompanied recitatives, reserved for the scenes of greatest pathos, bring the full tonal resources to masterly effect.

[22] GMB no. 258/259.

The overtures to the early operas were fashioned almost without exception after the orchestral church sonata in four movements. The so-called Neapolitan overture consisting of two fast movements and a slow, often transitional, middle part was completely dependent on continuo-homophony. Form and style of the Neapolitan overture were obviously derived from the concerto; we find here even the mannerism of the three-fold hammerstroke beginning and the tutti-solo contrast, for example in the overture to Scarlatti's oratorio *Sedecia*.[24] The single movements of Scarlatti's overtures are still undeveloped—they do not exceed about twenty measures [25]—and are hardly comparable in scope to a concerto movement.

The first movement of the overture gained its formal independence only after 1720 with the rise of the younger generation of Neapolitan composers in whose hands continuo-homophony was slowly transformed to the homophony of the early classic style. It comprised two pupils of Provenzale: Sarro and Fago, and in addition the brilliant Porpora, Feo, Leo (a pupil of Fago), Vinci, and the Italianized German Hasse (a pupil of Scarlatti). The da-capo aria assumed in the works of these composers the dimensions of a vocal sonata or concerto and the excessive use of coloratura and cadenzas indicated that the opera had become the absolute domain of the castrato. With Hasse the transition to the early classic style was an accomplished fact.

The development of the late Venetian opera closely paralleled that of the Neapolitan school. Except for its propensity for lavish orchestrations the Venetian opera did not differ stylistically from the Neapolitan. The *opera seria* was international in scope and style and its repertory triumphed not only in Venice, Rome, and Naples, but also in the European centers of opera, notably Vienna, Dresden, and London. The influence of the concerto style on the overture and the ritornello of the aria was as obvious in the Venetian school as in the Neapolitan. The da-capo aria assumed its vastest dimensions in the grand da-capo form in which the first and main part was subdivided into two units both consisting of a ritornello and a long vocal section. The first of these modulated to the dominant while the second expanded the main idea of the aria and reversed the modulation. This aria became the vehicle of vocal *bravura* which vied with the instrumental "divisions" of the concerto. We know from the testimony of Agricola that the stupendous cadenzas, sung without accompaniment at the end of each part of the da-capo aria, originated after 1710, that is shortly

---

[24] Botstiber, *Geschichte der Ouvertüre*, Ex. 7.
[25] Haas B, 207; HAM no. 259.

after the solo concerto had been established. The trend toward homophony came to the fore in the arias *all'unisono* in which the violins or even the entire orchestra accompanied the voice in unison and octaves throughout. Even the instrumental idioms of the concerto style were forced on the voice. The arias of the time abound with rapidly repeated notes, sweeping sequential scale patterns, extreme skips, and triadic motives which until the late days of the opera have remained the earmark of the *aria di bravura*.

The composers active in the international centers of the Venetian school are so numerous that only a selective list of names can be given here. It includes Carlo Pollaroli and his son Antonio, the prolific, but often dull, Caldara and the theorboe-player Conti (both active in Vienna), Agostino Steffani and Torri [26] (both brilliant composers, active mainly in Munich), Lotti (a pupil of Legrenzi) whose operas were performed all over Europe, Albinoni, Vivaldi, Pistocchi (the founder of an influential school of singing in Bologna), Perti (likewise in Bologna), Ariosti, the theorist and composer Gasparini, and the brothers Marc-Antonio and Giovanni Battista Bononcini (the sons of Giovanni Maria).[27] Giovanni Battista Bononcini (1670–c. 1748) was so highly regarded for the captivating lyricism of his melodious operas that he could become the serious rival of Handel in London.

The formal establishment of the *opera buffa* cannot be dissociated from that of the *opera seria*. Although comic scenes were a traditional feature of Italian opera in the seventeenth century, the *opera buffa* did not become a form in its own right before the early eighteenth century. Only with the relegation of the comic elements from the *opera seria* to the burlesque intermezzo, played between its three acts, was the contrast between the two types recognized in principle. The rising *opera buffa* precipitated important social changes (see Chapter XII) and gained momentum by its conscious opposition to the stilted conventions of the *opera seria*.

Unlike the *vaudeville* and the ballad opera which were based essentially on traditional music, the *opera buffa* belonged to art music. Consisting of arias and recitatives, it was composed in a deliberately popular tone that matched perfectly the stereotyped characters of the *commedia dell'arte*

[26] For Steffani see Chapter IX; DTB 6:2, 11:2, and 12:2; for Torri DTB 19/20.
[27] The three Bononcinis have created a good deal of confusion in modern publications. See note 33, and Parisotti, *Anthology of Italian Song*. In the latter publication the ascription of an aria to Giovanni Maria Bononcini must be changed on stylistic grounds to Giovanni Battista, or possibly his brother. See HAM no. 262.

which populated its librettos. It was in the *opera buffa* that the *style galant* made its first inroads on the baroque style. With complete disregard for polyphony the continuo-homophony was reduced to a plain homophony and its typical harmonic periods. Brief and repetitive phrases formalized in melodic clichés such as the harmonically static feminine cadence with an anticipatory triplet, characteristic of many *buffo* melodies; they even forced their way into the serious operas and oratorios of Pergolesi and Hasse. Drum basses merely dissembled the rhythmic motion that the *basso continuo* had previously actually provided. The rapid parlando effect which had already been employed by Landi became the main means of comic effect. The most important musical innovation of the *opera buffa* was the ensemble finale [28] in which the characters sang short snatches of phrases in quick alternation with drastic humor.

Neither Provenzale's *Schiavo* nor Scarlatti's two comic operas (*Dal male il Bene* and *Il Trionfo dell' Onore*) had yet abandoned the elevated style of the serious opera. The typical *buffo* style emerged first in *Patre Calienno* (1709) by the Neapolitan composer Orefice and in Vinci's masterly *Zite'n galera* (1722) which may be regarded as the first fully developed example of the *opera buffa*. With Pergolesi (1710–1736), the extremely gifted pupil of Durante and Feo, the *opera buffa* reached its first peak. His intermezzo *La Serva Padrona* (1733) owes its fame more to the sensation it made during the War of the Buffoons in Paris than to its refreshing musical qualities. They are in fact easily surpassed not only by Vinci's works but also by Pergolesi's own *Livietta e Tracollo* and the Neapolitan dialect comedy *Frate 'nnamorato* which contains an amusing parody of the conventional *aria di bravura*.

The Italian chamber cantata, also known as serenata, chamber duet or trio, represented by far the most valuable vocal music of the late baroque because it was written for a select audience of connoisseurs irrespective of popular success. It was strictly musician's music in which the composer was free to indulge in harmonic experiments and to test novel constructive methods at his heart's content. The chamber cantata had not changed formally since the middle baroque. It still presented in operatic manner a dramatic, purely lyrical, or pastoral scene, but its arias were now fully grown da-capo forms and its recitatives had assumed corresponding dimensions and had gained in harmonic depth. In the Italian "acàdemies," the

[28] See Dent, SIMG XII, 116, and Lorenz, *op. cit.* II, no. 42.

meeting place of connoisseurs and professional musicians, cantatas were often extemporized by the poet, immediately set to music by the composer and performed—a practice in which both Alessandro Scarlatti and Handel excelled. In the absence of the stage the cantata depended entirely on musical characterization and, as a result, achieved a musical intensity that the opera rarely attained.

The tremendous output of Scarlatti—more than 600 cantatas—makes him the leading composer of the form.[29] Only in his cantatas does the full range of his musicianship really become apparent. They are full of the most audacious harmonic progressions, especially the recitatives; his boundless imagination manifests itself in his superb melodic characterizations which have set the model for the last generation of baroque composers. He imbued his arias with the complex harmonies of the tonal idiom achieving startling, yet most convincing melodic progressions. The aria *Per un momento* (Ex. 76), taken from one of his unpublished cantatas,

Ex. 76. Alessandro Scarlatti: Aria from a chamber cantata.

illustrates not only the plastic realization of the idea of torment (see the coloratura on *tormentar*) but also the use of the stereotyped motto beginning. Scarlatti and Gasparini exchanged experimental cantatas written on the same text, of which *Andate o miei sospiri* is the best known example.[30] Scarlatti composed it twice, once *in idea humana* in his best operatic vein and a second time *in idea inhumana* in experimental fashion,

---

[29] ICMI 30, GMB no. 260, HAM no. 258.
[30] Dent, *Alessandro Scarlatti*, 140–43.

deliberately designed to confuse the performer by its remote modulation and bizarre accidentals which puzzle even a modern musician. Also *La Stravaganza* by Marcello [31] belongs to the group of studiously "extravagant" cantatas. Nearly all opera composers of the time wrote cantatas; it must suffice here to mention only those of Agostino Steffani, d'Astorga, Porpora, and Francesco Durante. Steffani is best known for his noble chamber duets [32] the smoothly finished counterpoint of which even Handel could only imitate but not surpass.

The Italian oratorio was completely under the spell of the late baroque opera. Serving as an opera substitute for the Lenten season it faithfully observed Zeno's opera reform. Only in the occasional use of chorus did the oratorio differ from the opera. The prominent oratorio composers whose works were performed at all European centers were Giovanni Bassani, Giovanni Battista Bononcini,[33] Ariosti, Marcello, Lotti, and the Neapolitans Alessandro Scarlatti (fourteen oratorios), Feo, Vinci, and Pergolesi.

However progressive in their operas and oratorios, these masters adhered in their church music to a dignified contrapuntal texture which gradually became the earmark of sacred music altogether. Lotti returned at times to the strict Palestrina style with doubling instruments, deploying the old contrapuntal artifices in calculated archaism. The masses of Caldara [34] and other Italian masters in Vienna were written in luxuriant counterpoint which did not lose its severity by the absorption of the concerto style and the aria with obbligato instruments. Even the strictly liturgical music displayed lavish orchestral settings but it made little use of the da-capo aria and recitative. Church music became the bulwark of a retrospective style, the sole domain where contrapuntal writing could retreat to, and here it survived as the "learned" or "strict" style of the classic era.

LATE BAROQUE AND ROCOCO STYLE IN FRANCE

ENSEMBLE AND CLAVECIN MUSIC

At the beginning of the late baroque period, instrumental ensemble music in France stood under the sign of the struggle between national self-preservation and submission to the Italian style. The clear recognition of

[31] Haas B, 212.
[32] DTB 6:2, GMB no. 242.
[33] See Schering, *Geschichte des Oratoriums*, App. (the composition is erroneously ascribed here to Giovanni Maria Bononcini).
[34] GMB no. 273.

the national differences in style gave French musicians solid ground to stand on and they tenaciously refused to surrender it. After the death of Lully they stripped his music of its heavy armor, broke his massive and unwieldy lines into small and flexible units, and repeated and varied them with innumerable *agréments*. The austere baroque style disintegrated to the intricately chiselled and ornamented rococo style which rose to its height during the Régence (1715–1723) and the subsequent reign of Louis XV.

Nothing can illustrate better the deeply ingrained conservatism of the French composers than the fact that their reluctance to take over the Italian concerto style even surpassed that of the Italians to adopt the French overture. Instrumental music, traditionally bound up in France with the dance and the opera, could hardly find an independent place. The concerto was very slow to gain a foothold in French music, and even when it did—more than a generation later than in Italy—it played only a secondary role. It is symptomatic that Brossard's *Dictionnaire de musique* (1703), one of the first musical dictionaries of the period, does not list the term *concert* at all, but only *concertato*, and only in the supplement is concerto explained as "approximately the same as *concertante*." It should be noted that the French term *concert* denoted not a concerto, but ensemble music in general; for the concerto proper the Italian spelling was retained, clearly indicating the Italian background of the form.

Characteristically enough, it was the Italian Mascitti who published the first concertos in Paris (1727). Only two important Frenchmen followed his model: Jean Aubert (d. 1753) and Jean Marie Leclair l'Aîné (1697–1764) whose concertos, the first French example of the kind, appeared in 1735 and 1737 respectively. Both composers were dependent on Vivaldi, as the *allegro* themes, notably those of Aubert clearly show. However, the delicately embroidered themes of the slow movements reveal the French penchant for the *air tendre*.

The trio and solo sonata was cultivated by two generations of composers of which the first began to compose in the late seventeenth and early eighteenth centuries. It comprised Marais, François Couperin, Jean Ferry Rebel (the member of a large dynasty of composers), Loeillet, and Duval. The celebrated gambist Marin Marais (d. 1728), a pupil of Lully, wrote one of the first *Pièces en trio* (1692) ever to be published in France. The characteristic titles show how closely the French instrumental music was associated with program music. His witty description of a gall-stone operation in a solo sonata for gamba and continuo (see Lavignac E II: 3, 1776) represents probably the *non plus ultra* of the illustrative trends of the time. The playfully programmatic titles that abound in French instrumental music did not always designate a concrete program but, as Couperin pointed out, often served merely the same function as a general marking like *tendrement*.

François Couperin le Grand (1668–1733), the famous clavecinist to the French court, has been extolled so exclusively for his harpsichord music that his important contribution to chamber music has been unduly minimized. His *Concerts Royaux*, quartet sonatas for violin, flute, oboe, and a continuo for bassoon and clavecin, were composed for the chamber concerts of the *Roi Soleil*. His other ensemble sonatas include *Les Nations, Les Goûts réunis,* and the *Apothéose de Lully*. All of them are works of the highest rank. As suggested by the title of the second collection Couperin strove for a union of the French and the Italian taste which would, in his opinion, bring about "the perfection of music."

The "United Tastes" contain a musical apotheosis of Corelli: *Le Parnasse* which bespeaks the high personal admiration of Couperin for the Italian master. It may seem strange that a composer whose keyboard works are the very essence of French style was the first to open the door to Italian music. He imitated Corelli's style with surprising self-effacement and even went so far as to pass off his first trio sonata as an Italian composition, admitting his authorship only after it had been favorably received. Certain movements of the *Parnasse, e.g.* "Corelli's arrival at Parnassus" and "The Thanks of Corelli," could well be mistaken for a work of Corelli. The final grand *sonade en trio* in four movements represents the "Peace at Parnassus." It begins, significantly, with a French overture—a token of the partial victory of French music—but the rest of the sonata is more Italian than French in style. Except for his church music Couperin has not written anything that can compare with the dignified and carefully wrought counterpoint of this sonata which seems to belie the thin texture of the rococo style. The *Apothéose de Lully,* Couperin's monument in honor of Lully, clearly discloses that the Florentine had by this time attained an almost legendary position in French music. In this work also Corelli makes an appearance, this time as the delegate of the muses who welcomes Lully among the exalted spirits. In a delightful contest between Italian and French music, far more elaborate than Lully's *Ballet de la Raillerie* (see p. 153), Corelli and Lully match forces and accompany each other in alternation. Here again we can see how profoundly Couperin had penetrated into the secrets of the Italian idiom.

The Belgian composer Loeillet (d. 1728), a little-known, but important master of chamber music, stood outside of the French tradition as his progressive style indicates. During his residence in London he came in contact with the Italian concerto style. His sonatas for flute, viola d'amore and other instruments carry the indelible stamp of the concerto style and also the ritornello form of certain movements bespeaks this influence. His music is noteworthy for the Handelian solidity of his themes, the fine workmanship of his counterpoint, and for Bachian touches in his harmony which distinguish also his harpsichord suites.[35]

The rococo style came to the fore in the chamber music of the second generation: Anet (a pupil of Corelli), Senaillé (a pupil of Tommaso Vitali), Aubert, Dieupart, Rameau, Leclair, Corrette, and the flutists La Barre, Blavet, Boismortier and Hotteterre. Although tinged with the Italian style their music upholds the French tradition, as can be seen in the graceful curves of their rococo melodies. Aubert very nearly succumbed to the influence of Corelli, but in the preface to his *Concerts de Symphonies* he pointed out that the Italian style was not everybody's taste, especially not "that of the ladies whose judgment has always determined the pleasures of the nation." Aubert's numerous "concerts" are actually delicate trio sonatas in suite form, composed in the "neatness and nice simplicity of the French taste." It is very characteristic of his French attitude that he faithfully retained in his sonatas the *agréments* of vocal music. We see here the exact opposite of the Italian instrumentalization of the vocal idiom.

Dieupart and Rameau also contributed to chamber music with clavecin suites arranged *en concert* as ensemble sonatas. Rameau included in his *Pièces de clavecin en concerts* (1741) arrangements of famous harpsichord pieces like *La Poule* which recalls the programmatic canzonas of Poglietti, and *L'Enharmonique*, noteworthy for its harmonic audacities. Boismortier made a name for himself by his *galanteries* for flute or even such instruments as the bagpipe and the hurdy-gurdy the vogue for which was due to the rococo period's enthusiasm for rustic naïveté.

The greatest French master of the solo and trio sonata, Jean Marie Leclair (a pupil of Somis), actually achieved the fusion of the French and Italian style of which Couperin had only dreamed. His sonatas (five books, 1723 ff.) [36] contain remarkably few programmatic hints—quite exceptional for a French composer—and adopt Italian tempo markings. Leclair ad-

---

[35] See the sonatas ed. by Béon (Lemoine), and the harpsichord suite in *c* in *Monumenta Musicae Belgicae* I, and Oesterle, *Early Keyboard Music* I, 181.
[36] Eitner PAM, 27; HAM no. 278.

hered to the late baroque sonata form with rudimentary recapitulation of a single theme and occasionally tied the movements together by means of similar thematic material. His advanced violinistic technique calls for multiple stops in high positions, perfect control of the bow, left-hand tremolo, and even such eccentricities as the use of the thumb for low triple stops. Leclair's music is distinguished for the sustaining power of its long sequential phrases, the graceful tenderness of its melodies, its rhythmic subtlety, and the fiery pathos of its harmonies. Leclair fused the outstanding virtues of the two national styles into an imaginative style of his own, unmatched either in French or in Italian music.

The French school of clavecinists culminated in the works of François Couperin, justly called "the Great." The four books of *Pièces de clavecin* (1713-30) consist of suites or *ordres* (as the author called them) the length of which varied from a few to as many as twenty compositions. The flexible contents of the suites corresponds to their flexible length. Although Couperin continued to utilize traditional dance patterns, he abandoned dance titles and replaced them by fanciful designations or names of allegorical or real persons that the music allegedly portrayed. Such collections of aristocratic and intimate genre miniatures and highly stylized dances scarcely deserved the name *ordre,* particularly since they were only superficially held together by one key. Even the unity of key was observed laxly enough to allow of the opposite mode and relative keys. Many of the character portraits formed part of a semi-operatic program, such as the various "acts" of *Les Fastes de la grande Ménestrandise* or *Les Folies Françaises ou les Dominos.* Only exceptionally did Couperin transfer the French opera overture to the clavecin as D'Anglebert had done before him.

That Couperin was fully conscious of the possibilities inherent in the harpsichord idiom is convincingly proved by his *L'Art de toucher le clavecin* (1716) in which he advocated a modernized and rational fingering. Although not the first method of keyboard playing it was the most authoritative book on the subject. The *style brisé* of the lute or, in Couperin's terminology, *les parties lutées* formed by now an integral part of the harpsichord idiom. The two manuals of the instrument became an absolute essential for his music. Couperin criticized the excessive use of arpeggiated figures in the left hand, which were in his opinion characteristic of the Italian sonata rather than of French music. Symptomatically, he put the greatest emphasis on the correct realization of the symbols for the *agré-*

ments. The significance of the ornaments can justly be appraised only in connection with his musical style in which late baroque and rococo traits are inseparably joined together.

In his clavecin miniatures he dismantled the expansive sequences of the severe baroque style and reduced them to short repetitive phrases typical of the early rococo style. These phrases, always overlaid with the gilt of an intricate ornamentation, were often repeated for color effect in different registers of the instrument. In Couperin's art intimate elaboration of detail mattered more than the great outline. He wisely limited himself to the small forms most suitable for his genius, and though some of them stemmed from the opera, notably the *air tendre* or *gracieux,* he thoroughly instrumentalized them by means of his ornamentation. The most extended form was the *rondeau.* This favorite French form gained length by the repetition of the refrain rather than by internal extension. *Les bergeries,* a fine example of the form from the sixth *ordre,* found its way even into the *Clavierbüchlein* of Anna Magdalena Bach. His remarkably vigorous passacaglia, one of his most weighty clavecin pieces, also adopts the *rondeau* form. This piece clearly demonstrates that he did not yet sacrifice solidity of harmony and texture to the scintillating sonorities of the instrument.

The clavecinists and organists after Couperin hardly surpassed his decorative imagination; only the wider scope of their harmonies disclosed that tonality finally was victorious also in French music. We meet here with a number of superior masters: [37] Marchand, well-known through the anecdote of his projected meeting with Bach; Clérambault, a pupil of Raison; Dieupart whose works Bach found worth his while to copy; the Belgian masters Fiocco and Boutmy,[38] both strongly indebted to Couperin; D'Agincourt, noteworthy for his pronounced interest in complex harmonic progressions; Dandrieu, the author of an important treatise on accompaniment; Daquin, a pupil of Marchand, famous for his *rondeau Le Coucou;* and finally Rameau.

The three books of *Pièces de Clavecin* by Jean-Philippe Rameau (1683–1764) sum up the entire development of clavecin technique in France. In the prefaces Rameau codified the fingering and the *agréments* in definitive form. It is hardly surprising that the author of the *Traité de l'harmonie* was preoccupied with harmony, as his calculated modulations and modestly chromatic experiments show. He subordinated his melodic invention to the invention of harmonic progressions which, elaborately figurated by precise

[37] Farrenc, *Trésor,* TAM X–XII, and numerous recent editions.
[38] *Monumenta Musicae Belgicae* III and V.

rhythmic motives, bestowed on his clavecin pieces a hitherto unknown consistency, if not uniformity, of structure. In his contention that melody was not more than an outgrowth of harmony Rameau merely rationalized the virtues and defects of his own talent, which was inspired by harmony and rhythm rather than melody.

Following the path of D'Anglebert he expanded the keyboard technique by quasi-orchestral and percussive *batteries,* extreme skips, crossing of the hands, and measured tremolos. Although these innovations closely parallel those of Domenico Scarlatti both composers arrived at them independently. Moreover, the fact that they used them in entirely different manner strikingly illustrates the conspicuous contrast between the Italian and the French conception of instrumental music: Scarlatti applied them to the absolute music of his sonatas, Rameau made them subservient to coloristic and illustrative purposes. Deeply affected by French aesthetics, Rameau conceived instrumental music primarily in terms of the opera, the dance, and the representation of non-musical objects.

OPERA AND CANTATA IN FRANCE

The domineering position which vocal music traditionally held in France could only be weakened, not upset in the late baroque period. Characteristically, the opera resisted the Italian influence even more stubbornly than instrumental music. The vocal idiom did not become as thoroughly instrumentalized as it did in Italy. The Italian concerto style was gradually recognized, but only as one possible style which, for the sake of variety, was used side by side with the traditional French one.

The interim period between Lully and Rameau saw the disintegration of the towering edifice that Lully had built. Lully's operas still dominated the stage, but it is significant that they were modernized in performance by means of profuse ornaments that forcibly softened the stiff lines to a more flexible rococo style. The leading composers of the interim: Colasse, Desmarets, Campra, and Destouches [39] could not rid themselves of Lully's overwhelming influence but they substituted for his frigid melodies short-breathed airs in rococo style which lacked dramatic significance. Only Marais (*Alcyone,* 1706) and Montéclair (*Jephté,* 1732) achieved a dramatic grandeur worthy of their predecessor. The incidental music (recitatives and choruses) to Racine's tragedies by Moreau (1656-1733), the

---

[39] Reprinted in COF.

teacher of Dandrieu, Clérambault, and Montéclair, should also be mentioned here.

André Campra (1660–1744), the most successful opera composer before Rameau captivated his audiences by his extraordinary lyrical talent. His graceful airs were ill suited for his ponderous *tragédies lyriques;* significantly, he earned his greatest fame with his opera-ballets *L'Europe galante* (1698) and *Les Fêtes Vénitiennes* (1710).[40] The opera-ballets reduced the opera to rococo dimensions and so laxly observed the demands of dramatic unity that the whole became only a pretext for a succession of incoherent danced and sung divertissements. Here was the place where Campra could show off with his tunes. One of his popular airs from the *Fêtes* (Ex. 77) almost literally anticipates the pseudo-folksong *Si des galans*

Ex. 77. Campra: Air from *Les Fêtes Venitiennes.*

from the *Devin de Village* by Rousseau (compare also Ex. 38). It is one of the many examples that prove the affinity between the rococo and the "return-to-nature" movement.

With all his French features Campra was also thoroughly familiar with the concerto style which he slavishly imitated in arias that were Italian not only in style but even in their texts (*Fêtes,* IV, 2).[41] Vividly contrasting with his French recitatives they bore all the traits of the Italian opera: extended da-capo form, motto beginning, and fiery instrumental coloraturas. These imitations of Italian arias were known in France by the name of *ariette.* It is most confusing that the brief *air tendre* in rondo form was called "air" while the full-fledged da-capo aria was given the diminutive term. However illogical, the distinction at least implies how clearly the French perceived the national differences in style.

The French opera entered its most glorious phase with Rameau whose operas represent one of the highest achievements of French music altogether. Deeply stirred by the performance of Montéclair's *Jephté* Rameau came later to the stage than perhaps any other opera composer. The fact

[40] Reprinted in COF.

[41] Campra was of Italian extraction which may account for his facile imitation of the Italian style.

that he did not begin to compose operas before he was fifty explains why his first opera, *Hippolyte et Aricie,* was a fully mature work and why his operas on the whole show a regressive rather than progressive development. His first opera period (1733-39) comprises his most significant works, notably the *tragédies lyriques Hippolyte et Aricie* (1733), *Castor et Pollux* (1737), *Dardanus* (1739), and the opera-ballet *Les Indes Galantes* (1735). The second opera period began with Rameau's appointment to the court of Louis XV (1745). In this period he turned to a less demanding and entertaining rococo style that seems shallow in comparison with his first operas.

Rameau composed *Hippolyte* with infinite care and patience. Its performance in the house of La Pouplinière, a gentleman composer influential for the development of symphonic music, prompted a typically French reaction: it released the paper war between the Lullistes and Ramistes which came to an end only with the Buffoon War. By that time Rameau was recognized as the genius of French opera although the Lullistes had formerly denounced him as the destructive element in French music. Rameau was convinced that he followed the precepts of Lully much more closely than the Lullistes wanted to admit. With the perpetual metrical changes in his recitatives, dance airs, airs with doubled continuo, and choral or instrumental chaconnes he unquestionably upheld the tradition of Lully, but he was not, as he put it, "a servile copyist." He filled the formal shell of Lully's operas with his coloristic and harmonic imagination and realized scenes of overwhelming human pathos by turning the harmonic innovations of the late baroque to startling stage effects. The dramatic intensity of his music is due to the wide scope of his harmonies, the frequent use of the diminished-seventh chord (denounced by the Lullistes as Italian), the chord of the added sixth, and the extreme range of his modulations which encompassed keys with five or more accidentals, generally avoided in his day. Unable to grasp the march of his harmony the contemporaries called Rameau "the distiller of baroque chords," a name that, aside from its derogatory implication, still remains valid today. His early operas do indeed contain more musician's music than any other opera of the period. His *tragédies lyriques* stand like erratic blocks isolated in a rococo surrounding.

In the dance air and the Italian *ariette,* sometimes also designated as *air gracieux* (*Dardanus,* Prologue), the harmonic rhythm moves at a relatively slow pace. The other airs and the recitatives, however, are steeped in the rich idiom of tonality. The prelude to *Puissant maître* from *Hip-*

polyte (Ex. 78) unfolds over the well-defined and steady harmonies of the bass a restlessly shifting melodic line that produces a great number of iridescent harmonies and a very fast harmonic rhythm, not shared by the underlying bass. The double-barrelled effect of his harmonic style parallels

Ex. 78. Rameau: Excerpt from *Hippolyte.*

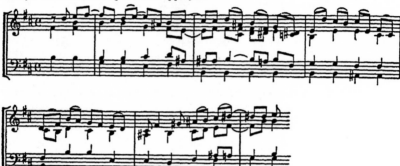

his theoretical distinction between the fundamental bass and the actually realized harmony. It reveals the dependence of the melody on harmony and a sparseness of counterpoint that characterizes all his music. It was this harmonic richness that Campra had in mind when he admiringly exclaimed that the music of *Hippolyte* was enough for ten operas.

True to the French operatic tradition the airs stand very close to the arioso, so close in fact that according to an anecdote of the time an Italian sat through an entire opera waiting in vain for the beginning of the first aria. Unforgettable beginnings like that of *Tristes apprêts* from *Castor et Pollux* (I, 3) show Rameau's rational economy of means, his sober and harmonically conceived melody, and his cautious handling of counterpoint.

Also his choral or solo ensembles emphasize chordal effects at the expense of counterpoint. This point is best illustrated by the awe-inspiring trio of the Fatal Sisters from *Hippolyte* (II, 5); far surpassing a similar trio in Lully's *Isis,* it contains enharmonic modulations that presented, like Wagner's *Tristan,* unsurmountable difficulties at the time. His ensemble scenes assume at times gigantic proportions. The dream sequence in *Dardanus* (IV), for example, is designed on so large a scale for an ensemble of chorus, soloists, and orchestra that the ensemble scenes of Lully seem diminutive in comparison.

With his superb coloristic sense Rameau managed the orchestration more adroitly than any of his contemporaries. The important function of the instruments comes to light not only in his accompanied recitatives but particularly in the numerous programmatic symphonies and overtures of the operas. Following the path of his predecessors, especially that of Campra, Rameau gradually abandoned the Lullian form and designed his overtures as grand landscapes or as representations of elemental events (sea storms, earthquakes). These overtures lead into the opera without a break. His orchestration standing at the threshold of the modern coloristic technique calls for woodwinds, horns, and even the modern clarinets. Sustained chords of the wind instruments coupled with sweeping scale passages of the strings conjure up tone pictures of unwonted realism. Singers and critics alike objected to the overbearing role of the instruments and Rousseau ridiculed it in the bon mot that in Rameau's operas the voice formed merely "the accompaniment of the accompaniment." But it is precisely the simultaneous use of extremely rhythmic instrumental patterns and sustained vocal sections that accounts for his most powerful musico-dramatic effects.

Even before the establishment of the *opera buffa* in Italy the French developed a comic counterpart to the *tragédie lyrique* in the *vaudeville* comedy. Its development began with the Italian comedians at the time of Lully who performed low Scaramouche comedies with inserted Italian and French songs. Because of their political aggressiveness the Italian troupes were expelled from Paris in 1697, but their tradition was continued by French comedians who supplied civil songs, operatic airs, and *brunettes* with topical and satirical words. The music of these *vaudevilles* appeared in Gherardi's *Théâtre Italien* (1694 ff.), the numerous *brunettes* collections of Ballard (1703 ff.), and *La Clef des Chansonniers* (1717). The French comedians, too, were severely restricted by political censorship, but they cleverly outwitted the censor.

Unlike the *opera buffa* the *vaudeville* comedy had spoken dialogue and its music consisted of traditional material borrowed indiscriminately from respectable and lowly sources. After 1715 the *vaudeville* became also known as *opéra comique*—a term that had originally a parodistic connotation since it applied to parodies of serious operas. Lesage's *Télémaque* (1715),[42] for example, parodies the opera of the same name by Destouches. The extensive repertory of the *vaudeville* comedy was published under the significant title *Le Théâtre de la Foire ou L'opéra comique* by Lesage and Dorneval (1722). The *vaudeville* comedy which set the precedent to the ballad opera in England, entered a new phase with the poet Favart. In his time specially

[42] Ed. by Calmus, *Zwei Opernburlesken der Rokokozeit.*

composed music gradually superseded borrowed tunes. However, the rise of the *opéra comique* in the modern sense belongs to the early classic period.

It is characteristic that France never developed an important song literature apart from the opera. The only forms of vocal music that continued to flourish beside the omnipotent opera were the cantata and the motet. The cantata was cultivated by Morin, Campra, Montéclair, Boismortier, Rameau, and, above all, by Clérambault (d. 1749). They all betray a strong Italian influence which is frankly admitted in Montéclair's *Cantates françaises et italiennes.* Clérambault's five books of cantatas (1710 ff.) represent the most valuable French contribution to the cantata. Clérambault favored mythological subjects which he set to music in masterpieces like *Orphée, Héro et Léandre,* and *Pigmalion.* Like Campra he deliberately juxtaposed recitatives in French style with arias in Italian style. This contrast comes clearly to light in the excerpt from *Pigmalion* (Ex. 79) in which

Ex. 79. Clérambault: Recitative and Air from *Pigmalion.*

the *simphonie* to the *air de mouvement* bears witness to Clérambault's mastery of the concerto style.

Hardly any of the French composers mentioned in this chapter neglected church music, but none of them made it his specialty. As the only exception Lalande (d. 1726) must be mentioned, whose requiem, motets, and lessons with orchestral accompaniment were recognized at the time as exemplary. Written in luxuriant counterpoint they afford the most conservative aspect of the period. It is noteworthy that even in sacred music the vocal lines were overcharged with rococo ornaments. Couperin's carefully wrought *Leçons de Ténèbres*[43] (Lessons for Holy Week) give a good idea of the extremely florid, yet dignified, part-writing in French church music.

[43] Music Press edition.

CHAPTER EIGHT

Fusion of National Styles: Bach

THE STATE OF INSTRUMENTAL MUSIC IN GERMANY
BEFORE BACH

THE FATE of late baroque music hung in the balance between the Italian and the French style, recognized by theorists and composers alike as the two poles of late baroque music. The harmonic resources of tonality, the concerto style in instrumental and vocal music, and the concerto and sonata forms of "absolute" music passed as the characteristics of the Italian style; the coloristic and programmatic trends in instrumental music, the orchestral discipline, overture and dance suite, and the highly florid ornamentation of the melody passed as the characteristics of the French style. The German style, universally recognized as the third in the group of national styles, was characterized by its marked proclivity for a solid harmonic and contrapuntal texture. Serving as the mediator between the two poles it brought the reconciliation of the opposed Italian and French techniques in a higher unity. The music that finally culminated in Bach attained its universality and distinction through the deliberate fusion of national styles.

Both the French and the Italian style exerted a decisive influence on the formation of late baroque style in Germany. The essential factors of the former were the orchestral innovations of Lully and the keyboard technique of Couperin, those of the latter the concerto style in instrumental music and the instrumentalized bel canto of the opera. The influence of Lully comes most strongly to light in the orchestral suites of three composers who were all pupils of the Florentine: Cousser, the Austrian Georg Muffat (d. 1704), and Johann Fischer (d. 1721). Cousser whose collection bears the symptomatic title *Composition de Musique suivant la méthode Françoise* (1682 ff.) [1] enriched the German suite by the French overture which since

---

[1] One overture reprinted in *Nagels Musikarchiv*.

his day was frequently used as a pompous introduction to the subsequent chain of dances. Muffat's *Florilegium* (I, 1695; II, 1698) [2] which contains an illuminating discourse about the difference between the French and German style of violin playing, and Johann Fischer's *Tafelmusik* (1702) [3] are likewise obligated to Lully. The *Journal de Printemps* (1695) [4] by Ferdinand Fischer must be regarded as one of the finest documents of German Lullianism. This Fischer (not to be confused with Lully's *notiste* Johann Fischer) commanded great melodic inventiveness and solid workmanship—see for example the overture and chaconne of his suite in *g*—that put such minor composers as Aufschnaiter, Schmicorer [5] and Mayr [6] to shame. The orchestra suite was also cultivated by Erlebach,[7] Philipp Krieger (a pupil of Rosenmüller and Pasquini), Fasch (a pupil of Kuhnau and Graupner), and Telemann. Philipp Krieger wrote his delightful suites *Lustige Feldmusik* [8] for wind ensembles in the vein of Pezel. Telemann's *Musique de Table* [9] displays the graceful French style more pronouncedly than do the ponderous overtures of Fasch whose contrapuntal style was highly esteemed by Bach. The Austrian Fux showed in the weighty fugues of his orchestral music [10] that his contrapuntal proficiency was not merely theoretical paper knowledge. Like all composers of the south he kept always close to Italian rather than French style.

The Italian concerto, especially the solo concerto, became known in Germany through the works of Vivaldi which were imitated by Heinichen, Pisendel, Graupner, Fasch, Hurlebusch, and Telemann.[11] These concertos represent the most progressive music of the Bach period in which the incipient disintegration of baroque style is at times unmistakable.

The role of Lully as an exemplar in the field of orchestral music was paralleled by that of Corelli in the field of chamber music. To the German composers the two national styles were not alternatives that precluded one another, as is convincingly shown by Georg Muffat who studied first with Lully and then with Corelli. Muffat was the first German to follow Corelli

[2] DTOe I:2 (vol. 2) and II:2 (vol. 4).
[3] Ed. by Engel, Bärenreiter.
[4] DDT 10.
[5] *ibid.*
[6] See Ulrich, *Die Pythagorischen Schmids-Füncklein*, in SIMG IX, 75.
[7] Two overtures in *Organum*.
[8] ER XIV, GMB no. 236 b; see also *Organum*.
[9] *Chamber Suites* (Longmans), 318; see also Schering, *Perlen alter Kammermusik*.
[10] DTOe IX:2 (vol. 19); see also the *Concentus musico-instrumentalis* in DTOe XXIII:2 (vol. 47).
[11] DDT 29/30.

in the field of the trio sonata. In his *Armonico tributo* (1682) [12] he paid a "harmonic tribute" to his second teacher, whom he imitated not only in this sonata collection but also in his valuable, if conservative, concerti grossi (1701).[13] The *Hortus musicus* (1687) [14] by the Hamburg organist Jan Reinken must also be mentioned here, from which Bach transcribed two sonatas for the keyboard. In his two sets of trio sonatas (1696) [15] Buxtehude turned the concise movements of the Corelli type into profound contrapuntal studies, drawing frequently on ground basses which appear at times even in rhythmic transformation. One of his chaconnes on a descending fourth is marked *concitato* (II, 2) which almost symbolizes the unruly imagination of the composer and also indicates the Italian background of his style. The remarkably rhapsodic interludes which disclose strong affinity to his organ toccatas have no equal in the music of his time. Pachelbel's trio sonatas call for the violin *scordatura*. While Telemann preferred to write his innumerable sonatas [16] in a facile French style, Fux, Fasch,[17] and Graupner adhered to a fugal, if not actually canonic, style which thoroughly Germanized the Italian counterpoint of Corelli. It is significant that Bach was especially fond of the works of Graupner, a pupil of Kuhnau and one of the best German composers of the Bach period.

In the field of orchestra and chamber music the Germans faithfully followed the trends of Italian and French music; while they were imitators they were not eclectics since they Germanized the forms they took over and assimilated them into the rich harmonic and contrapuntal idiom of the German style. However, in the field of keyboard music, especially organ music, they held the leading position. In Germany the organ was afforded the highest rank in the hierarchy of instruments. This predilection for keyed instruments was a natural outgrowth of the contrapuntal bent in German music which forced even the violin, an instrument hardly suited for polyphonic playing, into submission. The polyphonic style of violin playing remained throughout the period an essentially German characteristic.

With the impressive development of the school of German harpsichordists and organists from Froberger to Bach, the distinction between

[12] DTOe XI:2 (vol. 23).
[13] *ibid.*
[14] VNM 13.
[15] DDT 11.
[16] Reprints in *Nagels Musikarchiv, Collegium Musicum,* and *Perlen alter Kammermusik;* HAM no. 271.
[17] See *Nagels Musikarchiv* and *Collegium Musicum.*

the harpsichord and organ idioms crystallized mainly through the mediation of the French clavecinists, but it did not come to an absolutely final
separation, even as late as Bach. Although the harpsichord music was
oriented primarily toward France the organistic background of the German harpsichordists remained strong enough to give their music a decidedly
German flavor. The decisive stimuli for the development of the keyboard
sonata and suite came, as they had done so often before, from other media.
It was now the Italian sonata and the French overture that was transferred
to the keyboard. Johann Kuhnau (1660–1722), Bach's predecessor in Leipzig, was the first German composer to transfer the Italian church sonata to
the harpsichord, as can be seen in Part II of his *Clavierübung* (1689–92)
and even more clearly in the *Frische Clavierfrüchte* (1696).[18] The latter
collection consists of church sonatas in four or five movements in which
free-voiced keyboard style alternates with the contrapuntal texture of the
trio sonata. Some of the fugal movements can be considered as fully grown
fugues. With his *Biblische Historien* (1700) Kuhnau continued and expanded the French tradition of program music. These amusing sonatas
draw on all the instrumental forms from the dance to the chorale prelude.
Kuhnau's manner of introducing the chorale at widely spaced intervals
sounds sometimes surprisingly like Bach, for example in the sonata "The
Agonizing and Recuperated Hezekiah (Hiskia)," in which the chorale
appears twice, the second time in rhythmic transformation. The music
vividly "represents" various biblical incidents and in order to remove any
possible doubt about its "meaning" Kuhnau has added an elaborate and
informative preface which expounds the baroque conception of program
music.

The newly established keyboard sonata influenced the other forms,
notably the prelude. Its development can best be studied in the *Clavierübung* by Kuhnau, the suite collection *Musikalisches Blumenbüschlein* [19]
by Ferdinand Fischer, and Johann Krieger's *Anmutige Clavierübung*,[20]
a collection of ricercars, preludes, and fugues of which Handel was especially fond. Kuhnau's preludes elaborate one technical problem at a time
and are in this respect related to Domenico Scarlatti's sonatas. The preludes
of Fischer and Krieger, too, are not bound by the stereotyped forms of the
dance but freely unfold a pregnant harmonic or rhythmic idea. In these
works the ground was laid for the preludes of the Bach type.

The late baroque suite was known in Germany as *partie* or *partita*, a

[18] DDT 4. For the Hezekiah sonata quoted below see HAM no. 261.
[19] Ed. by Werra, 1901; compare HAM no. 248.
[20] DTB 18.

rather ambiguous term because it was used to denote not only suite, but also variation (the original meaning of the term). To add to the confusion the French term overture was universally adopted as synonymous with suite. We have seen in the preceding chapter that D'Anglebert and Couperin transferred the overture to the keyboard; Böhm and Johann Krieger were among the first to follow this example in Germany.

The list of suite composers includes Pachelbel (*Hexachordum Apollinis*),[21] Johann Krieger, Böhm,[22] Buxtehude,[23] Reinken,[24] Buttstedt,[25] Gottlieb Muffat (*Componimenti*),[26] Hurlebusch,[27] Telemann, and others. These composers paid their tribute to profusely embellished *à-la-mode* dances but at the same time did not neglect the traditional patterned variation. Both the French and the German aspects of the suite are clearly represented by Böhm, a composer noteworthy equally for his thorough command of the French *agréments* and of the resources of tonal harmony. Buxtehude's suites and variations, which have only recently been discovered, do not quite come up to the high level of his organ works. Arranged strictly according to the four main dance types: allemande, courante, saraband, gigue, which became the rule only in the late baroque suite, they contain a few *doubles* but none of the inserted dances which gave variety to the main types. The French influence in Buxtehude's harpsichord works is confirmed by the variations, one theme of which is based on Lully's famous *brunette* (see Ex. 43). On the other hand, the German background of the patterned variation is unmistakable. His *partite La Capricciosa* seem like a modest prefiguration of Bach's *Goldberg Variations*. We do not know whether or not Bach knew this work, but at any rate the key of both sets is the same, there are thirty-two variations, and—most important— Buxtehude's theme reappears as the tune *Kraut und Rüben* in Bach's final *quodlibet*.

The latest generation of harpsichord composers, notably Gottlieb (Theophil) Muffat, Telemann, and Mattheson, tended to merge forms that earlier composers had kept distinct. Gottlieb Muffat (the son of Georg and

---

[21] DTB 4:1; see also HAM no. 250.
[22] CE by Wolgast.
[23] Ed. by Bangert, 1944.
[24] VNM 14.
[25] He is said to have been the first (?) to adopt the term suite in his *Musikalische Vorrathskammer*, 1713.
[26] DTÖe III:3 (vol. 7), also *Handel Gesellschaft*, Suppl. 5; HAM no. 280. The collection contains a valuable preface discussing harpsichord playing and the execution of ornaments.
[27] VNM 32.

a pupil of Fux) introduced the sonata finale into the suite and thus prepared the ground for the fusion of suite and sonata in the classic period. The toccata-like recitatives of his *fantaisies* which sometimes take the place of the prelude bespeak a composer of great individuality. The facile Telemann showed his versatility in the three dozen *fantaisies* [28] in which he combined the French *galanterie* style with the Italian concerto style. Unlike Leclair, Telemann did not succeed in fusing the styles into a higher unity, and also his attempt to arrive at an extended cyclic form by means of dovetailed repeats remained an interesting, but isolated experiment.

The three leading composers of organ music: the Swedish-born Dietrich Buxtehude (1637–1707) in Lübeck, Johann Pachelbel (1653–1706) in Nuremberg, and Georg Böhm (1661–1733) in Lüneburg, were surrounded by a host of remarkable organists belonging to the north or central German school, notably Johann Christoph Bach, Nikolaus Bruhns (a pupil of Buxtehude), Buttstedt, Ferdinand Fischer, Johann Krieger, Kuhnau, Vincent Lübeck (a pupil of Buxtehude), Vetter (a pupil of Pachelbel), Gottfried Walther (a cousin of Bach), and Zachow (the teacher of Handel).[29] The Austrian school of Catholic organists: Georg Muffat (who had studied also with Pasquini), Murschhauser (a pupil of Kerll), Gottlieb Muffat, Richter, and Reutter stood apart from the German school. The Catholic liturgy called only for toccatas and versets such as can be found in Georg Muffat's important *Apparatus musico-organisticus* (1690) [30] and the works of his son Gottlieb Muffat.[31] The multipartite toccatas of Georg Muffat betray the growing influence of the church sonata.

Buxtehude [32] who was to take a decisive influence on the musical development of Bach endowed both the free forms of organ music (toccata, and fugue) and the *obbligo* forms (passacaglia, and organ chorale) with the fire of his impassioned individuality. His toccatas disclose in their harmonic ventures, their sweeping pedal solos, and their phantastically shaped melodic contours a composer of a restive and profoundly stirring imagination. His fugues are still imbedded in the rhapsodic flow of his toccatas and are frequently tied together through thematic transformation in the manner of

[28] Reprint *Veröffentlichungen, Musikbibliothek Paul Hirsch*, 4, also Broude Bros.
[29] See Straube, *Alte Meister des Orgelspiels* (two sets), *Choralvorspiele alter Meister*, and Dietrich, *Elf Orgelchoräle*, 1932.
[30] Ed. by de Lange, 1888, also *Liber Organi* V (Schott, 1933); HAM no. 240.
[31] DTOe XXIX:2 (vol. 58).
[32] Organ works ed. by Spitta, a more complete edition by Seiffert; HAM nos. 234 and 235.

the variation ricercar. The fugue themes frequently affect tone repetitions and sometimes outline tonal harmonies by means of diminished sevenths.

Pachelbel [33] transmitted the virtuoso style of keyboard playing that prevailed in the Austrian school to central Germany, and thus brought about the rapprochement between the Catholic and Protestant organists. His toccatas lack elaborate fugal sections and are built on monumental pedal points which support a dazzling display of virtuoso figuration in the two manuals. A less profound musician than Buxtehude, he was concerned with playfully ingenious rhythmic patterns rather than with stirring harmonies. That his harmonic idiom was markedly less absorbing than that of Buxtehude is shown in his ninety-four (!) magnificats for the organ. They are short-winded fughettas composed as functional music for the service. Like Johann Krieger, Pachelbel was still clearly dependent in his fugues on the transformation technique of the variation ricercar.

Pachelbel's music also heralds the coming of the "well-tempered" tuning which had in Werckmeister one of its most ardent advocates. One of his sets of suites calls for seventeen of the twenty-four keys theoretically available. Ferdinand Fischer brought the number up to nineteen in his *Ariadne Musica* (1715). This collection of preludes and fugues represents the most important document in the evolution of the temperament before Bach. It served as the direct model for the Well-Tempered Clavier, not only with regard to the order of keys, but sometimes even with regard to the fugue themes. [34] The title of the collection indicates that Fischer wanted to give the organist an "Ariadne thread" through the labyrinth of remote keys, rarely, if ever, adopted before his time.

Of the "bound" forms of organ music the organ chorale was closest to the hearts of the Protestant organists. Four types can be distinguished, all of which were ultimately perfected and transformed by Bach. The first type, the chorale partita or chorale variation, was obligated to the secular variation technique of the German suite. The fact that the chorale took the place ordinarily held by a secular aria or dance reveals the close interactions between the secular and sacred spheres in Protestant music. Böhm, Pachelbel (*Musikalische Sterbensgedanken*), and Buxtehude, all wrote chorale partitas, and Buxtehude even went so far as to present the chorale in form of a variation suite in which the chorale melody appeared successively as allemande, courante, saraband, and gigue, treated each time

---

[33] DTOe VIII:2 (vol. 17), DTB 2:1, 4:1; HAM no. 251.
[34] GMB no. 265. Bach borrowed the theme of this fugue for his fugue in *E* in the Well-Tempered Clavier; compare also HAM no. 247.

in the strictly patterned figuration of the German tradition. Böhm's contribution to the partita was that he furnished the chorale with a multitude of French *agréments* with which he was more familiar than any other German organist; however he disciplined them in typically German fashion by the use of rigid ground basses. Also Johann Krieger, Johann Bernhard Bach, Buttstedt, and Gottfried Walther contributed to the chorale partita.

The second type, the chorale fantasy, flourished especially in the north German school (Buxtehude, Lübeck, Bruhns, and Reinken). After Scheidt it had become a large rhapsodic composition of virtuoso character. Buxtehude's visionary fantasies stand very close to the toccata and introduce only fragments of the chorale melody that emerge and disappear amidst the turbulent activity of the other parts. Reinken stressed in his excessively long fantasies the virtuoso attitude, notably in the use of double pedal which bespeak at the same time the German predilection for polyphony.

The third type, the chorale fugue, was at home in the central German school and had its main representatives in Johann Christoph Bach, Pachelbel, and Zachow. Here the initial phrase of the chorale served as the theme of a fugue, after which the entire melody was either introduced in *cantus firmus* fashion (a practice most characteristic for Pachelbel) or else presented phrase by phrase in a chain of fughettas. This type, obviously derived from the chorale motet, assumed in the hands of Pachelbel a thoroughly instrumental character. Gottfried Walther endowed it with his strong late-baroque harmonies and created the only examples of the type that can be compared with those of Bach. Not unjustly did Mattheson praise Walther as "a second Pachelbel, if not the first in art."

The fourth type, the chorale prelude, served in the liturgy as the instrumental introduction for the congregational chorale singing. While the first three types are often loosely referred to as chorale preludes, the fourth type must be recognized as the chorale prelude proper. It served the liturgical function best because it stated the melody in songlike manner, usually in the soprano so that it could be easily heard and remembered. Related in its technique to the chorale partita the chorale prelude can be regarded as an extension of a single chorale variation. The melody in either plain or ornamented form was set in figurative harmony or in contrapuntal fashion and the other parts moved against it with independent rhythms and motives. Each line of the chorale was usually introduced by a short, often anticipatory, imitation of the other voices. Buxtehude and Pachelbel, the first important masters of the chorale prelude proper, laid the ground for the future development of the form with Bach. Buxtehude's preludes are of particular interest because they give a highly personal interpretation of the chorale—a trend that Bach led to consummation. Walther evolved distinctive melodic patterns in his preludes that served as a consistently running counterpoint to the melody.

THE STATE OF PROTESTANT CHURCH MUSIC BEFORE BACH

The late baroque period of Protestant church music may be said to begin with the emergence of a new form, the church cantata, which quickly assumed the leading role in vocal music. The motet increasingly lost ground as an independent form and survived only on the periphery in music for special occasions, weddings, funerals, etc. In the cantata two traditions merged that had existed side by side in the middle baroque: the dramatic *concertato* of the Schütz tradition and the chorale *concertato* of the Weckmann-Tunder tradition. What had formerly been known as dialogue, *concertato, symphonia sacra,* or simply motet (with instrumental accompaniment) was assimilated into the cantata, a term coined by the Hamburg pastor Neumeister, a staunch orthodox and Pietist hater. In his cycles of cantata texts (1700 ff.) he shifted the emphasis from the biblical words to their poetic, sententious, or edifying interpretation. Whereas the *concertato* was based essentially on scriptural words the reform cantata consisted of freely composed paraphrases that either replaced the scriptural text or served as poetic insertions. These paraphrases have been improperly called "madrigalian." Actually, however, they have nothing to do with madrigal poetry because they were admittedly modeled after the forms of the Italian opera and the secular cantata which gave the church cantata its name. Neumeister cast his devout contemplations in form of recitative and aria, each of which was based on a single affection. He described his reform, significantly, with the words: "In short, a cantata looks like a piece from an opera, composed of *stylo recitativo* and arias."

The creation of the church cantata after the most secular of all secular models naturally aroused the opposition of the Pietists. The clamor against "operatic" church music did not subside until the end of the baroque period. For the Pietists the cantata meant an abominable secularization, the ultimate desecration of sacred music. For the orthodox Lutherans it meant conversely the consecration of secular music since they did not conceive the sacred and secular spheres as opposed. This attitude explains why church music in the modern form flourished only in centers of orthodoxy.

As the reform movement in church music did not begin before 1700 it is clear that the composers of the generation before Bach were either not yet affected by it, or came to it only very late. Johann Christoph Bach, the uncle of Johann Sebastian, entitled his vocal compositions still lamento or arioso rather than cantata. His dramatic arioso *Ach dass ich Wassers genug hätte* is thoroughly steeped in the tradition of Schütz's plastic recitative and fully justifies the epithet "the great and expressive composer" that the chronicle of the Bach family bestowed upon him. The "cantatas" of Buxtehude, the visionary power of which exerted so deep an impression on Bach, still belong to the older *concertato* type.[35] They contain no recitatives or dacapo arias, but remarkable accompanied ariosi which disclose Buxtehude's subjective fervor. In the monumental cantata *Wachet auf* he utilizes the chorale text, but almost completely disregards the melody; however in *Gott hilf mir* he "presents" the chorale *Durch Adams Fall* as *cantus firmus* in instrumental *unisono* against which the chorus "interprets" the text in Bachian fashion. This differentiation between chorale and figurative accompaniment was suggested by the techniques of the organ chorale. In his brilliant choral writing Buxtehude was obligated to Carissimi whose influence is especially noticeable in the Latin cantatas. In other cantatas he made use of strophic variation for solo or chorus, and of ground basses. His celebrated *Abendmusiken* composed for the Christmas season, consist of allegorical dialogues of which only very few have come down to us. In contrast with the predominantly lyrical, if not subjective, cantatas they are dramatic compositions of an oratorical nature.

Outstanding cantata composers besides Buxtehude were Böhm, Pachelbel, Philipp Krieger, Kuhnau, and Zachow and, among the direct contemporaries of Bach, Graupner and Telemann. Nearly all of these cultivated the cantata *per omnes versus* in which the various stanzas of the chorale appeared as a series of vocal variations. The cantatas of Böhm and Pachelbel [36] are conceived either as *concertato* or as chorale variation. That Philipp Krieger [37] was one of the first composers to adopt the reform cantata is not surprising because his operas had prepared him for the forms that he applied to the cantata. In his works Italian influence is particularly strong. Kuhnau [38] and Zachow [39] more nearly approach the cantata of the Bach type than any of their contemporaries. Kuhnau began his career with works in *concertato* style, but in his later years the Thomas cantor wrote reform

---

[35] DDT 14, see also CE.
[36] DTB 6:1.
[37] DDT 53/54 and DTB 6:1. It should be noted that in the latter volume the solo cantata *Wie bist Du* is erroneously ascribed to Krieger. The composer is Johann Christoph Bach.
[38] DDT 58/59.
[39] DDT 21/22.

cantatas with *secco* and *accompagnato* recitatives, ariosi, and arias, that give a contemplative interpretation of the biblical text. Kuhnau showed his strong sense for balanced form in the impressive cantata *Wie schön leuchtet der Morgenstern*. It opens with a massive and elaborate chorale chorus and closes with a simple chorale setting so that a highly variegated structure is framed by means of the chorale—a device that became exemplary for Bach. Kuhnau's St. Matthew Passion (1721) also makes ample use of chorales.

Zachow excelled both in chorale variations and in reform cantatas. In the solo sections of his chorale variations he sometimes abandoned the chorale melody so as to allow for a free musical interpretation of the chorale text. His reform cantata *Das ist das ewige Leben* deserves particular attention because it represents the formal and even the inner features of the Bach cantata. The free paraphrase (recitatives and da-capo arias) and the biblical text (*concertato* and fugue) are set off in sharp relief and the whole is rounded off by a simple chorale setting. Graupner [40] and, especially, Telemann [41] lean in their cantatas toward the *style galant* which became fashionable during the years Bach wrote his passions and cantatas in Leipzig.

BACH: THE EARLY PERIOD

The brilliant development of instrumental and sacred music in the late baroque culminated in the works of Bach, the greatest genius of baroque music. Johann Sebastian Bach (b. March 21, 1685 in Eisenach; d. July 28, 1750 in Leipzig) was steeped in a twofold tradition, that of the local musical milieu in Thuringia, and that of the Bach family which made it natural for him to uphold staunchly the highest standards of musicianship and to be receptive to musical influences from abroad. Broadly speaking, Bach could count all the leading masters of European music among his teachers; he studied their works by copying—the traditional mode of "study" for a musical apprentice. The oldest of the Italian masters that served him as example was Frescobaldi whose *Fiori musicali* Bach copied out in its entirety. It seems significant that he selected of all of Frescobaldi's works the one most closely bound up with the (Catholic) liturgy. The observance of liturgy, whether Catholic or Protestant, obviously mattered more to him

[40] DDT 51/52.

[41] Telemann composed twelve (!) complete cantata cycles for the liturgical year, none of which has been reprinted.

than the difference in denomination. The list of other Italian masters whom Bach imitated and copied includes Legrenzi, Albinoni, Corelli, Lotti, Caldara, Vivaldi, Marcello, and Bonporti. The French were represented by D'Anglebert, Couperin, Dieupart, Grigny, Raison, and Marchand, the German Catholic masters by Froberger and Kerll, and finally the Protestant masters by Reinken, Buxtehude, Pachelbel, Böhm, Strungk, Bruhns, Ferdinand Fischer, Handel, Fasch, Graupner, Telemann, and many others. Bach's desire to learn from others, his unceasing zeal to perfect himself even in the years of fullest maturity, is well documented. It was he who made the determined, though unsuccessful, attempt to meet his greatest contemporary, Handel.

Bach learned the fundamentals of music from his father, a town musician in Eisenach. After the death of his father he received instruction from his elder brother who had learned his craft with Pachelbel and lived as organist in Ohrdruf. It was here that Bach was initiated into the German literature for organ. As boy soprano at the school in Lüneburg he came in contact with the organists Loewe (a pupil of Schütz) and Böhm (a pupil of Reinken); from the latter he learned the style of north German and French organ music. After the mutation of his voice Bach journeyed on foot to Hamburg, the center of the flourishing opera, to visit the organists Reinken and Vincent Lübeck. We know very little about this "journeyman period," but it seems likely that Bach was interested more in deepening his organistic background than in frittering away his time in the opera house. From Lüneburg he also visited the court in Celle several times where he became acquainted with orchestral music in French style.

In the creative development of Bach five periods can be distinguished that roughly correspond to the positions he held during his life.[42] Throughout his artistic career Bach remained absorbed in his main instrument, the organ, though he was also an accomplished violinist; it is symbolic of his organistic background that he served in his first two important positions as organist: first in Arnstadt (1703) and then in Mühlhausen (1707). These positions mark off the first period in which the young composer was groping for a personal style. It was from Arnstadt that Bach undertook the famous pilgrimage on foot to Lübeck (1705) in order to study vocal *concertato* and organ music with its best representative, Buxtehude. Bach's creative imagination caught fire upon contact with the music of the aged master and so deeply stirring was the impression that he long overstayed his leave to the chagrin of his superiors. The journey to Buxtehude, which

---

[42] See Gurlitt, *Bach*, 28 ff.

can be considered as the last phase of Bach's journeyman period, released the pent-up creative energies that manifest themselves in the works of the early period.

As successor to Georg Ahle in the post of organist in Mühlhausen Bach was drawn inevitably into the quarrels between Orthodoxy and Pietism in which he, true to his personal conviction and his family tradition, sided with the orthodox faction even against the pastor of his own church. It was the only course for him to take since the Pietists, opposed in principle to figural music in the service, tolerated only simple devotional or sickly sentimental songs. Paradoxically enough, these songs were more often than not derivatives of shallow operatic airs and betrayed the very same secular influence that the Pietists attacked so vehemently in theory. Bach felt too uncomfortable in Mühlhausen to stay there for more than a year. In his letter of resignation, a highly significant document of his musical and religious beliefs, he stated in his typical blunt fashion that his "final goal" was "a regulated church music in the honor of God"—regulated, that means: in accordance with the precepts of art music which governed both sacred and secular music. For a composer who conceived music as "the reflection and foretaste of heavenly harmony" (Werckmeister) it was no sacrilege to use in the church the *concertato* style or even opera style. Bach still shared the old Lutheran conviction that God should be praised in a ceaseless effort by means of the most "artificial" music.

The works of the early period are characterized by excessive length, superabundance of ideas, unbridled exuberance, and inconclusiveness with regard to harmony. Youthful effervescence manifests itself also in extravagant flourishes [43] of the early chorale accompaniments for which Bach was reprimanded by the church superintendent in Arnstadt.

Three early chorale partitas, the only examples that Bach contributed to this form, treat the chorale in strictly patterned figuration with independent counter-motives in the manner of Pachelbel, Buxtehude, and Böhm. They are uncouth in their harmonies except for the partita *Sei gegrüsset Jesu* which suggests by the more advanced harmonic style in some of its variations that it may have been revised at a later date. In view of Bach's observance of the relation between text and music it is

[43] Printed in Spitta, *Bach* III, 400. The book is quoted here after the rather faulty English translation.

significant that the partitas contain as many variations as the chorale had stanzas.

The early church sonatas for harpsichord are either direct adaptations of sonatas from Reinken's *Hortus musicus* or independent imitations of the form. The playful canzona theme of the sonata in *D* which combines the cackling of a hen with a cuckoo call obviously stems from the south German and Italian schools. The delightful "Capriccio on the Departure of the Beloved Brother," a secular complement to Kuhnau's programmatic Biblical Histories, reflects in its intimacy the family incident on which it is based. It contains several descriptive movements like "the flattering of the friends," or a "general lamento" on a chaconne bass (third type), elaborated with less naïveté and greater plasticity than was customary with Kuhnau. The concluding fugue on the horn call of the postillion suffers from lack of conciseness, but already points to the keen humor that distinguishes so many of Bach's secular works. The preludes and fugues, toccatas, and fantasias of the early period stand close to the visionary and erratic style of Buxtehude. The preludes and toccatas are hardly distinguishable and display dramatic life and youthful unruliness; the fugues lack the pregnant concise themes and the planned organization of the later works though the rambling counterpoint takes often surprising turns that have an appeal of their own. A fugue and prelude in *E*-flat (CE v. 36, no. 12) which presents in Froberger's manner a theme with changing countersubjects has passed for many years as a composition of Bach's early period though its author is actually his distinguished forbear Johann Christoph. The author of another spurious work of the period, the passacaglia in *d* (CE v. 42, no. 15), has been identified as Witt. Bach betrays in the early keyboard works a sure sense for virtuoso effects and a flair for idiomatic keyboard writing, especially in such a typically organistic device as the breaking of the scale into a pattern of alternating notes that lie easy in the hand and are particularly suitable for the pedal. Bach did not grow tired of it, not even in later works (Ex. 80.)

Ex. 80. Bach: Idiomatic keyboard patterns from fugue in *g* and toccata in *C*.

Bach's early cantatas reflect the state of the church cantata around 1700. They preserve the traits of the chorale *concertato* and contain multipartite vocal and instrumental ensembles, but no recitatives. Such recitatives as can be found in the earliest extant cantata *Denn du wirst meine Seele* (no. 15)

are the result of later revision. The grand "motetto" *Gott ist mein König* (no. 71), composed for the inauguration of a new city council in Mühlhausen, is the only cantata ever printed during Bach's lifetime, and this honor was due not to Bach's music, but to the political prestige of the city council. The cantata opens with a ponderous *concertato* chorus with full orchestral accompaniment and emphatically repeated invocations "God, God, God" which anticipate the opening chorus of the *St. John Passion*. The choral writing of the early cantatas has a strong instrumental flavor and is crowded with organistic patterns and ornamentation. In his arias Bach employs already the modulating quasi-ostinato bass with characteristic steps which was to become the outstanding means of his consistent musical organization. Even at this early stage Bach proved his unique ability to seize upon the fundamental idea of the cantata text and to realize it symbolically in music. In *Gott ist mein König* the central idea is that of old age and youth presented in metaphorical terms as the contrast between the Old and the New Testament. This contrast underlies the duet *con chorale in canto* in which the tenor solo "I am now eighty years old" symbolizes the Old Testament while the chorale *Ach Gott Du frommer Gott,* intoned simultaneously by the soprano, symbolizes the New Testament. Both aspects are reconciled in the dignified choral fugue "Thy old age be like thy youth" which stands, significantly, in the center of the cantata.

A similar interpenetration of musical and religious ideas obtains in the *Actus tragicus* or *Gottes Zeit* (no. 106), the most mature cantata of the early period (1707?). Written for a funeral service it reflects in its deeply serious and personal tone the private occasion. A moving "sonatina" for recorders and gambas serves as introduction. Its melody consists of typical "sigh" figures representing mourning and consolation. The idea of this cantata is based, too, on the conflict of the Old and New Covenant. The fugal chorus "It is the old decree" stands here for the inexorable law of the Old Testament by virtue of its strict contrapuntal structure which Bach always used to represent ideas of constraint and law. Against this chorus the recorders play the chorale tune *Ich hab mein Sach* in tacit allusion to the New Testament and a soprano solo makes this allusion explicit by its message from the gospel. This ensemble is only one of many examples of Bach's symbolic methods. As a rule, he represented the contrast of extra-musical ideas by superimposing different musical ideas in counterpoint. Music was capable of projecting into simultaneity what language could produce only in succession; only in music did the abstract opposition of divine law and divine grace become a concrete reality. In the course of this cantata Bach introduces two other chorales in similarly symbolic manner. They naturally complicate the structure of the ensemble. Solo and choral sections, as yet undivided, preserve the old-fashioned continuity of the *concertato*. We do not find in the early cantatas the clearly designed architecture of his later works, but the lack of formal control is amply compensated by the abundance of unbridled ideas that characterize his youthful works.

BACH THE ORGANIST: WEIMAR

The second period of Bach's creative career comprises the years he resided in Weimar (1708–1717), first as court organist and later as concert master of the orchestra. It is the period of his great organ compositions, especially those not connected with the chorale. Bach showed himself in this phase primarily as the great organist, as the virtuoso of his chosen instrument. His fame as organist spread from Weimar all over Germany and when he received the honorable offer to become the successor of Zachow in Halle he could afford to decline it. Praised especially for his marvellous performing ability, his stupendous pedal technique, and his art of registration, he was sought after as the expert in organ building and as the severe adjudicator of newly-built instruments. In Gottfried Walther he found a worthy colleague in Weimar to whom he was bound by ties of family relations and friendship.

The organ for which Bach composed in Weimar had been rebuilt by Compenius. His organs stood midway between the north German type of baroque organ, brought to perfection by Schnitger, and the central German type, brought to perfection by Silbermann. The sharply differentiated stops and rugged mixtures of the Schnitger organ contrasted markedly with the somewhat more blending stops and brilliant mixtures of the Silbermann organ, but both types had a powerful and completely independent pedal. Only on these baroque organs do the works of Bach disclose their true radiance and kaleidoscopic richness.

After the close atmosphere of Arnstadt and Mühlhausen the courtly spirit in Weimar was like a complete change of musical climate for Bach. The Weimar court was, like many other petty courts in Germany, open to the stimulating French and Italian innovations in secular music. The stream of compositions that began to flow during the Weimar period attests to a second creative encounter in Bach's life: the Italian music in general, and the concerto style in particular. While the first encounter, that with Buxtehude, had released his creative energies the second guided them into the channels of European music. It gave his music the decisive and final stamp that marks the second period as that of his early maturity. Like many other great German artists Bach found himself only by going through an Italian phase.

Bach set out again to learn, as usual, by imitation. In a first group of imitative works he seized with enthusiasm on the violin concertos of Vivaldi and transferred them to the organ and harpsichord. These arrangements—another proof of the German preference for keyed instruments—draw not only on Vivaldi but also on German composers, notably the Duke of Weimar, Telemann, and some unidentified composers who wrote in Vivaldi's style. They are highly illuminating documents of skilful adaptation in which the violin figuration is either literally preserved or transformed to mechanical organ patterns. While Bach rarely altered the concertos with regard to form, he supplied ornaments (which the Italians did not care to write down), fortified the counterpoint, and even added new middle parts so convincingly that they seem to belong to the original composition, as can be seen in the second concerto in G after Vivaldi (op. 7, 2). Walther also arranged concertos by Torelli, Albinoni, Taglietti, and others; his remarkable set of variations on a *basso continuo* by Corelli assumes the importance of an independent composition.[44] By means of arrangements Bach made himself thoroughly familiar with the form and style of the concerto and thus gained a new stylistic element which he amalgamated with his German contrapuntal technique.

In a second group of imitative works Bach studied the melodic and harmonic principles that governed the construction of the Italian themes. The monumental conciseness and the gestic pathos that the themes of Corelli and other Italian masters attained through the directive force of tonality cannot be found in Bach's early themes. Far superior to the Italians in contrapuntal workmanship he lacked as yet melodic clarity and balance. Bach overcame this obstacle by borrowing Italian themes and working them out independently. The results were the well-known fugues on themes of Corelli, Legrenzi, and Albinoni.[45] By virtue of their length and their imaginative contrapuntal treatment these imitations rise actually to the level of compositions in their own right. Bach also wrote in Weimar a

---

[44] DDT 26/27, 301.
[45] For Albinoni see Spitta, *op. cit.* III, 364; the Corelli theme has been borrowed from op. 3, 4.

variation canzona in *d* pursuing the old-fashioned style of Frescobaldi or that of his German follower Froberger, but imbuing it with the modern tonal idiom.

The profound effect of Bach's creative reaction to Italian music is clearly manifested in the new thematic incisiveness and the lucidity of form that distinguish the instrumental music of the Weimar period. The exuberant wealth of ideas is now disciplined by Italian simplicity. The mechanically patterned, long-winded, and sequentially spun-out themes of the Buxtehudes and Pachelbels are supplanted by plastic Italianate themes, unified by a single affection and the strong centripetal force of tonality—in short, a type of theme that we are apt to call "typically Bachian." The comparison between the theme of the multipartite prelude and fugue in *C* (or *E*) from the early period and that of the fantasy and fugue in *c* emphatically demonstrates the tremendous artistic growth from the first to the second period (Ex. 81). The second theme represents with its characteristic di-

Ex. 81. Bach: An early and a mature fugue theme.

minished seventh the type of sturdy and gestic theme that can be found in the organ fugues in *c* and *f,* and later also in the fugues of the *Well-Tempered Clavier.*

Another type retained the continuous motion of the old-fashioned themes, but instead of rambling on unchecked it was now exquisitely shaped and harmonically balanced by a strong and clear harmonic foundation. These themes show how Bach assimilated the continuo-homophony of the concerto style to his contrapuntal technique. As an example of continuo-homophony in a polyphonic setting the prelude and fugue in *D* may be quoted, a sparkling virtuoso piece with dashing pedal solos, typical of many organ compositions of the Weimar period. The fugue theme (Ex. 82),

Ex. 82. Bach: Fugue theme in *D* in concerto style.

which could easily serve as a concerto beginning, is harmonized by the typical running bass in concerto style; not by accident is the prelude to this particular fugue designated in one of the sources as *concertato* (= "in concerto"). The famous toccata and fugue in *d*, which has been catapulted to fame through a dramatized arrangement for symphony orchestra, also belongs to this group. The fact that the fugue dissolves at the end in fireworks of rhapsodic passages is an indication that it still forms an integral part of the toccata.

The exact chronology of many organ compositions has not yet been established with accuracy so that it is difficult to separate the works of the second period from those of the subsequent ones. The grand prelude and fugue in *a* goes back, at least in its first version, to the Weimar period. The lengthy theme of this fugue (Ex. 83) falls into two unequal sections the

Ex. 83. Bach: Theme of the organ fugue in *a* in "realized" form.

second of which carries on the continuous motion in sixteenth notes. In spite of its length it shows a hitherto unprecedented melodic precision and balance resulting from the interpenetration of melodic and harmonic factors. Harmonically, it is no more than an inspired realization of the stereotyped formulas of the concerto style; the first section is based on the three hammerstroke chords I-V-I that set the key, the second on the complete diatonic circle of fifths, ingeniously utilized in the further course of the fugue. Even the concerto form has left its mark on the fugue. The toccata, *adagio*, and fugue in *C* correspond to the three movements of the concerto, and this similarity is enhanced by the fact that the *adagio* is a highly ornamented aria on a rhythmic ostinato in the pedal.

In the organ works of the subsequent periods both the Italian concerto style and the German polyphonic style are inextricably interwoven, as shown in the great fantasia and fugue in *g*, composed probably in the Cöthen period for Bach's visit to Hamburg. The fantasia brings the rhapsodic type of the north German toccata to its consummation. The alternation of poignant solo recitatives and powerful tutti chords represents a further adaptation of the concerto principle to the organ. The fugue theme, universally admired even in Bach's time, was printed in an inferior version by Mattheson who quoted it probably from memory. With its plastic shape and harmonic lucidity, which are no longer Italian or

German but thoroughly Bachian, it illustrates the peak of thematic invention in baroque music altogether. A composition of equal importance and perfection is the passacaglia in *c,* fashioned after Buxtehude's chaconnes and passacaglias, and based in part on a passacaglia theme by Raison. The twenty variations are organized in strictly symmetrical groups, each of which is unified by corresponding rhythmic patterns. The axis of symmetry is formed by the tenth and eleventh variations in which the bass theme is carried in double counterpoint to the highest voice. It then returns step by step to the original position. The cycle closes with a variation for five voices and is crowned by a fugue. Bach imbued the quasi-mathematical permutations of the mechanical patterns which appealed so strongly to baroque speculation with visionary life and elevated what was at the time a mere vehicle for invention to an eternal work of art.

With regard to cantata composition also, Bach reached his early maturity in Weimar. It was here that he took the significant step to the reform cantata of Neumeister. Fully conscious of the secular roots of the cantata Bach did not hesitate to expand the traditional forms of the church *concertato* by the formal innovations of the Italian cantata and opera which make their first appearance in the cantatas composed not before 1712 and not later than 1714. These works stand apart from the cantatas of all other periods by virtue of their strongly mystical and subjective tone that prevails in both words and music. Struggling for his personal style Bach went through a phase of creative subjectivity in Weimar which manifested itself outwardly in the virtuoso attitude of his organ music; turned inwardly it took the form of introspective mysticism and self-centered devotion. These traits have often been explained as symptoms of pietistic influence on Bach's religiosity. Indeed the language of Bach's poet Salomon Franck (a follower of Neumeister in Weimar) makes use of pietistic phraseology, but it must be remembered that the cantata as such, being figural music, was diametrically opposed to the tenets of Pietism. It is true that the religious and artistic subjectivity of Bach resembles externally the devotional fervor of Pietism, but they could hardly be more different in origin and purpose.

Neumeister, avowedly, had conceived the cantata in analogy to a sermon. Since it paraphrased the topic of the sermon in art poetry it was sung directly before the sermon, or if there were two parts, before and after it. The ideas presented in the two parts of the cantata were often so pronouncedly divergent that their inner connection would have been incomprehensible without the sermon. This can be seen in the cantata *Ich hatte viel Bekümmernis* (no. 21) which presents in its first part the sorrow of the soul, and in its second part consolation and confidence while the sermon mediates between the two ideas. Old-fashioned and modern forms coexist side by side in this cantata. It is obviously a work of transition, and since it can be dated in 1714 we know at what time Bach turned to the reform cantata and how he effected the change. The variegated structure of the first two choral ensembles are obvious survivals of the old *concertato*. The beginning of the first chorus with its forceful reiterations "I, I, I had much grief" vividly recalls the beginning of *Gott ist mein König* but, significantly, the emphasis is now purely subjective. Mattheson in his *Critica Musica* has ridiculed this passage as an example of false emphasis, but the profoundly personal fervor is not the defect but the virtue of the cantatas of early maturity. The first chorus anticipates the opposition of ideas that underlies the cantata and gives literally and figuratively the "keynote" of the whole work. Sorrow and consolation are set off in sharp relief by means of contrasting melodic material and different tempi. Also the second chorus "Why art thou cast down," notable for its superb rhythmic flexibility and harmonic poignancy, contains violent changes in mood, tempo, dynamics, and equally violent solo and tutti contrasts. Bach reserved the modern forms for the solo sections of the cantata. The first aria "Sighing, Weeping" adopts the fashionable siciliano rhythm of the opera, and the second aria "From my eyes salt tears are flowing," memorable for its graphic violin accompaniment, is a fully developed da-capo aria with motto beginning. Uncanny as the masterly assimilation of these forms was, with Bach it cannot compare with the assuredness with which he handled his recitatives. The very first *accompagnato* recitative is replete with the keenest and most fervent verbal interpretations. Diminished sevenths in melody and harmony, sudden outcries, and weirdly twisted melodic fragments lend the recitative a high-strung intensity which seems like a last reverberation of Bach's youthful exuberance. The concerted dialogue between the soul and the savior "Come my Jesus," which can be described as a vocal trio sonata on a running bass, is fashioned after the passionate love duets of the opera. The introductory sinfonia, a somber duet between violin and oboe with languishing harmonies, also shows in its steady bass the influence of Corelli's trio sonata. Of all the movements of the cantata only the penultimate chorus makes use of a chorale; it is a chorale prelude transferred to the vocal medium in which the voices move in independent counterpoint against the *cantus firmus*. The last chorus, a monumental fugue with a full orchestra of three trumpets (and timpani), oboe, and strings, is written in the broad and sweeping oratorio style of Handel which rarely reappears in Bach's later works. However, its theme and its running counterpoint are indebted to the archaic organistic patterns of Pachelbel.

Yearning for death and profound mysticism pervades *Komm du süsse Todesstunde* (no. 161), perhaps the most subjective of all cantatas (text by Franck). It opens very quietly with a tender aria for alto, two obbligato flutes, and organ continuo. In symbolic reference to the first words of the aria the organ suddenly intones the melody of the death chorale *Herzlich tut mich verlangen*. This chorale was a favorite with Bach, as the numerous settings in the St. Matthew Passion witness. The famous accompanied recitative and arioso of the cantata depicts by means of string *pizzicato* and flute figures the tolling of the death bell which the alto is longing for so ardently. At the end the chorale reappears in a fully harmonized setting with a marvellous flute obbligato that hovers over the tune like a blessed spirit released from human bondage—a symbol of the central idea of the cantata.

In complete contrast to the subdued atmosphere of death stands the brilliant Easter cantata *Der Himmel lacht* (no. 31), known only in the revised form in which it has come down to us. It discloses Bach's resourcefulness and originality in adapting the concerto style to the cantata. The introductory "sonata" for an exceptionally full orchestra (three trumpets, timpani, five woodwinds, strings, and organ) is actually not a sonata, but a brilliant tripartite concerto movement with the typical unison beginning in all voices. Such unison passages are comparatively rare in his works since they are not consistent with his wonted love for polyphony, but whenever they appear they unmistakably point to the influence of the concerto. Also the tenor aria "Adam must be dead within me" adheres not only to the concerto style but even to the ritornello form of the concerto.

In view of Bach's subjective attitude in Weimar it is hardly surprising that he favored the free secular forms, best suited to individual expression. It is for this reason that the chorale figures less prominently in the cantatas of the second period than in those of any other. Bach often merely alluded to the chorale, or even abstained from it completely, as he did, for example, in *Tritt auf die Glaubensbahn* (no. 152). He combined it also with other secular forms; in *Nun komm der Heiden Heiland* (no. 61), for example, he even imposed it on the French overture.

BACH THE MENTOR: CÖTHEN

The third period in Bach's life coincides with his employment at the court in Cöthen (1717–1723) as capellmeister and director of chamber music. This position was remarkable in several respects. Socially, it meant for Bach the highest social prestige he ever attained, a fact he could not forget in the subsequent years in Leipzig. Artistically, it created a unique situation for him. The court belonged to the Reformed Church so that his official duties involved neither church music nor even the organ. Far removed from his "final goal," a regulated church music, Bach became now a composer of secular chamber and house music. It was in Cöthen that he wrote the bulk of his music for clavier (clavichord and harpsichord), and chamber ensembles. The composition of church cantatas stopped abruptly. He devoted his efforts to instrumental music in which he set up perfect models and "guides" to tyros, advanced students, and music lovers. The final goal was still one of "regulation," but it was now a didactic one, as is clearly apparent from the prefaces to the various music-books for members of his family, the *Well-Tempered Clavier*, the *Inventions*, and the *Orgelbüchlein*. Bach appears in the Cöthen period as the great mentor who by personal example dictates objective standards of technical craftsmanship. This could only be done in the "secular," that is worldwide, sphere. The *Clavierbüchlein* for Friedemann (1720) and that for Anna Magdalena (first version, 1722) contain in rudimentary form and unsystematic order material for the great cycles of keyboard music, notably the *Well-Tempered Clavier*, the *Inventions*, and suites. None of these didactic cycles appeared in print during Bach's lifetime, but they were nevertheless widely disseminated through manuscript copies of his pupils who felt free to add or omit ornaments. The superior craftsmanship and imagination of Bach the mentor raised these models far above the level of similar pedagogical pieces of the time.

The first important cycle of the Cöthen period is the *Orgelbüchlein* which Bach had already begun in Weimar. Originally planned to include 164 chorale preludes it contains only forty-five compositions, arranged in the order of the liturgical year. Bach's aim is succinctly stated by the title: "Guide . . . to the beginning organist to work out a chorale in sundry ways, serving also to perfect him in the pedal-study since the pedal is treated strictly as an obbligato voice." The chorale preludes give on the smallest possible scale the sacrosanct melody, nearly always stated in the soprano, to the accompaniment of three obbligato voices which weave independent motives in strictest counterpoint around it and hardly ever interrupt the flow of the melody by interludes. Bach treated the chorale like a single variation of a partita, but with a hitherto unknown severity of contrapuntal elaboration which in itself assured the proper dignity of liturgical music. He invented the rhythmic or melodic shape of the contrapuntal figure either abstractly, as Scheidt had done, or concretely in strict conformity with the affections or the pictorial ideas of the chorale text. We know from a pupil of Bach that he admonished his students to play the chorale "according to the tenor of the words." Once established, the figures governed the structure of the entire composition regardless of whether they belonged to the treasure of stereotyped figures or whether they were intellectually derived by means of metaphorical or symbolical references to motion or other concepts in the text. The unique musical intensity of the preludes resulted from the interpenetration of three unifying factors: the unity of the rhythmic figure, the unity of the melodic motive, and the unity of affection. Bach gave here in highly condensed form the essence of his musical philosophy; he reduced to simultaneity the "presentation" of the dogma (the chorale) and its "interpretation" (the contrapuntal setting). In the much-quoted chorale prelude *Durch Adams Fall* the fall of Adam from the state of innocence into sin is depicted by the "falling" seventh in the bass; since it was a fall into sin and since sin was conventionally represented by chromaticism, Bach made the sevenths not diatonic but diminished. Not satisfied with these two references Bach introduced a third meaning in the chromatically winding middle part representing the "snake," another symbol of sin to which the text expressly refers.

The most drastic symbolical or pictorial references occur, significantly, in the obbligato voice: the pedal. Nobody can mistake the forcefully rising fifths or fourths in the chorale of resurrection *Erstanden ist,* or the pealing rhythmic ostinati in *In dir ist Freude* and *Heut triumphieret* which seem to ring the change to the exultant accompaniment of the other parts. Without reference to the words and without knowledge of the doctrine of figures and affections the true meaning, or rather meanings, of the chorale prelude could not be properly understood. Like the baroque emblems which imposed non-pictorial and allegorical meanings on pictures, music too, was able to realize extra-musical meanings that, however intellectually

contrived, enhanced the meaning of the music. They actually supplied
the composer with the raw material (intervals and rhythms) out of which
he built his composition. Although these metaphorical procedures may
seem utterly mechanical and far-fetched today, they formed an essential
part of all baroque arts. They were common property in baroque music,
but assumed vital importance with Bach because he was able to make them
subservient to an artistic purpose. He forged the intellectual artifices into
a self-contained work of art, but without them the preludes would not
have taken the form in which they now exist.

On the other hand, it should not be forgotten that the pictorial and
emblematic references gave only one aspect of the music. As Bach said himself, he set the chorales in "sundry ways." The pictorial "interpretation"
of the chorale was only one extreme which had its complement in another
extreme: abstract "elaboration" by means of stereotyped figures that had
no other than their inherent musical meaning. The danger of reading meanings into the music that Bach did not have in mind has not always been
avoided, quite understandably because a significant part of the music does
call for metaphorical understanding. It would however be a fatal error
to apply the metaphorical interpretation to all of his compositions. The
origin and meaning of many pictorial motives will perhaps never be
as clear as they are in certain cantatas and chorale preludes; but even when
the motives were definitely conceived pictorially the idea of abstract elaboration obtained at the same time. This can be shown in a great number
of preludes. For example, the descending bass line in *Vom Himmel kam*
which graphically represents the "descent from heaven" appears in the
course of the composition in inversion in complete repudiation of its original meaning. The same is true of the rising intervals in *Erstanden ist*.
This conflict of meanings was not illogical for Bach because every figure
was as such subject to the doctrine of figures, which regarded inversion
as one of its most important devices.

A comparison between Walther's and Bach's preludes discloses how high
Bach towered even above the best of his contemporaries. Walther employs
in *Erschienen ist der herrlich Tag* (Ex. 84a) a rhythmic and melodic idea

Ex. 84a. Walther: Chorale prelude *Erschienen ist.*

that appears in strikingly similar fashion in Bach's setting of the same chorale (Ex. 84b); however, Bach uses it more consistently, elaborates it

Ex. 84.b. Bach: Chorale prelude *Erschienen ist.*

with richer harmonies, and, moreover, presents the melody in canon, the symbol of constraint, in reference to the last line of the text "he leads his enemies in chains."

Only rarely did Bach follow in the *Orgelbüchlein* the practice of Böhm and state the melody in profusely ornamented form. For Bach ornamentation was another method of subjective interpretation and it is significant that he used it with especially affective chorale texts, such as *Wenn wir in höchsten Nöten, Das alte Jahr,* and *O Mensch bewein.* In the latter prelude Bach gave the ultimate that was possible in subjective affection and ornamental treatment. The French *agréments* are completely spiritualized; they are no longer extraneous embellishments but integral parts of the musical structure. The rich harmonization is mapped out strictly in keeping with the words. The abrupt turn to chromaticism in the bass occurs exactly when the text refers to "sacrifice," and the reference to "crucifixion" in the final line is rendered in an ineffably poignant *adagissimo* cadence. All these features bespeak Bach's intensely personal attitude toward the liturgy, an attitude that does not prevail in the later series of chorale preludes. In this respect the preludes of the *Orgelbüchlein* are unique; they are in fact a last reflection of the subjectivism of the Weimar period.

The clavier works of the Cöthen period show that Bach avoided the danger of succumbing to the powerful Italian and French influences by assimilating them with his German polyphonic tradition. The fusion of national styles in what became the unique Bachian style is the most remarkable single factor in Bach's mature instrumental music. Whatever might formerly have been brilliant tinsel or mere mannerism was transformed through his superior craftsmanship into pure gold. In the toccatas for harpsichord Bach drew with sovereign freedom on such widely divergent techniques as the variation ricercar and the concerto style. The toccata in f-sharp, for example, evolves its fugue theme from the slow movement by a process of thematic transformation. In the dazzling and rhapsodic toccatas in c and a it is essentially the influence of the concerto style that contributes to the inexorable drive of the music; the repetitive triadic theme of the fugue in c would actually be more suitable for a concerto beginning than a fugue.

The great cycle of preludes and fugues that Bach combined for didactic purposes in the *Well-Tempered Clavier* (I, 1722) gives in systematic order the Ariadne thread through all the keys of the circle of fifths which the "well-tempered" tuning had made practicable for the first time. Bach borrowed the term "well-tempered" directly from Werckmeister. The newly attained freedom to modulate through the most distant keys led inevitably to enharmonic modulations. Bach did not need them in the fugues of the *Well-Tempered Clavier,* but he used them in the third English suite (saraband) and later also extensively in the *Chromatic Fantasy.* The contention, frequently voiced,[46] that the preludes and fugues are thematically related is unfounded; in fact, the documentary evidence of the *Clavierbüchlein* and other preliminary sources speaks definitely against it. Such accidental similarities between prelude and fugue as can be observed in no. 23 in B are rare exceptions that confirm the rule.

The immense variety of forms and textures in the cycle reflects Bach's intention of supplying models for the "youth anxious to learn." Each prelude is unified by consistent motivic treatment; only the contrasts between the motives themselves create the variety of types. Some of the preludes are ultimate stylizations of dances, such as the saraband (no. 8 in e-flat), others belong to the etude or *perpetuum mobile* type (no. 2 in c, no. 5 in D), or to the aria type (no. 10 in e). Still others belong to the transfer type. They are patterned after distinct forms of instrumental music, such as the trio sonata (no. 24 in b), the toccata (no. 7 in E-flat), the invention (no. 11 in f), and even the fugue (no. 19 in A). In the last case a fugue with countersubject serves exceptionally as "prelude" to another fugue.

Not in any of his fugues did Bach adhere to exactly the same pattern. He made the *Well-Tempered Clavier* the inventory of all previous types of fugue with strong emphasis on the monothematic fugue. While Bach

---

[46] Most has been made of the alleged relation by Werker, *Bachstudien.* He imposes on Bach's music a pseudo-mathematical analysis, as absurd in its method as in its results. Steglich, *Bach,* although opposed to Werker, applies a similarly forced analysis, and matters are scarcely improved by a strange admixture of Nazi ideology.

did not invent a single new type he made of the fugue what it stands for today: a contrapuntal form of the highest concentration in which a single characteristic subject in continuous expansion pervades a thoroughly unified whole. Bach heightened the unification of fugue writing by deriving the material for the episodes either from the second part of the fugue subject itself (no. 16 in *g*), or from the counterpoint to the subject (no. 12 in *f*). That Bach was fully conscious of the historical types of fugues is clearly evident in his retrospective fugue no. 4 in *c*-sharp which brings the ricercar to consummation. He uses here a typical slow ricercar theme, introduces new countersubjects in the manner of Sweelinck and Froberger, and finally combines them in a climactic finish. On the other hand, we find "modern" themes with rich tonal implications or even modulations (no. 12 in *f*, no. 24 in *b*). Also the technical treatment varies from the strictest contrapuntal artifices (no. 8 in *e*-flat) to a rhapsodic fugal style (no. 5 in *D*). What sets Bach's fugues apart from those of any other composer is the superb configuration of his themes which give the indelible stamp to each work. The themes stand firmly as though hewn from granite; their strong and characteristic shapes are the immutable entities of Bach's music. Even his counterpoints and countersubjects participate in the personal characterization and, consequently, many of Bach's countersubjects have more character than the primary subjects of his predecessors. The elevation of the fugue to a "character piece" embodying a single affection must be regarded as the culmination of the form. It was the ultimate step in the development that could be taken without breaking through the framework of baroque music altogether.

The *Inventions*, another didactic cycle of two- and three-part compositions, have been designated by Bach as an "honest guide to the lovers of the clavier" (1723). They are arranged like the *Well-Tempered Clavier* in the ascending order of keys but with the omission of those involving more than four accidentals. While Bach probably borrowed the title from the inventions of Bonporti the form was completely his own. Written in fugal style without being fugues the inventions represent the triumph of obbligato part-writing, specifically mentioned in the preface. Bach wanted to give the student "a strong foretaste of composition" and teach him how to "play neatly" and "in singing manner." The technical purpose becomes especially clear in the three-part sinfonie which challenge the musicianship and proficiency of the performer more severely than a four- or five-part fugue does.

The solidification of the fugue in the sphere of "absolute" music had its complement in the sphere of dance music in the ultimate stylization of the keyboard suite. The titles of the so-called "English" and "French" suites are not only not authentic but actually misleading if regarded as clues to their style. In both sets the ties with dance music proper are severed; only the shells of rhythmic patterns survive, raised by means of stylization into the rarefied atmosphere of abstract art music. As to the date of the suites we know only that they belong to the Cöthen period, but on stylistic grounds it seems certain that the English suites were composed first. Far from being "English" in style the first set reveals the radical assimilation of the Italian and the French style, but it is significant that, at this stage, they are kept apart in the different movements. The preludes follow Italian models, especially those to the second and third suites in which the concerto grosso and the ritornello form is bodily transferred to the harpsichord. The other movements betray French influence: there is more than one courante in a single suite; the sophisticated rhythms of the French courante type are prevalent; and several dances appear with *doubles,* separately written out with a typically German thoroughness in the use of *agréments* which no Frenchman would ever have applied. In the allemande of the first suite in *A* the "broken style" of the clavecinists is presented in its most refined form. Bach still adheres to the arpeggio figure of the lute, but injects so much motivic treatment into the thin texture that its free-voiced effect appears as though it had been produced by an artificial thinning out of a contrapuntal texture in complete reversal of the original procedure.

In the "French" suites Italian, French, and German styles no longer stand side by side but wholly merge with Bach's personal style. This fusion is in itself internal evidence for the later date of the second set. Moreover, the conciseness of all movements bespeaks the economy of maturity. In their melodic rather than motivic character the dances of the French suites lean toward the Italian style and also the fact that the fast Italian *corrente* occurs more frequently than the slower French type points in the same direction.

Bach's chamber music must be regarded as the highest manifestation of the Cöthen period. It is noteworthy that he wrote the majority of his sonatas not for two melody instruments and continuo but for a single melody instrument (violin, flute, or gamba) and obbligato harpsichord. It is indicative of his German proclivity for keyed instruments that Bach was not satisfied with using the harpsichord merely for the continuo; he made it a concerting instrument and provided the right hand with a fully independent part that would otherwise be taken by the second melody instrument. His "solo" sonatas are actually trio sonatas condensed for two instruments, and, characteristically, one of the gamba sonatas is actually only a condensation of an original trio sonata for two flutes. That the sonatas are strongly indebted to concerto style can be proved not only by the concerto character of the themes, the frequent use of da-capo and ritornello forms, but, especially, by the masterly handling of continuo-homophony that underlies even the fugal movements. While the flute sonatas contain, like the concerto, only three movements the violin sonatas usually follow the four-movement pattern of the church sonata. The first version of the sixth violin sonata—there exist altogether three versions—carries the da-capo principle to its highest point. The first movement, in itself a da-capo form, must be bodily repeated as a giant da-capo at the end and thus flanks three slow movements of pronounced lyrical affections. The manner in which Bach combined in his sonatas fugal writing with concerto style will always remain a marvel. Their contrapuntal brilliance and their wide range of affections have no equal in the entire literature of the trio or solo sonata.

The most monumental documents of polyphonic string music are without question the six suites for cello solo [47] and the six sonatas for violin solo *senza continuo* consisting of three church sonatas and three chamber sonatas. Their tremendous technical difficulties, especially the persistent use of multiple stops,[48] are not just virtuoso features but are the natural result of the complexity of his musical ideas. With his desire to produce polyphony at any cost Bach seems to break through the technical limitations of the instrument. The suggested rather than real polyphony on the violin recalls the suggestive methods that Gaultier had used on the lute, only that they appear here raised to infinite power. Bach relied on the hearer to supply the voice-leading that he could only imply on the violin. Mattheson quoted without mentioning Bach's name the gigantic fugue of the violin sonata in *C*, probably the longest of all of Bach's fugues, and justly praised the fugue in *a* for its inspired ingenuity. It is most revealing to compare the various fugues for violin with the organ transcriptions that Bach made at a later time. They demonstrate that the implied polyphony

[47] The last suite was written for *viola pomposa* or *violoncello piccolo*.
[48] The theory that the violinist could instantly regulate the pressure of the bow by his thumb to which Schweitzer has given wide currency has been questioned, apparently on good evidence, by Beckmann, *Das Violinspiel.* It seems that in Bach's time also the multiple stops had to be executed in arpeggiated form.

is grounded on strict part-writing, fully realized in the transcription. The celebrated chaconne in *d*, built on a combination of the first and second type of chaconne bass in the traditional saraband rhythm, unfolds a magnificent series of patterned variations. As in the chaconnes of Lully and Purcell, the sudden turn to the opposite mode at the beginning of the middle part gathers the diversified variations into a grand tripartite form.

The orchestral compositions of the third period disclose how well Bach had learned his lesson in Italian concerto style. That his creative imagination had been immeasurably enriched by the concerto clearly transpires in the chamber music. However, what had lain here under the surface came out into the open in the solo concertos, concerti grossi, and orchestra overtures. Of Bach's numerous violin concertos only three have survived in their original form: the solo concertos in *E* and *a*, and the double concerto in *d*. Almost all of the harpsichord concertos for from one to four instruments, composed probably for the *Collegium Musicum* in Leipzig, are arrangements of Bach's own or Vivaldi's concertos for violin or other instruments. Only the concerto for two harpsichords in *C* and two concertos for three harpsichords appear to be exceptions that prove the rule.

Bach took as his model the modern concerto type of Vivaldi with which he had familiarized himself in Weimar; however, the Italian model seems no more than a mere skeleton in view of what Bach made of it. In his hands it became a thoroughly personal composition, distinguished by incisive themes, perspicuity of form, and profuse contrapuntal texture. The admixture of polyphony inevitably tended to obscure the tutti-solo contrast but this increase in formal complexity was counterbalanced by the da-capo form which transformed the diversified ritornello form into a highly unified tripartite structure, as can be seen in the first movement of the violin concerto in *E* and several *Brandenburg Concertos*. The inner complexity of the concertos is also reflected in the occasional use of thematic contrast. The slow movements are often built, again in imitation of Vivaldi, on a more or less strict ground bass which supports a highly ornamented cantilena of the solo instrument.

The complete interpenetration of continuo-homophony and contrapuntal texture can be shown nowhere as clearly as in the six *Brandenburg Concertos* (1721) which represent in their exultant optimism courtly entertainment music at the highest level. Their greatly variegated instrumental combinations continue the coloristic tradition of Venice and of Vivaldi's concertos; however, the emphasis on wind instruments is a typically German heritage of the music for *Stadtpfeifer*. Bach calls for the silvery tone of the clarino trumpet (second concerto), recorders (fourth concerto), and the penetrating *violino piccolo* (tuned a minor third above normal pitch) in combination with horns and oboes (first concerto). The fifth concerto coordinates the flute and violin with the harpsichord but so distinctly emphasizes the keyboard part that it must be regarded as the first important harpsichord concerto on record. With their marvelously balanced concerto themes, their coloristic, yet solid, counterpoint, and their rhythmic exuberance the *Brandenburg Concertos* are the most inspired and complex concerti grossi of the baroque era.

The four orchestral "overtures" for strings and various combinations of wind instruments bring the chamber suite to perfection. Each of them opens with a grand French overture the fugal sections of which are ingeniously modified by the concerto principle. They parallel the fugal concerto movements of the *Brandenburg Concertos*. In his dances Bach presented his most buoyant affections, best exemplified by the irresistible *Badinerie* for solo flute and strings of the second suite. The celebrated *Air* from the third suite, a composition of deceptive simplicity, is built on an octave motive in the bass that recalls the technique of the organ pedal. That Bach thought very highly of his orchestral and chamber music can be seen in the fact that he returned to it time and again during the Leipzig period. In urgent need for new music in his weekly cantatas he rearranged it for other media; sometimes he incorporated a cantata chorus into the densely woven fabric of the music with an ingenuity that defies any attempt at description.

BACH THE CANTOR: LEIPZIG

The fourth period of Bach's artistic development begins with his employment as cantor at St. Thomas' in Leipzig (1723) and closes with the year of the last cantatas (c. 1745). As early as 1720 he had applied for the post of organist in Hamburg at the church where Neumeister was pastor, but he was not chosen. He was not the first choice in Leipzig either. Fasch had not even applied for the position though he had been asked to do so; Telemann and Graupner, both famous composers at the time and former pupils of the Thomas school, were considered first, and only after Telemann had decided to stay in Hamburg and Graupner could not get his dismissal, was Bach unanimously elected. Bach was reluctant to make the change from a court musician to a cantor, because he did not relish the idea of becoming the subordinate of a municipal council. Petty quarrels with his superiors in which Bach showed himself contentious and irascible embittered the later years of his life.

In Leipzig Bach returned to his "final goal" for which he had already aimed when he applied for the position in Hamburg. His official duties as cantor called for a cantata for every Sunday and feast day of the liturgical year. Of the five complete cantata cycles he has written (c. 300 works) only about 200 have been preserved. They disclose how Bach, now in his full maturity, expanded and deepened the cantata composition. Mature integration of old and new forms characterizes the cantatas of the fourth period. It must suffice to draw attention to one of the finest examples of the type, *Herr gehe nicht ins Gericht* (no. 105), composed in the early Leipzig years (c. 1725). It begins with a great multipartite *concertato* chorus in which the despair of the sinner is depicted in somber colors, jagged counterpoint, and poignant harmonies. In the famous soprano aria "We tremble and stumble" the rhythmic patterns of the accompaniment vividly suggest "trembling"; in addition, the idea that the sinner has no firm ground under his feet is symbolized by the conspicuous absence of the continuo, only the viola furnishes a "shaky foundation" to the music. The penultimate tenor aria with obbligato horn which opposes the spiritual world to the vanity of earthly pleasures is cast in grand da-capo form. Written in the instrumental idiom of the concerto style it presents great technical difficulties to the singer. The final chorale, a stanza of *Jesu der du meine Seele,* recapitulates in one concentrated movement the idea that underlies the whole cantata: the accompaniment starts out with the trembling figures of the first aria, but they gradually subside, and the instruments move at the end in uniform rhythm with the melody—a symbol of quiet and undisturbed faith.

In the years after 1730 when Bach had only a few singers at his disposal—the discipline at the school had noticeably deteriorated—he turned to the composition of solo cantatas. In these works he allowed himself more vocal virtuosity than in other cantatas and, naturally, favored the secular forms at the expense of the chorale. One of the outstanding examples of the solo cantata, *Ich will den Kreuzstab* (no. 56), is written for bass and a small orchestra. In the first aria, fashioned after the ritornello form of the concerto, Bach does not forgo the pleasure of representing the word "cross" by a sharp. This pun is intelligible only in German because "cross" and "sharp" are identical words only in this language. The celebrated recitative of the *Kreuzstab* cantata narrates the parable that likens life to a voyage; the undulating motive of the bass (the waves of the sea) stops exactly at the point where the text runs "thus I leave the ship," that is when the voyager reaches firm ground. The restrained manner in which Bach now employed highly pictorial motives bespeaks his mature mastery of tonal suggestions. The second aria with oboe obbligato is cast again in the grand da-capo form of the opera, very frequent in the late works. A simple four-part chorale concludes the cantata.

Important as the previously discussed cantatas are, they take second place beside the chorale cantata which became increasingly more prominent in the fourth period. The more Bach progressed in years, the more he tried to make his music subservient to the liturgy, the more he imbued the secular elements of the reform cantata with liturgical spirit. He effected this inner transformation by basing the entire cantata text on the words of the chorale which were in themselves quasi-liturgical. The first stanza now usually took the form of a monumental chorale fantasy, the last one that of a simple four-part setting. The intermediate stanzas of the chorale were either retained or paraphrased in form of recitative and aria. The spiritual unity of the cantata was thus assured by both text and melody of the chorale. The interchange of instrumental and vocal media and the penetration of all forms with the substance of the chorale melody are the outstanding characteristics of the chorale cantata. We find now chorale recitatives, chorale arias, chorale concertos, chorale chaconnes, chorale sinfonie, and the various types of the organ chorale in vocal form. Bach had no real model for the chorale cantata; he evolved it himself with the aid of the Leipzig poet Picander. It is usually regarded as the archetype of the Bach cantata, but it is actually not typical of the first three periods; only in Leipzig, in the phase of liturgical observance, did it become the main type.

The most radical realization of the chorale cantata, the well-known *Christ lag in Todesbanden* (no. 4), goes back probably to an earlier model, now lost. Written as a variation *per omnes versus* it continues the tradition of the chorale *concertato* and the organ variation, but includes also chorale arias in concerto style. In all verses text and melody of the chorale are retained. The cumulative effect of contrapuntal virtuosity, abstract consistency, and concrete pictorialism in this cantata staggers the imagination. Bach has never attempted to write another cantata in this essentially archaic form.

The typical chorale cantata can be exemplified by *Ein feste Burg* (no. 80), *Jesu der du meine Seele* (no. 78), *Christ unser Herr* (no. 7), and many others. The first of these, a revision of a Weimar cantata, opens with one of the magnificent chorale fantasies that usually head the larger works of the Leipzig period. Bach symbolized the dogmatic significance of the chorale by stating it in strict canon between the highest and the lowest instruments. These canonic *cantus firmi* enclose like gigantic steel braces a brilliant fugue the theme of which is derived also from the chorale. The second great chorus of the cantata which paints in sweeping manner the struggle between the faithful and the devil is a monumental chorale fantasy in concerto style. Here is one of the rare occasions where all voices sing the chorale in unison and octaves against the ceaselessly running counter-motives of the orchestra. The *cantus firmus* stands like a firm rock of faith against the temptations of the world. The movement breathes the spirit of defiance and conjures up a grandiose picture of apocalyptic vision.

Jesu der du meine Seele, composed around 1740, exemplifies Bach's most mature cantata style. The great introductory chorus of this cantata is a chorale chaconne, perhaps the most inspired example of the form. Bach combined the third type of the chaconne bass with the chorale in a double *obbligo* and though neither melody was Bach's property he joined them so convincingly as if they had been conceived as subject and countersubject. It is hard to decide what should be most admired: the plastic and suggestive gestures of the music, the intensely dramatic recitatives, the sweeping concerto style of the grand da-capo arias, or the wealth of melodic and harmonic ideas.

The melodic substance of the chorale also pervades the few but important motets (for one chorus or double chorus) of the Leipzig period. In the five-voice motet *Jesu meine Freude* chorale verses alternate with words from the epistles in a strictly symmetrical order. The underlying idea, the opposition of flesh and spirit, is most pointedly concentrated in a fugue that stands in the exact center of the composition.

Bach's choral compositions reach their absolute peak in the four monumental works of the Leipzig period: the two *Passions* according to St. John and St. Matthew, the *Magnificat,* and the Great Mass in *b*-minor. Bach began the composition of the *St. John Passion* (1723) in Cöthen and finished it in Leipzig. Its present form is the result of several revisions in the course of which the great da-capo choruses at the beginning and end were added. For parts of the text Bach relied on the rather tasteless *Passion Oratorio* by Brockes which Keiser, Telemann, Handel, and Mattheson also set to music, but he retained the Lutheran text of the Gospel for the part of the Evangelist. That Bach composed in great haste we can infer from the fact that the same music recurs several times with changed words. The dramatic realism and conciseness of the *St. John Passion* contrasts conspicuously with the contemplative tone and epic composure of the *St. Matthew Passion* (1729) though the latter does not lack dramatic qualities. A comparison between the wonderfully quiet arioso for bass *Am Abend* (St. M.P. no. 74) and the restive arioso *Betrachte meine Seele* (St. J.P. no. 31) gives an idea of the difference in atmosphere though both ariosi are similar externally. In the *St. Matthew Passion* Bach emphasized the scriptural words by surrounding the words of Christ with a halo of string chords and by entering all scriptural quotations in red ink in the fair copy of the score. The introductory chorus, a complex chorale fantasy for double chorus, two orchestras, and continuo, introduces the *cantus firmus* in a separate unison chorus of boy sopranos. In this movement the organ prelude of Bach's late period appears, transferred to the vocal medium, in its final glorification. In both Passions the same chorales are used more than once, each time harmonized differently in accordance with the text. They comment on the stages of the action and appear either in juxtaposition or even in superimposition with the arias and ariosi. In the bass aria *Mein teurer Heiland* (St. J.P. no. 60) two independent and self-contained compositions, the one a chorale setting, the other a continuo aria for bass, are sounded together simultaneously. Only Bach could create a composition of such bewildering intensity.

The *Magnificat,* the most exuberant and concise of the great choral works, was written for the Christmas Vespers (1723). It anticipates in its D-major splendor and exultation the jubilant choruses of the *b*-minor Mass. Also the use of the Gregorian *tonus peregrinus* as *cantus firmus* points in the direction of the latter work.

Bach composed his Great Mass in *b*-minor for the Catholic court in Dresden in the hope of being rewarded with the title of court composer, a distinction he finally received. He rose above religious denomination in this work. The ordinary of the Mass still existed in the Protestant service, as Bach's smaller Masses prove, but this work transcended in its vast dimensions any liturgical function, be it Protestant or Catholic. Nevertheless Bach underlined the dogmatic importance of certain sections of the ordinary by using the Gregorian melodies for the *Credo* and the *Confiteor* as *cantus firmi* in augmentation or canon. Several movements draw on music from earlier cantatas. The *Crucifixus,* for example, has been borrowed from the vocal chaconne of the cantata *Weinen Klagen* (no. 12), but the sublime turn to major by means of an augmented sixth at the final cadence is a masterly afterthought that occurred to Bach only during the revision for the Mass. The twelve variations on the chaconne bass (third type) represent the *ne plus ultra* of baroque chaconne writing. In no other chorale work of Bach does the luxuriant counterpoint reach such heights, are harmonic richness and contrapuntal density so completely fused together. The tortuous fugue theme of the first *Kyrie*[49] with its infinite harmonic and contrapuntal possibilities sets the tone of the entire work. In view of the dimensions of the work it should not surprise us that the grand da-capo form prevails not only in the arias and duets, but even at times in the choruses.

The *Christmas Oratorio,* frequently counted among the large-scale works, consists of a cycle of independent cantatas for six successive feast days. It is pieced together almost entirely of secular cantatas and thus leads to the secular works or serenades, composed for birthdays, weddings, welcomes, and other occasions in Weimar, Cöthen, and Leipzig. It has often been regretted that Bach had no occasion to write an opera; the closest he ever came to it are the secular cantatas and not by accident are many of them designated as *dramma per musica.* Far from treating them lightly or as inferior works Bach created in his secular cantatas a great treasure of dramatic and humorous music, unfortunately little known. For graceful counterpoint, dramatic characterization, and pictorial representation of nature they challenge comparison with Handel's works in the same genre. Only a list of the outstanding examples can be given here: *The Wedding Cantata, The Peasant Cantata, The Coffee Cantata, Phoebus and Pan, The Satisfied Aeolus,* and *Hercules at the Crossroads.* The last four are unsurpassed masterpieces. The fact that Bach borrowed so frequently from his secular cantatas for his church music (hardly ever the other way around) has been explained by the categorical statement that Bach could not help writing in sacred style, that his secular works were "not genuinely secular" (Spitta). Nothing could be farther from the truth. Firstly, there were no absolute criteria for what was sacred and secular in baroque music, as the constant interchange between the two functions proves; secondly, the reform cantata was itself derived from a secular model; and thirdly, the *contrafactum* represented so essential an element

---

[49] Compare the fugue theme of the same key in the *Well-Tempered Clavier* (I, no. 24).

in baroque music because basic affections governed music, be it secular or sacred. It is most revealing that Bach was careful to retain the basic affection in his adaptations of secular music to his church cantatas; only when pressed for time did he disregard the affections with the inevitable result that the pictorial references of the music became completely unintelligible.

In the instrumental music of the fourth period Bach reaped the fruits of his sustained efforts to give all types a degree of stylization that carried them to the peak of baroque characterization. What distinguishes the later works from the earlier ones are certain traces of modernism that modify the style of Bach, otherwise thoroughly conservative. Not only does the clavieristic virtuoso technique of Domenico Scarlatti come into prominence, especially the crossing of hands, but there are even hints of periodic phrase structure and suggestions of structural thematic contrast, especially in the Partitas and the "Trinity" prelude in E-flat for organ.

The publication of the *Clavierübung* (1731 ff.) confronts us with the anomaly that the *opus 1* of a composer reveals him in his most mature phase. Of the four parts of the collection only the first, second, and fourth belong to the harpsichord: the Partitas, the *Italian Concerto* and the *French Overture* (suite in *b*), and the *Goldberg Variations*. The gigantic *Chromatic Fantasy and Fugue,* the fantasy (and fugue) in *c,* and the second part of the *Well-Tempered Clavier* were not printed during Bach's lifetime. In the partitas and the French Overture the process of stylization is completed: the fact that one movement is entitled *tempo di Minuetta* indicates that even the dance patterns have lost significance. In addition, we find freely inserted character pieces, such as Burlesca, Scherzo, Echo, etc. The introductory movements cover all important forms from the toccata, praeambulum, French overture, and fantasia to the Italian sinfonia. Bach alternated in his courantes between the French and the Italian types, carefully designating each one as courante or corrente[50] respectively. Stylistically the partitas belong to the most advanced works that he ever wrote.

The *Goldberg Variations* sum up the entire history of baroque variation. Written on a chaconne bass in saraband rhythm they are arranged

[50] The stylistic significance of this illuminating distinction has not been grasped by the editors of the *Bach Gesellschaft* edition. Here, and in all subsequent editions, the titles of the second and fourth courante have been "corrected" to *corrente.*

strictly in the order of two free variations and one in canon. The dazzling variety of formal types (canon, fugue, *quodlibet*, dances, overture, trio sonata, etc.) and the inspired complexity of the music is surpassed only by the intricate clavieristic problems and coloristic devices, not commonly associated with Bach's music. In the *Italian Concerto* he adapted in brilliant fashion an orchestral form to a keyboard instrument; it represents the ultimate realization of what he had already attempted in the preludes to the English suites.

The stirring fantasy in *c* raises the bipartite sonata type of Scarlatti to absolute perfection. It is most unfortunate that the fugue to which the fantasy originally served as the prelude has come down to us only in fragmentary form. The second part of the *Well-Tempered Clavier* (1744) [51] collects many of the late and also some of the early works in systematic order. Modern features such as the free-voiced Scarlatti style and the monothematic sonata form (see the prelude in *D*, II, no. 5) distinguish the second part from the first part of the collection. Many fugue themes, *e.g.* the fugue in *a* (II, no. 20), now attained a measure of individuality characteristic only of the most mature Bach style.

The organ music of the Leipzig period begins with the celebrated six trio sonatas [52] which Bach wrote for his son Friedemann. Some movements go back to earlier works, others served in turn as material for later ones. Bach succeeded here in combining concerto form and style with the strictest polyphonic part-writing. By condensing the trio sonata to a solo composition he made his most significant contribution to the secular "chamber music" for organ. In the so-called "great" preludes and fugues in *C, b, e*, and *E*-flat Bach actually achieved the impossible: he brought two heterogeneous forms, the concerto and the fugue, into a higher unity. In these "concerto fugues" the da capo invades the form (see the fugue in *e*), the interludes assume the character of solos, the expositions that of tuttis, and also in the preludes the tutti-solo contrast comes to the fore (see the preludes in *b* and *E*-flat).

[51] Title, content, and order of the *Well-Tempered Clavier* have been imitated by the organist Weber whose cycle was once thought to have been the model for Bach (ed. by the *Neue Bach Gesellschaft*, 1933). It dates, however, from c. 1750 and is musically rather weak. Another imitation was *ABC Musical* by Kirchhoff, a pupil of Pachelbel.

[52] Spitta held with Rust that these sonatas (and also the passacaglia in *c*) were written not for the organ, but for pedal harpsichord. However, the autograph assigns them to "two claviers and pedal," a designation very common in Bach's organ works. Moreover, the manuscripts of the time transmit the sonatas together with organ fugues, and Bach himself inserted several slow movements of the sonatas into organ compositions. Spitta's contention that the term clavier denoted clavichord is erroneous.

Also the liturgical organ music of the Leipzig period is characterized by Bach's attempt to sanctify the concerto form. Under the impact of the concerto the chorale preludes gain a decisively new aspect. They develop into large movements with vastly extended interludes in which the chorale *cantus firmus* appears often subordinate to the free material, worked out independently in concerto style. In view of their internal and external weight these passages are only improperly described as "interludes." The remarkable trio *Allein Gott in der Höh'* in *A* [53] illustrates the extreme of this type: it is really a concerto movement the theme of which anticipates the chorale, but in which the chorale itself is not heard before the very end, and here only in fragmentary form.

The chorale preludes of the late period comprise the six Schübler chorales, the eighteen great preludes that Bach revised and collected shortly before his death, and the third part of the *Clavierübung*. The first set, which appeared also in print, contains only literal transcriptions of cantata movements which disclose the stylistic affinity between Bach's cantata and organ music. The famous "Eighteen" transcend by their magnitude and depth all previous types of chorale prelude. We find here, on the one hand, extensions of the subjective type, known from the *Orgelbüchlein*, with intense pictorial representation of the various stanzas, but, on the other hand, chorale fugues, chorale fantasies, and preludes in concerto style. In the latter group the subjective interpretation is supplanted by a dignified abstract elaboration to which Bach felt himself more and more attracted toward the end of his life. The third part of the *Clavierübung* is perhaps the most impressive monument of Bach's strict observance of the liturgy. It gathers the chorales of the Lutheran Catechism in a highly meaningful order. In correspondence with the Longer and Shorter Catechism each chorale is presented in a longer and a shorter setting, except for the Trinity chorale which must needs appear three times. While the long arrangements belong to the concerto type of prelude, the short ones are mostly chorale fugues. The high technical demands of the preludes become particularly obvious in the six-voice *Aus tiefer Not* which calls for an obbligato double pedal. After the chorales follow four "duets" in form of gigantic inventions to be played during the Communion. The whole collection is framed at the beginning and end by the grandiose "Trinity" or "St. Anne" prelude and fugue in E-flat symbolizing the trinity in the three flats of the key signature and the three themes of the "triple fugue." Consistent with the trend

---

[53] Compare this prelude with the arrangement in *G* of the same chorale in the *Clavierübung* III.

toward archaism Bach turned in this fugue to the tripartite ricercar of the Sweelinck and Froberger type with progressively accelerated themes.

BACH, THE PAST MASTER

The fifth and last period of Bach's creative career comprises the last five years of his life. In this phase the aging master withdrew more and more from the outer world to create in highest maturity his works of solitude and abstraction: the *Canonic Variations* for organ on the chorale *Vom Himmel hoch*, the *Musical Offering*, and the *Art of the Fugue*. These works give the sum and substance of the contrapuntal art of baroque music. All of them penetrate into the last mysteries of polyphony, all of them are contrapuntal variations on a single theme, all of them summon forms from the past but fill them with the spirit of the present. In their conspicuously retrospective attitude they show Bach in the light in which his contemporaries saw him; they regarded him as a consummate master of the past, a past master in the literal and figurative sense.

In the *Canonic Variations* Bach combined the chorale *cantus firmus* in archaic manner with a set of free voices, bound in turn by the strictest of all musical forms, the canon. In the last variation he even introduced all four lines of the chorale simultaneously. The *Musical Offering* (1747) was occasioned by Bach's visit to the court of Frederick II in Potsdam where his son Emanuel served as harpsichordist. The king gave Bach a "truly royal" theme to improvise on. After his return home Bach worked out the possibilities of the subject in a cycle of self-contained contrapuntal variations which covers the entire development of fugal forms from the ricercar—even the title is an acrostic of the word ricercar—to the canonic fugue. The two extended ricercars that flank the cycle enclose two groups of canons of which the first is restricted to canonic variations upon the theme while the second elaborates the theme itself in canon. They disclose supreme mastery of thematic transformation and of such artifices as cancrizans motion and mirror canon. The grand trio sonata which forms the exact centerpiece of the cycle is the most modern composition of the *Musical Offering*, both formally and stylistically. The second movement, a monumental da capo in concerto style, introduces the royal theme at widely spaced intervals in very much the same manner as the late type of chorale prelude does the *cantus firmus*. This trio sonata is by far the best example of the form that Bach ever wrote.

Like many of Bach's earlier works the *Art of the Fugue* also had a didactic purpose. It is a course in fugue writing, designed to unveil step by step the infinite contrapuntal possibilities inherent in a neutral subject and in the fugal procedure as such. By virtue of its profoundly artistic imagination it has become the eternal monument of polyphony altogether. The cycle contains eighteen fugues and canons [54] in roughly symmetrical order. Since Bach seems to have changed the plan of the whole as he progressed in the composition some details of the order, especially the position of the canons, cannot be determined with certainty. Systematically exhausting all the resources of fugue writing from the simplest to the most complicated Bach begins with the simple fugue, then progresses to the inversion of the subject, the counterfugue (in which both subject and its inversion are presented), the double fugue, the triple fugue, the mirror fugue, and ends with the quadruple fugue. Even more impressive than his formidable technical mastery is his art of thematic transformation; he extracts from the neutral theme (Ex. 85a) highly characteristic ideas such as the theme of the first mirror fugue (Ex. 85b). The quadruple fugue has remained a torso.

Ex. 85. Bach: Themes from the Art of the Fugue.

It breaks off just after the completion of the third part in which Bach introduced the letters B A C H (B-flat A C B) for the first time as a fugue subject, thus giving his work also literally the personal stamp for which he had been striving all his life. The fourth part of the fugue that was to contain the combination of the three subjects with the fourth and original one death forced him to leave unfinished. [55]

Stricken with blindness Bach dictated to his son-in-law and pupil his last composition, the chorale prelude *Vor deinen Thron*. For sentimental reasons this organ chorale has been edited as the finale to the *Art of the Fugue* with which it has nothing whatsoever to do. It is actually no more

[54] There are actually twenty compositions, but one double fugue and one mirror fugue are merely revisions or arrangements. For the *Art of the Fugue* and the *Musical Offering* the scholarly editions of David should be consulted (Peters and G. Schirmer respectively). The editions of the *Bach Gesellschaft* give a distorted picture of the order. See also Tovey's edition of the *Art of the Fugue*, 1931.

[55] The fact that the original theme does not appear in the fugue has misled Rust (the editor of the work in the *Bach Gesellschaft*), Schweitzer, and others, to believe that the fugue did not belong to the cycle.

than a revision (though a highly illuminating one) of the chorale *Wenn wir in höchsten Nöten* from the *Orgelbüchlein*. In the ultimate version Bach retained the original harmonization, but sheared the melody of the French embellishments in Böhm's manner and inserted, in keeping with his latest style, extended but strictly thematic interludes. He turned from the youthful subjective interpretation to an objective presentation of the liturgical melody, a change that symbolizes the essence of his artistic development.

The thoroughly personal character that distinguishes Bach's music although it embodies at the same time the typical baroque features in their most powerful concentration is due essentially to three factors. The first of these is the fusion of national styles. The best that the German, Italian, and French styles had to offer appears in his music transformed to a higher unity. The second factor is his almost superhuman technical craftsmanship. It is consistent with baroque psychology in general that technical constrictions stimulated rather than impeded his creative imagination. This is the reason why his allegorical and emblematic references, however intellectual they may be, never cease to be music and serve on the contrary as vehicles of inspiration. So great was his facility in bound forms that it is at times difficult to detect by ear the presence of an *obbligo* like canon. In the sixth canon of the *Goldberg Variations* (Ex. 86) Bach writes his

Ex. 86. Bach: Canon from the Goldberg Variations.

voices at the distance of only a half note (one of the most difficult forms of canon), yet they move as though they were the freely conceived voices of a trio sonata. Another aspect of Bach's craftsmanship is offered by the countless revisions of his own works. The various states of cantatas or instrumental works attest to his critical mind and his tenacious efforts at self-improvement. Only a genius like himself could discover new possibilities in a composition that must have appeared perfect to any other composer.

The third factor, perhaps the most important, is the balance between polyphony and harmony. Bach lived at a time when the declining curve of polyphony and the ascending curve of harmony intersected, where vertical and horizontal forces were in exact equilibrium. This interpenetration of opposed forces has been realized only once in the history of music and Bach is the protagonist of this unique and propitious moment. His melodies have the maximum of linear energy, but are at the same time saturated with harmonic implications. His harmonies have the vertical energy of logical chord progressions, but are at the same time linear in all their voices. Hence, whenever Bach writes harmonically the parts also move independently, and whenever he writes polyphonically the parts move also in tonal harmony. The interpenetration of the two concepts had far-reaching effects on dissonance treatment, melodic design, and texture. Since the harmonic progressions were at any point clearly defined, the voices were free to clash in amazing dissonances. Direct successions of dissonances including even simultaneous cross-relations are not rare in Bach's music, as can be seen in the first three-part invention (Ex. 87), to select a very

Ex. 87. Bach: Excerpt from the first three-part Invention or Sinfonia.

familiar example. They are felt, however, less as dissonances than as accidental results of independent part-writing.

The strict logic of Bach's chord progressions always entailed a fast harmonic rhythm. His harmonic vocabulary was essentially diatonic; Neapolitan and augmented-sixth chords (the only two outstanding chromatic combinations) appear only exceptionally at especially emphatic cadences. In the works of the fifth period chromaticism became slightly more prominent, as can be seen in the first ricercar of the *Musical Offering* or the second triple fugue of the *Art of the Fugue* in which the B-A-C-H-motive appears in passing.

Bach's melodies owe their linear energy to the consistency of rhythmic patterns that are as yet free from the regularity of accent because the melodic climaxes occur successively in the various contrapuntal voices, not simultaneously as they do in music dominated exclusively by harmony. The intervallic structure of his melodies is based on the scale or on free intervallic progressions, not yet as strongly subordinated to the triad as classic themes are. The melodic succession of two thirds was to Bach just one of the numerous intervallic progressions; it is for this reason that non-triadic themes appear much more often with Bach than with any classic composer.

The equilibrium between polyphony and harmony becomes apparent nowhere more clearly than in what may be called his "hidden" or "implied" polyphony. His melodic thinking was so thoroughly imbued with polyphony that he could not help suggesting polyphony even when he wrote a single line. Quite in contrast with classic and romantic composers who divided melodies or chord progressions into several lines in order to produce a sham-polyphony, Bach condensed two independent voices into a single line. The sonatas for violin and cello solo furnish astonishing examples of implied polyphony, but we find it also time and again in other works, for example in the allemande from the second partita (Ex. 88). In the quoted

Ex. 88. Bach: *Allemande* from the second *Partita.*

example the upper voice is reproduced in two forms, first as the single line that Bach wrote and then in a notation that realizes the implied interplay of two sequential voices. Since both the upper and lower line of the allemande follow the same pattern they actually imply a four-part setting within a two-part counterpoint. The polyphonic design of the melody was all the more effective because it lay under the surface of the music and immeasurably enriched its texture. This is the reason why a thin texture in Bach's music sounds often more complex than a thick texture does in the music of his contemporaries. Even when Bach wrote in the style of continuo-homophony, as he did in his concertos, implied polyphony raised the solo part far above a mere spinning-out of figurative harmonies which was the rule with other composers. Implied polyphony and the

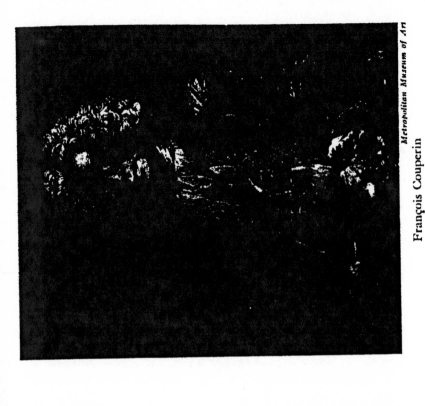

Henry Purcell
from a sketch by J. B. Closterman

François Couperin

George Frederick Handel

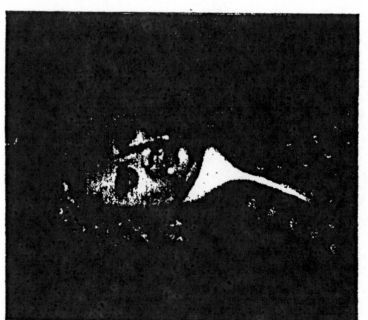

Johann Sebastian Bach
from a painting by Elias Gottlieb Haussmann

fullest independence of part-writing appear in Bach's music paradoxically united with the fullest dependence on tonal harmony. In their unique combination these traits bestow on his music the complex intensity that is the secret of his personal style.

CHAPTER NINE

Coordination of National Styles: Handel

THE STATE OF SECULAR VOCAL MUSIC IN GERMANY
BEFORE HANDEL

THE GERMAN church cantata and the music for keyboard, the decisive factors in the artistic development of Bach, have a far less important function in the creative career of the young Handel. They were to Handel merely part and parcel of a general technical training that he later applied to other musical fields. A survey of secular music in Germany, notably the opera, chamber cantata, and continuo song, forms the appropriate background for the discussion of the music of Handel.

The Italian opera exerted so potent an influence on the opera in Germany and Austria that attempts to establish an opera in the German language remained at first isolated ventures. Italian opera left its mark even in the theatre; several of the German historical tragedies, the so-called *Haupt- und Staatsactionen,* have turned out to be adaptations of Venetian opera libretti. The established centers of Italian opera in Germany continued to flourish in the late baroque period thanks to the efforts of Italian composers or German musicians, well versed in the Italian idiom. The court in Munich was supplied with operas by Steffani, and later by his pupil Torri; in Hanover we find Steffani and later Handel; in Dresden Strungk, Lotti, and later Hasse; Vienna, the main center of the opera, could boast of such masters as Caldara, Conti, the brothers Bononcini, and the Austrian Fux. The operas of Handel and Hasse were performed at the Austrian court together with many others by Italian composers.

The operas of Agostino Steffani (1654–1728) set a standard as exemplary and binding in Germany as those of Lully did in France. Several of Steffani's operas abandon the customary subjects taken from Roman mythology and turn instead to German history, for example, *Alarico*.[1] Since Steffani received his musical education in Germany (though from Italian masters) it is not surprising that his eighteen operas, written mostly for Hanover, show the German propensity for counterpoint and for combining features of the Italian and the French style. They are headed by Lullian overtures, frequently punctuated by trio episodes and rounded off by a minuet movement. Use of the ground bass, and consistently contrapuntal texture of the duets and trios are highly characteristic traits of his opera music though it must be admitted that the opera duets cannot compete in elegance and inspiration with his chamber duets,[2] in which Steffani reached his greatest stature. The concise aria forms, the stereotyped motto beginnings, the quasi-ostinato patterns in the bass, and the instrumental obligatos in a somewhat tentative concerto style belong to the heritage of the modern Venetian opera; but, on the other hand, the comparatively numerous arias with continuo accompaniment indicate Steffani's conservative leanings toward the middle baroque opera. The predilection for wind instruments in the orchestration, later also shown by Handel, reflects German practice whereas the accompanied recitatives with their full orchestral settings point toward French rather than Italian models. The smooth coordination of national styles that Steffani effected in his operas was to become a decisive factor in Handel's music.

The Italian opera rose to perfection at the Viennese court where Zeno watched over the inner reform of the *opera seria*. The Austrian *opera seria* differed from the Italian in its orchestral splendor and contrapuntal dignity, recognized at the time as a Viennese specialty. This was the result of the historically unique influence of the oratorio on the opera. Throughout the baroque period it was the opera that ordinarily served as model for the oratorio. In Vienna, however, the luxuriant counterpoint, extensively cultivated in the oratorio, gained a firm hold on the opera style, as can be seen in the careful workmanship of the choral writing and the prominent position of the chorus, paralleled only in the works of Lully and Purcell. In the operas of Fux (1660–1741) the artistic weight lies on the soloistic ensemble, the chorus for four or five voices, and the grand da-capo aria with obbligato accompaniment. The learned and conservative opera style of Fux, which puts his reputation as a dry-as-dust theorist to shame, enriches the accompaniment by contrapuntal devices including even fugue and canon. The single scenes of the operas are organized as large rondo struc-

[1] DTB 11:2; see also HAM no. 244.
[2] DTB 6:2.

tures by means of recurrent choral sections, as can be seen in *Costanza e Fortezza*,[3] written for the coronation of the Emperor in Prague (1723). Also *Elisa* dealing with the story of Dido and Aeneas excels in choral settings of vast dimensions. Like most Germans Fux was partial to obbligatos for wind instruments, including the *chalumeaux*, the early form of the clarinet. The stylistic conservatism of Fux is most pronounced in his overtures; he follows the old Italian practice instead of the French model and writes church sonatas or even canzonas in a thick, unwieldy texture.

After sporadic attempts during the seventeenth century at introducing opera in the German language the German opera came to full flowering not before the late baroque period. The courts of Brunswick-Wolfenbüttel and Weissenfels were centers of the German court opera. In Brunswick, German operas became famous with Cousser who performed his own works along with those of Erlebach and Philipp Krieger. These composers were, however, later overshadowed by Schürmann, the last German composer of baroque opera. The court of Weissenfels, the only place where the customary intermixture of Italian and German arias was not tolerated, relied primarily on Philipp Krieger's operas in which simple songs predominated.

German opera found vigorous support also in the German cities; the opera in Leipzig was founded and directed by Strungk. The leading and easily the most influential institution of German opera was the public opera house in the Hansa city of Hamburg, founded in 1678 by a number of enterprising burghers and senators. Hamburg, the "Venice on the Elbe," emulated the commercial opera in Venice. The opera "at the Goosemarket" soon attracted the most promising composers of German opera. The essentially popular background of the Hamburg opera is evident in the choice of local subjects, the appearance of dialect songs, and the rejection of castrato singing. Market women and dames of more than questionable reputation sang the female roles in the absence of castrati. The comic intermezzi of the operas soon aroused the ire of the pious merchants, and for a number of years a heated controversy raged in which Pietists and orthodox Protestants clashed once more, this time over the purely worldly issue of the opera. Naturally, the Pietists took an inimical attitude toward opera; they succeeded in banning it for a short time, but their opposition was ultimately overridden. The Hamburg opera flourished for sixty years in the course of which about 250 works were produced. The earliest operas in Hamburg, still indebted to middle baroque style, rose from humble be-

[3] SCMA 2, also DTOe XVII (vol. 34–35).

ginnings, such as *Singspiele* and school dramas with spoken dialogue which, based on biblical subjects, were performed for the edification of the Hamburg merchants. Similar sacred subjects were presented in *Singspiel* form by Löhner in Nuremberg. The Hamburg opera was inaugurated by the *Singspiel Adam und Eva* by Theile, a pupil of Schütz and a respectable contrapuntist. After Theile's hurried withdrawal Nikolaus Strungk and Johann Wolfgang Franck,[4] who also belong to the early period of the Hamburg opera, took his place.

The period knew only three prominent composers of German opera: Johann Sigismund Cousser (1660–1727), Reinhard Keiser (1674–1739), and Georg Kaspar Schürmann (c. 1672–1751). All of these were, at various times, affiliated with the Hamburg opera. Cousser (or Kusser), a man of restless and impetuous character, had a most adventurous career which began in Paris where he learned the craft from Lully, continued in Brunswick and Hamburg (1693–95) where he earned his greatest fame, and ended in Dublin. Cousser's operas, which are only fragmentarily preserved,[5] display a motley of styles of which Lully and Steffani form the most notable single ingredients. His vocal music is obligated to the Italian master. We find concise da-capo arias in Italian bel-canto style, sometimes with obbligato accompaniment, and sometimes with ostinati. On the other hand, airs in dance rhythm and simple duets bespeak French influence as clearly as strophic continuo songs do that of the popular German *Singspiel*. An English serenata composed in Dublin is so far the only extant example of Cousser's recitative style. Cousser never succeeded in unifying the various styles, but his personal influence was nevertheless a stimulating one. Under his directorship the Hamburg opera rose above the prevailing provincialism since he opened the doors to the Italian bel canto and the French instrumental style. Cousser's spirited musicianship aroused the enthusiasm of his fellow-musicians and Mattheson portrayed him as the model of the *Vollkommene Kapellmeister* (1739). Cousser performed Italian, French, and German operas in exemplary fashion true to the style and spirit of the composer, as Mattheson expressly states. Both as conductor and composer Cousser stimulated the budding talents of Keiser and Schürmann.

With Keiser the Hamburg opera passed through the most brilliant phase of its history. Lavishly praised by his contemporaries as the greatest opera composer, admired by both Steffani and Handel, Keiser still commands today the highest respect as a master of lyric and dramatic affections. His

---

[4] See *Die drey Töchter Cecrops* in EL.
[5] See the arias from *Erindo* in EL, also GMB no. 250.

extravagant conduct during his affluent years in Hamburg reflects the colorful conditions under which the public opera flourished and of which it became finally a victim. Keiser found a congenial poet of sure dramatic instinct in the librettist Feind whose *Gedancken von der Opera* (1708) give a well-reasoned account of the dramaturgy of the opera. In this treatise Feind discussed the poetic form of the da-capo aria for which he required a simile or a sententious moral. In view of the later development of the opera in Hamburg it is significant that he deplored the growing popularity of coarsely comic characters on the opera stage.

Of Keiser's alleged 116 operas only about two dozen have come down to us. Like the Venetians Keiser interpolated songs in local dialect into his operas, in this case songs in the Low German of the Hamburg variety. Beginning with *Claudius* (1703) Keiser mixed Italian arias and German ones, a fashion that Feind continued in the libretti to *Octavia* (1705), *Lucretia,* and *Masagniello furioso,* the last of which deals with the subject of the *Muette de Portici.* The score of *Octavia* [6] is important with regard to Handel who incorporated sections from it into his own music. Keiser's *Almira* (1706) was written in direct rivalry with Handel's first opera by the same name which proved so successful that Keiser feared to lose his supremacy on the Hamburg stage. After the bankruptcy of the opera under Keiser's extravagant management the composer fled from Hamburg, but returned later to write a number of new operas, notably *Croesus, L'Inganno fedele,* and *Jodelet.* [7]

A fine flair for palpably popular, yet artistic, musical effects runs through all of Keiser's music. Its earthy simplicity may be in part a re-flection of the popular demands of the audience, but it is at the same time a thoroughly personal characteristic. Although Steffani's concise aria style still obtained, Keiser's general attitude was more advanced: he brought to the German opera the innovations of the fully developed Italian con-certo style with electrifying violin passages in unison and running basses, handled by him in a somewhat angular fashion. He very clearly anticipated the "Handelian" type of melody in which a pregnant motive is placed upon a sequentially running bass and in which characteristic sudden halts and speaking rests interrupt the flow of the melody, as can be seen in the aria ritornello from *Croesus* (Ex. 89).

Keiser required from the singer Italian agility in strongly rhythmical

[6] Supplement to the *Handel Gesellschaft.*
[7] For the first two operas see DDT 37-38, for the last one, Eitner PAM 18; see also HAM no. 267.

coloratura passages which betray the unmistakable influence of the violin idiom. Many arias call for elaborate orchestral accompaniments, which may include the *chalumeaux*, trumpets, and other wind instruments. The less frequent, but important, continuo arias are generally reserved for songs

Ex. 89. Keiser: Ritornello from *Croesus*.

in the popular style of the German *Singspiel*. With their catchy melodies and their homespun humor they became the song hits of the day. In highly dramatic scenes Keiser preferred the arioso to the da-capo aria; but the latter form also is dramatically represented in such excellent arias as *Götter übt Barmherzigkeit* (Gods, have mercy), sung by Croesus when he is led to the stake. This aria unfolds on a quivering bass with quasi-ostinato patterns suggesting most vividly the affection of fear. The choruses are written in the grand oratorical manner exemplified by the opening chorus of *Croesus* in which the styles of Keiser and Handel come amazingly close to each other. One of Keiser's peculiarities is the use of ensemble recitative, by this time not very frequent in Italian opera. His recitatives have on the whole a highly individual tone; in their flawless declamation, their rhythmic vitality, and their emphatic, if slightly uncouth, power they are often reminiscent of the English recitative.

Although Keiser was strongly indebted to Italian opera style its features assumed in his hands a Germanized and personalized form. Keiser was too independent a musician to imitate slavishly. As was customary with every German composer, he retained features of the French style, especially the Lullian overture, the concluding rondeau, the dance suite, and refrain sections in the recitative. Yet the trend in Germany toward the Italian opera is clearly exposed by the two overtures to *Croesus:* the first version has a French overture, the final version an Italian sinfonia.

Mattheson and the indefatigable Telemann must be mentioned beside Keiser as the last composers of the Hamburg stage. Telemann who wrote about forty operas produced in his witty *Pimpinone* [8] a comic opera that anticipates *La Serva Padrona* by eight years. Telemann's career belongs to the declining phase of the Hamburg opera during which coarsely

[8] ER VI.

comic subjects prevailed. The oncoming *opera buffa* superseded these attempts to establish a comic opera in German.

The importance of Keiser for the public opera parallels that of Schürmann for the German court opera. With Schürmann the German opera at the court of Brunswick-Wolfenbüttel reached the peak of its development. Schürmann had learned his craft in Hamburg while serving as singer under Cousser. Although Schürmann's melodic invention is more restrained and less in the popular vein than that of Keiser, he surpasses Keiser in the noble finish of his arias. The stylistic contrast between the two composers corresponds to the difference between a public and a court opera. Many of Schürmann's numerous operas deal with subjects of German history as does, for example, *Ludovicus Pius* (1726).[9] In Schürmann's music, too, the characteristically German mixture of French and Italian styles can be observed. While his instrumental forms, especially the overtures and the ballets, point toward France, his vocal music leans toward Italy. Schürmann is perhaps the only composer of German opera able to beat the Italians on their own ground, namely in the grand da-capo aria. The expansion of the first part of the aria into two distinct sections recurs with Schürmann more regularly than in any of his fellow composers. In his dignified pathos, his rich harmonic resources, and his solid workmanship he had no rival except Bach. In the remarkably fine aria of Judith in *Ludovicus* [10] his melodic style holds midway between Bach's melodic complexity and Handel's broad cantilena. However, his numerous unpretentious, songlike arias foreshadow the coming of the *style galant*.

In spite of the promising strides of the German opera it was doomed to failure for lack of support from the educated middle classes. Shortly after 1730 the German opera houses ceased to produce operas and either closed down or were taken over by Italians. The opera in Germany became again what it had been in the beginning: a courtly importation. The semi-secular oratorios and passions which flourished in the cities, especially Hamburg, were the only outlet for dramatic music of high standards. Keiser, Handel, Telemann,[11] and Mattheson [12] composed works of this genre, notably a Passion Oratorio, based on the theatrical poetry of the Hamburg senator Brockes. Like Brockes himself, all four composers dealt

[9] Eitner PAM 17; see also the three books of arias ed. by Gustav F. Schmidt.
[10] GMB no. 293.
[11] DDT 28; HAM no. 272.
[12] GMB no. 267.

with the biblical subjects in an operatic rather than devotional spirit. True to the new ideas of enlightenment Brockes and his circle interpreted the passion as an individual tragedy that could be told in the poet's own words in a series of edifying experiences. Thus deprived of liturgical objectivity the passion became suitable more to the concert hall than the church. The semi-secular oratorio had a direct bearing on Handel's ethical conception of oratorio which interpreted biblical subjects as great examples of eternal human experience. The oratorios of Telemann form the transition from the baroque to the period of enlightenment. Telemann approached the biblical stories in the modern spirit of sensibility. The contemplative attitude toward nature, then newly discovered, is clearly manifested in his oratorio *Die Tageszeiten* which in many ways directly anticipates *The Seasons* by Haydn.

The secular cantata and the continuo song of the late baroque period were completely overshadowed by the opera, as the numerous cantatas of Telemann, Keiser, and many smaller talents show. Telemann's "monodrama" *Ino* and Keiser's collection *Gemüths-Ergötzung* (1698) deserve special mention as outstanding examples of the secular solo cantata. Franck, equally distinguished as composer of opera and sacred music, tended to merge the style of his sacred continuo songs and that of his opera arias so that they became practically undistinguishable. The most eminent composer in the smaller forms was Erlebach (1657-1714) whose *Harmonische Freude* (I. 1697, II. 1710) [13] must be regarded as the most attractive collection of continuo songs of the period. Strong operatic influence comes to light not only in the fact that Erlebach called his songs "arias," but also in such features as motto beginnings, obbligato accompaniments, use of coloratura, and interpolated arioso sections that raise certain arias to the level of small cantatas. Erlebach excelled in the graphic representation of affections of gaiety and gravity by purely melodic means, such as rippling coloraturas [14] or plaintive sighs (Ex. 90).

The innumerable collections of secular songs for the homes of the urban middle class either emulated the opera as best they could or relapsed into unpretentious songs in à-la-mode dance rhythms. In song collections like the *Tafelkonfekt* (Augsburg 1733 ff.) [15] by Rathgeber, and the *Sing, Spiel,*

[13] DDT 46-47; see also HAM no. 254.
[14] See the coloraturas in GMB no. 262.
[15] ER XIX, also Lindner, *Geschichte des deutschen Liedes*, 1871.

und Generalbassübungen (1734) [16] by Telemann the *style galant* began to encroach on baroque style and definitely triumphed in Sperontes' famous collection *Die Singende Muse an der Pleisse* (1736 ff.) [17] in which elegant and trifling French songs of the rococo appear supplied with German words.

Ex. 90. Erlebach: Aria from *Harmonische Freude*.

HANDEL: GERMAN APPRENTICE PERIOD

Secular music in Germany was stylistically much more closely allied with the modern strands in French and Italian music than was sacred music. This progressive attitude prevails also in the works of Handel, the last great master of baroque music and the exact contemporary of Bach and Domenico Scarlatti. Unlike Bach, George Frideric Handel [18] (b. February 23, 1685 in Halle; d. April 14, 1759 in London) came from a family indifferent to music and chose his musical career against the wishes of his father, a surgeon and barber who wanted his son to become a lawyer. Handel's musical talent showed itself early and proved irrepressible. In 1696, Handel found in Zachow, organist at the Liebfrauenkirche in Halle, a thorough and congenial teacher, "a man very strong in his art" to whom Handel, according to his own admission, owed very much. Under Zachow's guidance Handel perfected himself on the keyboard, the violin, and the oboe and received a fine grounding in counterpoint. He became especially proficient in the Italian type of "double fugue," *i.e.* fugues with counter-subjects which figured prominently in his much-admired improvisations.

[16] Reprint 1927.
[17] DDT 35-36.
[18] This is the Anglicized spelling that Handel adopted, his name was spelled originally Georg Friedrich Händel.

Like Bach he acquired solid craftsmanship through diligent copying of compositions by German cantors and Italian masters. He copied not only cantatas by Zachow but also keyboard music by Froberger, Kerll, Strungk, Ebner, Johann Krieger, Pachelbel, and others. Significantly, most of these masters belonged to the south German school which depended on Italian style. As though by a process of natural selection Handel, from the very beginning, kept allegiance to the facile Italian approach to counterpoint. Although he learned the ponderous organist's manner it hardly suited him temperamentally, if we can judge by the scant use he made of it in his later works. It has been claimed that the young Handel visited Berlin and its Italian opera which was flourishing there with Ariosti, Pistocchi, and Giovanni Battista Bononcini. If this visit really took place, it would represent Handel's first contact with Italian opera. As early as 1701 Handel met Telemann who, like Handel, was supposed to pursue the study of law, and from Telemann's autobiography we learn that Handel was regarded as important even at this early time. At the age of seventeen he attained his first musical position, that of organist at the cathedral in Halle. Although the cathedral belonged to the Reformed Church, the Lutheran Handel was chosen since no "reformed subject" could be found.

The creative career of Handel falls, like that of Bach, into several periods that correspond more or less closely to the phases of his life. In the case of Handel we can distinguish three periods which may be named after the successive stages that a guild craftsman traditionally went through. The first, the German apprentice period, ended in 1706; the second, the Italian journeyman period, ended in 1710; the third, the English master period, extended from 1711 to 1759. It comprised two distinct, though actually overlapping, phases: the opera period (1711–c. 1737) which ended with Handel's physical breakdown, and the oratorio period which began as early as 1720, but which was fully established not before 1738.

Of Handel's innumerable compositions none can be definitely dated to the beginning of the apprentice period in Halle. Three German arias,[19] a sonata for gamba, and the first version of *Laudate pueri,* later revised in Italy, may possibly go back to his student years. A church cantata *Ach Herr, mich armen Sünder*[20] has been ascribed to Handel, however without sufficient proof. The decisive event of the apprentice period was Handel's resolution to abandon the study of law and to move to Hamburg, the center of German secular music (1703). As violinist and later as harpsi-

[19] Not included in the CE; see Seiffert in *Festschrift für Liliencron,*
[20] *Organum,* I, 12.

chordist at the Hamburg opera Handel came in contact with Keiser, just then at the zenith of his fame, and with the young Mattheson whose report in the *Ehrenpforte* is the main source of information about Handel's life during this period. When he came to Hamburg Handel was at the crossroads of his musical career. Mattheson's and Handel's journey to Lübeck, which they undertook to present themselves as possible successors to Buxtehude's position, proves that Handel at least toyed with the idea of following the German organistic tradition. That Handel did not neglect the organ in Hamburg we know through Mattheson, but no organ compositions have survived from the period.

Mattheson also reports that Handel, before he came to Hamburg, had "perfect harmony," that he was "stronger than Kuhnau in counterpoint, especially in extemporized counterpoint, but knew little of melody." Several sonatas for either violin or viola da gamba and continuo or *cembalo concertato* [21] can give us an idea of Handel's early chamber-music style. They evince both a conservative and progressive attitude. The mechanically spun sequential patterns perpetuate the conservative German organistic routine, while the obbligato accompaniment, in itself a progressive feature, is written in a modern, if rather stiff, concerto style.

Handel's first major contribution to church music was his *St. John Passion* (1704), written to words by Postel, the celebrated librettist of Keiser. Postel belonged to the circle of Neumeister, Hunold-Menantes, and Brockes, all well-known for their reform of the church cantata, oratorio, and passion after the model of the opera and the secular cantata. It is significant in view of Handel's oratorio compositions that he, at this early stage, came in touch with this movement. In the *St. John Passion* he took the first step toward an oratorical work in which the liturgical ties were loosened though not yet severed. Postel went less far in the elimination of scriptural words that Hunold-Menantes did in Keiser's oratorio "The Bloody and Dying Jesus" (1704), famous for its revelling in bloodcurdling and sensational pictures. It is, however, characteristic that there are no chorales in Handel's passion. The whole is a colorful mixture of short *concertato* choruses in archaic style, *secco* and *accompagnato* recitatives, ensembles, and arias in opera style. There is no trace of the thorough *cantus-firmus* elaboration that distinguishes Zachow's church cantatas. Obviously, it was now Keiser's,

---

[21] CE 48, 112, Seiffert's edition (Breitkopf) no. 21, and one thus far unpublished sonata, described by Coopersmith (*Papers, International Congress of Musicology* [AMS], 1939, 218). We owe more than ten volumes of unknown or unpublished music by Handel to the painstaking research of Dr. Coopersmith.

not Zachow's path that Handel was following, a path that led directly to the opera.

The self-assured and brilliant fashion in which Handel established himself in the opera leaves no doubt about the true nature of his genius. With uncanny adaptability he deliberately composed his first opera in Keiser's style. Although it does not surpass Keiser, it makes it evident why the older master feared that his own success might be on the wane. Of the four operas that Handel wrote for Hamburg only the first, *Almira* (1705), has survived. The highly diversified score literally bristles with youthful ideas. The mixture of German and Italian in the libretto is faithfully reflected in the style of the music. Handel poured out a stream of Italian arias with motto beginnings and with obbligatos in concerto style. He turned the stereotyped motto to thrilling musical effect by interrupting the voice-part with rushing string passages that seem to snatch the notes away from the singer. Like the early Bach, Handel did not treat the voice very idiomatically; at this time he could not yet "hide the pedant," as Mattheson puts it. The lack of melodic suppleness and the overemphasis on rhythmic crispness in Handel's early concerto style imply that he learned it from a German, not an Italian master. The German arias in *Almira* are not formally stereotyped and breathe the captivating lyricism of Keiser. Also in Keiser's vein are the simple street songs demonstrating Handel's gift for the popular. Ostinato basses occur in *Almira* more frequently than in the later operas; often the ground bass is strictly applied only in the principal part of the aria while the middle part develops it as a patterned bass. Except for the French overture, the fairly numerous instrumental pieces lean more toward the Italian than the French style. The modest saraband from the third act must be mentioned because it contains the essence of one of Handel's most famous melodies (Ex. 91). It appeared in revised form as

Ex. 91. Handel: *Saraband* from *Almira*.

Lascia ch'io pianga in *Rinaldo*. This melody established a personal melodic type on which Handel fell back time and again but which remained essentially unchanged because it was perfect. In the accompanied recitatives and ariosi Handel rose at times even above Keiser. On the whole, Handel proved by his first opera that the pupil had learned what he could from the master and that in order to develop further he would have to turn to the European center of the opera: Italy.

ITALIAN JOURNEYMAN PERIOD

The stimulus Handel received during his journeyman period can be compared with Bach's creative encounter with Buxtehude. However, whereas Buxtehude's music released in Bach for the first time decisive creative energies, the Italian experience merely gave the final stamp to Handel whose imagination was already vividly active. What Handel still lacked was neither contrapuntal skill nor melodic inventiveness, but the *cantabile* style of the melody, the unmistakable idiom of the Italian bel canto.

The journeyman period led Handel through the important musical cities of Italy: Florence, Rome, Naples, and Venice. It brought him in touch with Alessandro Scarlatti, Pasquini, Corelli, Marcello, Lotti, Gasparini, Steffani, and Domenico Scarlatti. In Rome he was drawn into the exclusive circle of noblemen, artists, and musicians, gathered in the *Arcadia,* originally a literary academy for the improvement of artistic taste. The Arcadians assumed pastoral sobriquets and affected to live in an idyllic atmosphere remote from reality. Handel gained his entrée to this assembly of the most brilliant spirits of the time merely by virtue of his recognized talent without becoming a formal member of the group. In these refined surroundings Handel became familiar with what later emerged as one of the fundamental features of his music: the idyllic pastoral and the contemplation of nature. In the *Arcadia* Handel could also display his marvellous talent for improvisation in extemporized cantatas. The encounter with Domenico Scarlatti in Rome in which the two friends matched forces on the harpsichord and the organ was also primarily a contest of improvisatory and instrumental virtuosity. To interpret the outcome as the victory of German over Italian music, as some writers have done, seems unwarranted, especially since we do not know what the contestants played and since neither had as yet published any keyboard music. If we can judge from the organ music known to date from the period, Handel tried to assimilate Italian features and avoided German characteristics.

Once arrived in Italy Handel began to compose furiously. He directed the flood of composition into four channels: the secular cantata, Catholic church music, the oratorio, and the opera. The chamber cantata, on which Handel centered his attention, served him as proving ground. Here he could experimentally explore the whole range of his music from the idyllic to the dramatic without being handicapped by the consideration of the popular demands of the opera. The majority of Handel's cantatas, numbering more than a hundred, belongs to the Italian period; about a quarter call for more or less elaborate accompaniments, the rest are continuo cantatas. They contain some of Handel's most difficult arias both from the musical and technical point of view. Using the cantatas of Alessandro Scarlatti as a starting point Handel enlarged the dimensions and deepened the affective power of his models. They served him at the same time as exercises in bel-canto style and as vehicles to the complete mastery of the Italian style. Not by accident did he, in later years, fall back so often on material assembled in his Italian period.

The unrestrained exuberance of the youthful Handel reigns supreme in the fiery and unruly cantata *Lucrezia,* quoted in Mattheson's *Generalbass-Schule* because of its outlandish keys and its difficult continuo part. It requires stupendous vocal virtuosity though it is made subservient to a musical purpose. Handel expressed the affection of fury by means of an extraordinary melodic line showing that he did not hesitate to write intervals considered unsingable at the time. The cantata stands in the tradition of experimental works, such as Scarlatti and Gasparini exchanged. However, unlike Scarlatti, Handel was interested in melodic rather than harmonic experiments. He bestowed even on the continuo part breath-taking melodic agility, exploiting for this purpose the idiomatic arpeggio style of the harpsichord. The cantata *Armida abbandonata,* notable for the fact that Bach took a copy of it, begins with an unusual recitative *senza basso* in which only two violins provide the accompaniment. It contains also an impassioned recitative with *furioso* accompaniment, a designation of which Handel was very fond in this period. *Arresta il passo* and *Apollo e Dafne* are imposing dramatic scenes, designed on a large scale. The first of these utilized sections from *Almira,* and, in turn, both scenes repeatedly furnish material for later works. The siciliano aria in *Apollo e Dafne* is an outstanding example of the pastoral idyl which in Handel's later works invariably took the form of a siciliano. Arcadian spirit pervades also the cantata *Händel, non può mia musa* [22] in which the poet Cardinal Panfili extols the composer as the "new Orpheus." The work was probably extemporized

---

[22] See Coopersmith, *op. cit.* 219; Example in Streatfeild, *Musical Antiquary* 2 (1911), 223. Not included in CE.

by Panfili and Handel at one of the meetings of the *Arcadia*. The chamber
cantata *Agrippina* surprises by its firm delineation of rapidly changing
affections. It contains an interesting early example of Handel's typical
bel-canto style, the *adagio* aria *Come o Dio* (Ex. 92). Here a hymnic melody

Ex. 92. Handel: Bel-canto aria from the cantata *Agrippina*.

of simple gestic pathos slowly flows forth upon a steady bass support,
interrupted in highly characteristic fashion by affective halts or rests.
Although this example seems clumsy compared with such perfect bel-
canto arias as *Cara sposa* from *Rinaldo* it indicates that the melodic type,
which reappears time and again in the later works, was now firmly rooted
in Handel's music. These deceptively simple melodies draw their strength
from the conjunction of a sustained melody and the continuo-homophony
of the bass. They are vocal counterparts to the instrumental concerto style.
Both late baroque bel-canto and concerto style are based on continuo-
homophony, but they exploit it in their own way: the instrumental style
by the fire of the *allegro* passages, the bel canto by the power of sustained
notes that permit the voice to gather momentum and to unfold its sensuous
sonority.

In the measure in which Handel learned to master the Italian bel canto
he assimilated and developed another influence: the concerto grosso. He
strove for a close rapprochement between concerto grosso and aria in large-
scale compositions in which the voice not merely competed with the obbligato instruments, but, in addition, formed a concertino with them while the
aria ritornello functioned as *ripieno*. The cantata *Delirio amoroso* offers a
very obvious example of the concerto-grosso aria, an aria type that was to
play an important role in the opera and the oratorio.

The pastoral serenata *Aci, Galatea e Polifemo*, composed in Naples
(1708), brings us to the larger forms, the oratorio and the opera. The
serenata is chiefly remarkable for skilful obbligatos and the extensive
sequential part-writing in the duets. On the whole, Handel turned the

German organistic routine to good advantage, though it sometimes ran away with him as it often did in the early Italian cantatas. The tremendous bass arias deserve special attention, likewise the unbridled continuo parts which participate in striking manner in the affective characterization and call for a virtuoso like Handel himself.

With *Il Trionfo del Tempo* (1707) and *La Resurrezione* (1708) Handel made his first contributions to the secular and sacred oratorio respectively. Since the opera in Rome was forbidden at the time by Papal decree the oratorio enjoyed a great vogue differing from the opera only in its moral and devout subjects. It is therefore not surprising that certain pieces from the *Resurrezione* found their way into Handel's later operas. The solos predominate in these oratorios, and, although there are choruses, they play a subordinate role and appear in simple settings at the end of the acts as in the opera. The *Trionfo,* an allegorical solo oratorio on a moral subject, reveals how deeply Handel entered the spirit of the concerto grosso, just then all the rage in Rome. Obviously, he swam with the stream of fashion. His work contains highly developed concerto-grosso arias with rich orchestral accompaniments, and an orchestral "sonata" that would be more properly designated as concerto grosso. In this "sonata" a concertino of violins and oboes alternates with the solo organ. We have here the earliest example of the organ concerto, later brought to fame in England. In connection with the *Trionfo* the anecdote has been told that Corelli failed to play a passage of the French overture in the appropriate fiery and rhythmic French style. Whether true or not, the story illustrates an indubitable fact, namely that Handel by dint of his German background was as a matter of course familiar with the French style while it was still something new and out of the ordinary in Italy. Handel discarded the French overture and composed a concerto grosso instead, employing in it the typical formulas and mannerisms of Corelli to such a degree that the whole could be taken for a calculated parody of the Corelli style, were it not for the pathetic slow movement that only Handel could write. The score of the *Trionfo* was twice revised by Handel, first in 1732, and again in 1757. The latter revision, representing at the same time Handel's last important composition, gave the work the English form in which it is known today.

The Catholic church music in Latin, mostly psalms for solos, chorus, and orchestra, displays the customary pomp and circumstance of the Roman style. The psalms interest mainly as documents of Handel's adaptability. With the greatest of ease did the Lutheran composer take up the luxuriant counterpoint and the choral virtuosity typical of Catholic church music of the late baroque. The psalm *Dixit Dominus* elaborates a solemn *cantus firmus*, later used again in the tenth *Chandos Anthem* and in *Deborah*. It appears here to the jubilant accompaniment of fanfare motives and a terse anapestic rhythm to which Handel gave the final stamp in the Hallelujah chorus of the *Messiah*.

Handel's early contributions to Italian opera were so signally successful that they proved decisive for his future career. The first work, *Rodrigo*, of which only fragments have been preserved, borrows heavily both from Handel's own *Almira* and Keiser's *Octavia*, and has furnished in turn material for *Agrippina* (1709). The latter opera, written for the carnival in Venice, proved to the world that Handel had become a composer of European stature, equal to the most famed masters in the field: Alessandro Scarlatti, Giovanni Battista Bononcini, Porpora, and Lotti. In *Agrippina* the extensive studies in the dramatic and lyric Italian style bore rich fruit. The score is shot through with borrowings from cantatas, the two oratorios, the pastoral serenata, and *Rodrigo;* but Handel showed his matured judgment by telling revisions which usually shorten the first versions. The experimental stage of Handel's music was now overcome.

An amazing variety of types and forms unfolds in *Agrippina* ranging from flawlessly set solo and ensemble recitatives, affective *accompagnato* recitatives, vast coloratura arias in grand da-capo form, to simple dance songs in a catchy popular tone. Handel is known to have been interested even in such lowly material as street cries as possible melodies for his music.[28] The immediate success of *Agrippina* was due to the freshness of melodic invention and to the deliberately playful manner in which Handel seized upon conventional ideas. They were in themselves common property of eighteenth-century composers and gained musical interest only through his imaginative treatment. He gave them a new individual turn by varied repetition of short phrases, and a startling and unexpected continuation of the melody which seems cadential, but time and again postpones the actual cadence. The ritornello from the last aria of *Agrippina* exemplifies such continual deferment of the cadence and illustrates at the same time the

[28] See Streatfeild, *Handel*, 254.

sweeping and irresistible drive that Handel bestowed on the concerto style (Ex. 93). In the aria *Bel piacere* (III, 10) Handel's youthful playfulness is evident in the consistent alternation between 3/8 and 2/4 meter. It is one

Ex. 93. Handel: Ritornello from the opera *Agrippina*.

of the numerous examples in which he treated meter more freely than any other baroque composer (Ex. 94). This melody, which appears again in *Rinaldo*, is stated without continuo accompaniment in unison with the violins. It belongs to the *all'unisono* type of arias, very common in the late

Ex. 94. Handel: Unison aria from *Agrippina*.

Bel pia - ce-re   è go-   de-re fi-do a - mor

Venetian and Neapolitan opera. The numerous unison arias in *Agrippina* occur in two forms: either the melody is doubled by the violins only while the bass and the continuo are silent, or it is reinforced in unison and octaves by the whole orchestra including the bass. In the latter case the harpsichord continuo would possibly provide a thin chordal accompaniment, but in either case a practically monophonic aria results in which the melody alone carries the entire weight of the composition. Such melodic emphasis is a harbinger of the *style galant* although the consistent patterns of Handel's monophonic arias imply a fast harmonic rhythm, inconsistent with the homophony of the *style galant*. Arias in bel-canto style and lyrical sicilianos stand side by side with the modern monophonic arias. On the other hand, we find the severe baroque style preserved in stately arias with a concise fugal accompaniment. The score gives in its variety a summary of both the old and new aspects of Italian opera, seen through the individuality of a young composer who was to lead baroque opera to perfection.

A German interlude separates the Italian journeyman period from the English master period. Recognized as a master, Handel left Italy to become the successor of Steffani at the court of the Elector of Hanover (1710). The interlude did not last very long because Handel took a leave from his position without returning to it, though he was not spared the embarrassment of having his former employer ultimately follow him to England as King George I. The famous anecdote that the reconciliation between the king and Handel was brought about by the *Water Music* is probably legendary; at any rate there is no historical evidence that Handel ever incurred the royal displeasure.

In Hanover Handel learned from Steffani the last secrets of bel-canto writing and paid homage to him in his masterly Italian chamber duets and trios (c. 1712). In these works the contrapuntal texture is kept fluid and is completely subordinated to the sensuous splendor and even flow of the bel canto. Handel proved that he had rid himself of the conventional organistic routine. Besides the chamber duets Handel composed only two other German works, both on words by Brockes. The first is the Passion Oratorio (c. 1715), written in rivalry with Keiser and Telemann and later set also by Mattheson. Bach found it worth his while to copy the score although it is only an occasional work in which Handel drew, as usual, on previously composed music, both secular and sacred. Handel came back to this music in such widely different compositions as the *Chandos Anthems, Giulio Cesare, Deborah,* and the keyboard fugues. The other German work is a set of nine arias with obbligato instruments (1729) [24] which represents together with the works of Erlebach the finest contribution to the devotional or moral song literature of the late baroque period.

ENGLISH MASTER PERIOD: THE OPERAS

When Handel went to England for the production of *Rinaldo* (1711) he came there, paradoxically enough, as the true representative of Italian art. Before Handel's arrival several futile attempts had been made to establish an English opera, especially by Clayton (*Arsinoë,* 1706) who pillaged

[24] Not in CE; ed. by Roth (Breitkopf).

Italian operas and presented them in English translation. *Thomyris,* another operatic compilation for which Motteux had written the libretto, used arias by Alessandro Scarlatti and Giovanni Battista Bononcini; only the recitatives had been specially composed by Pepusch. As in Hamburg, polyglot operas were the order of the day in London. The only really English opera of the time, *Rosamond* (1707) with words by Addison and music by Clayton, was doomed to failure because of the incompetence of its composer. A successful performance of Scarlatti's *Pyrrhus and Demetrius,* aided by the virtuoso singing of the castrato Nicolini, paved the way for the Italian domination of the London stage.

The violent ups and downs of Handel's opera period (1711–1737) clearly reflect the vicissitudes of the commercial opera companies of the time. During the first phase (1711–1715) Handel composed four operas. In the following five years he rested from his main concern and wrote no opera. This "creative rest" is comparable to Bach's rest from his "final goal," the composition of church cantatas, during the Cöthen period. With the foundation of the Royal Academy of Music (1720) under the management of the crafty Heidegger the second phase began in which Handel found himself in rivalry with Ariosti and Bononcini. This phase took a disastrous turn because of internal squabbles among the singers, especially between the two prima donnas Faustina and Cuzzoni, and the paralyzing success of *The Beggar's Opera* (1728). Three further attempts followed; first the New Royal Academy, then the struggle between Handel's own company and the "Opera of Nobility" (1733) which boasted such celebrities as the castrati Senesino and Farinelli. It was the most brilliant, if short-lived, phase of the London opera in the course of which Handel was pitted against Porpora and Hasse, the leading Italian composers of the time. The issues involved were actually not artistic but political ones. The Prince of Wales and the anti-German faction of the English nobility who backed the Opera of Nobility sought to gain ground against the German court by attacking the foreigner Handel, little concerned about the paradoxy of the situation: the nationalistic faction fought with the weapon of the foreign Italian opera and summoned the aid of foreigners such as Hasse, himself an Italianized German like Handel. After the struggle had inevitably ruined both companies, the fifth and last phase of the opera was merely satyric drama after the tragedy. It began after Handel's physical breakdown (1737) and lasted to 1741 when Handel had already definitely turned to the oratorio.

Rinaldo (1711) taking London by storm opens the chain of forty operas, composed over a period of thirty years. Its phantasmagorical subject lent itself particularly well to the greatly variegated character of the music which is a motley of many successful pieces from previous operas, oratorios, and cantatas. *Teseo* and *Amadigi* (1715) are likewise grand magic show pieces. After the pause in opera production Handel began his series for the Academy with *Radamisto,* a dramatically conceived work, and continued with an unprecedented number of successful operas: *Ottone* (1723), *Giulio Cesare, Tamerlano* (both 1724), *Rodelinda* (1725), and *Admeto* (1727). The first of these has become, next to *Rinaldo,* one of Handel's most popular operas while the other four belong to his most dramatic and lasting creations. *Mucio Scevola* is one of the numerous collective ventures of the time for which Handel wrote only the third act, Ariosti (or Mattei?) and Bononcini the other two acts. The operas for the New Academy include *Poro* and *Ezio,* both based on libretti by Metastasio, and *Orlando Furioso* (1733), the boldest of Handel's works, anticipating in its famous mad-scene the vast dramatic sweep of Gluck's reform operas. In *Orlando* and later again in *Alcina* Handel returned to his favorite magical subjects, but the magical props were now made subservient to profound human characterizations. During the rivalry with the Opera of Nobility Handel payed tribute to the French ballet opera in *Ariodante* and *Alcina* (1735). The turn to French models was prompted by the presence of a troupe of French dancers in London, but possibly also by the sensation created by Rameau's first opera *Hippolyte* although there are no direct stylistic ties between Handel and Rameau. The last phase of Handel's opera production includes *Serse* (1738) containing the best known of all of his bel-canto arias: the "Largo" *Ombra mai fu.* This hymnic melody, designated in the original as larghetto, has been insidiously changed by later editors to a dragging *largo* which robs the melody of its strength and gives it an undeserved pseudo-religious flavor. *Serse,* and also *Deidamia* (1741), Handel's last operatic work, curiously revert to the seventeenth-century type of opera in which humorous and serious scenes are intermixed. Both works breathe the wisdom of maturity; their subdued and subtle humor has nothing in common with the parodistic wit of the *opera buffa.* Like Verdi, Handel took his farewell from the opera on a note of humor.

The colossal production of Handel's opera period does not show any distinct internal direction or development. It centers around an ideal of *opera seria,* realized by the single operas with a varying degree of perfection. In his best creations Handel enlivened his heroic characters by a tragic individualization that made him the true successor of Racine. In the weaker ones he closely adhered to the conventional types of dramatic affections. Handel always struck a balance between the progressive monophonic and the retrospective contrapuntal arias leaning sometimes more to the modern style, as in *Ottone,* sometimes more to the grand manner, as in *Orlando,* but never completely upsetting the balance. Handel's penchant for the "modern" style has been attributed to the influence of Bononcini and Porpora, but we need not assume such influence because Handel had full control of this style as early as *Agrippina.*

Throughout his career Handel remained essentially faithful to the basic forms of the *opera seria:* recitative, arioso, aria, and occasional duets and larger ensembles for the soloists. Only in one respect did he transcend the operatic convention, namely in the creation of the dramatic grand *scena.* The grand *scena* is a musically continuous complex in which *secco* and *accompagnato* recitatives and ariosi alternate with arias or fragments thereof in free succession, dictated only by the dramatic exigencies of the situation. These scenes actually foreshadow the ideals of the classic opera and stand in the baroque opera as gigantic isolated blocks,—monuments of Handel's dramatic genius. The mad-scene that concludes the second act of *Orlando* stands out as the most memorable grand *scena.* The hero imagining himself in Hades is torn between visions of wildly contrasting affections. With bold abruptness Handel pitted them against one another in form of *accompagnato* recitatives, ariosi, and an uncanny gavotte. The recitative contains passages in 5/8 meter which composers hardly dared to write before the twentieth century. The gavotte returns three times in rondo fashion, thus lending musical unity to the otherwise rhapsodic scene. One of the interludes of the rondo is cast in form of a chaconne on a chromatic fourth—one of the rare occasions when Handel used a strict ground in his later operas.[25] Another grand *scena,* the death of Bajazet in the third act of *Tamerlano,* is in no way inferior to *Orlando's* mad-scene though it lacks the musical unity of the latter. The scene leads with increasing tension to the tragic climax showing how the poison is slowly taking effect on Bajazet. In his last halting breaths the hero curses his enemy in choked accents, set by Handel in a realistic recitative. If this scene

---

[25] Another strict ground extending over one measure only can be found in *Poro* (III, 12)

is compared with the last section of Monteverdi's *Combattimento,* very similar in its pathetic *pianissimo* ending, the entire range of dramatic realization in baroque music is clearly encompassed.

Similarly dramatic, though less expansive scenes, cast mostly in the form of ariosi, deserve special attention, such as the two monologues in *Giulio Cesare:* the meditation of Cesar at the tomb of Pompeo and the superb image of nature which reflects the thoughts of Cesar at the seacoast; or the apparition of furies at the beginning of *Admeto;* or the dungeon scene in *Rodelinda,* highly reminiscent of *Fidelio.* In all these scenes the orchestration is handled with imagination and care, quite in keeping with the important pictorial function assigned to the orchestra.

The arias fall into the established types of Italian opera. As a rule only a single affection governs the aria, first announced by the orchestra, then taken up by the inevitable motto of the singer and subsequently maintained in the musical elaboration. The middle part of the aria, frequently set off from the fully accompanied main part by a thin continuo accompaniment, presents a different shade of the basic affection; however, in highly dramatic scenes Handel did not hesitate to substitute a free *accompagnato* for the middle part. There are a few exceptional arias in which two distinct affections are juxtaposed by means of contrasting motives, tempi, and dynamic marks. In the masterly *Empio, perverso cor* from *Radamisto* Zenobia whispers in passionate accents to her disguised husband and utters furious defiance to the tyrant, quickly alternating between *ardito e forte* and *adagio e piano.* A similar aria occurs in *Amadigi.* It is noteworthy that Handel conceived the antithesis of affections in baroque manner and kept them both static. The two contrast motives depend on and complement each other, but the one does not generate the other in a continuous development—a device that a classic composer would have adopted. It is as though Handel had condensed two different arias into a single one.

In spite of the enormous number of arias Handel's imagination revolved round relatively few types which appear time and again in ever-new modifications. The influence of the dance and the concerto style are the two most prominent single factors in Handel's arias. The driving rhythm that pulsates in all arias discloses how strongly Handel was stimulated by patterns of dance music; like Bach, he stylized them according to the affections to such a degree that the ascription of a particular aria to any one of the stereotyped patterns may at times become difficult. At least four aria types related to dance music can be distinguished. The first is the siciliano, one of Handel's favorites, employed for idyllic affections and situations, but also for the representation of oppressive inner conflicts, as can be seen in the subdued aria *Affani di pensier* from *Ottone*.

The second type is characterized by a slowly flowing bel-canto cantilena, usually associated with dances in triple time, such as the saraband and the slow minuet, but sometimes also with the slow allemande. In the case of *Lascia ch'io pianga* from *Rinaldo*, the derivation of the melody from a saraband can be proved on Handel's own authority, but *Ombra cara* from *Radamisto* and *Cara sposa* from *Rinaldo*, the two bel-canto arias that Handel himself considered his best, also move in stylized dance rhythms, as does the ineffably gentle *Ombre pallide* from *Alcina*. In all of these the orchestra weaves a dense texture around the voice part although the accompaniment is not always worked out as contrapuntally as in *Tanti affanni* from *Ottone*.

A third type is formed by the *allegro* arias which tend to maintain a single pattern with the consistency of a rhythmic ostinato, used primarily for affections of triumph and agitation. In this type the rhythms of the bourrée, allemande, or gavotte are most frequently suggested, as they are for example in the monophonic aria *Già lo stringo* from *Orlando* (Ex. 95).

Ex. 95. Handel: Gavotte aria from *Orlando*.

The fourth type, the simple arietta with a popular melody, prefers the rhythms of the courante and the minuet. In these arias Handel approached the *style galant* more nearly than in any other form.

The arias in concerto style, written either *all'unisono* or with obbligato accompaniment, belong to a fifth category, the only one not dependent on the dance. The arias of this type befitted the most spectacular affections. Handel naturally displayed in them all the splendor of vocal bravura and all the resources of the concerto grosso. In *Rinaldo* he even provided for an improvised concertino of the harpsichord, indicated merely by blank spaces in the original score.[26]

None of the five categories [27] implies a definite form. Although the

---

[26] CE 58, 117.
[27] Handel's arias should not be classified according to the five categories of John Brown (*Letters on the Italian Opera*, 1789), as they are in Grove's *Dictionary*. These

da-capo aria holds the leading position in Handel's opera bipartite forms, composite arias with contrasted tempi, or simple through-composed cantilene appear at prominent places. *Ombra mai fu* from *Serse* is an example of the latter form. The celebrated bel-canto aria *Verdi prati* from *Alcina* is cast in simple rondo form, possibly the reason why the conceited castrato Carestini refused at first to sing it. As has been pointed out above, the strict ground bass takes second place beside the rhythmic ostinato, the most prominent device of bass organization with Handel. It serves to heighten the affective intensity of the bass which often rivals that of the voice part. Handel liked to state the bass pattern first in the continuo alone and then work it out against the voice achieving a close interrelation between vocal and instrumental parts that was unrivalled in the earlier phase of opera.

Handel's ensembles often assume vast proportions. The duets range from "doubled arias" in parallel motion to dramatic contrapuntal settings. Many of the ensembles for three and more singers still adhere to the primitive ensemble technique of Scarlatti, but there are also admirably wrought trios and quartets that project the conflict of characters directly into the music, for example, the trios of *Tamerlano* and *Alcina*. In the duet from *Orlando* the rage of the hero and the plaint of his beloved are synchronized by means of a stereotyped contrapuntal device, turned by Handel to surprising dramatic use: a chain of slow suspensions is set against the excited parlando of the other voice.

There can be little doubt that Handel very carefully observed in his works a subtle distinction between the opera chorus and the oratorio chorus. The main stylistic difference lies in the primarily decorative function of the opera chorus and the primarily structural function of the oratorio chorus. This functional difference comes to light also in the musical texture; in the typical Italian opera there is no place for choral polyphony. While it would be an exaggeration to classify Handel's operas as solo operas, it is true that not any of the opera choruses ever approaches the vast choral polyphony of the oratorio choruses, not even the later operas which are coeval with the oratorios. As a matter of fact, the opera choruses are frequently not truly choral pieces at all, but soloistic ensembles in choral settings. All the "choruses" in *Giulio Cesare* belong to this type. The relative prominence of chorus and ballet in *Alcina* is due to the influence of

---

categories belong to the post-baroque phase of the Neapolitan opera. They show that by this time the affections had become technical formulas, such as *portamento, cantabile,* etc. See also Flögel, *Die Arientechnik.*

the French opera. It should be noted that the exceptionally full first chorus from *Alcina* is based on an instrumental composition, the organ concerto op. 4, 4.

Purely instrumental music occurs in the operas many times, not only as processional and dance music, but also in the concerto-grosso sections of the arias. The overtures consist of several movements, usually a ponderous French overture and one or several dance movements. This combination of the French and the Italian overture is best exemplified by the overture to *Rinaldo,* praised by Mattheson as a happy union of the two national styles.

Viewed as an artistic whole each single opera gives the impression of tremendous variety in spite of its adherence to type. The musical and dramatic uniformity that results if all operas are lumped together is due to the recurring typical situations in the plots, and even more to the fact that the arias do not represent the active part of the drama. Dramatic action is reserved to the recitative and the grand *scena,* the arias merely reflect on or even retard the action. If the operas are taken, as they most frequently are, as collections of arias, the essential function of the recitative is ignored— an attitude that gives as one-sided a picture of the opera as if in an evaluation of *Hamlet* only the monologues would be considered.

That Handel's opera, in spite of its artistic perfection, was ultimately a failure was caused by social, not musical reasons. The nobility in London was too weak to support one, let alone two, opera companies and the court was, as in Purcell's time, not directly associated with the opera. On the other hand, the middle class was not interested in a musical entertainment designed primarily for the nobility and presented in a foreign tongue. Handel's turn from the opera to the oratorio should not be interpreted as a tacit admission on his part that the opera was an artistically deficient form. Rather does it represent a change in the social background to Handel's art: he turned from the nobility to the middle class, the class from which Handel himself had sprung.

The reluctance of the middle class to put up with the Italian opera was voiced in the trenchant criticism of Addison and Steele in the *Spectator* and *Tatler.* The precarious position of the opera in London is illuminated as though by a flash of lightning by *The Beggar's Opera* (1728), written by John Gay with the musical assistance of Pepusch. The success of this "Newgate Pastoral" (Swift) was due primarily to its political satire which cleverly exposed the "Similitude of Manners in high and low life." The

political point of the opera is revealed at its very beginning by the French
overture which introduces the ballad tune "Walpole, or the Happy Clown"
in obvious reference to the corrupt Prime Minister Walpole. Compared with
the social critique, the parody of Italian opera is a less significant, though
characteristic feature, which the ballad opera had in common with the
opera buffa and its various national parallels. The ballad opera, which had
grown out of the seventeenth-century plays with inserted songs, had its
direct model in the French *vaudeville* or *Théâtre de la Foire* both with
regard to its political sarcasm and its modest musical means. Its music was
borrowed from pre-existing tunes, such as traditional songs, fashionable
dance music, or even the opera. Gay exploited a number of contemporary
tune collections, especially Durfey's *Wit and Mirth* the "old and new" civil
songs of which he often merely paraphrased. Aside from the overture
Pepusch's musical contribution was rather meager: he supplied merely the
basses and not too successfully either since he was not always aware of the
fact that some of the tunes were variations on famous grounds, such as
Greene Sleeves (*romanesca*), *Joy to Great Cesar* (*folia*), and *Lumps of
Pudding* (*passamezzo antico*). The indebtedness to France is expressly
acknowledged by the use of several French tunes. Composers of art music
have contributed to *The Beggar's Opera* more extensively than is generally
known. The list includes such names as Akeroyde, Bononcini, Carey,
Eccles, Handel, Leveridge, and Purcell. The tunes appear sometimes in
simplified, but very skilful, variants for which Pepusch may have been
responsible. Gay did not pass up the opportunity of poking fun at the
quarrel between Faustina and Cuzzoni in a prison scene "which the
Ladies always reckon charmingly pathetick." In this most entertaining
scene Gay cleverly wove fragments of many tunes into one continuous
grand *scena*. Compared with the political wit of the *Beggar's Opera* the
musical parodies seem mild and good-humored and designed to appeal to
friends rather than enemies of the *opera seria*. Gay's work did not, as has
often been contended, deal the death blow to the Italian opera, nor did
the author, a friend of Handel, intend to do so. The most intense period
of the Italian opera began actually after the success of the *Beggar's Opera*.
The vogue of ballad opera that followed its wake brought a flood of imitations of which Coffey's *The Devil to Pay* was the most influential for the
development of the German *singspiel*. The ballad opera was soon superseded by musical comedies of sensibility for which the music was no
longer borrowed from traditional sources but newly composed in *style
galant*.

THE ORATORIOS

Handel's oratorio period which comprises also his contributions to Anglican church music reaches back to his first years in England. For a long time the composition of oratorios formed a secondary line of activity. With *Israel in Egypt* (1738) the oratorio assumed its definitive form. Handel's slow inner development toward the oratorio can only be understood in view of a new musical stimulus: the English tradition of choral music. Nothing reveals his genius more clearly than the modest and yet self-assured method of incorporating the English choral polyphony into his own style. Although recognized at the time as an Italian master he became a student again, seized with great insight upon the essentially polyphonic style of English music and raised it to his own level. The odes and welcome songs, the choral anthems, and the English masque represent the three main points of contact with the English tradition. Handel's first compositions with English words were the *Te Deum* and *Jubilate* (1713) celebrating the Peace of Utrecht and the *Birthday Ode* for Queen Anne (1714?). The *Te Deum* and the odes of Purcell obviously served as models for Handel, less with regard to borrowings of thematic material than to the distribution of solo and chorus, key arrangement, and the formal design of the whole. Handel's occasional clumsiness in English declamation contrasts with Purcell's excellence in this respect, but Handel easily surpasses him in the vast dimensions and the pathos of the melodic gestures. He replaced the boyish pace of Purcell's dotted rhythms by his heavy-footed pomp and expanded the dimensions by the wide range of his late baroque harmonies. Even in these tentative works the English choral idiom is carried far beyond the limited technical means of the middle baroque and the chorus is deployed in the monumental fashion ever since associated with Handel's choral writing. It goes without saying that Handel revised some earlier compositions for his first English works, especially for the *Jubilate,* and in turn borrowed from them later on.

Handel laid the cornerstone for his future choral compositions in the twelve *Chandos Anthems,* composed before 1720. Handel served at the time as private chapel-master to the Duke of Chandos whose immense fortune, though amassed by reckless methods, enabled Handel to spend the most carefree years of his life. The *Chandos Anthems* bring the Anglican church music of the baroque to its consummation. They are great orchestral cantatas in which the choruses form the solid pillars, and the solos, duets, and recitatives the lofty arches of a grand and imposing architecture. Although forced to write for only three or four voices Handel tested in the choruses all aspects of the choral idiom: the choral fugue, the dramatic fugato, chordal hammerstrokes, and even the gradual choral *decrescendo*, expressly marked by the composer. It is noteworthy that Handel anticipated here the continuous dynamics that were to assume prime importance in the storm and stress of the Mannheim school. The anthems are preceded by trio sonatas many of which appeared later in the printed sets of chamber music. The fifth anthem is of particular interest with regard to the close interrelations between instrumental and vocal music. In this work he transformed a trio sonata (later published as op. 5, 1) into a vocal setting, used again as the final chorus in *Belshazzar*. Handel repeatedly came back to the music of the *Chandos Anthems* in later works— an indirect indication of his esteem for it.

The style of the *Chandos Anthems* appears transposed to the largest possible scale in Handel's later church music: the famous *Coronation Anthem*, composed for the coronation of George II (1727) partly on texts that Purcell had set before; the two wedding anthems; the anthem for the Foundling Hospital; and the colossal *Dettingen Te Deum* (1734) which borrows heavily from a *Te Deum* by Urio. With the emphasis on choral music it is not surprising to see Handel fall back occasionally on the cantor's music he learned under Zachow, especially chorale arrangements. Only rarely did Handel elaborate chorale *cantus firmi,* and wherever they occur they do not bear in the Angelican context the liturgical dignity of Bach's settings, but merely serve to enhance the splendor by austerity. The "canto fermo" of the sixth *Chandos Anthem,* left unidentified by Handel, is actually the chorale *Christ lag in Todesbanden,* supplied here with English words and treated in Zachow's manner. In the *Foundling Hospital Anthem* the chorale melody *Aus tiefer Not* furnishes the scaffold for a sumptuous choral movement. Among other works in which Protestant chorales are quoted or at least suggested the *Funeral Anthem, L'Allegro,* and the *Occasional Oratorio* may be mentioned.

The first works in which Handel approached the oratorio proper were, significantly, descendants of the English masque: *Acis and Galathea,* and *Haman and Mordecai,* later known in revised form as *Esther* (words by Pope and Arbuthnot after Racine). Both works, composed ca. 1720 for the Duke of Chandos, were called masques at the time and were probably presented in scenic form. *Acis and Galathea,* for which Gay wrote the libretto, is perhaps the most delightful of Handel's secular serenatas in which the best features of the baroque pastoral are transfigured. Musically, the English version bears no relation to the Italian serenata of the same title, though Handel made an unsuccessful attempt to combine the two versions (1732). In *Esther,* the first English oratorio in both language and form, Handel turned to the Old Testament, the source of most of his oratorios. Both *Acis and Galathea* and *Esther* differ in principle from the Italian operas in the emphatic use of the chorus, a typical feature of the English tradition. This emphasis manifested itself not only in the almost equal numerical balance between chorus and aria, but particularly in the artistic weight of the choral sections. The role of the chorus became increasingly more important in the later oratorios, and is in fact the crucial factor in the distinction between opera and oratorio. Handel arrived logically but vicariously at a type of choral oratorio that is still valid today. The trend of the development can be seen in the revision of *Esther* (1732) performed by Handel with scenery but without action. With the artistic concentration on choral settings stage action became difficult, if not impossible, so that drama and music could no longer appeal to the eye. It now presented an idealized action divorced from the stage and directed only toward the imagination of the audience.

The oratorios of Handel fall into three classes: the choral opera, the choral cantata, and the choral drama. It is scarcely necessary to point out that a hard and fast classification cannot always be made because the oratorios share with the opera such external features as the division into three acts and the conventional types of the aria. But the inner pictorial power of oratorio music is also derived from the opera and often comes close to calling for the stage. The particular group of oratorios classed as "choral operas" includes works in which the proximity to the opera is most conspicuous. Because of their subject matter and form they could be called English operas. In style they are comparable with the Italian operas of the Viennese court, which are notable for their choruses. The first class comprises secular oratorios dealing not with biblical subjects but with incidents of ancient mythology. Among these *Semele* (1743), a work of the highest order, is actually based on an opera libretto by Congreve; it is more worthy of revival than perhaps any other of Handel's neglected oratorios. *Hercules* (1744) is a personal tragedy of jealousy, called by Handel himself a "musical drama." In its intensity it compares favorably with *Tamerlano.* Certain oratorios of the same group, notably *Susanna, Theodora, Alexander Balus,* and *Joseph and His Brethren,* draw on biblical sources but deal with their heroes as individual characters in the manner of an opera. *Susanna* belongs to the Italian type of *oratorio erotico,* and *Theodora* to that of the martyr legend, very frequent in the Catholic oratorio. The number of solo arias is relatively higher in these works than in those of the other categories, and the choruses have sometimes merely the decorative function of the opera chorus.

The choral cantatas forming the second group continue the line of the English odes and deal with allegorical subjects without dramatic action. This group includes such famous works as *Alexander's Feast, Ode for St. Cecilia's Day* (both after Dryden); *L'Allegro* (after Milton), related in subject matter to a cantata by Carissimi; the *Occasional Oratorio;* and the *Triumph of Time and Truth,* the last oratorio of Handel.

Most oratorios belong to the third class, the choral drama. The baroque ideal, the revival of the Greek tragedy, has been more nearly realized in the choral drama than in the opera although the latter owes its origin to this ideal. In these monumental oratorios the chorus acts as the idealized protagonist of the inner action in which tragedy and triumph are strangely intermingled. Wherever the hero of the choral drama is an individual he is presented essentially as the spokesman of his people. The Old Testament was the ideal source for the choral drama because it provided Handel with exactly what he needed: monumental characters in a monumental setting. Handel's grand manner, his broadly sweeping style, are peculiarly fitting for these massive choral dramas so that subject matter and musical style are in perfect harmony. The amazingly numerous choral dramas, each of which Handel tossed off in about a month's time, include: *Deborah, Athalia* (both 1733), *Saul, Israel in Egypt* (both composed in 1738), *Samson* (1743), *Belshazzar* (1745), *Judas Maccabaeus* (1747), *Joshua* (1748), and *Jephtha* (1751). In these works Handel brought to fruition what he had began in the revision of *Esther.* It is significant that in an early oratorio, such as *Deborah,* the musical importance of the chorus outweighs that of the solo numbers. The most radical work in this respect is *Israel in Egypt,* an intensely dramatic oratorio though its text is, like that of the *Messiah,* exclusively biblical. The chorus in *Israel in Egypt* actually usurps almost all functions otherwise reserved for the soloists: twenty choruses stand opposed to only seven arias and duets, and four recitatives. In the other choral dramas Handel achieved a more satisfactory balance and avoided the danger of giving only a series of unrelated pictures without dramatic continuity.

From Majer's Emblematic Book "Atalanta fugiens"

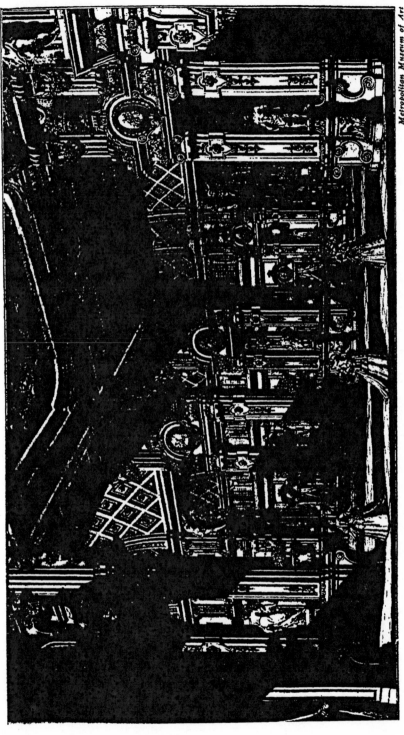

Stage set by Galli Bibiena

The *Messiah* (1741), the most celebrated and universally known composition by Handel, does not fall into any one of the three categories. It holds in splendid isolation a unique place among all other oratorios. Although it has become the archetype of the Handelian oratorio by virtue of its tremendous popularity, it is actually a highly individual work standing outside of the general trend of Handel's oratorio composition. The *Messiah* can be described as an oratorical epic devoid of outward dramatic action and dedicated entirely to devotional contemplation. The spirit of religious edification, prevalent in the Hamburg oratorio, manifests itself here in its most sublime form. Even though its words are selected exclusively from the Scriptures, the *Messiah* is as far from a liturgical function as the other oratorios are. The three parts of the *Messiah* cover all phases of the life of the Savior and thus encompass the liturgical year in its entirety. The story is told in genre pictures, vivified by Handel's unique ability to draw a dramatic spark from the words. As a whole, it is not musically superior to the best choral dramas and its fame is due more to its universal religious appeal than to its musical excellence. This appeal has created the mistaken notion that all of Handel's oratorios are church music. Actually Handel dealt with his subjects, whether sacred or secular, in the spirit of an ethical humanism which overrides the boundaries of the denominations. For this reason there is no inner or stylistic difference between the sacred and the secular oratorios. They are equally remote from the individual emotionalism of the German oratorio and from the liturgical observance of Bach's passions. The pathos of Handel's oratorios is an ethical one, they are hallowed not by liturgical dignity but by the moral ideals of humanity.

In view of the close stylistic ties between opera and oratorio it is to be expected that the solo numbers in the oratorios do not differ essentially from those of the operas. As a general rule it can be stated that the number of da-capo arias decreases in the oratorios in favor of arias in unorthodox forms. This development was partly caused by the fact that the oratorical texts were not bound by operatic conventions, but partly also by musical considerations which made the da capo impractical, though Handel frequently suggested it musically by the return of an instrumental ritornello. However, the thoroughly operatic style of the oratorical arias is undeniable, and is confirmed by Handel's numerous borrowings from his operas. Even the *Messiah* forms no exception. *Why do the nations* can be quoted as a typical example of the rage aria in grand da-capo form,[28] and the bass-solo *The people that walked in darkness,* remarkable for its pictorial diminished intervals, exemplifies the modern *all'unisono* aria. The classic bel-canto aria *I know that my redeemer liveth* very successfully avoids the da capo and presents the main idea in various keys in the manner of the concerto. The solo ensembles of the oratorios, though not very numerous, sometimes go above the operatic ensembles, in their contrapuntal demands. The impassioned quartet from *Jephtha* deserves special attention as one of the most dramatic quartets that Handel ever wrote. The ariosi and *accompagnato* recitatives are quickened by the dramatic breath of the opera, as for example the solo *O Jove, what land is this* from *Hercules,* a worthy complement of the operatic grand *scena.*

However valuable the solo numbers in the oratorios may be, they fade in comparison with the choruses which show in their dimensions and variety alone their structural importance. Handel's choral technique which triumphs in his oratorios coordinates four distinct influences: the German cantata, the Italian opera, the English choral tradition, and the oratorio of Carissimi. The choral oratorio of Carissimi from which Handel is known to have borrowed presents the prototype of the form. In the hands of Handel it was developed far beyond its originally limited scope. He forced the disparate stylistic elements into a new whole by merging them with the English choral tradition. The fact that Handel himself referred to his oratorio choruses as "anthems" seems symbolic of the English share in the formation of the oratorio.

In a broad synthetic process Handel took vocal techniques from practically every field and transferred them to his massive choral idiom. Only a few examples of his transfer forms can be listed here. There is the archaic motet style transposed to the large scale. There are sumptuous Venetian double-choruses pitting a-cappella sections against fully accompanied tuttis. There are choruses in the airy texture of the continuo madrigal, paralleled only by works of Fux and Caldara in the Viennese oratorio. In the magnificent da-capo chorus *Pleasure submits* from the *Triumph of Time* the madrigal style is applied to a full chorus, written for the rare combination of five or more real voices. There are gigantic *cantus-firmus* choruses, based sometimes on Protestant chorales, but more frequently on a *cantus firmus* of Handel's own invention. There are choral da-capo arias and choral dance songs in simple setting, frequently preceded by a solo statement of

---

[28] For dramatic reasons Handel exceptionally omitted the repeat, but the aria adheres to the typical formal pattern in all other respects.

the melody. There are huge choral chaconnes, written either on the familiar descending fourth or on a short rhythmic ground bass, such as occurs in the sinister "Envy" chorus from *Saul*. There are choral recitatives, perhaps the most interesting of Handel's transfer forms, in which the chorus functions as collective narrator. A famous example of the choral recitative can be found in the ominous plague chorus *He sent a thick darkness* from *Israel in Egypt* which actually ends with the stereotyped recitative cadence and vividly represents the fall of darkness by harmonic means. There are, finally, the innumerable choruses in concerto style with or without the accompaniment of a concerto grosso. They represent the most progressive side of Handel's choral idiom and favor the melodic types of the Italian concerto, as can be seen in the chorus *His yoke is easy* from the *Messiah*, based, significantly, on one of his Italian chamber duets.

Handel's choral writing is distinguished by a terse pictorial plasticity, less recondite and detailed than that of Bach, and is bent on sweeping effects which have set the standard for our modern choral idiom. Sometimes the chorus and the orchestra share equally in the pictorial representation, as, for example, in the "Flies and Lice" chorus from *Israel in Egypt*. The vocal recitation of this chorus is literally taken from a serenata by Stradella(?), only the bustling accompaniment of the orchestra, which strongly recalls the orchestral technique of Rameau's operas, seems to be Handel's share in the composition. The drastic dramatic impact of his choruses is due to the unique flexibility of his choral style, achieved primarily by the interpenetration of polyphonic and chordal textures. Handel abruptly juxtaposed on the narrowest space fugal sections and gigantic chordal blocks. The sovereign freedom with which he took up and abandoned the one or the other device for dramatic emphasis is strikingly illustrated by the chorus *Fall'n is the Foe* from *Judas Maccabaeus*. Although he sometimes resorted in his contrapuntal settings to such artifices as the quadruple fugue (*Alexander's Feast*), consistently polyphonic choruses are comparatively rare in the oratorios. Handel's free-voiced contrapuntal style stands diametrically opposed to Bach's uniformly polyphonic approach to choral writing. Handel's counterpoint does not grow out of long-spun lines which intertwine in ever-new linear combinations, but works with pregnant motives and terse countersubjects, conceived in double counterpoint. These are presented in new keys but rarely in new contrapuntal combinations. Motive and countersubject form in Handel's music small contrapuntal cells that enable him to transform instantly the contrapuntal contrast into the contrast of two melodic ideas and conversely. The Hallelujah chorus from the *Messiah* furnishes the best known example of this technique. Two distinct melodic ideas are presented first singly and are then combined in a contrapuntal cell (Ex. 96). This ingenious application of contrapuntal

Ex. 96. Handel: Hallelujah chorus from *Messiah*.

cells accounts for the amazing flexibility of the choral texture and explains at the same time Handel's liking for the improvisation of "double fugues," based invariably on countersubjects.

The simultaneous use of motive and counter-motive and free-voiced texture reflects the Italian heritage in Handel's counterpoint, most clearly manifested in his keyboard fugues. The interrelations between the instrumental and vocal fugue are often so close as to resolve to complete identity. In *Israel in Egypt* several keyboard fugues have been transformed into vocal fugues with only a few alterations. The choral fugues of the oratorios, which lead the style of the *Chandos Anthems* to perfection, consist more often than not of a series of fugal expositions, dissolving at the end into continuo-homophony. The numerous Amen and Hallelujah fugues that usually conclude major parts of the oratorios and anthems belong to this type.

The growth of Handel's conception of the oratorio from the Italian solo oratorio to the monumental choral drama can be most palpably summarized by a comparison of the *Trionfo del Tempo* and its English version *The Triumph of Time*, Handel's *opus ultimum*. Stricken by blindness Handel dictated his last work to his pupil John Christopher Smith, Jr. While the first version lacks choruses altogether, the third version has eleven, some of which Handel borrowed from Karl Graun and his own works. The newly composed choruses reveal Handel in his maturest phase; they curiously contrast with the youthful da-capo arias, retained from the first version. Thus the last oratorio encompasses the fire of youth and the wisdom of old age and marks the stations of the long road which Handel had travelled.

INSTRUMENTAL MUSIC

The instrumental music of Handel cannot be assigned to definite periods because all of it was published, if at all, after 1720 though much of it is known to go back to earlier periods. The uneven quality of some instrumental works is due to the close affiliation of improvisation and composition in Handel's music. True to the Italian tradition he left a wide margin for the ingenuity of the improvising performer giving in his notation merely a rough sketch of the music. A very significant portion of Handel's instrumental works is irretrievably lost, namely his keyboard improvisations for which he was universally praised at the time. Only a faint reflection of them has come down to us in those keyboard works that still bear the traces of written-down improvisations. All of his instrumental music is heavily indebted to the Italian style.

Of the four keyboard collections, the first *suite de pièces* (1720) contains not only suites but a mixture of practically all forms and styles of the time. We find side by side: Italian church sonatas, sonatas in the concerto style of Domenico Scarlatti, French overtures and chaconnes, patterned variations in German style, and preludes and fugues. The fugal works follow in their free-voiced texture Italian models. Several pieces of the first collection exist in very primitive early versions that illuminate Handel's artistic growth of which so little is known. The third suite in *d* shows in its first version obvious survivals of the archaic variation suite, but, significantly, the final revision preserves only traces of it. The fifth suite contains the famous set of patterned variations known by the spurious title "The Harmonious Blacksmith." The seventh suite in *g* brings in its *passacaille* what can be regarded as the consummate form of the chaconne bass (Ex. 97). By a stroke of genius Handel transformed the conventional

Ex. 97. Handel: *Passacaille* bass.

pattern of the descending fourth (marked by asterisks) into the familiar formula of fifths which circumscribes the full tonality of late baroque music. Although the formula was used by every composer of the period it took a

Handel to discover in it the possibility of a chaconne. The second and third sets of keyboard pieces, and the six "fugues or voluntarys," printed without the permission of Handel, do not essentially alter the picture of the first set. They bring more chaconnes, the last of which gives in its sixty-two variations an example of a written-down improvisation.

The chamber music comprises fifteen sonatas for either flute, oboe, or violin and continuo (op. 1), and two sets of trio sonatas (op. 2 and 5). A further set of trio sonatas for oboe, and some separate solo and trio sonatas were not published in Handel's time, and are in part not even included in the edition of the *Händel Gesellschaft.* The potent influence of Corelli on Handel can be traced nowhere as clearly as in the chamber music, especially in such typical traits as running basses and the stereotyped harmonic formulas. It goes without saying that Handel's melodic inventiveness is more advanced and therefore more characteristic than that of Corelli. In form, content, and technical demands, however, the sonatas are conservative except for the merging of the borderlines between the chamber and church sonata. Most sonatas are patterned after the church sonata, but both the number of movements and the occasional addition of dances break through the limits of the form. In many *allegro* movements Handel easily surpasses Corelli by his superb handling of lightly fugal textures and his complete mastery of the concerto style. In others we find dance patterns, as, for example, in the flute sonata op. 1, 9, the second movement of which disguises a hornpipe by the neutral designation *allegro.* Hornpipes and country dances (which occur also in the concerti grossi) are the only definitely English elements in Handel's instrumental music. There is also a strong French element, particularly in the chamber overtures which consist of a French overture and a dance suite. This type is illustrated by the trio sonata op. 5, 2, in part identical with the prelude to the first *Chandos Anthem.*

Handel's concerti grossi represent his most significant contribution to instrumental music: six for woodwinds and strings, often summarily called "oboe concertos" (op. 3), twelve for strings alone (the famous set op. 6), the organ concertos (op. 4 and 7), and a great number of individual concertos, including the *Water Music, Firework Music,* and the concertos for two and three *cori.* The massive accumulation of wind instruments in these works was called for by open-air performance. There are many close resemblances in form and even melodic material between the sonatas and the concertos, so much so that the concertos sometimes seem like large projections of small originals. Handel raised the Italian concerto grosso to the highest level of baroque entertainment. In their adherence to the church sonata form his concerti grossi are obligated to the conservative vein of Corelli although they lean in respect to dimensions and thematic precision toward the progressive school of Vivaldi. The merging of styles and forms that can be observed in Handel's famous set op. 6 characterizes it as a typical "late" collection. We find here not only concerti grossi but also perfect examples of the two other types: the orchestral concerto and the solo concerto. Only exceptionally did Handel adopt Vivaldi's modern concerto form in three movements; as a rule he wrote only single movements in concerto style, as, for example, the imposing third movement of op. 6, 3, characterized by bustling unison passages. The fourth movement of op. 6, 6 is really a solo violin concerto. The *all'unisono* practice of the orchestral concerto in which concertino and tutti merely double each other is most skilfully manipulated in the fifth movement of op. 6, 5 and in op. 6, 7. They must be regarded as the most finished examples of the orchestral concerto. The last movement of op. 6, 11 makes use of the dacapo form. Handel enriched the church sonata form of the concerto grosso by pompous French overtures, subdued sicilianos, and inspired bel-canto airs, but he was, like Corelli, conservative in the solo sections. His concertinos consist of episodic figurative passages that rarely assume thematic independence.

The organ concertos which can be considered a personal innovation of Handel combine the German predilection for the organ and the Italian vogue of the concerto grosso. Performed as special attractions between the acts of the oratorios, they served primarily as vehicles for Handel's brilliant improvisations. Although we find an early example in the *Trionfo* the organ concerto belongs essentially to the English master period. In the organ concerto of the *Trionfo* the organ as yet functions as one concertino instrument among others; only in the later concertos does it take the lead. Handel depended on the Italian organ style which favored the manual to the virtual exclusion of the pedal. This was the result of the influence of the harpsichord idiom on organ playing, clearly manifested in the frequent use of arpeggios, Alberti basses, and similar figurations. Indeed Handel's concertos were designated for "Harpsichord or Organ." Very exceptionally do they call for a pedal; it must be remembered that only a few English organs were equipped with pedals in Handel's time, the organ at St. Paul's being one of the exceptions. With its brilliant passage work in continuo-homophony and its superficially handled, improvisatory polyphony Handel's organ music represents the direct opposite of the severe German organ style with obbligato pedals. The scores of the concertos do not give us a true picture of their musical value because they are merely skeletal outlines to be dressed up by the improvising performer. Many of Handel's organ concertos are, like the harpsichord concertos by Bach, arrangements; they prove in most spectacular fashion the close interrelations between the various fields of his instrumental music. In his arrangements Handel drew not only on orchestral concerti grossi, but also on the trio sonata, and even the solo sonata.

Handel's countless borrowings bring us to the much-discussed question of his "plagiarism." Handel took his ideas from wherever he pleased without ever acknowledging his debt. His characteristic laxness in these matters was the result of his improvisatory attitude toward composition which explains at the same time the breakneck speed with which he habitually composed. The borrowings began very early in his life with the operas of Keiser, noticeably increased after his physical breakdown in 1737, and took on major proportions in such famous works as *Israel in Egypt, Ode for St. Cecilia's Day,* and *Jephtha.* The standards of the baroque period permitted extensive use of borrowed material, but, as Mattheson put it, the composer was supposed to pay back his debt "with interest," that is he was expected to improve on the original. Yet Handel was often satisfied with taking over integral parts from works of other composers without any modification although, at other times, he performed veritable strokes of genius by greatly improving on the originals, whether borrowed or his own. Among the names of composers whom Handel exploited we find famous ones like Carissimi, Stradella, Kerll, Keiser, Gottlieb Muffat, and Perti, but also more obscure ones like Erba, Urio, Karl Graun, Habermann, and others. The compositions of Urio, Erba, and Stradella may possibly be early works of Handel himself since their ascription to these composers has not been established beyond doubt. It is remarkable that Handel should have borrowed from composers several years his junior like Graun, Habermann, and Muffat whose ideas were not intrinsically superior to anything Handel was capable of writing. Yet even more remarkable is the fact that the borrowed sections always fit into the whole without any stylistic incongruity. Handel took only what he found congenial or what he could render "Handelian" by revision, and he incorporated the borrowings so smoothly and unobtrusively in his works that many of them have only recently been discovered and others may well have remained unnoticed to the present day. In justice to Handel it must be pointed out that he has borrowed more from himself than from all other composers taken together. The highly complex relations between the various states of the same music in different works, which offer valuable clues to the chronology, and the intricate interchange between his vocal and instrumental music have not yet been systematically investigated. They represent one of the main obligations of the future Handel research.

BACH AND HANDEL, A COMPARISON

The musical style of Handel must be seen in the general perspective of late baroque music, and must be evaluated in relation to its opposite pole: the style of Bach. There are many striking similarities between these two ultimate representatives of baroque music: both were born in the same part of Germany, both were reared in the atmosphere of cantors and organists, both were famous for their improvisations, both preferred the organ to any other instrument for their own playing, both were stricken with blindness, both dictated their respective last work, which was in either case a revision of a composition from an early period. However, these external parallels lose significance in view of the fundamental polarity between Handel and Bach. The work in which Handel most nearly approached Bach's musical style is the *Passion Oratorio,* the text of which was in part also set to music in Bach's *St. John Passion.* The stylistic rapprochement becomes quite clear in the ritornello to the aria "Sinners behold with fear" which Handel wrote as a tortuous "Bachian" melody with rich harmonic implications (Ex. 98). Settings of the same text by both Bach and

Ex. 98. Handel: Ritornello from the *Passion Oratorio.*

Handel can claim particular attention. If we compare the two compositions of the aria *Eilt ihr angefocht'nen Seelen* [29] in the *Passion Oratorio* and the

[29] Compare also Keiser's music for the same aria, printed in Bücken, *Musik des Rokokos und der Klassik,* 63.

St. John Passion respectively striking similarities come to light: not only is the key the same and the pictorial representation of "haste" very similar, but in either case the chorus bursts in dramatically with its interjections. However much the two versions may have in common, Handel's music is inferior because it lacks the highly individual stamp that distinguishes Bach from all other composers. Also the four chorales of the *Passion Oratorio*, indifferently treated by Handel as devotional songs without liturgical significance, do not reach the level of Bach's chorale movements.

It would be patently unfair to contrast the weakest side of Handel with the strongest of Bach, particularly if the comparison attempts to be more than an indication of a difference of approach. In the music of both composers certain musical ideas, typical of the late baroque, recur time and again. While Bach transformed these types in a personal way, Handel clung closer to convention, treating the same type more often, but in less individual a fashion. Due to his improvisatory attitude, evinced in his customary haste to finish a work, Handel used pre-existing types as springboards for his music. As in every improvisation his aim was not so much the transformation of the type as its animation by means of a great variety of solutions. The recurrence of types lends to Handel's music a certain uniformity which may be criticized as a defect, but which has the virtue of enabling Handel to borrow extensively from himself. In his borrowings and revisions Handel usually observed the underlying affections, as can be shown in the two basses taken from the *Passion Oratorio* and the sixth *Chandos Anthem* respectively (Ex. 99). These basses belong to two different compositions though they actually represent only variants of the traditional chaconne bass. In either case the composition is associated with pathetic affections.

Ex. 99. Handel: Basses from (a) *Passion Oratorio;* (b) *Chandos Anthem.*

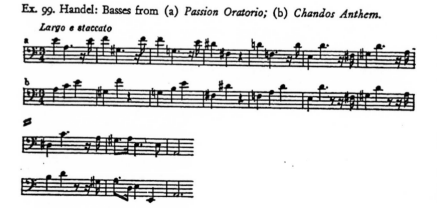

Largo e staccato

As musicians of the baroque, both Handel and Bach were equally in-debted to the doctrine of affections, but their methods of representation differ widely and reveal a sharp contrast with regard to melodic design. Handel excels in broad and gestic motives, Bach in complex and intricate lines; Handel's melodies are extensive, Bach's melodies are intensive. This antithesis is borne out by the arioso part of the aria *He was despised* from the *Messiah* and the recitative *Erbarm' es Gott* from the *St. Matthew Passion*. In both compositions the scourging of Christ is represented by means of chords in heavily heaving rhythms. Although the pictorial background is practically the same the musical results are hardly comparable. Bach traces in his melodic design and his tight harmonic progressions the affections of each word; Handel seizes only upon the basic affection and writes a melody of wide arches. Handel's penchant for improvisation manifests itself in his sweeping melodic lines, designed in bold strokes as if painted with a thick brush in fresco manner; Bach's penchant for the luster of scrupulous workmanship manifests itself in his consistently patterned melodies, de-signed as if engraved with a fine cutting tool. The two-dimensional in-tricacies of Bach's implied polyphony lie below the surface of the melody; Handel's one-dimensional melodies sweep the hearer off his feet by the sheer force of their drive. In their sensuous and immediate appeal the arias of Handel stand diametrically opposed to the abstract appeal of the lines of Bach. Even in their dance melodies the contrast between Bach's and Handel's melodic conception can be observed. For reasons of comparison the theme of the *Goldberg Variations* (Ex. 100a), written upon the same bass as Handel's chaconne in *G* of the second set of suites, has been hypo-thetically adapted (Ex. 100b) to Handel's famous saraband rhythm of *Lascia ch'io pianga* in bel-canto style. The extensive quality of Handel's

Ex. 100.a. Bach: Theme of the Goldberg Variations.
Ex. 100.b. The same theme in Handel style.

melody explains why his music lends itself to amplification by massed ensembles. The monumental effects of Handel's music actually gain strength by reasonable reinforcement whereas the same practice would ruin Bach's music because it would obscure the transparency of the contrapuntal web.

Bach's and Handel's divergent conception of melody entails an equally sharp contrast with regard to counterpoint. It can best be grasped if the second movement of Handel's suite in g is compared with Bach's two-part invention in a. Both compositions utilize the identical motive. It is quite possible that Bach deliberately borrowed the beginning from Handel to show what he could do with it. Bach gives a thoroughly consistent elaboration of the theme whereas Handel loses himself in the sequential spinning-out of new material only occasionally returning to the theme. Although Handel, like Bach, employs double counterpoint, his movement seems loose and improvisatory by comparison. Here again the fundamental polarity of the two composers comes to light: to Handel, who is always close to improvisation, the flow of ideas is more important than their elaboration, whereas to Bach the elaboration is more important than the number of ideas. Handel regards counterpoint only as a means to a dramatic end, as can be seen in the quickly changing textures of his choral writing. Bach takes it as an end in itself which must of necessity be consistent. Because of its dramatic conception Handel's counterpoint reaches its greatest heights in the vocal medium. Even his keyboard fugues seem to call for text and seem to acquire their final impetus in vocal form; it is for this reason that Handel was so successful in transferring his ideas from the instrumental to the vocal medium. Bach's counterpoint is designed essentially as the interplay of abstract lines and is ultimately instrumental in nature. Bach does not hesitate to submit his choral polyphony to an instrumental standard. In the flexibility of his choral idiom Handel surpasses Bach in the same measure as Bach surpasses Handel in contrapuntal consistency. The free-voiced choral polyphony of Handel and the strictly linear, instrumentally conceived polyphony of Bach form the two poles of late baroque music.

In respect to form and instrumental idiom also Bach and Handel stand at opposite poles. In his instrumental music Handel shares the Italian conservatism and hardly goes beyond Corelli so far as form is concerned although the simplicity of his instrumental melodies points toward the innovations of the classic period. Bach, on the other hand, is conservative in his adherence to polyphonic texture, but progressive in his adoption of modern forms, such as the concerto form of Vivaldi. Likewise, the organ style of Handel is as clearly influenced by the idiom of the harpsichord as the harpsichord style of Bach is by the idiom of the organ.

The polarity of Bach and Handel can in the last analysis be explained as that of two great individualities of fundamentally different psychological attitudes. Handel belongs to the extrovert, Bach to the introvert type. This typological difference emerges most convincingly in the manner in which both composers reacted to the musical styles of the period. Handel assimilated the various national styles so that they became his second nature. He thus arrived at a complete coordination of national styles enabling him to master each one equally well. Bach, conversely, assimilated the various influences with his own personal style and thus arrived at a fusion of national styles in which the single elements are inseparable. The two methods are incommensurable and cannot be weighed against each other, but they explain why Handel's works center round his operas, written from a world-wide perspective for an international public, and his oratorios, the monuments of his ethical humanism; and why Bach's works center round his cantatas, written for the local churches of Saxony, and his passions, the monuments of his liturgical severity. In this light, the life of Handel and Bach symbolizes their respective artistic significance: Handel, always bent on success, passed through the international centers of music; Bach, unconcerned about worldly success, began and ended his career within the narrowness of central Germany. Both composers are universal in their appeal. The worldly grand manner of Handel and the spiritual attitude of Bach represent the two essential and at the same time complementary aspects of baroque music which cause the curious paradox that Bach and Handel are equals only where they are incomparable.

CHAPTER TEN

Form in Baroque Music

FORMAL PRINCIPLES AND FORMAL SCHEMES

THE DISCUSSION of form in baroque music is beset by a serious obstacle. It has become the custom to regard form as a formal scheme or mold that can be filled by various ideas or what is usually referred to as the "content" of the music. The imaginary contrast between form and content, which grew out of the antipathy that the romantic era had against formal schemes, still survives in our way of thinking and that is why baroque music is either ignored or inadequately treated in modern treatises on form. This fact in itself is a tacit admission that the underlying formal principles have not been genuinely understood, chiefly because they do not necessarily crystallize into formal schemes. Form ought not to be regarded as something external, divorced from the inner organization of the music; structure and texture are functions of the melodic, harmonic, and rhythmic elements, and these in turn assume and exercise different functions in different styles even if their external manifestations be the same. Form, taken in this sense, covers the manifold interrelations of all these aspects, not only the external scheme, but also the principle that governs the inner organization of a particular composition.

The interdependence of form and style is one of the most difficult and also one of the most neglected problems in music history. It can be shown concretely only within definite stylistic eras. The evolution of musical style from the early to the late baroque period which has been discussed in the preceding chapters is faithfully mirrored in a parallel evolution of formal principles. This chapter surveys the history of baroque music from the viewpoint of form, the two subsequent chapters from the viewpoints of theory and of sociology.

The music of the early baroque, especially that of Italy, presents an ostensible discrepancy between style and form which seems to belie the interrelations that have just been proclaimed. It is indeed striking that the forms of the renaissance, such as the madrigal, the motet, the canzona, ricercar, the dance, the bass variation, outwardly persisted well into the baroque era. This indisputable fact indicates that the early baroque composers were interested in stylistic rather than formal innovations. Preponderance of style over form is a general characteristic of all "early" (*i.e.* formative) periods in the history of a style. Significantly, the two outstanding innovations of the early baroque, the recitative and the *concertato* style, appeared first in the medium of conventional forms. Gabrieli evolved the *concertato* within the motet, and Caccini wrote the recitatives of his *Nuove Musiche* in forms that he himself called madrigals. We have seen that Monteverdi published the majority of his works in madrigal books, and that Frescobaldi observed the forms of his predecessors in his collections. Yet this apparent conservatism signified only that the composers were preoccupied with a new stylistic idiom. The fact that a conventional form was written in a new idiom involved necessarily a transformation of the form; it is this inner transformation that must occupy our attention.

Seen in the perspective of the renaissance the new idiom was destructive because it brought about the internal and external disintegration of conventional forms. It must, however, be realized that the destructive force contained at the same time latent formal principles that later emerged as constructive elements. The most general formal and stylistic principle that distinguishes renaissance from early baroque music is discontinuity. Discontinuity obtains in nearly all forms of early baroque music. The contrast motive, one of the earliest symptoms of the incipient baroque style in the music of Gabrieli, abandoned both rhythmic and melodic continuity. The disintegration of the madrigal was effected internally by the new dissonance treatment, externally by the addition of the continuo. Although both the renaissance and the baroque madrigal were through-composed forms, only the former had musical coherence and continuity by virtue of its contrapuntal texture. In the madrigals of Gesualdo a growing tendency toward discontinuity can be observed. The monodic "madrigals" of Caccini and Peri were completely discontinuous and rhapsodic in melody, harmony, and rhythm. The recitative can really be called amorphous from the strictly musical point of view since the only element of continuity left was an extra-musical one, the text. However, this lack of form was not the primary aim of the composer but merely the logical by-product of the subordination of music to the words.

The means of formal differentiation in the opera recitative were naturally also dependent on the text; we find attempts as early as Monteverdi to relieve the rhapsodic discontinuity through refrain sections and repeated choruses. These were highly effective, if primitive, factors of unification which operated by simple juxtaposition of unrelated sections. The strophic variation, on the other hand, tried to overcome the extreme of discontinuity through internal organization. Variation appears so consistently as an element of baroque music that the whole era may justly be called one of variation. The strophes or repeats of the strophic variation were at first almost inaudible because the bass line lacked a recognizable rhythm and contour, and because the melody was each time so fundamentally varied as to become practically a through-composed composition. Strophic variation was the leading aria form of early baroque opera; also the other aria types were usually strophic, in contrast with those of the late baroque opera. Each repeat of the melody became an ornamental variation since the singer was supposed to improvise ornaments.

In instrumental music the toccata, the most discontinuous form, stood close to the recitative. However, it did not serve an extra-musical idea and received at least some degree of unity through consistent scale figures. The juxtaposition of contrapuntal and rhapsodic sections which we find in the renaissance toccata was intensified in the early baroque form to calculated contrasts, and the discontinuity of textures was condensed on a small space. The fugal forms, the ricercar (and fantasia), and canzona (and capriccio), became emancipated from their vocal models, motet and chanson. In both forms discontinuity prevailed. Frescobaldi's ricercars fell into a number of distinct sections set off by *rubato* cadences; the *tempo rubato* sharply contrasted with the even and continuous flow of the renaissance ricercar. The written-out trills at the cadences adduced further discontinuity. Also the change from smooth diatonic subjects to chromatic themes with "false" intervals brought in an element of unrest which reflected the pretonal idiom of the harmony. Sweelinck's fantasias, less venturesome in harmonic respect, loosened up the uniformity of the old ricercar by climactic drives of rhythmic patterns.

In the canzona the discontinuity was even more pronounced. The multi-sectional patchwork or quilt canzona consisted of short sections of contrasting rhythm, tempo, meter, melodic material, and texture. The few-voiced ensemble canzonas were even more radically multisectional than the keyboard canzonas. The solo sonata, a descendent of the canzona, shared the multisectional structure with its parent and showed in addition the influence of the recitative, especially in rhapsodic solo passages which instrumentalized the *gorgia* technique. Solo passages for alternating instruments occurred also in the few-voiced ensemble sonatas by Neri which experimented with tutti-solo contrasts. They appeared first in Gabrieli's canzonas and finally led to the concerto.

The foregoing analysis warrants the conclusion that nearly all early baroque forms had one formal trait in common: multisectional structure. This feature must be understood as the formal corollary of the discontinuity that characterizes early baroque style. The nervous and erratic flow of early baroque music merely reflects its intensely affective nature.

Variation could be used either to reinforce or to mitigate discontinuity. It was of special importance for dance music and forms related to it, such as the continuo song, and elaborations on ground basses. Dance music was of necessity rhythmically continuous because of its function. The arrangement of dances in rhythmically contrasted pairs or varied couples was extended in the German variation suite to the suite as a whole. Variation served here as a means of unification. However, in the chaconne variation the rhythmic patterns changed after every fourth measure producing a highly discontinuous result in spite of the uniformity of tempo and meter. The prevalence of discontinuity did not mean that all musical elements were necessarily discontinuous—this would be impossible for a musically coherent composition—but that its presence in a single element sufficed to convey the effect. In the ostinato forms the principle of variation actually crystallized in a formal scheme that may be called chain form. The same principle functioned in the variation canzona and variation ricercar only as an important formal element, and while it served to achieve variety in the chaconne, it served to unify the fugal forms. In the variation canzona and ricercar the number of subjects was naturally reduced to one or two, and their thematic transformations always assured a certain degree of coherence, however contrasting the various sections were. The canzona preserved in addition a heritage of the French chanson, namely a short da-capo section at the end that unified the form by either literally repeating or slightly varying the first section. In the ricercar this return was not used, but consistent adherence to contrapuntal texture made it one of the most highly unified forms of early baroque music altogether.

In the music of the middle baroque we can witness a reaction to the discontinuity of the preceding phase. The variegated forms became more unified internally and externally. The number of sections decreased in the same measure as their dimensions grew. Middle baroque music favored multipartite rather than multisectional structure. Although the question of what constitutes a part and what a section in a composition is one of relative weight and can therefore hardly be determined with certainty, the distinction is valid as a tendency of the development. Toward the end of the middle baroque the parts grew, also almost imperceptibly, into independent movements. While there are exceptions in every phase of baroque music the generalization may be made that sections, parts, and movements are the three units of organization that correspond respectively to the early, middle, and late periods of baroque music.

The process of formal stabilization was closely paralleled by a process of stylistic stabilization. Experiments with pre-tonal harmony that distinguish early baroque style were supplanted by the emphatic use of simple cadences that betrayed a rudimentary key feeling, clearly evidenced in the bel-canto style. Together with the toning down of the harmony went the simplification of melody, cautious use of "false" intervals, and, particularly, the smoothing out of the rhythmic flow by means of a continuous triple rhythm.

The stylistic change found its most conspicuous formal expression in the differentiation of the monody into *secco* recitative, arioso, and aria. Here again formal and stylistic factors can hardly be separated because the differentiation was as much a question of style as one of form. The strophic variation, the representative aria form of the early baroque opera, was at first retained in the middle baroque opera, but it now became a fully audible form since the bass line was as distinctly organized as the melody so that the strophic repeats could be perceived by ear. In Cavalli's operas we meet with complex strophic variations that are internally expanded to comprise a sequence of arioso, recitative, and aria, repeated several times with unchanged bass but varied melody. However, the brief da-capo aria soon superseded the strophic variation. This tripartite form became possible only through the support it received from the harmony. The absence of stabilized harmony explains why the form could not develop sooner. The first part, unified by a clearly stated key and sequential motives, could now be juxtaposed with another key area, the middle part, after which the first part was repeated, usually with ornamental variations.

The areas were naturally diminutive since the sustaining power of harmony was as yet restricted.

Not by any means was the brief da capo the preferred aria form. At least equally important was the bipartite aria which consisted of only A and B, or A A′ B B′, or A B B′. The last alternative, the varied repeat of the second part, was most commonly used, and still prevailed in the early operas of Scarlatti.

Strophic variation, brief da-capo, and bipartite aria, all of which had more than one strophe, account for practically all forms of the opera and cantata since duets and ensembles were also cast in one of the aria forms. The manner in which they were combined in composite forms of higher order (opera and cantata) depended of course on the text. In contrast with the late baroque opera and its rigid alternation of recitative and aria the middle baroque opera retained great formal flexibility because its forms were small and comparatively undeveloped. In Lully's operas and Carissimi's oratorios, aria and recitative were not yet clearly set off, but this lack of formal differentiation was counterbalanced by the choruses that punctuated the scenes or acts in a most emphatic fashion. In the cantata of the middle baroque three types can be distinguished, the aria cantata, refrain cantata, and rondo cantata, the formal characteristics of which have been discussed in Chapter IV. All composite forms of the middle baroque involved many more repeats than was customary in both early and late baroque music. In the former the desire for discontinuity was averse to repeats, in the latter repeats were less feasible because of the vast dimensions of the form.

In sacred music the forms of the dramatic *concertato* deserve particular attention. Basically the motet served as point of departure, but the form gained great flexibility through juxtaposed tutti and solo ensembles and instrumental ritornelli. The early works of Schütz were governed by the multisectional structure of the early baroque *concertato,* but as early as Gabrieli we find inserted ritornelli and repeated *tripla* sections that strongly suggest a free rondo form. Even if the words did not call for extended repeats the composer deliberately took up a previously stated section or repeated the same music with changed words. In either case the repeats set off the sections and balanced the formal structure of the whole.

The *concertato* never crystallized into stereotyped musical schemes as the various aria forms did. Nevertheless, the great formal variety can be reduced to three types which do not necessarily exclude each other. The first is the through-composed type of *concertato,* most closely allied with the formal principle of the motet. The second is the arch form consisting of several sections or parts arranged in the order of A B C D X . . B'A'. Here A and B recur in inverted order at the end; the center of the arch is usually the most important part, both textually and musically. We find also *concertato* pieces that stand halfway between the first two types; they are essentially through-composed except for a return of A or a varied A' at the end. The third and most common type may be described as a free rondo structure in which the A part, and sometimes also the B part, returns from time to time in the same or in varied form. The contrast between the various parts may be emphasized by means of alternating solo and tutti ensembles or instrumental ritornelli, very frequent in Schütz's *Symphoniae sacrae* and Purcell's anthems. As in all compositions in which the words influenced or determined the form, the *concertato* also made use of the rondo as a formal principle rather than as a formal scheme.

The attempt has been made to explain the structure of the *concertato* by imposing on it the so-called bar form of the meistersinger which consisted of two *Stollen* and an *Abgesang* (A A B). In order to accommodate the formal variety, ostensible derivatives of the bar form had to be artificially created, such as "inverted bar" etc., and even through-composed sequences like A B C were forcibly interpreted as a variation of the bar. Such unhistorical methods of analysis accomplish little and confuse rather than clarify; they waver between a consideration of the text and self-contained musical schemes, often invented for the nonce.[1] The formal principles that governed the *concertato* should not be confused with formal schemes.

In the chorale *concertato* we are confronted with a different situation. Here the *cantus firmus* presented a voice that tied all parts, however contrasted, together. If the chorale was treated not as a *cantus firmus* but as a freely ornamented voice, the setting differed little from the dramatic *concertato* so far as form is concerned. It is, however, significant that the *can-*

---

[1] This wavering accounts for the incorrect use of the term bar by Lorenz (*Das Geheimnis der Form bei Richard Wagner,* 4 vols. 1924 ff.) who utilized the bar as the main tool in his attempt to reveal the formal "secret" of Wagner's operas. Strictly speaking bar form is a misnomer because, according to the theory of the meistersinger, the form *Stollen, Stollen,* and *Abgesang* was a *Gesätz.* Bar form pertained to poetry and consisted of three *Gesätze.* What Lorenz calls a bar form should be called *Gesätz* form, but even this term seems unnecessary because the form is only an imitation of the French *ballade.* Both forms were musically identical (including the musical rhyme at the end) though they differed textually since the *ballade* had a refrain. Lorenz's method of formal analysis was applied to Schütz by Schuh, *Formprobleme,* and Moser, *Schütz.*

tus firmus furnished only abstract rather than concrete unity because it was usually cut up into phrases, each of which received an independent contrapuntal elaboration. It is interesting to note that although the chorale melodies themselves were mostly composed in *Gesätz* form the *concertato* setting did not necessarily retain it, as can be seen in Schein's *Opella nova*. On the other hand, the chorale variations *per omnes versus* of the Tunder tradition usually preserved the form of the chorale. The juxtaposed stanzas were differentiated by rhythmic and contrapuntal patterns and resulted in a simple chain form that can be found also in instrumental compositions based on a *cantus firmus* or a bass melody, as, for example, the organ variation or the *passamezzo* variation.

In instrumental music the change from multisectional to multipartite structure was particularly obvious. The variation canzona and ricercar in the middle baroque dealt with only a few thematic transformations, each of which was, however, extensively developed in a part of its own. The fugal forms of Froberger—they furnish the best examples of the type—contained as a rule not less than three and not more than five parts. The stabilization of harmony of the bel-canto style was reflected in the stable key areas of each part. The same observation can be made in the chaconne variations, both vocal and instrumental. The modulating ground bass moved through closely related keys, and the bass repetitions in each key established harmonically unified parts through which the form gained both harmonic expansion and unity. A further means of harmonic unification were the sudden turns to the opposite mode and equally sudden returns to the original one which made the chaconne a large tripartite form. They became common with Lully and Purcell.

The distinction between *sonata da chiesa* and *sonata da camera* which was a functional one in the early baroque did not take on a formal significance before the middle baroque period. However, contrary to common belief, neither form consisted as yet of four movements. The church sonata fell as a rule into five parts that freely alternated between contrapuntal and chordal texture. We can glean from the sonatas of the Bologna school that harmonic stability, the melodic influence of bel-canto style, thematic transformation, and the reinstatement of counterpoint gave the parts inner consistency and some measure of independence which led finally to the development of independent movements.

The French suite was a free anthology of dances and characteristic miniatures in one key with frequent ornamental *doubles;* the German suite contained only three basic movements, allemande, courante, and saraband, with the gigue appearing optionally either between the first two or the last two dances. The stylized introductory movements of the suite, such as prelude, overture, sinfonia, sonatina, assumed increasing importance in the German suite and began to outweigh the dances proper, while on the other hand the German variation suite survived only in rudimentary form as the traditional varied couple in Froberger's suites. It is odd that the technique of thematic transformation which was so prominent in the fugal forms of the middle baroque declined in the suite after the short spurt it had taken in the early baroque. Apparently the desire to create contrasting types of dances made the composers abandon the device.

The overture which originated in the French *ballet de cour* also crystallized as a form only in the middle baroque. The sinfonie of the early baroque opera were patterned either after the canzona, as with Landi and the later Venetian opera composers, or after the varied couple of the dance, as with Monteverdi and Cavalli. The richly contrasted type of sinfonia, preferred in the Venetian opera, ran parallel with the French form that Lully coined. Like the dances it preceded, the French overture was originally a bipartite form with a dominant cadence separating the slow first part in dotted rhythm from the fast second part in a fugal texture and ternary rhythm. Only in the late baroque did the return to the beginning become a stereotyped feature which made the overture a tripartite form.

Late baroque music brought the direct reversal of the situation we found at the beginning of the period. We are now confronted with a preponderance of form over style, typical of all "late" periods of musical history. With the final consolidation of style, the establishment of tonality, luxuriant counterpoint, and continuo-homophony, definite formal patterns emerged which usually pass as the forms of baroque music in general. Actually they characterize only late baroque music. The tendency to mistake the features of late baroque style for those of baroque style in general (discussed in Chapter I) is at this point particularly noticeable. Coincident with the growth of parts into movements, the order of the movements became stereotyped in the cyclic forms. The church sonata crystallized as a four-movement form in the order of slow-fast-slow-fast. It can be found not only in solo and trio sonatas, but also in certain concerti grossi and Italian overtures. The suite also assumed, at least in German music, the features of a four-movement form in the order of allemande, courante, saraband, and gigue, though it could be expanded by inserted dances. The main type of three-movement form in the order of fast-slow-fast was represented by the concerto. It should not be regarded as a reduction or segment of the church-sonata pattern because the movements themselves were dependent on continuo-homophony which called for a novel type of form. The concerto pattern also obtained in many sonatas, the Neapolitan opera overture, and even the da-capo aria, the parts of which became almost independent movements. The two-movement form was consolidated in recitative and aria, and prelude (toccata, fantasy) and fugue.

While the movements of the cycle followed a fixed scheme the internal organization of the single movement depended on a highly flexible formal principle. The inner growth of the movement was the direct result of the establishment of tonality and luxuriant counterpoint. The sequence through the complete diatonic circle of fifths, the classic formula of tonality, served as scaffold for the expansion of a single motive and enabled the composer to sustain extended tonal areas which now formed the inner units of the form. Rapid harmonic rhythm and contrapuntal texture made for continuous motion without clear-cut incisions or a palpable formal scheme. The discontinuity of the early baroque gave way to a highly integrated continuity. Since late baroque music was essentially monothematic and continuously developed a short motive, it has often been considered as "formless," except for the fugue which even modern treatises discuss as a special form. Yet actually the opposite is true: of all formal types of late baroque music the concerto, the aria, and the sonata came close to evolving an internal formal scheme while the fugue did not even come near it. The continuity of late baroque music was correctly observed, but its interpretation as a "formless" process was obviously tainted by the conception of development in the classic sonata form. The late baroque type of development lacked the dramatic and psychological qualities of the sonata and must be clearly distinguished from the classic type. It is best defined as "continuous expansion." Being a formal principle and not a scheme, it lent itself to infinite variation as to formal patterns.

In its most consistent manifestation, continuous expansion produced a movement that elaborated a single motive in an unbroken series of rhythmic figures, running from beginning to end without a break like a *perpetuum mobile*. Examples of this radical type can be found in the preludes of the *Well-Tempered Clavier*, e.g. no. 1 in C, no. 6 in *d*, and no. 15 in G. More commonly, however, there were several incisions in the movement. The motive was distinctly stated and then consistently expanded in modulatory fashion; when a new key had been confirmed by a cadence the same beginning was restated in the new key, further expanded, and so on to the end. The basic pattern was what may be called an open form; it can be represented by the diagram A X', A' X'', A'' X''', etc., in which A stands for the motive, X for its continuous expansion, and ' for the various keys. The whole movement consisted of a series of departures in different keys in which neither the number of departures nor the sequence of keys was fixed by the formative principle. The last A did not necessarily return to the original key. If it did, the rudimentary recapitulation of the baroque sonata resulted; if it did not, the return to the tonic was effected in the last X. In either case the form revolved within itself in a series of formally equivalent departures. It is noteworthy that the dominant key, which was to assume a primary role in the classic sonata, did not yet "dominate," but was coordinated with the submediant, subdominant, and supertonic—the keys in which the departures were most frequently made. The preludes of the *Well-Tempered Clavier*, notorious for their ostensible "lack of form," furnish abundant examples of continuous expansion with few or numerous incisions or departures. The prelude no. 13 in *F*-sharp has a great many departures on a small space, no. 16 in *g* only three; no. 17 (second part) in *A*-flat brilliantly illustrates the principle on a larger scale. It begins four times anew with the same motive in the order of *A*-flat, *E*-flat, *f,* and *D*-flat, and in each departure the motive is expanded in different manner.

It can be readily seen that the principle of continuous expansion underlay all forms of late baroque music. The ritornelli of the concerto form were merely a more or less stereotyped application of it. The monothematic sonata, the prelude, the invention, the aria, and even the dance forms carried it out, each in its own fashion. The inversion of the motive, a typical feature marking the beginning of the second part in the suite movement, did not, of course, affect the formative principle. The typical concerto movement consisted of a more or less regular alternation of tutti and solo (T S T S T S T). Consistent with the principle of continuous expansion, neither the number of tuttis nor their tonal order was fixed. The tutti ritornelli circumscribed the key and determined the form. It is characteristic that also in the ritornello form the dominant was just one of the eligible keys; significantly enough, the ritornello of concertos in minor keys frequently appear in the minor dominant which lacked the most important characteristic of the dominant: the leading tone. It is also characteristic that thematic contrast did not essentially alter the structure of the ritornello form. It was an accessory contrast, reserved for the solo, as can be seen in the concertos of Vivaldi, Bach, and Handel. Bach's *Italian Concerto* which, as legend has it, anticipates the classic sonata form, is actually written in typical ritornello form; it lacks the dramatic juxtaposition of keys and themes of the sonata and the idea of development in the modern sense. However, the formal scheme of the classic sonata may accidentally be realized in the ritornello form. This is actually the case in the *Polonaise* of Handel's famous set of concerti grossi (op. 6, 3). We find here an "exposition" with two themes in tonic and dominant respectively, a modulating "development" of both themes, and a "recapitulation" of both themes in the tonic. Yet the contrast of themes is only an accessory feature; significantly, it is conceived in terms of the concerto as tutti and solo contrast— the second idea occurs only as solo—and there is no hint of dramatic "development." The movement, written in the familiar bipartite dance form, coincides with the formal scheme of the classic sonata but not with its style. However, the coincidence discloses that the concerto established the point of contact between the baroque and classic styles. It is not surprising that this was done by the form most closely associated with continuo-homophony, since the development of the classic sonata form was premised upon the reduction of continuo-homophony to homophonic style.

The late baroque opera and cantata relied primarily on the contrast of recitative and aria. Only the grand *scena* of Handel's operas must be mentioned as an exception. In this gigantic composite form, unaccompanied and accompanied recitatives, ariosi, and arias were dramatically joined together. The vast dimensions that the single form attained through continuous expansions is best illustrated by the grand da-capo aria. The da-capo fell into two major divisions each consisting of ritornello and aria; while the first division set out in the tonic and ended emphatically on the dominant, the second departure began in the dominant with the same idea, reversed the modulation and ended in the tonic. This scheme was identical with that of the bipartite sonata form except for the repeat sign in the middle which the aria lacked. Since the coloraturas imitated violin style, the da-capo aria could be regarded as a vocal sonata (or even concerto), both stylistically and formally.

Whether applied to figurative harmony, continuo-homophony, chordal texture, or contrapuntal texture, continuous expansion always served as the same formal principle. The fugue, the most famous of the late baroque "forms," illustrates its application to contrapuntal texture. The statements of the textbooks notwithstanding, the fugue was not a form, tripartite or other, nor was it a texture. Motet and canon had contrapuntal texture in common with the fugue, but this did not make them fugues. Strictly speaking, the fugue was a contrapuntal procedure in which *dux* and *comes* were stated in tonic and dominant respectively; it comprised a number of contrapuntal devices, such as double counterpoint, augmentation, diminution, inversion, stretto, cancrizans motion, mirroring, etc., which were, however, optional. The one formal feature that all fugues had in common was continuous expansion, realized in a chain of fugal exposition. However, the number of departures and their tonal order varied. Even if each departure started in the same key ("rondo fugue") the principle of expansion entailed a different contrapuntal combination each time. Neither stretto nor interlude nor any of the abovementioned contrapuntal devices was indispensable. This is the reason why there is such infinite variety of fugue "form," and why none of the Bach fugues follows exactly the same pattern. Since the fugue was a procedure, it could be, and actually has been, used in different styles. The classic fugues observed the procedure of the baroque fugue, but not its style. The monothematic fugue originated from the application of the procedure to late baroque style.

STYLE AND FORM

The lack of dramatic development in late baroque music which manifested itself in the uniform continuity of the movements has often been commented upon. That the dramatic function of music was not unfamiliar to the baroque era is amply attested by the opera and oratorio, but its conception of drama was different from the modern one. The unity of affection which prevailed in late baroque music (and only here) precluded a psychological development that presented a theme as a new entity in dramatic fashion; the motive never lost its identity in the process of continuous expansion, and the juxtaposed climaxes of the sonata form did not exist. However, we do find in Bach's music, for example in the prelude no. 22 in *b*-flat of the *Well-Tempered Clavier* and the first fugue of the *Art of the Fugue,* a gradual drive to a powerful chord of the diminished seventh in which the motion is suddenly halted shortly before the end. Here all energies are pent up in a "speaking" rest and then immediately released in the final cadence. This emphatic preparation for the cadence is one of the many devices of intensification that we find in late baroque forms. At this point the intensive contrapuntal forms of the baroque style stand clearly opposed to the extensive forms of the homophonic style. In contrapuntal style the function of the form was essentially a process of intensification through expansion. Of all devices of intensification the stretto illustrates the function best because in the stretto the intensity mounted in exactly the same measure as the space shrank within which the voices were condensed. Not all baroque forms were equal in this respect. It is significant that the concerto approached the extensive forms of the homophonic style by virtue of its continuo-homophony.

The development of the concerto shows the interactions between style and form with particular clarity since it took place within a short time at the beginning of the late baroque period. In order to understand the development we must discriminate between three factors. The first is the device of opposed bodies of sound which first appeared in the *concertato* style and then, as tutti-solo contrast, became an important element of the late baroque concerto. The second is the concerto style which originated only with the rise of continuo-homophony. The third, finally, is the ritornello form which crystallized shortly after the concerto style had been established. The earliest concerti grossi of Corelli made great use of the device of opposed groups, only small use of concerto style, and practically no use of the ritornello form. Here then, we have the earliest and most primitive stage of the development. Formally, Corelli's concerti grossi were dependent on the church or chamber sonata. The orchestral concertos of Torelli, Taglietti, Abaco, and Handel dispensed completely with the device of tutti-solo contrast, but utilized all the more emphatically concerto style, and also ritornello form. Although these works looked like sonatas they were concertos as their title indicates. In the concertos of Vivaldi, Albinoni, and Bach we find all three factors united in complete harmony. Here the peak of the development is reached. The decisive factor in the development was the concerto style; it is for this reason that neither the concerti grossi of Stradella nor the canzonas of Gabrieli can be regarded as concertos though they make use of contrasted groups. The device in itself was only a neutral musical technique that was applicable to many styles. It was not conducive to the evolution of a formal scheme. Only with the preponderance of form over style in the late baroque period did the concerto style soon formalize, but even here the stylistic innovation preceded the formal innovation.

The interrelations between style and form were especially complex in the transfer forms which owed their prominence in baroque music to the scarcity of stereotyped formal schemes. The essentials of musical structure were carried by style and texture so that the form could be transferred from one medium to another. Since many of the baroque "forms" were actually procedures like variation, fugue, and canon, they could be realized both in the vocal and instrumental medium, and be adapted to the idiom of the voice or the particular instrument. The transfer of idioms and that of forms were complementary aspects of the same attitude.

At the beginning of the early baroque vocal idioms were transferred to instruments and *vice versa*. The appearance of the *gorgia* in the early violin sonatas of Fontana and Marini testifies to the influence of the recitative. Similarly, the chorale motet influenced the organ fantasies of Scheidt, and after the vigorous development of the organ chorale it was transferred back to the vocal medium in the late baroque cantata, as the first chorus of the *St. Matthew Passion* shows. While the transfer in the early and middle baroque was mostly one of style and idiom, we find in the late baroque transfers of formal patterns. The da-capo aria was exemplary for vocal and instrumental forms alike. The great chorus *Et resurrexit* from Bach's B-minor Mass can be cited as one of the most striking examples of this transfer. Although a chorus, it is patterned after the grand da-capo aria: the two statements of the first part stand in *D* and *A* respectively, the middle part is set off in *b*, and the da-capo is condensed into one choral statement and a concluding ritornello. The da capo was also superimposed on the sonata and, especially, on the ritornello form of the concerto, as can be seen in Bach's violin concerto in *E* (first movement).

No composer of the baroque era could rival Bach in the skilful handling of transfer forms. Bach's preferred transfer form was the concerto. The transfer of the concerto to the chorale prelude entailed a rapprochement between the ritornello form and the *cantus-firmus* form. The prelude to the "St. Anne" fugue in E-flat very clearly illustrates the absorption of the concerto into the "free" forms. It consists of four tutti ritornelli for *organo pleno* in E-flat, B-flat, A-flat, and E-flat. These four departures enclose three "solos," scored mainly for the manuals alone. The first two solos present independent ideas while the third restates and expands the first two solo ideas in transposed keys. In spite of its length and wealth of ideas the prelude is a closely knit and superbly balanced composition.

Bach pressed the transfer of the concerto to its limit in his late "concerto fugues" in which he treated exposition and interlude like tutti and solo. Conversely, he infused elements of the fugue into the ritornello form, as the fugal concerto movements of the *Brandenburg Concertos* disclose. The great organ fugue in *e*, the so-called Wedge fugue, even adopts the strict da-capo form. Such repeats emphasized the idea of return inherent in the ritornello form, but they were extraneous to the idea of intensification inherent in the fugue.

We meet with a different situation in cycles like the *Art of the Fugue* in which Bach superimposed the principle of the variation ricercar on that of the fugue, but employed them on different levels. Each movement is a self-contained fugue, but each presentation of the subject is based on thematic transformation. Here it is literally true that the various parts of the variation ricercar have grown into independent movements. They are in themselves no longer ricercars, but they preserve the idea of it on a higher level in the sequence of movements. The same observation can be made of the *Musical Offering* which Bach himself called a ricercar though it does not consist exclusively of fugal movements.

AUDIBLE FORM AND INAUDIBLE ORDER

We do not know whether Bach ever envisaged the performance of the *Art of the Fugue* as a cycle, that is as a composite form of higher order. It is very doubtful that he did, but there can be no question that in such a performance, whether authorized or not, we are able to perceive by ear the intricate thematic transformations that tie all fugues together. The inner unity of the cycle is a direct aesthetic experience. This is, however, not true of all composite forms and collections that have come down to us from the baroque era. The order of musical collections could either be fortuitous or be designed according to a distinctive, though not necessarily musical, plan. The first kind, represented by aria collections that included only the "favorite" arias of an opera, does not interest us. The second kind offers some interesting problems.

One of the most widely used principles was what may be called the architecture of keys. In composite vocal forms of dramatic character, such as the cantata, opera, and oratorio, the choice of keys was significant because the doctrine of affections coordinated certain keys with certain affections. We find in baroque books on music theory lists expounding the affective qualities of each mode or key. The idea for such coordination goes back to the speculative theory of antiquity which connected the tones with planets, and planets in turn with the various states of mind and soul. In the baroque era the coordinations had become stereotyped and conventional key characteristics the survival of which we can see even in Mozart's operas. Whether the characteristics were conditioned by acoustical reasons, the meantone temperament for example, or whether they were, what is more likely, faded survivals of speculative references no longer clearly understood, does not matter. Even if the key characteristics were rendered imaginary in practice by the variations in absolute pitch, the well-tempered tuning and, especially, transpositions, they were believed in and at least ostensibly observed by the composers.

Since the cantata had a limited dramatic scope and only one or two protagonists, the range of characteristic keys was consequently also restricted. The keys employed show a definite order and a conscious desire for tonal unity. Most of the cantatas, secular and sacred, and also corresponding forms, such as Purcell's odes, begin and end in the same key and touch in the middle movements on closely related keys. Bach's cantata *Jesu, der du meine Seele* (no. 78) consists of five movements (choruses, arias, and a chorale) in the tonal order of *g, B-flat, g, c,* and *g* with the modulatory recitatives serving as transitions. The key architecture, in this case strictly symmetrical, uses the tonic key as the pillars and the other keys as the arches of the architecture. It is a debatable question to what extent this symmetry can be realized by ear since it presupposes a vast orientation that comprises the work as a whole and actually transcends direct musical experience. To put it differently: is the symmetry something that transpires only in retrospect as the result of an analysis that looks "symmetrical" on paper? Is it an audible form or an inaudible order? All that can be stated with certainty by way of an answer is that, if known beforehand, the symmetry enhances, at least indirectly, the aesthetic pleasure. On the other hand, tonal unity, which is not necessarily "symmetrical," occurs so consistently in the cantata that its formal function cannot be mistaken. Although it may not have been of great import for listeners without absolute pitch it was an eminent formal factor and formed an audible and integral part of the aesthetic experience.

In the monumental forms, such as the opera, oratorio, and passion, the wide dramatic range of affections made a wide range of keys necessary that precluded tonal unity, quite aside from the fact that the idea of maintaining it would make well-nigh superhuman demands on musical understanding. The keys freely alternated in keeping with the dramatic situation and only within scenes of similar or unified affections were closely related keys used. It is clear that no key architecture could develop on this basis. We find tonal unity only in smaller forms, such as the *entrées* of the *ballet de cour* and also the acts of Purcell's chamber opera *Dido and Aeneas*, which was formally dependent on the masque.

Of late it has become fashionable in German musicology to discover key architectures in Handel's operas and the Bach *Passions*,[2] but these rationalizations try to establish relations that cannot exactly be called convincing. It goes without saying that among the hundreds of acts from Handel's operas a few can be found that display, at least in certain scenes, the key architecture of a cantata, but the great majority of the acts begin and end in different keys. The Bach *Passions* which have been "explained" as a series of cantatas (which in itself would need an explanation) do not adhere to tonal unity. In addition, both Bach and Handel betray in their revisions, many of which introduce new keys, what would have to be considered as a deplorable lack of appreciation for their own key architecture, had it really existed.

An entirely different aspect of the problem comes to light in the collections of instrumental music which usually observe a distinct order if not a balanced architecture of keys. Keyboard collections arranged according to the series of modes go back to the renaissance and can be found throughout the seventeenth century. Klemme's *Tabulatura italica* (1631) is only one of many collections that systematically present all twelve modes. In later collections the keys took the place of the modes. In the suites of the *Neue Clavier Übung* Kuhnau utilized the ascending series of diatonic keys first in major (*C-B flat*) and then in minor (*c-b*); also Ferdinand Fischer adopted in *Ariadne Musica* the ascending order, which Bach (and after him Weber) took over and extended to all keys of the circle in the *Well-Tempered Clavier*. The Inventions which also observe the ascending order were planned originally in symmetrical fashion in an ascending and descending series of keys in which major and minor modes corresponded to each other.[3] In Sorge's *Clavierübung* the twenty-four keys are arranged in two ingeniously interlocked circles of fifths (see p. 385). The aim to provide for all diatonic or even all chromatic degrees of the scale cannot be mistaken in any of these collections. It may not be coincidental that the two first parts of Bach's *Clavierübung*, which was named after Kuhnau's collection, presents exactly the same degrees as its model.

It should not be inferred from the tonal order of the collections that the pieces they contained were supposed to be performed as cycles. The order was dictated by pedagogical considerations which gave the collection a logical and didactic, but hardly an aesthetic unity. It is noteworthy that

[2] For Handel see Steglich, Adler HMG, 664 and ZMW III; and Müller-Blattau, *Händel*, 112. For Bach see the articles in the *Bach Jahrbuch* by Smend (23, 25), and Moser (29).

[3] See Spitta, *Bach*, II, 60; and David, BAMS no. 3.

many of these collections were works of instruction from which each piece could be selected at will. The scalewise order of keys was in itself just as mechanical an arrangement as an alphabetical order according to title. The change from one key to another, which was a calculated musical effect that differentiated the movements of the sonata or cantata, did not apply here. The didactic arrangement was abstract and extra-musical, it was an inaudible order, not an audible form; but this does not mean that it was negligible.

We find different types of extra-musical or supra-musical arrangements in the works of Bach. The *Orgelbüchlein,* for example, is ordered according to the liturgical year, and if it were taken as a musico-liturgical cycle it would take a whole year to hear it in its entirety. Both the liturgical and the didactic order grew out of the function of the music and bestowed on the collection an inner, if inaudible, unity. In the third part of the *Clavierübung* Bach went even a step further. Here the chorale preludes follow again a liturgical order, that of the Lutheran Mass service, but the fact that each one appears in a long and a short setting in correspondence with the Long and Short Catechism can be understood only as a purely intellectual reference. In addition, Bach superimposed on the two ideas of order a third one: the prelude at the beginning and the fugue at the end flank the whole and give it the appearance of a cycle. The work has actually been performed as a cycle though its liturgical function does not bear out this interpretation. However, the amazing inner unity of the collection is beyond question and this was the aim of Bach when he published it in so sophisticated an order.

Only intellectual playfulness can account for the order of the nine canons in the *Goldberg Variations.* The first one is a canon at the prime, the second a canon at the second, the third a canon at the third, and so on to the ninth. While it is of course true that the sequence of canons at different intervals can be grasped by ear, the idea of correlating the numerical order of the canons with their intervallic order is a clever intellectual pun, possible only because musical intervals happen to be called by numerals. These puns are typical of baroque psychology and essential for the understanding of baroque art. We know that the individual movements of the *Goldberg Variations* were supposed to be selected at random, but the fact that Bach added at the end "Aria da capo" proves that he considered the set also as a gigantic cycle of thirty chaconne variations.

The didactic, liturgical, and intellectual principles were all extra-musical devices to secure inner unity and consistency that in themselves were not audible because they were extraneous to the music. They materialized at times only on the printed page, like certain puzzle canons, written in form of a cross. The devices were logical, but their logic was not a musical logic. They could be intellectually understood but not intuitively experienced. While in modern aesthetics these two processes have been almost completely severed they complemented each other in the baroque era. Music was more than something audible, it was not merely an "aggregation of auditory stimuli," to put it in the modern jargon of a pseudo-scientific theory. Abstract principles of order were as yet undivorced from aesthetic pleasure and actually enhanced it; like the allegorical and emblematic references in the music they contributed to the intensification of musical understanding. We have grown unfamiliar with these concepts, but even we have not yet become impervious to the special aesthetic pleasure we can derive from hearing the canons of the *Goldberg Variations* unfold in their musical and supra-musical order.

The distinction of audible form and inaudible order did not exist in baroque music. Music reached out from the audible into the inaudible world, it extended without a break from the world of the senses into that of the mind and intellect. We would make a fatal mistake if we tried to deny the intellectual nature of inaudible order because intellect is in ill repute today, or if we tried to "prove" its audibility by means of a far-fetched and unhistorical analysis. It would, however, be equally fatal to ignore it because it can only be known and not heard. We must recognize the speculative approach to music as one of the fundamentals of baroque music and baroque art in general without either exaggerating or belittling its importance. If abstract thoughts could be enhanced through poetic form, as we see in the philosophical poetry of the baroque era, then by the same token concrete works of art could be enhanced through abstract thought. Audible form and inaudible order were not mutually exclusive or opposed concepts, as they are today, but complementary aspects of one and the same experience: the unity of sensual and intellectual understanding.

CHAPTER ELEVEN

Musical Thought of the Baroque Era

MORE THAN any other period of musical history the baroque era was partial to vivid, if often painfully loquacious, treatises on music. The value of these theoretical sources is naturally uneven not only because of their immense number, but especially because many merely repeated what former authorities had written. Certain important theory books of the period do not discuss baroque music at all but deal either with the music of antiquity or with that of the renaissance. To this group belong the works of Zacconi and Cerone which summarize in encyclopedic and authoritative fashion the whole of renaissance music; such references to baroque music as may be found in them tend to be critical rather than descriptive.

The treatises on baroque music can be grouped according to the three so-called "disciplines" of music, *musica theorica, musica poetica,* and *musica practica,* which reflect an old Aristotelian classification, still valid for baroque writers. The meaning of these disciplines must not be interpreted in the modern sense of the terms. *Musica theorica* refers to theoretical speculation; *poetica* not to "expressive music," as many modern writers believe, but to the art of composition (the word is derived from the Greek meaning "to create"); and *practica* to the performance or rendition of music. Modern music theory with its characteristic shift of emphasis toward the "practical" side of music disregards the speculative aspects of theory and comprises essentially only what would be called in the baroque *musica poetica.* The three groups of baroque treatises are listed here in an order that exactly reverses the baroque sequence and proceeds from the concrete to the abstract. The first group then consists of practical guides designed for instruction and performance; they give simple rules and elementary explanations of terms and deal with aspects of performance, ornamentation, singing, etc. The second group is formed by books of what is nowadays called "music theory," containing beside practical rules more or less systematic elucidations of counterpoint, thorough-bass, and the general method of composition. The third group finally includes treatises on the nature of sound and music, aesthetic discussions of the position and function of music in the entire system of human knowledge, and metaphysical speculations on the harmony of the universe.

CODE OF PERFORMANCE

In the discussion of baroque musical thought we begin at the lowest level, most closely allied with musical practice. The aspects of performance raise a great number of perplexing questions because we have become unfamiliar with the fundamental fact that in baroque music notation score and performance score did not, as a rule, coincide. The notation presented merely a skeletal outline of the composition; its structural contour had to be filled in, realized, and possibly ornamented by an extemporizing performer. This practice bears witness to the intimate ties between composer and performer, between composition and improvisation, which make a clear distinction between the two almost impossible. The division of labor had not yet developed to a point where performing and composing were recognized as fields of specialization, as they are today. Significantly the great virtuosi of the baroque, like Domenico Scarlatti, Handel, and Bach, were also the great composers of the period. A code of performance, partly codified in books, but partly unwritten, obtains in baroque music; it must be known and observed in order that a faithful and undistorted rendition of the music be accomplished. The books on performance, ornamentation, thorough-bass realization, and related subjects give us an enormous amount of information which must be complemented in turn by the musical documents themselves demonstrating the stylistically correct application of the code. Isolated findings ought not to be hastily generalized as standard practice because they may range from modest additions to the music to most spectacular changes, justified only by an extraordinary occasion. Moreover, the stylistic contrast between the early, middle, and late phases of baroque music applies also very definitely to the code of performance, so that a realization of a bass by Bach according to the continuo practice of Monteverdi would be as misleading as that according to the practice of Emanuel Bach. Also the various styles of embellishments faithfully mirror the three phases of baroque music.

At the beginning of the seventeenth century the number of treatises on "diminution" and ornamentation, either vocal or instrumental, is noticeably higher than in the middle and late baroque periods. The emphasis on ornamentation must be understood as a symptom of the structural importance assigned to the melodic ornament, especially in the early baroque monody. The distinction between "essential" and "arbitrary" ornaments, prevalent during the early classic period, is foreign to the baroque era. Although the baroque embellishments at first merely perpetuated the practice of renaissance diminutions, the trend toward affective ornaments can be found in such features as the strikingly discontinuous rhythm, the *tempo rubato* or *sprezzatura,* as Caccini calls it, the *messa di voce,* and the affective Lombard rhythm—all highly characteristic of early baroque ornamentation. Among the early baroque authors describing the vocal ornamentation or *gorgia* practice, Zacconi and Cerone may be mentioned as transitional figures, while the important ones are Caccini (Preface to his *Nuove Musiche*), Conforto,[1] Praetorius, Banchieri (*Cartella musicale*), Francesco Rognone (*Selva di varii passaggi*), Mersenne, and Bernhard. Rognone flaunts his progressive attitude by referring to "modern use" on the title page of his book and modern ornaments do indeed appear in his rules for the ornamentation of cadences by means of *gorgia* (Ex. 101). In the quoted

Ex. 101. Rognone: Diminutions of the cadence (after Kuhn).

example the first variation of the cadence begins in Lombard rhythm and ends with a written-out *groppo* or shake; and the second begins with free *passaggi* and ends with a written-out *trillo* or tremolo, sometimes referred to as "goat's trill."

In comparison with the exuberant *gorgia* of the early baroque the belcanto ornamentation of the middle baroque was restrained because it subordinated the embellishments to the even flow of the melody. The famous castrato and teacher Tosi summarized in his *Opinioni de'Cantori antichi e moderni* the salient traits and virtues of bel-canto singing at a time when the virtuoso ornamentation of the late baroque had already become the latest fashion. The multitude of ornaments was by now stereotyped in a few patterns, notably the *appoggiatura,* the shake, the *portamento* and *messa di voce,* and the *tempo rubato.* Tosi vigorously defended the *cantabile* and the pathetic style of the bel canto, supplanted in his day by fast

---

[1] For the sake of brevity only names are given here and exceptionally also important titles. For the full titles see the checklist of baroque books on music in the appendix.

divisions, which he viewed with disfavor and which he tried to restrict stringently. The fast ornamentation is typical of late baroque music and its fiery concerto style; its strictly measured scale passages and its long unaccompanied cadenzas are dependent on instrumental models, especially the violin concerto. Tosi bitterly objected to the indiscriminate application of fast divisions not only because it blotted out the distinction between church, chamber, and theatre styles, but also because it disregarded the proper affections. He remarked sarcastically: "the grand *Mode* demands that he [the singer] be quick, and ready to burst himself in his Lamentations, and weep with Liveliness." He likewise criticized the aria *all'unisono* in which "the Sopranos . . . sing in the manner of the Bass, in Spight of a thousand *Octaves.*" Although he required improvised ornaments and cadenzas in the da-capo aria himself he castigated the excessive practice of the time with grim humor: "Every *Air* has (at least) three *Cadences* [cadenzas] . . . Generally speaking, the Study of the Singers of the present Time consists in terminating the *Cadence* of the first Part with an overflowing of *Passages* and *Divisions* at Pleasure, and the *Orchestre* waits; in that of the second the Dose is increased, and the *Orchestre* grows tired; but on the last *Cadence,* the Throat is set going, like a Weathercock in a Whirlwind, and the *Orchestre* swears." Some extraordinary vocal cadenzas, for example those sung by the "divine" Farinelli,[2] have come down to us. They look as though they had been lifted bodily out of a violin concerto, but cadenzas of this type should not be taken as the rule.

It must also be remembered that the directions for extensive ornamentation apply only to music for soloists, especially castrati and the exceptional female singers. Both Tosi and Mancini compared the individual virtues of the two most famous prima donnas of Handel's day: Cuzzoni and Faustina. The first excelled in the *cantabile* style, in *portamento* and *legato* singing, and was praised for her sweet tone quality and for her ability to extemporize affective ornaments, which strikingly contrasted with the often ridiculed habit of singers of always inserting the same divisions in different arias. Faustina, the wife of Hasse, distinguished herself in the amazing agility of her divisions, a "granitic" firmness in the execution of trills, perfect intonation, and a breath control that enabled her to phrase and articulate superbly. Tosi nostalgically speculated how beautiful the mixture between the two "angelick creatures" would be, could "the Pathetick of the one and the *Allegro* of the other" ever be united. The tone quality of the castrato voice combined the penetrating, bell-like sonority of a boy soprano

[2] See Haas, *Aufführungspraxis,* 185.

with the fully developed breath control and strength of a man, which gave it a somewhat instrumental flavor, heightened by tremendous range and sustaining power. The fascinating and intense color of the castrato voice embodied an ideal of stylized voice production which differs as distinctly from our modern ideal of vocal quality as the penetrating sonorities of the baroque organ do from the orchestral organ.

In choral ensemble music the solo embellishments, just described, were considered out of place. When more than one singer sang a part, only carefully rehearsed ornaments could be tolerated though references to the confused rendition of choral music because of ornamental singing imply that the rule was not always observed. We know of rehearsed embellishment through Allegri's famous *Miserere,* sung a-cappella in the Sistine Chapel. In this case the rehearsed embellishments actually gave distinction to a simple and otherwise hardly memorable composition in *falso-bordone* style. The influence of the soloistic *messa di voce* on the a-cappella music of the early baroque can be seen in the experiments with dynamic gradations, such as *crescendo* and *decrescendo.* This collective *messa di voce* was destined to become one of the most hackneyed means of the a-cappella idiom. Dynamic gradations constitute practically the only form of embellishment in choral music. The absence of figurative ornamentation in choral compositions became even more pronounced in the *concertato* style in which the full chorus (*cappella*) and the *concertato* were differentiated by an unadorned rendition and a highly florid style respectively; symptomatically, the latter was reserved for the soloists or *favoriti,* as Schütz calls them.

The development of instrumental ornamentation parallels that of vocal ornamentation and is similarly restricted to solo music or ensembles of soloists. As in vocal ornamentation, three phases can be distinguished which coincide with early, middle, and late baroque styles. The early baroque practice is characterized by a lively interchange between the discontinuous vocal and instrumental embellishments. Even Rognone, writing primarily for singers, remarks that the ornaments could be used by instrumentalists desirous to "imitate the human voice." The violin tremolo, first employed by Marini, Usper, and Monteverdi, is merely an instrumental adaptation of the familiar vocal tremolo or goat's trill, which Scheidt transferred in turn to the organ under the designation *imitatio violistica*. And in his interesting treatise on trumpet playing Fantini transferred the *messa di voce* to the brass instrument. The middle baroque style of instrumental ornamentation is represented by the early Bologna school whose composers show as much restraint toward embellishments as the bel-canto style does. The late baroque phase is characterized by rapid divisions and unaccompanied cadenzas. The slow movements of the sonatas and concertos were the special domain of extensive graces which in effect turned a sustained melody into a rapidly moving filigree, as can be seen in the chamber music of Corelli and Handel (compare Exs. 71 and 102). In those sections of a concerto grosso in which *concertino* and *ripieno* played in unison no embellishments were intended, not even in slow movements. The broad cantilena that distinguishes the third movement of Handel's concerto grosso op. 6, 12, would ordinarily call for rich ornaments, but the unison orchestration definitely precludes it because Handel at this place deliberately set off an unadorned bel-canto line against the subsequent written-out variation of the melody.

The methods of embellishment changed not only with the different phases of the baroque era but also with the various countries. In the course of the seventeenth century the three leading national styles developed three different methods of ornamentation: the Italians notated hardly any embellishments at all, leaving them to the performer; the French devised a system of symbols as a sort of shorthand for the *agréments;* the Germans, finally, tended to write out the ornaments in full and availed themselves also of some of the French symbols. The French and German methods both curtailed the improvisatory additions of the performer, typical of Italian practice. Characteristically, Lully, Couperin, and Bach do not call for additional ornamentation whereas Corelli, Vivaldi, and the Italian opera composers do. Handel clearly illustrates, as he usually does, the Italian attitude. An early version of his harpsichord suite in *d* (first set) contains an "aria" without any written ornaments, but for its publication in England Handel thought it necessary to write them out. Significantly, he changed the title to "air" and added profuse ornaments in small print (Ex. 102). These ornaments seem, however, tame in comparison with the fantastically exuberant harpsichord arrangements of Handel's opera arias by his pupil Babell which reflect in their interminable cadenzas the divisions of castrato singing.

The ready resolution of the French ornamental symbols into notes was a special art [8] with which every French and German musician was supposed to be familiar. The French composers took pains to compile numerous tables of *agréments*, and Bach followed their example in the *Clavierbüchlein* for his son Friedemann. In certain modern "instructive" editions

Ex. 102. Handel: Two versions of an air for harpsichord.

all symbols have been transcribed in full notation—a deplorable practice not so much because of the rhythmic confusion that inevitably results, but especially because it annihilates the fundamental distinction between harmonically essential and unessential notes, implied in the notation by smaller print of the ornamental notes. Since only essential notes could carry ornamental symbols, the notation gave actually a musically intelligent, if elementary, melodic analysis.

The techniques of the individual instruments were discussed in the numerous methods or tutors. They cover practically all instruments (and the voice) and range from simple instructions to elaborate treatises. The viol was treated by Christopher Simpson and Jean Rousseau; the trumpet by Fantini; the lute by Mersenne, Mace, and Baron; the flute by Hotteterre; the cello by Corrette; the harpsichord by Couperin and Maichelbeck; the organ by Diruta, Correa, Samber, and Justinus. The violin, the new and coming instrument, received more attention than any other. Violin methods begin with the humble books by Francesco Rognone, da Cruz, and Zanetti and later continue with the more extensive treatises by Merck, Montéclair, Geminiani, Tessarini, and Corrette.

[8] For a discussion of ornamentation see the introduction to Ralph Kirkpatrick's edition of the *Goldberg Variations* (G. Schirmer).

Of the many questions arising from instrumental techniques only a few can be touched upon here, notably the bowing and tonguing of the strings and winds, the fingering on keyboard instruments, and the effect of the fingering on musical articulation. As to bowing and tonguing the general rule can be stated that all notes were separately bowed or tongued unless the opposite was expressly indicated by slurs which occur as early as Marini (1617). According to Tartini the violin sonatas of Corelli must be played in *détaché* bowing, not *legato* as some modern violinists are given to believe. Not before the time of Lully did a distinct French style of bowing develop, which in many ways forms the basis of our modern bowing. The French manner spread rapidly over Germany but found only a slow response in Italy. In the preface to his *Florilegium* the German Lullist Georg Muffat explained at length the difference between the rhythmically pointed style of the French and the less precise German and Italian styles. Lully introduced rhythmic precision by the rule that all rhythmically strong notes, regardless of their position in the measure, should be taken on the down-bow. This was, according to Muffat, "the secret of bowing" and "the principal and indispensable rule of the Lullists." In the German and Italian style the bowing consisted of a mechanical alternation of down- and up-bows, hardly able to do justice to an intelligent articulation of the music. In one of Muffat's examples the two procedures are clearly juxtaposed (Ex. 103). The French bowed with short and precise strokes while the Italians

Ex. 103. Georg Muffat: German and French style of bowing.

liked the long strokes or the full bow. Muffat also explains the French habit of playing passages in even eighth-notes in dotted fashion, the practice of the so-called *notes inégales* which was also taken over by the French masters of the *clavecin*. Lully insisted on the meticulous observation of his rules and thus achieved in his orchestra the brilliant uniformity and precision of bowing which won him the admiration of Europe.

There is no place in baroque music for the perpetual string *vibrato* that "graces" modern violin playing. The references to the *vibrato* which appear first in the lute instructions of Mersenne and Mace, and later in Merck's violin tutor, bear unequivocal proof that the *vibrato* was, like the *crescendo,* a special ornament, indicated by a symbol of its own and to be used with discretion only at the proper places. The manner of holding the violin against the chest precluded in itself extensive use of the *vibrato*. The idea of playing continually with *vibrato* would be as preposterous to baroque musicians as that of always pulling the tremulant stop on the organ. The *bebung* of the clavichord and the tremulant stop of the baroque organ roughly correspond to the *vibrato* ornament and are likewise singular effects and refinements among many others. The production of an even tone was foremost in the minds of the instrumentalists (and singers), and the *vibrato* must be understood as a deliberate, but only occasional, abandonment or variation of what would today be considered a "lifeless" tone. Being the regular way of producing a tone nowadays the *vibrato* has ceased to function as an ornament whereas the *non-vibrato* has in turn become a special ornament the composer must prescribe if he wishes it, as Bartók does in his Second Piano Concerto.

The fingering of the keyboard instruments observed during the early and middle baroque periods was the traditional "three-finger playing," in general use except in England. It favored the index, middle, and ring finger to the virtual exclusion of the thumb and the small finger. Ascending scales were played with characteristic crossings or skips of the third finger over the fourth or even the fifth. The frequent slidings of the same finger from one key to the next were greatly facilitated by the light touch of the old instruments. From the many extant examples of original fingering a ricercar by Erbach may be quoted which shows that even in the octave the thumb was often avoided (Ex. 104). Thirds were always fingered with

Ex. 104. Erbach: Ricercar with original fingering.

the second and fourth fingers so that parallel thirds could be rendered only *staccato*. This *staccato* style of playing persisted well into the late baroque period. Couperin proposed in his *Art de toucher le clavecin* several reforms that approach modern principles of fingering, notably the use of the small finger and thumb for the smooth playing of scales, and the *legato* rendition of two parallel thirds. Bach built his remarkably advanced fingering on Couperin's method and expanded it in systematic fashion. However, both composers recognized the old as well as the new fingering and used them side by side.

The fingering throws some light on the important, if highly vexing, question of musical articulation. First of all, we learn from it that the customary smooth *legato* style of the modern "tradition" is, to put it mildly, a distortion. While it would be senseless to advocate a reinstatement of the old fingering for the sake of correct articulation, its musical effect should be carefully studied in order to reproduce it by modern fingering. The correct articulation must be regarded as the most essential aspect of performance because it is the decisive, and for instruments such as the organ the only, means of phrasing. Its importance for polyphonic music cannot easily be overestimated since only by articulation can the contrapuntal texture be rendered with the proper transparency. In order to achieve this goal, each single motive must be given relief, and in a succession of two or more motives they must be set off by a *staccato* in order to make the internal structure of the phrase audible. The ricercar by Erbach, quoted above, proves beyond doubt that the first motive, ending on the first note of the second measure, is definitely separated by a *staccato* from the continuation. The fundamental rule of articulation requires that the unity of the motive be reinforced by the uniformity of articulation. Thus within a *legato* motive no change to *staccato* should be made except for the shortening of the last note for the sake of clearly perceptible separation. The resulting overlaps of different articulations are an inherent trait of polyphonic music that should not be obscured. It goes without saying that the motivic complexities of Bach's music admit more than one articulation each of which may be consistent with the fundamental rule. However, once chosen, the articulation must be maintained throughout in order to make all voices equally distinct. Inconsistent articulation, such as can be found in Czerny's edition of Bach's keyboard works, betrays a blatant lack of understanding for the Bach style. The objection, frequently met with, that the motivic articulation disrupts the flow of the phrase is based on ideas of phrase structure typical of the classic but not of the baroque period. A clear conception of baroque articulation will bring out the fact that the almost omnipresent upbeat patterns, the development of which has been traced in previous chapters, usually straddle the bar line and play havoc with an accentual or strictly metrical rhythm, especially in the music of Bach. In the rhapsodic sections of his compositions Bach sometimes implied articulation by judiciously distributing the line between the two hands so as to clarify the motivic structure of the melody.

One of the main reasons for the disparity of notation and performance score in baroque music lies in the realization of the thorough-bass. As the innumerable treatises on the subject show its mastery formed the main pillar of a well-rounded musicianship. Thorough-bass realization is so wide a field as to fill a voluminous book [4] so that it must suffice here to point out the development of the continuo realization from utmost simplicity in the Italian early baroque to highly imaginative, contrapuntal realizations in the German late baroque period. The main sources for the early baroque continuo and *basso seguente* practice are the prefatory remarks of Cavalieri, Peri, and Caccini and the brief rules set down by Viadana, Agazzari, Bianciardi, Bottazzi, and Banchieri, on which the German treatises by Praetorius, Aichinger, and Staden are largely based. The middle baroque stage is summarized for Italy in Penna's important book *Li Primi Albori Musicali* and for England in the short rules by Locke and Blow. Of the many excellent books on the highly advanced continuo practice of the late baroque period only a few can be mentioned. Gasparini codified the thorough-bass techniques applicable to Corelli and Handel; St. Lambert that of the French opera; and Niedt, Heinichen, and Mattheson that of Bach. Heinichen's inexhaustible *Der Generalbass in der Composition* is heavily indebted to Gasparini's valuable *L'Armonico Pratico al Cimbalo*, especially in the discussion of the *acciaccatura*.

The written-out organ accompaniments in certain sections of Monteverdi's sacred music prove that the early continuo practice relied heavily on the doubling of voices, especially in church music. In this early phase the figures of the bass ran from 2 to 15 and higher because they indicated the actual distance from the bass. The last chord of the cadence was understood to be always major unless figured to the contrary. In the Italian opera and cantata the unfigured basses, in themselves an indication of the laxity of Italian practice, present a perpetual difficulty. Many editors have sinned in making their realizations of early baroque music too ostentatious and too advanced harmonically. A comparison between the editions of Monteverdi's *Orfeo* by Eitner, d'Indy, and Malipiero is highly instructive in this respect; only the last one is, in spite of many shortcomings, stylistically acceptable. The realizations represent a constant challenge to present-day musicianship and scholarship, but so far neither has made a brilliant showing. All editions should observe one simple rule of honesty: the original score, including the bass figuring, should always be made distinct from editorial accretions by means of variation in type or other devices; unfortunately, though, only a small number of reprints of old music adhere to this policy.

[4] Arnold, *The Art of Accompaniment from a Thorough-Bass*.

By the end of the baroque period continuo playing had risen to such a refined art that it became virtually identical with improvised composition. The average accompanists and amateur musicians could not keep abreast with this advance which led to a parting of the ways between simple and learned accompaniment. In his *règle de l'octave* the theorboe player Delair (1690) formulated a simple style of accompaniment in keeping with the modest possibilities of his instrument. Originally set down as a rule of thumb for the realization of unfigured basses, the "rule of the octave" soon became the vehicle for beginners, and its widespread use in the later eighteenth century heralds the decline of the thorough-bass.

The *basso-continuo* practice had a profound influence on the baroque conception of orchestration. The division of the orchestra into fundamental and ornamental instruments, first made by Agazzari, would obviously have been impossible without the advent of the thorough-bass. In baroque orchestration three types may be distinguished that roughly correspond to the three phases of baroque style: cumulative orchestration, continuo orchestration, and contrapuntal orchestration. Early baroque music is characterized by the almost unbelievable accumulation of fundamental and, to a lesser degree, also ornamental instruments. This practice is illustrated by the score of Monteverdi's *Orfeo* or by Praetorius' interesting arrangements of motets by Lasso and others, which transform renaissance compositions into baroque pieces by the addition of a great many fundamental instruments. In his highly informative treatise *Syntagma musicum* Praetorius fully expounded the principles of cumulative orchestration and explained how the reinforcing instruments were selected according to the clefs indicating the range, and how the greatest possible mixture of sonorities could be achieved. Except for France, the orchestral doublings by instruments of the same type was not common. By way of exception Monteverdi suggested in his *Ballo delle Ingrate* that the strings could be doubled according to the size of the hall.

During the middle baroque the continuo orchestration came to the fore which remained in favor throughout the baroque era. This type consists of a continuo fundament and a superstructure of from one to four ornamental instruments. It relied primarily on the strings, best fitted to furnish an appropriate background for the bel-canto with which it was ordinarily used in the opera. The dualistic conception of the continuo orchestration emphasized the structural contour of the composition: the outermost lines were heavily reinforced while the middle was less essential and could be left to the improvised harmonies of the continuo player. This practice explains why extant middle parts were often designated as optional, and why the superstructure of the upper voices contained instruments of the same range, such as three violins, frequent in the Italian opera orchestra of the middle baroque.

The contrapuntal orchestration, brought to perfection in the late baroque, especially in the works of Bach, is based on the equality of all voices that prevails in a contrapuntally highly integrated composition. In this type all parts, whether instrumental or vocal, could be doubled, as often happens with Bach. Contrapuntal orchestration is dominated by the consideration of obbligato part-writing which allows no instrument to drop out entirely during a movement. The terraced orchestration of the concertos, which derives its effects from a juxtaposition rather than a combination of instruments of different color, is modeled after the terraced dynamics of the organ. Bach's conception of orchestration is in many ways as strongly indebted to the organ as the romantic organ is to the orchestra.

The orchestration was not always rigidly prescribed. Especially in soloistic ensemble music the performer was given a certain freedom to choose his instruments, yet the selection was not arbitrarily made but depended on the affection of the piece. Each instrument was associated with certain affections and wherever obbligatos for flute, trumpet, viola d'amore, and other instruments appear in the opera, oratorio, or cantata, they serve to emphasize the affection. The modern coloristic orchestration which can be reconciled with neither the continuo nor the contrapuntal orchestration began with the French rococo and took its first strides in the operas of Rameau.

THEORY AND PRACTICE OF COMPOSITION

The treatises on *musica poetica* clearly disclose in the organization of their material that counterpoint and thorough-bass were regarded at the time as the two essential aspects of musical composition. It may seem strange that "harmony books," the type of theory book most familiar today, did not exist in the baroque period. Harmonic theories were conceived and presented in terms of the thorough-bass practice, and they did not become independent until Rameau. The chordal "continuo thinking" pervaded all aspects of theory. Even the approach to counterpoint was governed by harmonic considerations. Treatises dealt more extensively with questions concerning which notes were allowed to sound together than with problems of linear or melodic design. This peculiarity accounts not only for the absence of harmony treatises but also for the fact that a densely woven contrapuntal texture was referred to at the time as "rich harmony." The *Rules How to Compose* (c. 1610) by Coperario very clearly demonstrate the intrusion of chordal thinking into contrapuntal theory, especially in the manner of reckoning all voices from the bass. In spite of the Italian propensity of its author the treatise gives a highly informative account of the state of counterpoint in the period of the English madrigalists and far surpasses that of Morley with regard to the musical practice, then current.

The baroque theorists teach counterpoint and thorough-bass either in separate chapters of the same books or specialize in either one field. It can hardly surprise that the books on counterpoint evince on the whole a more conservative attitude than do those on thorough-bass. The contrapuntal instructions of the early baroque period, such as Sweelinck, Crüger, Ravenscroft, and Coperario, follow the model set by Zarlino, but expand it by the inclusion of new intervallic or chordal combinations. The four outstanding treatises on counterpoint were written by Bontempi, Giovanni Maria Bononcini, Berardi, and Fux. The treatise by Fux became famous for its deliberate restoration and glorification of the Palestrina style, but similar tendencies can be found also in the earlier ones. The instruction in "strict style" or *stile antico* was regulated by the so-called species, all five of which appeared as early as Berardi; they are today always associated with Fux though he merely codified them in the order in which they became universally known. Although Palestrina was repeatedly quoted as the ultimate authority and model, the rules of the *stile antico* were not actually drawn from renaissance music but codified a chordally conceived a-cappella style that embodies the baroque conception of renaissance music rather than the true renaissance style. The highly illuminating treatise on composition by Bernhard, the pupil of Schütz, significantly subdivides counterpoint into two categories: *gravis* and *luxurians* which correspond to the distinction of *stile antico* and *moderno*. Freedom of dissonance treatment, characteristic of "modern" counterpoint, was justified according to Bernhard only by the text or the appropriate affection. Bernhard himself stood obviously on the side of the *stile moderno,* but even he expected the composers to be familiar with both styles. The bearing of the "duplicity of styles" on the history of music in general has been discussed in Chapter I.

The books on the theory of thorough-bass deserve special study because they actually epitomize the general theory of baroque composition. They represent the progressive strand in the theoretical thought of the period. Little concerned with the *stile antico,* they go far beyond the ordinary rules of thorough-bass realization and give valuable directions for improvised and written composition. With regard to improvisatory ability Mattheson went further than any other composer and theorist. In his *Grosse Generalbass-Schule* he presented a series of forty-eight "test pieces" in unusually remote keys, consisting of figured basses, arranged and graded in order of difficulty. If correctly realized, these basses could pass as self-contained compositions. Also Gasparini and, especially, Heinichen called for the addition of improvised melodies against the figured bass, a practice that Bach carried in his realizations to the highest level. The treatises teach the structural elements of composition by means of cadential patterns, typical bass progressions, and amusing recipes as to how to put them together. Spiridion and Niedt gave many examples of such formulas, and Bach also used them in his thorough-bass instructions. In view of the high quality of baroque music the directions seem surprisingly mechanical as though composition consisted of nothing more than the word implied, namely the putting-together or "com-position" of formulas. However, these methods help us understand why bass patterns like the chaconne and others found such universal favor. They furnished the basic formulas which by stereotyped methods of elaboration could be easily turned into full-fledged written or extemporized compositions. The close interaction between improvisation and composition becomes nowhere more clearly apparent than here. Also the general practice of ornamentation must be understood as part and parcel of the improvisatory element in composition. This baroque type of improvisation was closely confined within restricted but flexible boundaries; it was a strictly patterned or guided improvisation not an arbitrary rambling through keys.

The handling of modulation was taught by similarly mechanical means. With the establishment of tonality and a roughly equal temperament in the late baroque period the whole circle of keys was open to composers and it is interesting to see how they wrestled with the problem. Both Heinichen and Mattheson proposed different circles of keys as guides to modulation through all the keys. While Heinichen merely placed the major and their relative minor keys in the circle of fifths, Mattheson (*Kleine Generalbass-Schule,* 1735) more nearly approached an order of modulation that was actually observed in the compositions of the late baroque. His circle (see the diagram) is actually identical with the order of keys that Sorge adopted in his *Clavierübung* (1730).

It should be noted that in Mattheson's circle the keys of *D* and *d* stand rather far removed from each other, quite in keeping with late baroque music which treated the two opposite modes as less closely related than the relative minor and major.

The most momentous harmonic innovation of the baroque period was unquestionably the concept of tonality which slowly evolved in the Italian middle baroque and did not appear fully established until Provenzale and Corelli at the beginning of the late baroque period. The transition from modal to tonal concepts entailed a crisis of musical thought, manifested in the harmonic experimentations of the early baroque. The thorough-bass proved to be a most valuable tool for these experiments because it lent itself equally well to both contrapuntal and chordal music. The change from the preoccupation with intervallic combinations to that with chords is the symptom of the transition from renaissance to baroque theory. The early baroque treatises of Lippius, Baryphonus, and Crüger, which are essentially based on Zarlino, expand the concept of the triad, learnedly called at the time *trias harmonica*. The thorough-bass was premised upon a diatonic scale and the principle of triadic harmony. For this reason triads were left unfigured and assumed major or minor form according to their position in the scale. Only those chords needed figures that were either not triads or did not automatically fall into the diatonic pattern. This accounts for a curiously primitive rule of the early continuo practice prescribing that all bass notes modified by an accidental should be realized as sixth chords, even if not thus figured.

Although chordal thinking was greatly furthered by the continuo practice, it must not be forgotten that in the thorough-bass two principles were in constant conflict, one progressive and one retrospective. Progressive was the tendency to reduce all voices to chords which could be figured from the bass. This method of chord formation ultimately led to the recognition of tonality. Retrospective was the method of chord progression. Before the establishment of tonality chord progressions were regulated not by a harmonic, but as yet by a melodic principle, namely by the actual bass line itself. This method points back to renaissance music, even though the baroque bass line was no longer governed by modality. The chordal thinking overthrew the modes and led to the recognition of keys. The incipient tonal principle was brought out as early as Lippius, Crüger, and Carissimi. They reduced the multiplicity of modes to only two (major and minor) or to what was called at the time the "sharp" and "flat" keys. The only real mode to survive was Phrygian. The independence of the Phrygian mode is clearly evident as late as Ferdinand Fischer who presented in his *Ariadne Musica* three preludes and fugues successively in Phrygian, *e*, and *E*. The retention of just one and, for that matter, the most characteristic of the old modes is significant with regard to the chords of the "Neapolitan sixth" and augmented sixth, the only two chords in the regular harmonic vocabulary of the baroque period that would be called chromatic today. Both chords owe their origin not to any chordal "alteration," but to the fusion of the Phrygian mode with the key of *E* (major or minor) which became possible only after the rudiments of key feeling had been established by the harmonic practice of the middle baroque. Indeed, they appear exactly at this time in the works of the three great C's: Cavalli, Carissimi, and Cesti. The "Neapolitan" sixth, which would more properly be called the Phrygian-sixth chord, is derived from the cadential progression II6-V-I, in which the Phrygian supertonic is followed by the dominant of the key; and the augmented sixth results from the insertion of a chromatic passing note into the ordinary Phrygian cadence, which reinforces the effect of a half cadence. This effect persists even in the usage of the classic period. Both chords (Ex. 105) would require many special symbols in our current harmonic

Ex. 105. "Neapolitan" and augmented-sixth chord in typical context.

analysis, but they could be expressed in the continuo system by a very simple set of figures.

The contrast of major and minor, discussed as early as Glareanus and Zarlino, assumed universal importance only with the advent of baroque music. Carissimi represented cheerfulness and sadness by abruptly juxtaposing the two modes in his cantata *I Filosofi*, quoted by Kircher as a rare artifice, known only to the initiated. In the writings of Masson and Brossard major and minor had become the only surviving modes of which all keys were only transpositions. Brossard stated clearly even before Rameau that the major and minor thirds "form the soul and fundament of harmony." The so-called Dorian notation of the key of *g* with only one flat and similar survivals of modal habits in late baroque music do not necessarily imply what has been called "modal harmony," but often represent merely an archaic form of notation.

While the theoretical recognition of keys must be credited to the middle baroque period, the honor of having realized their harmonic implications goes unquestionably to Rameau. His *Traité de l'harmonie reduite à ses principes naturelles* and later treatises, in which the author fundamentally amended his view, laid the foundation for modern harmonic theory by the recognition of a tonal center (*centre harmonique*), the discovery of the chord inversions, and the postulate that chords must be built up in thirds. By reducing all chords to three functions, the tonic, dominant, and subdominant, he designed a system of chordal relations that prescribed the progression of chords by a "fundamental bass." This bass reduced all harmonic progressions to a theoretical line that was independent of the actually sounding bass. With the functional determination of chord progressions and the emancipation of the fundamental bass from the thorough-bass Rameau actually exploded the continuo system, which recognized neither inversions nor the third structure of chords, and which knew of no harmonic direction of chords. It is strange that in the presentation of his system Rameau fell into inconsistencies which show him still imprisoned in continuo thinking. His manner of figuring the fundamental bass and that of "adding" tones to triads (*Sixte ajoutée*) represent vestiges of the continuo practice which have survived even to the present day in such terms as sixth chord. In spite of its inner contradictions, however, Rameau's system of functional harmony represents the beginning of a new era of harmonic thought. His emphatic subordination of melody to harmony, which cannot be reconciled with contrapuntal music, forms the transition to the theory of the classic period.

The technical aspects of the theory of composition must be complemented by the doctrine of affections which set stringent rules to all baroque composers. The wealth of baroque affections was stereotyped in an infinite number of "figures" or *loci topici* which "represented or depicted" the affections in music. The elaborate systematization of these figures must be regarded as the main contribution of the baroque era to the doctrine of affections. If we can judge by the great number of books on this subject, it was especially attractive to German theorists although it occurred, of course, with writers of other nationalities. Discussions of the doctrine of affections and figures in the baroque era began with the works of Nucius, Crüger, Schönsleder, and Herbst; they continued in the more explicit treatise of Bernhard, and finally crystallized in definitive form with Vogt, Mattheson, and Scheibe. *Der Vollkommene Capellmeister* by Mattheson contains the most lucid and musically most fruitful account of the subject, but indicates in its critical approach the advent of the age of enlightenment.

The doctrine of affections was based on the ancient analogy between music and rhetorics and elaborated it by figures in a peculiar manner. The innovation of the recitative especially gave the theorists ample occasion to observe the parallelism between music and speech, and theorists of the monody, especially Doni, began to evolve concrete musical figures for such "figures of speech" as question, affirmation, emphatic repetition, and others. Toward the middle of the century Bernhard could already state that "because of the multitude of figures music nowadays has risen to such height that it may well be likened to a *rhetorica*." Mattheson also held forth that music was a form of "sound speech." According to him the two outstanding *loci topici* were the *locus notationis* and the *locus descriptionis*, designated respectively as "the richest" and "the most essential" vehicles of invention and composition. The first *locus* dealt with such abstract musical figures as imitation, inversion, repetition, and other means of musical organization. They are particularly arresting because they demonstrate how intimately the doctrine of affections and figures was bound up with the technical aspects of the musical craft. The *locus descriptionis* depicted extra-musical ideas by means of metaphorical and allegorical figures and similes which, according to baroque thinking, were as essential to music as they were to the emblems, in which pictorial and figurative meaning were inseparable. Not by accident do emblematic books of the time contain music, as does for example Majer's *Atalanta fugiens* (see plate 11).

The whole system of "topics" was conceived as a "guide to invention" or *ars inveniendi* which facilitated the selection of a particular figure for the appropriate representation of an affection. The unity, achieved by consistent elaboration of the chosen figure, vouched at the same time for the unity of affection that governed the piece. The maintenance of a single affection throughout a composition began tentatively in the middle baroque and became increasingly more rigid toward the end of the period. The motto beginning of the aria very clearly illustrates the use of a figure that summarized the whole composition by its concise shape. Mattheson asserted that the arias "have almost all a short theme or subjectum wherein the whole content and affection must be contained as much as possible." He was fully aware of the danger that non-essential figures might depict only single words and not the sense of the entire passage; he ridiculed such practices with the punning remark—he never missed a chance for a pun— that they "turn music into a monkey-business." Consistent with the practice of Bach, Handel, and Telemann, he advised the composer to relegate secondary figures to the accompaniment where they could be of good service.

It must be strongly emphasized that the musical figures were in themselves necessarily ambiguous, and took on a definite meaning only in a musical context and by means of a text or title. Since they did not "express" but merely "presented" or "signified" the affections, musically identical figures lent themselves to numerous and often highly divergent meanings. It is therefore misleading to isolate certain figures and classify them in a system of absolute meanings as motives of joy, steps, beatitude, and so forth.[5] Nor should these procedures be misrepresented as emotional program music or as the psychological expression of feelings. The affections were non-psychological, static attitudes and were therefore peculiarly fitted for musical representation. Not by any means does the presence of metaphorical figures distinguish the music of Bach from that of other baroque composers, nor does it make any music automatically good. It is the masterly and highly refined integration of musical structure and metaphorical meaning that bestows on Bach's music its unique intensity.

The distinctly rational and intellectual connotation of the doctrine of figures was a direct outgrowth of the highly characteristic attitude toward concrete and abstract concepts in baroque thought, which tried to render

[5] This is the principal objection to the method of Schweitzer who popularized the metaphorical interpretation that Pirro put on a solid scholarly basis; see Bukofzer, *Allegory in Baroque Music.*

abstract ideas concretely and concrete things abstractly. A strictly musical idea was therefore at once concrete and abstract, it presented an abstract affection in concrete form, and for this reason the figure had a structural significance for the entire composition. The profound respect for the figures in music is solemnly affirmed by Bernhard who bluntly puts it like this: "What cannot be justified by figures should be banished from music as a monstrosity."

MUSICAL SPECULATION

With the discussion of the doctrine of affections and figures we have actually risen to the third and highest level of musical thought. Books on *musica theorica,* referred to today as speculative with a somewhat derogatory overtone, form an integral part of baroque thinking, and they alone can give us the proper perspective for the discussion of any particular aspect of music theory. They elucidate how the doctrine of affections and figures and the classifications of music according to styles fitted into the general aesthetics of the period, which was dominated by the concept of the imitation of nature.

The two most impressive and typical books on musical speculation were written by two clerics and polyhistors: Mersenne (*Harmonie universelle*) and Kircher (*Musurgia universalis*). As the similarity of the titles implies, both authors approached their subject in a truly encyclopedic and universal fashion. While the information they give cannot be accepted without many reservations their books nevertheless represent historical documents of the first order. They touch on all subjects of music, practical and theoretical, including solmisation, temperament, and music history.

The solmisation of music by means of hexachords had become obsolete through the modern system of keys, but it persisted to the days of Buttstedt and Mattheson who finally buried the question in a heated controversy.

Discussions of temperament occupied the best minds of the time (Werckmeister, Rameau, Loulié, and Neidhardt) and ended with the victory of a "well-tempered" tuning which broke through the narrow limits of the meantone temperament and made all keys of the complete circle of fifths available for musical practice. It is not surprising that it was accepted only after the fully established tonality had made it a musical necessity. The three "well-tempered" tunings that Werckmeister proposed were, contrary to common belief, only approximations of equal temperament. Although Werckmeister, Kuhnau, and Rameau recognized and, at least at times, advocated strict equal temperament they did so mainly in theory and not always consistently.

It is highly significant that the awakening of interest in music history coincides with the beginnings of the baroque era. Aside from Kircher and Mersenne, the historical approach to music found devotees in Calvisius, Praetorius, Printz, Bontempi, and Bourdelot, none of whom wrote "critical" music histories in the modern sense. The musical historiography of the baroque must be recognized as another symptom of the growing historical style-consciousness that distinguishes the baroque era from preceding periods. Kircher's disquisition on musical styles in the *Musurgia universalis* is especially noteworthy because it discloses the interdependence of the system of stylistic classifications and the doctrine of affections within the general framework of baroque philosophy. Kircher presented a threefold order of classification: individual styles, social or national styles, and functional styles. The individual styles corresponded to the "four humors" which go back to Galen's ancient theory of the individual temperaments. The social or national styles were thought to express the national characteristics and idiosyncrasies of the various countries. The Italian, French, and German style, the three leading national styles of the period, found different characterizations with the different theorists, but they made them generally without nationalistic bias. The specific virtues of each national style were impartially recognized and, contrary to nationalistic thinking, the combination of Italian and French styles, typical of the German late baroque style, was praised, not censored. The third stylistic order of Kircher was a set of nine styles distinguished according to functions, such as dance, theatre, church music, but also according to technical principles, such as canonic or melismatic style, and according to forms, such as motet and madrigal style. These styles were later incorporated into the leading musical dictionaries of the time, notably those of Janowka, Brossard, and Walther.

The Italian classification of music according to church, chamber, and theatre style, first established by Scacchi, found even wider acceptance then that of Kircher, especially among practical musicians. Scacchi tended to distinguish styles by means of formal and technical criteria as did also Monteverdi in his distinction between *prima prattica* and *seconda prattica* which served Scacchi as a point of departure. In the writings of Mattheson the technical classification of Scacchi and the functional one of Kircher were combined in a form that has served as the basis of our modern concept of musical style.

The works of Bacon, Descartes, and Leibniz testify to the fact that music held an important place in the philosophical treatises of the baroque era. In accordance with his metaphysical system Leibniz defined music as "the unconscious counting of the soul," convinced that the unconscious realization of mathematical proportions was the ultimate cause of the sensuous effect of music. In this manner Leibniz, and with him many music theorists, reconciled the senses and the intellect, the audible and the inaudible. *Sensus* and *ratio* were the two basic factors in the judgment and evaluation of music, and, for that matter, of all other baroque arts. The two factors complemented each other and, as we have seen in the discussion of form, their interactions had a direct bearing not only on the theory but also the practice of music.

The aspect of *ratio* was greatly furthered by Sauveur's discovery of the overtone series or what has been termed the "chord of nature." Like tonality and gravitation this was a discovery of the late baroque period; it revolutionized the science of music and led to the substitution of the physical properties of sound for mathematical or purely speculative rationalizations. Ever since, musical theorists have tried to find the answer to questions of music theory in acoustical laws. The first attempt in this direction was made by Rameau. Although he had arrived at his theory of tonality before he knew of the existence of overtones, he utilized them later to consolidate his system, however, with questionable success. Experiments in acoustics were favorite subjects of such baroque authors as Fludd, Mersenne, and Kircher. In their treatises they correlated the field of music with all fields of human knowledge and placed it among the sciences. These included not only mathematics, represented by the specialized treatises of de Chales and Euler, but also such "sciences" as geomantics and astrology, which were discussed by Fludd on the same level as geometry and music.

Music was regarded as an imitation of the music of the universe, a simile of heavenly music, so that Praetorius felt justified in placing music next to theology in the order of disciplines. Like other abstract concepts the music of the universe was a concrete and real thing even to the scientists of the period. Kepler's discovery of the laws of planetary motions grew out of his sincere belief in the actual existence of mundane harmony and his desire to prove it scientifically. In his *Harmonices Mundi* he not only treated music in a competent technical manner, but actually "applied" the Kepler Laws in strictly musical terms. The physical science of music, regarded at the time as senseless in itself, derived its meaning only from metaphysical speculation. Only if we realize this spiritual unity of matters physical and metaphysical do we understand how Berardi could seize on such concrete technical terms as *cantus firmus* and *cantus figuratus* and interpret them abstractly as symbols of divine and human law respectively. The symbolism of music was seen and actually experienced as the direct reflection of the parallelism between divine and human order which, according to the social philosophy of the time, formed the foundation of human society.

CHAPTER TWELVE

Sociology of Baroque Music

COURTLY MUSICAL INSTITUTIONS: PRIVATE PATRONAGE

THE STYLISTIC unity of baroque music which has been discussed in the previous chapters primarily from a technical point of view cannot be severed from the ideas that created it. The investigation of music history is a live and fruitful pursuit only if the changes in musical style and in the conception of music are seen as integral parts of a general history of ideas. The knowledge of the spiritual and social background of former musical styles is an essential factor in musical understanding.

The transition from renaissance to baroque coincides in religious respect with the counter-reformation by which the revitalized Catholic church successfully retrieved the political influence it had lost under the onslaught of the reformation. It coincides in political respect with the triumph of absolutism and the consolidation of national states, which expressed itself musically in the increased interest in national styles. It coincides in economic respect with the rise of mercantilism, which recognized gold as the only true source of wealth. In view of the virtual identity of state and church during the absolutism it cannot surprise that both institutions used the arts as means of representing power, the power of God and his earthly representatives: the nobility and the clergy. Display of splendor was one of the main social functions of music for the counter-reformation and the baroque courts, made possible only through money; and the more money spent, the more powerful was the representation. Consistent with the mercantile ideas of wealth the sumptuousness in the arts became actually an end in itself. Like all baroque arts music too was bound socially to the aristocracy; both the nobility and clergy served in equal measure as patrons. However, viewed from the social angle the shining lights of the flowering arts cast the blackest shadows. Hand in hand with the brilliant development of court and church music went the inquisition and the ruthless exploitation of the lower classes by means of oppressive taxes.

The basic classification of music according to church, chamber, and theatre styles applies also to the main social functions of court music. The opera must be considered as the most courtly and representative of all musical institutions. Three types of opera can be distinguished in social respect: court opera, commercial opera, and middle-class opera. The opera originated as an exclusive courtly institution; indeed Gagliano calls it "truly the spectacle of princes." Performed only for the representatives of the nobility, the opera knew no box office; admission was gained only by invitation. Designed to be a feast for eye and ear, the musical stage attracted attention more with regard to the sets and the singers than to the music, and many reports of the time gave lengthy descriptions of the productions without even mentioning the composer. The libretti also clearly indicated the courtly purpose in their themes as well as in their form. Heroes of mythology or ancient history were shown in the stereotyped conflict between honor and love as thinly disguised allegories of the ruling monarch, especially so in France. The customary prologues addressed the ruler directly in the so-called *licenza* which established the link between the occasion and the topical action. Since the hero represented the monarch, a tragic ending would not have corresponded to the *bienséance* so that the tragedy was usually brought to a happy ending by the sudden appearance of a *deus ex machina*. This device occurs so frequently in the libretti of Zeno and Metastasio that Gay could jeer in his *Beggar's Opera* "an opera must end happily . . . no matter how absurdly things are brought about."

Many petty courts were unable to vie with the operas of the large courts and could not afford the luxury of a standing opera. To satisfy the demand of the smaller noblemen the court opera was commercialized by professional companies. These opera companies developed very early in mercantile centers like Venice, Naples, Hamburg, and London. Here the nobility and the wealthy patricians jointly backed the enterprise by a system of shareholder-ship that entitled subscribers to admission. The boxes of the Venice opera were held by noblemen from all over Europe who met for a gay carnival season in this proverbially "free" city. The stalls were sold through a box office at four *lire* a piece. The Venetian gondoliers, whose famed musical judgment may often have determined the success or failure of an opera, were admitted free of charge to the empty seats as claque, and they often volunteered additional entertainment by their outspoken, if not unprintable, comments on the singers. A special charge was made for the printed libretto which was sold with a little candle enabling the buyer to read in the darkened theatre. The libretti have come down to us stained with wax—an indication that even in the Venetian audience many people needed the crutch of the libretto to guide them through the intricate plots. The opera companies were speculative ventures like other famous speculations of the mercantile period, such as the South Sea Company in England, the Tulip Swindle in Holland, and John Law's companies in France. They were extremely profitable for a certain time but ruinous in the long run. Efforts to make opera "a paying proposition" were not successful, as the fate of the opera in Hamburg, Venice, and London shows.

The libretti of both the court and commercial operas presented not individual characters but fixed psychological types driven by two affections: ambition and love. The plots of the commercial opera stressed especially the love intrigue, the *inganno in amor,* which furnished an endless variety of perplexing situations. Since Monteverdi's *Poppea* the commercial opera preferred characters taken from history to the mythological heroes of the court opera. The historical subjects were modernized in a piquant anachronistic manner by sensational events of the day, the so-called *accidenti verissimi,* which disclosed the protagonists in a number of embarrassing situations (in bed, in women's clothes, etc.). Whether gods or heroes, they always behaved like Venetians of the seventeenth century. The mixture of comic and heroic scenes was a typical feature of the commercial opera, but burlesque as many situations may appear today, they were not intentional parodies of the heroic opera. The comic operas in the strict sense, rare in the seventeenth century, took their heroes from the peasant or middle class. Political criticism too raised its head in the Venetian opera, as can be seen in the libretti of the painter, composer, and poet Salvatore Rosa whose bitter comments would not have been tolerated in the court opera.

Musically, the court opera differed from the other types in several respects. It used large orchestras and choruses and emphasized ensembles, contrapuntal splendor, and elaborate sets and machines. In the commercial opera the chorus was reduced to an ornamental function and sometimes omitted altogether. The costs of large orchestras and involved machines were prohibitive for the commercial opera, but economic considerations cannot explain why choruses, ensembles, and contrapuntal style were not favored. The recruiting of chorus personnel from the music-loving Venetians could have been done at small or no expense, and moreover, since many operas did have a few choruses, it would have been no costlier to use them more frequently in the same work.

Actually, the aversion to the demanding forms of the court opera had sociological reasons. The city audiences were primarily interested, as they still are today, in star singers and fast action, and little concerned with the refined musical pleasures of madrigal choruses and sophisticated ensembles. The works of Cavalli, Cesti, and Pallavicino show how conscious the Venetian composers were of the fact that court and city audiences varied greatly in their taste. Their operas written for Venice display the features of what has been called, somewhat misleadingly, "solo opera" while those written for the courts in Vienna and Paris adhere to the lavish choral style of the court opera. The stylistic features of the chorus and solo opera were not bound up with particular schools—usually the "Roman" chorus opera is contrasted with the "Venetian" solo opera—rather do they reflect the sociological difference between the court opera and the commercial opera.

After the formal establishment of the *opera seria* and the *opera buffa* at the turn of the seventeenth century the comic opera became the opera of the middle class. Symptomatically, it was not connected with a court and was organized by commercial companies which frequently travelled around. In contrast with the public operas in Venice and London, which had all the earmarks of a commercialized court opera, the middle-class opera belonged unmistakably to a non-courtly atmosphere. The *opera seria* was a courtly and international affair, the comic opera a national one. The Neapolitan *opera buffa* had its parallels in the French *vaudeville* comedy (the forerunner of the *opéra comique*), the English ballad opera (the forerunner of the comic opera), the Spanish *tonadilla escénica,* and the German *Singspiel.* As a matter of course these operas were performed in the native tongue of the country or even in local dialects.

The drastic change in social respect can be most clearly seen in the libretti. The protagonists of the action were no longer mythological or historical heroes but members of the middle class. Current events appeared on the stage and replaced historical subjects. Comical effects were derived from the parody of the *opera seria,* especially the pompous mannerisms of the castrati, who never gained a foothold in the comic opera. The nobility was ridiculed and the lower classes often won out at the end, quite in contrast with the courtly comedies.

The musical resources of the comic opera were at first extremely modest, most markedly so in the *vaudeville* and the ballad opera. The rise in artistic quality, which marks the later development of the comic opera, coincides with the social rise of the third estate.

The extravagant expenses of the court opera could only be covered if the patron received a steady revenue. In the budgets of German sovereigns who ruled a small country opera and ballet formed the largest single item of the expense account. The Duke of Brunswick, for one, relied not only on the most ingenious forms of direct and indirect taxation but resorted even to slave trade. He financed his operatic amusements by selling his subjects as soldiers so that his flourishing opera depended literally on the blood of the lower classes.

The two most costly factors in opera production were the sets, designed by special theatre architects, and the singers. The movable sets of the baroque stage were supplemented by intricate contraptions and machines that transported the godlike heroes through the air and provided mechanical means for the apparitions, sea storms, conflagrations, and miracles, that crowd the librettos. Nicola Sabbatini gives us a detailed account of the theatrical props, the lighting, and other effects of the baroque stage. The famous Italian stage architects drew fabulous salaries, notably Giacomo Torelli in Paris, and Burnacini and the brothers Galli Bibiena in Vienna. The brothers Galli Bibiena introduced an innovation in the handling of the perspective. Torelli and Burnacini designed their sets in a heavily overdrawn perspective and strict frontal symmetry which is typical of the early and middle baroque opera. The brothers Galli Bibiena shifted the axis of symmetry at an angle to the audience and thus achieved sweeping effects that seem to break through the picture frame of the stage. This novel style of stage design corresponds with the stylistic innovations of late baroque music. It is characteristic of the curious relation between art and life in the baroque that stage designs actually exerted a strong influence on the architecture of the time. All the world was, literally, a stage.

The prodigious sums that the sets and machines devoured can only be compared with those spent on the singers. All the unhealthy characteristics of the star system that we associate with the theatre and cinema of today almost pale in comparison with the baroque opera. The newly arrived stars were the female singers and the castrati. During the renaissance women were not expected to sing in public and only with the beginning of the baroque did female virtuosi like Archilei, Baroni, and Francesca Caccini appear. They were feted with incredible adulation by both the nobility and the clergy. The latter were so enchanted by the sensuous vocal virtuosity of the opera that they did not want to do without it in the church, but here women were not tolerated because of the time-honored injunction *mulier tacet in ecclesia* (women are silent in the church). The regulation was, however, neatly circumvented by the castrato singing which was, like the thorough-bass, essentially a baroque practice although it persisted well into the classic period. The desire for stylization, which forced the natural growth of trees and shrubs by means of artificial trimming into geometrical patterns, was so extreme that one did not shrink from imposing a similar procedure on the natural growth of the male voice. The beginnings of the castrato practice were intimately connected with the Papal chapel in Rome where castrati appeared for the first time as early as 1562. Previously, the soprano parts had been performed either by boys or men falsettists, but their voices lacked the desired sensuous appeal and were not fitted for the new affective style. It is most revealing of the baroque conception of "nature" that Pietro della Valle actually called castrati *soprani naturali* in contrast to the "artificial sopranos," the falsettists. The production of castrati became a veritable industry in Italy; they were available "in abundance" and the normal development of innumerable boys was sacrificed on the mere chance that they might become highly paid stars. Although they grew very fat as a result of the operation, they were praised not only for their singing but also for their acting. In his "Comparison between the French and Italian Music" the Abbé Raguenet gave vent to his raptures with the assertion that the castrati not only "touched the soul" with their fine voices but impersonated female roles with more grace and beauty than women themselves. The powerful *messa di voce,* the "placing" or "sending of the voice," literally "sent" the audiences of the time, especially the women, and the mass hysteria they provoked did not differ from the obnoxious adulation on which modern "crooners" are thriving.

The castrati had to be treated in a specially polite manner. A secret budget of the court in Parma lists the singers in the order of their importance and notes for each one how he should be honored. The castrato-composer Vittori heads the lists with the remark "should be paid more by presents than by money." Men like Carestini, Senesino, and Farinelli amassed great wealth and became pawns in the international diplomacy of the time. Their conceited behavior was the inevitable result of the privileged treatment they were afforded.

It is to be expected that the lavishness and social abuses of the opera were just as much censored as its artistic achievements were praised. Kuhnau bluntly stated in his highly entertaining musical novel *Der Musikalische Quacksalber* that "persons of high degree who patronize music do it for reasons of state in order to distract the people and to prevent them from looking into their cards." Mazarin sponsored the opera precisely for this reason and the enormous sums he spent on it figure prominently in the attacks of the *fronde*. Gala productions, such as Cavalli's *Ercole* in Paris or Cesti's *Pomo d'Oro* in Vienna, could indeed upset the annual budget of even a royal or imperial household. Marcello's *Teatro alla Moda* stands out as one of the most amusing and trenchant documents of operatic criticism. Being an opera composer himself, he directed his satire not against the opera as such but only against the slovenly routine and the abuse that had crept into opera production. He spared nobody and attacked composers, singers, directors alike, down to the last stage hand. The vivid picture he draws would in many ways apply also to the modern operatic "tradition" which according to Gustav Mahler is identical with *Schlamperei*. Marcello presented his vitriolic suggestions in an ostensibly serious tone and revealed by implication more about the musical and social aspects of opera than other authors did by factual reports. The bitterest attacks were leveled against the castrati who visibly embodied the most abusive side of opera. Their singing was derisively called "capon's laughter." Outside of Italy they were sometimes beaten up in the streets, not because of their singing but because of economic jealousy and the social injustices for which they stood.

Chamber and church music were courtly institutions also and whenever the court travelled musicians formed an indispensable part of the retinue. Chamber music served as entertainment, or as background for pageants, banquets, and other social occasions. With the close relation between state and church, the court musicians also provided music for the official church services. The functions of court music were either carried out by a single court musician or divided between different composers. In the latter case quarrels about the division of responsibilities were unavoidable. Since the higher clergy belonged to the nobility they supported, like other dignitaries, their private orchestras, primarily for purposes of entertainment.

As members of a courtly household the musicians were exposed to the vicissitudes of political life. Very often the bursar did not know how to pay even for the victuals, and the musicians were usually the first to suffer from the periodic lacks of money in the treasury. They frequently received only a fraction of their allotted salary, or none at all. The backlog of salaries accumulated over years. During the Thirty Years' War the situation for German musicians grew so desperate that Schütz was forced to write a number of deeply moving supplications on behalf of his completely destitute fellow musicians at the court of Saxony. Likewise the petitions of Captain Cooke to Charles II show that, in spite of orders to the contrary, no salaries were being paid and that the gowns of the chapel boys had become so ragged that he refused to let the singers appear in public, much to the indignation of the officials. At affluent courts, composers could sometimes amass fortunes, as, for example, Lully whose shrewdness in real estate speculation further increased his wealth. But in contrast, the salary that Monteverdi received in Mantua was exceedingly low. Money was not the only form of salary, however, because musicians were paid in kind, such as exactly specified quantities of wood, wine, and grain, free housing, or even such special prerogatives as a fire in winter time in the assembly hall. Imponderables, too, entered into the computation of salaries. Employment at court carried a high social prestige regarded at the time as an asset well worth money.

CIVIC MUSICAL INSTITUTIONS: COLLECTIVE PATRONAGE

Employment by a private nobleman was the most common position in the baroque era. The only comparable positions were offered by collective patrons, notably the free cities which controlled the music life of the burghers and their churches. The distribution of jobs was organized by bureaucratic councils of patricians such as existed in the republic of Venice and the Hansa cities in Germany. By means of recommendations and a system of try-outs and examinations every applicant was given an equal chance. The regulations for the tests prove that the standards of musicianship were very high. At San Marco in Venice the ultimate election was made democratically by secret ballot on the basis of majority vote. If accepted, the musician became part of the municipal hierarchy for life and was thus protected against the whims of private noblemen, free to "hire and fire" at will. As members of princely households the musicians were not at liberty to quit their position, but had to petition humbly for their dismissal, while the civic musicians were free to cancel their contracts. That the musicians were well aware of the security afforded by public employment transpires from many sources, for example from the writings of Beer to whom the positions in "republics" rated higher than those at courts because of their security and their more "orderly" organization. However, even in the cities, it was not the best applicant who was necessarily chosen but the one willing to put up the customary graft or to acknowledge his "gratitude" by "kick-back" money—a practice that amounted to the selling of the job to the highest bidder. Bach failed to be chosen organist in Hamburg because an inferior organist was, as Mattheson sarcastically puts it, "better at preluding with his thalers than his fingers."

In the Protestant cities of north and central Germany the most important positions were those of the cantor and organist. The cantor headed the church choir or *Kantorei*, consisting of indigent youths of the public schools. The cantors taught Latin or other subjects in the schools as regular part of their job. Originally, the *Kantorei* had been recruited from the burghers themselves, but they bought themselves off more and more by supplying free meals to needy school boys. Being in close contact with vocal music and the *stile antico* the cantors were despised as reactionaries by the organists who prided themselves on a progressive attitude. The organists were the chief supporters of the *concertato* style with instruments. Protracted squabbles between cantors and organists fill the archives of the seventeenth century.

The salaries included not only free housing and *naturalia,* but also legitimate prospects of making extra money. The main sources of the so-called *accidentia* were weddings and funerals, which were unthinkable without music. In one of his few personal letters Bach complained that the "healthy air" in Leipzig had substantially decreased his income because of the disappointingly small number of "corpses." As cantor of St. Thomas in Leipzig he held one of the most distinguished posts in Protestant church music, yet Bach had at first hesitated to accept it. We can understand this reluctance only if we realize that the change from a courtly *capellmeister* to a municipal cantor meant a loss of caste; how acutely Bach was aware of this is not only evinced in his letter,[1] but in his eagerness to recapture social prestige through the title of court composer to the Elector of Saxony. A similar sentiment was implied by Schütz at a time when the conditions in Dresden had become so miserable that civic employment seemed to him, in spite of its lower social prestige, more attractive than his present court position. He exclaimed in hot indignation: "God knows I would rather become a cantor or organist in a small city than put up with this situation any longer, which makes my dear profession insufferable to me."

The organization of musical life was as a matter of course directly dependent on the higher classes, the nobility, the clergy, and the wealthy merchants who took particular pride in imitating the nobility. The forms

---

[1] For the full text see David-Mendel: *The Bach Reader,* 125.

in which music was heard closely corresponded to the strata of society. Aristocratic music addressed by definition a restricted audience, and only on such representative occasions as entries in cities, welcomes, and public receptions, would courtly music be heard by the people, and here only incidentally. The church was the only place where music was regularly accessible to the citizens, and a good church concert upheld the reputation of a city as firmly as a famous opera did that of a court. For this reason the city councils were eager to appoint famous musicians.

The private music of the middle class was organized in consorts of trained amateurs and convivial music clubs. The students at the universities met for music and carousals in the so-called *collegium musicum*. The *collegia musica* in Switzerland (Winterthur) and Germany [2] were the forerunners of the modern concert hall. Music for the students was recognized by the composers as an important market for their music, as the titles of the collections by Widman, Schein, Vierdanck, Loewe, Kindermann, and Rosenmüller show. Burghers and students met regularly in their clubs for rehearsals to which only members and guests were admitted. Travelling virtuosi had to make contacts with these groups in order to be heard.

Concerts of individual artists and travelling virtuosi were called academies after the literary and musical clubs in Italy. These were originally aristocratic societies, like the *Arcadia* in Rome, before which Handel was given a chance to appear. Some of them soon became professional societies open only to such trained musicians as were able to pass the difficult entrance tests. The most distinguished musical society was founded in Bologna (1675) under the name of *Accademia dei Filarmonici* whose fame spread over all Europe in the eighteenth century. Next to the courts and churches the private academies of the middle class represent the most important centers of musical life.

The first traces of public academies on a commercial basis, *i.e.* our modern concerts, appeared, significantly, in England, economically the most advanced of all European countries. During the Restoration period John Banister arranged public concerts in ale-house fashion for an entrance fee of one shilling. The famous concerts of Britton, the small-coal man, were organized as club meetings rather than as public concerts. Commercialized academies became more frequent in the eighteenth century and dominated concert life until the arrival of the modern concert manager. Public

[2] The two most famous *collegia musica* in Germany (Hamburg and Leipzig) were founded by Weckmann and Telemann respectively.

academies were arranged by the artist at his own risk and expense on the basis of advance subscriptions and ticket sale. Handel's oratorios were thus performed as public academies in which the composer appealed primarily to the middle class. The unprecedented success of the oratorios had unmistakably political overtones. The Anglican audience identified itself with the histories of the Chosen People, enacted in the music. The glorification of liberty, so frequent in the oratorios, appealed strongly to the optimistic spirit of awakening English nationalism, and after 1739 the annual performance of an oratorio by Handel was recognized as a truly national institution. They were financially so successful that Handel, after two bankruptcies in the opera, could retrieve most of his losses.

The Continent lagged behind the example of England. The only public musical institutions of the middle class that still fall within the limits of the baroque period were the public concerts founded by Telemann in Hamburg (1722), and the *Concerts Spirituels* (1725) in Paris. The latter took place during the Lenten season when the opera was closed and only "spiritual" entertainment was permitted. The musical institutions of the baroque era can best be described negatively by the lack of the public concert hall and the concert audience. The distribution of music relied almost entirely on private circles; the few exceptions to the rule foretell the coming of the classic period.

SOCIAL AND ECONOMIC ASPECTS OF MUSIC AND MUSICIANS

Consistent with the predominantly private organization of musical life, the social position of the musician was in principle dependent on a patron. Self-supporting composers who made their living from the proceeds of their music did not exist. Toward the end of his life Handel lived as an independent composer, but even he received a life annuity from the English court. The dependence on an aristocratic patron put the musician in the servant class. Like bakers and tailors he had to wear livery, and depositions about livery were important items of the contract. Under the collective patronage of the churches and cities the musician enjoyed the same independence as did the craftsman of the middle class. Civic employment in a prosperous city carried almost as much social prestige as court employment. Like the rest of the *tiers état,* the musicians were organized in guilds, corporations, or unions which rigidly regulated musical training, defined the rights, prerogatives, and responsibilities of their members, and saw to it that a high standard was maintained. Expulsion from the corporation because of poor musicianship was tantamount to economic ruin.

The history of musicians' unions is especially well documented in Italy, Germany, France, and England. In Venice the musicians of San Marco stood directly under the Council of the Ten and were not unionized, a fact that led to "union trouble" with the other musicians of the city, organized in the union of San Silvestro. Even Monteverdi was drawn into these quarrels and on one occasion had his beard pulled in public. The musicians' union accused the San Marco instrumentalists of unfair competition because they played not only for the church, but also for weddings. Wedding music was the prerogative of the union and the case was finally settled in its favor.

In Germany the guilds of musicians were organized after the pattern of the guilds of the craftsmen. Musicians had to pass through the stages of apprentice, journeyman, and master. The youngsters were given room and board as apprentices to a master, who taught them his craft and at the same time made use of them in his household. An intricate system of tests and advancements provided for certain shortcuts; the apprentice could, for example, have his journeyman period waived if he married the daughter of the master; the succession to certain master positions was directly tied up with a marriage clause. Handel and Mattheson were confronted with this situation in Lübeck, but apparently they both preferred the short years of the journeyman period to the long years of marriage with Buxtehude's daughter. Buxtehude, who had himself married the daughter of his predecessor Tunder, did finally manage to find a successor willing to take a wife into the bargain.

The trumpeters and kettledrum players formed of old an exclusive guild, endowed with special privileges and a salary scale considerably above that of other musicians. Their high position was an outgrowth of the traditional association of trumpets with persons of high degree. In warfare, trumpeters were treated like officers in the exchange of prisoners. The use of trumpets was originally restricted only to the nobility and church, and commoners were allowed trumpets in their wedding music only by special permission. The trumpeters cultivated and jealously guarded as their prerogative their special *clarino* technique, namely, the art of playing without valves the diatonic scale in the high register, which Bach so frequently requires in his music. This art declined with the decline of the guilds at the beginning of the classic period. The classic composers had no use for the high register so that this unique and dazzling *clarino* technique became a lost art some time before the invention of the valve trumpet. The high social position of the trumpeters is symbolized even in such external features as the notation of the music. As a matter of prerogative, trumpets always stood at the top of the score, a practice to which the cantatas of Bach still testify; whenever Bach assigned a solemn chorale *cantus firmus* to this instrument of highest social prestige he gave at once a spatial, social, and musical allegory of God's supremacy. The social status of the instruments varied in different countries. In Germany, the winds were considered more noble than the strings; the survival of this conception can be seen in the orchestration of the banquet scene in *Don Giovanni*. In Italy the strings were regarded as socially more prominent than the winds.

The perpetual quarrels between musicians to which the long-winded minutes of the archives amply testify resulted from actual or imagined encroachments on prerogatives. Prerogative was the watchword of all organized musicians. Although the issues were as a rule petty, they were fought with bitterness and passion. Bach's life is full of such quarrels, whether it was the question of who was to determine which chorale should be sung on a particular Sunday, or who had the right to appoint the prefect or assistant. In the argument between Görner (the musical director of the university in Leipzig) and Bach, the latter violated Görner's prerogative by composing an ode of mourning for the university. Görner tried to make Bach sign an injunction that this would not establish a precedent, but Bach stubbornly refused to comply. Times of official mourning proclaimed at the death of a member of the court entailed substantial reductions in the income of the musicians because music was entirely banished for months. These dire periods were dreaded by all city musicians; Kuhnau caustically remarked: "nobody will pray more devoutly for a long life of his sovereign than the instrumentalists."

Individual talent sometimes gave the artist great social distinction. Both Schütz and Lully are outstanding examples of composers who rose from a humble station to an aristocratic position. Telemann was greatly honored in Hamburg and Rudolph Ahle even rose to mayoralty. Salomone Rossi Ebreo, the Jewish violinist, was granted the special right to appear in public without the yellow badge that other Jews were forced to wear. Like the two Scarlattis, Handel gained access to the highest circles in Italy only by virtue of his individual talent. Agostino Steffani served, like many other musicians, on important diplomatic missions; but only very few were actually knighted, as, for example, Hassler, Kerll, and Biber.

Music education in the baroque was very thoroughly and efficiently organized. As in the other crafts, education began early and was guided by a master. Thorough instruction in singing, instruments, and the rules of composition was taken for granted; the most effective pedagogical method consisted in the conditioning of the young musicians to a musical climate by means of ceaseless copying and performing. Bach did not differ from the general rule when he brought his pupils up on his own keyboard works. He started the students of composition with written thorough-bass realizations in strict four-part writing, then proceeded to chorales, and only when they were well grounded in harmony did he progress to contrapuntal compositions in two and more parts. From the beginning he discouraged students who showed no aptitude.

Italian music education held practically a monopoly for vocal training. The great demands for singers were filled by the conservatories, the most famous of which were located in Venice and Naples. The directorship of a conservatory was one of the most coveted positions in Italy. Originally the conservatories had been non-musical institutions of charity (*conservatorio*-orphanage), but they soon developed into musical institutions in which poor children were educated for music. They were run as boarding schools by the clergy. Instruction was gratuitous, and the training excellent. Bontempi gave a precise report about the daily instruction; the schedule included in the morning: one hour devoted to difficult passages, one hour of trill studies, one hour of scales and ornaments, one hour of literature, one hour of vocal exercises in the presence of the master (singing in front of a mirror was used as a device to break bad habits); in the afternoon: one hour of theory, one hour of contrapuntal practice, another hour of literature. The rest of the day was spent playing, composing, or listening to famous singers. After eight years of such training the singer was a well-rounded musician, able to cope with any musical problem, however inadequate his general education may have been.

Musicians were one of the most valuable "export articles" in Italy's national economy. The artistic leadership of the Italian opera in all countries except France had its economic counterpart in the fact that the key positions in opera and orchestra were held by Italians, much to the chagrin of the local musicians. The foreign influx was strongly resented not so much because of artistic competition as for economic reasons. According to the extant budgets of the time the Italians received as a rule twice as much salary as a native musician, even though he was officially equal to the foreigner in rank and title. The courts were willing to pay the high prices customarily associated with imported goods. Kuhnau very cleverly satirized the Germans for their adoration of everything foreign. He portrayed in his "Musical Quack" a bumptious and mediocre German musician who Italianized his name and fooled the gullible German audiences by his pompous arrogance.

The flourishing Italian export trade in musicians, especially castrati, was only one of the many musical trades of the baroque era. One of the most lucrative industries was the building of musical instruments. In violin building Cremona was the undisputed world center, the home of the celebrated workshops of Amati, Stradivari, and Guarneri. These masters made of their craft a consummate art which coincides with the significant development of violin music in the Bologna school. The Tyrolese workshop of Stainer was a branch of the Italian school. The northern countries concentrated on the building of organs, a craft which had its chief representatives in Compenius, Casparini, Schnitger, and Silbermann. The Ruckers family in Antwerp built the best harpsichords in the seventeenth century.

Music printing and publishing gradually developed into an industry. The publishers were bound neither by a code of ethics nor a copyright law. Pirated editions were the order of the day, and even when composers were paid for publication the remuneration was small in comparison with the profits. Music publishing houses were founded in the great commercial cities, such as Venice (Vincenti), Bologna, Paris (Ballard), London (Playford, Walsh), Amsterdam (Roger), Nuremberg, Frankfort, and Leipzig. The trade catalogues of the annual fairs in Leipzig and Frankfort during the seventeenth and eighteenth centuries list a great deal of printed music of which no other record is extant.

The production and consumption of music in the baroque period must be seen in the perspective of patronage. Its virtues and defects can be justly appraised only if we keep in mind that music had not yet become a free commodity on a free market. In spite of its social drawbacks patronage, either private or collective, assured the composer of a basically sound relation between producer and consumer. He composed not for a vacuum nor for an ideal, yet non-existent, audience, but for clearly defined purposes and groups: the court, the church, the consort, or the *collegium musicum*.

Most compositions must therefore be classified as "occasional" works, written for a temporal purpose, and usually forgotten thereafter. This statement applies to Bach's *St. Matthew Passion* as well as to Handel's operas. Since each special occasion called for new music, composers were naturally prolific in their artistic pursuits. As a result of the ever-present demand for new compositions incredible quantities of music have come down to us of which printed music forms only a small part. In the Italian opera the disproportion between printed and manuscript music is particularly obvious. Operas were composed for one season as articles of fashion, outmoded after one run. It therefore hardly paid to print the full score. Successful operas were disseminated in the form of aria selections, and only exceptionally did fully printed scores appear, notably in France where they were engraved for gala occasions at the expense of the court. The bulk of Italian opera remained in manuscript—one of the reasons why the literature is so little known today.

Music production was regulated primarily by contract or court order. The composer wrote continually because he was under contract to supply a cantata for each Sunday, or an opera for a specified date. Young composers, eager to make a name for themselves and on the lookout for a position, started out by dedicating their opus 1 (usually a collection of madrigals, motets, or an instrumental set) to a patron, be it a nobleman, a city council, or a church. They paid for the costs of the printing themselves, but this was a comparatively safe investment because the patron, honored by the dedicatory preface in flowery language, would acknowledge the compliment with a substantial token of gratitude. If the expected present was not forthcoming, it was not improper to remind the patron of his duties, as Scheidt once did. Commercial opera companies commissioned operas from year to year by the so-called *scrittura*, usually paid for by a lump sum. Likewise, innumerable wedding, funeral, and other occasional compositions were commissioned by wealthy burghers who not only paid a fee to the composer, but liked to see their personal music in print. From no other period of music have so many printed occasional compositions been preserved. Contract or court order, dedication, and commission, were the three chief forms of music production. Works written for purposes of instruction, such as the *Well-Tempered Clavier* or the *Art of the Fugue*, confirm the rule.

The composer had no other way of assuring that nobody but he himself reaped the fruits of his labors except to keep the composition in manuscript form, or to acquire a monopoly of printed music, such as Lully was granted by the French king as a special prerogative. Even Lully could not stop publishers from printing his music outside of France. Schütz published his *Christmas Oratorio* in continuo reduction only, but advertised that the full parts could be rented "for a moderate fee." Although preserved only in manuscript form the compositions had a wide dissemination because the pupils copied the works of their masters as a regular part of their musical education. Many of Bach's works are extant only through the diligence of his disciples—a mode of preservation that gives valuable indirect hints as to the local distribution of styles.

Because of the close contact between composer and his audience the question of inspiration and artistic freedom could never become a serious issue. As a matter of course, the music was "custom-made" because the composer adapted himself to the available means. When Handel was confronted with the delicate task of satisfying the conflicting demands of Cuzzoni and Faustina in the opera *Alessandro* he carefully balanced the number of arias and took advantage of the individual talents of each singer. Revisions were constantly made in order to meet the exigencies of the moment. Since the concert hall and an anonymous audience were just in the process of formation in the late baroque period, there was no need as yet for music critics to formulate public opinion. It is characteristic that the first traces of music criticism appeared in such magazines of general information, as the *Mercure galant* and the *Spectator,* later imitated by Mattheson's *Critica Musica* and Scheibe's *Der Critische Musikus,* the first examples of professional music criticism. The writings of Mattheson and, especially, Scheibe already show a growing influence of the ideas of enlightenment.

The fatal gap between composer and audience that characterizes modern musical life did not exist in the baroque period. The composers wrote as a matter of course in an idiom that was "modern" at the time. They did not fear, as our contemporary composers sometimes do, that their genius might be recognized only after they had been safely dead long enough to be recognized as "classics." The aristocrats and the patricians had sufficient technical training in music to keep abreast with the musical innovations of the time. This high level of musical understanding was taken for granted although the unschooled common people were obviously far removed from it. In view of the restricted social background of baroque music it is not surprising that the common man was given no consideration. Complaints that the common people did not understand the elaborate church music were quite frequent. It is interesting to see how these justified objections were countered. In his *Psalmodia Christiana* Mithobius disposed of the argument in a highly significant fashion. He admitted that the common man was unable to understand "all tricks and artifices of the musician," but he did not conclude from this fact that music should be composed on a lower level within the grasp of the untrained. He maintained on the contrary that the common people should rise to the music by "exercise" because the more labor and artifice was devoted to the praise of God the better: "God cannot be praised artificially enough." Even though the people did not quite follow the composer, it was, according to Mithobius, enough for them to know that a sacred piece was being performed. He clearly disclosed the strong ethical reason why patterned elaborations and contrapuntal complexity held so central a place in music. It did not occur to the composers to "write down" to an audience, nor were they bothered by the idea of writing for eternity. Bach's works were composed for the various occasions of the liturgical year and these called for his best efforts. Precisely because Bach wrote for the day as elaborately and "artificially" as he could, he composed music that was not of an age, but for all time.

Appendices

ABBREVIATIONS

Adler HMG	Adler, G. *Handbuch der Musikgeschichte*, 2nd ed., 1930
AM	*Acta Musicologica*
AMF	*Archiv für Musikforschung*
AMW	*Archiv für Musikwissenschaft*
BAMS	*Bulletin, American Musicological Society*
CE	Complete edition
Chrysander D	*Denkmäler der Tonkunst*, ed. by Chrysander, 1869–71
COF	*Chefs-d'oeuvre classiques de l'opéra français*
CW	*Das Chorwerk*, ed. by Blume
DDT	*Denkmäler deutscher Tonkunst*, 1892–1931
DTB	*Denkmäler der Tonkunst in Bayern*, 1900–31
DTOe	*Denkmäler der Tonkunst in Oesterreich*, 1894–1938
Eitner PAM	Gesellschaft für Musikforschung. *Publikationen älterer . . . Musikwerke*, ed. by Eitner, 1873–1905
EL	*Das Erbe deutscher Musik, Landschaftsdenkmale*
ER	*Das Erbe deutscher Musik, Reichsdenkmale*
Haas B	Haas, R. *Musik des Barocks*, 1928 (in Bücken: *Handbuch der Musikwissenschaft*)
GMB	*Geschichte der Musik in Beispielen*, ed. by Schering, 1931
HAM	*Historical Anthology of Music*, ed. by Davison-Apel, 1946
ICMI	*I Classici della Musica Italiana*, ed. by D'Annunzio
ICMIB	*I Classici Musicali Italiani*, Fond. Bravi
IM	*Istituzione e Monumenti dell'Arte Musicale Italiana*
JMP	*Jahrbuch der Musikbibliothek Peters*
Lavignac E	Lavignac—La Laurencie, *Encyclopédie de la musique*, 1913 ff.
MA	*The Musical Antiquary*
MfM	*Monatshefte für Musikgeschichte*
ML	*Music and Letters*
MQ	*Musical Quarterly*
OCM	*Old Chamber Music*, ed. by Riemann, Augener
OHM	*Oxford History of Music*, 2nd ed.
PAMS	*Papers, American Musicological Society*
PMA	*Proceedings, Musical Association*, London

RdM	*Revue de Musicologie*
Riemann HMG	Riemann, H. *Handbuch der Musikgeschichte*, 1904–13
RM	*La Revue Musicale*, 1920– (an older periodical of the same title 1901–1910)
RMI	*Rivista Musicale Italiana*
SCMA	*Smith College Music Archives*
SIMG	*Sammelbände der internationalen Musikgesellschaft*
StzMW	*Studien zur Musikwissenschaft* (Beihefte der DTOe)
TAM	Tagliapietra, G. *Antologia di musica . . . per pianoforte*, 1931–32
Torchi AM	Torchi, L. *L'Arte Musicale in Italia*
VfM	*Vierteljahrsschrift für Musikwissenschaft*, 1884–93
VNM	*Vereeniging voor Nederlandsche Muziekgeschiedenis. Uitgabe van oudere Meesterwerken*
ZIMG	*Zeitschrift der internationalen Musikgesellschaft*
ZMW	*Zeitschrift für Musikwissenschaft*

Anonymous. *The Self-Instructor on the Violin*, Bologna[?], 1695.

———. *Vermehrter . . . Wegweiser . . . die Orgel recht zu schlagen*, Augsburg, 1693.

Adlung, J., *Anleitung zur musikalischen Gelahrtheit*, 1758.

———. *Musica mechanica organoedi*, 1768; facs. repr. 1931.

L'Affilard, M. *Principes tres-faciles pour bien apprendre la musique*, 2nd ed., Paris, 1697.

Agazzari, A. *Del sonare sopra 'l basso*, 1607; facs. repr. Milan, 1933.

———. *La musica ecclesiastica*, 1638.

Ahle, J. R. *Anleitung zur Singekunst*, 1704 (4th ed. by J. G. Ahle).

———. *Brevis et perspicua introductio in artem musicam*, 2nd ed. 1673 (1st ed. 1648).

Alardus, L. *De veterum musica liber singularis*, 1636.

Albrecht, J. W. *Tractatus physicus de effectibus musices in corpus animatum*, Leipzig, 1734.

d'Alembert, J. *Elemens de Musique . . . suivant les principes de Rameau*, Paris, 1752.

Alstedt, J. H. *Scientiarum omnium Encyclopaedia*, 1610 (1649). Partial Engl. translation in J. Birchensha, *Templum musicum*, London, 1664.

———. *Elementale mathematicum*, Frankfort, 1611.

André, Y. M. *Essai sur le beau*, Paris, 1741.

Andrea di Modena. *Canto harmonico*, 1690.

Andrien, J. F.[?]. *Kurtze anführung zum general-bass*, 2nd ed., Leipzig, 1733.

Angleria, C. *Regola del contraponto*, Milan, 1622.

Antegnati, C. *Arte organica*, 1608 (Preface to *L' Antegnata*); reprint 1938.

Arresti, G. C. *Dialogo tra un maestro et un discepolo desideroso d'approfitare nel contrapunto*, 1663.

Arrhenius, L. *Dissertatio mythologico-historica de primis musicae inventoribus . . .* , Upsala [1729].

Artusi, G. M. *L'arte del contraponto*, 1598.

———. *L'Artusi overo delle imperfettioni della moderna musica*, 1600; 2nd ed., 1603.

Asola, G. M. *Canto fermo sopra Messe*, Venice, 1607.

Avella, G. d'. *Regole di Musica*, Rome, 1657.

Avison, Ch. *An Essay on Musical Expression*, London, 1752.

Bacilly, B. de. *Remarques curieuses sur l'art de bien chanter*, Paris, 1668.

Bacon, Fr. *Sylva Sylvarum*, 1626.

Baillie, A. [?]. *An Introduction to the Knowledge and Practice of the Thoro'-bass*, Edinburgh, 1717.

Banchieri, A. *Conclusioni nel suono dell'organo*, 1609; facs. repr. Milan, 1934.

——. *Cartella musicale*, Venice, 1614.

——. *Lettere armoniche*, Bologna, 1628.

——. *Organo suonarino*, Venice, 1638.

Bann, J. A. *Dissertatio epistolica de musicae natura*, 1637.

Barnickel. *Kurtzgefasstes musicalisches Lexicon*, Chemnitz [1737], 1749.

Banister, J. *The Most Pleasant Companion*, London, 1681.

Baron, E. G. *Historisch-Theoretisch und Practische Untersuchung des Instruments der Lauten*, 1727.

Bartoli, D. *Del suono de' tremori armonici*, Rome, 1679.

Bartolus, A. *Musica mathematica*, Altenburg, 1614.

Baryphonus, H. *Isagoge musica*, 1609[?].

——. *Plejades musicae*, Halberstadt, 1615.

——. *Ars canendi*, Leipzig, 1630.

Bedford, A. *The Temple Musick*, London, 1706.

——. *The Great Abuse of Music*, London, 1711.

Bedos de Celles, F. *L'Art du facteur d'orgues*, Paris, 1766–78; repr. Kassel, 1934.

Beer (Bähr), J. *Bellum musicum*, 1701.

——. *Musicalische Discurse*, 1719; repr. in *Kirchenmusikalisches Jahrbuch*, 1885.

Bendeler, J. Ph. *Organopoeia*, 1690[?].

——. *Orgelbau-Kunst*, Frankfort, 1739.

Berardi, A. *Ragionamenti musicali*, Bologna, 1681.

——. *Documenti armonici*, Bologna, 1687.

——. *Miscellanea Musicale*, Bologna, 1689.

——. *Il Perchè musicale*, Bologna, 1693.

Beringer, M. *Der freyen, lieblichen Singkunst erster und anderer Theil*, Nuremberg, 1610.

Bernardi, St. *Porta Musicale . . . regole del contrapunto*, Venice, 1639.

Bernhard, Chr. *Von der Singe-Kunst, Tractatus compositionis*, c. 1650; printed in J. Müller-Blattau *Die Kompositionslehre H. Schützens*, 1926.

Bertalotti, A. *Regole facilissime . . . per apprendere . . . li Canti fermo e figurato*, Bologna, 1698.

Besard, J. B. *Isagoge in artem testudinariam*, Augsburg, 1617.

Bevin, E. *A Briefe and Short Introduction of the Art of Musicke to Teach how to Make Discant*, London, 1631.

Bianchini, F. *De tribus generibus instrumentorum musicae veterum organicae dissertatio*, Rome, 1742.

Biermann, J. H. *Organographia Hildesiensis*, 1738; facs. repr. 1930.

Birchensha. *See* Alstedt.

Blankenburg, Qu. van. *Elementa musica of niew licht tot het welverstaan van de musiec en de bas-continuo*, The Hague, 1739.

Blow, J. *Rules for Playing of a Through Bass*, in F. T. Arnold *The Art of Accompaniment from a Thorough-Bass*, 1931, 163 ff.

Boiseul, J. *Traitté contre les danses*, La Rochelle, 1606.

Bollioud-Mermet, L. *De la corruption du goust dans la musique françoise*, Lyon, 1746.

Bona, G. *De divina psalmodia*, Paris, 1663.

Bona, V. *Essempi delli passaggi*, Milan, 1596.

Bonanni, F. *Gabinetto Armonico*, Rome, 1722.

Bonini, S. *Discorsi e Regole sovra la Musica* (MS c. 1641). excerpts in Solerti *Le origine del melodramma*, 1903.

Bonlini, G. C. *Le glorie della poesia e della musica*, Venice, 1730.

Bonnet, J. (see Bourdelot).

————. *Histoire générale de la danse*, Paris, 1724.

Bononcini, G. M. *Il musico prattico*, Bologna, 1673.

Bontempi, G. A. *Nova quatuor vocibus componendi methodus*, Dresden, 1660.

————. *Historia Musica*, Perugia, 1695.

Borjon de Scellery, Ch. E., *Traité de la musette*, Lyon, 1672.

Bottazzi, B. *Choro et Organo*, Venice, 1614.

Bourdelot, P. and Bonnet, J. *Histoire de la musique et de ses effects*, 1715.

Bottrigari, E. *Il Desiderio*, 1594 ff.; facs. repr. 1924, Veröffentl. Bibl. Paul Hirsch.

Bovicelli, G. M. *Regole, Passagi di musica*, 1594.

Boyvin, J. *Traité abrégé de l'accompagnement*, Amsterdam, c. 1700.

Braccino, A. *Discorso secondo musicale*, Venice, 1608; facs. repr. Milan [193–?].

Brizeño, L. de. *Método para aprender a tañer la guitarra*, Paris, 1626.

Brossard, S. de. *Dictionnaire de musique*, Paris, 1703 (Engl. transl. by Grassineau, 1740).

Bruce, Th. *The Common Tunes; or, Scotland Church Musick Made Plain.* Edinburgh, 1726.

Brun(n)elli, A. *Regole . . . per li scolari*, 1606.

————. *Regole . . . di contrappunti*, 1610.

Bruschi, A. F. *Regole per il contrapunto*, Lucca, 1711.

Burette, P. J. *Dissertation sur la mélopée de l'ancienne musique*, Paris, 1729.

Burman, E. *Specimen academicum de Triade harmonica*, Upsala, 1727.

————. *Dissertatio musica, de basso fundamentali*, Upsala, 1728.

————. *Elementa musices*, Upsala, 1728.

Burmeister, J. *Musica autoschediastike*, Rostock, 1601.

————. *Musica poetica* . . . , Rostock, 1606.

Butler, Ch. *The Principles of Musik, in Singing and Setting (Ecclesiastical and Civil)*, London, 1636.

Buttstedt, J. H. *Ut, mi, sol, re, fa, la, tota musica*, Leipzig, 1717.

Caccini, G. *Le Nuove Musiche*, 1601 [1602]; facs. repr. Rome, 1934.

Cahusac, L. de. *La danse ancienne et moderne*, Paris, 1754.

Caldenbach, Ch. *Dissertatio musica*, 1664.

Callachius, N. *De Ludis scenicis*, 1713.

Calvisius, S. *Exercitationes musicae*, Leipzig, 1600–11.

————. *Melopoia sive Melodiae condendae ratio*, Erfurt, 1592.

Campion, F. *Traité d'accompagnement* . . . *selon la règle de l'octave*, Amsterdam, 1716.

Campion, Th. *A New Way of Making 4 Parts*, London, 1610; reprinted in CE.

Caramuel de Lobkowitz, J. *Mathesis audax*, Louvain, 1644.

Carissimi, G. *Ars cantandi*, Augsburg, 1693. (The Italian version is not extant.)

Caroso, M. F. *Nobiltà di dame*, Venice, 1600.

————. *Raccolta di varie balli*, Rome, 1630.

Casali, L. *Generale invito alle grandezze, e maravigli della musica*, Modena, 1629.

Casoni, G. A. *Manuale Choricanum*, 1649.

Caus, S. de. *Institution Harmonique*, Frankfort, 1615.

Cavalliere, G. F. *Il scolare principiante di musica*, Naples, 1634.

Cazzati, M. *Risposta alle oppositioni*, 1664.

Cerone, D. P. *El melopeo y maestro*, Naples, 1613.

Cerreto, S. *Della prattica musica vocale et instrumentale*, Naples, 1601.

Chales, C. F. de. *Mundus mathematicus*, Lyon, 1674.

Chiavelloni, V. *Discorsi della musica*, Rome, 1668.

Chiodino, G. B. *Arte practica latina e volgare di far contrappunto*, Venice, 1610; German transl. by J. A. Herbst, Frankfort, 1653.

Coferati, M. *Il cantore addottrinato*, 1682.

Colonna, F. *La sambuca lincea*, 1618.

Conforto, G. *Breve et facile maniera* . . . *a far passaggi*, 1603[?]; facs. repr. Veröffentl. Musikbibl. Paul Hirsch, 1922.

Coperario, G. *Rules how to compose*, c. 1610 (MS in Huntington Lib.).

Corre(i)a de Araujo, F. *Facultad organica*, Alcala, 1626; ed. by Kastner, *Instituto Espagnol de Musicologia*, VI.

Corette, M. *L'Ecole d'Orphée, Méthode* . . . *du violon dans le goût français et italien*, 1738.

————. *Méthode* . . . *pour* . . . *le violoncelle*, Paris, 1741.

————. *Méthode pour apprendre aisément à jouer de la flute traversiere*, c. 1730.

————. *Le maître de clavecin,* Paris, 1753.

Couperin, F. *L'Art de toucher le clavecin,* 1716 ff.; repr. CE.

Cousu, A. *La musique universelle,* Paris, 1658.

Crisanio, G. *Asserta Musicalia nova,* Rome, 1650.

Crivellati, C. *Discorsi musicali,* Viterbo, 1624.

Crome, R. *The fiddle new model'd,* London [174–?].

Crousaz, J. P. de. *Traité du beau,* Amsterdam, 1715.

Crüger, J. *Synopsis musica,* Berlin, 1630; rev. ed. 1654.

————. *Musicae practicae Praecepta,* Berlin, 1660.

Cruz, A. da. *Lyra de Arco ou Arte de tanger rabeca,* Lisbon, 1639.

Cruz, J. Ch. da. *Methodo breve e claro . . . da arte de musica,* Lisbon, 1745.

Cruz, A. de la. *Médula de la musica theorica,* 1707.

Curson, H. *The Theory of Sciences . . . Principles of the 7 liberal Arts,* London, 1702.

Dandrieu, J. F. *Principes de l'Accompagnement du clavecin,* 1719.

David, F. *Methode nouvelle . . . pour apprendre facilement la musique,* Paris, 1737.

De La Fond, J. F. *A new system of Music,* 1725.

Delair, D. *Traité d'accompagnement pour le théorbe et le clavessin,* 1690.

Delphinus, H. *Eunuchi conjugium oder die Capauner Hochzeit,* Halle, 1685.

Demantius, J. Ch. *Isagoge artis musicae,* Freiberg, 1607 ff.

Démotz de la Salle, J. F. *Méthode de musique selon un nouveau système,* Paris, 1728.

Denis, J. *Traité de l'accord de l'espinette,* 1650.

Descartes, R. *Musicae compendium,* 1650 (Engl. transl. 1653).

Diruta, G. *Il Transilvano,* Venice, I, 1597; II, 1610.

Doisi, N. *Nuevo Método de Cifra,* Naples, 1630.

Doni, G. B. *Compendio del trattato de'generi e de'modi della musica,* Rome, 1635.

————. *Annotazioni sopra il compendio,* 1640.

————. *De praestantia musicae veteris libri tres,* Florence, 1647.

————. *Lyra Barberina,* Florence, 1763.

Douwes, K. *Grondig ondersoek van de toonen der musijk,* 1699.

Drexel, J. *Rhetorica coelestis,* 1636.

Dufort, G. *Trattato del ballo nobile,* Naples, 1728.

Dukes, N. *A Concise . . . Method of Learning the Figuring Part of Country Dances,* London, 1752.

Dumanoir, G. *Le mariage de la musique avec la dance,* Paris, 1664 (repr. by J. Gallay, Paris, 1870).

Dupont, H. B. *Principes de musique,* Paris, 1718.

————. *Principes de Violon,* Paris, 1740.

Dupuit, J. B. *Principes pour toucher de la vièle,* Paris, 1741.

Effrem, M. *Censure . . . sopra il sesto libro de madrigali di Marco da Gagliano,* Venice, 1622.

Eisel, J. P. *Musicus autodidaktos,* Erfurt, 1738.

Eisenhut, Th. *Musikalisches Fundamentum,* 1682.

Elsmann, H. *Compendium musicae,* Wolfenbüttel, 1619.

Elst, J. van der. *Notae Augustinianae,* Gand, 1657.

———. *Den ouden en de nieuwen grondt van de Musicke,* Gand, 1662.

Erhard, L. *Compendium Musices,* 1660.

Erculeo, M. *Il canto ecclesiastico,* Modena, 1686.

Erythraeus, J. *Pinacotheca imaginum . . . illustrium . . . virorum,* 1647.

Esquivel Navarro, J. de. *Discursos sobre el arte del dançado,* Sevilla, 1642.

Euler, L. *Tentamen novae theoriae musicae,* 1739; printed in *Opera omnia* III, 1, 1926.

Fabbrizi, P. *Regole generali di canto ecclesiastico,* Rome, 1651.

Fabricius, H. *De Visione, Voce, Auditu,* Venice, 1600.

Falck, G. *Idea boni cantoris,* Nuremberg, 1688.

Fantini, G. *Modo per imparare a sonare di tromba,* Frankfort, 1638; facs. repr. Milan, 1934.

Feijoo, B. G. *La musica de los templos,* 14. discourse in E. Cerbéllon: *Teatro critico universal,* Madrid, 1726.

Feind, B. *Gedancken von der Opera,* Hamburg, 1708.

Fernandes, A. *Arte de musica de canto dorgam,* Lisbon, 1626.

Fernandes de Huete, D. *Compendio numeroso de cifras armónicas,* 1702.

Ferriol, B. *Reglas utiles . . . a danzar,* 1745.

Feuillet, R. A. *Choréographie, ou l'art de décrire la danse,* Paris, 1700 ff. (Engl. transl. 1710, 1715).

Fischer, J. Ph. A. *Kort en grondig onderwys van de transpositie,* Utrecht, 1728.

Fludd, R. *Utriusque cosmi metaphysica,* Oppenheim, 1617.

Freher, P. *Theatrum virorum eruditione clarorum,* 1688.

Freillon Poncein, J. P. *La veritable manière d'apprendre à jouer . . . du hautbois,* Paris, 1700.

Frezza dalle Grotte, G. *Il Cantore ecclesiastico,* 1698.

Friderici, D. *Musica Figuralis oder Newe Singe Kunst,* Rostock, 1614 (printed by Langelütje, Graues Kloster Gymnasium, 1901).

Fries, J. H. H. *Abhandlung vom sogenannten Pfeifer-Gericht,* Frankfort, 1752.

Frovo, J. A. *Discursos sobre a perfeição do Diathesaron,* Lisbon, 1662.

Fuhrmann, M. H. *Musikalischer Trichter,* 1706.

———. *Musica vocalis in nuce,* Berlin, 1715.

Furetiere, A. *Dictionnaire universel,* 3rd ed., Rotterdam, 1708.

Fux, J. J. *Gradus ad Parnassum,* Vienna, 1725. German transl. L. C. Mizler, 1742; abbrev. Engl. transl. by A. Mann: *Steps to Parnassus,* New York, 1943.

Galilei, V. *Dialogo della musica antica e della moderna*, 1581; facs. repr. Rome, 1934; Milan, 1946.

Gantez, A. *L'entretien des musiciens*, 1643; ed. by Thoinan, 1878.

Gasparini, F. *L'Armonico pratico al cimbalo*, 1708.

Gebst, V. *Corona musices*, Jena, 1611.

Geminiani, F. *The Art of Playing on the Violin*, London, 1731 (anonymously published in Prelleur).

———. *Rules for Playing in a True Taste on the Violin*, 1739.

———. *The Entire . . . Tutor for the Violin*, 1747.

———. *A Treatise of Good Taste in the Art of Musick*, London, 1749.

Gengenbach, N. *Musica nova*, Leipzig, 1626.

Gervais, L. *Méthode pour l'accompagnement du clavecin*, 1734.

Gesius, B. *Synopsis musicae practicae*, Frankfort, 1609.

Ghezzi, I. *Il Setticlave Canoro*, 1709.

Gibelius, O. *Seminarium modulatoriae*, 1645.

———. *Introductio musicae theoreticae didacticae*, Bremen, 1660.

———. *Propositiones mathematico-musicae*, Minden, 1666.

Giustiniani, V. *Discorso sopra la musica de' suoi tempi*, MS, 1628, ed. by S. Bongi, Lucca, 1878. Excerpts in Solerti: *Le origini del melodramma*, 1903.

Goretti, A. *Dell' Eccellenze . . . della musica*, 1612.

Gradenthaler, H. *Horologium Musicum*, Nuremberg, 1687.

Grandval, N. R. *Essai sur le bon goust en Musique*, 1732.

Grassineau, J. *A musical dictionary*, London, 1740 (see Brossard).

Gresset, J. B. L. *Discours sur l'harmonie*, Paris, 1737.

Grimarest, J. L. *Traité du récitatif dans la lecture*, Paris, 1707.

Guerau, F. *Poema Harmonicó*, Madrid, 1684.

Gugl, M. *Fundamenta partiturae*, Salzburg, 1719.

Gumpeltzhaimer, A. *Compendium musicae*, 1st ed. 1591; 13th ed. 1681.

Hafenreffer, S. *Monochordon symbolico-biomanticum*, 1640.

Haltmeier, C. J. F. *Anleitung: wie man einen general-bass . . . in alle töne transponieren könne*, Hamburg, 1737.

Harnisch, O. S. *Artis Musicae delineatio*, Frankfort, 1608.

Hartong. *Musicus theoretico-practicus*, Nuremberg, 1749.

Hase, W. *Gründliche Einführung in die edle Singekunst*, Goslar, 1657.

Heinichen, J. D. *Der Generalbass in der Komposition*, 1728.

Herbst, J. A. *Musica Moderna Prattica overo Maniera del Buon Canto*, Frankfort, 1641; 2nd ed., 1653.

———. *Musica poetica*, Nuremberg, 1643.

Herrando, J. *Arte . . . del Modo de Tocar el Violín*, Paris, 1756.

Hitzler, D. *Newe Musika oder Singkunst*, Tübingen, 1628.

Holder, W. *A Treatise of the Natural Grounds and Principles of Harmony*, London, 1694.

Hotteterre, J. *Principes de la flute traversière*, 1708.

————. *Methode pour la musette*, Paris, 1738.

Hudgebut, J. *A vade mecum for the Lovers of Musick, Shewing the Excellency of the Recorder*, London, 1679.

Hunold-Menantes, C. H. *Die allerneuste Art zur reinen und galanten Poesie*, Hamburg, 1712.

Huygens, C. *Ghebruik, en onghebruik van 't orghel*, Amsterdam, 2nd ed., 1660.

Ivanovich, C. *Minerva al Tavolino*, Venice, 1688.

Janowka, Th. B. *Clavis ad thesaurum magnae artis musicae*, 1701.

João IV of Portugal. *Defensa de la Musica Moderna*, Lisbon, 1649.

Jumilhac, Dom P. B. de. *La science et la pratique du plain-chant*, Paris, 1673.

Pater Justinus (Carmelita). *Musicalische arbeith und Kurtz-weil*, Augsburg, 1723.

————. *Chirologia organico-musica, Musikalische Handbeschreibung*, Nuremberg, 1711.

Keller, G. *A Compleat Method for . . . a Thorough Bass*, London, 1707.

Kellner, D. *Treulicher Unterricht im General-Bass*, Hamburg, 1732.

Kepler, G. *Harmonices Mundi*, 1619; printed in *Opera omnia*.

Kircher, A. *Musurgia universalis*, Rome, 1650.

————. *Phonurgia nova*, 1673.

Kraftius, J. *Musicae practicae rudimenta*, Copenhagen, 1607.

Kretzschmar, J. *Musica latina germanica*, Leipzig, 1605.

Kuhnau, J. *Der Musikalische Quacksalber*, 1700 (repr. by Benndorf, 1900).

————[?]. *Musicus Vexatus*, Freyberg, 1690.

————[?]. *Musicus Curiosus*, Freyberg, 1691.

————[?]. *Musicus Magnanimus*, Freyberg, 1691.

Lambranzi, G. *Nuova . . . scuola de balli theatrali*, 1716.

Lampe, J. F. *The Art of Musick*, London, 1740.

————. *A Plain and Compendious Method of Teaching Thorough-Bass*, London, 1737.

Lange, J. C. *Methodus nova et perspicua*, Hildesheim, 1688.

Lanze, F. de. *Apologie de la Danse*, 1623.

La Voye, M. de. *Traité de musique pour bien et facilement apprendre et chanter et composer*, Paris, 1656.

Lebeuf, J. *Traité . . . sur le chant ecclésiastique*, 1741.

Le Blanc, H. *Défense de la Basse de Viole*, 1740; repr. in RM IX, 1928.

Le Cerf de la Viéville, J. L. *Comparaison de la musique italienne et de la musique françoise*, Bruxelles, 1704 (2nd ed., 1705/06).

Lenton, J. *The Gentleman's Diversion, or the Violin Explained*, London, 1694.

[Léris, A. de.] *Dictionnaire portatif des théatres*, 1754.

Levens. *Abrégé des règles de l'harmonie*, 1743.

Le Vol, C. *Philomea Gregoriana*, Venice, 1669.

Liberati, A. *Due lettere . . . in difesa d'un passo dell'opera seconda d'Arcangelo Corelli*, MS Liceo Music., Bologna.

Lippius, J. *Disputatio musica prima-tertia*, Wittenberg, 1609–10.

——. *Synopsis musicae*, 1612.

Locke, M. *Observations upon . . . an Essay to the Advancement of Musick*, 1672.

——. *The Present Practice of Musick Vindicated*, 1673.

——. *Melothesia, or Certain Rules for Playing upon a Continued Bass*, London, 1673.

Lorbeer, J. K. *Lob der edlen Musik*, Weimar, 1696.

Lorente, A. *El porque de la musica*, 1672.

Loulié, E. *Elements ou principes de musique*, Paris, 1696.

——. *Nouveau système de musique*, 1698.

——. *Musique théorique et pratique*, 1722.

Lustig, J. W. *Inleiding tot de Muzykkunde*, Groningen, 1751.

Mace, Th. *Musick's Monument*, London, 1676.

Magirus, J. *Artis musicae legibus logicis . . . compendiumque rationem*, 1611 (1st ed., 1596).

——. *Musicae rudimenta*, 1619.

Magius, H. *De tintinnabulis liber*, Amsterdam, 1689.

Maichelbeck, F. A. *Die auf dem Klavier lehrende Cäcilia*, 1738.

Maier, J. F. B. *Hodegus musicus*, 1718.

——. *Museum musicum*, 1732 (1st ed. of subsequent title).

——. *Neu-eröffneter Theoretisch- und Pracktischer Music-Saal*, Nuremberg, 1741.

Maillart, P. *Les tons ou discours sur les modes de musique*, Tournay, 1610.

Majer, M. *Atalanta fugiens*, 1618.

Malcolm, A. *Treatise of Music*, Edinburgh, 1721.

Mancini, G. B. *Pensieri e riflessioni pratiche sopra il canto figurato*, Vienna, 1774; 3rd ed., 1777, Milan (reprinted in A. della Corte: *Canto e bel canto*, 1933).

Marais, M. *Nouvelle méthode de musique pour servir d'introduction aux acteurs modernes*, 1711.

Marcello, B. *Il teatro alla moda*, 1722 (new ed., 1913 [Fondi], French, 1890 [David], German, 1917 [Einstein]).

Marinelli, G. C. *Via retta della voce corale*, Bologna, 1671.

Martin y Coll, A. *Arte de canto llano*, Madrid, 1714.

Martins, J. *Arte de canto chão*, Coimbra, 1603.

Masson, Ch. *Nouveau Traité des règles pour la composition*, Paris, 1694; 3rd ed., 1705.

Matteis, N. *The False Consonances of Musick*, 168–?

Mattheson, J. *Das neu-eröffnete orchestre*, Hamburg, 1713.

——. *Critica Musica*, Hamburg, 1722–25.

——. *Grosse General-Bass-Schule*, 1731.

——. *Kleine General-Bass-Schule*, 1735.

——. *Kern melodischer Wissenschaft*, 1737.

——. *Der vollkommene Capellmeister*, 1739.

——. *Grundlage einer Ehrenpforte*, 1740; reprint 1910.

Maugars, A. *Response . . . sur le sentiment de la musique d'Italie*, Rome, 1639 (ed. by Thoinan, 1865; German transl. in *MfM* 10, 1878).

Meckenheuser, J. G. *Die sogenannte allerneueste, musikalische Temperatur*, Quedlinburg, 1727.

Mei, G. *Discorso sopra la musica antica e moderna*, 1602; facs. repr. Milan, 1933.

Meibom, M. *Antiquae Musicae auctores*, 1652.

Menestrier, C. F. le. *Des représentations en musique ancienne et moderne*, Paris, 1681.

——. *Des ballets anciens et modernes*, Paris, 1682.

Mengoli, P. *Speculationi di musica*, Bologna, 1670.

Merk, D. *Compendium musicae instrumentalis chelicae*, 1695.

Mersenne, M. *Harmonie Universelle*, 1636–37.

Meyer, J. *Unvorgreiffliche Gedancken über die neulich eingerissene theatralische Kirchen-music*, 1726.

Michele, A. di. *La nuova chitarra di regole*, Palermo, 1680.

Milioni, P. and Monte, L. *Vero . . . modo d'imparare a sonare . . . la Chitara*, 1647.

Minguet, P. *Academia Musical de los instrumentos*, Madrid, 1752.

Mithobius, H. *Psalmodia christiana*, 1665.

Mizler, L. C. *Neu eröffnete musikalische Bibliothek*, 1736–54.

——. *Musikalischer Staarstecher*, 1739–40.

——. *Anfangs-gründe des Generalbasses*, Leipzig, 1739.

Montéclair, M. P. de. *Méthode pour apprendre la musique*, 1700.

——. *Méthode facile pour apprendre à jouer du violon*, 1712.

——. *Principes de musique*, 1736.

Montserrate, A. de. *Arte breve de las dificultades*, 1614.

Murschhauser, F. X. A. *Fundamentalische Handleitung*, 1707.

——. *Academia musico-pratica*, 1721.

Muscovius, J. *Bestrafter Missbrauch der Kirchenmusik*, 1694.

Nasarre, P. *Fragmentos musicales*, 1683.

——. *Escuela musica*, 1724.

Negri, C. *Le Gratie d'amore*, Milan, 1602.

——. *Nuove inventioni di balli*, Milan, 1604.

Neidhardt, J. G. *Die beste und leichteste Temperatur*, 1706.

——. *Gäntzlich erschöpfte mathematische Abtheilungen des . . . Canonis Monochordi*, 1732.

Niedt, F. E. *Handleitung zur Variation*, 1706.

——. *Musicalisches A B C*, 1708.

——. *Musikalische Handleitung*, I–III, 1700; 1706; 1717.

Nivers, G. G. *Dissertation sur le chant gregorien*, Paris, 1683.

———. *La gamme du si, nouvelle méthode pour apprendre à chanter*, 1646.

———. *Traité de la composition*, Paris, 1667.

North, R. *The Musical Gramarian*, MS (ed. by H. Andrews, 1925).

Nucius, J. *Musices poeticae*, 1613.

Nunes da Silva, M. *Arte minima*, Lisbon, 1685.

Orgosinus, H. *Musica nova*, Leipzig, 1603.

Osio, T. *L'armonia del nudo parlare*, 1637.

Ottonelli. *Della christiana moderatione del theatro*, Florence, 1652.

Pacichelli, J. B. *De Tintinnabulo*, 1693.

Paolucci, G. *Arte pratica di contrappunto*, 3 vols. 1765–72 [contains examples of renaissance and baroque music].

Paradossi, G. *Modo facile di suonare il sistro*, Bologna, 1695; facs. repr. Milan, 1933.

Parran, A. *Traité de la musique théorique et pratique*, Paris, 1646.

Pasquini, B. *Regole per ben suonare il cembalo*, MS 3002 Bibl. Santini, Münster; also Liceo Musicale, Bologna.

———. *Saggio di contrapunto*, Berlin, Staatsbibl. Mus. MS L. 214.

Peacham, H. *The Compleat Gentleman*, 1622.

Pellegrini, C. *Museum Historico-Legale*, 1665.

Pemberton, E. *An Essay for the Further Improvement of Dancing*, London, 1711.

Penna, L. *Li primi albori musicali*, Bologna, 1672.

Pepusch, J. C. *A Treatise on Harmony*, 2nd ed. London, 1731.

Perego, C. *La regola del canto fermo ambrosiano*, Milan, 1622.

Pexenfelder, M. *Apparatus eruditionis . . . per omnes artes*, 1670.

Picerli, S. *Specchio . . . di musica*, Naples, 2 vols. 1630–31.

Piovesana, F. S. *Misure harmoniche*, 1627.

Pisa, A. *Battuta della musica dichiarata*, Rome, 1611.

Pitoni, G. A. *Guida armonica*, n.d. [before 1700].

Playford, J. *A Briefe Introduction to the Skill of Musick*, 1654 ff.

———. *The Division Violin*, 1685.

———. *An Introduction to the Skill of Musick; Corrected and Amended by Mr. Henry Purcell*, 12th ed. 1694.

Praetorius, M. *Syntagma Musicum*, I–III, 1615–1619; v. II facs. repr. 1884 and 1929; v. III repr. 1916.

Prelleur, P. *The modern Musick-Master*, London, 1731.

Preus, G. *Grundregeln von der Struktur . . . einer untadelhaften Orgel*, Hamburg, 1729.

Prinner, J. J. *Musicalischer schlissl* (1677). MS, Library of Congress.

Printz, W. C. *Phrynis Mytilenaeus*, 1676–77.

———. *Musica modulationis vocalis*, 1678.

————. *Historische Beschreibung der Edelen Sing- und Klingkunst,* Dresden, 1690.

Profe, A. *Compendium musicum,* 1641.

Prynne, W. *Histriomastix,* London, 1633.

Pure, M. de. *Idée des spectacles anciens et nouveaux,* Paris, 1658.

Puteanus, E. *Musathena* (2nd ed. of *Modulata Pallas*), Hanover, 1602.

Quirsfeld, J. *Breviarium musicum,* Dresden, 1675.

Quitschreiber, G. *Musikbüchlein für die Jugend,* Jena, 1607.

Raguenet, Abbé F. *Parallèle des Italiens et des François,* 1702. Engl. transl. 1709; repr. MQ 32 (1946), 411.

Ralph, J. *The Taste of the Town,* 1731.

Rameau, J. P. *Traité de l'harmonie,* Paris, 1722.

————. *Nouveau système de musique théorique,* 1726.

————. *Generation harmonique,* 1737.

————. *Démonstration du principe de l'harmonie,* 1750.

————. *Nouvelles Réflexions sur sa démonstration,* 1752.

————. *Observations sur notre instinct musical,* 1754.

Rameau, P. *Abrégé de la nouvelle méthode dans l'art d'écrire . . . danses de ville,* Paris, 1725.

————. *Le maître à danser,* Paris, 1725.

Ravn, H. M. *Heptachordum danicum, ad canendum,* 1646.

Ravenscroft, Th. *A Briefe Discourse of the True (but Neglected) Use of Charact'ring the Degrees,* 1611.

Reimann. *Musikbüchlein,* Erfurt, 1644.

Rémond de Saint-Mard, T. *Reflexions sur l'opera,* The Hague, 1741.

Riccoboni, L. *Reflexions historiques sur les differens théâtres de l'Europe,* 1740.

Robinson, Th. *The Schoole of Musicke,* 1603.

Rodio, R. *Regoli di musica,* Naples, 1609.

Roel del Rio, A. V. *Institución harmonica,* Madrid, 1748.

Rognone Taegio, F. *Aggiunta dello scolaro di violino,* 1614.

————. *Selva di varii passaggi secondo l'uso moderno,* 1620.

Rognone Taegio, R. *Passaggi . . . nel diminuire,* 1592.

Rosa, S. *Satire,* 1664.

Rossi, G. B. *Organo de Cantori,* Venice, 1618.

Rossi, L. *Sistema musico overo musica speculativa,* Perugia, 1666.

Rousseau, J. *Méthode . . . pour apprendre à chanter,* 1678 ff.

————. *Traité de la Viole,* 1687.

Ruffa, G. *Introduttorio musicale,* 1701.

Ruiz de Ribayaz, L. *Luz y norte musical,* Madrid, 1677.

Sabbatini, G. *Regola facile e breve per sonare sopra il basso continuo,* Venice, 1628; 3rd ed. Rome, 1669.

Sabbatini, N. *Pratica di fabricar scene,* Ravenna, 1638 (German transl. by W. Flemming, Weimarer Bibliophilengesellschaft, 1926).

Sabbatini, P. *Toni ecclesiastici. Modo per sonare il basso continuo*, Rome, 1650.

St. Evremond, Ch. de. *Dissertation sur l'opéra*, in *Oeuvres*, London, 1705.

St. Hubert, de. *La manière de composer et faire réussir les ballets*, Paris, 1641.

Saint-Lambert, M. de. *Les principes du clavecin*, 1697.

――――. *Nouveau traité de l'accompagnement*, Paris, 1707.

Salmon, Th. *An Essay to the Advancement of Musick*, 1672.

Salter, H. *The Genteel Companion; . . . Directions for the Recorder*, 1683.

Samber, J. B. *Manuductio ad organum, Anleitung zur edlen Schlagkunst*, Salzburg, 1704.

――――. *Continuatio ad Manuductionem organicum*, Salzburg, 1707.

Sangiovanni, G. *Primi emmaestramenti della musica*, 1714.

Sanz, G. *Instrucción de música sobre la guitarra*, Saragossa, 1674 (1697).

Sartorius, E. *Institutionum Musicarum Tractatio*, Hamburg, 1635.

――――. *Musomachia, id est: Bellum musicale*, Rostock, 1642 [1st ed. 1622].

Sauveur, J. *Principes d'acousticque et de musique*, Paris, 1701.

――――. *Système general des intervalles, des sons*, Paris, 1701.

――――. *Méthode générale pour former des systèmes tempérés*, 1707.

Scacchi, M. *Cribrum musicum*, Venice, 1643.

Scaletta, O. *Scala della musica*, 1598 ff.; 24th ed. 1685.

――――. *Primo scalino della scala di contrapunto*, 1622.

Scarlatti, A. *Discorso sopra un caso particolare* (printed in Kirnberger: *Die Kunst des reinen Satzes*, 1771).

――――. *Regole per principianti*, MS Add. 14244 and 31517 of the British Museum.

Scheibe, J. A. *Der critische Musikus*, 1737–1740.

――――. *Eine Abhandlung von den Musikalischen Intervallen*, 1739.

Schmidt, J. M. *Musico-theologia*, 1754.

Schönsleder, W. (Volupius Decorus) *Architectonice musices universalis*, 1631.

Schott, K. *Magia Universalis*, pt. II, *Acustica*, 1657 ff.

――――. *Organum mathematicum*, 1668.

Schreyer, B. *Musica choralis theoro-practica*, Munich, 1663.

Schwenter, D. *Deliciae physico-mathematicae*, 1636–1653.

Scorpione, D. *Riflessioni Armoniche*, 1701.

Secchi, A. *De ecclesiastica hymnodia libri tres*, 1634.

Serré, J.-A. *Essais sur les principes de l'harmonie*, Paris, 1753.

Simpson, Chr. *The Division Violist*, 1659 ff.

――――. *A Compendium or Introduction to Practical Musick*, 1667 ff.

Sieffert [Syfert], P. *Anticribatio musica*, 1645.

Siris, P. *The Art of Dancing*, London, 1706.

Sorge, G. A. *Vorgemach der musicalischen Composition*, 1745–47.

Spadi, G. B. *Passaggi . . . con madrigali diminuiti per sonare*, Venice, 1609.

Speer, D. *Grundrichtiger . . . Unterricht der musikalischen Kunst oder Vierfaches musikalisches Kleeblatt*, 1697.

Sperling, J. P. *Principia musicae,* 1705.

Spiess, M. *Tractatus musicus compositorio-practicus,* Augsburg, 1746.

Spiridion. *Neue Unterweisung, wie man in kurzer Zeit nicht allein zu vollkommenem Orgel- und Instrumentenschlagen, sondern auch zu der Kunst der Komposition gänzlich gelangen mag,* 1670.

Steffani, A. *Quanta certezza habbia da suoi principii la Musica,* Amsterdam, 1695.

Stierlein, J. C. *Trifolium musicae consistens in Musica theorica, practica et poetica,* Stuttgart, 1691.

Strozzi, G. *Elementorum musicae praxis,* Naples, 1683.

Tans'ur, W. *A New Musical Grammar,* 1746.

Tartini, G. *Trattato di Musica,* 1754.

Taubert, G. *Rechtschaffener Tantzmeister,* Leipzig, 1717.

Tessarini, C. *Grammatica di musica . . . a suonar il violino,* 1741.

Tettamanzi, F. *Breve metodo per fondamente . . . apprendere il canto fermo,* Milan, 1686.

Tevo, Z. *Il Musico Testore,* 1706.

Thalesio, P. *Arte de canto chão,* Coimbra, 1628.

Tigrini, O. *Il compendio della musica,* Venice, 1602.

Torres, J. de. *Reglas generales di acompañar en organo,* 1702.

Tosi, P. F. *Opinioni de' cantori antichi e moderni,* 1723; repr. in della Corte: *Canto e bel canto,* 1933. Engl. transl. by J. E. Galliard: *Observations on the Florid Song,* London, 1742 (facs. repr. London, 1926).

Treiber, J. P. *Der accurate Organist im General-Bass,* Jena, 1704.

Trew, A. *Lycei musici theorici practici,* 1635.

Trümper, M. *Epitome oder Kurtzer Auszug der Musik,* 1668.

Tufts, J. *A Very Plain and Easy Introduction to the Whole Art of Singing Psalm Tunes,* 1720.

Turner, W. *Sound Anatomiz'd,* 1724.

Uberti, G. *Contrasto musico,* Rome, 1630.

Ulloa, P. de. *Musica universal,* Madrid, 1717.

Ureña, P. de. *Arte nueva de musica,* Rome, 1669 (ed. by J. Caramuel de Lobkowitz).

Valle, P. della *Discorso della musica dell'età nostra,* 1640 (repr. in Solerti: *Le origini del melodramma,* 1903).

Valls, F. *Respuesta . . . a la censura,* Barcelona, 1716.

Vaz Barradas Muitopão, J. *Flores musicaes,* 1735.

Veracini, F. M. *Il Trionfo della practica musicale,* op. III; MS in Conservatory, Florence.

Verato, G. M. *Il Verrato insegna . . . per imparare per tutte le Chiave,* 1623.

Vogt, M. *Conclave thesauris magnae artis musicae,* 1719.

Voigt, C. *Gespräch von der Musik,* Erfurt, 1742.

Wagenseil, J. C. *De Germanicae Phonascorum, Von der Meister-singer Origine,* Nuremberg, 1697.

Wallerius-Retzelius, *De Tactu musico,* Upsala, 1698.

Walliser, Th. *Musicae figuralis praecepta,* Strasbourg, 1611.

Walter, Th. *Grounds and Rules of Music,* 1721.

Walther, J. G. *Musikalisches Lexikon,* 1732.

Warren, A. *The Tonometer,* 1725.

Weaver, J. *An Essay Toward an History of Dancing,* London, 1712.

Werckmeister, A. *Orgelprobe,* 1681 (facs. repr. of 2nd ed. 1698, Kassel, 1928).

———. *Musicae mathematicae hodegus curiosus,* 1687.

———. *Musikalische Temperatur,* 1691.

———. *Hypomnemata musica,* 1697.

———. *Organum Gruninge redivivum,* 1705 (repr. 1932).

———. *Musicalische Paradoxal-Discourse,* 1707.

Zacconi, L. *Prattica di musica,* 2 vols., Venice, 1592, 1622.

Zanetti, G. *Il Scolaro per imparar a suonare di violino et altri stromenti,* Milan, 1645.

Zerleder, N. *Musica figularis oder . . . Singkunst,* Bern, 1658.

Zondarini, F. G. *Riflessioni . . . nell'apprendere il canto con l'uso d'un solfeggio,* Venice, 1746.

Zumbag, C. *Institutiones Musicae of Korte onderwyzingen,* Leyden, 1743 (based on MS 70.J.11 of his father Lothar Zumbag in Royal Library of The Hague).

————. "Commemorazione della Riforma melodramatica," *Atti dell' Accademia del R. Instituto Musicale di Firenze*, Anno XXXIII, Florence, 1895.

Abbiati, Fr. *Storia della Musica*, II (*Seicento*), III (*Settecento*), Milan, 1941.

Abert, A. A. *Die stilistischen Voraussetzungen der Cantiones Sacrae von H. Schütz*, 1935.

Abert, H. "Händel als Dramatiker," *Gesammelte Schriften*, 1931.

Adams, H. M. "Passion Music before 1724," *ML* VII.

Adler, G. "I 'Componimenti musicali per il Cembalo' di Teofilo Muffat e il posto che essi occupano nella storia della 'Suite' per il Pianoforte," *RMI* III, 1896.

————. *Handbuch der Musikgeschichte*, 1930 (see especially the contributions by Einstein, Wellesz, Schering, Fischer, and Haas).

————. "Zur Geschichte der Wiener Mess-Komposition," *StzMW*, 4.

Ademollo, A. *I teatri di Roma nel secolo XVII*, Rome, 1888.

Adrio, A. *Die Anfänge des geistlichen Konzerts*, Berlin, 1935.

————. "Die Matthaeus-Passion von J. G. Kühnhausen (um 1700)," *Festschrift Schering*, 1937.

Alaleona, D. *Studi su la storia dell'oratorio musicale in Italia*, Turin, 1908.

————. "Le laudi spirituali italiane nei secoli XVI e XVII e il loro rapporto coi canti profani," *RMI* XVI, 1909.

————. *Storia dell'oratorio musicale in Italia*, Milan, 1945.

Albini, E. "Domenico Gabrielli, il Corelli del Violoncello," *RMI* XLI, 1937.

Alewyn, R. *Der Kapellmeister J. Beer*, 1932.

Allen, W. D. *Philosophies of Music Histories*, New York, 1939.

Altmann, W. "Thematisches Verzeichnis der gedruckten Werke Vivaldis," *AMW* IV, 263 (see also Rinaldi).

Ambros, A. W. *Geschichte der Musik*, v. 4, 3rd ed. by Leichtentritt, Leipzig, 1909.

Angeli, A. d'. *Benedetto Marcello*, Milan, 1940.

Anglès, H. "Orgelmusik der Schola Hispanica," *Festschrift Peter Wagner*, 1926.

Apel, W. "Neapolitan Links between Cabezon and Frescobaldi," *MQ* 24, 1938.

Arger, J. "Le rôle expressif des 'agréments' dans l'école vocale française de 1680 à 1760," *RdM*, 5.

Arienzo, N. d'. "Salvator Rosa musicista e lo stile monodico da camera," *RMI* I, 1894.

————. "Origini dell'opera comica," *RMI* II, IV, VI, VII.

Arkwright, G. E. P. "Purcell's Church Music," *MA* I, 1910.

————. "An English Pupil of Monteverdi," *MA* IV (1913), 236.

Arnheim, A. "Ein Beitrag zur Geschichte des einstimmigen weltlichen Kunstliedes in Frankreich im 17. Jahrhundert," *SIMG* X, 399.

Arnold, F. T. *The Art of Accompaniment from a Thorough-Bass*, London, 1931.

————. "A Corelli Forgery," *PMA*, 1921.

Arundell, D. *Henry Purcell*, London, 1927.

Auerbach, C. *Die deutsche Clavichordkunst des 18. Jahrhunderts*, Diss. Freiburg, 1928; Kassel, 1930.

Bacher, J. *Die Viola da Gamba*, 1932.

Baehrens, C. E. *The Origin of the Masque*, Groningen, 1929.

Bairstow, E. *The Messiah*, London, 1928.

Barblan, G. *Un musicista trentino, F. A. Bonporti*, 1940.

Barbour, J. M. *Equal Temperament, Its History from Ramis to Rameau*, Diss. Cornell, 1932 (typewritten).

————. "Bach and the Art of Temperament," *MQ* 33 (1947), 64.

Becker, C. F. *Die Tonwerke des 16. und 17. Jahrhunderts*, 2nd ed. Leipzig, 1855.

Beckmann, G. "Johann Pachelbel als Kammerkomponist," *AMW* I (1918–1919), 267.

————. *Das Violinspiel in Deutschland vor 1700*, Leipzig, 1918.

Benn, F. *Die Messkomposition des J. J. Fux*, Diss. Vienna, 1931.

Benvenuti, G. "Il manoscritto veneziano della 'Incoronazione di Poppea,'" *RMI* XLI, 1937.

Berend, F. *N. A. Strungk*, Diss. Munich, 1913.

Berger, A. V. "The Beggar's Opera, The Burlesque and Italian Opera," *ML* XVII, 93.

Bessaraboff, N. *Ancient European Musical Instruments*, 1941.

Betti, A. *La vita e l'arte di F. Geminiani*, Lucca, 1933.

Blume, F. *Das monodische Prinzip in der protestantischen Kirchenmusik*, Leipzig, 1925.

————. "Eine unbekannte Violin-Sonate von J. S. Bach," *Bach Jahrbuch*, 1928, 96.

————. "Fortspinnung und Entwicklung," *JMP*, 1929.

————. *Michael Praetorius Creuzburgensis*, 1929.

————. *Die Evangelische Kirchenmusik* (*Handbuch der Musikwissenschaft*), 1931.

————. "Das Werk des Michael Praetorius," *ZMW*, 17.

————. "Das Kantatenwerk D. Buxtehudes," *JMP*, 1940.

Böttger, F. *Die Comédie-ballets von Molière und Lully*, Diss. Berlin, 1930.

Boghen, F. *L'arte di B. Pasquini*, 1931.

Bolte, J. "Die Singspiele der englischen Komödianten," *Theatergeschichtliche Forschungen*, 7 (1893).

———. "Von Wanderkomödianten und Handwerkerspielen des 17. und 18. Jahrhunderts," *Sitzungsberichte, Preussische Akademie der Wissenschaften*, Phil. Hist. KL. 1934, 19.

Bonaccorsi, A. "Contributo alla storia del Concerto grosso," *RMI* XXXIX, 1932.

Bonaventura, A. *B. Pasquini*, Rome, 1923.

Bontoux, G. *La chanson en Angleterre aux temps d'Elisabeth*, 1936.

Born, E. *Die Variation als Grundlage handwerklicher Gestaltung im musikalischen Schaffen Joh. Pachelbels*, Berlin, 1941.

Borrel, E. "La basse chiffré dans l'école française au XVIIIe siècle," *RdM*, 7.

———. "L'interprétation de Lully d'après Rameau," *RdM*, 29.

———. "Les notes inégales dans l'ancienne musique française," *RdM*, 40.

———. "Un paradoxe musical au XVIII siècle," *Mélanges Musicologie, La Laurencie*, 1933.

Borren, Ch. van den. *Les origines de la musique de clavier dans les Pays-Bas*, Brussels, 1914.

———. *A. Scarlatti et l'esthétique de l'opéra napolitaine*, 1922.

———. *Il Ritorno*, Brussels, 1925.

———. "Le livre de clavier de Vincentius de la Faille (1625)," *Mélanges de Musicologie, La Laurencie* (1933), 85.

Bosquet, E. "Origine et formation de la sonate allemande de 1698 à 1742," *La Revue Internationale de Musique*, 1939, 853.

Botstiber, H. *Geschichte der Ouvertüre*, 1913.

Bouvet, C. "Un musicien oublié: Charles Piroye," *RdM*, 28.

———. *Musiciens oubliés (Piroye, Fouquet, Du Buisson)*, Paris, 1932.

Boyden, D. "Ariosti's Lessons for Viola d'Amore," *MQ* 32 (1946), 545.

Brenet, M. "Les 'Oratoires' de Carissimi," *RMI* IV, 1897.

———. "French Military Music in the Reign of Louis XIV," *MQ*, 1917, 340.

Bridge, J. C. "A Great English Choir-Trainer, Captain H. Cooke," *MA* II (1911), 61.

Bridge, J. F. "Purcell and Matteis," *SIMG* I, 623.

———. *Twelve Good Musicians from Bull to Purcell*, London, 1920.

Bronson, B. H. "The Beggar's Opera," *Studies in the Comic, Univ. of California Public. in English*, v. 8 no. 2, 1941.

Brotanek, R. "Die englischen Maskenspiele," *Wiener Beiträge zur englischen Philologie*, 15, Vienna, 1902.

Brunold, P. "Trois livres de pièces de clavecin de J. F. Dandrieu," *RdM*, 43.

———. *Traité des signes et agréments employés par les clavecinistes*, 1935.

Buchmayer, R. "Drei irrtümlich J. S. Bach zugeschriebene Klavierkompositionen," *SIMG* II, 253.

Büttner, H. *Das Konzert in den Orchester-Suiten Telemann's*, Diss. Leipzig, 1931.

Bukofzer, M. F. "Allegory in Baroque Music," *Journal of the Warburg Institute* III (1939–40), 1.

——. "On the Performance of Renaissance Music," *Proceedings MTNA*, 1941, v. 36,225.

——. "The Neo-Baroque," *Modern Music* XXII (1945), 152.

Burney, C. *A General History of Music*, 1776–89 (ed. by Mercer, 1935).

Buszin, W. E. "D. Buxtehude on the Tercentenary of his Birth," *MQ* 23 (1937), 465.

Caffi, F. *Storia della musica sacra*, Venice 1854/55; repr. Milan, 1931.

Calmus, G. "Die Beggar's opera," *SIMG* VIII, 286.

——. "Drei satirisch-kritische Aufsätze von Addison über die italienische Oper in England," *SIMG* IX (1908), 131.

——. *Zwei Opernburlesken der Rokokozeit (Lesage-Gay)*, 1912.

Cametti, A. "Orazio Michi 'dell'Arpa' virtuoso e compositore di musica della prima metà del seicento," *RMI* XXI (1914), 203.

Cannon, B. C. *Johann Mattheson, Spectator in Music*, New Haven, 1947.

Carse, A. *The History of Orchestration*, 1925.

Casimiri, R. "G. Frescobaldi e un falso autografo," *Note d'archivio* 19 (1942), 130–31.

Catelani, A. *Della opera di Alessandro Stradella*, Modena, 1866.

Cecil, G. *The History of Opera in England*, 1930.

Cellier, A. "Les Motets de La Lande," *RM* 22 (1946), 20.

Cesari, G. "L' 'Orfeo' di Claudio Monteverdi all'Associazione di Amici della Musica di Milano," *RMI* XVII, 1910.

Chase, G. *The Music of Spain*, New York, 1941.

Chilesotti, O. "Trascrizioni da un codice musicale di Vincenzo Galilei," *Atti del Congresso Int. di Scienze Storiche* (1903), V. 8, 1905, 135.

——. "Gli Airs de Cour di Besard," *Atti del Congresso Int. di Scienze Storiche* (1903), V. 8, 1905, 131.

——. "La chitarra francese," *RMI* XIV, 1907.

——. "Canzonette del Seicento con la Chitarra," *RMI* XVI, 1909.

——. "Notes sur le guitariste Robert de Visée," *SIMG* IX, 1908, 62.

Chrysander, F. *G. F. Händel*, 3 vls., Leipzig, 1858–67; repr. 1919.

——. "Händel's Instrumentalkompositionen für grosses Orchester," *VfM* III (1887), 1; 157; 451.

——. *Händel's biblische Oratorien*, Hamburg, 1897.

Clercx, S. "Johann Kuhnau et la sonate," *RdM*, 15.

——. "Les clavicinistes Belges," *RM* 20, 1939.

Coopersmith, J. M. "Handelian Lacunae," *MQ* 1935.

———. "Unpublished Music by Handel," *Papers Internat. Congress of Musicology*, New York, 1939 (1944), 213.

Corte, A. della. *L'opera comica italiana nel '700*, 1923.

———. *Canto e bel canto*, Turin, 1933.

Corte, A. della, and Pannain, G. *Storia della Musica*, I (*Il seicento e il settecento*), Turin, 1936; 1944.

Cotalero, E. *Historia de la Zarzuela*, Madrid, 1934.

Crussard, C. *Un musicien inconnu, Marc-Antoine Charpentier*, Paris, 1945.

Cucuel, G. *Les créateurs de l'opéra comique français*, 1914.

Cummings, W. H. *Handel*, London, 1905.

———. *Purcell*, London, 1911.

———. "J. Blow," *SIMG* X, 421.

Daffner, H. *Die Entwicklung des Klavierkonzerts bis Mozart*, 1906.

Danckert, W. *Geschichte der Gigue*, 1924.

Dannreuther, E. *Musical Ornamentation*, 1893–95.

Davey, H. *History of English Music*, 2nd ed. 1921.

David, H. T. "Die Gestalt von Bach's chromatischer Fantasie," *Bach Jahrbuch* 1926, 23.

———. "Zu Bach's Kunst der Fuge," *JMP*, 1928.

———. "The Structure of Musical Collections up to 1750," *BAMS*, 3.

———. *J. S. Bach's Musical Offering*, New York, 1945.

David, H., and Mendel, A. *The Bach Reader*, New York, 1945.

Day, C. L. *The Songs of John Dryden*, Cambridge, Mass., 1932.

———. *The Songs of T. D'Urfey*, Cambridge, Mass., 1933.

Deffner, O. *Über die Entwicklung der Fantasie for Tasteninstrumente bis Sweelinck*, 1927.

Dent, E. J. "The operas of A. Scarlatti," *SIMG* IV, 143.

———. *Alessandro Scarlatti*, 1905.

———. "Italian Chamber Cantatas," *MA* II (1911), 143, 185.

———. "Ensembles and Finales in 18th-Century Italian Opera," *SIMG* XII (1911), 112.

———. *Foundations of English Opera*, Cambridge, 1928.

———. "English Influences on Handel," *Monthly Musical Record* 49 (1929), 167 (also *Händel Jahrbuch*, 1929).

———. "La Rappresentazione di Anima e di Corpo," *Papers Intern. Congress of Musicology*, New York, 1939 (1944), 52.

———. "Italian Opera in London," *PMA* 71 (1945), 19.

Dickinson, G. S. *The Pattern of Music*, 1939.

Dietrich, F. "J. S. Bachs Orgelchoral und seine geschichtlichen Wurzeln," *Bach Jahrbuch*, 1929, 1.

————. "Analogieformen in Bachs Tokkaten und Präludien für die Orgel," *Bach Jahrbuch* 28 (1931), 51.

————. *Geschichte des deutschen Orgelchorals im 17. Jahrhundert,* 1932.

Dilthey, W. "Die Affektenlehre des 17. Jahrhunderts," *Gesammelte Schriften* II, 1929.

Dodge, J. "Ornamentation as indicated by signs in lute tablature," *SIMG* IX (1908), 318.

————. "Lute Music of the 16th and 17th centuries," *PMA,* 34.

Dolmetsch, A. *The Interpretation of Music of the 17th and 18th Centuries,* new ed. 1944.

Dorian, F. *The History of Music in Performance,* New York, 1942.

Dreger, C. O. "Die Vokalthematik J. S. Bachs, dargestellt an den Arien der Kirchenkantaten," *Bach Jahrbuch,* 31 (1934), 1.

Dulle, K. *A. Destouches,* Diss. Leipzig, 1909.

Dufourq, N. *Esquisse d'une histoire de l'orgue,* 1935 (Bibliogr. in *RdM,* 1934).

————. *La musique d'orgue française de Titelouze à Alain,* Paris, 1941.

Dupont, C. *Geschichte der musikalischen Temperatur,* 1935.

Dupré, H. *Purcell,* Paris, 1927; Engl. transl. New York, 1928.

Echorcheville, J. *De Lulli à Rameau, l'Esthétique musicale,* Paris, 1906.

————. *Corneille et la musique,* Paris, 1906.

Ehrichs, A. *Giulio Caccini,* Diss. Leipzig, 1908.

Ehrlinger, F. *Händel's Orgelkonzerte,* Diss. Erlangen, 1934.

Eimert, H. *Musikalische Formstrukturen im 17. und 18. Jahrhundert,* Diss. Cologne, 1932.

Einstein, A. "Zur deutschen Literatur für Viola da Gamba im 16. und 17. Jahrhundert," *Beihefte IMG,* II. Folge, 1, 1905.

————. "Ein unbekannter Druck aus der Frühzeit der deutschen Monodie," *SIMG* XIII (1912), 286.

————. "Die Aria di Ruggiero," *SIMG* XIII, 444.

————. "Ancora sull'Aria di Ruggiero," *RMI* XLI, 1937.

————. "Agostino Steffani," *Kirchenmusikalisches Jahrbuch,* 23, 1910.

————. "Ein Concerto grosso von 1619," *Festschrift Kretzschmar,* 1918, 26.

————. *Heinrich Schütz,* Kassel, 1928.

————. "Ein Emissär der Monodie in Deutschland: Francesco Rasi," *Festschrift Johannes Wolf,* 1929, 31.

————. "Die Anfänge des Vokalkonzerts," *AM* III, 1931.

————. "Firenze prima della Monodia, Animuccia, Corteccia, Striggio," *La Rassegna Musicale,* VII (1934), 253.

————. "Das Madrigal zum Doppelgebrauch," *AM* VI, 1934.

Eisenschmidt, J. "Die szenische Darstellung der Opern Händels auf der Londoner Bühne seiner Zeit," *Schriftenreihe des Händel-Hauses,* 1940, 1941.

Emsheimer, E. *Joh. Ulr. Steigleder, sein Leben und seine Werke,* Diss. Freiburg, 1927; Kassel, 1928.

Engel, H. *Das Instrumentalkonzert,* Leipzig, 1932. (*Führer durch den Konzertsaal,* Kretzschmar).

Epstein, E. *Der französische Einfluss auf die deutsche Klaviersuite im 17. Jahrhundert,* 1940.

Epstein, P. "Zur Rhythmisierung eines Ritornells von Monteverdi," *AMW* VIII, 416.

———. "Heinrich Litzkau, ein früher deutscher Violinmeister," *ZMW,* 12 (1930), 225.

Erlebach, R. "William Lawes and His String Music," *PMA* 1932–33.

Evans, W. M. *Henry Lawes,* 1941.

Evelyn, J. *The Diary* (ed. Bray), 1906.

Fassini, S. *Il melodrama italiano a Londra,* Turin, 1914.

Fehr, M. A. *Zeno und seine Reform des Operntextes,* Zürich, 1912.

Fellerer, K. G. "J. S. Bach's Bearbeitung der Missa sine nomine von Palestrina," *Bach Jahrbuch* 1927, 123.

———. *Der Palestrinastil und seine Bedeutung in der vokalen Kirchenmusik im 18. Jahrhundert,* 1928.

———. "Rupert Ignaz Mayr (1646–1712) und seine Kirchenmusik," *AMF* I (1936), 83, 200.

———. "Zur italienischen Orgelmusik des 17. und 18. Jahrhunderts," *JMP,* 1938.

Fellowes, E. H. "The Philidor Manuscripts," *ML* XII, 116.

Ferand, E.-T. *Die Improvisation in der Musik,* Zürich, 1939.

Fischer-Krückeberg, E. "Johann Krüger als Musiktheoretiker," *ZMW* 12, 609.

———. "Johann Krügers Choralbearbeitungen," *ZMW* 14, 248.

Fischer, K. "Gabriel Voigtländer," *SIMG* XII (1911), 17.

Fischer, L. H. "Fremde Melodien in H. Alberts Arien," *VfM* II, 467.

Fischer, M. *Die organistische Improvisation,* Kassel, 1939.

Fischer, W. "Zur Entwicklungsgeschichte des Wiener klassischen Stils," in *StzMW,* 3.

Fleischer, O. "Denis Gaultier," *VfM* II, 1.

Flemming, W. *Oper und Oratorium im Barock,* 1933.

Fleury, L. "The Flute . . . in the French Art of the 17th and 18th Centuries," *MQ* 1923, 515.

Flögel, B. "Studien zur Arientechnik in den Opern Händels," *Händel Jahrbuch,* 1929, 50.

Florimo, F. *La scuola musicale di Napoli,* Naples, 1880.

Flower, N. *G. F. Handel, His Personality and His Times,* London, 1929.

———. "Händels 'Jupiter in Argos,'" *Händel Jahrbuch* 1928, 60.

Forster, K. *Über das Leben und die kirchenmusikalischen Werke des G. A. Bernabei*, Diss. Munich, 1933.

Frati, L. "Attilio Ottavio Ariosti," *RMI* XXXIII, 1926.

Friedländer, M. *Das deutsche Lied im 18. Jahrhundert,* 2 vls. 1902.

Frotscher, G. "Die Affektenlehre als geistige Grundlage der Themenbildung J. S. Bachs," *Bach Jahrbuch* 1926, 90.

———. *Geschichte des Orgelspiels*, 2 vls. Berlin, 1935.

———. *Orgeldispositionen aus 5 Jahrhunderten*, 1939.

Fuller-Maitland, J. A. *Bach's Brandenburg Concertos*, 1928.

———. "The Age of Bach and Handel," *OHM*, v. 4, 2nd ed. 1931.

Gagey, E. M. *Ballad Opera*, New York, 1937.

Garnault, P. *Histoire et influence du tempérament*, 1929.

Gaspari, G. *Musicisti Bolognesi nel sec. XVII*, Modena, 1875–80.

———. *La Musica in San Petronio*, 1868–70.

Gastoué, A. *Les Messes Royales de Henri Dumont*, Paris, 1912.

———. "Notes sur . . . M. A. Charpentier," *Mélanges de Musicologie, La Laurencie* (1933), 153.

Gehrmann, H. "Johann Gottfried Walther als Theoretiker," *VfM* VII, 468.

Geiringer, K. "Paul Peuerl," *StzMW*, 16.

Georgii, W. *Klaviermusik, Geschichte der Musik für Klavier*, 1941.

Gerber, R. "Wort und Ton in den Cantiones sacrae von Schütz," *Abert-Gedenkschrift*, 1928.

———. *Das Passionsrezitativ bei H. Schütz*, 1929.

———. *Die deutsche Passion von Luther bis Bach*, 1931.

Gerhartz, K. "Die Violinschule in ihrer musikgeschichtlichen Entwicklung bis Leopold Mozart," *ZMW* 7, 553.

Gerheuser, L. *Jacob Scheiffelhut und seine Instrumentalmusik*, Augsburg, 1931.

Gérold, Th. *L'Art du chant en France au XVIIe siècle* (*Publ. de la Faculté des Lettres de L'Université*), Strasbourg, 1921.

Gerstenberg, W. *Die Klavierkompositionen Dom. Scarlattis*, Diss. Leipzig, 1931

Gleason, H. *Method of Organ Playing*, Rochester, 1940 (Bibliography).

Ghisi, F. *Del fuggilotio musicale di Giulio Romano (Caccini)*, Rome, 1934.

———. *Alle fonti della monodia*, Milan, 1940.

Giazotto, R. *Tommaso Albinoni (1671–1750)*, Milan, 1945.

Goldschmidt, H. *Die italienische Gesangsmethode im 17. Jahrhundert*, 1890.

———. "Cavalli als dramatischer Komponist," *MfM*, 1893.

———. "Zur Geschichte der Arien- und Symphonienform, *MfM*, 1901.

———. *Studien zur Geschichte der italienischen Oper*, 2 vls., 1901–04.

———. "Cl. Monteverdis Oper Il ritorno d'Ulisse," *SIMG* IV; IX.

———. "Fr. Provenzale als Dramatiker," *SIMG* VII, 608.

———. *Die Lehre von der vokalen Ornamentik*, 1907.

———. *Die Musikaesthetik des 18. Jahrhunderts*, 1915.

Gombosi, O. "Italia: Patria del Basso Ostinato," *La Rassegna Musicale* VII (1934), 14.

———. "Ein neuer Sweelinckfund," *Tijdschrift VNM* XIV (1933), 1.

———. "The Cultural and Folkloristic Background of the Folia," *PAMS*, 1940, 88.

Grace, H. *The Organ Works of Bach*, 1922.

Gräser, H. *Telemanns Instrumental-Kammermusik*, Diss. Frankfort, 1925.

Gräser, W. "Bach's Kunst der Fuge," *JMP*, 1924.

Gras, Ch. le "J. J. Mouret, 'le musicien des graces,'" *Académie de Vaucluse, Mémoires*, Avignon, 1939, ser. 3, t. 3, 115.

Graupner, F. *Das Werk des Thomaskantors J. Schelle*, Wolfenbüttel, 1929.

Gress, R. *Die Entwicklung der Klaviervariation von A. Gabrieli bis zu J. S. Bach*, 1929.

Grout, D. J. *The Origins of the Comic Opera*, Harvard Diss. 1939 (typewritten).

———. "Seventeenth-Century Parodies of French Opera," *MQ* 27 (1941) 211, 514.

———. "The Music of the Italian Theatre at Paris 1682–97," *PAMS*, 1941.

———. "German Baroque Opera," *MQ* 32 (1946), 574.

Grunsky, K. "Bachs Bearbeitungen und Umarbeitungen eigener und fremder Werke," *Bach Jahrbuch*, 1912, 61.

Gurlitt, W. *Leben und Werke des M. Praetorius*, Diss. Leipzig, 1915.

———. "Über Prinzipien und zur Geschichte der Registrierkunst in der alten Orgelmusik," *Kongressbericht Deutsche Musikgesellschaft*, Leipzig, 1926.

———. *J. S. Bach*, Berlin, 1936 (2nd ed. 1947).

Haas, R. "Zamponis Ulisse nell'Isola di Circe," *ZMW* 3, 385; 5, 63.

———. *Die Wiener Oper*, Vienna, 1926.

———. *Die estensischen Musikalien*, Regensburg, 1927.

———. "Wiener deutsche Parodieopern um 1730," *ZMW* 8, 201.

———. "Zur Neuausgabe von Monteverdis Il Ritorno," *StzMW*, 9.

———. "Das Generalbassflugblatt Francesco Bianciardis," *Festschrift Johannes Wolf*, 1929, 48.

———. *Musik des Barocks*, (*Handbuch der Musikwissenschaft*), 1928.

———. *Aufführungspraxis*, (*Handbuch der Musikwissenschaft*), 1931.

———, "Dreifache Orchesterteilung im Wiener Sepolcro," *Festschrift Koczirz*, 1930.

Haberl, F. X. "Ludwig Grossi da Viadana," *Kirchenmusikalisches Jahrbuch*, 1889, 59.

Haböck, F. *Die Kastraten und ihre Gesangskunst*, Stuttgart, 1927.

Haefner, W. E. *Die Lautenstücke des Denis Gaultier*, Diss. Freiburg, 1939.

Hagen, M. D. *Buxtehude*, Copenhagen, 1920.

Halm, A. "Über J. S. Bachs Konzertform," *Bach Jahrbuch* 1919, 1.

Hamburger, P. "Die Fantasien in E. Adriansens Pratum musicum, 1600," ZMW 12.

Hamel, F. *Die Psalmkompositionen Joh. Rosenmüllers*, Diss. Giessen (1930), 1933.

Handschin, J. "De différentes conceptions de Bach," *Schweizerisches Jahrbuch für Musikwissenschaft*, IV, 7.

——. "Die Grundlagen des a capella-Stils," *Hans Häusermann und der Häusermannsche Privatchor*, Zürich, 1929.

Hausswald, G. *Johann David Heinichens Instrumentalwerke*, Diss. Leipzig, 1937.

Hawkins, J. *General History of Music*, London, 1776, (Novello 1875).

Hayes, G. R. *Musical Instruments and Their Music*, 2 vls. London, 1928 ff.

——. *King's music*, 1937.

——. *The Lute's Apology*, London, 1938.

Hernried, R. "F. Geminianis Concerti grossi op. 3," *AM* IX, 1937.

Herz, G. "Bach's Religion," *Journal of Renaissance and Baroque Music* I (1946), 124.

Hess, H. "Die Opern Alessandro Stradellas," in *Beihefte IMG* II, 3, Leipzig, 1906.

Heuss, A. "Die Instrumentalstücke des Orfeo," *SIMG* IV, 175.

——. "Die venezianischen Opernsymphonien," *SIMG* IV.

——. *Die Matthäuspassion*, Leipzig, 1909.

——. "Das Semele-Problem bei Händel," *ZIMG* XV, 143.

——. "Zachow als dramatischer Kantaten-Komponist," *ZMW* 10, 228.

Hirschmann, K. F. *W. C. Briegel 1626–1712*, Marburg, 1934.

Hirtler, F. "Neu aufgefundene Orgelstücke von Johann Ulrich Steigleder und Johann Benn," *AMF* II, 1937.

Hjelmborg, B. "Une partition de Cavalli," *AM* XVI–XVII, 1944–45.

Hörner, H. *G. P. Telemanns Passionsmusiken*, Diss. Kiel (1930), 1933.

Holland, A. K. *H. Purcell: The English Musical Tradition*, London, 1932.

Horneffer, A. *Johann Rosenmüller*, 1898.

Howard, J. T. *Our American Music*, 3rd ed., New York, 1946.

Huard, G. "Les ballets de 'Tancrede' et de 'Psyche' . . . en 1619," *Société de l'histoire de l'art français, Bull.* 1936, 36.

Hudemann, H. *Die protestantische Dialogkomposition im 17. Jahrhundert*, Freiburg i. Br., 1941.

Huggler, H. *J. S. Bach's Orgelbüchlein*, Diss. Berne, 1930.

Hughes, C. W. "Porter, Pupil of Monteverdi," *MQ* 20 (1934), 278.

——. "Richard Deering's Fancies for Viols," *MQ* 27, 1941.

——. "The Music for Unaccompanied Bass Viol," *ML* XXV, 1944.

——. "John Gamble's Commonplace Book," *ML* XXVI, 1945.

Hull, A. E. *Bach's Organ Works*, London, 1929.

Ilgner, G. *Matthias Weckmann*, Diss. Kiel, 1939.

Iselin, D. J. *Biago Marini*, Diss. Basle, 1930.

Johandl, R. "D. G. Corner und sein Gesangbuch," *AMW* II, 447.

Juncker, H. "Zwei Griselda Opern," *Festschrift Sandberger*, 1918, 51.

Kade, O. *Die ältere Passionskomposition bis 1631*, Gütersloh, 1893.

Kade, R. "Christoph Demant," *VfM* VI, 469.

Kahle, F. *Händels Cembalosuiten*, 1928.

Kamienski, L. "Zum Tempo rubato," *AMW* I, 108.

Kastendieck, M. M. *England's Musical Poet, Thomas Campion*, 1938.

Kastner, S. *Música Hispánica, O Estilo do Padre Coelho*, 1936.

———. *Contribución al estudio de la musica española y portuguesa*, Lisbon, 1941.

Katz, E. *Die musikalischen Stilbegriffe des 17. Jahrhunderts*, Diss. Freiburg, 1926.

Kaul, O. *A. Kircher*, 1932.

Keller, H. *Die musikalische Artikulation, insbesondere bei J. S. Bach*, 1926.

———. *Generalbassschule*, 1931.

Kendall, R. "The Life and Works of Samuel Mareschall," *MQ* 30 (1944), 37.

Kidson, F. *The Beggar's Opera: Its Predecessors and Successors*, Cambridge, 1922.

Kinkeldey, O. "L. Luzzaschis Solomadrigale," *SIMG* IX, 538.

———. *Orgel- und Klavier in der Musik des 16. Jahrhunderts*, Leipzig, 1910.

———. "Thomas Mace and His Tattle de Moy," *A Birthday Offering to Carl Engel*, New York, 1943, 128.

Kiwi, E. "Die Triosonate von ihren Anfängen bis zu Haydn," *Zeitschrift für Hausmusik* 3 (1934), 37.

Klotz, H. *Über die Orgelkunst der Gotik, Renaissance und Barock*, 1934.

Köchel, L. v. *J. J. Fux*, Vienna, 1872.

Köhler, W. E. *Beiträge zur Geschichte und Literatur der Viola d'amore*, Diss. Berlin, 1937.

Koletschka, K. "Esaias Reussner Vater und Sohn und ihre Choralbearbeitungen für Laute," *Festschrift Koczirz*, 1930.

Krabbe, W. "Zur Frage der Parodien in Rists 'Galathea,'" *Festschrift Kretzschmar*, 1918.

———. "Das Liederbuch des Johann Heck (1679)," *AMW* IV, 420.

Kreidler, W. *H. Schütz und der stile concitato von Monteverdi*, 1934.

Kretzschmar, H. "Das 1. Jahrhundert der deutschen Oper," *SIMG* III, 270.

———. "Die venetianische Oper und die Werke Cavallis und Cestis," *VfM* VIII (1892), 1.

———. "Monteverdis Incoronazione di Poppea," *VfM* X (1894), 483.

———. "Beiträge zur Geschichte der venetianischen Oper," *JMP* 1907, 71; 1910, 61.

———. "Das Notenbuch der Zeumerin," *JMP* 1909, 57.

———. "Allgemeines und Besonderes zur Affektenlehre," *JMP* 1911.

———. *Geschichte des neueren deutschen Liedes*, Leipzig, 1911.

———. *Geschichte der Oper*, 1919.

———. *Bachkolleg*, Leipzig, 1922.

———. *Führer durch den Konzertsaal*, 6th ed. 1921; see also Engel, Mersmann, Noack, Schnoor.

Kroyer, Th. "A cappella oder conserto?" *Festschrift Kretzschmar*, 1918.

———. "Zwischen Renaissance und Barock," *JMP*, 1927.

———. "Die barocke Anabasis," *ZMW*, 1933.

Krüger, L. *Die Hamburgische Musikorganisation im 17. Jahrhundert*, 1933.

Krüger, W. "Das Concerto grosso Joh. S. Bachs," *Bach Jahrbuch*, 1932, 1.

———. *Das Concerto grosso in Deutschland*, Diss. Berlin, 1932.

Kuhn, M. "Die Verzierungskunst in der Gesangsmusik," *Beihefte IMG*, I, 7, Leipzig, 1902.

Kunz, L. *Die Tonartenlehre des Pier Francesco Valentini*, (*Münsterische Beiträge zur Musikwissenschaft* 8), 1937.

Kurth, E. *Grundlagen des linearen Kontrapunkts*, 3rd ed. 1922.

Lacroix, P. *Ballets et Mascarades de Cour (1581–1651)*, Geneva, 1868–70.

La Laurencie, L. de. *Le Goût musical en France*, Paris, 1905.

———. "Un musicien Piémontais en France au XVIIIe siècle (Guignon)," *RMI* XVIII, 1911.

———. "Les pastorales en musique au XVIIe siècle en France," 4th Congress *IMG*, London, 1911, 139.

———. *Lully*, Paris, 1911.

———. "Un émule de Lully, Pierre Gautier de Marseille," *SIMG* XIII (1912), 39.

———. "André Campra," *L'Année musicale*, 1913.

———. "Un musicien dramatique du XVII. siècle français: Pierre Guedron," *RMI* XXIX, 1922.

———. "Le rôle de Leclair dans la musique instrumentale," *RM* IV, 1923.

———. *L'Ecole française de violon de Lully à Viotti*, 3 vls., 1922–24.

———. *Rameau (Les Musiciens Célèbres)*, 1926.

———. *Les Créateurs de l'Opéra français (Maîtres de la Musique)*, 1930.

———. *Les Luthistes (Les Musiciens Célèbres)*, Paris, 1928.

———. "Quelques luthistes français du XVIIe siècle," *RdM*, 8.

———. "L'Orfeo nell' inferni d'André Campra," *RdM*, 27.

———. "Un opéra inédit de M.-A. Charpentier, 'La descente d'Orphée aux enfers,'" *RdM*, 31.

———. "Les débuts de la musique de chambre en France," *RdM*, 49–52. (see also Lavignac, E.)

Lamson, R., Jr. "English Broadside Ballad tunes of the 16th and 17th centuries," *Papers Intern. Congress of Musicology*, New York, 1939 (1944), 112.

Landshoff, L. "Über das vielstimmige Accompagnement," *Festschrift Sandberger*, 1918.

Lang, P. H. *Music in Western Civilization*, New York, 1941.

———. "The Formation of the Lyric Stage," *A Birthday Offering to C[arl] E[ngel]*, New York, 1943, 143.

Lange, M. *Die Anfänge der Kantate*, Diss. Leipzig, 1938.

Langer, G. *Die Rhythmik der J. S. Bachschen Präludien und Fugen für die Orgel*, Diss. Leipzig, 1937.

Lawrence, W. J. "Music and Song in the Eighteenth Century Theater," *MQ* 2, 1916.

———. "Early Irish Ballad Opera," *MQ*, 1922.

———. "Foreign Singers and Musiciens at the Court of Charles II," *MQ* 1923, 217–25.

Leichtentritt, H. *R. Keiser in seinen Opern*, Diss. Berlin, 1906.

———. "Cl. Monteverdi als Madrigal-Komponist," *SIMG* XI, 255.

———. *Geschichte der Motette*, Leipzig, 1908.

———. *Händel*, Stuttgart, 1924.

———. "Handel's Harmonic Art," *MQ*, 1935.

Lesser, E. "Zur Scordatura der Streichinstrumente, mit besonderer Berücksichtigung der Viola d'amore," *AM* IV, 123, 148.

Levarie, S. *Fugue and Form*, 1941.

Liess, A. *Die Triosonaten von J. J. Fux*, Berlin, 1940.

Lightwood, J. T. *Methodist Music in the 18th Century*, 1927.

Lindner, E. O. *Die erste stehende deutsche Oper*, Berlin, 1855.

———. *Geschichte des deutschen Liedes*, 1871.

Lindsey, E. S. "The music of the Songs in Fletcher's Plays," *Studies in Philology* XXI, No. 2, 1924.

Litterscheid, R. *Zur Geschichte des basso ostinato*, Diss. Marburg, 1928.

Loewenberg, A. *Annals of Opera*, 1943.

Lorenz, A. *Alessandro Scarlattis Jugendopern*, 2 vls., Augsburg, 1927.

———. "Das Relativitätsprinzip in den musikalischen Formen," *Festschrift Adler*, 1930, 179.

———. "Homophone Grossrhythmik in Bach's Polyphonik," *Die Musik*, 22, 1929–30.

Lott, W. "Zur Geschichte der Passionskomposition von 1650 bis 1800," *AMW* III, 285.

Luciani, S. A. "Alla scoperta degli autografi di D. Scarlatti," *Archivi*, Rome, 1935. ser. 2, 2, 298–304.

Luedtke, H. "Bachs Choralvorspiele," *Bach Jahrbuch*, 1918, 1.

446 Bibliography

Mahrenholz, Ch. *Samuel Scheidt, sein Leben und sein Werk,* Leipzig, 1924.

Malipiero, G. F. *Cl. Monteverdi,* Milan, 1929.

Martin, B. *Untersuchungen zur Struktur der 'Kunst der Fuge,'* Diss. Cologne, 1941.

Martin, H. "La 'Camerata' du Comte Bardi et la musique florentine du XVIe siècle," *RdM* 42, 43, 44, 46, 47.

Martin, J. C. *Die Kirchenkantaten J. Kuhnaus,* 1928.

Masson, P. M. "Les Brunettes," *SIMG* XII (1911), 347.

――――. " 'Les Fêtes vénitiennes' de Campra (1710)," *RdM,* 43, 44.

――――. *L'Opéra de Rameau,* Paris, 1930 (2nd ed. 1932).

Maxton, W. *Johann Theile,* Diss. Tübingen, 1926.

――――. "Mitteilungen über eine vollständige Abendmusik Dietrich Buxtehudes," *ZMW* 10 (1928), 387.

Meissner, R. *Georg Ph. Telemanns Frankfurter Kirchen-Kantaten,* Diss. Frankfort, 1928.

Mellers, W. "The Clavecin Works of François Couperin," *ML* XXVII (1946), 233.

Menke, W. *History of the Trumpet of Bach and Handel,* 1934.

――――. *Das Vokalwerk Georg Philipp Telemanns. Überlieferung und Zeitfolge,* Kassel, 1942.

Mersmann, H. "Ein Weihnachtsspiel des Goerlitzer Gymnasiums von 1668," *AMW* I, 244.

――――. *Die Kammermusik* I, Leipzig, 1933 (*Führer durch den Konzertsaal,* Kretzschmar).

Meyer, E. H. *Die mehrstimmige Spielmusik des 17. Jahrhunderts in Nord- und Mitteleuropa,* Kassel, 1934.

――――. "Die Vorherrschaft der Instrumentalmusik im niederländischen Barock," *Tijdschrift VNM* 15, 1939.

――――. "Form in the Instrumental Music of the 17th century," *PMA* 65 (1939), 45.

――――. *English Chamber Music,* London, 1946.

Meyer, K. "Das Officium und seine Beziehungen zum Oratorium," *AMW* III, 1921.

Mies, P. "Die Chaconne (Passacaille) bei Händel," *Händel Jahrbuch* 1929, 13.

Mishkin, H. G. "The Italian Concerto before 1700," *BAMS* no. 7.

――――. "The Solo Violin Sonata of the Bologna School," *MQ* 29 (1943), 92.

Mitjana, R. C. *Monteverdi y los origines de la ópera italiana,* Málaga, 1911.

Mohr, E. *Die Allemande,* Diss. Basle, 1932.

Moser, A. "Johann Schop als Violinkomponist," *Festschrift Kretzschmar,* 1918.

――――. "Zur Frage der Ornamentik und ihrer Anwendung auf Corellis Op. 5," *ZMW* 1, 287.

――――. "Zur Genesis der Folies d'Espagne," *AMW,* I, 358.

——. "Die Violin-Skordatur," *AMW* I, 573.

——. *Geschichte des Violinspiels*, Berlin, 1923.

Moser, H. J. "Aus der Frühgeschichte der deutschen Generalbasspassion," *JMP*, 1920, 18.

——. "Die Zeitgrenzen des musikalischen Barock," *ZMW* 4, 253.

——. *Geschichte der deutschen Musik*, 3 vls., 5th ed. 1930.

——. *Der Junge Händel und seine Vorgänger in Halle*, 1929.

——. *Die mehrstimmige Vertonung des Evangeliums*, 1931–34.

——. "Eine Augsburger Liederschule im Mittelbarock," *Festschrift Kroyer*, 1933.

——. *Corydon* 1–2, 1933.

——. *J. S. Bach*, 1935 (2nd ed. 1943).

——. *Heinrich Schütz*, 1936.

——. "Daniel Speer," *AM* IX, 1937.

Müller, G. *Geschichte des deutschen Liedes*, München, 1925.

Müller, K. F. *Die Technik der Ausdrucksdarstellung in Monteverdis monodischen Frühwerken*, Berlin, 1931.

Müller-Blattau, J. *Die Kompositionslehre H. Schützens in der Fassung seines Schülers Chr. Bernhard*, Leipzig, 1926.

——. "Bach und Händel," *JMP* 1926, 45.

——. *H. Alberts 'Kürbishütte,'* 1932.

——. *Grundzüge einer Geschichte der Fuge*, 2nd ed. 1931.

——. *Händel (Die grossen Meister der Musik)*, 1933.

Nagel, W. *Geschichte der Musik in England*, 2 vls., 1894/97.

——. "Daniel Purcell," *MfM* 1898, 51.

Naldo, A. R. "Un Trattado inedito ignoto di F. M. Veracini," *RMI* XLII (1938), 617.

Naylor, E. W. "Three Musical Parson-Poets of the XVII century," *PMA* 54 (1928), 93.

Neemann, H. "Philipp Martin, ein vergessener Lautenist," *ZMW* 9, 545.

——. "Die Lautenhandschriften von S. L. Weiss," *ZMW* 10, 396.

——. "Die Lautenistenfamilie Weiss," *AMF* IV (1939), 157.

Nef, K. "Zur Geschichte der deutschen Instrumentalmusik in der 2. Hälfte des 17. Jahrhunderts," *Beihefte IMG* I, 5; Leipzig, 1902.

——. *Geschichte der Sinfonie und Suite*, Leipzig, 1921.

——. "Das Petrusoratorium von M. A. Charpentier und die Passion," *JMP* 1930, 24.

——. "Schweizerische Passionsmusiken," *Schweizerisches Jahrbuch für Musikwissenschaft*, V, 113.

Neisser, A. *Servio Tullio, eine Oper (1685) von Steffani*, Leipzig, 1902.

Nettl, P. "Ueber ein handschriftliches Sammelwerk von Gesängen italienischer Frühmonodie," *ZMW* 2, 83.

———. "Eine Sing- und Spielsuite von A. Brunelli," *AMW* II, 385.

———. "Die Wiener Tanzkomposition," *StzMW*, 8.

———. "Beiträge zur Geschichte des deutschen Singballets," *ZMW* 6, 608.

———. "Giovanni Battista Buonamente," *ZMW* 9, 528.

———. *Musikbarock in Böhmen und Mähren*, 1927.

———. "Eine Wiener Tänzehandschrift um 1650," *Festschrift Koczirz*, 1930.

———. *Das Wiener Lied im Zeitalter des Barock*, 1934.

———. "The Austrian Baroque Lied," *Journal of Renaissance and Baroque Music* I (1946), 101.

Neuhaus, M. "A. Draghi." *StzMW*, 1.

Neumann, W. *J. S. Bachs Chorfuge*, Diss. Leipzig, 1938.

Newton, R. "English Lute Music of the Golden Age," *PMA* 65 (1939), 63.

Niessen, W. "Das Liederbuch des Studenten Clodius," *VfM* VII, 579.

Noack, E. "Ein Beitrag zur Geschichte der älteren deutschen Suite," *AMW* II, 275.

Noack, F. *Chr. Graupners Kirchenmusiken*, Leipzig, 1916.

———. "W. C. Briegel als Liederkomponist," *ZMW* 1, 523.

———. "Johann Sebastian Bach und Christop Graupner: Mein Herze schwimmt im Blut," *AMW* II, 85.

———. "Die Musik zu der Molièreschen Komödie M. de Pourceaugnac von Lully," *Festschrift J. Wolf*, 1929, 139.

———. *Sinfonie und Suite*, 1932 (*Führer durch den Konzertsaal*, Kretzschmar, 7th ed.)

Norlind, T. "Zur Geschichte der Suite," *SIMG* VII (1906), 172.

Nowak, L. *Grundzüge einer Geschichte des basso ostinato*, 1932.

Nuelsen, J. L. *John Wesley und das deutsche Kirchenlied*, 1938.

Nuitter, Chr. and Thoinan, E. *Les origines de l'opéra français*, Paris, 1886.

Oberst, G. *Die englischen Orchester Suiten um 1600*, Wolfenbüttel, 1929.

Osthoff, H. *Adam Krieger*, 1929.

Otto, I. *Deutsche Musikanschauung im 17. Jahrhundert*, Diss. Berlin, 1937.

Ottzenn, K. *Telemann als Opernkomponist*, Diss. Berlin, 1902.

Pannain, G. *Le origini e lo sviluppo dell'arte pianistica in Italia*, Naples, 1917.

———. "Francesco Provenzale e la lirica del suo tempo," *RMI* XXXII, 1925 (see also Corte, A. della).

Paoli, D. de. *Claudio Monteverdi*, Milan, 1945.

Parry, H. *J. S. Bach: The Story of the Development of a Great Personality*, 1909 (1934).

———. "The Music of the 17th century," *OHM*, v. 3, 3rd ed. 1938.

Pasquetti, G. *L'Oratorio musicale in Italia*, Florence, 1906.

Payne, M. de Forest. *Melodic Index to the Works of J. S. Bach*, 1938.

Pedrell, F. "La festa d'Elche," *SIMG* II, 203.

————. "La Musique indigène dans le théâtre espagnol du XVII siècle," *SIMG* V, 46.

————."L'Eglogue 'Le forêt sans amour' de Lope de Vega et la musique du théâtre de Calderon," *SIMG* XI, 55.

Pereyra, M.-L. "La musique de la Tempête, par Pelham Humfrey," *RdM*, 7.

————. "Les livres de virginal de la bibliothèque du Conservatoire de Paris," *RdM*, 20, 21, 24, 28, 29, 37, 42, 45.

Pessl, Y. "Secular Patterns in Bach's Secular Keyboard Music," *PAMS*, 1941.

Petzoldt, R. *Die Kirchenkompositionen und weltliche Kantaten R. Keisers*, Diss. Berlin, 1934.

Pfau, S. *Die Violinmusik in Italien, 1600–50*, Diss. Berlin, 1931.

Piersig, F. *Die Einführung des Horns in die Kunstmusik*, Halle, 1927.

Pincherle, M. *Les Violinistes*, Paris, 1924.

————. *Corelli*, Paris, 1933.

Pirro, A. *L'Orgue de J. S. Bach*, 1897; Engl. transl. 1902 (*Bach the Organist*).

————. "Louis Marchand," *SIMG* VI (1905), 136.

————. *Bach*, Paris, 1906 (1924).

————. *Descartes et la Musique*, 1907.

————. *L'esthétique de Bach*, Paris, 1907.

————. *D. Buxtehude*, Paris, 1913.

————. *H. Schütz* (*Les Maîtres de la Musique*), Paris, 1913, (1924).

————. "Deux danses anciennes," *RdM*, 9.

————. *Les Clavecinistes* (*Les Musiciens Célèbres*), Paris, 1925 (see also Lavignac, E.).

Plamenac, D. "An Unknown Violin Tablature of the Early 17th Century," *PAMS*, 1941.

Poladian, S. *Handel as an Opera Composer*, Diss. Cornell, 1946 (typewritten).

Pougin, A. *Les vrais créateurs de l'opéra français*, Paris, 1881.

Pratella, F. B. "G. Carissimi ed i suoi oratori," *RMI* XXVII, 1920.

Preussner, E. "Die Methodik im Schulgesang der evangelischen Lateinschulen des 17. Jahrhunderts," *AMW* VI, 407.

Propper, L. *Der Ostinato als technisches und formbildendes Prinzip*, Diss. Berlin, 1926.

Prout, S. "Graun's 'Passion-Oratorio' and Handel's knowledge of it," *Monthly Mus. Record* XXIV, 97, 121.

Prüfer, A. *J. H. Schein*, Leipzig, 1895.

————. "J. H. Schein und das weltliche deutsche Lied des 17. Jahrhunderts," *Beihefte IMG*, II, 7, Leipzig, 1908.

————. "Scheins Cymbalum Sionium," *Festschrift Liliencron*, 1910, 176.

Prunières, H. "Lecerf de la Viéville et le classicisme musical," *SIMG* IX, 1908.

————. *Lully*, Paris, 1910.

——. "Notes sur les Origines de l'Ouverture française," *SIMG* XII (1911), 565.

——. "Jean de Cambefort," *Année musicale,* 1912.

——. *L'Opéra italien en France avant Lully,* Paris, 1913.

——. *Le ballet de cour en France avant Lully,* Paris, 1914.

——. "Notes bibliographiques sur les cantates de L. Rossi au Conservatoire de Naples," *ZIMG* XIV, 109.

——. "P. Lorenzani à la Cour de France," *RM,* 1922.

——. "Notes sur une partition faussement attribuée à Cavalli," *RMI* XXVII, 1920.

——. "Bénigne de Bacilly," *RdM,* 8.

——. "The Italian Cantata of the 17th century," *ML* VII.

——. *La vie et l'œuvre de C. Monteverdi,* Paris, 1924, (1931); Engl. transl. London, 1926.

——. *Cavalli et l'opéra vénitien,* Paris, 1931.

——. "A. Barberini," *Mélanges de Musicologie, La Laurencie,* 1933, 117.

——. *A New History of Music,* New York, 1943.

Pulver, J. *A Dictionary of Old English Music,* 1923.

——. "Music in England during the Commonwealth," *AM* VI, 1934.

Quervain, F. de *Der Chorstil H. Purcells,* Diss. Berne, 1935.

Quittard, H. "Orphée descendant aux enfers. Cantate de M.-A. Charpentier," *RM,* 1904.

——. "L'Air de Cour: Guesdron," *RM,* 1905.

——. *Henry du Mont,* 1906.

——. "Un musicien oublié: G. Bouzignac," *SIMG* VI, 356.

——. *Les Couperins,* Paris, 1913.

Rapp, E. *Beiträge zur Frühgeschichte des Violoncell-Konzerts,* Diss. Würzburg, 1934.

Rau, K. A. *Loreto Vittori,* Diss. Munich, 1913.

Raugel, F. *Les organistes,* Paris, 1923.

Rebling, E. *Die soziologischen Grundlagen der Stilwandlung der Musik in Deutschland um die Mitte des 18. Jahrhunderts,* 1935.

Redlich, H. F. *Das Problem des Stilwandels in Monteverdis Madrigalwerk,* Diss. Frankfort, 1931.

——. "Monteverdi's Religious Music," *ML* XXVII (1946), 208.

Reimann, M. *Untersuchungen zur Formgeschichte der französischen Klaviersuite,* Diss. Cologne, 1941.

Reitter, L. *Doppelchortechnik bei H. Schütz,* Diss. Zürich, 1937.

Reuter, F. *Die Beantwortung des Fugenthemas, dargestellt an den Themen von Bachs Wohltemp. Klavier,* 1929.

Reyer, P. *Les masques anglais,* Paris, 1909.

Ricci, V. "Un melodramma ignoto della prima metà del 600," *RMI* XXXII, 1925.

Richter, W. "Liebeskampf 1630 und Schaubühne 1670," *Palaestra* 78 (1910).

Rieber, K. Fr. L. *Die Entwicklung der deutschen geistlichen Solokantate im 17. Jahrhundert*, Diss. Freiburg, 1932.

Riemann, H. *Handbuch der Fugenkomposition*, 1890–94 (1914–21); Engl. transl. 1893, 3 vls. (includes *Well-Tempered Clavier* and *Art of the Fugue*).

———. "Die Triosonaten der Generalbassepoche," *Präludien und Studien*, v. 3, Leipzig, 1901.

———. "Zur Geschichte der deutschen Suite," *SIMG* VI (1905), 501.

———. "Der Basso ostinato und die Anfänge der Kantate," *SIMG* XIII, 531.

———. "Eine siebensätzige Tanzsuite von Monteverdi," *SIMG* XIV, 26.

———. "A. Steffani als Opernkomponist," *DTB* XII:2.

———. "Basso ostinato und Basso quasi ostinato," *Festschrift Liliencron*, 1910, 193.

———. *Geschichte der Musiktheorie*, 2nd ed. 1921.

———. *Handbuch der Musikgeschichte*, II:2. *Das Generalbasszeitalter*, 2nd ed. Leipzig, 1922.

Riemer, O. E. *Bodenschatz und sein Florilegium Portense*, Diss. Leipzig, 1928.

Rietsch, H. "Der Concentus von J. J. Fux," *StzMW*, 4.

———. "Bachs Kunst der Fuge," *Bach Jahrbuch*, 1926.

Rinaldi, M. *Antonio Vivaldi*, Milan, 1943.

Ripollès, V. *El Villancico i la cantata del segle XVIII a València; Inst. d'Estudis Catalans, Bibl. de Catalunya* XII, (1935).

Ritter, A. G. *Geschichte des Orgelspiels*, 1884 (for a revised edition see Frotscher).

Robbins, R. *Beiträge zur Geschichte des Kontrapunkts von Zarlino bis Schütz*, Diss. Berlin, 1938.

Robinson, P. *Handel and His Orbit*, London, 1908.

———. "Handel, or Urio, Stradella and Erba," *ML* XVI, 269.

———. "Handel up to 1720: A New Chronology," *ML* XX, 55.

Rokseth, Y. "Un Magnificat de Marc-Antoine Charpentier," *Journal of Renaissance and Baroque Music* I, 1946.

Rolandi, U. "Emilio de'Cavalieri, il Granduca Ferdinando e l' 'Inferigno,'" *RMI* XXXVI, 1929.

Rolland, R. *L'histoire de l'opéra en Europe avant Lully et Scarlatti*, Paris, 1895; new ed. 1931.

———. *Musiciens d'autrefois*, 1908, (1919); Engl. transl. 1915.

———. *Händel*, Paris, 1910; Engl. transl. 1916.

———. *Voyage musical au pays du passée*, Paris, 1920; Engl. transl. 1922.

———. (see also Lavignac E.)

Roncaglia, G. *La Rivoluzione Musicale Italiana*, Milan, 1928.

———. "Di insigni musicisti modenesi," *Atti e memorie della R. Deputazione di storia . . . modenesi*, Ser. VII, v. II. Modena, 1929.

———. "Il Tirinto di B. Pasquini," *La Rassegna musicale*, 1931.

———. *Il melodioso settecento italiano*, Milan, 1935.

———. "Le composizioni strumentali di A. Stradella," *RMI* XLIV (1940), 81, 337.

———. "Le composizioni vocali di Alessandro Stradella," *RMI* XLV (1941); XLVI (1942).

Roncalio, A. C. "Unaccompanied violin music before Bach," *Journal of Musicology*, I, 1940.

Ronga, L. G. *Frescobaldi, organista Vaticano*, Turin, 1930.

Rosenthal, K. A. "Über Sonatenformen in den Instrumentalwerken Joh. Seb. Bachs," *Bach Jahrbuch*, 1926, 68.

Rumohr, E. V. *Der Nürnbergische Tasteninstrumentstil im 17. Jahrhundert*, Diss. Münster, 1938.

Sachs, C. "Barockmusik," *JMP*, 1919, 7.

———. *World History of the Dance*, New York 1937 (the German edition of 1932 has a better bibliography).

———. *The History of Musical Instruments*, New York, 1940.

———. *The Commonwealth of Art*, New York, 1946.

Sandberger, A. "Zur Geschichte der Oper in Nürnberg," *AMW*, I, 85.

———. "Zur venezianischen Oper," *JMP*, 1924, 61; 1925, 53.

Sander, H. A. "Beiträge zur Geschichte der Barockmesse," *Kirchenmusikalisches Jahrbuch*, 1933, 77.

———. "Ein Orgelbuch der Breslauer Magdalenen-Kirche aus dem 17. Jahrhundert," *Festschrift Max Schneider*, 1935.

Sawyer, F. H. "The Music in 'Atlanta Fugiens,'" in John Read: *Prelude to Chemistry*, New York, 1937, 281–9.

Schaefer-Schmuck, K. G. P. *Telemann als Klavierkomponist*, Diss. Kiel, 1934.

Scheide, A. *Zur Geschichte des Choralvorspiels*, 1930.

Schenck, E. "Über Begriff und Wesen des musikalischen Barock," *ZMW* 17.

———. "Johann Theiles 'Harmonischer Baum,'" *Festschrift Seiffert*, 1938.

Schering, A. "Zur Bachforschung," *SIMG* IV, 234; V, 565.

———. *Geschichte des Instrumental-Konzerts*, Leipzig, 1905, 2nd ed. 1927.

———. "Zur instrumentalen Verzierungskunst im 18. Jahrhundert," *SIMG* VII (1906), 365.

———. "Die Lehre von den musikalischen Figuren," *Kirchenmusikalisches Jahrbuch* 21, (1908), 106.

———. "Zur Geschichte der Solosonate in der ersten Hälfte des 17. Jahrhunderts," *Festschrift Riemann*, 1909, 309.

———. "Zur Geschichte des begleiteten Sologesanges im 16. Jahrhundert," *ZIMG* XIII, 190.

———. *Geschichte des Oratoriums* (*Kleine Handbücher der Musikgeschichte*, 3), Leipzig, 1911.

———. "Die Kantaten der Thomas-Kantoren vor Bach," *Bach Jahrbuch,* 1912.

———. "Zur Metrik der Psalmen von Schütz," *Festschrift Kretzschmar,* 1918.

———. "Über Bachs Parodieverfahren," *Bach Jahrbuch,* 1921, 49.

———. "Geschichtliches zur 'ars inveniendi' in der Musik," *JMP* 1925, 25.

———. "Historische und nationale Klangstile," *JMP* 1927.

———. "Bach und das Symbol," *Bach Jahrbuch,* 1928, 119.

———. "Händel und der protestantische Choral," *Händel Jahrbuch,* 1928, 27.

———. "Musikalische Analyse und Wertidee," *JMP,* 1929.

———. *Aufführungspraxis alter Musik,* 1931.

———. *J. S. Bachs Leipziger Kirchenmusik,* 1936.

———. *Das Symbol in der Musik,* Leipzig, 1941.

———. *Über Kantaten J. S. Bachs,* Leipzig, 1942.

Schiedermayr, L. "Die Anfänge der Münchener Oper," *SIMG* V, 442.

———. "Zur Geschichte der früh-deutschen Oper," *JMP* 1910, 29.

Schild, E. *Geschichte der protestantischen Messkomposition im 17. und 18. Jahrhundert,* Diss. Giessen, 1934.

Schilling, H. *T. Eniccelius, F. Meister, N. Hanf, ein Beitrag zur Geschichte der evangelischen Frühkantate in Schleswig-Holstein,* Diss. Kiel, 1934.

Schlossberg, A. *Die italienische Sonate für mehrere Instrumente im 17. Jahrhundert,* Diss. Heidelberg, 1932.

Schmidt, G. F. "Die älteste deutsche Oper in Leipzig," *Festschrift Sandberger,* 1918.

———. "Zur Geschichte der frühdeutschen Oper," *ZMW* 5; 6.

———. *Die frühdeutsche Oper und die musikdramatische Kunst G. K. Schürmanns,* 2 vls. 1933–34.

———. "Joh. W. Franck's Singspiel 'Die drey Töchter Cecrops,'" *AMF* IV (1939), 257.

Schmitz, A. "Psalterium harmonicum. Ein Kölner Jesuitengesangbuch," *ZMW* 4, 18.

———. "Monodien der Kölner Jesuiten," *ZMW* 4, 266.

Schmitz, E. "Zur Geschichte des italienischen Kontinuomadrigals im 17. Jahrhundert," *SIMG* XI, 509.

———. "Zur musikgeschichtlichen Bedeutung der Harsdörferschen Frauenzimmergesprächsspiele," *Festschrift Liliencron,* 1910, 254.

———. "Zur Frühgeschichte der lyrischen Monodie Italiens im 17. Jahrhundert," *JMP* 1911, 35.

———. *Geschichte der Kantate und des geistlichen Konzertes,* (1. *Geschichte der weltlichen Solokantate*), Leipzig, 1914.

———. "Zur Geschichte des italienischen Kammerduetts im 17. Jahrhundert," *JMP* 1916, 43.

Schneider, C. "Biber als Opernkomponist," *AMW* VIII, 281.

Schneider, M. "Der Generalbass J. S. Bachs," *JMP* 1914/15, 27.

———. *Die Anfänge des Basso continuo und seiner Bezifferung*, Leipzig, 1918.

———. "Die Besetzung der vielstimmigen Musik des 17. und 18. Jahrhunderts," *AMW* I, 205.

———. "Zum Weihnachtsoratorium von H. Schütz," *Festschrift Kroyer*, 1933.

Schnoor, H. *Oratorien und weltliche Chorwerke (Führer durch den Konzertsaal,* Kretzschmar), Leipzig, 1939.

Scholes, P. *The Puritans and Music*, London, 1934.

Scholz, H. *S. Kusser*, Leipzig, 1911.

Schrade, L. "Ein Beitrag zur Geschichte der Toccata," *ZMW* 8, 610.

———. " 'Choro et Organo' di B. Bottazzi," *RMI* XXXVI, 1929.

———. "Studien zum Alexanderfest," *Händel Jahrbuch*, 1932.

———. "Bach: The Conflict between the Sacred and the Secular," *Journal of the History of Ideas* VII (1946), 151.

Schreiber, I. *Dichtung und Musik der deutschen Opernarien 1680–1700*, 1935.

Schrijver, K. de "Zuidnederlandsche Muziek in de Baroktijd," *Vlaamsch Jaarboek vor Muziekgeschiedenis* IV, 1942.

Schünemann, G. *Geschichte des Dirigierens*, 1913.

Schuh, W. *Formprobleme bei H. Schütz*, Leipzig, 1928.

Schultz, W. E. *Gay's Beggar's Opera*, New Haven, 1923.

Schulz, W. *Studien über das deutsche, protestantische monodische Kirchenlied des 17. Jahrhunderts*, Diss. Breslau, 1934.

Schulze, W. *Die Quellen der Hamburger Oper (1678–1738)*, Oldenburg, 1938.

Schwartz, E. P. *Die Fugenbeantwortung vor Bach*, Diss. Vienna, 1932.

Schwartz, R. "Das erste deutsche Oratorium," *JMP*, 1898.

Schweitzer, A. *J. S. Bach*, 1905; Engl. transl. 1911 (1923), new ed. 1935.

Seidler, K. *Untersuchungen über Biographie und Klavierstil J. J. Frobergers*, 1930.

Seiffert, M. "Zu Händels Klavierwerken," *SIMG* I, 131.

———. "Weckmanns Collegium musicum," *SIMG* II, 76.

———. "F. J. Habermann," *Kirchenmusikalisches Jahrbuch*, 1903.

———. "Pachelbels Musikalische Sterbensgedanken," *SIMG* V, 476.

———. "Die Verzierung der Sologesänge im Messias," *SIMG* VIII, 581.

———. "J. P. Sweelinck und seine direkten deutschen Schüler," *VfM* VII.

———. "Händels deutsche Gesänge," *Festschrift Liliencron*, 1910, 297.

———. "G. Ph. Telemanns Musique de Table als Quelle für Händel," *Bulletin Union Musicologique* VI, 1925; also *Beihefte* II, *DDT*.

Seiffert, M., and Weitzmann, K. F. *Geschichte der Klaviermusik*, 1899.

Serauky, W. *Die musikalische Nachahmungsaesthetik 1700–1850*, 1929.

———. "Werckmeister als Musiktheoretiker," *Festschrift Max Schneider*, 1935.

Shaw, H. W. "John Blow's Anthems," *ML* XIX, 429.

———. "The Secular Music of John Blow," *PMA* 63 (1936–37), 1.

———. "Blow's Use of the Ground Bass," *MQ* 1938.

Shedlock, J. S. *The Pianoforte Sonata*, London, 1895.

———. "Handel and Habermann," *Musical Times*, 1904, 805.

———. "The Harpsichord Music of A. Scarlatti," *SIMG* VI (1905), 160, 418.

Shirlaw, M. *The Theory of Harmony*, London, 1917.

Sigtenhorst Meyer, B. van den *Jan P. Sweelinck en zijn instrumentale muziek*, The Hague, 1934.

Silin, Ch. I. *Benserade and his Ballets de Cour*, Baltimore, 1940.

Sirp, H. "Die Thematik der Kirchenkantaten J. S. Bachs in ihren Beziehungen zum protestantischen Kirchenlied," *Bach Jahrbuch* 1931, 1, and 1932, 51.

Sittard, J. "S. Capricornus contra P. F. Böddecker," *SIMG* III, 87.

Sitwell, S. *A Background for D. Scarlatti*, London, 1935.

Sleeper, H. J. "John Jenkins and the English Fantasia-Suite," *BAMS* 4, 34.

Smend, F. "Die Johannes-Passion von Bach," *Bach Jahrbuch*, 1926, 105.

———. "Bachs Matthäus-Passion," *Bach Jahrbuch*, 1928, 1.

———. "Die Tonartenordnung in Bachs Matthaeus-Passion," *ZMW* 12, 336.

———. "Bachs Kanonwerk über 'Vom Himmel hoch da komm ich her,' " *Bach Jahrbuch*, 1933, 1.

Smijers, A. (ed.) *Algemeene Muziekgeschiedenis*, Utrecht, 1938.

Smith, L. *Music of the Seventeenth and Eighteenth Centuries*, Toronto, 1931.

Solerti, A. "Laura Guidiccioni Lucchesini ed Emilio de'Cavalieri. I primi tentativi del melodramma," *RMI* IX, 1902.

———. *Le origini del melodramma*, Turin, 1903.

———. *Gli Albori del melodramma*, 3 vls., Milan, 1905.

Sonneck, O. G. "Italienische Opernlibretti des 17. Jahrhunderts," *SIMG* XIII.

———. "Dafne the first opera," *SIMG* XV, 102.

Sostegni, A. *L'opera e il tempo di G. Frescobaldi*, 1929.

Souchay, M.-A. "Das Thema in der Fuge Bachs," *Bach Jahrbuch* 1927, 1; and 1930, 1.

Spitta, F. *Die Passionen von Heinrich Schütz*, 1886.

———. "Die Passionen von Schütz und ihre Wiederbelebung," *JMP*, 1906, 15.

———. *Heinrich Schütz, ein Meister der Musica sacra*, 1925.

Spitta, Ph. *J. S. Bach*, Leipzig, 1873–1880; Engl. transl. 1899.

———. "Sperontes 'Singende Muse an der Pleisse,' " *VfM* I, 35, 350.

———. "Die Anfänge madrigalischer Dichtung in Deutschland," *Musikgeschichtliche Aufsätze*, Berlin, 1894.

Spitz, Ch. " 'Ottone' von Händel und 'Teofane' von Lotti," *Festschrift Sandberger*, 1918, 265.

———. *A. Lotti . . . als Opernkomponist*, Diss. Munich, 1918.

Springer, H. "Sizilianische Volksmusik in Settecentoüberlieferung," *Festschrift Kretzschmar*, 1918.

Squire, W. B. "Purcell's Music for the Funeral of Mary II," *SIMG* IV, 225.

———. "Purcell's Dramatic Music," *SIMG* V, 489.

———. "Purcell as Theorist," *SIMG* VI, 521.

———. "An Index of Tunes in the Ballad Operas," *MA* 1910.

———. "The Music of Shadwell's 'Tempest,'" *MQ* 1921, 565.

Stahl, W. *Dietrich Buxtehude*, Kassel, 1937.

Stege, F. "Constantin Christian Dedekind," *ZMW* 8, 476.

Steglich, R. "Die Händel-Opern-Festspiele in Göttingen," *ZMW* 3, 615.

———. "Händels Oper Rodelinde und ihre neue Göttinger Bühnenfassung," *ZMW* 3, 518.

———. *J. S. Bach (Die grossen Meister der Musik)*, 1935.

Stein, F. "Ein unbekannter Evangelienjahrgang von Augustin Pfleger," *Festschrift Max Schneider*, 1935.

Steinecke, W. *Die Parodie in der Musik*, 1934.

Stephan, H. "Der modulatorische Aufbau in Bachs Gesangswerken. Ein Beitrag zur Stilgeschichte des Barock," *Bach Jahrbuch* 1934, 63.

Storz, W. *Der Aufbau der Tänze in den Opern und Ballets Lullys*, Göttingen, 1928.

Streatfeild, R. A. *Handel*, London, 1909.

Striffling, L. *Esquisse d'une histoire du goût musical en France au XVIIIe siècle*, Paris, 1912.

Striggio, A. *L'Orfeo di Monteverdi*, Bologna, 1928.

Strom, K. *Beiträge zur Entwicklungsgeschichte des Marsches in der Kunstmusik*, 1926.

Subirá, J. *Pergolesi y la Serva Padrona*, 1922.

———. *La Musica en la Casa de Alba*, 1927.

———. *La Participación Musical en el Antiguo Teatro Lírico Español*, 1930.

———. *El Operista Español J. Hidalgo*, 1934.

Taylor, S. *The Indebtedness of Handel to Works of Other Composers*, Cambridge, 1906.

Terry, C. S. "The Spurious Bach 'Lucas Passion,'" *ML* XIV, 207.

———. *Bach, a Biography*, London, 1928; 2nd ed. 1933.

———. *Bach: The Historical Approach*, 1930.

———. *Bach's Orchestra*, 1932.

———. *The Music of Bach*, 1933.

Tessier, A. "Les deux styles de Monteverdi," *RM* III, 1922.

———. "Les Messes d'orgue de Couperin," *RM* VI, 1925.

———. *Couperin (Les Musiciens Célèbres)*, 1926.

———. "Une Pièce inédite de Froberger," *Festschrift Adler*, 1930, 47.

Thiele, E. *Die Chorfugen J. S. Bachs*, Diss. Berne, 1936.

Thorp, W. *Songs from the Restoration Theater*, 1934.

Tiersot, J. "Les chœurs d'Esther et d'Athalie de Moreau," *RM*, 1903.

———. *La musique dans la comédie de Molière*, 1921.

——. *Les Couperins* (*Les Maîtres de la Musique*), 1926.

——. "Les Nations, Sonates en trio de François Couperin," *RdM,* 2.

Toni, A. "Sul basso continuo e l'interpretazione della musica antica," *RMI* XXVI, 1919.

Torchi, L. *La musica istrumentale,* 1901; also *RMI* I, IV, V, VI.

——. "Canzoni ed arie italiane ad una voce nel secolo XVII," *RMI* I, 1894.

——. "L'accompagnamento degli istromenti nei melodrammi italiani," *RMI* I, 1894.

Torrefranca, F. "Poeti minori del clavicembalo," *RMI* XVII, 1910.

Tovey, D. F. *A Companion to the Art of Fugue,* 1931.

——. *Essays in Musical Analysis,* London, 1935 ff.

——. *Musical Articles from the Encyclopaedia Britannica,* 1944.

Treiber, F. "Die thüringisch-sächsische Kirchenkantate z. Zt. des jungen Bach (1700–1723)," *AMF* II (1937), 129.

Uldall, H. "Beiträge zur Frühgeschichte des Klavierkonzerts," *ZMW* 10, 139.

Ulrich, B. "Die Pythagorischen Schmidsfünklein," *SIMG* IX, 75.

Ulrich, E. *Studien zur deutschen Generalbasspraxis in der ersten Hälfte des 18. Jahrhunderts,* Kassel, 1932.

Unger, H. J. *Die Beziehungen zwischen Musik und Rhetorik im 16.–18. Jahrhundert,* Würzburg, 1941.

Ursprung, O. "Vier Studien zur Geschichte des deutschen Liedes. IV. Der Weg von den Gelegenheitsgesängen und dem Chorlied über die Frühmonodisten zum neueren deutschen Lied," *AMW* VI, 262.

——. *Die katholische Kirchenmusik* (*Handbuch der Musikwissenschaft*), 1931.

——. "Celos aun del aire matan—die älteste erhaltene spanische Oper," *Festschrift Schering,* 1937.

Valabrega, C. *D. Scarlatti, il suo secolo, la sua opera,* Modena, 1937.

Valentin, E. *Die Entwicklung der Toccata im 17. und 18. Jahrhundert,* 1930.

Vatielli, F. *La Lyra Barberina di G. B. Doni,* Pesaro, 1908.

——. "Il Corelli e i maestri bolognesi," *RMI* XXIII, 1916.

——. "Les Origines de l'art de violoncelle," *RM* IV, 1923.

——. *Arte e vita musicale a Bologna,* 1927.

——. "La scuola musicale bolognese," *Strenna storica bolognese,* 1928.

——. "L'oratorio a Bologna," *Note d'archivio per la storia musicale,* 1938.

——. "L'Ultimo liutista," *RMI* XLII, 469.

——. "Primizie del Sinfonismo," *RMI* XLVII (1943), 117.

Vega, C. "La Musica de un codice colonial des siglo XVII," *Inst. de Literatura Argentina,* sec. Folklore, Ser. I, 2, No. 1, Buenos Aires, 1931.

Veinus, A. *The Concerto,* New York, 1945.

Velten, R. *Das ältere deutsche Gesellschaftslied unter dem Einfluss der italienischen Musik,* Heidelberg, 1914.

Vetter, W. *Das frühdeutsche Lied*, 2 vls., 1928.

Vogel, E. "Cl. Monteverdi," *VfM* III, 315.

——. "M. da Gagliano," *VfM* V, 396.

——. *Bibliothek der gedruckten weltlichen Vokalmusik Italiens 1500–1700*, Berlin, 1892. New edition (in progress) by Einstein in *Notes, Music Library Association*.

Vogel, H. "Zur Geschichte des Oratoriums in Wien," *StzMW*, 14.

Vogl, E. *Die Oratorientechnik Carissimis*, Diss. Prague, 1928.

Vogt, W. *Die Messe in der Schweiz im 17. Jahrhundert*, Diss. Basle, 1937.

Volkmann, H. *Emanuele d'Astorga*, 2 vls., 1911; 1919.

Völsing, E. *Händel's englische Kirchenmusik*, Diss. Giessen, 1940.

Wagner, P. *Geschichte der Messe*, Leipzig, 1913.

——. "Die konzertierende Messe in Bologna," *Festschrift Kretzschmar*, 1918.

Waldersee, P. Graf "Antonio Vivaldis Violinconcerte unter besonderer Berücksichtigung der von Johann Seb. Bach bearbeiteten," *VfM* I, 356.

Walker, E. "An Oxford Book of Fancies," *MA* III.

——. *A history of music in England*, 2nd ed. 1924.

Wallner, B. "J. Kuen und die Münchener Monodisten," *ZMW* 2, 445.

Walther, L. *Die konstruktive und thematische Ostinatotechnik in den Chaconne- und Arienformen des 17. und 18. Jahrhunderts*, 1940.

Warlock, P. *The English Ayre*, London, 1926.

Wasielewski, J. W. v. *Die Violine im 17. Jahrhundert*, Bonn, 1874.

——. "Die Collection Philidor," *VfM* I, 531; (see Fellowes).

——. "Ein französischer Musikbericht aus der ersten Hälfte des 17. Jahrhunderts (André Maugars)," *MfM* 10, 1878.

Weitzmann, C. F. *A History of Pianoforte Playing and Pianoforte-Literature*, New York, 1897; (see Seiffert).

Wellesz, E. "Die Ballet-Suiten von J. H. und A. A. Schmelzer," *Sitzungsberichte, Akademie der Wissenschaften*, Phil.-hist. Kl., Vienna, 1914.

——. "Cavalli und der Stil der venezianischen Oper 1640–1660," *StzMW*, 1.

——. "Die Opern und Oratorien in Wien 1660–1708," *StzMW*, 6.

——. *Der Beginn des musikalischen Barocks und die Anfänge der Oper in Wien*, 1922.

——. "Renaissance und Barock, *ZMW* 11, 37.

Welsford, E. *The Court Masque*, Cambridge, 1927.

Werker, W. *Bachstudien*, 2 vls. 1922–23.

Werner, A. "Samuel und Gottfried Scheidt," *SIMG* I, 401.

——. *Vier Jahrhunderte im Dienste der Kirchenmusik. Geschichte des Amtes und Standes der evangelischen Kantoren, Organisten und Stadtpfeifer seit der Reformation*, Leipzig, 1932.

Wesely, W. *Die Entwicklung der Fuge bis Bach*, Diss. Prague, 1928.

West, J. E. "Old English Organ Music," *SIMG* XII (1911), 213.

Westrup, J. A. "The Originality of Monteverdi," *PMA*, 1933–34.

———. "Monteverdi and the Orchestra," *ML XXI*, 230.

———. *Purcell*, London, 1937.

———. "Monteverdi's Lamento d'Arianna," *Music Review* I, 144.

———. "Amateurs in 17th-century England," *Monthly Musical Record*, LXIX, 1939.

———. "Foreign Musicians in Stuart England," *MQ* 27 (1941), 70.

———. "Domestic Music under the Stuarts," *PMA* 68 (1942), 19.

Whittaker, W. G. "Some Observations on Purcell's Harmony," *Musical Times*, Oct. 1934.

———. "A Lost Bach Magnificat," *ML XXI*, 312.

Wiel, T. *I Codici musicali Contariani del sec. XVII nella R. Bibl. di S. Marco*, Venice, 1888.

Wilson, S. "The Recitatives of the St. Matthew Passion," *ML XVI*.

Winter, C. *R. Giovanelli, Nachfolger Palestrinas*, Munich, 1935.

Winterfeld, K. v. *Gabrieli und sein Zeitalter*, 3 vls. Berlin, 1834.

———. *Zur Geschichte heiliger Tonkunst*, 2 vls. Leipzig, 1850; 1852.

Wintersgill, H. A. "Handel's Two-Length Bar," *ML XVII*.

Wittwer, M. *Die Musikpflege im Jesuitenorden*, Greifswald, 1936.

Wójcikówna, B. "Johann Fischer von Augsburg (1646–1721) als Suitenkomponist," *ZMW* 5, 129.

———. "Un disciple de Jean-Baptiste de Lully: Johann Fischer," *RdM*, 32.

Wolff, H. C. *Die Venezianische Oper in der zweiten Hälfte des 17. Jahrhunderts*, 1937.

Wood, A. *Life and Times*; ed. by Clark, Oxford, 1891.

Wotquenne, A. *Etude bibliographique sur Luigi Rossi*, Brussels, 1909.

Wurzbach, W. "Eine unbekannte Ausgabe und eine unbekannte Aufführung von Calderons 'El secreto a voces,'" *Homenaje a Bonilla y San Martin*, Madrid, I, (1927), 181.

Zander, E.,—Steglich, R. "Der Schlusschor von Händels 'Acis und Galathea,' Ergänzung und Analyse," *Händel Jahrbuch*, 1930, 145.

Zelle, F. *Beiträge zur Geschichte der ältesten deutschen Oper (Franck, Theile, Strungk, Förtsch)*, 1889–93.

Zulauf, M. *Die Harmonik J. S. Bachs*, Berne, 1927.

———. "Die Musica figuralis des Kantors Niklaus Zerleder," *Schweizerisches Jahrbuch für Musikwissenschaft*, IV, 57.

LIST OF EDITIONS

(This is a selective list. For fuller quotations and additional items see the bibliographies of Eitner (MfM 1871); Hofmeister; Altmann; Lott (Verzeichnis der Neudrucke 1936–   ); McColvin-Reeves (Music Libraries, 1937–38); Heyer (Check-List, 1944); Bukofzer (Proc. MTNA 1946); and, especially, *Acta Musicologica, Novae editiones.*)

1. GENERAL ANTHOLOGIES

della Corte: *Scelta di Musiche,* 1928
————: *Antologia della storia della musica,* 2 vls., 2nd ed., 1933/40; 4th ed., in one v., 1945
Davison-Apel: HAM
Einstein: *A Short History of Music* (Appendix of Examples), 1938; [Beispielsammlung, 1930]
Riemann: *Musikgeschichte in Beispielen,* 3rd ed., 1925
Schering: GMB
Wolf: *Music of Earlier Times (Sing- und Spielmusik),* Broude

2. HISTORICAL COLLECTIONS

Antiqua (Schott)
Archives des maîtres de l'orgue (Guilmant)
Cathedral Music (Boyce)
Chrysander D
COF
Collegium Musicum (Riemann)
Concerts spirituels, Schola Cantorum (Ch. Bordes)
CW
DDT
Denkmäler altpolnischer Tonkunst (Chybinski)
DTB
DTOe
Eitner PAM
EL
ER
Harmonia Sacra (Page, repr. by Rimbault)

Hispaniae Schola Musica Sacra (Pedrell)
ICMI
ICMIB
IM
Institut d'Estudis Catalans, Bibl. de Catalunya, Publicacions
Lira Sacro-Hispana (Eslava)
Mestres de L'Escolania de Montserrat (Pujol)
Monumenta Musicae Belgicae
Musikalische Formen in historischen Reihen (Martens)
Musikalische Werke schweizerischer Komponisten (Nef)
Nagels Musikarchiv
The Old English Edition (Arkwright)
Organum (Seiffert)
Perlen alter Kammermusik (Schering)
A Polyfonia Classica Portuguesa (dos Santos, 1938)
Praeclassica
Publications, Société Française de Musicologie
SCMA
Torchi AM
Trésor des Pianistes (Farrenc)
Veröffentlichungen, Musikbibl. Paul Hirsch
VNM

3. SMALLER COLLECTIONS AND PERFORMING EDITIONS

A. VOCAL MUSIC

Ameln-Mahrenholz-Thomas: *Handbuch der deutschen evangelischen Kirchen-musik,* 1932 ff.
Aroca: *Cancionero de Sablonara*
Bal y Gay: *Trienta canciones de Lope de Vega,* 1935
Benvenuti: *35 Arie di vari autori del sec. XVII,* Ricordi
Dolmetsch: *English Songs and Dialogues*
Expert: *Airs français des XVIe et XVIIe siècles*
————: *Répertoire de musique religieuse*
Fellowes: *Songs and Lyrics from the plays of Beaumont and Fletcher,* 1928
Gevaert: *Les Gloires de l'Italie,* 2 vls.
Landshoff: *Alte Meister des Bel Canto,* 1927
Moser: *Alte Meister des deutschen Liedes,* 1931
Ouseley: *Cathedral Services by English Masters*
Parisotti: *Anthology of Italian Song* (*Arie antiche,* 3 vls.)
————: *Piccolo Album*
Ricci: *Antiche gemme italiane,* Ricordi

Riemann: *Kantatenfrühling*
Torchi: *Eleganti canzoni ed arie italiane*
Vatielli: *Antiche cantate spirituali*, Capra
——: *Antiche cantate d'amore*, Bologna
Warlock-Wilson: *English Ayres, Elizabethan and Jacobean*, Oxf. Univ. Press
Wolff: *Deutsche Barockarien aus Opern Hamburger Meister*, 1944
Zanon: *Raccolta di 24 Arie di vari autori del sec. XVII*
——: *Piccola Antologia musicale italiana*

B. INSTRUMENTAL ENSEMBLE MUSIC

——: *Das Musikkränzlein*
Alard: *Les Maîtres classiques du violon*
Beck: *Nine fantasias in four parts*, N.Y. Public Library, 1938
Beckmann: *Das Violinspiel in Deutschland, Beispielsammlung*, Simrock, 1921
Cartier: *L'Art de violon*, 1798
David: *Hohe Schule des Violinspiels*, 2 vls.
——: *Vorstudien zur Hohen Schule*, 2 vls.
Debroux: *L'Ecole du violon aux 17e et 18e siècles*, Lemoine
Ecorcheville: *Vingt suites d'orchestre du XVIIe siècle*, 1906
Jensen: *Klassische Violinmusik*
Komma: *Gruppenkonzerte der Bachzeit*, ER 11
Mangeot: *Three Fancies for String Quartet*, 1936
Meyer: *Spielmusik des Barock, Englische Fantasien*, 1935
Moffat: *Meisterauswahl der Violoncello Literatur*, Simrock
——: *Klassische Violinsonaten*
——: *Trio-Meisterschule*
——: *Kammersonaten des 17. und 18. Jahrhunderts*
Moser: *Haus- und Kammermusik aus dem XVI–XVIII Jahrhundert*, 1930
Riemann: *Old Chamber Music* [OCM] Augener
Schering: *Alte Meister des Violinspiels*, Simrock
Vatielli: *Antichi maestri bolognesi*
Wasielewski: *Instrumentalsätze vom Ende des 16. bis zum Ende des 17. Jahrhunderts*, 1905
Wier: *Chamber Suites and Concerti Grossi*

C. KEYBOARD AND LUTE MUSIC

——. *Les clavecinistes français*, Durand
Apel: *Concord Classics for the Piano*
——: *Musik aus früher Zeit*, Schott
Boghen: *Antichi maestri italiani*
Bonnet: *Historical Organ Recitals*, G. Schirmer
Bruger: *Alte Lautenkunst aus 3 Jahrhunderten*, Simrock

Dietrich: *Elf Orgelchoräle des 17. Jahrhunderts*, 1932
Expert: *Les maîtres du clavecin*
Fischer-Oberdorffer: *Deutsche Klaviermusik des 17. und 18. Jahrhunderts*
Frotscher: *Orgelchoräle um J. S. Bach*, ER 9
Fuller-Maitland: *Contemporaries of Purcell*, 1921
Gargiulo and Rosati: *Raccolta di composizioni di clavicembalisti*, 1938
Hennefield: *Masterpieces of Organ Music*, 1945
Herrmann: *Lehrmeister und Schüler J. S. Bachs*
Kaller: *Liber Organi*, Schott
Kastner: *Cravistas portuguezes*
Neemann: *Alte Meister der Laute*, Vieweg; see also ER 12
Oesterle: *Early Keyboard Music*, 2 vls.
Pauer: *Alte Meister*
Pedrell: *Antologia de organistas*, 1908
Peeters: *Oudnederlandsche Meesters vor het Orgel*, 1938
Redlich: *Meister des Orgelbarock*
Rehberg: *Alte Hausmusik für Klavier*
Schweiger: *A Brief Compendium of Early Organ Music*, 1943
Stahl: *150 Choralvorspiele alter Meister*
Straube: *Alte Meister des Orgelspiels*, 2 vls.
————: Same, Neue Folge, 2 vls. 1929
————: *Choralvorspiele alter Meister*, 1907
Tappert: *Sang und Klang aus alter Zeit* [1906]
Villalba: *Antologia de organistas*, 1914
Vitali: *Clavicembalisti italiani*, Ricordi
Werner: *Deutsche Klaviermusik aus dem Beginn des 18. Jahrhunderts*, Nagel
West: *Old English Organ Music*

4. COMPLETE OR COLLECTED EDITIONS OF INDIVIDUAL COMPOSERS

(This list is designed to guide the reader through the labyrinth of reprints of baroque music. It is based primarily on the large historical editions but includes also single titles if the music is not otherwise available. For reasons of space extreme brevity has been necessary. Where no titles appear, the analytical index of the *Harvard Dictionary of Music, s.v.* Editions, must be consulted. The names of editors are given in parentheses.)

Abaco: DTB 1 and 9:1
Ahle, J.R.: DDT 5
Albert: DDT 12/13
Albicastro: Sonata in A, ed. Henn, Genève, 1931
Albinoni: Sonatas in Nagels Musikarchiv; Schott; Violin Concerto, Vieweg; see also J. G. Walther, DDT 26/27
Ariosti: Sonatas for Viola d'Amore, Schott

Bach, Johann Christoph: 44 Choräle zum Präambulieren (Fischer) Bärenreiter;
Wie bist Du DTB 6:1; *Ach dass ich Wassers,* Breitkopf; ER 1–2

Bach Family Archive: ER 1/2

Bach J. S.: CE, Bach Gesellschaft, also Veröffentlichungen der Neuen Bach
Gesellschaft

Bassani, G. B.: ICMI 2; Torchi AM 7; Wasielewski, Instrumentalsätze

Benevoli: DTOe X:1 (V. 20)

Bernardi: DTOe XXXVI:1 (V. 69)

Bernhard: DDT 6; see also Bärenreiter: CW 16

Biber: DTOe V:2, XII:2, XXV:1, XXX:1 (V. 11, 25, 49, 59)

Blow: *Venus and Adonis,* Oiseau-Lyre; two trio sonatas (Whittaker) Oiseau-
Lyre; Selected Organ Music (Butcher) Hinrichsen

Böhm: CE (Wolgast); DDT 45

Bonporti: Sonatas (Moffat)

Boutmy: Monumenta Musicae Belgicae V

Bruhns: CE (Stein), also EL

Buxtehude: CE (Ugrino Gemeinde); organ works (Spitta; a more complete edition by Seiffert, Breitkopf); keyboard works (Bangert); DDT 11, 14

Cabanilles: CE of organ works (Anglès)

Caccini: Eitner PAM 10; *Nuove Musiche,* ICMI 4; Facs. reprint Rome 1934

Caldara: DTOe XIII:1, XXXIX (V. 26, 75)

Cambert: COF

Campion, Fr.: Pièces de son livre de tablature, (Baille) Senart

Campion, Th.: Old English Edition 1; English School of Lutenist Song-writers
(Fellowes)

Campra: COF

Carissimi: Chrysander D 2; ICMI 14; Concerts Spirituels, Schola Cantorum;
Jephtha, Novello; (Landshoff) Alte Meister des Bel Canto; Torchi
AM 5

Cavalieri: ICMI 10; *Anima e Corpo,* vocal score (Tebaldini) 1929, Facs. reprint
Rome 1912 (Mantica)

Cavalli: Eitner PAM 12; Goldschmidt, Studien, I; 20 Arie (Schmidl, 1908); 23
Arie (Zanon)

Cererols: Mestres de l'escolania di Montserrat (Pujol) I–III

Cesti: Eitner PAM 12; DTOe III:2, IV:2 (V. 6, 9); (Vatielli) Antiche Cantate
d'amore

Chambonnières: CE (Brunold-Tessier) 1925; (Quittard) 1911; Farrenc: Trésor, 2

Charpentier: *Histoires sacrées,* Concerts spirituels, Schola Cantorum, sér.
anc. III.

Chaumont: Monumenta Leodiensium Musicorum I

della Ciaja: Sonatas (Buonamici) Bratti

Clérambault: Guilmant, Archives 3; Pièces de clavecin (Brunold) Oiseau-Lyre; *Symphonia,* (Fendler) Music Press

Coelho: *Tentos* (Kastner), 1936

Colasse: COF

Comes: Obras musicales (Guzmán)

Corelli: Chrysander D 3; ICMI 9

Couperin, Fr.: CE (Cauchie) Oiseau-Lyre; Chrysander D 4

Couperin, Louis: CE (Brunold) Oiseau-Lyre

Cousser: *Erindo,* EL

Dandrieu: Guilmant, Archives 7

D'Anglebert: Publications, Soc. Franç. de Musicologie 8

Destouches: COF

Dieupart: CE (Brunold) Oiseau-Lyre

Draghi: DTOe XXIII:1 (V. 46)

Durante: ICMI 11

Erbach: DTB 4:2

Erlebach: DDT 46/47

Falconieri: 17 Arie (Benvenuti)

Ferdinand III: Works (Adler) 1895

Fiocco: Monumenta Musicae Belgicae III

Fischer, Johann: Suites, Bärenreiter; Sonatas, (Beckmann) Simrock

Fischer, J. K. Ferdinand: Keyboard works (Werra); DDT 10

Franck, J. W.: *Drey Töchter Cecrops,* EL

Franck, M: DDT 16

Frescobaldi: *Fiori* (Guilmant), Les grands maîtres (Haberl) 1913, (Germani) 1936; ICMI 12; *Toccate* (Germani); *Arie* (Boghen) 1933; *Canzoni,* Antiqua

Froberger: DTOe IV:1, VI:2, X:2 (V. 3, 12, 21)

Fromm: Oratorio, Denkmäler der Musik in Pommern, 5

Fux: DTOe I:1, II:1, IX:2, XVII, XXIII:2 (V. 1, 3, 19, 34/35, 47), also SCMA 2

Gabrieli, G.: IM 2; Antiqua; Winterfeld 3

Gagliano: Eitner PAM 10

Gaultier: *Rhétorique,* Publications Soc. Franç. de Musicologie 6/7; Fleischer VfM II

Geminiani: Sonatas, SCMA 1; David, Hohe Schule; Concerti grossi, (Hernried) Eulenburg; (Beck) New York Public Lib.; Perlen alter Kammermusik

Gigault: Guilmant, Archives 4

Grandi: CW 40

Gr(i)eco: (Shedlock) 1895

Grigny: Guilmant, Archives 5

Hammerschmidt: DTOe VIII:1 (V. 16); DDT 40

Handel: CE Deutsche Händelgesellschaft (Chrysander); Sonata in G for Vln and Cembalo conc. (Seiffert) Breitkopf; Deutsche Arien (Roth) Breitkopf; Harpsichord Pieces (Squire and Fuller-Maitland) Schott

Hassler: Eitner PAM 15; DTB 4:2, 5:2, 11:1; DDT 2, 7, 24/25

Hausmann: DDT 16

Herbst: EL

Hidalgo: *Celos* (Subirá), Inst. d'estudis catalans, 1933

Hurlebusch: VNM 32

D'India: ICMIB 9

Jenkins: Fantasia, N.Y. Public Lib. 1934; (Grainger) G. Schirmer, 1944

Keiser: DDT 37/38; Eitner PAM 18; Sonatas, Nagels Musikarchiv; *Octavia*, Handel CE, Suppl. 6

Kerckhoven: Monumenta Musicae Belgicae II

Kerll: DTOe XXV, XXX (V. 49, 59); DTB 2:2

Kindermann: DDT XIII, XXI–XXIV

Knüpfer: DDT 58/59

Krieger, A.: DDT 19

Krieger, Johann: DTB 6:1, 18

Krieger, J. Philipp: DDT 53/54; DTB 6:1, 18; Arien (Moser)

Kuhnau: DDT 4, 58/59

Landi: Torchi AM 5; Goldschmidt, Studien I

Lawes, H.: *Comus* (Visiak-Foss) 1937

Le Bègue: Guilmant, Archives 9

Leclair: Eitner PAM 27; Sonatas, Antiqua; (Beck) Music Press; Concertos, Peters

Legrenzi: Sonatas, Wasielewski, Instrumentalsätze

Leopold I: Works (Adler) 1895

Locatelli: ICMI 16; Perlen alter Kammermusik

Locke: *Macbeath* (Loder) 1934; Suites, (Beck) N.Y. Public Lib. 1942; (War-lock-Mangeot) 1932

Loeillet: Monumenta musicae Belgicae I; Sonatas, (Béon) Lemoine; (Mann) Music Press

Lotti: DDT 60

Lübeck: CE (Harms) 1921

Lully: CE (Prunières) 1930; COF

Marcello: *Arianna*, Biblioteca di rarità 4 (Chilesotti); ICMIB 6, 8; (Vatielli) Antiche Cantate d'amore

Marini: Sonatas, Torchi AM 7

Milanuzzi: 22 Arie (Benvenuti) Ricordi

Monteverdi: CE (Malipiero) 1926; *Orfeo,* Facs. repr. Augsburg 1927; ICMIB 10; *Incoronazione,* Facs. repr. Milan 1937; vocal score (Benvenuti) 1937, also Goldschmidt, Studien II; *Ritorno,* DTOe XXIX:1 (V. 57); see also Paoli, App.

Mouret: *Suite de Symphonies,* (Viollier) Schneider, 1937

Muffat, Georg: Farrenc, Trésor 2; (de Lange) 1888; Liber Organi V; DTOe I:2, II:2, XI:2 (V. 2, 4, 23)

Staden, G.: *Seelewig*, MfM 13.

Staden, J.: DTB 7:1 8:1

Stadlmayr: DTOe III:1 (V. 5)

Steffani, A.: DTB 6:2, 11:2, 12:2

Stradella: *La Forza*, vocal score (Gentili) 1931; Handel CE, Suppl. 3; Concerto grosso (Gentili); Sonatas, Schmidl, Trieste; (Riemann) Kantatenfrühling

Straus: DTOe XXX (V. 59)

Sweelinck: CE (1st volume in 2nd ed.), VNM 1894

Telemann: ER 6; DDT 28, 29/30, 49/50, 57, 61/62; cantatas, Bärenreiter; sonatas Nagel, E. C. Schirmer, Collegium Musicum, Perlen alter Kammermusik, Antiqua; concertos (Upmeyer) Vieweg; fantasies for keyboard, Broude, for solo violin [1735] (Küster), Kallmeyer

Tessarini: trio sonatas, N. Y. Public Lib. 1934

Theile: CW 16; DDT 17

Torelli: (Jensen) Klassische Violinmusik; (Toni) Milan 1927; N.Y. Public Lib. 1942; Perlen alter Kammermusik; Wasielewski, Instrumentalsätze; Nagels Musikarchiv

Torri: DTB 19/20

Trabaci: Torchi AM 3; IM 5

Tunder: DDT 3

Veracini: ICMI 34

Vitali, G. B.: Torchi AM 7

Vivaldi: Concertos, Schott, Assoc. Music Publ., Music Press, Oxford Univ. Press, N.Y. Public Lib., Antiqua, Eulenburg, Ricordi, ICMI 35; Sinfonie, (Landshoff) Peters; CE

Walther, J. Gottfried: DDT 26/27

Walther, J. Jacob: ER 17; (Beckmann) Simrock

Weckmann: DDT 6, EL

Woodcock: Concerto (Beck), N.Y. Public Lib. 1942

Young: Sonatas, suites, Oxf. Univ. Press

Zachow: DDT 21/22

Zipoli: ICMI 36

30. Luigi Rossi: Chamber cantata (after Dent).
31. Carissimi: Chamber duet (after Landshoff).
32. Carissimi: Bel-canto aria from *Lucifer* (unpublished).
33. Cavalli: Lamento on a ground from *Egisto* (after Prunières).
34. Cesti: Terzetto from *Semiramide* (unpublished).
35. Cesti: Comic aria with motto beginning (after Eitner).
36. Legrenzi: Aria from *Totila* (after Wolff).
37. Pallavicino: Excerpt from *Demetrio* (after Abert).
38. Pallavicino: Popular song from *Gerusalemme liberata* (after Abert).
39. Cavalli: Canzona theme (after Schlossberg).
40. Legrenzi: Trio sonata *La Cornara* (after Wasielewski).
41. Giovanni Battista Vitali: Violin sonata (after Torchi).
42. Mersenne: *Air de cour* with embellishments (after original).
43. Lully: *Brunette* (after Masson).
44. Lully: Plaint from *Fêtes de Versailles* (after Prunières and Böttger).
45. Lully: Accompanied *Récit* from *Armide* (after Eitner).
46. Lully: Accompanied Air from *Armide* (after Eitner).
47. Charpentier: Air on a ground (unpublished).
48. Gaultier: *Pavane* (after Tessier and Fleischer).
49. Chambonnières: *Courante* (after Brunold-Tessier).
50. Hidalgo: Bass from *Celos* (after Subirá).
51. Lanier: Monody *Hero and Leander* (unpublished).
52. Henry Lawes: *More than most fair* (unpublished).
53. Blow: Recitative of Venus from *Venus and Adonis* (after Lewis).
54. Blow: Excerpt from *Venus and Adonis* (after Lewis).
55. *Greensleeves* for harpsichord (unpublished).
56. Humfrey: Sacred solo cantata (unpublished).
57. Blow: Elegy on Queen Mary (unpublished).
58. Purcell: Excerpt from a full anthem (all exs. of Purcell's after CE).
59. Purcell: Excerpt from *I will give thanks*.
60. Purcell: Excerpt from *Arise my Muse*.
61. Purcell: Excerpt from *'Tis natures voice*.
62. Purcell: Ritornello from *The Tempest*.
63. Purcell: Bell chorus from *The Tempest*.
64. Purcell: *Alleluja* from *My heart is inditing*.
65. Purcell: Ground basses.
66. Corelli: Excerpt from violin sonata op. 5, 7 (after Chrysander).
67. Corelli: Excerpt from Concerto grosso XI (after Chrysander).
68. Corelli: From Concerto grosso XII (after Chrysander).
69. Grossi: Trumpet sonata (after Schlossberg).
70. Vivaldi: Concerto themes.
71. Corelli: Violin sonata with embellishments (after Chrysander).

INDEX

Printed in the United Kingdom
by Lightning Source UK Ltd.
132959UK00001B/41/A

9 781406 739336